MAYO CLINIC
Guide to
Your Baby's First Year

Da Capo

LIFE
LONG

A Member of the Perseus Books Group

Image credits

MAYO CLINIC

Medical Editors
Walter J. Cook, M.D.
Robert V. Johnson, M.D.
Esther H. Krych, M.D.

Managing Editor
Karen R. Wallevand

Senior Product Manager, Books
Christopher C. Frye

Director, Health Information
John (Jay) W. Maxwell

Creative Director
Michael (Wes) C. Weleczki

Art Directors
Richard A. Resnick

Illustrator
Kent McDaniel

Editorial Research Librarians
Anthony J. Cook, Amanda K. Golden,
Deirdre A. Herman, Erika A. Riggin

Proofreaders
Miranda M. Attlesey, Donna L. Hanson,
Julie M. Maas

Indexer
Steve Rath

Contributors
Rachel Bartony; Julie A. Buchholtz, R.D.;
Dawn Marie R. Davis, M.D.; Lee Engfer;
Jennifer L. Jacobson; Robert M. Jacobson,
M.D.; John Karapelou; Tara K. Kaufman,
M.D.; Cynthia C. Leonard; Mark S. Mannen-
bach, M.D.; Sarah Moran; Debra I. Mucha,
R.N, C.N.P.; Jodi O'Shaughnessy Olson;
Stephanie R. Starr, M.D.; Ruth E. Stoeckel,
CCC-SLP; Cheryl L. Stuhldreher, I.B.C.L.C.;
Megha M. Tollefson, M.D.; Allison C. Van
Dusen; Myra J. Wick, M.D., Ph.D.

MAYO, MAYO CLINIC and the Mayo
triple-shield logo are marks of Mayo
Foundation for Medical Education and
Research.

Cataloging-in-Publication data for this book
available from the Library of Congress.

ISBN: 978-1-56148-750-9

Published by Da Capo Press
A member of the Perseus Books Group
dacapopress.com

Note: The information in this book is true
and complete to the best of our knowledge. This book is intended only as an
informative guide to those wishing to know
more about health issues. In no way is this
book intended to replace, countermand,
or conflict with the advice given to you by
your own physician. Information in this
book is offered with no guarantees on the
part of the authors or Da Capo Press. The
authors and publisher disclaim all liability in
connection with the use of this book. The
names and identifying details of people
associated with events described in the
book have been changed. Any similarity to
the actual person is coincidental. The
individuals pictured in the lifestyle photos
are models. There is no correlation
between the individuals portrayed and the
condition or subject being discussed.

For bulk sales to employers, member
groups and health-related companies,
contact Mayo Clinic, 200 First St. SW,
Rochester, MN 55905; 800-430-9699;
SpecialSalesMayoBooks@mayo.edu

Printed in the United States of America.
LSC-C

Introduction

Raising a child is one of the most challenging, yet rewarding, experiences you will ever have. There is perhaps nothing more special than the lifelong bond that forms between a parent and a child. But be prepared that as with everything else in life, there will be ups and downs.

Information from authoritative parenting resources, such as the information in this book, can help satisfy your need for baby-care details and provide reassurances about the health of your baby and your own health.

Mayo Clinic Guide to Your Baby's First Year is an easy-to-use yet comprehensive how-to manual that provides answers and explanations to the questions and concerns of new mothers and fathers. The book is your one-stop resource for caring for a newborn. From baby-care basics to month-by-month development to common illnesses to health and safety, this book covers it all. There's also a wealth of tips and advice for couples coping with the many changes to daily life that come with parenthood.

Mayo Clinic Guide to Your Baby's First Year is the work of a team of pediatric experts at Mayo Clinic who find nothing in medicine more exciting, fascinating and satisfying than caring for young children.

Parenthood is a personal journey. How you deal with all of the changes that come with raising a child will likely reflect your expectations and hopes of what life with your newborn will be like. The pages that follow provide information to help you prepare for and deal with many of the routine events, issues and tasks of life with a newborn. However, you are the one who makes it all happen. A positive attitude, a good support system and plenty of love can go a long way in making the years ahead truly enjoyable.

A project of this scope requires the teamwork of many individuals. A special thanks to all of the people who helped make this book possible.

The Editors

Meet the Editors

Esther H. Krych, M.D., (left) is a specialist in general pediatric care within the Department of Pediatrics, Mayo Clinic, Rochester, Minn. She is the mother of three young children and can relate to parenting from both a mother's and doctor's perspective.

Robert V. Johnson, M.D., (center) is a specialist in the Department of Pediatrics and chair of the Division of Neonatology, Mayo Clinic, Rochester, Minn. He is also an assistant professor at College of Medicine, Mayo Clinic. A father of two and grandfather of two, Dr. Johnson has spent more than 25 years caring for newborns.

Walter J. Cook, M.D., (right) is a specialist in general pediatric care within the Department of Pediatrics, Mayo Clinic, Rochester, Minn., and an assistant professor at College of Medicine, Mayo Clinic. A father of three, including twins, he has cared for thousands of babies in more than 20 years of pediatric practice.

How to use this book

To help you easily find what you're look-ing for, *Mayo Clinic Guide to Your Baby's First Year* is divided into six sections.

Part 1: Caring for Your Baby

From how to feed your newborn to de-veloping a sleep schedule to comforting a crying baby to clothing your young one, you'll find basic baby-care tips in this de-tailed section. You'll also find information on identifying your child's temperament and learning to understand his or her specific traits.

Part 2: Baby's Health and Safety

Part 2 covers all of the key elements to keeping your child from injury and ill-ness. You'll read about doctor checkups and vaccinations, as well as suggestions for childproofing your home.

Part 3: Growth and Development Month by Month

This section provides monthly insights into your baby's growth and develop-ment. It covers a range of topics includ-ing toys and games, separation anxiety, sign language, and sitting, standing and walking.

Part 4: Common Illnesses and Concerns

Here you'll find helpful tips for managing conditions that commonly affect young children, such as fever, colds, ear infec-tions, pink eye and others. You'll also learn when medication may be appropri-ate and when it may be best to avoid it.

Part 5: Managing and Enjoying Parenthood

For first-time parents, caring for a new-born can be nerve-racking and exhaust-ing. The information in Part 5 can help you get through the first year with the reassurance that you're doing well.

Part 6: Special Circumstances

Most children are born healthy, but sometimes problems can develop. Dis-eases and disorders that can affect new-borns, and how they're treated, are dis-cussed here.

Contents

Fever • Febrile seizures • Fifth disease • Flu (influenza)
Hand-foot-and-mouth disease • Hives • Impetigo • Insect bites and
stings • Jaundice • Lazy eye • Pink eye (conjunctivitis) • Pneumonia
Reflux • RSV • Roseola • Stomach flu (gastroenteritis) • Sty
Sunburn • Swollen scrotum • Teary eyes • Teething • Thrush
Urinary tract infection • Vomiting • Whooping cough

PART 1

Caring for your baby

CHAPTER 1

Welcome to parenthood!

Congratulations! You are now entering one of the greatest phases of your life — parenthood. There is perhaps nothing in life more special than the bond that forms between a parent and a child. It's a relationship that will bring endless years of joy, laughter, admiration and satisfaction. The time you spend raising your children will be time that you will cherish forever. In the years to come, you'll learn more about attachment, love and protectiveness than you ever thought possible.

But be prepared that not every day in your parenthood journey will be grand and glorious. Like everything else in life, there will be ups and downs. You may find that some of the more stressful and exhausting days of being a parent will come early on, when you first bring your new son or daughter home.

Bringing a baby into your house can literally turn your life upside down. The routine you once knew — having time to yourself, getting together with friends, going out for a relaxing dinner or spending the day indulging in your favorite hobby — has been put on hold. In its place is a reality that may feel totally foreign to you. That's because children don't arrive with instruction manuals, and parenting is somewhat of a trial-by-fire experience. If you've never had to care for a young child before, you may feel nervous, unsure of yourself and a bit lost. That's to be expected — and is perfectly normal.

PARENTING 101

Many parents describe their first year with a new baby as a roller coaster ride. As one new mom put it, "One minute you're laughing and joking; the next minute you're crying, not really knowing why." You may go from adoring your baby and marveling at tiny fingers and toes to grieving your loss of independence and worrying about your ability to care for a newborn, all in the space of a single diaper change.

Given all these changes, the first few weeks after you bring your baby home are likely to be one of the most challenging times of your life. The changes in the daily rhythms of your life can feel chaotic, but you will learn to adapt. It may take months or even a year, but you'll get there — in your own way, in your own time, and with your own missteps and successes.

Relish the time As chaotic as it may seem, this is a special time in your life. Appreciate the joy your new son or daughter brings to your life, and don't let your worries overshadow your joys. Newborn days won't last long. Step back and appreciate the moment. For all the strain associated with the first year, parenthood brings an incredible richness to daily living. Nothing can quite compare to the joy of seeing a newborn's smile or the wobbly first steps of a toddler.

Trust your instincts Caring for a baby may be totally new territory for you, but have confidence in yourself. You'll quickly learn the things you need to know to take great care of your child. Also realize that you aren't expected to know it all. It's OK to ask questions and seek guidance from friends, family and medical professionals. If you get unsolicited advice, take the advice that "fits" with your parenting style and feel free to forget the rest.

Check your expectations Many new parents start out with unrealistic expectations — that life won't be much different from before, that parenting is going to be fun every minute of the day, that the new baby will mostly eat and sleep, that they'll be able to manage everything perfectly. The gap between expectations and reality can lead to stress and disappointment. Throw out any preconceived notions about what life with a new baby should be like, and be realistic about the increased demands on your time. That cute, little 8-pound addition to your household can create a lot of extra work.

Be patient For the first few weeks, your life may seem limited to round-the-clock feeding, bathing, diapering and soothing — all on shortened amounts of sleep. You may find it difficult to fit in a shower and do a load of laundry, let alone make dinner. You may fear this is what your life is going to be like forever! It won't be. Over time you'll adjust to the new normal, revive old routines and create new ones. As your baby gets older, you'll find you have more time for yourself.

Take care of yourself Childhood care also extends to parents. Taking good care of your baby includes taking good care of yourself. The better you feel, the better able you'll be to care for and enjoy your new son or daughter. Sneak in as much sleep as possible, eat well and get some exercise. Most of all, don't be afraid to ask for help when you need it.

Take care of your relationship Babies, while wonderful, can be hard on a relationship. You and your partner may miss your life as a couple. You may also find that you have differences of opinion on issues related to caring for your child. Be patient with yourself and your partner. Take time to admire his or her relationship with your baby, and you will likely find great inspiration, not only as a parent, but also as a couple.

THIS BOOK

As you maneuver the ins and outs of parenting, a little guidance and reassurance can be of great help. *Mayo Clinic Guide to Your Baby's First Year* is designed to help you find answers to common questions during the first year of a baby's life. The book is also intended to provide you with reassurance that you're doing well, and that the emotions and concerns you may be experiencing are the same as those of many other first-time parents.

Dig in by whatever manner works best for you. You can turn the page and begin reading, or you can selectively choose those chapters or sections that are most important to you right now. Keep the book handy so you can turn to it whenever a concern arises or to prepare yourself for what may be in store in the month ahead.

Remember that parenting is an adventure; enjoy the journey!

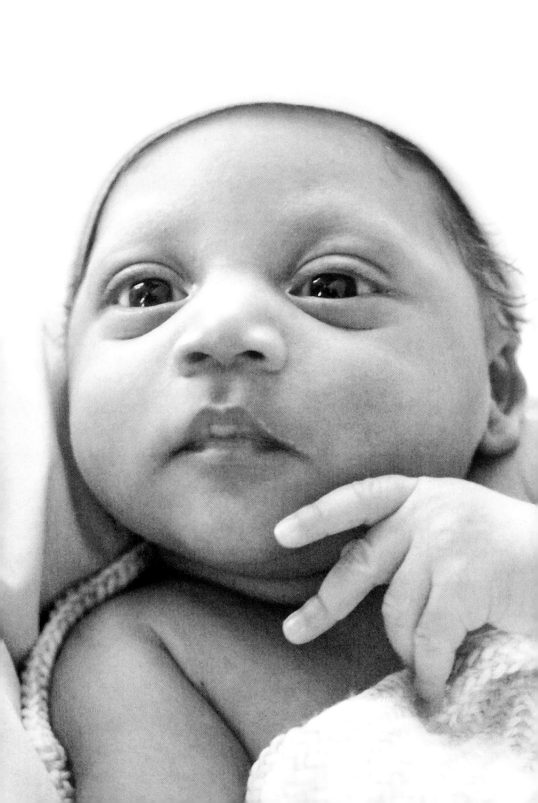

CHAPTER 2

Baby's first days

From the moment you first learned you were pregnant, you've been eagerly anticipating one thing: the day you could hold your baby and look into his or her face. And now that day is here!

Your labor and delivery — whether it was a marathon session or shockingly short — is behind you. Now is the time to enjoy that precious little person you've been waiting so long to meet.

The mental picture you have of your baby — the product of thousands of advertisements and television shows — is of a plump, cuddly infant announcing his or her arrival with a lusty cry. In reality, the tiny person you greet may not be the perfect little cherub you imagined.

Newly born babies generally emerge somewhat messy looking, often with misshapen heads and blemished skin. Take heart, though. It won't be long before the baby you envisioned is the one you're holding in your arms.

In this chapter, you'll learn about your newborn's first days of life — what he or she may look like and standard examinations and screenings. You'll also learn about conditions often seen in newborns.

BABY BONDING

As soon as babies are born, they need and want you to hold, cuddle, touch, kiss, talk and sing to them. These everyday expressions of love and affection promote bonding. They also help your baby's brain develop. Just as an infant's body needs food to grow, his or her brain benefits from positive emotional, physical and intellectual experiences. Relationships with other people early in life have a vital influence on a child's development. Some parents feel an immediate connection with their newborn, while for others the bond takes longer to develop. Don't worry or feel guilty if you aren't overcome with a rush of love at the very beginning. Not every parent bonds instantly with a new baby. Your feelings will become stronger with time.

Bonding moments During those first weeks, most of your time with your new son or daughter is likely to be spent feeding him or her, changing diapers, and helping him or her sleep. These routine tasks present an opportunity to bond. When babies receive warm, responsive care, they're more likely to feel safe and secure. For example, as you feed your baby and change diapers, gaze lovingly into his or her eyes and talk gently to him or her.

Babies also have times when they're quietly alert and ready to learn and play. These times may last only a few moments, but you'll learn to recognize them. Take advantage of your baby's alert times to get acquainted and play.

Talk, read and sing to your baby Even infants enjoy music and being read to. These early "conversations" encourage your baby's language capacity and provide an opportunity for closeness. Babies generally prefer soft, rhythmic sounds.

Cuddle and touch your baby Newborns are sensitive to changes in pressure and temperature. They love to be held, rocked, caressed, cradled, snuggled, kissed, patted, stroked, massaged and carried.

Let your baby watch your face Soon after birth, your newborn will become accustomed to seeing you and will begin to focus on your face. Allow your baby to study your features, and provide plenty of smiles.

Play music and dance Put on some soft music with a beat, hold your baby's face close to yours, and gently sway and move to the tune.

Establish routines and rituals Repeated positive experiences provide children with a sense of security. Be patient with yourself in these first weeks. Caring for a new child can be daunting, discouraging, thrilling and perplexing — all in the same hour! In time, your skills as a parent will grow, and you will come to love this little one far more than you could have imagined.

Don't worry about spoiling your newborn Respond to your child's cues and clues. Among the signals babies send are the sounds they make — which will be mostly fussing during the first week or two — the way they move, their facial expressions, and the way they make or avoid eye contact. Pay close attention to your baby's need for stimulation as well as quiet times.

BABY'S LOOKS

Considering what they've just been through during labor and childbirth, it's no wonder newborns don't look like the little angels seen on television. Instead, your newborn may first appear wrinkled and pale. If your baby is like most, his or her head will be a bit misshapen and larger than you expected, and the eyelids may be puffy. His or her arms and legs may be drawn, and the hands and feet may be bluish or purplish in color. He or she may be somewhat bloody and likely wet and slippery from amniotic fluid.

In addition, most babies will be born with what appears like skin lotion. Called vernix, it's most noticeable under your baby's arms, behind the ears and in the groin. Most of this vernix will be washed off during your baby's first bath.

Head At first, your baby's head may appear flat, elongated or crooked. This peculiar elongation is one of the common features of a newly born baby.

A baby's skull consists of several sections of bone that are flexibly joined so that the head shape can change to correspond to the shape of your pelvis as your baby moves through the birth canal during childbirth. A long labor usually results in an elongated or tall skull shape at birth. The head of a breech baby may have a shorter, broader appearance. If a vacuum extractor was used to assist in the birth, your baby's head may look particularly elongated.

Fontanels When you feel the top of your baby's head, you'll notice two soft areas. These soft spots, called fontanels, are where your baby's skull bones haven't grown together yet.

The fontanel toward the front of the scalp is a diamond-shaped spot roughly the size of a quarter. Though it's usually flat, it may bulge when your baby cries or strains. In seven to 19 months, this fontanel will be filled in with hard bone. The smaller fontanel at the back of the head is less noticeable. Some parents don't even realize it's there. This fontanel is about the size of a dime and it closes much quicker — around six weeks after birth.

Some parents are anxious about touching baby's soft spots, partly because they don't like the way they feel. Don't worry. You won't hurt your baby if you do touch a fontanel.

Skin Most babies are born with some bruising, and skin blotches and blemishes are common.

A rounded swelling of the scalp is usually seen on the top and back of the baby's head when a baby is born the usual way — headfirst. This puffiness of the skin disappears within a day or so.

Pressure from your pelvis during labor can cause a bruise on your baby's head. The bruise may be noticeable for several weeks, and you might feel a small bump that persists for several months. You may also see scrapes or bruises on your baby's face and head if forceps were used during delivery. These bruises and blemishes should go away within a couple of weeks.

The top layer of a newborn's skin flakes off shortly after birth. Because of this, you may notice plenty of dry, peeling

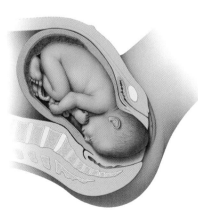

Head elongation

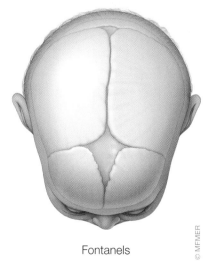

Fontanels

© MFMER

skin the first few weeks. In general, this "peeled" look gets better on its own. If the skin should crack or bleed, apply some petroleum jelly to the area.

Following are other skin conditions common in newborns. For pictures and more information on these conditions, see Chapter 5.

Erythema toxicum It may sound scary, but erythema toxicum is the medical term for a common newborn rash that typically appears within the first few days after birth and lasts up to two weeks. It's characterized by little reddish splotches that may or may not have a white center and that come and go. The splotches tend to flare up where baby has been snuggled or held. The condition causes no discomfort and it's not infectious.

Milia These are tiny white spots that may look like pimples, but are not. They're usually located on the nose and chin. Although they appear to be raised, they're nearly flat and smooth to the touch. Milia disappear in time, and they don't require treatment.

Baby acne Baby acne refers to the red bumps and blotches similar to teenage acne that are seen on the face, neck, upper chest and back. It's generally most noticeable the first few months and typically disappears without treatment. Having baby acne doesn't necessarily mean that a child will have acne later in life.

Pustular melanosis This is another condition whose name may sound scary, but the rash is typically mild and it usually disappears soon after birth. Pustular melanosis is characterized by small spots that look like small yellowish-white sesame seeds. The spots are present at birth,

and they quickly dry and peel off. The spots may look similar to skin infections (pustules), but pustular melanosis isn't an infection, and it disappears without treatment. Pustular melanosis is more common in dark-complected babies.

Birthmarks Contrary to their name, birthmarks aren't always present at birth. Some, such as a hemangioma, develop weeks later. And though most are permanent, a few types fade as a child grows. Most birthmarks are harmless, but some may require treatment for cosmetic reasons or because of rapid growth or risk of future health problems. See pages 30 and 31 for pictures of common birthmarks.

Salmon patches Salmon patches are sometimes affectionately called stork bites or angel kisses. They are reddish or pink patches that are often found just above or below the hairline at the back of the neck. Salmon patches may also be found on the eyelids, forehead or upper lip. These marks are caused by collections of tiny blood vessels (capillaries) close to the skin. Salmon patches on the forehead, eyelids or between the eyes usually fade with time, though they may flare with increased blood flow to the head, such as when crying, straining or pushing. Salmon patches on the nape of the neck may not fade, but they're often covered by hair. Salmon patches don't require any type of treatment.

Slate gray nevus A slate gray nevus, previously called a mongolian spot, is a large, blue-gray birthmark that's sometimes mistaken for a bruise. It's more common in darker skinned babies, especially those of Asian heritage. This birthmark may disappear later in childhood and requires no treatment.

Cafe au lait spot As the name implies, these permanent birthmarks are light-brown, or coffee, colored. Cafe au lait birthmarks are very common, and they can occur anywhere on the body. Usually, no treatment is needed. However, if your child has more than six cafe au lait spots, ask his or her care provider whether further evaluation is warranted.

Hemangioma Hemangiomas are caused by an overgrowth of blood vessels in the top layers of skin. They appear as a bright red, raised spot that may resemble a strawberry. Usually not present at birth, a hemangioma may begin as a small, pale spot that becomes red in the center. The birthmark enlarges during the baby's first few months and most often disappears without treatment by school age. Large hemangiomas may cover an entire segment of the face or body. Some fast-growing hemangiomas may require laser treatment or medication. Babies with several hemangiomas may need evaluation for an underlying condition.

Congenital nevus A congenital nevus is a large, dark-colored mole that typically appears on the scalp or trunk of the body. It can range in size from less than 0.4 inches to more than 5 inches across, covering large areas. Children with a large-sized congenital nevus are at an increased risk of developing skin cancer as adults. If your child has this type of birthmark, consult your child's care provider so that he or she can check for skin changes.

Port-wine stain A port-wine stain is a permanent birthmark that starts out pink, but turns darker red or purple as a child grows. Most often, a port-wine stain appears on the face and neck, but it can affect other areas. The involved skin may thicken and develop an irregular, pebbled surface. The condition can be treated, often with laser therapy.

Facial appearance When you first look at your baby, his or her nose may seem flattened. This is from pressure inside the birth canal. Within a day or two, the nose will take on a more normal appearance. His or her cheeks may also have marks or bruises if forceps were used during the delivery. This, too, will improve in a short time.

Eyes It's perfectly normal for your newborn's eyes to be puffy. Some infants have such puffy eyes that they aren't able to open their eyes wide right away. This will improve within a day or two.

You may also notice that your baby sometimes looks cross-eyed. This, too, is normal, and your child will outgrow the condition within several months.

BIRTHMARKS

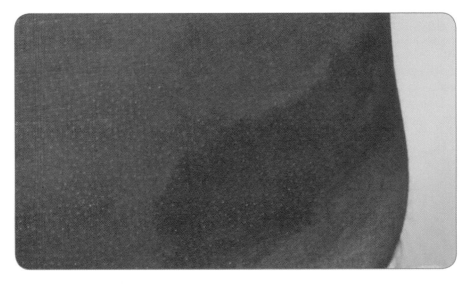

Cafe au lait spot Cafe au lait spots are pigmented birthmarks that are often oval in shape. Their name is French for "milky coffee," which refers to their light-brown color. Cafe au lait spots usually are present at birth, but they may develop in the first few years of a child's life.

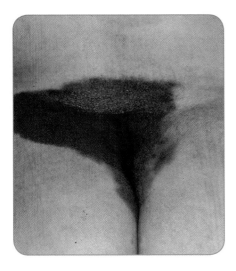

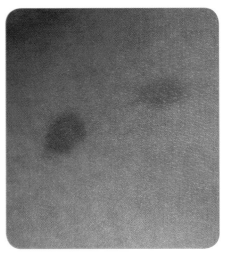

Congenital nevus A congenital nevus is a mole present at birth that may vary in size from small to large. It typically appears as light brown- to black-colored patch. It can occur on any part of the body.

Slate gray nevus Also known as a mongolian spot, this blue-gray birthmark is sometimes mistaken for a bruise. It's more common in darker skinned babies, especially those of Asian heritage.

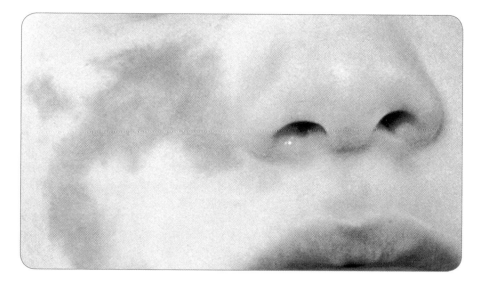

Port-wine stain A port-wine stain is a birthmark in which swollen blood vessels create a reddish-purplish discoloration of the skin. Early port-wine stains are usually flat and pink in appearance. As the child gets older, the color may deepen to a dark red or a purplish color.

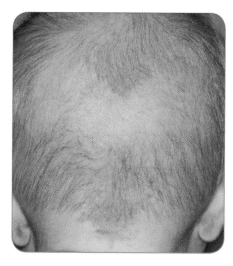

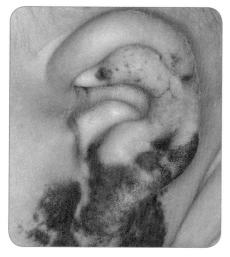

Salmon patches Also called stork bites, these marks are small blood vessels (capillaries) visible through the skin. Salmon patches are most common on the forehead, eyelids, upper lip and back of the neck.

Hemangioma A hemangioma is an abnormal buildup of blood vessels in the skin. The marks are bright red and often raised. They often appear on the neck or facial area.

Sometimes babies are born with red spots on the whites of their eyes. These spots result from the breakage of tiny blood vessels during birth. The spots are harmless, and they won't interfere with your baby's sight. They generally disappear in a week to two.

Like a newborn's hair, his or her eyes give no guarantee of their future color. Although most newborns have dark bluish-brown, blue-black, grayish-blue or slate-colored eyes, permanent eye color may take six months or even longer to establish itself.

Hair Your baby may be born bald, with a full head of thick hair — or almost anything in between! Don't fall in love with your baby's hair too quickly. The hair color your baby is born with isn't necessarily what he or she will have six months down the road. Blond newborns, for example, may become darker blond as they get older, or their hair may develop a reddish tinge that isn't apparent at birth.

You may be surprised to see that your newborn's head isn't the only place he or she has hair. Downy, fine hair called lanugo covers a baby's body before birth and may temporarily appear on your newborn's back, shoulders, forehead and temples. Most of this hair is shed in the uterus before the baby is born, making lanugo especially common in premature babies. It disappears within a few weeks after birth.

FIRST EXAMINATION

From the moment your little one is born, he or she is the focus of much activity. Your care provider or a nurse will clean his or her face. To make sure your baby can breathe properly, the nose and mouth are cleared of fluid as soon as the head appears — and again immediately after birth.

While baby's airway is being cleared, his or her heart rate and circulation can be checked with a stethoscope or by feeling the pulse in the umbilical cord. All newborns look somewhat bluish-gray for the first several minutes, especially on their lips and tongue. By five to 10 minutes after birth they become pinker, though baby's hands and feet may still remain bluish, which is normal. Your baby's umbilical cord is clamped with a plastic clamp, and you or your partner may be given the option to cut it.

In the next day or two, many things will take place. The medical team will conduct newborn examinations, administer screening tests and give some immunizations.

Apgar scores One of the first examinations of your baby will be determining his or her Apgar scores. Apgar scores are basically a quick evaluation of a newborn's health, which are given at one minute and five minutes after a baby is born. Developed in 1952 by anesthesiologist Virginia Apgar, this brief examination rates newborns on five criteria: color, heart rate, reflexes, muscle tone and respiration.

Each of these criteria is given an individual score of zero, 1 or 2. The scores are totaled for a maximum possible score of 10. Higher scores indicate healthier infants, but don't get too caught up in the numbers. Your care provider will tell you how your baby is doing, and even those babies with lower scores often turn out to be perfectly healthy.

Other checks and measurements Soon after birth, your newborn's weight,

CORD BLOOD BANKING

During your pregnancy, you may have heard or read about what's called cord blood banking. At this point in time, cord blood banking is not common procedure, and you shouldn't feel pressured to take part. However, if you think this is something you may want to do, here's some information to help you make a decision.

The blood within a baby's umbilical cord is a rich source of stem cells, the cells from which all other cells are created. Cord blood banking is a procedure in which cord blood is taken from a baby's umbilical cord shortly after delivery and preserved for possible future use in a stem cell transplant. Collecting a baby's cord blood poses few, if any, risks to either mother or baby. If the cord blood isn't collected for preservation or research, it's simply discarded.

Public vs. private There are two main ways to bank cord blood. The first is using a public cord blood bank. Public banks collect and store cord blood for use by any individual who has a medical condition in which cord blood might provide a cure. The second type is a private bank. It oversees the collection and storage of cord blood for families who are willing and able to pay for the service, and the blood is saved for use by that family.

Should you consider it? Donating cord blood to a public cord blood bank is a tremendous opportunity to help others. Cord blood transplants from unrelated donors can be used to treat many conditions, including leukemia and various metabolic problems. You won't be charged any fees to donate cord blood to a public bank. However, you may need to give birth at one of the limited number of hospitals or other facilities equipped to handle public cord blood donations.

Donating cord blood to a private facility for possible personal use is controversial. The cost is often considerable, and the chance that your child will use his or her own banked cord blood in the future is remote. Also, should your child need a stem cell transplant, there's no guarantee that his or her banked cord blood will remain viable or be suitable for a transplant.

The American Academy of Pediatrics (AAP) encourages donation to public cord blood banks but discourages private donation. In recommending against private donation, the AAP states: "The chances of a child needing his or her own cord blood stem cells in the future are estimated to range from 1 in 1,000 to 1 in 200,000. Private cord blood banks target parents at an emotionally vulnerable time when the reality is most conditions that might be helped by cord blood stem cells already exist in the infant's cord blood. However, the AAP does recommend private cord blood banking for parents who have an older child with a condition that could potentially benefit from transplantation, such as a genetic immunodeficiency."

If you're considering cord blood banking, talk to your care provider. He or she can help answer any questions you may have and help you better understand the options so that you can make an informed decision.

length and head circumference are measured. Your baby's temperature may be taken, and breathing and heart rate measured. Usually within 12 hours after birth, a physical exam is conducted to detect any problems or abnormalities.

Your child's blood sugar (glucose) also may be checked within the first hour or two after birth, especially if your baby is somewhat larger or smaller for his or her age or if he or she seems overly sleepy or has trouble getting started eating.

A baby whose blood sugar is too low may be more sleepy than normal and won't feed well. Assistance may be given to encourage eating and improve the baby's blood sugar (see page 536 for more information).

Treatments and vaccinations The following steps are generally taken shortly after birth to prevent disease.

Eye protection To prevent the possibility of gonorrhea being passed from mother to baby, all states require that infants' eyes be protected from this infection immediately after birth. Gonorrheal eye infections were a leading cause of blindness until early in the 20th century, when treatment of babies' eyes after birth became mandatory. An antibiotic ointment or solution is placed onto his or her eyes. These preparations are gentle to the eyes and cause no pain.

Vitamin K injection In the United States, vitamin K is routinely given to infants shortly after they're born. Vitamin K is necessary for normal blood coagulation, the body's process for stopping bleeding after a cut or bruise. Newborns have low levels of vitamin K in their first few weeks. An injection of vitamin K can help prevent the rare possibility that a

newborn would become so deficient in vitamin K that serious bleeding might develop. This problem is not related to hemophilia.

Hepatitis B vaccination Hepatitis B is a viral infection that affects the liver. It can cause illnesses such as cirrhosis and liver failure, or it can result in the development of liver tumors. Adults contract hepatitis through sexual contact, shared needles or exposure to the blood of an infected person.

Babies can contract hepatitis B from their mothers during pregnancy and birth. For most newborns, protection against hepatitis B begins with a vaccine given shortly after birth.

NEWBORN ISSUES

Some babies have a bit of trouble adjusting to their new world. Fortunately, most of the problems they experience in the first few days after birth are generally minor and soon resolved.

Jaundice More than half of all newborn babies develop jaundice, a yellow tinge to the skin and eyes. Signs generally develop after the first 24 hours and peak about five to seven days after birth. The condition may last several weeks.

A baby develops jaundice when bilirubin, which is produced by the breakdown of red blood cells, accumulates faster than his or her liver can break it down and pass it from the body.

Your baby may develop jaundice for a few reasons:
▶ Bilirubin is being produced more quickly than the liver can handle.
▶ The baby's developing liver isn't able to remove bilirubin from the blood.

◗ Too much of the bilirubin is reabsorbed from the intestines before the baby gets rid of it in a bowel movement.

Treatment Most newborns are screened for jaundice, either by visual inspection or with laboratory testing. Mild jaundice generally doesn't require treatment, but more-severe cases can require a newborn to stay longer in the hospital. Jaundice may be treated in several ways:

◗ You may be asked to feed the baby more frequently, which increases the amount of bilirubin passed out of the body via bowel movements.

◗ A doctor may place your baby under a bilirubin light. This treatment, called phototherapy, is quite common. A special lamp helps rid the body of excess bilirubin.

◗ Rarely, if the bilirubin level becomes extremely high, intravenous (IV) medications or a specialized blood transfusion may be required.

Eating problems Whether you choose to breast-feed or bottle-feed, during the first few days after your baby's birth you may find it difficult to interest your newborn in eating. The first feedings can sometimes be difficult. If this is the case, you're not alone. Remember, your baby is learning and so are his or her parents. See the next chapter for advice on how to reduce the stress of early feedings.

If things aren't going well, or you're concerned that your baby isn't getting enough nourishment, talk to your baby's nurse or care provider. Some babies are slow eaters the first few days, but soon they catch on and breast-feed or bottle-feed with enthusiasm.

Over the first week, a newborn may lose about 10 percent of his or her birth weight and will gradually gain that weight back, and more!

Infection A newborn's immune system isn't adequately developed to fight infection. Therefore, any type of infection can be more critical for newborns than for older children or adults.

If things don't seem right — if your newborn seems too fussy or too sleepy — or if your newborn has a fever, don't delay seeking care. This may mean going to the emergency room if the illness occurs in the middle of the night.

Serious bacterial infections, which are uncommon, can invade any organ or the blood, urine or spinal fluid. Prompt treatment with antibiotics is necessary, but even with early diagnosis and treatment, a newborn infection can be life-threatening.

For this reason, care providers are often quick to treat a possible or suspected infection. Antibiotics often are given early and stopped only when an infection doesn't seem likely. Although the majority of the test results come back showing no evidence of infection, it's better to err on the side of safety by quickly treating a baby than to risk not treating a baby with an infection soon enough.

Hernias It's not unusual for a baby to be born with a hernia. Hernias can occur either in the groin area (inguinal hernia) or near the baby's bellybutton (umbilical hernia).

Inguinal hernia An inguinal hernia may occur in boys or girls but is more common in boys. An inguinal hernia is caused by a weakness in the lower abdominal wall that allows the intestines to bulge outward. The hernia appears as a swelling in the lower abdomen or groin and is generally painless. Sometimes the hernia is visible only when an infant is crying, coughing or straining during a bowel movement.

An inguinal hernia may be small at first, but it tends to gradually enlarge so that an operation is eventually needed to repair the weak spot. An inguinal hernia usually won't go away by itself.

Umbilical hernia An umbilical hernia occurs when part of the intestine protrudes through an opening in the upper abdominal muscles near the bellybutton. It may be especially evident when an infant cries, causing the baby's bellybutton to protrude. This is a classic sign of an umbilical hernia.

Most umbilical hernias close on their own by baby's first birthday, though some take longer to heal. Umbilical hernias that don't disappear by age 4 or those that appear later in a person's life may require surgical repair to prevent complications.

CIRCUMCISION

If you have a baby boy, one of the decisions you'll face soon after birth is whether to have him circumcised. Circumcision is an elective surgical procedure performed to remove the skin covering the tip of the penis. Knowing about the procedure's potential benefits and risks can help you make an informed decision.

Issues to consider Although circumcision is fairly common in the United States, it's still somewhat controversial. There's some evidence that circumcision may have medical benefits, but the procedure also has risks. The American Academy of Pediatrics doesn't recommend routine circumcision of all male newborns, saying there isn't enough evidence of benefit.

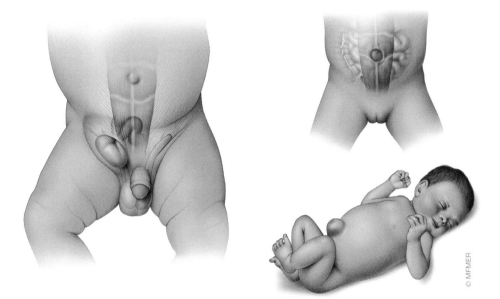

An inguinal hernia (left) results when a portion of the small intestine protrudes through the lower abdominal wall. With an umbilical hernia (right), the small intestine protrudes through an opening in abdominal wall near the bellybutton.

Consider your own cultural, religious and social values in making this decision. For some people, such as those of the Jewish or Islamic faith, circumcision is a religious ritual. For others, it's a matter of personal hygiene or preventive health. Some parents choose circumcision because they don't want their son to look different from his peers.

As you decide what's best for you and your son, consider these potential health benefits and risks.

Benefits of circumcision Some research suggests that circumcision provides certain benefits. These include:

▶ *Decreased risk of urinary tract infections.* Although the risk of urinary tract infections in the first year is low, studies suggest that such infections may be up to 10 times more common in uncircumcised baby boys than in those who are circumcised. Uncircumcised boys are also more likely to be admitted to the hospital for a severe urinary tract infection during the first three months of life than are those who are circumcised.

▶ *Decreased risk of cancer of the penis.* While this type of cancer is very rare, circumcised men show a lower incidence of cancer of the penis than do uncircumcised men.

▶ *Slightly decreased risk of sexually transmitted infections.* Some studies have shown a lower risk of human immunodeficiency virus (HIV) and human papillomavirus (HPV) infections in circumcised men. However, safe sexual practices are much more important in the prevention of sexually transmitted infections than is circumcision.

▶ *Prevention of penile problems.* Occasionally, the foreskin on an uncircumcised penis may narrow to the point where it's difficult or impossible to retract (phimosis). Circumcision may be needed to treat the problem. A narrowed foreskin can also lead to inflammation of the head of the penis (balanitis).

▶ *Ease of hygiene.* Circumcision makes it easy to wash the penis. But even if the foreskin is intact, it's still quite simple to keep the penis clean. Normally the foreskin adheres to the end of the penis in a newborn, then gradually stretches back during early childhood.

Risks of circumcision Circumcision is generally considered a safe procedure, and the risks related to it are minor. However, circumcision does have some risks. Possible drawbacks of the procedure include:

▶ *Risks of minor surgery.* All surgical procedures, including circumcision, carry certain risks, such as excessive bleeding and infection. There's also the possibility that the foreskin may be cut too short or too long, or that it doesn't heal properly.

▶ *Pain during the procedure.* Circumcision does cause pain. Typically a local anesthetic is used to block the nerve sensations. Talk to your care provider about the type of anesthesia used.

▶ *Cost.* Some insurance companies don't cover the cost of circumcision. If you're considering circumcision, check whether your insurance company will cover it.

▶ *Complicating factors.* Sometimes, circumcision may need to be postponed, such as if your baby is born prematurely, has severe jaundice or is feeding poorly. It also may not be feasible in certain situations, such as in the rare instance when baby's urethral opening is in an abnormal position (hypospadias). Other conditions that may prevent circumcision include ambiguous genitalia or a family history of bleeding disorders.

Circumcision doesn't affect fertility. Whether it enhances or detracts from sexual pleasure for men or their partners hasn't been proved. Whatever your choice, negative outcomes are rare and mostly minor.

How it's done If you decide to have your son circumcised, his care provider can answer questions about the procedure and help you make arrangements at your hospital or clinic. Usually, circumcision is performed before you and your son leave the hospital. At times, it's done in an outpatient setting. The procedure itself takes about 10 minutes.

Typically, the baby lies on a tray with his arms and legs restrained. After the penis and surrounding area are cleansed, a local anesthetic is injected into the base of the penis. A special clamp or plastic ring is attached to the penis, and the foreskin is cut away. An ointment, such as petroleum jelly, is applied. This protects the penis from adhering to the diaper.

If your newborn is fussy as the anesthetic wears off, hold him gently — being careful to avoid putting pressure on the penis. It usually takes about seven to 10 days for the penis to heal.

Circumcision care The tip of your son's penis may seem raw for the first week after the procedure. Or a yellowish mucus or crust may form around the area. This is a normal part of healing. A small amount of bleeding is also common the first day or two.

Clean the diaper area gently, and apply a dab of petroleum jelly to the end of the penis with each diaper change. This will keep the diaper from sticking while the penis heals. If there's a bandage, change it with each diapering. At some hospitals, a plastic ring is used instead of a bandage. The ring will remain on the end of the penis until the edge of the circumcision has healed, usually within a week. The ring will drop off on its own. It's OK to wash the penis as it's healing. See page 97 for cleansing instructions.

Problems after a circumcision are rare, but call your baby's care provider in the following situations:

▶ Your baby doesn't urinate normally 12 to 18 hours after the circumcision.

▶ Bleeding or redness around the tip of the penis is persistent.

▶ The penis tip is significantly swollen.

Before circumcision (left), the foreskin of the penis extends over the end of the penis (glans). After the brief operation, the glans is exposed (right).

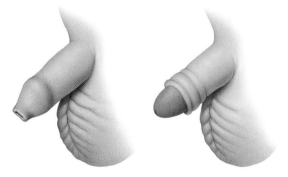

© MFMER

- A foul-smelling drainage comes from the penis tip, or there are crusted sores that contain fluid.
- The ring is still in place two weeks after the circumcision.

SCREENING TESTS

Before your baby leaves the hospital, a small amount of his or her blood is taken and sent to the state health department or a private laboratory working in collaboration with the state laboratory. This sample, which may be taken from a vein in your baby's arm or a tiny nick made on the heel, is analyzed to detect the presence of rare but important genetic diseases. This testing is referred to as newborn screening. Results are generally available in one to two weeks.

Occasionally, a baby needs to have the test repeated. Don't be alarmed if this happens to your newborn. To ensure that every newborn with any of these conditions is identified, even borderline results are rechecked. Retesting is especially common for premature babies.

Each state independently operates its newborn screening program, resulting in slight differences between the tests offered. The American College of Medical Genetics recommends a panel of tests to check for about 40 targeted diseases. Some states check for additional diseases. You also may request a specific genetic test if you feel your child may be at risk of a certain genetic disorder.

Some of the diseases that can be detected by the panel include:

Biotinidase deficiency This deficiency is caused by the lack of an enzyme called biotinidase. Signs and symptoms of the disorder include seizures, developmental delay, eczema and hearing loss. With early diagnosis and treatment, all signs and symptoms can be prevented.

Congenital adrenal hyperplasia (CAH) This group of disorders is caused by a deficiency of certain hormones. Signs and symptoms may include lethargy, vomiting, muscle weakness and dehydration. Infants with mild forms are at risk of reproductive and growth difficulties. Severe cases can cause kidney dysfunction and even death. Lifelong hormone treatment can suppress the condition.

Congenital hypothyroidism About 1 in 3,000 babies have a thyroid hormone deficiency that slows growth and brain development. Left untreated, it can result in mental retardation and stunted growth. With early detection and treatment, normal development is possible.

Cystic fibrosis Cystic fibrosis causes the body to produce abnormally thickened mucous secretions in the lungs and digestive system. Signs and symptoms generally include salty-tasting skin, poor weight gain and, eventually, persistent coughing and shortness of breath. Affected newborns can develop life-threatening lung infections and intestinal obstructions. With early detection and treatment, infants diagnosed with cystic fibrosis often live longer and in better health than they did in past years.

Galactosemia Babies born with galactosemia can't metabolize galactose, a sugar found in milk. Although newborns with this condition typically appear normal, they may develop vomiting, diarrhea, jaundice and liver damage within a few weeks of their first milk feedings. Untreated, the disorder may result in mental disabilities, blindness, growth failure

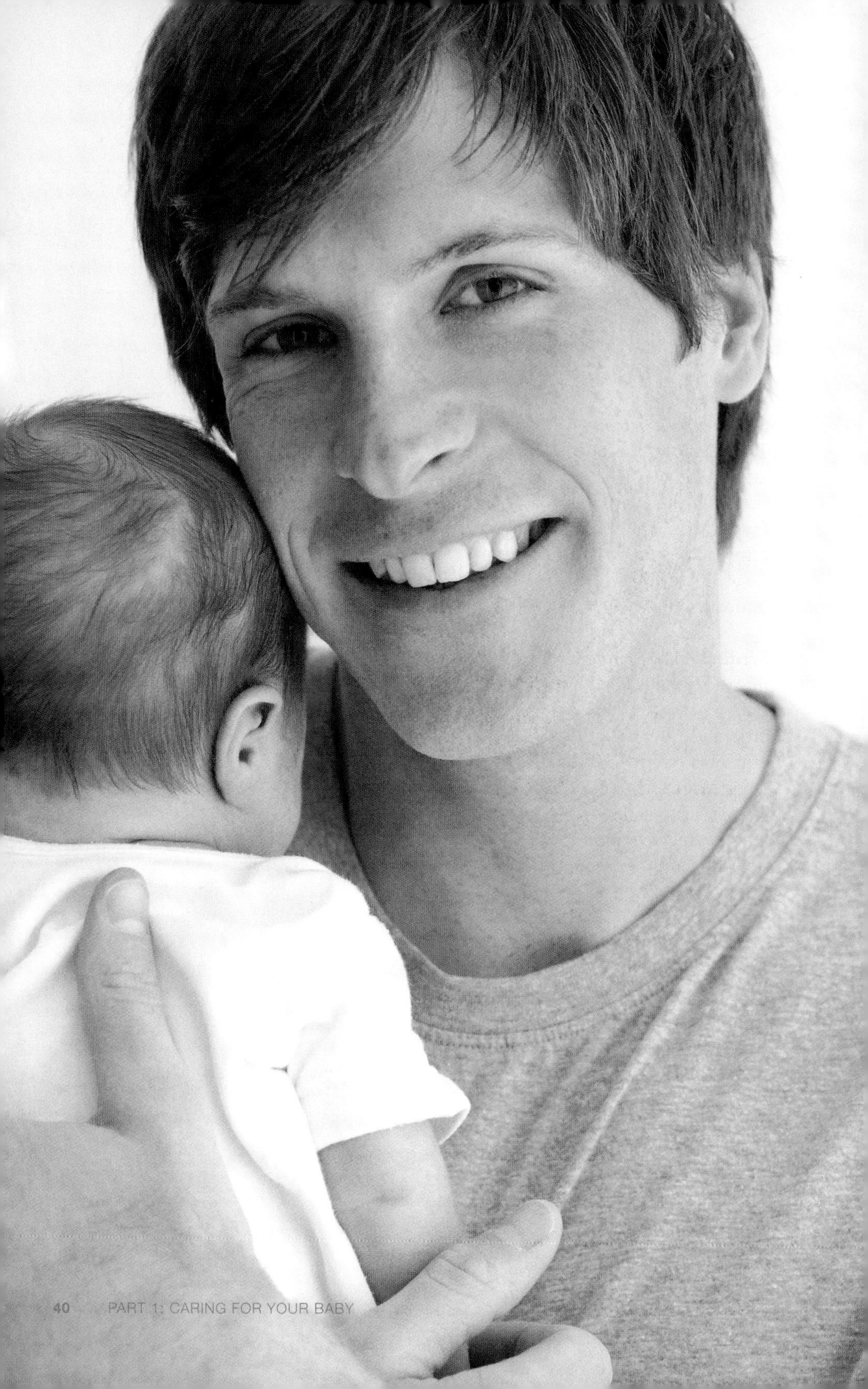

and, in severe cases, death. Treatment includes eliminating milk and all other dairy (galactose) products from the diet.

Homocystinuria Caused by an enzyme deficiency, homocystinuria can lead to eye problems, mental disabilities, skeletal abnormalities and abnormal blood clotting. With early detection and management — including a special diet and dietary supplements — growth and development should be normal.

Maple syrup urine disease (MSUD) This disorder affects the metabolism of amino acids. Newborns with this condition typically appear normal, but by the first week of life they experience feeding difficulties, lethargy and poor growth. Left untreated, MSUD can lead to coma or death.

Medium-chain acyl-CoA dehydrogenase (MCAD) deficiency This rare hereditary disease results from the lack of an enzyme required to convert fat to energy. Babies with MCAD deficiency develop serious vomiting, lethargy that can worsen into coma, seizures, liver failure and severely low blood sugar. With early detection and monitoring, children diagnosed with MCAD deficiency can lead normal lives.

Phenylketonuria (PKU) Babies with PKU retain excessive amounts of phenylalanine, an amino acid found in the protein of almost all foods. Without treatment, PKU can cause mental and motor disabilities, poor growth rate, and seizures. With early detection and treatment, growth and development should be normal.

Sickle cell disease This inherited disease prevents blood cells from circulating easily throughout the body. Infants with sickle cell disease experience an increased susceptibility to infection and slow growth rates. The disease can cause bouts of pain and damage to vital organs such as the lungs, kidneys and brain. With early medical treatment, the complications of sickle cell disease can be minimized.

Hearing screening While your baby is in the hospital, he or she may have a hearing test. Although hearing tests are not done routinely at every hospital, newborn hearing screening is becoming widely available. The testing can detect possible hearing loss in the first days of a baby's life. If possible hearing loss is found, further tests may be done to confirm the results.

Two tests are used to screen a newborn's hearing. Both are quick (about 10 minutes), painless and can be done while your baby sleeps. One test measures how the brain responds to sound. Clicks or tones are played through soft earphones into the baby's ears while electrodes taped on the baby's head measure the brain's response. Another test measures specific responses to sound waves that enter a baby's ear. As clicks or tones are played into a baby's ear, a probe placed inside the ear canal measures the response.

CHAPTER 3

Feeding baby

If it seems like all you do these days is feed your baby, you know what? You're right! Newborns may not eat a lot, but they eat often. And in those first few weeks with your new son or daughter, your life will revolve around satisfying his or her hunger. Just when you think you have a moment to relax or perhaps get some laundry done, wouldn't you know it, baby wants to eat again!

At first, all of these feedings may seem like a real chore. For almost every new parent, early days with a newborn are often demanding and exhausting. Both you and your baby are adapting to a new reality, and that takes time.

Throughout this adjustment, remember that feeding your newborn is about more than just nourishment. It's a time of cuddling and closeness that helps build the connection between you and your baby. You want to make every feeding a time to bond with your baby. Cherish this time before your baby is old enough to start feeding himself or herself. That time will come soon enough.

BREAST VS. BOTTLE

Some women know right from the start what they'll do — breast-feed or bottle-feed — while others struggle.

Most child health organizations advocate breast-feeding, and "breast is best" is a commonly used phrase. There's no doubt, breast-feeding is a wonderful way to nourish a newborn — breast milk provides numerous benefits. Mayo Clinic experts agree.

However, care providers also realize that not all women are the same, and people's life situations are different. Depending on your circumstances, certain factors may lead you to choose infant formula instead of breast milk. Or you may opt for a combination of both breast milk and formula.

Some women who choose the bottle instead of the breast are bothered by their decision. They worry they're not being a good mother or putting the needs of their child first. If you're among this group, don't shower yourself in guilt.

Such negative thinking isn't good for you — or for your baby.

Feeding, regardless of how it's delivered — breast milk or formula, breast or bottle — promotes intimacy.

Know that both options will provide your child the nutrition he or she needs to grow and thrive.

Questions to ask If you haven't had your baby yet and you're debating whether to breast-feed or bottle-feed, you might consider these questions:

▶ *What does your care provider suggest?* Your care provider will likely be very supportive of breast-feeding unless you have specific health issues — such as a certain disease or disease treatment — that make formula-feeding a better choice.

▶ *Do you understand both methods?* Many women have misconceptions about breast-feeding. Learn as much as you can about feeding your baby. Seek out expert advice if needed.

▶ *Do you plan to return to work?* If so, how will that impact breast-feeding? Does your place of work have accommodations available where you can use a breast pump, if that's your plan?

▶ *How does your partner feel about the decision?* The decision is ultimately yours, but it's a good idea to take your partner's feelings into consideration.

▶ *How have other mothers you trust and respect made their decisions?* If they had it to do over again, would they make the same choices?

BREAST-FEEDING

Breast-feeding is highly encouraged because it has so many known health benefits. The longer you breast-feed, the greater the chances that your baby will experience these benefits, and the more likely they are to last.

Benefits for baby Breast milk provides babies with:

Ideal nutrition Breast milk has just the right nutrients, in just the right amounts, to nourish your baby completely. It contains the fats, proteins, carbohydrates, vitamins and minerals that a baby needs for growth, digestion and brain development. Breast milk is also individualized; the composition of your breast milk changes as your baby grows.

Protection against disease Research shows that breast milk may help keep your baby from getting sick. Breast milk provides antibodies that help your baby's immune system fight off common childhood illnesses. Breast-fed babies may have fewer colds, ear infections and urinary tract infections than do babies who aren't breast-fed. Breast-fed babies may also have fewer problems with asthma, food allergies and skin conditions, such as eczema. They may be less likely to experience a reduction in the number of red blood cells (anemia). Breast-feeding, research suggests, might also help to protect against sudden infant death syndrome (SIDS), also known as crib death, and it may offer a slight reduction in the risk of childhood leukemia. Breast milk may even protect against disease long term. As adults, people who were breast-fed may have a lowered risk of heart attack and stroke — due to lower cholesterol levels — and may be less likely to develop diabetes.

Protection against obesity Studies indicate that babies who are breast-fed are less likely to become obese as adults.

Easy digestion Breast milk is easier for babies to digest than is formula or cow's milk. Because breast milk doesn't remain in the stomach as long as formula does, breast-fed babies spit up less. They have less gas and less constipation. They also have less diarrhea, because breast milk appears to kill some diarrhea-causing germs and helps a baby's digestive system grow and function.

Benefits for mother For mothers, the benefits include:

Faster recovery from childbirth The baby's suckling triggers your body to release oxytocin, a hormone that causes your uterus to contract. This means that the uterus returns to its pre-pregnancy size more quickly after delivery than it does if you use formula.

Suppresses ovulation Breast-feeding delays the return of ovulation and, therefore, your period, which may help extend the time between pregnancies. However, breast-feeding is not a guarantee against pregnancy. You can still become pregnant while breast-feeding.

Possible long-term health benefits Breast-feeding may reduce your risk of getting breast cancer before menopause. Breast-feeding also appears to provide some protection from uterine and ovarian cancers.

Other issues Beyond potential health benefits, other benefits of breast-feeding include:
- *Convenience.* Many mothers find breast-feeding to be more convenient than bottle-feeding. It can be done anywhere, at any time, whenever your baby shows signs of hunger. Plus, no equipment is necessary. Breast milk is always available — and at the perfect temperature. Because you don't need to prepare a bottle and you can nurse lying down, nighttime feedings may be easier.
- *Cost savings.* Breast-feeding can save money because you don't need to buy formula, and you may not need bottles.

However, breast-feeding can also present some challenges and inconveniences. Drawbacks to breast-feeding for some parents include:
- *Exclusive feeding by mom.* In the early weeks, parenting can be physically demanding. At first, newborns nurse every two to three hours, day and night. That can be tiring for mom, and dad may feel left out. Eventually, you can express milk with a breast pump, which will enable your partner or others to take over some feedings. It may take about a month before your milk production is well established so that you can use a pump to express and collect breast milk.
- *Restrictions for mom.* Women who are breast-feeding generally should avoid alcohol. However, it may be OK to have a minimal amount occasionally. Alcohol can pass through breast milk to the baby.
- *Sore nipples.* Some women may experience sore nipples and, at times, breast infections. These can often be avoided with proper positioning and technique. A lactation consultant or your care provider can advise you on proper positioning.
- *Other physical side effects.* When you're lactating, your body's hormones may keep your vagina relatively dry. Using a water-based lubricating jelly can help treat this problem. It may also take time for your menstrual cycle to once again establish a regular pattern.

WHAT GOES IN, COMES OUT

While you're breast-feeding, keep in mind that the foods and other items you ingest can be passed on to your baby through your breast milk.

A couple of things to remember while breast-feeding:

- *Avoid or limit alcohol.* If you do have an occasional drink, keep it to a minimal amount.
- *Limit caffeine.* Drink mainly decaffeinated beverages.
- *Check your medications.* Most are safe to take, but consult your child's care provider first.

Only rarely do the foods you eat cause your baby to be fussy or gassy. Babies can get fussy for many reasons, and they can experience gas from the air they swallow when they cry or eat. However, if you suspect your child may be intolerant to something you ate, try eliminating the food for a while and see how your baby responds.

Milk production Early in your pregnancy, your milk-producing (mammary) glands prepare for nursing. By about the sixth month of your pregnancy, your breasts are ready to produce milk.

Your milk supply gradually increases between the third and fifth days after your baby's birth. As the milk-producing glands fill with milk, your breasts will be full and sometimes tender. They may also feel lumpy or hard.

Milk is released from the glands when a baby nurses. The milk is propelled down milk ducts, which are located just behind the dark circle of tissue that surrounds the nipple (areola). The sucking action of the baby compresses the areola, forcing milk out through tiny openings in the nipple.

Your baby's sucking stimulates nerve endings in your areola and nipple, sending a message to your brain to release the hormone oxytocin. Oxytocin acts on the milk-producing glands in your breasts, causing the ejection of milk to your nursing baby. This release is called the let-down reflex, which may be accompanied by a tingling sensation.

The let-down reflex makes your milk available to your baby. Although your baby's sucking is the main stimulus for milk let-down, other stimuli may have the same effect. For example, your baby's cry — or even thoughts of your baby or the sounds of rippling water — may set things in motion.

Regardless of whether you plan to breast-feed, your body produces milk after you have a baby. If you don't breast-feed, your milk supply eventually stops. If you do breast-feed, your body's milk production is based on supply and demand. The more frequently your breasts are emptied, the more milk they produce.

Getting started If this is your first experience at breast-feeding, you may be nervous, which is normal. If it goes easily for you right from the first feeding, that's wonderful. If not, be patient. Like most anything new, it often takes some practice to get it right.

Breast-feeding may be a natural process, but that doesn't mean it comes easily to all mothers. Breast-feeding is a new skill for both you and your baby. Nothing can really prepare your nipples for a nursing baby. If this is your first child, you may not be comfortable holding a baby — let alone putting a baby to your breast. It may take a few attempts before you and your baby get the hang of it.

The time to begin breast-feeding is right after the baby is born. If possible, put baby to your breast in the delivery room. Early skin-to-skin contact has been shown to improve breast-feeding outcomes.

While you're in the hospital, ask a lactation consultant or other medical staff to assist you. These experts can provide hands-on instruction and helpful hints. After you leave the hospital or birthing center, you might want to arrange for a public health nurse who is knowledgeable about infant feeding to visit you for additional one-on-one instruction.

It's a good idea to take a class on breast-feeding. Often, information on breast-feeding is offered as part of childbirth classes, or you may be able to sign up for a class. Most hospitals and birthing centers also offer classes on feeding a newborn.

Supplies to have on hand Purchase a couple of nursing bras. They provide important support for lactating breasts. What distinguishes nursing bras from regular bras is that both cups open to the front, usually with a simple maneuver that you can manage unobtrusively while you hold your baby.

You'll also need nursing pads, which can absorb milk that leaks from your breasts. Slim and disposable, they can be slipped between the breast and bra to soak up milk leakage. Avoid those with plastic shields, which prevent air circulation around the nipples. Nursing pads can be worn continuously or on occasion. Some women don't bother with the pads, but most women find them helpful.

Feeding positions When it's feeding time, find a quiet location and take

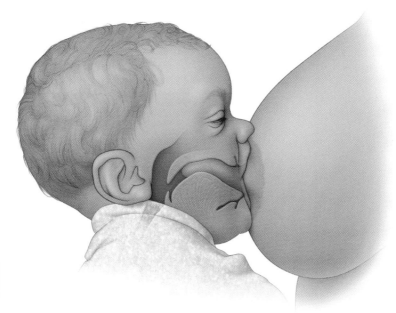

© MFMER

advantage of this time with your baby. Have a drink of water or juice at hand because it's common to feel thirsty when your milk lets down. Put the phone nearby or turn it off. If you would like, place a book or the TV remote control within reach.

Get into a comfortable position. Both you and baby should be comfortable. Whether in your hospital bed or a chair, sit up straight. Put a pillow behind the small of your back for support. If you opt for a chair, choose one with low armrests, or place a pillow under your arms for support.

Move your baby across your body so that he or she faces your breast, with his or her mouth near your nipple. Make sure your baby's whole body is facing you — tummy to tummy — with ear, shoulder and hip in a straight line. Begin by placing your free hand up under your breast to support it for breast-feeding.

Support the weight of your breast in your hand while squeezing lightly to point the nipple straight forward.

Different women find different nursing positions most comfortable. Experiment with these positions to see which works best for you:

Cross-cradle hold Bring your baby across the front of your body, tummy to tummy. Hold your baby with the arm opposite to the breast you're feeding with. Support the back of the baby's head with your open hand. This hold allows you especially good control as you position your baby to latch on. With your free hand, support your breast from the underside in a U-shaped hold to align with baby's mouth.

Cradle hold Cradle your baby in your arm, with your baby's head resting comfortably in the crook of the elbow on the

Cross-cradle hold

© MFMER

same side as the breast you're feeding with. Your forearm supports your baby's back. Use your free hand to support your breast.

Football (clutch) hold In this position, you hold your baby in much the same way a running back tucks a football under his arm. Hold your baby at your side on one arm, with your elbow bent and your open hand firmly supporting your baby's head faceup at the level of your breast. Your baby's torso will rest on your forearm. Put a pillow at your side to support your arm. A chair with broad, low arms works best.

With your free hand, support your breast from the underside in a C-shaped hold to align with baby's mouth. Because the baby isn't positioned near the abdomen, the football hold is popular among mothers recovering from C-sections. It's also a frequent choice of women who have large breasts or who are nursing premature or small babies.

Side-lying hold Although most new mothers learn to breast-feed in a sitting position, at times you may prefer to nurse while lying down. Use the hand of your lower arm to help keep your baby's head positioned at your breast. With your upper arm and hand, reach across your body and grasp your breast, touching your nipple to your baby's lips. After your baby latches on firmly, you can use your lower arm to support your own head and your upper hand and arm to help support your baby.

Nursing basics If your baby's mouth doesn't open immediately to accept your breast, touch the nipple to your baby's mouth or cheek. If your baby is hungry and interested in nursing, his or her mouth should open. As soon as your

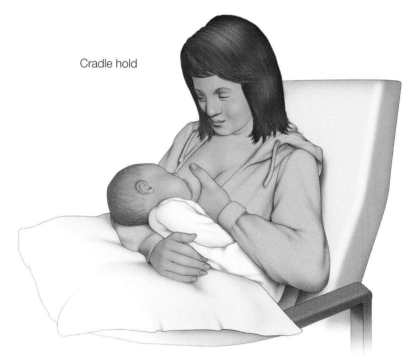

Cradle hold

© MFMER

baby's mouth is opened wide, like a yawn, move his or her mouth onto your breast. You want your baby to receive as much nipple and areola as possible. It might take a few attempts before your baby opens his or her mouth wide enough to latch on properly. You can also express some milk, which may encourage baby to latch on.

As your baby starts suckling and your nipple is being stretched in your baby's mouth, you may feel some surging sensations. After a few suckles, those sensations should subside a bit. If they don't, sandwich the breast more and draw baby's head in more closely.

If that doesn't produce comfort, gently remove baby from your breast, taking care to release the suction first. To break the suction, gently insert the tip of your finger into the corner of your baby's mouth. Slowly push your finger between your baby's gums until you feel the re-

lease. Repeat this procedure until your baby has latched on properly. You want there to be a firm bond of suction.

You'll know that milk is flowing and your baby is swallowing if there's a strong, steady, rhythmic motion visible in your baby's cheek. If your breast is blocking your baby's nose, elevating your baby slightly, or angling the baby's head back and in, may help provide a little breathing room. If your baby attaches and sucks correctly — even if the arrangement feels awkward at first — the position is correct.

Once nursing begins, you can relax the supporting arm and pull your baby's lower body closer to you.

Frequency Because breast milk is easily digested, breast-fed babies usually are hungry every few hours at first. During those early days, it may seem that all you do is breast-feed!

Football hold

© MFMER

Side-lying hold

© MFMER

Most newborns eat eight to 12 times a day — about every two to three hours. By six to eight weeks after birth, your baby will probably begin to go longer between feedings. During growth spurts, your baby may take more at each feeding or want to breast-feed more often. Trust your body's ability to keep up with the increased demand. The more often your baby nurses, the more milk your breasts produce.

Length In general, let your baby nurse as long as he or she wants. The length of feedings may vary considerably. However, on average, most babies nurse for about half an hour.

Offer your baby both breasts at each feeding. Allow your baby to end the feeding on the first side. Then, after burping your baby, offer the other side. (See burping positions on page 68.) Alternate starting sides to equalize the stimulation each breast receives.

You want baby to finish one breast before switching to the other side because the milk that comes first from your breast, called the foremilk, is rich in pro-

tein for growth. But the longer your baby sucks, the more he or she gets the hind-milk, which is rich in calories and fat, and therefore helps your baby gain weight and grow. So wait until your baby seems ready to quit before offering him or her your other breast.

Amount A baby's need for frequent feeding isn't a sign that baby isn't getting enough; it reflects the easy digestibility of breast milk. If your baby is satisfied after feeding and is growing, you can be confident that you're doing well.

If you're concerned that baby may not be getting enough milk, ask yourself these questions:

▶ *Is baby gaining weight?* Steady weight gain is often the most reliable sign that a baby is getting enough to eat. Although most babies lose weight soon after birth, it's typically regained — and then some — within 10 days to two weeks.

▶ *Can I hear baby swallowing?* If you listen carefully, you'll be able to hear your baby swallowing. Also look for a strong, steady, rhythmic motion in your baby's lower jaw. A small amount of milk may even dribble out of your baby's mouth.

▶ *How do my breasts feel?* When your baby is latched on successfully, you'll feel a gentle pulling sensation on your breast — rather than a pinching or biting sensation on your nipple. Your breasts may feel firm or full before the feeding, and softer or emptier afterward.

▶ *What about baby's diapers?* By the fourth day after birth, expect your baby to have six to eight wet diapers a day. Also expect regular bowel movements. The stool will be dark and sticky for the first couple of days, eventually becoming seedy, loose and golden yellow.

▶ *Does baby seem healthy?* A baby who seems satisfied after feedings and is alert and active at other times is likely getting enough milk. Also look for a healthy skin tone.

Support If you're having problems breast-feeding, or you're worried that baby isn't getting enough milk, ask for help. You know your baby best. If you sense something isn't right, don't be afraid to contact your baby's care provider or a lactation consultant.

Most hospitals have lactation consultants on staff who can answer your questions or help you resolve any problems you may encounter.

Remember, however, just as your body knows what it's doing during pregnancy and childbirth, your body knows how to support a breast-feeding baby. Have faith in your body's ability to meet your baby's nutritional needs.

VITAMIN D

Talk with your baby's care provider about vitamin D supplements for your baby. While breast milk is the best source of nutrients for babies, it likely won't provide enough vitamin D. Your baby needs vitamin D to absorb calcium and phosphorus. Too little vitamin D can cause rickets, a softening and weakening of bones.

Since sun exposure — an important source of vitamin D — isn't recommended for babies younger than 6 months, supplements are the best way to prevent vitamin D deficiency in infants.

The American Academy of Pediatrics and the Institute of Medicine recommend that babies who are breast-fed receive 400 international units (IU) of liquid vitamin D a day — starting in the first few days after birth. Continue giving your baby vitamin D as long as you breast-feed.

As your baby gets older and you add solid foods to his or her diet, you can help your baby meet the daily vitamin D requirement by providing foods that contain vitamin D — such as oily fish, eggs and fortified foods. Keep in mind, however, that most babies won't consistently eat these foods during their first year.

When giving your baby liquid vitamin D, make sure you don't exceed the recommended amount. Carefully read the instructions that come with the supplement and use only the dropper that's provided.

PUMPING YOUR BREASTS

During the first several weeks of your child's life, it's best to nurse exclusively to help you and your baby learn how to breast-feed and to be sure your milk supply becomes well established.

Once your milk supply is established and you feel confident that the two of you are doing well with breast-feeding, you may give your baby an occasional bottle of breast milk. This allows others, such as your partner or a grandparent, an opportunity to feed the baby. And it provides you a break, if you need one.

Keep in mind that the feel of a bottle nipple in a baby's mouth is different from that of the breast. The way a baby sucks from a bottle nipple also is different. So it may take some practice for your baby to be comfortable with a bottle nipple. And beware that he or she may be reluctant to take a bottle from mom because baby associates mother's voice and scent with breast-feeding.

Most breast-feeding mothers find using a breast pump easier than expressing milk manually. A lactation consultant or your baby's care provider can help you determine what type of pump — manual or electric — is best for you, and offer help and support if problems arise.

In deciding on a pump, here are some factors to consider:

- *How often will you use the breast pump?* If you'll be away from the baby only occasionally and your milk supply is well established, a simple hand pump may be all you need. They're small and inexpensive. If you're returning to work full time, or planning to be away from your baby for more than a few hours a day, you may want to invest in an electric pump.
- *Will you need to pump as quickly as possible?* A typical pumping session lasts about 15 minutes a breast. If you'll be pumping at work or in other time-crunched situations, you may want to invest in an electric breast pump that allows you to pump both breasts at once. Double breast pumps can cut pumping time in half.
- *How much can you afford to spend?* While manual models generally cost less than $50, electric pumps that include a carrying case and insulated section for storing milk may cost more than $200. Some hospitals or medical supply stores rent hospital-grade breast pumps, and some health insurance plans cover the cost of buying or renting a breast pump.
- *Is the pump easy to assemble and transport?* If the breast pump is difficult to assemble, take apart or clean, it's bound to be frustrating, which may reduce your enthusiasm for pumping. If you'll be toting the pump to work every day, or traveling with the pump, look for a lightweight model. Some breast pumps come in a carrying case with an insulated section for storing expressed milk. Also keep noise level in mind. Some electric models are quieter than are others. If it's important to be discreet, make sure the pump's noise level is acceptable.
- *Is the suction adjustable?* What's comfortable for one woman may be uncomfortable for another. Choose a pump that allows you to control the degree of suction.

Storing breast milk Once you start pumping, it's important to know how to safely and properly store your expressed breast milk.

Container Store expressed breast milk in capped glass or plastic containers that

GOING BACK TO WORK

With a little planning and preparation, you can do both — breast-feed and return to work. Some mothers work at home, while some arrange to have their babies brought to them for feedings or they go to the babies. Most mothers, though, rely on the help of a breast pump.

You can provide your baby with bottled breast milk by expressing milk while at work, storing it and saving the milk for the next day. Using a double breast pump is the most effective. A double breast pump requires about 15 minutes of pumping every three to four hours. If you need to increase your milk supply, nurse and pump more often.

If you're worried that pumping at work may pose a problem or you prefer not to, brainstorm ways to make it convenient. For example, pump after the morning feeding and after the feeding when you return home. As long as all of your milk produced in 24 hours is removed either by your baby or from pumping, you'll maintain a good supply.

There are no rules set in stone. Go with whatever works best for you.

have been cleaned in a dishwasher or washed in hot, soapy water and thoroughly rinsed. Consider boiling the containers after washing them if the quality of your water supply is questionable.

If you store breast milk for three days or less, you can also use a plastic bag designed for milk collection and storage. While economical, plastic bags aren't recommended for long-term breast milk storage because they may spill, leak and become contaminated more easily than hard-sided containers. Also, certain components of breast milk may adhere to the soft plastic bags during long-term breast milk storage, which could deprive your baby of essential nutrients.

Method You can store expressed breast milk in the refrigerator or freezer. Using waterproof labels and ink, label each container with the date and time. Place the containers in the back of the refrigerator or freezer, where the temperature is the coolest. Use your earliest milk first.

To minimize waste, fill individual containers with the amount of milk your baby will need for one feeding. Also consider storing smaller portions — 1 to 2 ounces — for unexpected situations or delays in regular feedings. Keep in mind that breast milk expands as it freezes, so don't fill containers to the brim.

You can add freshly expressed breast milk to refrigerated or frozen milk you expressed earlier in the same day. However, be sure to cool the freshly expressed breast milk in the refrigerator or a cooler with ice packs for at least one hour before adding it to previously chilled milk. Don't add warm breast milk to frozen breast milk because it will cause the frozen milk to partially thaw. Keep milk expressed on different days in separate containers.

Be aware that during storage expressed breast milk will separate — causing thick, white cream to rise to the top of the container. Before feeding your baby, gently swirl the contents of the container to ensure that the creamy portion of the milk is evenly distributed.

Expiration The length of time you can safely keep expressed breast milk depends on the storage method.

- *Milk stored at room temperature.* Freshly expressed breast milk can be kept at room temperature — up to 77 F — for six hours. If you won't use the milk that quickly, store it in the refrigerator or freezer.
- *Milk stored in an insulated cooler.* Freshly expressed breast milk can be stored in an insulated cooler with ice packs for up to one day. Then use the milk, or transfer the containers to the refrigerator or freezer.
- *Milk stored in the refrigerator.* Freshly expressed breast milk can be stored in the refrigerator at 39 F for up to eight days.
- *Milk stored in the freezer.* Breast milk can be stored in a freezer compartment inside the refrigerator at 5 F for two weeks. If your freezer has a separate door and a temperature of 0 F, breast milk can be stored for three to six months. If you have a deep freezer that's opened infrequently and has a temperature of -4 F, breast milk can be stored for six to 12 months.

Generally, though, the sooner you use the milk, the better. Some research suggests that the longer you store breast milk — whether in the refrigerator or in the freezer — the greater the loss of vitamin C in the milk. Other studies have shown that refrigeration beyond two days may reduce the bacteria-killing properties of breast milk, and long-term freezer storage may lower the quality of breast milk's lipids.

Thawing Thaw the oldest milk first. Simply place the frozen container in the refrigerator the night before you intend to use it. You can also gently warm the milk by placing it under warm running water or in a bowl of warm water. Avoid letting the water touch the mouth of the container.

Never thaw frozen breast milk at room temperature, which enables bacteria to multiply in the milk. Also, don't heat a frozen bottle on the stove or in the microwave. These methods can create an uneven distribution of heat and destroy the milk's antibodies. Use thawed breast milk within 24 hours. Discard any remaining milk. Don't refreeze thawed or partially thawed breast milk.

Thawed breast milk may smell different from freshly expressed milk or taste soapy due to the breakdown of milk fats, but it's still safe for your baby to drink. The milk may separate, so you may need to gently swirl the thawed milk so it's mixed evenly.

KEEPING YOURSELF HEALTHY

If you're like most new mothers, your attention may be focused intently on the needs of your baby. Although this commitment is completely reasonable, don't forget about your needs. If your baby is to thrive, he or she needs a healthy mother.

Nutrition The best approach to nutrition while breast-feeding isn't unlike the best approach at other times in your life: Eat a healthy, balanced diet. There are no special foods to avoid when you're breast-feeding. (However, you may find it helpful to limit certain foods that can show up in breast milk if you feel your baby doesn't tolerate them well.) In addition, drink 6 to 8 cups of fluids each day. Water, milk and juice are good choices.

Small amounts of coffee, tea and soft drinks are fine.

As a new mother, it can be hard to prepare healthy meals each day. You may find it easier to snack on healthy foods throughout the day. Partners can help support a breast-feeding mother by bringing her refreshments while she's nursing.

Rest Try to get as much rest as you can, as hard as that may seem at times. You'll feel more energetic, you'll eat better, and you'll enjoy your new baby best when you're rested. Rest promotes the production of breast milk by enhancing the production of milk-producing hormones. The soothing effect of breast-feeding can

make you feel sleepy, so try and sleep on baby's schedule.

Don't be afraid to ask others to help out with daily chores so that you can rest. Young children may appreciate being able to help mother and baby by pitching in around the house.

Breast care As you start to breast-feed, you may experience some minor, occasional problems, which often can be easily treated.

Fullness A few days after your baby is born, your breasts may become full, firm and tender, making it challenging for your baby to grasp your nipple. This swelling, called engorgement, also causes congestion within your breasts, which makes your milk flow slower. So even if your baby can latch on, he or she may be less than satisfied with the results.

To manage engorgement, express some milk by hand before trying to breast-feed. Support with one hand the breast you intend to express. With your other hand, gently stroke your breast inward toward your areola. Then place your thumb and forefinger at the top and bottom of the breast just behind the areola. As you gently compress the breast between your fingers, milk should flow or squirt out of the nipple. Taking a warm shower may also result in let-down of milk and provide some engorgement relief. You can also use a breast pump to express some milk.

As you release your milk, you'll begin to feel your areola and nipple soften. Once enough milk is released, your baby can comfortably latch on and nurse. Frequent, lengthy nursing sessions are the best means to avoid engorgement.

Nurse your baby regularly and try not to miss a feeding. Wearing a nursing bra both day and night will help support engorged breasts and may make you feel more comfortable.

If your breasts are sore after nursing, apply an ice pack to reduce swelling. Some women find that a warm shower relieves breast tenderness. Fortunately, the period of engorgement is usually brief, lasting no more than a few days following delivery.

Nipple discomfort When you first begin breast-feeding, you may experience some initial nipple discomfort as baby latches on, but the discomfort should subside as your baby feeds.

Sore or cracked nipples are usually caused by incorrect positioning and latching. At each feeding, you want to make sure that the baby has the areola and not just the nipple in his or her mouth. You also want to be certain that the baby's head isn't out of line with his or her body. This position causes pulling at the nipple.

To care for your nipples, express milk onto your nipples and let them air-dry after each feeding. You don't need to wash your nipples after nursing. There are built-in lubricants around the areola that provide a natural salve. Soap and water with daily bathing is fine. Afterward, let your nipples air-dry.

Blocked milk ducts Sometimes, milk ducts in the breast become clogged, causing milk to back up. Blocked ducts can be felt through the skin as small, tender lumps or larger areas of hardness. Because blocked ducts can lead to an infection, you should treat the problem right away.

The best way to open up blocked ducts is to let your baby empty the affected breast, offering that breast first at each feeding. If your baby doesn't empty the affected breast, express milk from it

by hand or by breast pump. It may also help to apply a warm compress before nursing and to massage the affected breast. If the problem doesn't go away with self-treatment, call a lactation consultant or your care provider for advice.

Breast infection Infection (mastitis) may be caused by a failure to empty your breasts at feedings. Germs may also gain entry into your milk ducts from cracked nipples and from your baby's mouth. These germs are not harmful to your baby; everyone has them. They just don't belong in your breast tissues.

Mastitis starts with flu-like signs and symptoms such as a fever, chills and body aches. Redness, swelling and breast tenderness then follow. If you develop such signs and symptoms, call your care provider. You may need antibiotics, in addition to rest and more fluids.

Keep nursing if you're taking antibiotics. Treatment for mastitis doesn't harm your baby, and emptying your breasts during feedings will help to prevent clogged milk ducts, another possible source of the condition. If your breasts are really painful, hand express some milk from them as you soak your breasts in a bath of warm water.

WEANING

There will come a time when it's best for baby and you to transition from the breast to a cup. Your baby is growing up and he or she is ready to take the next big step. Or, if your child is not ready for a cup, you may need to transition your child from the breast to a bottle.

Breast-feeding is an intimate activity for you and your child. You may have mixed emotions about letting go. By taking a gradual approach to weaning — and offering plenty of love and affection — you can help your child make a smooth transition. Weaning doesn't have to be difficult. Choose the right time and do what you can to make it a growing experience.

Timing You may wonder when's the best time to start weaning. There really isn't a right or wrong answer.

Breast-feeding until your baby is 1 is recommended. Breast milk contains the right balance of nutrients for your baby and boosts your baby's immune system. Still, when to start weaning your child is a personal decision.

It's often easiest to begin weaning when your baby initiates the process — which may be sooner or later than you expect. Weaning often begins naturally at 6 months, when solid foods are typically introduced. Some children begin to gradually turn away from breast milk and seek other forms of nutrition and comfort at around age 1, when they've begun eating a wide variety of solid foods and may be able to drink from a cup. Other children may not initiate weaning until their toddler years, when they become less willing to sit still during breast-feeding.

You may also decide when to start the weaning process yourself. This may be more difficult than following your child's lead — but can be done with some extra care and sensitivity.

Whenever you start weaning your baby from the breast, stay focused on your child's needs as well as your own. Resist comparing your situation with that of other families, and consider rethinking any deadlines you may have set for weaning when you were pregnant or when your baby was a newborn.

You might consider delaying weaning if your child isn't feeling well or is teething. He or she will be more likely to handle the transition well if you're both in good health.

You might also consider postponing weaning if a major change has occurred at home, such as moving to a new home or the addition of a new family member. You don't want to add more stress at what may already be a stressful time for your child.

Some research also suggests that exclusive breast-feeding for at least four months may have a protective effect for children who have a family history of food allergies. If food allergies run in your family, talk to your child's doctor about the potential benefits of delaying weaning.

Method When you start the weaning process, take it slow. Eliminate one breast-feeding session a day every two to three days. Slowly tapering off the number of times you breast-feed each day will cause your milk supply to gradually diminish and prevent discomfort from engorgement.

Keep in mind that children tend to be more attached to the first and last feedings of the day, when the need for comfort is greater — so it might be helpful to drop a midday breast-feeding session first. You might also choose to wean your baby from breast milk during the day but continue breast-feeding at night. It's up to you and your child. When eliminating a breast-feeding session, try to avoid sitting in your usual breast-feeding spots with your child. Instead, offer a distraction, such as a book, toy or fun activity.

Depending on your approach, weaning could take days, weeks or months. Remember, however, that rushing the weaning process may be upsetting for your child and cause engorgement for you. Be patient.

Nutrition If you wean your child before age 1, substitute breast milk with iron-fortified formula. Ask your child's doctor to recommend a formula. Don't give your child cow's milk until after his or her first birthday. You can wean your child to a bottle and then a cup or, if your child seems ready, directly to a cup.

If you're introducing your child to a bottle for the first time, do so at a time when your child isn't extremely hungry and may have more patience. It also may help if another caregiver introduces the bottle, since some children may refuse a bottle when the breast is available.

Choose a bottle nipple with a slow flow at first. If you use a bottle nipple with a fast flow, your child may become frustrated with the slower flow of milk during breast-feeding.

BOTTLE-FEEDING

Some mothers prefer to bottle-feed their newborn with infant formula rather than breast-feed. This is a personal choice, and there are a variety of reasons why new mothers opt for the bottle rather than the breast. In a few cases, a mother isn't able to breast-feed her child.

If you choose not to or you aren't able to breast-feed, be assured that your baby's nutritional needs can be met with the use of infant formula. And your baby will still be happily bonded to you as a parent.

Pros vs. cons Parents who bottle-feed feel the main advantage of a bottle is:

▶ *Flexibility.* Using a bottle with formula allows more than one person to feed the baby. For that reason, some mothers feel they have more freedom when they're bottle-feeding. Partners may like bottle-feeding because it al-

lows them to share more easily in the feeding responsibilities.

▶ *Convenience.* Some mothers feel formula is more portable, especially on outings and in public places. They don't have to find an out-of-the-way location to breast-feed.

Bottle-feeding can also present some challenges, such as:

▶ *Time-consuming preparation.* Bottles must be prepared and warmed for each feeding. You need a steady supply of formula. Bottles and nipples need to be washed. If you go out, you may need to take formula with you.

▶ *Cost.* Formula is costly, which is a concern for some parents.

Supplies Make sure you have the right supplies on hand when you bring your baby home from the hospital. Staff at the hospital or birthing center also can provide bottle-feeding equipment and formula the first few days after your baby's birth and show you how to bottle-feed your newborn.

The equipment generally needed if you are going to bottle-feed your son or daughter includes:

▶ Four 4-ounce bottles (optional, but useful at the beginning)
▶ Eight 8-ounce bottles
▶ Eight to 10 nipples, nipple rings and nipple caps
▶ A measuring cup
▶ A bottle brush
▶ Infant formula

In addition to buying the right equipment, consider taking a class on infant feeding, if you haven't taken one already. Often, information on feeding a newborn is offered as part of childbirth classes. If you've never bottle-fed a baby before, taking a class will help you feel more comfortable when you bring your baby home.

Bottles Bottles generally come in two sizes: 4 ounces and 8 ounces. They may be glass, plastic or plastic with a soft plastic liner.

Nipples Many types of nipples are on the market, which have openings sized according to a baby's age: newborn, 3-month-old, 6-month-old, and so on. The flow rate from the nipple is appropriate to the baby's age.

It's important that formula flows from the nipple at the correct speed. Milk flow that's either too fast or too slow can cause your baby to swallow too much air, leading to stomach discomfort and the need for frequent burping. Test the flow of the nipple by turning the bottle upside down and timing the drops. One drop per second is about right.

INFANT FORMULAS

A wide variety of infant formulas are on the market. The majority of them are based on cow's milk. However, never use regular cow's milk as a substitute for formula. Although cow's milk is used as the foundation for formula, the milk has been changed dramatically to make it safe for babies.

Infant formula is treated by heat to make the protein in it more digestible. More milk sugar (lactose) is added to make the concentration similar to that of breast milk, and the fat (butterfat) is removed and replaced with vegetable oils and animal fats that are more easily digested by infants.

Infant formulas contain the right amount of carbohydrates and the right percentages of fat and protein. The Food and Drug Administration (FDA) monitors commercially prepared infant formula. Each manufacturer must test each batch of formula to ensure it has the required nutrients and is free of contaminants.

Infant formula is designed to be an energy-dense food. More than half its calories are from fat. Many different types of fatty acids make up that fat. Those that go into infant formula are specifically selected because they're similar to those found in breast milk. These fatty acids help in the development of your baby's brain and nervous system, as well as in meeting his or her energy needs.

Types If you're planning to feed your baby infant formula, you may have many questions. Is one brand of infant formula better than another? Are generic brands OK? Is soy-based formula better than cow's milk formula?

Commercial infant formulas are regulated by the FDA. Three major types are available:

MILK ALLERGY

A person of any age can have a milk allergy, but it's more common among infants.

A milk allergy occurs when the body's immune system mistakenly identifies the protein in milk as something the body should fight off. This starts an allergic reaction, which can cause fussiness and digestive problems.

Cow's milk is the usual cause of milk allergy; however, milk from sheep, goats and buffalo also can cause a reaction. And some children who are allergic to cow's milk are allergic to soy milk, too.

Because most formula is derived from cow's milk, infants who are formula-fed may have a higher risk of developing a milk allergy than those who are breast-fed. Researchers don't fully understand why some infants develop a milk allergy and others don't.

If you use formula and your son or daughter has a milk allergy, your doctor may advise you to switch to another type of formula that's less likely to cause an allergic reaction.

If you're breast-feeding, restrict the amount of dairy products you consume. The milk protein in dairy products that triggers the allergic reaction can cross into your breast milk. In addition to irritability, signs and symptoms of a milk allergy may include loose stools (possibly containing blood), vomiting, gagging, refusal to eat, excessive crying, and skin rashes. Fortunately, most children outgrow a milk allergy by age 3.

Cow's milk formulas Most infant formula is made with cow's milk that's been altered to resemble breast milk. This gives the formula the right balance of nutrients — and makes the formula easier to digest. Most babies do well on cow's milk formula. Some babies, however — such as those allergic to the proteins in cow's milk — need other types of infant formula.

Soy-based formulas Soy-based formulas can be useful if you want to exclude animal proteins from your child's diet. Soy-based formulas may also be an option for babies who are intolerant or allergic to cow's milk formula or to lactose, a sugar naturally found in cow's milk. However, babies who are allergic to cow's milk may also be allergic to soy milk.

Protein hydrolysate formulas These are meant for babies who have a milk or soy allergy. Protein hydrolysate formulas are easier to digest and less likely to cause allergic reactions than are other types of formula. They're also called hypoallergenic formulas.

In addition, specialized formulas are available for premature infants and babies who have specific medical conditions.

Forms Infant formulas come in three forms. The best choice depends on your budget and desire for convenience:

- *Powdered formula.* Powdered formula is the least expensive. Each scoop of powdered formula must be mixed with water.
- *Concentrated liquid formula.* This type of formula also is mixed with water.

▶ *Ready-to-use formula.* Ready-to-use formula is the most convenient type of infant formula. It doesn't need to be mixed with water. It's also the most expensive option.

Generic vs. brand name All infant formulas sold in the United States — both generic and brand name — must meet the nutrient standards set by the FDA. Although manufacturers may vary in their formula recipes, the FDA requires that all formulas contain the minimum recommended amount — and no more than the maximum amount — of nutrients that infants need.

Additional ingredients It's important to buy iron-fortified infant formula. Your baby needs iron to grow and develop, especially during infancy. If you're not breast-feeding, using iron-fortified formula is the easiest way to provide this essential nutrient.

Some infant formulas are enhanced with docosahexaenoic acid (DHA) and arachidonic acid (ARA). These are omega-3 fatty acids found in breast milk and certain foods, such as fish and eggs. Some studies suggest that including DHA and ARA in infant formula can help infant eyesight and brain development, but other research has shown no benefit.

In addition, in an effort to mimic the immune benefits of breast milk, some infant formulas now include probiotics — substances that promote the presence of healthy bacteria in the intestines. The data on probiotic-supplemented formulas is limited and long-term benefits or complications of the formula are unknown.

At this point, there's insufficient evidence to recommend the use of enhanced formulas. In addition, they tend to be more expensive than regular formula. If you think your child might benefit from formula supplemented with probiotics or another substance, talk to your child's care provider for additional information and guidance.

Preparation Whatever type and form of formula you choose, proper preparation and storage are essential, both to ensure the appropriate amount of nutrition and to safeguard the health of your baby.

Wash your hands before handling formula or the equipment used to prepare it. All equipment that you use to

---

LOOK BEFORE YOU BUY

Don't buy or use outdated infant formula. If the expiration date has passed, you can't be sure of the formula's quality.

While checking the expiration date, also inspect the condition of the formula container. Don't buy or use formula from containers with bulges, dents, leaks or rust spots. Formula in a damaged container may be unsafe.

measure, mix and store formula should be washed with hot, soapy water and then rinsed and dried before every use. Sterilizing bottles and nipples isn't necessary as long as you wash and rinse them well. Use a bottle brush to wash bottles. Brush or rub the nipples thoroughly to remove any traces of formula. Rinse well. You can also clean bottles and nipples in the dishwasher.

Whether using powder formula or liquid concentrate, always add the exact amount of water specified on the label. Measurements on bottles may be inaccurate, so pre-measure the water before adding it to the formula. Using too much or too little water isn't good for your baby. If formula is too diluted, your baby won't get enough nutrition for his or her growth needs and to satisfy his or her hunger.

Formula that's too concentrated puts strain on the baby's digestive system and kidneys, and could dehydrate your baby. Generally, you can store all prepared formula or liquid concentrate in the refrigerator for up to 48 hours. After that, throw away all unused formula.

Follow these steps to ensure proper nutrition and avoid food-related illness.

Wash your hands Before preparing formula, wash your hands thoroughly. Wet your hands with warm running water, then rub soap on your hands vigorously for at least 20 seconds.

Prepare your utensils Sterilize new bottles, nipples, caps and rings before using them for the first time. Boil the utensils in water for five minutes. Use a pot that's large enough to hold the utensils and cover them completely with water. Remove the utensils from the water using a clean set of tongs. Allow the utensils to air-dry.

After the first use, there's no need to sterilize your utensils. Simply wash these items with soap and water and allow them to air-dry. To help prevent fungal growth, you might want to rinse nipples daily in equal parts vinegar and water and allow them to air-dry.

Also make sure the nipples are open. Hold each nipple upside down and fill it with water, then look for the water to drip slowly out of the nipple.

Measure the formula For ready-to-use formula, shake the container of formula well before opening it. Pour enough formula for one feeding into a clean bottle.

For liquid-concentrate formula, pour the amount of formula for one serving into a clean bottle. For powdered formula:

▸ Use the scoop that came with the formula container. Make sure the scoop is dry.

▸ Determine the amount of formula you want to prepare, following instructions on the package. Note the number of scoops you'll need.

▸ Fill the scoop with powdered formula, shaving off any excess formula from the top of the scoop with the flat side of a knife — not a spoon or other curved surface.

▸ Repeat as needed, depending on how much formula you want to prepare.

Add water to liquid-concentrate or powdered formula If you're using liquid-concentrate or powdered formula, you'll also need to add water to the bottle. Follow the instructions on the container for how much water to mix with the formula, and then shake well. Adding too little water can put a burden on your baby's digestive system, and adding too much water may overly dilute the formula and deprive your baby of important calories and nutrients.

You can use any type of clean water — tap or bottled — to prepare liquid-concentrate or powdered formula. Consider the amount of fluoride in the water you use to prepare your baby's formula. If you use bottled water or well water, it may not contain fluoride. Mention this to your child's care provider. Exposure to fluoride during infancy helps prevent tooth decay during childhood and later in life.

Warm the formula, if needed Warming formula isn't necessary for nutritional purposes, but your baby may prefer it warm. To warm formula:

- Place a filled bottle in a bowl or pan of hot, but not boiling, water and let it stand for a few minutes — or warm the bottle under running water.
- Shake the bottle after warming it.
- Turn the bottle upside down and allow a drop or two of formula to fall on your wrist or the back of your hand. The formula should feel lukewarm — not hot.
- Don't warm bottles in the microwave. The formula may heat unevenly, creating hot spots that could burn your baby's mouth.

After warming, shake the bottle well and feed the formula to your baby immediately. Discard any formula that remains in the bottle after a feeding.

Store formula safely Store unopened formula containers in a cool, dry place. Don't store formula containers outdoors or in a car or garage, where temperature extremes can affect the quality of the formula.

If you're using ready-to-use formula, cover and refrigerate any leftover formula from a freshly opened container. Discard any leftover formula that's been in the refrigerator more than 24 to 48 hours.

If you prepare and fill several bottles of liquid-concentrate or powdered formula at once:

- Label each bottle with the date that the formula was prepared.
- Refrigerate the extra bottles until you need them — don't freeze them.
- Put the bottles toward the back of the refrigerator, where it's coldest.
- Discard any prepared formula that's been in the refrigerator more than 24 to 48 hours.

If you're unsure whether a particular container or bottle of formula is safe, throw it out.

Getting into position The first step to bottle-feeding is to make you and your baby comfortable. Find a quiet place where you and your baby won't be distracted.

Cradle your baby in one arm, hold the bottle with the other and settle into a comfortable chair, preferably one with broad, low armrests. You may want to put a pillow on your lap under the baby for support. Pull your baby in toward you snugly but not too tightly, cradled in your arm with his or her head raised slightly and resting in the bend of your elbow. This semi-upright position makes swallowing much easier.

Using the nipple of the bottle or a finger of the hand holding it, gently stroke your baby's cheek near the mouth, on the side nearest you. The touch will cause your baby to turn toward you, often with an opened mouth. Then touch the nipple to your baby's lips or the corner of the mouth. Your baby will open his or her mouth and gradually begin sucking.

When feeding your baby, position the bottle at about a 45-degree angle. This angle keeps the nipple full of milk. Hold the bottle steady as your baby feeds. If your baby falls asleep while bottle-feeding, it may be because he or she has had enough milk, or gas has made your baby full. Take the bottle away, burp your baby (see page 68), then start to feed again.

Always hold your baby while feeding. Never prop a bottle up against your infant. Propping may cause your baby to vomit and may lead to overeating. In addition, never give a bottle to your baby when he or she is lying on his or her back. This may increase your baby's risk of developing an ear infection.

Although your baby doesn't have teeth yet, they're forming beneath the gums. Don't develop a habit of putting your baby to bed with a bottle. Formula lingers in the mouth of a baby who falls asleep while sucking a bottle. The prolonged contact of sugar in milk can cause tooth decay.

Amount During the first few weeks, your baby will likely drink about 1 to 3 ounces per feeding. As he or she grows, the amount will gradually increase.

In general, during the first month, expect eight to 12 feedings in a 24-hour period — about every two to three hours.

You'll know that your young one is getting enough formula if by the end of the first week he or she has about six to eight wet diapers a day. He or she may also experience one or two bowel movements a day.

Weaning Infant formula is generally recommended until age 1, followed by whole milk until age 2 — but talk with your child's care provider for specific guidance. Reduced-fat or skim milk generally isn't appropriate before age 2 because it doesn't have enough calories or fat to promote early development.

FEEDING TIPS

As your baby matures, he or she will gradually need fewer daily feedings and eat more at each feeding. A feeding pattern and routine will begin to emerge after the first month or two. Whether you breast-feed or bottle-feed, here are a few pointers to keep in mind.

Feed on cue The size of your infant's stomach is very small, about the size of his or her fist, and the time it takes to become empty varies from one to three hours. Feeding on cue requires you to watch for signs that a baby is ready to eat: your baby makes sucking movements with his or her mouth or tongue (rooting), sucks on his or her fist, makes small sounds, and of course, cries. You will soon be able to distinguish between cries for food and those for other reasons, such as pain, fatigue or illness.

It's important to feed your baby promptly when he or she signals hunger. This helps your baby learn which kinds of discomfort mean hunger and that

hunger can be satisfied by sucking, which brings food. If you don't respond promptly, your baby may become so upset that trying to feed at this point may prove more frustrating than satisfying.

Let baby set the pace Try not to rush your baby during a feeding. He or she will determine how much and how fast to eat. Many babies, like adults, prefer to eat in a relaxed manner. It's normal for an infant to suck, pause, rest, socialize a bit and then return to feeding. Some newborns are speedy, efficient eaters, consistently whizzing through feedings. Other babies are grazers, preferring snack-sized feedings at frequent intervals. Still others, especially newborns, are snoozers. These babies may take a few vigorous sucks and blissfully doze off, then wake, feed and doze again intermittently throughout a typical feeding session.

Your baby will also let you know when he or she has had enough to eat. When your baby is satisfied, he or she will stop sucking, close his or her mouth or turn away from the nipple. Baby may push the nipple out of his or her mouth with his or her tongue, or your baby may arch his or her back if you try to continue feeding. If, however, your baby needs burping or is in the middle of a bowel movement, his or her mind may not be on eating. Wait a bit, and then try offering the breast or bottle again.

Be flexible Don't expect your baby to eat the same amount every day. Babies vary in how much they eat, especially if they're experiencing a growth spurt. At these times, your baby will need and demand more milk and eat more frequently. It may seem like your baby can't get full. During these times, you may need to put your baby to your breast or offer a bottle more often.

Babies often don't eat at precise intervals throughout the day. Most babies bunch (cluster) their feedings at various times of the day and night. It's common for a baby to eat several times within a few hours and then sleep for a few hours.

Stick with breast milk or formula
Don't give your newborn water, juice or other fluids. Introducing these liquids before your baby is 6 months is unnecessary and can interfere with his or her desire for breast milk or formula, which may lead to malnourishment.

Consider feedings a time to bond
For babies, feeding is as much a social activity as a nutritional one. Your baby's growth and development are based, in part, on the powerful bond that forms during feedings. Hold your baby close during each feeding. Look him or her in the eye. Speak with a gentle voice. Don't miss this opportunity to build your baby's sense of security, trust and comfort.

SPITTING UP

Does your baby spit up after every feeding? Spitting up is a rite of passage for many babies. Although it's messy, you probably don't need to worry. Spitting up rarely signifies a serious problem. As long as your baby seems comfortable and is gaining weight, there's generally little cause for concern.

If you keep a burp cloth within reach at all times, you're well prepared. About half of all babies experience infant reflux (gastroesophageal reflux) during the first three months after birth.

Reflux Normally a valve (lower esophageal sphincter) between the esophagus and the stomach keeps stomach contents where they belong. Until this valve has time to mature, spitting up may be an issue — especially if your baby eats too much or too quickly.

Minimal spitting up doesn't hurt. It isn't likely to cause coughing, choking or discomfort — even during sleep. Chances are your baby won't even notice the fluid dripping out of his or her mouth.

Spitting up tends to peak at age 4 months, and most babies stop spitting up by 12 months.

What you can do To reduce spitting up, consider these tips:

Keep your baby upright Position baby's head higher than the rest of the body when feeding. Follow each feeding with 15 to 30 minutes in a sitting position. Hold your baby in your arms, or try a front pack, backpack or infant seat. Avoid active play and infant swings while the food is settling.

Try smaller, more frequent feedings Feeding your baby too much can contribute to spitting up. If you're breast-feeding, limit the length of each nursing session. If you're bottle-feeding, offer your baby slightly less than usual.

Take time to burp your baby Frequent burps during and after each feeding can keep air from building up in your baby's stomach. Sit your baby upright, supporting your baby's head with one hand while patting his or her back with your other hand (see page 68).

Check the nipple If you're using a bottle, make sure the hole in the nipple is the right size (see page 60). If it's too large, the milk will flow too fast. If it's too small, your baby might get frustrated and gulp

BURPING POSITIONS

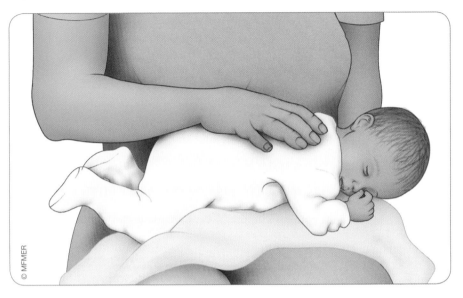

Lay baby facedown across your lap, and gently rub and pat baby's back.

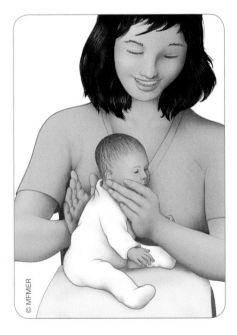

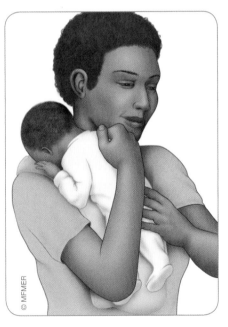

While sitting baby upright and supporting his or her chin and back, gently rub and pat baby's back.

Lay baby facedown across your shoulder, and gently rub and pat his or her back.

air. A nipple that's the right size will allow a few drops of milk to fall out when you hold the bottle upside down.

Experiment with your diet If you're breast-feeding, your baby's doctor might suggest that you eliminate dairy products or certain other foods from your diet.

Pay attention to baby's sleep position To reduce the risk of sudden infant death syndrome (SIDS), it's important to place your baby to sleep on his or her back. If this seems to aggravate reflux, it might help to slightly elevate the head of your baby's crib — although this can be difficult to maintain if your baby moves around in his or her sleep. Placing a baby to sleep on his or her tummy is rarely recommended to prevent spitting up.

When it's more serious Normal spitting up doesn't interfere with a baby's growth or well-being. More severe spitting up may indicate something more serious. Contact your baby's doctor if your baby:

- Isn't gaining weight
- Spits up so forcefully that stomach contents shoot out of his or her mouth (vomits)
- Spits up green or yellow fluid
- Spits up blood or a material that looks like coffee grounds
- Resists feedings
- Has blood in his or her stool
- Has other signs of illness, such as fever, diarrhea or difficulty breathing

These signs and symptoms might indicate an underlying condition. Some babies experience infant gastroesophageal reflux (GER). For more information on GER, see page 382.

Treatment depends on what's causing the problem. Special feeding techniques or medication may be helpful.

INTRODUCING SOLIDS

When a child is first born, breast milk or formula is the only food he or she needs. Eventually, though, your baby will begin to develop the coordination to move solid food from the front of the mouth to the back for swallowing. At the same time, his or her head control will improve so that he or she can sit with support. These are essential skills for eating solid foods.

So when are babies ready for solid foods? It varies and there's no specific time you have to introduce solids. The American Academy of Pediatrics recommends waiting until a child is at least 4 months old before introducing solids, and preferably holding off until a child is closer to 6 months old. Your child's readiness and nutritional needs also are key factors to be considered.

It's a good idea to check with your child's care provider or another member of the health care team before starting any solid foods. These individuals can give you some advice and practical tips.

Getting started When the time is right, begin with baby cereal. One way to make eating solids for the first time easier is to give your baby a little breast milk or formula first, then switch to very small half spoonfuls of food, and finish with more breast milk or formula. This will prevent your baby from getting frustrated when he or she is very hungry.

Use a small spoon — one that will fit into your baby's mouth — and begin with very small amounts. At first, your little one may frown, sputter and spit it out. This isn't necessarily because he or she doesn't like it, but rather because he or she may not be familiar with moving the tongue backward yet.

Expect that your baby may not eat much in the beginning. Give him or her time to get used to the experience. Some babies need practice keeping food in their mouths and swallowing.

Don't be surprised if your baby puts his or her fingers into his or her mouth to help swallow the food. He or she may also try to bat away the spoon. Expect it to be a messy experience!

Once your little one gets used to solids, he or she may be ready for a few tablespoons of food a day. When your child begins eating more, add another feeding.

Taste and texture Your baby's taste buds are continually maturing. As you begin with solids, keep in mind that babies are more likely to eat foods that are bland. They also react to how food feels and tastes in their mouths.

Introduce cereals and other solid foods one at a time so that your baby can get used to having a new taste, as well as a new texture, in his or her mouth.

Start with the blandest food at each feeding. It may take a couple of tries for a new food to gain acceptance.

Baby cereal Mix 1 tablespoon of a single-grain, iron-fortified baby cereal with 4 to 5 tablespoons of breast milk or formula. Many parents start with rice cereal. Even if the cereal barely thickens the liquid, resist the temptation to serve it from a bottle. Instead, help your baby sit upright, and offer the cereal with a small spoon once or twice a day.

Once your baby gets the hang of swallowing runny cereal, mix it with less liquid. For variety, you might offer single-grain oatmeal or barley cereals. Keep in mind that some babies eat cereal with gusto right from the start. Others are less enthusiastic. Be patient and keep trying.

Pureed meat, vegetables and fruits Once your baby masters cereal, gradually introduce pureed meat, vegetables and fruits. Offer single-ingredient foods at first, and wait three to five days between each new food. If your baby has a reaction to a particular food — such as diarrhea, rash or vomiting — you'll know the culprit.

Finely chopped finger foods At about 9 months, most babies can handle small portions of finely chopped finger foods,

HOMEMADE BABY FOODS

If you want to give your baby fresh food, use a blender or a food processor to puree the food. For softer foods, you may be able to simply mash them with a fork. You can feed your baby raw bananas that have been mashed, but most other fruits and vegetables should be cooked until they're soft. It's best not to add salt or seasoning.

Refrigerate any food you don't use, and look for signs of spoilage before giving it to your baby. Fresh foods are not bacteria-free, so they'll spoil more quickly than food from a can or jar.

Talk with your child's care provider about homemade foods you should avoid giving to your child before age 1.

OBESITY: PUTTING YOUR CHILD AT RISK

Can starting solids too soon increase your child's risk of obesity? According to one study, the answer is yes. A 2011 study published in the journal *Pediatrics* found that infants on formula who were fed solid foods before age 4 months had a higher risk of becoming obese than those starting solids later.

The study involved more than 840 young children, and it found that formula-fed infants who were introduced to solid food before 4 months had up to six times the risk of being obese at age 3 than did infants on formula who received solids after 4 months.

The results were not the same for breast-fed infants. There was no association between the timing at which solid foods were started and the development of obesity. Breast-feeding was linked to a more normal pattern of growth and to a slower introduction of solid foods.

such as soft fruits, well-cooked pasta, cheese, graham crackers and ground meat. As your baby approaches his or her first birthday, mashed or chopped versions of whatever the rest of the family is eating will likely become your baby's main fare. Continue to offer your child breast milk or formula with and between meals.

To help prevent food allergies, parents were once told to avoid feeding young children eggs, fish and peanut butter. Today, however, researchers say there's no convincing evidence that avoiding these foods during early childhood will help prevent food allergies.

Still, it's a good idea to check with your baby's care provider if any close relatives have a food allergy. You may consider giving your child his or her first taste of a highly allergenic food at home — rather than at a restaurant — with an oral antihistamine available, just in case.

Juice You can offer mild, 100 percent fruit juices when your baby is 6 months or older. Juice isn't a necessary part of a baby's diet, however, and it's not as valuable as the original fruit itself. If you offer juice to your baby, make sure it's pasteurized.

Limit the amount your baby drinks to 4 to 6 ounces a day. Too much juice may contribute to weight problems and diarrhea, as well as thwart your baby's appetite for more nutritious solid foods. In addition, sipping juice throughout the day or while falling asleep may lead to tooth decay.

Know what's off-limits Don't offer cow's milk, citrus, honey or corn syrup to your child before age 1. Cow's milk doesn't meet an infant's nutritional needs — it isn't a good source of iron and, for infants, it can lead to iron deficiency anemia. Citrus can cause a painful diaper rash, and honey and corn syrup may contain spores that can cause a serious illness known as infant botulism.

In addition, don't offer your baby foods that could pose a choking hazard. Such foods include:

▶ Small, slippery foods, such as whole grapes, hot dogs and hard candy
▶ Dry foods that are hard to chew, such as popcorn, raw carrots and nuts

▶ Sticky or tough foods, such as peanut butter and large pieces of meat

For babies younger than 4 months, if you do feed solids, it may be best to avoid home-prepared or canned spinach, beets, turnips and collard greens. These foods may contain high levels of nitrates, potentially harmful compounds naturally present in these foods.

Make meals manageable When your baby begins eating solid food, mealtime is sure to become an adventure. To help make it more enjoyable — for both you and your baby:

Stay seated At first, you may feed your baby in an infant seat or propped on your lap. As soon as your baby can sit easily without support, use a highchair with a broad, stable base. Buckle the safety straps, and keep other children from climbing or hanging on to the highchair.

Encourage exploration Your baby is likely to play with his or her food between bites. Although it's messy, hands-on fun helps fuel your baby's development. Place a dropcloth on the floor so you won't worry about falling food.

Introduce utensils Offer your baby a spoon to hold while you feed him or her with another spoon. As your baby's dexterity improves, encourage your baby to dip the spoon in food and bring it to his or her mouth.

Offer a cup Feeding your baby breast milk or formula from a cup at mealtime can help pave the way for weaning from a bottle. When your child reaches 9 months, he or she may be able to drink from a cup on his or her own. You may want to begin with a nonspill cup, often called a "sippy" cup.

Dish individual servings Your baby may eat just a few spoonfuls of food at a time. If you feed your baby directly from a jar or container, bacteria and saliva from the spoon can quickly spoil any leftovers. Instead, place 1 tablespoon of food in a dish. The same goes for finger foods. If your baby finishes the first serving, offer another.

Avoid power struggles If your baby turns away from a certain food, don't push. Simply try again another time. And again. And again. Repeated exposure can help ensure variety in your baby's diet.

Know when to call it quits When your baby has had enough to eat, he or she may turn away from the spoon, lean backward, or refuse to open his or her mouth. Don't force extra bites. As long as your baby's growth is on target, you can be confident that he or she is getting enough to eat.

Enjoy the mess Whether it be your baby's sloppy tray, gooey hands or sticky face, you're building the foundation for a lifetime of healthy eating.

Encourage good habits It's important for your baby to get used to the process of eating — sitting up, taking food from a spoon, resting between bites and stopping when full. These early experiences will help your child learn good eating habits throughout life.

And it's never too early to build good eating habits. As your child gets older, focus on eating three meals, with two to three snacks in between. Children who graze, or eat constantly, may never really feel hungry. And they can develop problems from eating too much or too little. In addition, feed your child a variety of healthy, nutrient-rich foods.

CHAPTER 4

Diapers and all that stuff

There's a lot to look forward to in your baby's first year, but changing diapers isn't exactly at the top of the list. It can seem like a daunting task — the average child goes through about 5,000 diaper changes before being toilet trained. You might wonder, what diapers are best? What should I do about diaper rash? And, is it normal that my sweet little baby has yellow or green or brown poop?

A little information and preparation can help make diaper duty more pleasant and less worrisome. You may even look upon diaper changing as another opportunity to bond with your baby. After all, caring for your child in this way, day after day, offers a time for you and your baby to pause, connect and communicate.

TYPES OF DIAPERS

There are several different types of diapers — cloth or disposable, brand name or generic — and they come in many sizes and styles. Some babies are comfortable and stay clean in a lot of different types of diapers, while others need a particular kind that works just right for their body. If your baby doesn't fit well in the diapers you have, or if he or she seems irritated by the diaper, don't be afraid to try something new.

Disposable These diapers are commonly used, and they're highly absorbent and convenient. However, the cost of using disposable diapers adds up, especially if you have more than one baby.

The materials used in disposables usually keep your baby's skin drier for a longer period of time. But the downside of this absorbency is it can be harder to monitor how much your baby has urinated, which may be important to know when your baby is a newborn.

Disposables are also convenient — you throw them away after each use. However, disposable diapers generally aren't considered biodegradable. At best, they may degrade over a very long period of time. An estimated 18 billion diapers a year are sent to landfills. Fortunately, more disposable diaper companies are making efforts to have less of a negative impact on the environment by using different materials, fewer dyes and better packaging.

Cloth Cloth diapers have become increasingly common in recent years, as new brands and styles offer more effective and convenient options. Cloth may be more comfortable on your baby, and cloth diapering also saves a lot of money over time. However, cloth diapers are typically less absorbent than are disposables, and they require more work.

Cloth diapers typically have two parts. There's an inner layer, which is usually made from a soft cotton material, as well as an outer cover that's made from a type of plastic, cotton or terry cloth. Some parents like that these materials don't contain chemicals, materials or fragrances that can irritate babies. Today's cloth diapers are usually fastened with snaps or fabric fasteners, not pins. Cloth diapers typically aren't as absorbent as disposables, so they need to be changed quickly after they become dirty to prevent irritation to your baby's skin.

Depending on how many diapers you buy, cloth diapers need to be washed anywhere from a couple of times a week to daily. Some people hire a diaper-washing service to drop off clean diapers and pick up dirty diapers for washing. Some cloth diapers also come with an optional disposable insert, so you can throw away the dirty part of the diaper. There are even some biodegradable disposable inserts that can be composted or flushed down the toilet.

With the rise in cloth diaper use, there also are more accessories to make it easier, including sprayers that attach to your toilet so that you can rinse off urine and stool from dirty diapers, and wet bags to contain the diapers and smell before they're washed.

Sizes Most disposable diaper packages are labeled with a size that corresponds to your baby's weight. Though the range varies based on the brand, newborn sizes typically go up to 10 pounds, and size 1 is for babies who weigh about 8 to 14 pounds. Preemie diapers are usually for babies who weigh less than 6 pounds.

Some cloth diapers come in different sizes — such as newborn, small, medium or large — while other styles have one-

---

SWIM DIAPERS

As your baby gets older, there may come a time you want to take him or her to the swimming pool. Infants in the pool with their parents often wear swim diapers or swim pants. It's not clear how well these products contain stools in a pool. Even if they appear to contain everything, some contaminants and germs can leak through. If your baby has diarrhea or is sick, he or she should not go into a pool. Doing so could contaminate the water and make other babies and children sick. If your baby is healthy and you take him or her to the pool, change the swim diapers as needed.

size diapers that can be adjusted to fit your growing baby.

Amount If you use disposable diapers, you'll need 80 to 100 a week, at least during the newborn period. If you plan to buy cloth diapers, the number you'll need depends on how often you plan to wash them. Some people buy enough that they only need to be washed every third day or so, and others buy a smaller quantity and wash daily.

GETTING EQUIPPED

Diaper changes will be easier if you have everything you need on hand.

Changing station It helps to have one or two places where you always change your baby's diaper. This way, you can keep all your materials together and readily available in the designated location. If you use a changing table, make sure it has a wide, sturdy base that has compartments for storing diaper supplies. Remember to always keep one hand on your baby during changes. Another option is to change your baby using a changing pad on the floor. You can store supplies in the lower drawer of a crib or in a nearby dresser for easy access.

Diapers Keep an adequate stock of diapers on hand. If you primarily use disposables, it may help to have some cloth diapers around in case you run out. If you mainly use cloth, keep a stack of disposables handy for those days when you haven't had a chance to do the wash.

Wipes You can buy pre-moistened baby wipes, use a moistened cloth, or make your own wipes using a homemade solu-

tion. If you use pre-moistened baby wipes, choose wipes for sensitive skin that don't contain alcohol or fragrance. This will help prevent irritation. It's not necessary to use wipes with every change. Urine is rarely irritating, so if your baby has only peed, letting the area dry or wiping it with a moist cloth may be sufficient. Remember that most pre-moistened wipes cannot be flushed. Unless your package of wipes specifies that they're flushable, wipes must be thrown away.

Dry cloths You may want to have some dry, soft cloths on hand so that after you're finished wiping your baby, you can gently pat his or her bottom dry if you don't have time to let it air dry. Air exposure can trigger babies to urinate, and your baby may urinate while you're changing the diaper. If your baby is a boy, you can avoid being sprayed with urine by covering his penis loosely with a dry cloth while you clean the rest of his bottom.

HOMEMADE BABY WIPES

Pre-moistened baby wipes are common in the United States, but they aren't always necessary, and they're often overused. Some pre-moistened wipes contain ingredients that can be irritating to babies' bottoms. One way you can eliminate your baby's exposure to these ingredients, and save money, is to make your own baby wipes.

There are a variety of ways to make homemade wipes, but here are some suggestions to get you started. After reading through the options, decide which approach you feel would work best for you.

Wipes There are a few different options you can consider for wipes. See what you like best:

 ⦚ Buy rolls of soft paper towels. Cut the rolls in half so that you have two shorter rolls. You'll have a nice size for wipes.
 ⦚ Buy a stack of reusable wipes, which are often made of flannel or some other form of cotton. Or, purchase some thin baby washcloths that you will use as wipes.
 ⦚ Make your own reusable wipes. Purchase soft flannel, terry cloth or fleece fabric and cut it into 5-inch squares. Then sew the edges so that the fabric won't unravel in the wash.

Moistener There are options on what you can use.

 ⦚ Water
 ⦚ Homemade solution. Here's one recipe:
   2 tablespoons baby wash
   2 tablespoons olive oil
   2 cups water

Container Use whichever method is easiest for you.

 ⦚ Round plastic storage container. Pour your homemade solution in the bottom of the container. Set a half roll of paper towels inside the container and place the cover on the container. The paper towels will absorb the liquid, and then you can tear off each sheet as you need it.
 ⦚ Spray bottle. Keep fresh water or your homemade solution in a spray bottle. If you use a solution, wet down your wipes with water first, and then spray each wipe with a couple of squirts of solution.

If you create your own baby-wipe solution, you may want to check with your baby's care provider to ensure the baby wash or other ingredients in the solution don't contain any potentially harmful or irritating substances. Products can be absorbed into your baby's body through the skin, so it's important that you're comfortable with all the ingredients.

Diaper pail or wet bag Diaper pails store dirty diapers and wipes, and wet bags are made to store dirty cloth diapers and reusable wipes before they're washed. There are a variety of types of pails and bags available. Look for one that's convenient, sanitary and holds in odors.

Ointment You don't need to apply baby ointments unless your baby tends to develop diaper rashes. But it's nice to have a product on hand so that if your baby develops a rash, you won't have to immediately run out to buy something.

CHANGING DIAPERS

By the time your child is potty trained, you'll be a diaper-changing pro. In the meantime, the following steps and pointers can help make diaper changing a successful venture for both you and baby.

Mindset Changing diapers is an unavoidable part of parenting, but it may help to think of this necessary task as an opportunity for closeness and communication with your baby. Your warm words, gentle touches and encouraging smiles help make your baby feel loved and secure, and soon your infant will be responding with gurgles and coos.

Frequency Because newborns urinate frequently, it's important to change your baby's diapers every two or three hours for the first few months. But you can wait until your baby wakes up to change a wet diaper. Urine alone doesn't usually irritate a baby's skin. However, the acid in a bowel movement can, so change a messy diaper as soon as your baby awakens.

Preparation Have your wipes and a new diaper ready and within arm's reach. It may help to pull out or prepare the number of wipes you think you'll need for the job, and open the diaper to lay it flat. Make eye contact and tell your baby that you're going to change his or her diaper. Lay your baby gently on his or her back. If you change the baby anywhere but the floor, remember to keep your hand on your baby at all times.

Remove old diaper Unfasten the fabric fastener, tape or snaps on the diaper your baby is wearing, and pull down the front side of the diaper. If your baby has had a bowel movement, you can use the clean inside front of the diaper to pull much of the stool off your baby's skin. Set the diaper off to the side beyond your baby's reach.

Clean baby's bottom During the cleaning, carefully grasp and hold your baby's legs at the ankles with one hand. Using a cloth that's been moistened with warm water or pre-moistened wipes, clean from baby's front to back. Remember to check and clean out folds, where hidden stool can hide. You can place dirty wipes in the middle of the inside of the dirty diaper to keep the mess consolidated. If you have a baby boy, you may want to place a loose cloth over his penis while you're cleaning his bottom to avoid being sprayed with urine.

Changing baby girls Remember to wipe from the front side to the back side to avoid getting stool (or more stool) in the vaginal area. Baby girls have more folds and places for poop to hide, so it's important to clean them thoroughly. However, girls also often have a normal white discharge in the folds of the labia, and it's

CHANGING A DISPOSABLE DIAPER

Step 1. When opening the diaper, make sure the tape, which is at the back of the diaper, is at the top, or away from you. Slide the diaper under your baby until the top edge (the edge with the tape) lines up with your baby's waist.

Step 2. Bring the front of the diaper up through the legs, without twisting it to one side.

© MFMER

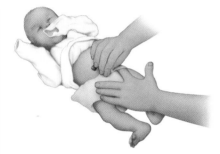

Step 3. Hold one side in position while removing the tab from the tape. Pull the tape forward and stick it to the diaper front. Repeat for the other side, making sure the diaper is snug around your baby's legs and not twisted to one side.

Step 4. For a newborn, fold down the top of the diaper so that it won't rub against the healing umbilical cord. Disposable diapers should fit snugly around the waist, with room enough for only one finger.

not necessary to remove that. Too much scrubbing can cause irritation.

Let dry When finished with the cleaning, gently pat your baby's bottom with a soft cloth so that the skin is dry when you put the new diaper on.

Place new diaper As you lift your baby's legs from the ankles, slide the new diaper underneath his or her buttocks. The side with tabs should be in the back, underneath your baby. Pull the front of the diaper up between your baby's legs, and place it so that the front side and back side of the diaper will be at about the same level around your baby's body. Then fasten the tape, fabric fastener or snaps so that the diaper fits snugly around your baby's waist. If you're using disposable diapers, make sure that none of the elastic around the legs has folded underneath itself. If you're using cloth, make sure the inner layer is tucked inside the outer layer.

Changing baby boys Baby boys can have a tendency to urinate up and out of their diapers, causing leaks and wet clothes. As you put a new diaper on your baby boy, try positioning his penis downward to prevent these leaks. Also, you may want to fold the diaper down and in for extra protection on his front side.

Discard old diaper If you're using disposables, you can roll up the dirty diaper from the front to the back — with any wipes in the middle of the diaper — and then fasten the tabs around the sides of the rolled up diaper. Toss the diaper in a diaper pail. If you're using cloth diapers and cleaning them yourself, dump any stool into your toilet, rinse the diaper off and place it in a designated holding spot — such as a wet bag or diaper pail — until you wash your load of diapers. Some families use diaper sprayers, which attach to the toilet. They can often be purchased in a baby store or online.

Wash your hands When you're finished with the diaper change and baby is in a safe place, wash your hands with soap and water. Hand-washing is important. It can prevent the spread of bacteria or yeast to other parts of your baby's body, to you or to other children.

WHAT'S NORMAL

New parents often wonder what's normal when it comes to their baby's urination and bowel movements. For newborns especially, there's a range of what's considered normal for color, consistency and frequency. But there also are guidelines that help you know what to expect and when there's cause for concern.

Urine In a healthy infant, urine is light to dark yellow in color. Sometimes, as highly concentrated urine dries on the diaper, it creates a chalky, pinkish color, which may be mistaken for blood. This is normal and not a cause for concern. Keep in mind that concentrated urine is different

THE UMBILICAL CORD

For the first few days that you're changing your baby's diapers, you'll need to work around baby's umbilical cord stump. It's best to expose the stump to as much air as possible as it dries up and eventually falls off. It's also important to keep the umbilical cord stump clean — from contact with urine and stool. Most newborn diapers are designed with a small cutout so that the diaper sits below the cord and doesn't rub it. If your diapers don't have this feature, fold the top down so that the diaper is positioned below the cord.

from blood in that it dries to a powder, and it's not as red in color.

By the time a baby is 3 or 4 days old, he or she should have at least four to six wet diapers a day. As your baby gets older, he or she may have a wet diaper with every feeding.

Stools Your baby's first soiled diaper, which will probably occur within 48 hours of birth, may surprise you. During these first few days, a newborn's stools will often be thick and sticky — a tar-like, greenish-black substance called meconium. After the meconium is passed, the color, frequency and consistency of your baby's stools will vary depending on how your baby is fed — by breast or bottle.

Color If you're breast-feeding, your baby's stools will likely resemble light mustard

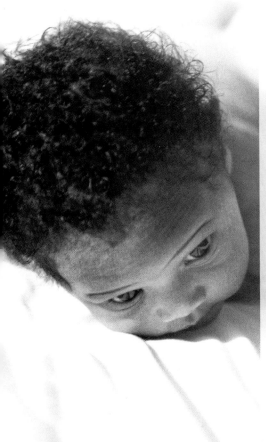

with seed-like particles. They'll be soft and even slightly runny. The stools of a formula-fed infant are usually tan or yellow and firmer than those of a breast-fed baby, but no firmer than peanut butter.

Occasional variations in color and consistency are normal. Different colors may indicate how fast the stool moves through the digestive tract or what the baby ate. The stool may be variations of the colors green, yellow, orange or brown.

The color isn't that significant unless the stool has blood — shown as red or coal-black streaks — or if it is a whitish-grey color instead of closer to yellow-brown. A whitish-grey color could be a sign that the stool is lacking bilirubin products, which are normal byproducts from the body breaking down excess red blood cells. These very pale stools could indicate that your baby's body isn't eliminating waste properly. If you see blood or whitish-grey stools, contact your child's care provider.

Consistency Mild diarrhea is common in newborns. The stools may be watery, frequent and mixed with mucus. Constipation is not usually a problem for infants. Babies may strain, grunt and turn red during a bowel movement, but this doesn't mean they're constipated. A baby is constipated when bowel movements are infrequent, hard and perhaps even ball shaped.

Frequency The range of normal is quite broad and varies from one baby to another. Babies may have a bowel movement as frequently as after every feeding or as infrequently as once a week, or they may have no consistent pattern.

Blood If your baby's stools appear to contain blood — whether you see red or coal-black coloring, streaks, flecks or

DIAPER SURPRISES

You might occasionally notice a surprising but often harmless substance in your baby's diaper. These substances may appear as:

Gel-like materials Clear or yellow-tinted beads or particles may come from diaper materials that have become overly wet with urine.

Small crystals A newborn baby's kidneys may make clear crystals if baby is relatively dehydrated. This can also leave a tinted orange or pink stain in the diaper.

Pink or small blood stains A newborn baby girl may have some pink or blood stains in her diapers in the first few weeks. This is generally from exposure to her mother's hormones right before birth. It isn't usually a problem, and it goes away with time.

otherwise — contact your child's care provider and have the problem checked out. Actual blood in stools is always a cause for concern, but don't panic; sometimes the problem isn't serious.

For example, newborns may have ingested some of their mother's blood during delivery, or they may be taking it in while breast-feeding if the mother has cracked or bleeding nipples. Flecks or streaks of blood in stools may also be a sign of an allergy to the protein in cow's milk, which may be found in formula or breast milk. For older babies, red or black in stools could be from certain foods, including tomatoes, beets, spinach, cherries and grape juice.

Diarrhea If you notice that your baby's stool becomes more watery than normal and you observe a gradual or sudden increase in how often or how much he or she is pooping, contact your child's care provider.

There are many possible causes of diarrhea. Some foods may cause diarrhea. Diarrhea may also be an indication of an illness. And antibiotics are a common cause. Antibiotics wipe out both the good and bad bacteria in the gut.

If antibiotics are the culprit and your child is 9 months or older, you might consider feeding your child foods that contain probiotics, such as yogurt. Probiotics, found in certain fermented foods, are microorganisms that contain "good bacteria." Probiotics may help bring a healthy bacterial balance back to your child's gut and improve digestion.

Probiotics are also available as over-the-counter supplements. However, because not a lot is known about the supplements, and studies with young children are limited, Mayo Clinic pediatricians generally don't recommend their use. If you have questions about probiotics, talk to your child's care provider.

DIAPER RASH

All babies get a red or sore bottom from time to time, even with frequent diaper

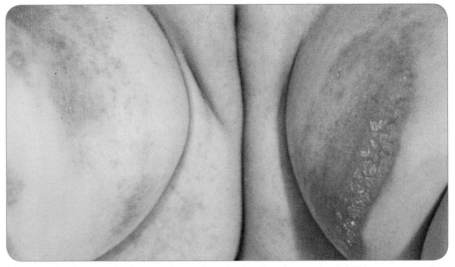

Diaper rash often results from prolonged contact with urine or stool. Mild cases can often be treated with over-the-counter products. Cases that are more severe may need to be treated with prescription medications.

changes and careful cleaning. Diaper rash is such a common condition that it happens to nearly every baby at some point. You certainly aren't a bad parent if your baby gets a diaper rash. Fortunately, diaper rash is usually easily treated and improves within a few days.

Appearance Diaper rash is marked by red, puffy and tender-looking skin in the diaper region — buttocks, thighs and genitals. The skin may have rashes or just look red and irritated. Your baby may seem more uncomfortable than usual, especially during diaper changes.

Causes Causes of diaper rash include the following:

Irritation from stool and urine Prolonged exposure to feces or urine can irritate a baby's sensitive skin. Your baby may be more prone to diaper rash if he or she has frequent bowel movements, because feces are more irritating than urine.

Irritation from a new product Disposable wipes, a new brand of disposable diaper, or a detergent, bleach or fabric softener used to launder cloth diapers can all irritate your baby's delicate bottom. Other substances that can add to the problem include ingredients found in some baby lotions, powders and oils.

Introduction of new foods As babies start to eat solid foods, the content of their stool changes, increasing the likelihood of diaper rash. Changes in your baby's diet can also increase the frequency of stools, which can lead to diaper rash.

Bacterial or yeast (fungal) infection The area covered by a diaper — buttocks, thighs and genitals — is especially vulnerable because it's warm and moist, making a perfect breeding ground for bacteria and yeast. These rashes generally start within the creases of the skin, and there may be red dots scattered around the edges.

Chafing or rubbing Tightfitting diapers or clothing that rubs against the skin can lead to a rash.

Use of antibiotics Antibiotics kill bacteria — both bad and good ones. Without the right balance of good bacteria, yeast infections can occur. This can happen when babies take antibiotics or when mothers who are breast-feeding their infants take antibiotics.

Treatment The most important factor in treating diaper rash is to keep your baby's skin as clean and dry as possible. This often means increasing "diaper-free" time and thoroughly but gently washing the area with water during each diaper change. Avoid washing the affected area with soaps and disposable, scented wipes. Alcohol and perfumes in these products can irritate your baby's skin and aggravate or provoke the rash.

If the rash is severe, it might help to clean your baby's bottom with warm water from a squirt bottle instead of using a moistened cloth or wipes, so you won't have to rub the tender skin. It's also important to allow baby's bottom to air-dry completely before putting on a new diaper. If possible:

▶ Let your child go without a diaper for longer periods of time.

▶ Avoid using plastic pants or tight-fitting diaper covers.

▶ Use larger sized diapers until the rash goes away.

In addition, use a mild ointment anytime pinkness appears in the diaper area. This can reduce friction and rubbing and block chemical irritants — from stools or from diaper materials — from contact with your baby's skin.

Apply the cream in a thin layer to the irritated region several times throughout the day to soothe and protect the baby's skin. You don't have to completely remove the cream at every diaper change if the area is clean — rubbing will only irritate the skin further.

Many effective creams contain zinc oxide, which helps sooth the skin. Look for a cream that doesn't contain fragrance, preservatives or other ingredients that could cause irritation or allergies, including neomycin. Products that are put on people's skin are absorbed into their bodies through the skin. And some creams contain ingredients that can be harmful for your baby, including boric acid, camphor, phenol, benzocaine and salicylates.

PREVENTING RASH: CLOTH OR DISPOSABLE?

When it comes to preventing diaper rash, there's no compelling evidence that cloth diapers are better than disposable diapers or vice versa, though disposables may keep baby's skin slightly drier. Because there's no one best diaper, use whatever works best for you and your baby. If one brand of disposable diaper irritates your baby's skin, try another.

No matter whether it's cloth or disposable, always change your baby as soon as you can after he or she soils the diaper, to keep the bottom as clean and dry as possible.

Also avoid creams that have steroids, such as hydrocortisone, in them, unless your baby's care provider specifically recommends such a product. Creams containing steroids can be harmful, and they usually aren't necessary. Also, don't use talcum powder or cornstarch on a baby's skin. An infant may inhale talcum powder, which can be very irritating to a baby's lungs. Cornstarch can contribute to a bacterial infection.

When to seek medical treatment
Contact your baby's care provider if:
▶ The rash is accompanied by a fever.
▶ The rash has blisters, boils, discharge or pus-filled sores.
▶ The rash isn't going away or improving after two to three days of home treatment.
▶ Your baby is taking antibiotics, and the rash is bright red with red spots around the edges. It could be a yeast infection, which needs additional treatment.
▶ The rash is severe.
▶ The rash is present on skin outside the diaper area.

Preventing diaper rash There are a variety of steps you can take to help prevent, or at least reduce the incidence of, diaper rash:
▶ Change your baby's diaper often so his or her skin is not in contact with urine or stools for very long.
▶ Let your baby's bottom air out once in a while by letting him go without a diaper for a brief period.
▶ Avoid using superabsorbent disposable diapers, because they tend to be changed less frequently.
▶ If you're using cloth diapers, be sure to wash and rinse them thoroughly. Pre-soak heavily soiled diapers, and use hot water to wash them. Use a mild detergent with no fragrance, and skip fabric softeners and dryer sheets, which can contain fragrances that irritate your baby's skin. Double-rinse the diapers.
▶ If you use cloth diapers, select snap-on plastic pants, instead of those with elastic bindings, to improve circulation.
▶ After changing diapers, wash your hands well. Hand-washing can prevent the spread of bacteria or yeast to other parts of your baby's body, to you or to other children.

CHAPTER 5

Bathing and skin care

Bathing your baby can be a sweet and fun experience. Don't worry if you feel a little awkward at first — it takes practice to get the hang of cleaning a slippery and squirmy baby. And don't be surprised if, at first, your son or daughter doesn't like being bathed. It's a whole new experience for him or her — and for you, too!

The tips that follow will help make your bath-time routine safe and smooth. You'll also learn how to identify and deal with skin conditions that are common in a baby's first year. Sometimes people expect new babies to have flawless skin, but that's rarely the case.

BATHING BASICS

As your child gets older, chances are he or she will enjoy taking a bath. Babies have fun splashing in the water and playing with bath toys. They'll often jump at the chance to suds up. Newborns, however, often don't like the bath experience.

They don't enjoy getting undressed or the cold feeling that comes with having no clothes on.

Fortunately, infants don't need much bathing. It's not until your child gets older and gets dirtier that baths become more of a regular ritual.

Frequency During your newborn's first couple of weeks, as the umbilical cord falls off and heals, one sponge bath a week is probably sufficient. Check his or her folds — in the thighs, groin, armpits, fists and double chins — to see if they need occasional spot cleaning in addition to a weekly sponge bath.

Generally, babies need only one to three baths a week in the first year. Once your baby starts crawling around and eating solid food, he or she might need up to three baths a week. Bathing more frequently than that can dry out a baby's skin.

Types of baths A sponge bath is often the gentlest and easiest way to introduce your new baby to bathing. A sponge bath basically involves using a warm washcloth to clean your baby instead of placing him or her in a tub of water. During a sponge bath, you can keep your baby covered with a dry towel so that he or she doesn't get cold. As you clean a part of baby's body, you move a small piece of the towel aside in order to get at that area. Once finished, pat that body part dry and cover it back up with the towel before moving onto another area of the body.

Sponge baths are a good alternative to a full bath for the first six weeks or so after your child is born. Once the umbilical cord has fallen off and the area is healed, you can try moving your baby into a full bath.

When you decide it's time to try a full bath, you might start out using a baby bathtub, which you can set inside your regular tub or on the floor or next to the sink. Put a few inches of water in the bottom of the baby bath, test the temperature, and then place your baby in the bath and start washing. The first few baths should be especially gentle and brief. If your baby doesn't like it, you might stick with sponge baths for a while longer before trying a full bath again.

When Find a time for bathing your baby that's convenient for both of you. Many people give their baby a bath before bedtime as a relaxing, sleep-promoting ritual. Others prefer a time when their baby is fully awake. You'll enjoy this time more if you're not in a hurry and aren't likely to be interrupted.

You may also want to wait a bit after your baby eats or drinks to give a bath in order to allow his or her stomach to settle. Waiting briefly may also reduce the chances of your baby peeing or pooping during the bath.

BATH ITEMS AND PRODUCTS

A little preparation can help make baths go a lot smoother. Think about all of the equipment you'll need and have it set out within arm's reach before you suds up.

Place for baby Some parents find it easiest to bathe a newborn in a bathinette, a sink or a plastic tub lined with a clean towel. Baby baths, which are often placed inside your tub, are commonly used as babies get a little older. Bathinettes are free-standing, portable bath stations that allow you to stand and bathe your baby inside a small tub. They're similar to changing tables in structure, and they often have compartments or shelves where you can keep washcloths, soap or anything else that you might need.

Water Of course you'll want warm water — not too hot — handy for washing and rinsing. Most of the time, soap isn't necessary, and plain water is all that's needed to clean your baby.

Soap Generally, it's best to use only water to bathe your baby. Soap can dry your baby's skin or contain ingredients that are irritating to your little one. As your baby gets older and starts eating solid foods, crawling around on the ground and playing outside, soap may be needed. If you sense that plain water won't do the trick, you can use a little mild baby soap or shampoo that's free of fragrances and deodorants, which can irritate your baby's skin.

Washcloths Soft washcloths can help you gently clean out those hard-to-reach places and folds, such as your baby's genital area, thighs, armpits and double chins.

Towels Have a couple of soft, dry towels on hand. Baby-sized towels are usually easier to use because you don't have to deal with all the excess material as you wrap up your little one.

Cotton balls While bathing your newborn, use two damp cotton balls to wipe each eye from the inside to the outside corner.

Soft scrubber Some people like to use a soft baby scrubber to wash their baby's hair. These scrubbers can be a handy accessory, though a washcloth will work fine, too.

Moisturizer Most babies don't need any moisturizer, even though their skin may be peeling and appear dry, especially in the first few days after birth. Some moisturizers, including those with fragrance, may irritate their skin and even cause rashes. But if needed, or if your baby's care provider recommends it, have a moisturizer on hand. Look for a brand that's fragrance-free and gentle to baby's skin.

Diaper-changing equipment Keep diaper-changing equipment nearby in case your baby poops or pees during the bath and so that you can put a diaper back on before dressing him or her.

Clothes or pajamas Have some clothes or pajamas ready for after the bath to keep your baby from getting cold.

Bath toys Bath toys aren't necessary early on — your baby will have plenty of excitement and stimulation from bathing alone. However, as your son or daughter gets older, he or she may enjoy having a toy or two in the bath to play with and keep him or her occupied throughout the bathing.

BATH SAFETY

A baby's bath time might conjure up images of bubbles, toys and fun, but it's also a time to exercise caution. Whether your baby is a newborn or a bathing veteran, it's important to be attentive to things like water temperature — too hot can burn your baby, and too cool can chill a little one. Ensure a safe, smooth bath by preparing the space ahead of time and staying focused on the task at hand.

Preparation Prepare the bath area with all the items you'll need. Place everything within arm's reach so that you can keep one hand on your baby at all times.

Temperature Take a cue from Goldilocks before you place your baby into bath water. Remember the temperature

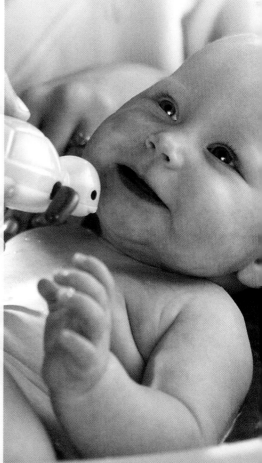

needs to be just right. For baby's safety, you don't want the water too hot — it could hurt or even burn your baby. And for his or her comfort, you also don't want the water so cold that your baby gets chilled. Generally, a temperature between 95 and 100 F is ideal for a baby's bath.

Before filling up the tub or basin, test the water temperature with your elbow or wrist. The water should feel warm but not hot. Once you fill the tub or basin, test the temperature again — water temperatures frequently change while the water is running. Never let the bath fill while your baby's sitting in it. Instead, fill the tub or basin and then test the water again. Once you're confident the temperature is right, place your baby in the tub. If you're not sure about the temperature, consider purchasing a bath thermometer to help guide you.

You also want to make sure that the water heater in your house is set at no higher than 120 F. This is a precautionary measure to protect your son or daughter. Many water heaters are set dangerously higher than that, to 140 or 150 F. Just three seconds of exposure to 140-degree water can cause third-degree burns on a child.

Attentiveness It's important to give your baby your full and undivided attention during baths. If the phone rings or someone rings the doorbell, ignore it. Babies can drown in less than an inch of water in an instant, so you don't want to be diverted from the task at hand. They can also roll and fall from high surfaces, or slip and hit their heads, even when they're seated. During a bath, keep your eyes on your little one at all times.

SAFE BABY CARE PRODUCTS

Finding baby care products that are absolutely safe and gentle seems like it should be an easy task, but unfortunately, that's not always the case. Baby products are generally marketed as safe, gentle, mild and natural, yet some of these products may contain ingredients that can be irritating to your baby.

Remember that whenever you put something on your baby's skin, the ingredients in the product can be absorbed into your baby's body through the skin. Here are some ways you can protect your baby from potentially harmful ingredients:

▶ Limit the number of products you use on your baby.

▶ Read labels to ensure you're comfortable with all the ingredients. This method has its limitations, however, since most people aren't familiar with the many names and types of chemicals. In addition, in the United States, the Food and Drug Administration doesn't require products to list the individual ingredients that are used to make a fragrance, and many products just list "fragrance" as the ingredient.

▶ Do your homework. Go online or check government and health resources to learn more about the ingredients in products you're using or are considering purchasing.

If you forgot something you need for the bath, take your baby out of the bath and take him or her with you, even if the item is just a step away.

BATHING STEP BY STEP

You'll fall into a bath-time routine soon enough, but in the meantime, here are a few tips on how to go about giving your child a bath and making it an easy and enjoyable event.

Prepare your baby Talk calmly and encouragingly to your baby about the upcoming bath. Even if your baby can't understand you, your tone of voice will be comforting, and eventually he or she will understand what's happening.

Place your baby Remove your baby's clothes and diaper. Whether you're cleaning your baby with a sponge bath or a full bath, gently lower him or her into position. Support his or her head and torso to help him or her feel secure.

Keep hold Babies can be slippery and can become suddenly squirmy, so keep a good hold on your baby during baths. It may help to keep your dominant hand free for reaching and cleaning and use the other hand to keep your baby steady and safe.

Eyes first Use a cloth or cotton ball dampened with water to wipe from the inside to the outside corner of your newborn baby's eye. Discard the used cotton ball and use a fresh, damp cotton ball for the other eye.

Start at the top Use a soft cloth to wash your baby's face with water and then pat the face dry. Wash your baby's head with water too, tipping his or her head back or cupping your hand over his or her forehead to keep any water or soap from running into baby's eyes. It's not necessary to shampoo your baby's hair every bath — once or twice a week is plenty. If your baby seems agitated by a wet head, save the hair wash for last. You can use a soft washcloth, your fingertips or a baby scrubber to wash his or her hair and scalp.

Wash and check folds Wash the rest of your child's body from the top down, including the inside folds of skin and the genital area. For a girl, gently spread the labia to carefully clean the area. For a boy, lift the scrotum to clean underneath. If your son is uncircumcised, don't try to retract the foreskin of the penis. Let your baby lean forward on your arm while you clean his or her back and bottom, separating the buttocks to clean the anal area.

Pat dry Once your baby is clean and rinsed off, carefully pick him or her up and into a towel — remember he or she will be slippery! You may set a towel vertically over your body so that part of it hangs over your shoulder. Bring your baby to your chest and then bring the bottom of the towel up and around your baby. Another option is to spread a towel out on the floor. Place your baby on the towel and then wrap the towel around him or her. Gently pat your baby dry with a towel. Patting the skin instead of rubbing it dry will help keep your baby's skin from getting irritated.

Diaper and clothe After you've dried baby off, place a fresh diaper on him or her, and put on some clothes or pajamas to keep your child warm.

BABY BATH

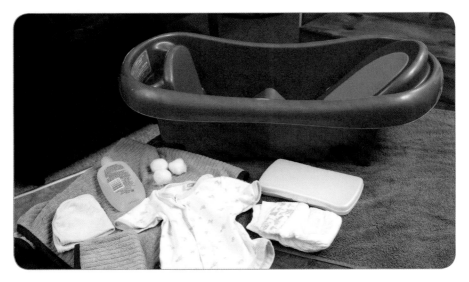

Breaking out the tub When you're ready to give your baby a tub bath — whether you do so right from the start or you try sponge baths first — you'll have plenty of choices. You can use a free-standing plastic tub specifically designed for newborns, a plain plastic basin or a small inflatable tub that fits inside the bathtub. Lined with a towel or rubber mat, the kitchen or bathroom sink might be another option.

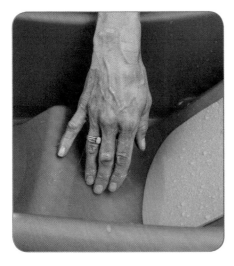

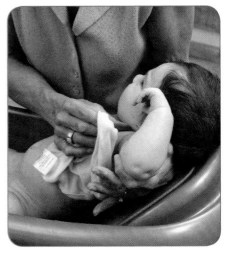

Checking the water temperature You need only a few inches of warm water. To prevent scalding, set your water heater thermostat to below 120 F. Check the temperature with your hand.

Use a secure hold A secure hold will help your baby feel comfortable and stay safe in the tub. Use one of your hands to support your baby's head and the other to hold and guide your baby's body.

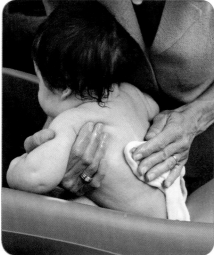

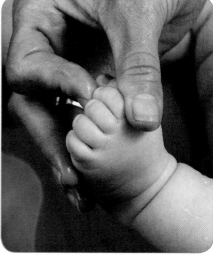

Washing baby's back When you clean your baby's back and buttocks, lean him or her forward on your arm. Continue to grasp your baby under the armpit.

Remember the creases Pay attention to creases under the arms, behind the ears, around the neck and in the diaper area. Wash between baby's fingers and toes.

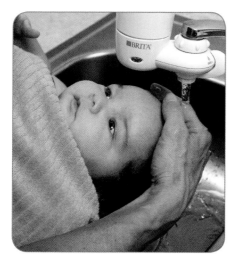

Rinsing baby's hair You might want to try a football hold under the faucet for washing hair. Support your baby's back with your arm, keeping a firm hold on your baby's head while you rinse.

When baby cries If your baby cries in the tub, stay calm. Clean what you can and then wrap your baby in a towel. Wait a few days and then try again. In the meantime, use sponge baths where needed.

UMBILICAL CORD CARE

After your newborn's umbilical cord is cut, all that remains is a small stump. In most cases, the remaining cord will dry up and fall off one to three weeks after birth. Until then, you want to keep the area as clean and dry as possible. It's a good idea to give sponge baths rather than full baths until the cord falls off and the navel area heals.

Traditionally, parents have been instructed to swab the cord stump with rubbing alcohol. But research indicates that leaving the stump alone may help the cord heal faster, so many hospitals now recommend against this practice. If you're unsure about what to do, talk to your baby's care provider.

Exposing the cord to air and allowing it to dry at its base will hasten its separation. To prevent irritation and keep the navel area dry, fold the baby's diaper below the stump. In warm weather, dress a newborn in just a diaper and T-shirt to let air circulate and help the drying process.

It's normal to see a bit of crusted discharge or dried blood until the cord falls off. But if your baby's navel looks red or has a foul-smelling discharge, call his or her care provider. When the stump falls off, you may see a little blood, which is normal.

Umbilical cord problems, including infections, aren't common. But have the area examined by your baby's care provider if you notice any of the following:

- The navel continues to bleed.
- The skin around the base of the cord is red.
- There's a foul-smelling, yellowish discharge from the cord.
- Your baby cries when you touch the cord or the skin near the cord.
- The cord hasn't dried up or fallen off by the time the baby is 2 months old.

Umbilical granuloma In some cases, the umbilical cord forms a small red mass of scar tissue (granuloma) that remains on the bellybutton even after the cord has fallen off. The granuloma usually drains a light yellow fluid. If you notice these signs, contact your baby's care provider to discuss whether your baby needs to be examined. Typically, an umbilical granuloma resolves on its own after about a week, but if it doesn't, your baby's care provider may need to remove the tissue.

Umbilical hernia If your baby's umbilical cord area or belly button protrudes or bulges when he or she cries, strains or sits up, he or she may have an umbilical hernia. In this common condition, part of the abdomen pushes through a hole in the abdominal wall when there's pressure. Umbilical hernias typically resolve on their own and don't need treatment. In rare cases, a baby may need surgery to close the hole. Taping the bulge down or taping a coin over the hernia is a potentially harmful practice and should be avoided. For more on umbilical hernias, see page 36.

CIRCUMCISION CARE

If your newborn boy was circumcised, the tip of his penis may seem raw for the first week after the procedure. Or a yellowish mucus or crust may form around the area. This is a normal part of healing. A small amount of bleeding also is common the first day or two.

Clean the area around the penis gently and apply a dab of petroleum jelly to the end of the penis with each diaper change. This will keep the diaper from sticking while the penis heals. If there's a bandage on the penis, change it with each diapering.

At some hospitals, a plastic ring is used instead of a bandage. The ring will remain on the end of the penis until the edge of the circumcision has healed, usually within a week. The ring will drop off on its own.

Problems after a circumcision are rare, but call your baby's care provider if you notice bleeding, redness or crusted sores containing fluid around the tip of the penis. Other signs to be aware of are swelling of the penis tip or a foul-smelling drainage coming from the penis tip.

Washing a circumcised penis It's OK to gently wash the penis as it's healing. And once it's healed, the circum-cised penis doesn't need special care. Wash your baby's penis with warm water and mild baby soap, just like you clean the rest of his bottom. Occasionally, a small piece of foreskin remains on the penis. If this occurs, gently pull back that skin to make sure the head of the penis is clean.

Caring for an uncircumcised penis During your baby's first few months, clean his uncircumcised penis with water and a bit of mild baby soap, just like you would clean the rest of his bottom. You don't need anything else such as antiseptic or cotton swabs. Don't try to pull back or retract the foreskin. Doing so can cause tearing, pain and bleeding. The foreskin will retract on its own, most likely after your baby is about 6 months or older.

It's important to watch your uncircumcised baby urinate once in a while. If you notice his urine stream isn't stronger than a trickle, or if he seems uncomfortable while he pees, contact your baby's care provider. It's possible that the hole in the foreskin is too small to allow a normal flow of urine.

Because the foreskin separation can take several months or longer, check with your baby's care provider to find out when the separation is complete. Once it is, you can gently retract the foreskin to clean the head of the penis. Then pull the foreskin back over the penis when you're finished.

Once your baby boy is older, it's important to teach him how to properly wash his penis using these three steps:

▶ Gently pull the foreskin back and away from the head of the penis.

▶ Use warm water and soap to clean the head of the penis and the fold in the foreskin.

▶ Pull the foreskin back to its original place over the head of the penis.

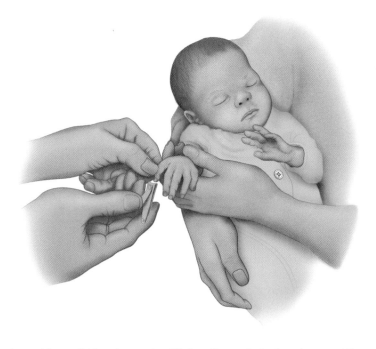

© MFMER

Two hints for making nail trimming easier: Wait until your baby is asleep and then work together, with one person holding the baby and the other person trimming the nails.

NAIL CARE

Your baby's nails are soft, but they're sharp. A newborn can easily scratch his or her own face — or yours. To prevent your baby from accidentally scratching his or her face, you will want to trim or file the fingernails shortly after birth. Then continue to trim his or her nails a few times a week.

Sometimes you may be able to carefully peel off the ends with your fingers because baby nails are so soft. Don't worry — you won't rip the whole nail off. You can also use a baby nail clippers or a small scissors. Here are some tips to make nail trimming easier for you and your baby:

▶ Trim the nails after a bath. They'll be softer, making them easier to cut.
▶ Wait until your baby is asleep.
▶ Have another person hold your baby while you trim his or her nails.
▶ Trim the nails straight across.

Don't bite your baby's nails as a method of keeping them trimmed — this can cause infection.

Your baby's toenails will probably grow much more slowly than his or her fingernails. They may need a trim only once or twice a month. Toenails are also softer than fingernails, so they may appear to be ingrown, but unless the skin around the nail looks red and inflamed, they're probably fine.

COMMON SKIN CONDITIONS

Many parents expect their newborn's skin to be flawless. But most babies are born with some bruising, and skin blotches and blemishes are common. Young infants often have dry, peeling skin, especially on their hands and feet, for the first few weeks. Some blueness of the hands and feet is normal and may continue for a few weeks. Rashes also are common. Most rashes and skin conditions are treated easily or clear up on their own.

Milia Milia is the name for tiny white pimples or bumps that appear on the nose, chin and cheeks. Although they appear to be raised, they are nearly flat and smooth to the touch. If your baby has milia, you can wash his or her face once a day with warm water and a mild baby soap, but avoid using lotion, oils or other products. It's also important to leave the skin alone — never scrub or pinch the bumps. Milia disappear in time, often within a few weeks, and they don't require treatment.

Acne Baby acne refers to the more pronounced red or white bumps and blotches (pimples) that are seen on the face, neck, upper chest and back. Among newborns who experience acne, the pimples are generally most noticeable within the first few weeks. To care for baby acne, place a soft, clean receiving blanket under baby's head and wash his or her face gently once a day with mild baby soap. Avoid lotions, oils and other treatments and never scrub, squeeze or pinch the affected skin. The condition typically disappears without treatment within the first couple of months. If it doesn't clear up after a few months, talk with your child's care provider.

Sometimes baby acne may not develop until later, occurring when babies are around 3 or 4 months old. In these cases, the acne usually clears up sometime within the first year, but it can last a few years. Talk with your child's care provider. The provider may recommend treatment if he or she is worried about possible scarring.

Having acne as a baby doesn't necessarily mean that your child will have acne later in life.

Erythema toxicum Erythema toxicum is the medical term for a skin condition that's typically present at birth or appears within the first few days after birth. It's characterized by small white or yellowish bumps surrounded by pink or reddish skin. The condition causes no discomfort and isn't infectious. Erythema toxicum disappears in several days, although sometimes it flares and subsides before completely clearing up. Treatment isn't necessary.

Pustular melanosis These small spots look like small yellowish-white sesame seeds that quickly dry and peel off. They may look similar to skin infections (pustules), but pustular melanosis isn't an infection and disappears without treatment. The spots are commonly seen in the folds of the neck and on the shoulders and upper chest. They're more common in babies with darker skin.

Cradle cap Cradle cap refers to a scaliness and redness that develops on a baby's scalp. It results when oil-producing sebaceous glands produce too much oil. Cradle cap is common in infants, usually beginning in the first weeks of life and clearing up over a period of weeks or months. It may be mild, with flaky, dry skin that looks like dandruff, or more severe, with thick, oily, yellowish scaling or crusty patches.

Shampooing with a mild baby shampoo can help with cradle cap. Don't be afraid to wash your baby's hair frequently.

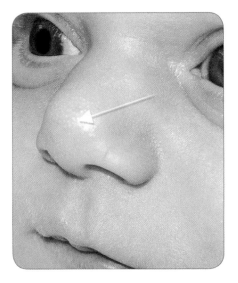

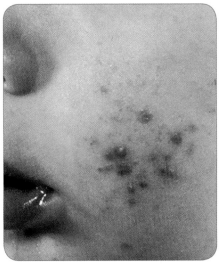

Milia Many babies are born with tiny white bumps that appear on the nose, chin or cheeks. This condition, called milia, occurs when skin flakes become trapped near the surface of the baby's skin.

Acne Acne typically appears as red or white bumps on a baby's forehead or cheeks. The condition often develops as a result of exposure to maternal hormones during pregnancy.

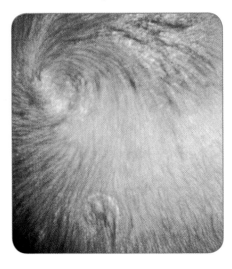

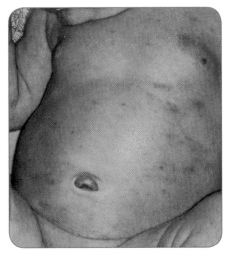

Cradle cap Cradle cap appears as thick, yellow, crusty or greasy patches on a baby's scalp. Cradle cap is common in newborns and usually appears within the first few weeks after birth.

Erythema toxicum The main symptom of this condition is a rash of small, yellow-to-white colored bumps (papules) surrounded by red skin. There may be a few or several papules.

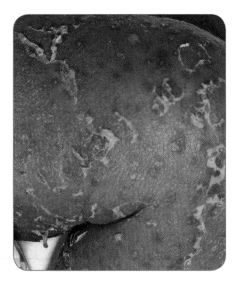

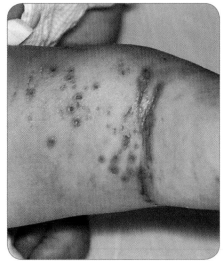

Pustular melanosis This condition involves small blisters that resemble seeds that dry up and peel away. The blisters leave behind spots, or "freckle" marks, that disappear in weeks to months.

Eczema Baby eczema is characterized by patches of red, scaly, itchy skin. Occasionally the patches ooze and crust over. Eczema often appears at the elbows and knees and on the cheeks.

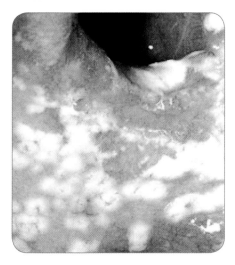

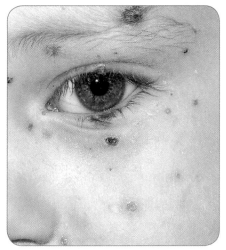

Oral thrush Oral thrush produces slightly raised, creamy white, sore patches on a baby's mouth or tongue. The patches may spread to the gums or the back of baby's mouth.

Impetigo Impetigo starts as a red sore that ruptures, oozes for a few days and then forms a honey-colored crust. Sores mainly occur around the nose and mouth and spread to other parts of the face.

This, along with soft brushing, will help remove the scales. If the scales don't loosen easily, rub a few drops of mineral oil onto your baby's scalp. Let it soak into the scales for a few minutes, and then brush and shampoo your baby's hair. If you leave the oil in your baby's hair, the scales may accumulate and worsen cradle cap.

If cradle cap persists or spreads to other parts your child's body, especially in the creases at the elbow or behind the ears, contact your baby's care provider, who may suggest a medicated shampoo or lotion.

Cradle cap isn't usually uncomfortable or itchy for your baby, but sometimes a yeast infection can occur in the affected skin. In this case, the skin will become very red and itchy. If you notice this, contact your baby's care provider.

Eczema Eczema, also known as atopic dermatitis, is marked by dry, itchy, scaly red patches of skin that are often found around babies' elbows or knees. Sometimes the affected area is small and doesn't bother a baby much, and treatment isn't necessary. Many babies outgrow eczema.

In other cases, eczema can cover a lot of skin and be extremely itchy and uncomfortable. In these cases, talk with your baby's care provider about whether treatment is needed. You can also try the following methods to prevent eczema from recurring:

▶ Use fragrance-free baby soaps to wash your baby and laundry detergents that are free of fragrances, dye and deodorants. Even "mild" baby soaps may have a small amount of fragrance that can irritate sensitive skin.

▶ Dress your baby in soft, cotton clothing, and avoid synthetic fabrics and wool.

▶ Bathe your baby daily with a fragrance-free hypoallergenic bath oil. This can help moisturize your baby's skin, in addition to help prevent skin infections, which are more common in babies with eczema.

▶ Use a fragrance-free moisturizer right after patting baby dry following a bath. This helps lock moisture from the bath into baby's skin.

▶ Keep your baby from environmental triggers for eczema, including heat and low humidity.

▶ Check your baby's sleeping conditions and ensure that the area is free of dust and upholstery that may contain dust mites.

Contact dermatitis and 'drool rash' Contact dermatitis is a kind of skin inflammation that occurs when substances touching your skin cause irritation or an allergic reaction. The resulting red, itchy, dry or bumpy rash isn't contagious or life-threatening, but it can be very uncomfortable. Culprits for babies could include soaps, laundry detergent, rough fabric or even your baby's own drool (sometimes referred to as drool rash).

If you can identify the offending agent and eliminate contact between it and your baby, the contact dermatitis should clear up. Often, using an absorbent bib and changing it frequently, as well as applying a barrier cream such as petroleum jelly to the area of irritation, can help prevent the rash from worsening. In the meantime, a wet compress may help comfort your baby. Contact your child's care provider if the rash is severe or gets worse or if your baby's skin is oozing or extremely itchy.

Impetigo Impetigo is a highly contagious skin infection that mainly affects infants and children. It usually appears as

A WORD ON SUNSCREEN

Remember that your baby's skin will sunburn easily. If you're going to be outside for any length of time, protect your baby's skin with clothing and a cap. Keep him or her in the shade to avoid overexposure to the sun.

As for sunscreen, recommendations differ for infants younger and older than 6 months. Consider these general guidelines from the American Academy of Pediatrics, the Food and Drug Administration and the American Cancer Society:

▶ *For babies younger than 6 months* Keep him or her out of direct sunlight. Protect your baby from sun exposure by dressing him or her in protective clothing, a hat with a brim and sunglasses. If sun exposure can't be avoided, most pediatric dermatologists recommend using a sunscreen. Look for one that's 100 percent zinc oxide or titanium dioxide. These are "physical blockers" as opposed to "chemical blockers" often found in other sunscreens. In addition to sunburn, infants don't sweat easily. If they're in the sun, they can easily become overheated.

▶ *For babies 6 months or older* Liberally use sunscreen. In addition, avoid exposing your baby to the sun during peak hours — generally 10 a.m. to 4 p.m. — and dress your baby in protective clothing, a hat with a brim and sunglasses.

The American Academy of Dermatology recommends using a broad-spectrum sunscreen with a sun protection factor (SPF) of 30 or more. To avoid irritating your baby's skin and eyes, use a sunscreen that contains only inorganic filters, such as zinc oxide and titanium dioxide. Avoid using products that combine sunscreen and the insect repellent DEET, since sunscreen must be regularly reapplied and insect repellent typically doesn't need to be reapplied. Apply sunscreen generously, and reapply every two hours — or more often if your baby is spending time in the water or is perspiring.

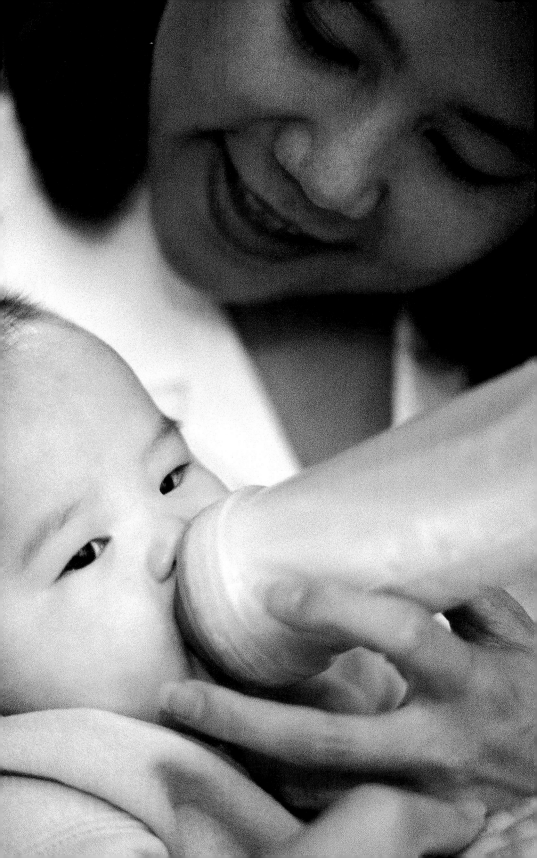

red sores on the face, especially around a child's nose and mouth. The sores may be covered with a yellow-brown scab or crust, or grow into blisters and pimples and weep pus. Although impetigo commonly occurs when bacteria enter the skin through cuts or insect bites, it can also develop in skin that's perfectly healthy.

Impetigo is seldom serious, and it usually clears on its own in two to three weeks. But because impetigo can sometimes lead to complications, your child's doctor may choose to treat impetigo with an antibiotic ointment or oral antibiotics.

Thrush Thrush, which is a yeast infection in the mouth, is a common infection in babies. You may notice creamy white lesions on your baby's cheeks or tongue. Sometimes thrush even spreads to the top of your baby's mouth, gums, tonsils or the back of the mouth. Aside from the white patches or lesions, your baby may not have any noticeable signs and symptoms. Other indications of thrush include:

▶ Pain or fussiness while eating and drinking
▶ Loss of appetite, including drinking less milk

If your baby only has a white tongue, it's probably not thrush. Drinking milk often results in a white tongue for babies before they start eating solid foods.

Your baby's care provider can determine if your baby has thrush by examining his or her mouth and tongue and scraping off a sample of the white lesions or patches. If your baby has thrush, he or she will probably be given an anti-yeast medicine.

Babies can pass the infection to their mothers during breast-feeding. The infection may then pass back and forth between a mother's breasts and a baby's

mouth. Women whose breasts are infected with the yeast may experience the following signs and symptoms:

▶ Unusually red, sensitive or itchy nipples
▶ Shiny or flaky skin on the areola
▶ Unusual pain during nursing or painful nipples between feedings
▶ Stabbing pains deep within the breast

If you're breast-feeding an infant who has oral thrush, you and your baby will do best if you're both treated with medication. Otherwise, you're likely to pass the infection back and forth. Your doctor may prescribe a mild antifungal medication for your baby and an antifungal cream for your breasts. If your baby uses a pacifier or feeds from a bottle, rinse nipples and pacifiers in a solution of equal parts water and vinegar daily and allow them to air-dry to prevent fungus growth. Additionally, if you use a breast pump, rinse any of the detachable parts that come in contact with your milk in a vinegar and water solution.

CHAPTER 6

Clothing baby

One of the things many new parents look forward to during pregnancy and after baby is born is going baby-clothes shopping! For years you may have walked by the baby section at clothing and discount stores and excitedly anticipated the day when you would be able to purchase such cute items for your son or daughter.

While it may be hard to resist the frilly dresses, designer blue jeans or miniature sports jerseys, you want to be practical in the clothes you buy. You'll be changing clothes a lot (yes, they get dirty), and undressing and dressing may not be one of your child's favorite activities. So why make it more complicated than you have to.

A FEW SHOPPING TIPS

If you haven't had a lot of experience in outfitting a baby, here are a few suggestions you may find helpful as you shop for baby clothing.

Size Almost all baby clothing is sized in three-month intervals. Sizes often begin with 0-3 months, followed by 3-6 months, 6-9 months and 9-12 months. It would make sense that a newborn would wear 0-3 months. But buying for baby often isn't quite that simple — as many parents who've had to return clothing to the store can attest!

When you're buying clothes for your newborn, don't go strictly by what's on the label. Look at the item and see if it appears to run small or about the right size for your child. You may find you want to size up, even if it means the item may be a little big to begin with.

Many babies fit into clothing long before what's indicated on the label. A newborn may wear a size 3-6 months within a few weeks of birth. And it's not uncommon for a 4-month-old to wear a size 6-9 months.

Many mothers will tell you about waiting until baby was 6 months old to wear the cute 6-9 month outfit, only to put it on and find out it was too small!

Some manufacturers include tags that list weight and height guidelines for each size. They may give you a better idea if the item will fit.

Fabric In general, look for soft, comfortable clothing that's washable. Your infant is just as likely to appreciate clothing that doesn't irritate, bind, twist or rub as you are. Select sleepwear that's labeled flame resistant or flame retardant, which can be either a synthetic fiber or cotton treated with flame-retardant chemicals.

Remember, babies make a mess! So purchase clothing that's stain-remover and washing-machine friendly. Also keep in mind that items made from cotton may shrink a bit.

Safety Keep it simple. Avoid clothes with buttons, which are easily swallowed, and ribbons or strings, which can cause choking. Don't buy garments with drawstrings, which can catch on objects and strangle a child.

Ease Because you may be changing your baby's clothing a few times a day — or at least changing diapers several times a day — make sure the outfits are uncomplicated and they open easily.

Look for garments that snap or open down the front, have loosefitting sleeves, and are made of stretchy fabric. Avoid items with zippers. You know what it feels like to zip your own skin in a zipper! You wouldn't want to accidently do the same to your baby.

Cost Since babies outgrow clothes so quickly, consider purchasing some clothes at thrift stores, garage sales or from other mothers. If someone offers you hand-me-downs, don't take it as an insult. Hand-me-downs are a great way to save money that you can put to use for other items you may want to purchase for baby.

WHERE TO START

You can fill your baby's closet with all sorts of clothes, but because babies grow so fast, you don't want to buy too much. You run the risk that your son or daughter will outgrow the clothes before he or she has a chance to wear them. It's often best to purchase a few outfits at a time every few months.

You'll also find there are certain clothes babies seem to wear more than others — often because of ease, comfort or convenience.

One-piece undershirts You want the kind that comes between the legs, fits up over the crotch and snaps in front. People often refer to these as Onesies. Onesies, however, is a registered trademark of Gerber Childrenswear. Other manufacturers make similar products but call them by a different name.

One-piece undershirts can be worn underneath clothing or, if the weather is hot or the indoor temperature a bit warm, by themselves. They provide an easy way to give your baby an extra layer of warmth, and they help keep your baby's other clothing from rubbing up against that new and delicate skin.

You'll go through a lot of these. Buy enough to last you between clothes washings.

One-piece outfits Footed one-piece outfits go by a lot of names, including stretchies, sleepers or rompers. When your baby is young, you may find them quite practical. The outfits generally snap in front and at the crotch and are easy to get on and off.

A gown resembles a stretchy or sleeper, but instead of having footed legs, it looks more like a sleeping bag at the bottom. A gown may have an open, elasticized bottom.

Again, because your newborn may wear one-piece outfits almost every day,

make sure you have enough to last you between washings.

Pajamas Depending on the weather, baby's pajamas may be of a lighter or heavier material. During hot summer months, a sleeper or gown may be all baby needs while sleeping. During the colder winter months, you may want to put baby in a heavier blanket sleeper. Blanket sleepers keep baby warm without the need for a comforter or blanket.

Don't purchase oversized pajamas, regardless of how comfortable you think they might look. If the garment rides up on the neck and head or is too loose around the shoulders, the extra space between the material and baby's skin may increase the risk of suffocation. With sleepwear, ignore the buy-big rule and purchase pajamas that fit snugly.

You'll likely want at least a couple of pajamas. Make sure the material is flame resistant or flame retardant.

Dress wear For occasions when you'll be taking baby out and you want more dressy clothing, look for outfits that are comfortable and easy to get on and off.

Two-piece outfits that snap at the waist help prevent the pants from falling off or the top from riding up. If the outfit has elastic at the waistline, legs or arms, make sure the elastic isn't too tight.

In the warm summer months, one-piece outfits with short sleeves and short pants are great day wear.

Socks As you well know, socks have a tendency to fall off! Look for those that are most likely to stay on, but also expect that you will lose some along the way. You don't need to worry about purchasing socks with nonskid bottoms until baby starts walking.

Winter wear During the cooler winter months, you need a winter cap to cover baby's head. His or her hands should also be covered. When baby is young, you may find a bunting to be convenient. However, these sac-like outer garments generally aren't recommended if baby is in a car seat. The extra material could prevent baby from being strapped in securely. A snowsuit, which has legs, often works best.

Summer hat or cap To help protect baby's skin and keep him or her from getting too warm, use a hat or cap during warm, summer months. A hat or cap also helps keep the sun out of baby's eyes.

Shoes Many babies don't walk until after their first birthday, but a few young ones get their legs under them early. If your son or daughter begins walking early, you may need to purchase a pair of shoes.

There's nothing wrong with baby walking in his or her bare feet — it's actually a great way to learn. Shoes are needed at times, though, to protect baby's feet, especially when outside. You don't want baby stepping on something sharp or in something unpleasant.

When shopping for shoes, look for shoes that are low-cut with flexible, nonskid soles. The upper part of the shoe should be made from material that's breathable and lightweight. Err on the side of buying shoes that are too big rather than ones that will soon be too small. However, you don't want the shoes so big that baby has difficulty walking in them.

WASHING BABY'S CLOTHES

After your baby arrives, it can seem as if you do laundry all of the time. To make the process as easy as possible, purchase

---

DRESS FOR THE WEATHER

New parents sometimes overdress their infants. A good rule of thumb is to dress your baby in the same number of layers that you would feel comfortable wearing, and possibly one more light layer. For example, you might put baby in a diaper and undershirt, covered by a sleeper or gown, and wrapped in a receiving blanket.

In hot weather — over 75 F — a single layer of clothing is often appropriate. Babies don't sweat easily and can become overheated. However, you may want an additional layer if the baby is in air conditioning or near drafts.

Remember that your baby's skin will sunburn easily. If you're going to be outside, keep baby out of the sun, and protect your baby's skin with clothing and a hat or cap. For more on sun protection, see page 103.

clothes that appear durable and that are likely to wash well. It's also a good idea to wash all clothes before baby wears them, in case during handling irritating substances got on the clothing. Here are a few other tips.

Stains Stains are inevitable. Breast milk, formula, spit-up, poop — these common offenders will more often than not wind up on your baby's clothes (and probably yours, too!).

If possible, wipe or rinse off the substance while it's still fresh and before it sets. You might soak stained clothes with a pre-soak before you wash them. At the very least, blast them with a good douse of stain remover before they're put in the washing machine.

Detergents Babies have sensitive skin, and some babies develop skin irritation from normal laundry detergents. If you think your baby's skin may be sensitive to normal laundry detergent, try a detergent without colors and fragrances. This might reduce the irritation. And don't use fabric softeners.

You might also consider washing baby's clothes in milder detergents that supposedly leave less residue and, therefore, don't cause as much skin irritation. The label on these products often indicates the detergent is intended for the clothing of babies and children and those who are sensitive to laundry soap residue. Be warned, though, these products tend to be more expensive.

Some parents run baby's clothes through an extra rinse cycle to ensure there's no soap residue left on the clothing. This may not be necessary, but if you would like, you can try it to see if it helps.

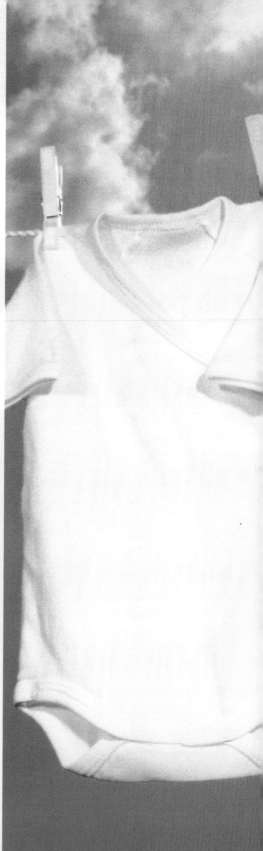

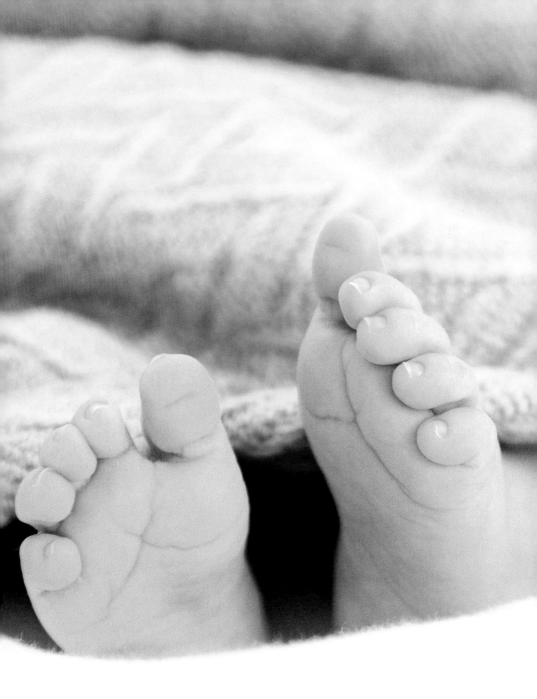

CHAPTER 7

Sleep and sleep issues

Oh, baby! There's nothing like getting a good night's sleep. While newborns usually sleep about 16 hours a day, it's frequently for only one or two hours at a time. Your baby can thrive on that schedule, but you may find it exhausting. If you haven't had a good night's sleep since your baby was born, you're not alone. Sleepless nights are a rite of passage for most new parents. But don't despair, your baby will learn to sleep better at night. Honestly! From the time your baby is born, you can encourage him or her to adopt good sleep habits.

This chapter also discusses common sleep-related issues such as colic and reviews prevention strategies to reduce the risk of sudden infant death syndrome (SIDS) and crib accidents.

SLEEP SCHEDULE

It takes a while for newborns to get on any kind of schedule for sleeping. During the first month, they usually sleep and wake round-the-clock, with relatively equal periods of sleep between feedings.

In addition, newborns don't know the difference between night and day. It takes time for them to develop circadian rhythms — the sleep-wake cycles and other patterns that revolve on a 24-hour cycle. As a baby's nervous system gradually matures, so do his or her phases of sleep and wakefulness.

Daily sleep Although newborns don't usually sleep for more than a few hours at a stretch, altogether they typically sleep 12 to 16 hours a day. They may stay awake long enough to feed, or for up to about two hours, before falling asleep again. The first few days home from the hospital don't be surprised if you feel exhausted. Remember, you just had a baby, and you're now trying to get adjusted to what it's like being up with a baby at night.

By the time your baby is 2 weeks old, you'll likely notice that the periods of sleeping and wakefulness are lengthening. By age 3 to 4 months, some babies sleep at least five hours at a time and shift more of their sleep to nighttime, much to the relief of their parents! By age 6 months, nighttime stretches of nine to 12 hours are possible.

Naps Many newborns nap frequently in one- to two-hour spurts. As baby gets older, nap times may lengthen and become more predictable. With some babies, though, napping remains completely random and they never fall into any type of pattern.

When baby is a few months old, you may find he or she will fall into a three-naps-a-day schedule: a morning nap, an early afternoon nap and an early evening nap. However, this, too, varies considerably with each baby.

Night vs. day Some babies clearly have their days and nights reversed, and they sleep more in the daytime than at night. For parents who are sleep deprived, this can be a stressful time. Generally, though, within a few weeks to a couple of months, days and nights will become more predictable and regular.

One way to help speed up this transition is to limit daytime naps to no more than three or four hours each. In addition, during the day, have baby sleep in a more active area of the house with the lights on and where noises can be heard. In contrast, at night, keep the bedroom dark and quiet.

During nighttime feedings and diaper changes, avoid stimulation. Keep the lights low, use a soft voice, and don't play or talk with your baby. This reinforces the message that nighttime is for sleeping.

NOISY BREATHING

The familiar phrase "sleeping like a baby," conjures up images of a baby lying quietly and breathing ever so softly. But babies — especially newborns — often aren't quiet when they sleep.

Newborns spend about half their time in an active phase of sleep, called rapid eye movement (REM) sleep. During REM sleep, baby may breathe irregularly, grunt, snort and twitch. During deeper sleep, called non-rapid eye movement (NREM) sleep, baby sleeps more peacefully. As babies get older, they spend more time in NREM sleep and less time in active sleep. So they generally become less noisy.

In addition, newborns are dominantly nose breathers — they breathe through their noses, not their mouths. This is so they can breathe at the same time they nurse. The slightest congestion or mucus in baby's tiny nasal passages as air flows in and out can make a lot of noise. If your baby's breathing sounds a bit stuffy, it doesn't necessarily mean that he or she has a cold or allergies.

Noisy breathing in infants can be very worrisome for parents. Most of the time, the noise is normal. However, if you're concerned that something isn't right, contact your child's care provider.

ADOPTING GOOD SLEEP HABITS

Some babies just sleep well from the start. They nap during the day and sleep for long stretches at night, only waking for feedings. Most babies aren't that easy. They may take only short catnaps, wake often at night and have trouble lulling themselves back to sleep.

If your baby doesn't sleep well, know that with time his or her sleep will improve. In addition, there are steps you can take to help him or her sleep better and learn how to fall asleep without your assistance.

Learning to fall asleep In the first few months, it's common for a pattern to evolve in which a baby is fed and falls asleep in a parent's arms. Many parents enjoy this closeness and snuggling. But eventually this may be the only way the baby is able to fall asleep. When the baby wakes up in the middle of the night, he or she can't fall asleep again without being fed and held.

Drooping eyelids, rubbing the eyes and fussiness are the usual signs that a baby is tired. When you notice these signs, put your baby in his or her crib while he or she is drowsy but still awake. You want to catch the signs of sleepiness early. The longer you wait, the more overtired and fussy your baby may become, and the harder it may become for him or her to fall asleep. If a baby can fall asleep in bed without assistance when first laid down, it's more likely that he or she will fall asleep on his or her own after waking in the middle of the night.

It's common for babies to cry when put down for sleep, but if left alone for a few minutes, most will eventually quiet themselves. If you leave the room for a while, your baby will probably stop crying after a short time. If not, try comforting him or her and allow for time for him or her to settle again.

If your baby wakes shortly after you put him or her to bed and isn't wet, hungry or ill, try to be patient with the crying and encourage self-settling. This may require soliciting support from a partner, family member or friend to keep you from not picking baby up.

During sleep, babies are often active, twitching their arms and legs, smiling, sucking and generally appearing restless. And while sleeping, infants may cry and move about when entering different sleep cycles. Parents sometimes mistake a baby's stirrings as a sign of waking up, and they begin unnecessary feeding. Instead, wait a few minutes to see if your baby falls back to sleep.

Sleep tips Here are some suggestions to help your baby learn how to "sleep like a baby."

Encourage activity during the day When your baby is awake, engage him or her by talking, singing and playing. Surround your baby with light and normal household noises. Stimulation during the day can help promote better sleep at night.

Monitor your baby's naps Regular naps are important — but sleeping for large chunks of time during the day may leave your baby wide awake at bedtime.

Follow a consistent bedtime routine Before bedtime take part in relaxing activities such as bathing, cuddling, singing or reading. Soon your baby will associate these activities with sleep. If you play bedtime music, choose the same tunes each time you put your baby in the crib. Avoid active play right before bedtime.

Put your baby to bed drowsy but awake This will help your baby associate bed with the process of falling asleep. The American Academy of Pediatrics (AAP) strongly advises that you place your baby on his or her back at bedtime. Putting babies to sleep on their backs reduces the risk of sudden infant death syndrome (SIDS). SIDS prevention is discussed later in this chapter.

Give your baby time to settle down Your baby may fuss or cry before finding a comfortable position and falling asleep. If the crying doesn't stop, speak to your baby calmly and stroke his or her back. Your reassuring presence may be all your baby needs to fall asleep.

Consider a pacifier If your baby has trouble settling down, a pacifier might do

the trick. Another possible benefit, as noted by the AAP, is that a pacifier may reduce the risk of SIDS. Is there a downside to using a pacifier? Yes — if it falls out of your baby's mouth during the night, he or she may let you know by crying loudly, and this can happen multiple times throughout the night. In addition, if you're breast-feeding, you may want to avoid pacifier use during the first month until you feel comfortable you have the process down and baby is eating well.

Expect frequent stirring at night Babies often wriggle, squirm and twitch in their sleep. They can be noisy, too. Sometimes fussing or crying is simply a sign of settling down. Unless you suspect that your baby is hungry or uncomfortable, it's OK to wait a few minutes to see what happens.

Keep nighttime care low-key When your baby needs care or feeding during the night, use dim lights, a soft voice and calm movements. This will tell your baby that it's time to sleep — not play.

Don't bed share Many new parents are tempted to take their newborn into bed with them — often because they're tired and don't want to get up, and because having baby in bed seems more convenient. Sometimes parents bed share for cultural or philosophical reasons. No matter the reason, this is not a good practice. It can make it harder for your baby to fall asleep on his or her own. In addition, adult beds aren't as safe for babies to sleep as are cribs. Bed sharing may increase your baby's risk of SIDS.

Expect setbacks Once your baby begins to sleep well during the night, don't take it as a sign that your sleep-deprived nights are gone for good. As babies grow and develop, there will be setbacks. For

FEEDING A SLEEPY BABY

You'll no doubt have times when your baby signals that he or she is hungry, only to doze off once you begin feeding. Try these tips to feed a sleepy baby:

- Watch for and take advantage of your baby's alert stages. Feed at these times.
- If your baby falls asleep while feeding, gently wake and encourage him or her to finish eating.
- Give your baby a massage by walking your fingers up his or her spine.
- Partially undress your baby. Because your baby's skin is sensitive to temperature changes, the coolness may wake him or her long enough to eat.
- Stroke a circle around your baby's lips with a fingertip a few times.
- Rock your baby in a sitting position. The baby's eyes often open when he or she is positioned upright.

example, as your child gets older, he or she may experience separation anxiety, which can affect sleep. Illness and increased motor development also may disrupt sleep.

Don't give up If you're having trouble getting your baby to sleep, remember that it's often not as easy as it may sound. Sometimes what you try works, sometimes it doesn't, and sometimes it works only some of the time. If you feel you need more help, call your doctor to ask for suggestions. Call a friend or a family member and ask for help and a little relief. Just even talking about it can help — you'll know you're not alone.

'BACK' TO SLEEP

Always place your baby on his or her back to sleep, even for naps. This is the safest sleep position for reducing the risk of sudden infant death syndrome (SIDS). Sometimes called crib death, SIDS is the sudden and unexplained death of a baby under 1 year of age.

Research shows that babies who are put to sleep on their stomachs are much more likely to die of SIDS than are babies placed on their backs. Infants who sleep on their sides are also at increased risk, probably because babies in this position can roll onto their stomachs. Since 1992, when the American Academy of Pediatrics began recommending the back-sleeping position for infants, the incidence of SIDS in the United States has declined significantly.

The only exceptions to the back-sleeping rule are babies who have health problems that require them to sleep on their stomachs. If your baby was born with a birth defect, spits up often after eating, or has a breathing, lung or heart problem, talk to your baby's care provider about the best sleeping position for your child.

Make sure that everyone who takes care of your baby knows to place baby on his or her back for sleeping. That may include grandparents, child care providers, baby sitters, friends and others.

Some babies don't like sleeping on their backs at first, but they get used to it quickly. Many parents worry that their baby will choke if he or she spits up or vomits while sleeping on his or her back, but doctors have found no increase in choking or similar problems.

Some babies who sleep on their backs may develop a flat spot on the backs of their heads. For the most part, this will go away after the baby learns to sit up. You can help keep your baby's head a normal shape by alternating the direction your baby lies in the crib — head toward one end of the crib for a few nights and then toward the other. This way, the baby won't always sleep on the same side of his or her head.

SIDS

Sudden infant death syndrome (SIDS) is the unexplained death, usually during sleep, of a seemingly healthy baby. Sudden infant death syndrome is sometimes referred to as crib death because the infants often die in their cribs.

Although the exact cause is still unknown, it appears that sudden infant death syndrome may be associated with abnormalities in the portion of an infant's brain that controls breathing and arousal from sleep.

Researchers have discovered some factors that may put babies at extra risk of sudden infant death syndrome. They've also identified some measures you can take to help protect your child from sudden infant death syndrome. The most important is placing your baby on his or her back to sleep.

Causes A combination of physical and sleep-related environmental factors can make an infant more vulnerable to SIDS. These factors may vary from child to child. Physical factors associated with SIDS include:

▶ *Brain abnormalities*. Some infants are born with problems that make them more likely to die of SIDS. In many of these babies, the portion of the brain that controls breathing and arousal from sleep doesn't work properly.

▶ *Low birth weight*. Premature birth or being part of a multiple birth increases the likelihood that a baby's brain hasn't matured completely, so he or she has less reliable control over such automatic processes as breathing and heart rate.

▶ *Respiratory infection*. Many infants who have died of SIDS have recently experienced a cold, which may contribute to breathing problems.

The items in a baby's crib and his or her sleeping position can combine with a baby's physical problems to increase the risk of SIDS. Examples include:

▶ *Sleeping on the stomach or side*. Babies who are placed on their stomachs or sides to sleep may have more difficulty breathing than those placed on their backs.

▶ *Sleeping on a soft surface*. Lying facedown on a fluffy comforter or a couch or water bed can block an infant's airway. Draping a blanket over a baby's head also is risky.

▶ *Sleeping with parents*. While the risk of SIDS is lowered if an infant sleeps in the same room as his or her parents, the risk increases if the baby sleeps in the same bed — partly because there are more soft surfaces (such as a soft mattress or a water bed) to impair breathing. Blankets or pillows also can interfere with breathing or make baby overly warm.

Risk factors Although sudden infant death syndrome can strike any infant, researchers have identified factors that may increase a baby's risk. They include:

- *Sex*. Boy babies are more likely to die of SIDS.
- *Age*. Infants are generally most vulnerable during the second and third months of life.
- *Race*. For reasons that aren't well understood, black, American Indian and Eskimo infants are more likely to develop SIDS.
- *Family history*. Babies who've had siblings or cousins die of SIDS are at higher risk of SIDS themselves.

The risk of SIDS is also affected by maternal factors associated with the pregnancy. Mothers under the age of 20, who smoke cigarettes or use drugs or alcohol, or who receive inadequate prenatal care are at increased risk of having a baby die of SIDS.

Prevention There's no guaranteed way to prevent SIDS, but you can help your baby sleep more safely by practicing the following recommendations.

Back to sleep Place your baby to sleep resting on his or her back, rather than on the stomach or side.

Select bedding carefully Use a firm mattress and avoid placing your baby on thick, fluffy padding, such as lambskin or a thick quilt. These may interfere with breathing if your baby's face presses against them. For the same reason, don't leave pillows, fluffy toys or stuffed animals in your infant's crib.

Don't overheat baby To keep your baby warm, try a sleep sack or other sleep clothing that doesn't require additional covers. If you use a blanket, make it lightweight. Tuck the blanket securely at the foot of the crib, with just enough length to cover your baby's shoulders. Then place your baby in the crib, near the foot,

covered loosely with the blanket. Don't cover your baby's head.

Keep baby out of your bed Baby should sleep alone. Adult beds aren't safe for infants. A baby can become trapped and suffocate between the headboard slats, the space between the mattress and the bed frame, or the space between the mattress and the wall. A baby can also suffocate if a sleeping parent accidentally rolls over and covers the baby's nose and mouth.

Offer a pacifier Sucking on a pacifier at nap time and bedtime may reduce the risk of SIDS. One caveat — if you're breast-feeding, wait to offer a pacifier until breast-feeding is well established. For some babies, this can be 3 to 4 weeks of age. If your baby's not interested in the pacifier, try again later. If the pacifier falls out of your baby's mouth while he or she is sleeping, don't pop it back in.

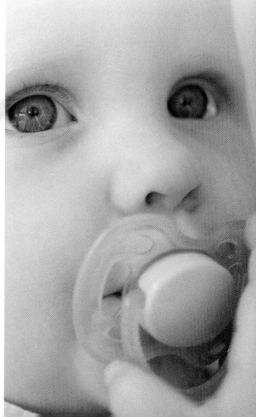

Make time for tummy time Just because your baby should sleep on his or her back doesn't mean baby should never spend any time on the tummy. While baby is awake and being supervised, place him or her on the floor on his or her tummy. Another option is to lay your baby tummy-down on your tummy or on your lap.

Being on the tummy is good for babies. It prepares them for the time when they'll be able to slide on their bellies and crawl by encouraging them to lift their heads and build strong head, neck and shoulder muscles. As babies grow older and stronger, they'll need more time on their tummies to build their strength.

Spending time on the stomach also helps a baby's head develop its conventional roundness, preventing it from becoming flat in the back. A baby's skull is soft and made up of several movable plates. If a baby's head is left in the same position for long periods of time, the skull may flatten. While it's recommended that you place your baby on his or her back to sleep to reduce the risk of sudden infant death syndrome (SIDS), tummy time helps reduce the risk of flat spots.

In addition, research suggests that babies who spend time on their tummies crawl on their stomachs earlier than do babies who don't practice tummy time. The more time babies spend on their tummies, the earlier they might begin to roll over, crawl on their stomachs, crawl on all fours and sit without support.

Make sure to make tummy time a part of your baby's daily activities. Start by laying your newborn on his or her tummy across your lap two or three times a day for short periods of time. As your baby grows stronger, place him or her on a blanket on the floor and increase tummy time.

Some babies may not like the tummy-time position at first. To help out, place yourself or a toy on the floor for baby to look at or play with. It also may be a good idea not to put baby on his or her tummy shortly after baby has eaten. Eventually your baby will become used to tummy time and enjoy play in this position.

CRIB SAFETY

An exciting time during your pregnancy was shopping for all of the items you would need for your new baby. Now they are being put to use!

In addition to being cute or decorative, your baby's gear needs to be safe. One item for which this is especially important is the crib. Make sure that your crib — the place where your baby will spend countless hours — meets all safety regulations.

Even if an old crib is in good shape, safety standards have improved over the years, so it's best to buy a new crib if you can. A crib should be the one place you feel comfortable leaving your child alone.

No more drop sides In 2011, the Consumer Product Safety Commission (CPSC) banned the manufacture and sale of drop-side cribs due to growing evidence that they played a role in the suffocation or strangulation deaths of dozens of infants over the past decade. The ban also includes the resale of drop-side cribs.

Drop-side cribs — the cribs which you probably slept in as a child — have a side rail that moves up and down, allowing a parent to lower the side and more easily lift baby from the crib.

These cribs came under scrutiny because of malfunctioning hardware, sometimes cheaper plastics, or assembly problems that can cause the drop-side rail to partially detach from the crib. When this happens, the drop side can create a dangerous "V-like" gap between the mattress and side rail where a baby can get caught and suffocate or strangle.

If you have a drop-side crib, or family or friends offer you one of theirs, don't use it. Knowing this type of crib poses a safety risk, it's best to avoid its use.

Other safety precautions In addition to the ban on drop-side cribs, other recent CPSC manufacturing regulations strengthen crib slats and mattress supports, improve the quality of crib hardware, and require more rigorous testing.

When purchasing and using a crib, follow these safety guidelines.

Check the slat spacing The crib's slats should be no farther apart than 2⅜ inches. This applies to bassinets, too. If you can fit a can of soda through the slats, the openings are too large. You're more likely to find this problem in older cribs, but you can't be too safe when it comes to your baby, so check any crib you put him or her in.

Check the corner posts If your crib has corner posts or knobs, they should stand at least 16 inches above the crib's end panels. This is so a child can't reach the top and get his or her pajamas caught. If the corner posts or knobs are shorter than this, unscrew or saw them off so that the corners are no more than 1⁄16 of an inch higher than the crib ends or side panels. Make sure to sand the crib corners to eliminate splinters and sharp ends.

Check the crib's paint If your crib is painted, make sure the paint isn't chipped or peeling. This is especially important with older cribs that may have been coated with paint that contains lead — another reason not to use an old crib.

Check the hardware Occasionally check the screws and bolts in your baby's crib to ensure nothing is loose, missing or damaged. Crib hardware can loosen over time and may need occasional tightening. If anything is missing or broken, contact the manufacturer for replacement parts.

Check the mattress supports Make sure that the system that supports the crib mattress isn't bent, broken or coming apart. If the mattress is suspended on hangers attached to hooks on the end panels, make sure the hangers are well connected.

Check that the mattress fits The mattress should fit tightly into the crib. There shouldn't be any cracks or openings between the crib and the mattress because a baby can get trapped in the smallest of spaces. If you can place more than two fingers between the mattress and the crib frame, the fit isn't snug enough.

Adjust the mattress height correctly Most cribs have a feature that allows the mattress to be placed at more than one level. The higher levels make it easier to take your infant out of the crib. However, this can become dangerous when your child is able to pull himself or herself to a standing position. Before your child reaches that stage, the mattress should be at its lowest setting.

Don't use a sleep positioner These are wedge-shaped pieces of foam designed to help babies sleep on their backs. The American Academy of Pediatrics says the devices haven't been tested sufficiently to show they're effective or safe.

Forget the bumper pads Crib bumpers are cute, but the American Academy of Pediatrics recommends that you don't use them. According to the organization, there's no evidence that bumper pads or similar products that attach to crib slats or sides prevent injury in young infants. However, bumper pads may increase the risk of entrapment and suffocation. They also need to be tied down with string, which can be hazardous if not properly secured.

Keep toys out of the crib Baby toys are cute and cuddly, and it can be difficult, if not impossible, to resist buying them. You will likely amass numerous baby toys. The main rule is to use them for play under parent supervision and keep them out of the crib. They can pose a small but nevertheless potential safety risk.

Remove crib mobiles early Crib mobiles typically include string and small attached pieces. Make sure your little one cannot reach the mobile so that he or she can't become entangled or pull anything off. When baby is able to push himself or herself onto the hands and knees, the mobile should be removed from the crib.

CHAPTER 8

Comforting a crying baby

The dream: Your baby starts sleeping through the night just a few weeks after birth, gurgles happily while you run errands and only fusses when hunger strikes. The reality: Your baby's favorite playtime is after a 2 a.m. feeding, and crankiness peaks whenever you're out and about.

Babies cry. The average newborn cries one to four hours a day — and for lots of reasons. Babies cry because they're tired, hungry, lonely, too hot, too cold or simply because it's that time of day. All this crying can be particularly baffling for first-time parents, who might think they should know what their screaming bundle of joy is trying to tell them — and be able to do something, quickly! Rest assured that if you can't figure out why your baby is crying or how to stop the tears, you haven't failed as a parent. Don't take the tears personally. If your baby's crying is causing you stress or anxiety, take a deep breath and try to relax. Ask for help if you feel you need it, and remember this stage won't last forever.

WHY BABIES CRY

When your baby cries, he or she is generally trying to tell you something. Crying is a baby's way of communicating that he or she is hungry, tired, uncomfortable, or simply has had too much stimulation for one day. There may be times when your baby needs to cry it out, but, in general, it's best to respond quickly to his or her cries — especially when your child is a newborn. Don't be afraid that by doing so you'll be spoiling your baby by giving him or her too much attention. Just the opposite, studies indicate that being responsive to a child's needs might help him or her cry less overall and show less aggressive behavior as a toddler.

Hunger Most newborns eat every few hours round the clock and usually wake for feedings during the night. Quiet babies may squirm and root around or fuss gently when they're hungry. More active babies can become almost frantic when hunger strikes. They may get so worked up by the time feeding begins that they gulp air with the milk. This can cause spitting up, trapped gas and more crying. Some babies are intensely bothered by having air in their stomachs, while for others it isn't as much of a problem.

Discomfort Just like adults, babies don't like to feel uncomfortable. A common cause of baby discomfort is a wet or soiled diaper. Some babies don't mind the warm, messy feeling they've created. Other babies can't tolerate a soaked or dirty diaper, and they let you know right away they're unhappy. Tummy troubles also are a common source of discomfort. Gas or indigestion can cause babies to cry. If your baby fusses after being fed, he or she may be feeling some sort of tummy pain. Often, after a burp or the passing of gas, the crying will stop. Temperature also can be a source of discomfort — if baby is too hot or too cold, it can trigger tears. So can tight, binding or

itchy clothing. Make sure the waistband around baby's stomach isn't too tight, the collar doesn't rub on baby's face, the legs or sleeves don't pull when baby moves, or the material itch. For some babies, these are no-nos.

Loneliness, boredom or fear Sometimes, babies cry simply because they're looking for attention — a little tender, loving care (TLC). Baby may be lonely or bored. Or he or she may be frightened. A baby seeking TLC will often calm down simply by seeing or hearing you, feeling your touch or being cuddled. As you'll find, babies like to be held. They like to see and hear their parents and listen to the sound of their parents' heartbeats.

Overtiredness or overstimulation When a baby is overtired or overly stimulated, crying becomes a way to unwind or release tension. Tired babies generally fuss. And you may find that your baby needs more sleep than you think. Newborns often sleep for 16 hours a day. Too much noise, movement or visual stimulation also might drive your baby to tears. In addition, many babies have predictable periods of fussiness. They cry at certain periods of the day and often for no apparent reason.

UNDERSTANDING BABY'S CRIES

What many new parents find is that with time — as they get to know their child and the child's developing personality — they come to understand what baby's different cries mean. With time, the same will be true for you. However, here are a few "crying cues" that may help you if you can't figure out what your little loved one is trying to tell you.

- A hungry cry might be short and low pitched.
- A cry of pain might be a sudden, long, high-pitched shriek.
- If your baby is making lip movements or rooting, hunger might be the problem.
- If your baby is rubbing his or her eyes, he or she might be tired and in need of some sleep.
- If your baby hears a loud noise and begins to cry, he or she may simply be startled.

Picking up on particular patterns can help you better respond to your baby's cries. Getting to know your child's crying triggers can also help you notice when your baby is experiencing unusual distress — crying for reasons he or she normally doesn't.

COMFORTING A CRYING BABY

OK. So my baby is crying. Now what do I do? Sometimes, the cause is obvious and you can quickly remedy the situation. In other cases, you may have to experiment with a couple of calming techniques until you find out what your baby likes — what brings comfort to him or her. Keep in mind that babies are different. What works for one baby doesn't always work for another.

Check baby's diaper Do a quick exam of your baby's diaper to make sure it's clean and dry. A new diaper may be the answer to the problem.

See if baby is hungry If your baby is hungry, he or she will likely stop crying when you offer the breast or a bottle. Keep in mind, however, that crying is a late sign of hunger that can interfere with

feeding. You might need to calm your baby before he or she can begin feeding. To avoid this situation, try to respond to early signs of hunger, such as lip smacking, rooting, facial grimaces or fussing. If your baby begins to gulp during the feeding, take a break. During and after each feeding, take time to burp your baby.

Look for signs of discomfort Feel your baby's hands and feet. If baby seems too hot or too cold, add or remove a layer of clothing. If your baby is cold, a warm bath might help calm him or her. You might also remove his or her clothing to see if tight elastic or irritating material might be the cause of the tears. If the culprit is air or gas, try to burp baby or gently massage the tummy. If your child remains warm, check his or her temperature to make sure he or she isn't running a fever.

Caress baby A gentle massage or light pats on the back can often help soothe a crying baby. You might do this while lying baby tummy-down across your lap.

Keep baby movin' Babies generally like movement. Sometimes, just that feeling of motion can help soothe baby. You might rock baby or walk through the house. Keeping safety precautions in mind, try placing baby in an infant swing or vibrating infant seat, or experiment with an infant sling. If the weather permits, head outdoors with the stroller or a baby carrier. You might even want to buckle up baby in the car seat and go for a ride in the car.

Sing or play music Quietly singing or humming a song to your baby may calm him or her and stop the tears. You might even play soft, soothing music. White noise — such as a recording of ocean waves — or even the monotonous sound of an electric fan or vacuum cleaner in a nearby room sometimes can help a crying baby relax. Babies often like soothing, muffled sounds similar to the amniotic fluid waves or pulsing sounds they heard in the womb.

Let baby suck Offer a clean finger or pacifier. Sucking is a natural reflex. For many babies, it's a comforting, soothing activity.

Seek quiet If your baby is overly tired or has had too much stimulation, move to a calmer environment. At times, baby just needs to get away from the noise and commotion.

Let baby cry it out If you've tried everything and your baby is still upset, consider letting your baby cry it out. While listening to your baby wail can be agonizing, keep in mind that sometimes babies cry to get rid of excess energy. And some babies can't fall asleep without crying. Your baby might go to sleep more quickly if he or she is left to cry for a little bit. Be sure to put your baby in a safe place — such as the crib or bassinet. If you've fed, burped and changed your baby and he or she appears otherwise all right, it's OK to let your baby cry for 10 or 15 minutes in the crib.

COLIC

All babies cry, but some cry more than others. And for a few babies, no matter what you try to do to stop the crying, nothing seems to work. If your son or

---

THE DISTRACTION TRICK

A common reaction to try and comfort a screaming baby is to place something in front of his or her face to try and distract baby's attention. Don't waste your time, especially early on. Holding up a toy to distract your newborn isn't likely to provide comfort. A crying baby isn't processing new information. He or she is too busy seeking attention. Offering a toy to change your baby's focus might actually make him or her more upset. As your baby gets older, however, you might be able to stop the tears by using this technique, provided it's something baby really wants or likes.

daughter fits this description, it's possible he or she many have colic. Colic is the term for periods of intense, inconsolable crying that last for three hours or more, at least three days a week (sometimes every day) and for at least three weeks. The crying episodes typically start a few weeks after birth and generally begin to improve by age 3 months.

Causes The big question when it comes to colic is what is it that causes an otherwise healthy child to cry so much? And the answer is, experts really don't know. There are a variety of theories, and not all doctors agree about what may or may not be potential triggers. It's possible the cause may be a combination of factors, and it may differ between infants.

Temperament Some babies are naturally irritable or sensitive, which might contribute to colicky behavior.

Immature nervous system If your baby has an immature nervous system, he or she might be unusually sensitive to stimulation. These babies become overloaded by all of the sights and sounds, and they aren't able to console themselves. As a result, they cry and they may have difficulty sleeping. Premature babies may exhibit their sensitiveness in the form of fussiness rather than crying.

Food sensitivities If you breast-feed your baby, colic might be a sign that your baby is sensitive to certain foods in your diet. If you feed your baby formula, colic could be an indication your baby is sensitive to milk protein in formula.

Other health problems Rarely, colic might be a sign that your baby has a health problem, such as a hernia or an infection.

Many other theories about what makes a child more susceptible to colic have been proposed, but none have been proved. Gas was long thought to be a cause because many colicky babies have gas. However, colicky babies may develop gas as a result of swallowing too much air while crying. What doctors do know is that birth order doesn't matter — colic doesn't occur more often among firstborns than in later children. Girls and boys experience colic in similar numbers. And there are no lasting effects or complications from the crying episodes. Babies with colic grow and develop normally, and they aren't any more likely to cry when they become older infants or toddlers than are infants who didn't have colic.

Common signs Some babies are fussy but they don't have colic. Although the behavior can vary, a baby with colic generally exhibits the following signs:

Predictable crying episodes A baby with colic often cries about the same time every day. These crying episodes can occur at any time during the day; however, they tend to be most common in the late afternoon or evening. The crying usually begins suddenly and for no clear reason. Your baby might have a bowel movement or pass gas near the end of the colic episode.

Intense or inconsolable crying Colic crying is intense and often high pitched. Your baby's face might flush, and he or she is extremely difficult to comfort.

Posture changes Among babies with colic, during crying episodes they tend to curl up their legs and clench their fists. You may also notice the baby has tensed abdominal muscles.

Diagnosis If you think your baby may have colic, it's a good idea to consult your child's care provider, especially if your baby is inconsolable or you notice signs of illness, such as fever, vomiting, or changes in eating or sleeping patterns, or other signs or symptoms that worry you. Your baby's care provider can help you tell the difference between normal tears and something more serious. To prepare for your appointment:

▶ Track your baby's crying episodes. Record when and how often they occur, how long they last, and any observations you've made about your baby's behavior before, during and after the episodes.

▶ Note your efforts to soothe your baby. Jot down the methods you've used and the results.

▶ Record your baby's diet and feeding schedule. What do you feed your baby and how often? Does baby seem to have gained or lost any weight?

Your baby's care provider may do a physical exam to identify any possible causes for your baby's distress. If your baby is otherwise healthy, his or her doctor may identify the problem as colic. Lab tests, X-rays and other diagnostic tests generally aren't needed to make a diagnosis. However, in unclear cases such a test can help exclude other health issues.

MANAGING COLIC

Caring for an infant who has colic can be exhausting, confusing and stressful — even for experienced parents. Colic isn't a result of poor parenting skills, so don't blame yourself for your baby's colic. Instead, focus on ways to make this difficult stage a little more bearable. Remember, this too shall pass.

Unfortunately, there are few treatment options for colic. Over-the-counter drugs, such as simethicone (Baby Gas-X, Mylicon), haven't proved helpful for colic, and other medications can have serious side effects. Some studies suggest that treatment with probiotics — substances that help maintain the natural balance of "good" bacteria in the digestive tract — might soothe colic. However, more research is needed to determine the effects of probiotics on infants. In general, Mayo Clinic pediatricians don't recommend the use of probiotics in infants.

Some parents also report trying alternative therapies, such as herbal teas, herbal remedies or glucose. Alternative therapies for colic haven't proved to be consistently helpful, and some might be dangerous. Before giving your baby any medication or substance to treat colic, consult your child's care provider.

While you might not be able to treat colic, there are things you can do to try and soothe your baby and reduce or lessen the severity of the crying episodes. Consider these suggestions:

Your feeding style Don't overfeed your baby. Try to make it at least two to two-and-a-half hours between feedings. During feedings, hold your baby as upright as possible and burp him or her often to reduce air swallowing.

If you feed your baby formula, use a curved bottle, or a bottle with a collapsible bag also might help. You might also consider giving him or her a hypoallergenic formula, such as whey hydrolysate formula, for one week. If your baby's symptoms don't improve, continue using the original formula. Avoid frequently switching your baby's formula. If bottle feedings typically take less than 15 to 20 minutes, consider using a nipple with a smaller hole.

If you breast-feed, try to empty one breast completely before switching sides. This will give your baby more hindmilk, the fattier and potentially more satisfying milk at the end of a feeding.

Your diet If you breast-feed and you suspect that a food or drink you consume may be making your baby fussier than usual, avoid it for several days to see if it makes a difference. Consider eliminating dairy products or other allergenic foods, which can cause allergic symptoms in breast-fed infants. Research suggests that in some special cases avoiding foods such as cow's milk, eggs, peanuts, tree nuts, wheat, soy and fish for a week can reduce infant fussiness. Also, try to eliminate or reduce the amount of caffeine in your diet. Caffeine in your breast milk can keep your baby awake for prolonged periods or cause agitation. Some moms say avoiding gassy or spicy foods can help — but this hasn't been proved.

Your lifestyle If you or your partner smoke, get serious about quitting. Research suggests that exposure to cigarette smoke can increase your baby's risk of colic.

Calming techniques For most babies with colic, soothing techniques can often help calm the child and lessen the crying — at least for a while. The trick is finding out which techniques your son or daughter likes. Experiment with the comforting

TUMMY HOLD

Some babies find comfort by being held on their tummies, a position sometimes referred to as the colic hold or colic carry. If your baby is fussy, you might try this position to see if it helps. Place baby facedown along your forearm with your arm firmly between his or her legs. Baby's cheek should be resting on your palm. Hold your arm close to your body, using it to brace and steady your baby. Don't let baby sleep in this position.

© MFMER

strategies discussed on pages 127-128 to see if they help.

Remember that babies with colic often like motion. Anything you can do to keep baby moving may help. Carry baby around the house in a baby sling, take a walk with your baby, or buckle baby in the car seat and go for a drive. In addition, babies with colic often find certain sounds calming. A steady background of soft noise or "shushing" sounds may help. Turn on the kitchen or bathroom exhaust fan, run the vacuum in the next room, use a white noise machine or play music of environmental sounds, such as ocean waves or a gentle rain. Sometimes, the tick of a clock or metronome does the trick.

You might also try holding your baby in a position that puts slight pressure on his or her abdomen (see "Tummy hold" on page 131). However be sure not to leave your child in this position when sleeping.

You may find you'll have to rely on a combination of techniques to get the job done. For example, consider giving your baby a pacifier, swaddling him or her, and shushing or swinging him or her — all at once.

ALWAYS BE GENTLE

When your crying baby can't be calmed, you might be tempted to try just about anything to get the noise and the tears to stop. But remember the importance of treating your baby gently. Never yell at, hit or shake your baby.

Newborns have weak neck muscles and often struggle to support their heads. Shaking your baby out of sheer frustration can have devastating consequences — including brain damage that leads to seizures, learning disabilities or mental retardation. And severe shaking can be life-threatening, or even fatal.

If you're worried about your ability to cope with a crying baby, contact your care provider, your baby's care provider, a local crisis intervention service or a mental health help line for support. If you need to, take your baby somewhere where you know he or she will be safe and cared for.

KEEPING YOUR COOL

Listening to a baby cry is stressful, especially when it seems to go on for hours on end. Even for the best of parents, coping with colic is tough. When you're all tensed up over your baby's crying, look for ways to calm yourself. Think about the happy moments you'll spend with your baby and the milestones ahead. And while taking care of your baby, remember to also take care of yourself.

Take a break If your baby's cries are getting to you, slow down. Take a deep breath and count to 10. Repeat a calm word or phrase, such as, "Take it easy." Imagine yourself in a calm, relaxing place. Play soothing music in the background. In some cases, the best thing to do may be to put baby down in his or her crib for a period of time while you walk into another room and give yourself a break.

Get out of the house Put your baby in the stroller or a baby carrier and take a walk. The exertion might take your mind off the tears — and the movement or change of scenery might soothe your baby. You might even buckle the baby into his or her car seat and take a short drive, provided you feel that you can concentrate on your driving.

Ask for help Let a loved one take over for a while. Take advantage of baby-sitting offers from trusted friends, neighbors or other close contacts. Use the time to take a nap or do something you enjoy. Even an hour on your own can help renew your coping strength. Expressing yourself can help, too. When you're getting frustrated, speak up. Saying the words out loud can help ease the tension. The more relaxed you are, the more able you'll be to handle and cope with baby's crying spells. It's also good for baby. Babies can sense when you're tense and stressed out.

CHAPTER 9

Understanding your baby's temperament

Every baby is different. Although all new babies like to sleep, eat and cry, if you get a group of them together, you'll soon start to notice that how they sleep, eat and cry can be very different from one another. One baby may be content to lie still in his crib, sleeping or taking in his surroundings with alert eyes. Another may lie in her crib, but she constantly fidgets and wiggles.

All of these differences in normal behavior are part of a baby's inborn temperament traits, qualities he or she acquired even before birth. Many of these traits continue on into adulthood and contribute to individual personalities.

As a parent, you have the opportunity to observe and discover your child's own temperament. Is she easygoing or ultra-sensitive? Does he voice his opinion loudly and strongly, or is he pretty happy with whatever comes along?

Often babies behave in ways their parents are not expecting. Depending on the situation, a temperament trait can be pleasing or frustrating to you as a parent.

For example, the same high energy that makes your baby so fun to play with — pleasing — can also make for difficult diaper changes or wriggly feedings — frustrating! This can be an adjustment in and of itself.

But if you keep an open mind and look for clues to your little one's unique traits, you can learn your baby's normal behaviors and adjust your parenting style to bring out the best in him or her. By meshing your parenting techniques with your baby's specific temperament (and this may vary from child to child even within the same family), you can achieve what child behavior experts call "goodness of fit," where the opportunities and demands of your child's environment fit with his or her inherent capabilities, characteristics and behavioral style.

A good fit between your child's temperament and his or her surroundings makes for optimal development. It also creates the foundation for a thoughtful, dynamic relationship between you and your child that can stretch and expand to meet the varying challenges of development over time.

YOUR CHILD'S TRAITS

Psychiatrists Dr. Stella Chess and Dr. Alexander Thomas began to explore the idea that every child has a natural behavioral style, or temperament, as early as the 1950s. Based on their observations, Chess and Thomas recorded nine different dimensions of temperament that describe how a child behaves: activity, regularity, initial approach, adaptability, sensitivity, intensity, mood, distractibility and persistence. Psychiatrists today still use these groupings to help parents understand their children and develop effective parenting strategies that suit their child's individual needs.

Each trait functions as a continuum, and traits may occur in clusters. For example, some kids are naturally easygoing. They quickly develop regular sleeping and eating schedules, fuss infrequently, smile easily and adapt well to new situations. Other babies are naturally more shy or slow to warm up. These babies may be less active and not too intense, approach new things slowly and with caution, and have a more difficult time transitioning from one activity to another.

Then there are children who are born to take the world head-on. They display fierce emotion, have tons of energy, and approach things and people with either avid curiosity or determined caution. They become easily frustrated and have difficulty making changes.

Many children have mixed traits. Their overall temperament may be moderate to easy, but they may score high on intensity, activity or persistence.

As you read through the different aspects of temperament, think about where your son or daughter may fall on the scale of each one. It can be a challenge to identify temperament traits in a sleepy newborn. But observe your baby closely, and as the months pass you'll better identify his or her temperament. By 4 months, many of your child's traits become apparent. Some are usually more dominant than others.

Activity

Low	Variable	High

Activity This is your baby's usual level of physical motion throughout the day, his or her "idle speed." It can range from low to high energy.

Watch your baby during daily routines such as feeding, diaper changing and bathing. Does your baby lie or sit still and watch quietly? Or does he or she wiggle and squirm a lot? When sleeping, does your child start out on one side of the crib and end up on the other, or does he or she remain relatively still? When you approach your son or daughter, does she or he wave arms and legs vigorously or wait quietly for you? As your child gets older and begins to crawl, is he or she in constant motion or content to sit and play in one spot?

Regularity

Regular	Variable	Irregular

Regularity In infants, this refers to the predictability of their bodily rhythms, such as when they get hungry or tired. Can you set the clock by your baby's nap schedule? Or maybe you can predict with a fair degree of accuracy at what time he or she will poop tomorrow. Babies who eat, sleep and poop on schedule have a high degree of regularity.

On the other hand, maybe you have a little one who keeps you guessing when he or she might be tired or hungry. One day, your baby is starving in the morning. The next, he or she doesn't want to nurse until later. Or maybe you've learned to have diapers and wipes always on hand because you never know when you might need them. Naps are all over the map.

If your child lies somewhere in between predictability and irregularity, note that, too.

Initial approach

Very cautious	Variable	Very curious

Initial approach What's your baby's usual first response to something new? Is she or he naturally curious, smiling and cooing at a new person or diving right in to taste new foods? Or does he or she resist, hanging back a little, waiting to see what will happen next before making his or her approach? Babies can range anywhere from being very cautious to very curious. Some kids are curious in some circumstances and cautious in others.

Adaptability

Adjusts easily	Variable	Adjusts slowly

Adaptability This trait concerns how easily your baby adapts to change and transition. Some babies adjust easily to switching from the crib at home to the car seat in the van, or to changing from pajamas to clothes. Others are less adaptable and need more time to adjust to a new situation, particularly to something such as a new child care center or a new baby sitter. Sometimes even changes in feeding positions can cause some children distress.

Sensitivity

Low	Variable	High

Sensitivity Some babies are highly perceptive of their environments and respond readily to external sources of stimulation, such as lights, sounds, tastes or even the way clothing feels on their skin. Does your baby fuss as soon as his or her diaper is wet, or could he or she really care less about the sagging load in the rear? Does your tyke have a strong opinion about breast milk versus formula? Does your son or daughter notice when you're wearing glasses or have your hair cut?

Some babies are more sensitive to certain factors than others. Your baby might dislike loud noises but isn't as picky when it comes to wearing a hat or not.

Intensity

Low	Variable	High

Intensity Intensity refers to the energy level of your child's response to different situations, whether positive or negative. Some babies seem to have strong feelings on just about everything. They squeal, laugh, scream, wail and flail. Less intense babies may smile, whimper or just turn away when they've had enough.

Mood

Sunny	Variable	Serious

Mood As with adults, babies can have various emotions throughout the day. But in general, think about whether your child has an overall sunny disposition or a more serious and grave outlook on the world. Is your child often happy and playful? Or does your little guy or gal require a bit more coaxing to smile and have fun?

Distractibility

Focused	Variable	Distractable

Distractibility This trait can range from focused to distractible. Some infants remain focused on an activity for some time, despite potential distractions. This trait is often tied to others, such as activity and curiosity. For example, when your focused baby settles down to nurse, that's all he or she is concerned about, for the most part. A distractible baby, on the other hand, may nurse briefly, turn away to look at a toy in the corner, nurse a little more, then pause to listen to a truck rumble by outside. Older focused babies may sit and play with one toy for a while, discovering all of its ins and outs, while another more distractible baby may flit from one thing to another, unable to resist the urge to move and curious to investigate.

Persistence

Low	Variable	High

Persistence or attention span Some babies persist in the face of obstacles, whereas others give up more easily when confronted with frustration. Does your baby persist in trying to fit the peg in the hole, or does he or she cry for help after a few unsuccessful tries? As your baby becomes more mobile, watch what happens when you start to set limits. Does your baby insist on trying to pull the cover off the electrical outlet, or can you persuade him or her to play with something else fairly easily?

YOUR CHILD'S BEHAVIORS

To get a better picture of your baby's unique temperament and how it might affect development, experts recommend taking notes for a short period of time on your baby's natural behavior. For each trait, write down your observations, and then rate your baby's behavior on the continuum of that trait. For example, you might note that your son or daughter whimpers when he or she is hungry, turns away when full, doesn't react much to bright lights or loud noises, smiles when happy and is generally mild in intensity. On the other hand, he or she isn't keen on trying new foods, dislikes drop-off time at child care, cries when you run too many errands at one time and is generally slow to adapt to changes in environment and caregivers.

Once you get a clear idea of how your child normally reacts under different cir-

---

TEMPERAMENT IN NEWBORNS

Although some parents are certain their child's temperament hasn't changed since day one, it's not always easy to distinguish your baby's predominant traits in the first several weeks of life. This is because those first three months are a big adjustment for every baby, and there's so much going on that's temporary. After the first three months, many babies who demanded constant care and attention settle into daily life and become much easier to manage. If your baby was born prematurely, it may take a little longer to discern his or her inborn traits.

cumstances, you can work on adjusting your schedule, daily routine or parenting tactics to minimize stress while still accomplishing overall goals, such as safety, good nutrition, proper care, and warm affection and support.

Following are some tips and tools for adapting parenting techniques to specific traits. But don't stop here. This is just a sampling. There are many books available to help you explore the subject of temperament and inspire you to new heights of creativity.

Highly active Highly energetic babies need lots of childproofed space within which to explore and move about. Try to let them roam as much as is safely possible within the house, rather than keeping them to a single room, crib or playpen. If you live in a small apartment, check out baby gyms or play spaces where your baby can have some extra room to play. Once your little mover and shaker learns to stand, that might be all he or she wants to do for the brief period until he or she learns to sit down. In the meantime, it may be easier to change diapers in a standing position or let your baby eat while standing at a low table.

Very curious If your baby loves to investigate new things and always seems to be into everything, make this trait enjoyable for both of you by ensuring your baby has a safe space to explore. Childproof, childproof and childproof again. If you've made certain there's nothing truly dangerous around, you'll feel more comfortable turning your son or daughter loose, and you won't have to rely so heavily on the power of "No!" (the effect of which is unreliable when it comes to active babies who are very focused on their mission).

Persistent This trait may become more prominent as your baby nears his or her first birthday. When you start to set limits on what your persistent child can and can't do, he or she may not comply as willingly as you'd like. Persistent children don't like giving up easily, and if you won't let them climb the bookshelves or fiddle with the electric outlet, you're bound to meet resistance. It's OK to pick your battles, but when it comes to safety and other rules you want to keep in place, enforce the rules kindly and consistently, and prepare to do so often! It may take a while to distract them with something else, but eventually they'll come along.

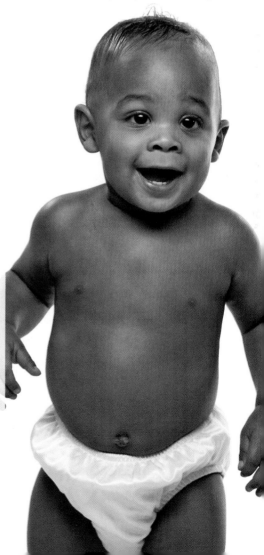

Intense You can expect strong reactions from an intense child. Just don't counter your little one's intensity with your own. When you see your child's emotions building, stay (or at least try to act) calm and soothing in return. Turn down the lights, make shushing sounds and avoid overstimulation. Sometimes a bath will help. Emotions can be especially volatile at the end of the day, so try to keep dinner and bedtime routines simple and predictable.

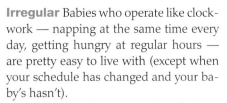

Irregular Babies who operate like clock-work — napping at the same time every day, getting hungry at regular hours — are pretty easy to live with (except when your schedule has changed and your baby's hasn't).

Babies who have irregular rhythms require a little more flexibility. Here's where the art of parenting comes into play, and you have to use knowledge of your child's temperament combined with a creative flair for getting the job done. Take sleep, for example. If your baby is irregular but adapts easily to changing circumstances, put him or her down to sleep as soon as eyes start to droop. But if your baby dislikes change or is slow to adapt, follow a steady nap and bedtime schedule. Although your son or daughter may not fall asleep right away, he or she has the comfort of knowing what to expect and will eventually drift off when drowsy enough.

Even if your baby tends toward irregularity, you can still coax him or her into something of a schedule that fits with the rest of the family. You might gradually extend the minutes between feedings to make them more regular or keep naps to a consistent length every day.

Quiet and content Babies who almost always appear content, regardless of household chaos and hectic schedules, can be so easy to live with that they sometimes get lost in the shuffle. This is especially true if you have other demands on your time, such as a busy work schedule or older children who require more active management. It can be easy to put off someone who isn't clamoring for attention. But check in regularly with your adaptable tyke, making sure you spend time with him or her and that all of his or her needs are met.

Easily frustrated Some babies are more easily frustrated than others. They become quickly upset when they can't quite grasp the peas on their tray, or a toy foils them yet again. These babies have smaller reserves of energy for dealing with stress and can only deal with frustration in small bits. Mornings are usually their best times, so try to reserve big activities for earlier in the day. As the day wears on, baby becomes emotionally worn out, less able to deal with frustration, and less able to entertain himself or herself. If you can keep afternoons and evenings simple and predictable, with a minimum of challenges, it will make it easier on both of you.

Slow to adapt A baby who adjusts slowly to change — whether it be to food, schedules, people or surroundings — finds comfort in rituals and routines. This doesn't mean you shouldn't expose your small creature of habit to new things; it just means it make take a while longer for your baby to get used to them. Weaning a less adaptable baby may come later than with others, and this is fine. Some babies may need to wean from the breast to a bottle first, rather than straight to a cup, for example.

It's also important to allow time for your baby to change tracks from one activity to another, especially as he or she gets older. You may sing a special song for different activities during the day, such as a wake-up song or a bath-time song. Instead of scooping your baby up without warning to take him or her from playtime to lunch, signal to your baby what's going to happen next. Several minutes before lunch is ready, point toward the highchair or use sign language to help your baby understand what's coming next. Use one activity to signal the next — for example, always bring the baby to play in the kitchen while you make lunch. Keeping your routine predictable will minimize anxiety and confusion in your little one's mind.

Distractible Around 4 or 5 months, a baby's vision begins to improve substantially. A baby that's easily distracted may all of a sudden have difficulty focusing on nursing when there are so many other interesting things to look at. If you notice this happening with your infant, try turning the lights down when feeding so distractions are less visible.

The advantage of having an easily distractible baby is that he or she is generally easier to soothe when upset, with a jingling set of keys or a look out the window. Babies who are less distractible aren't necessarily in greater distress; they may just need to voice their displeasure for a little longer.

Highly sensitive If your baby is highly perceptive of his or her surroundings, try to keep those surroundings comfortable to minimize unnecessary stress. For example, if your son or daughter is sensitive to noise, avoid eating at crowded restaurants. Or cut a wide berth from the live band at a local festival and head for calmer areas. Remove scratchy tags on shirts. If your child can't stand to wear shoes, skip them unless absolutely necessary. Even a well-intentioned bear hug may be too much for this little one. In general, avoid overstimulating your baby's highly attuned senses.

YOUR PARENTING STYLE

Depending on your baby's general temperament, you might find that parenting is easier or harder than you expected. If

your baby is naturally even-tempered, parenting might seem to be a piece of cake and you might wonder why you were so worried before the baby arrived. You might even wonder why other parents seem to have such a hard time with their children.

A spirited child, on the other hand, may cause parents to wonder what happened along the way that produced the whirlwind that now inhabits their home. A curious, highly active child requires more time, vigilance and physical space than a less curious or more slow-moving child. An easily frustrated infant requires more patience and creative thinking from a parent than a child who's more persistent or accepting of minor obstacles. And a child who resists change requires more advance planning than a child who easily swings from one activity to another.

A common cause of frustration in a parent-child relationship is parental expectations regarding how a child should behave. Things can be especially difficult if your temperament differs markedly from your child's. Perhaps you had envisioned sitting quietly with your little one, working on a puzzle or reading a book. But what happens when your rambunctious guy or gal has no patience for being still and wants to be constantly on the move? Or maybe you're outgoing and love to try new things and you're disappointed or even embarrassed that your baby is so cautious and reluctant. Parents often find it difficult to slow their schedules to accommodate a less-flexible child's need for extra time and preparation. Other parents feel inadequate because they don't feel capable of keeping up with their child's demands.

How you react to your child's temperament is a key part of parenting. Instead of looking at your child as a direct reflection of yourself or your parenting skills, try to look at him or her as a separate individual with his or her own unique perspective. This slight distance between yourself and your child allows you to look objectively at your child's needs and adapt your parenting style to meet those needs. Rather than trying to change your child's disposition, you can focus on creating the best possible environment in which your child can naturally thrive. As a result, and with no feelings of guilt or failure on your part, you can swap the puzzle (which may have been beyond your child's capability to begin with) for a swing or adjust your schedule so that you run errands before you pick your baby up from child care. With a little bit of trial and error, you'll be able to determine what works best for both of you.

If you have a child who requires a lot of time and skill, and you start to feel anxious, overwhelmed or just plain exhausted, schedule more frequent breaks so that you can recharge yourself. You might swap time off with your partner or engage a trusted baby sitter for regular hours where you're "off the clock." And if you feel you need professional help, talk to your care provider or a child mental health specialist who can help you find more effective parenting strategies.

Parenting skills don't come overnight, and some children require more of a learning curve than do others. But if you can learn to step back and appreciate your baby's temperament in a positive light, you're more likely to feel closer to your child and confident in your parenting role.

PART 2

Baby's Health and Safety

CHAPTER 10

Finding the right care provider

During your baby's first year, you and your baby will likely spend a lot of time with his or her care provider. Beyond the recommended checkups every couple of months, it's likely your son or daughter will get his or her first illness at some point this year. In addition, you may have questions about newborn care or your baby's health and development.

While finding a care provider for your baby might sound simple, it's worth the effort to find an individual who can best meet your baby's and family's needs. Determining what you're looking for in a care provider for your baby can help you find a pediatric care professional whom you feel comfortable with and whom you can build a good relationship with as your child grows and matures.

GETTING STARTED

If you haven't already chosen a care provider for your baby, now is the time to do

so. If possible, you want to choose your baby's care provider before your baby is born — such as during your third trimester. Settling on a care provider before your baby is born will make it easier for you to arrange your newborn's first checkup in the hectic first few days after his or her arrival. Visiting with your baby's care provider before your baby is born will also give you a chance to ask questions, talk about any problems during your pregnancy, discuss the practice's policies and fill out any necessary insurance forms without the distraction of having your new baby with you. It's also comforting to know that you already have a trusted source you can call with any questions you might have regarding newborn care — and most first-time parent have lots of questions!

In addition, if you choose your baby's care provider before your son or daughter is born and you deliver your baby at a hospital where the care provider works, you might be able to have the care provider examine your baby at the hospital.

Don't worry, though, if that's not possible. Your baby will still be seen at the hospital by qualified staff.

If you don't have a specific care provider in mind, start by asking for recommendations from trusted family members, friends or co-workers who have children. Your own care provider might be a good referral source, too. You may also be able to find information about care providers by calling a nearby hospital or other community health resources.

Keep in mind your health insurance company may require you to choose from its approved network of care providers. Check to see if the company provides information about the providers in the network to help you make your decision.

Whatever you do, don't put off finding a care provider for your baby. Even if you're about to move or change insurance providers, do your best to find a care provider as soon as possible. Waiting until your baby becomes sick can be stressful for you and might delay your baby's care. Establishing a relationship with a care provider for your baby will also make it easier for you to schedule regular visits and keep your child's immunizations up to date.

CARE PROVIDER OPTIONS

When it comes to choosing a care provider for your baby, you have options. Many types of medical personnel treat babies and children, including:

Pediatricians Many parents choose a pediatrician to be the care provider for their children because pediatricians specialize in the care of children from infancy through adolescence. After medical school, pediatricians go through a three-year residency program. Some pediatricians receive further training in subspecialties such as neonatology — the care of sick and premature newborns — or pediatric cardiology or dermatology. If your baby ever needs to be treated by a subspecialist, his or her regular care provider can provide a referral.

Family physicians Family physicians provide health care to people of all ages, including babies. They're trained in adult and pediatric medicine. A family physician can see your child from infancy all the way through adulthood. Family physicians take care of most medical problems. Also, if the rest of your family sees the same care provider, he or she will gain an overall health perspective of your family. If you already have a family doctor you trust, ask whether he or she will see infants.

Nurse practitioners Nurse practitioners are registered nurses who have ad-

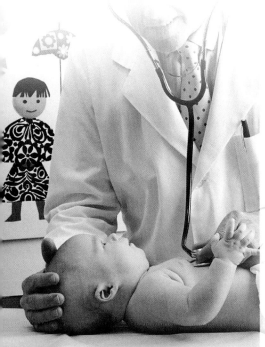

vanced training in a specialized area of medicine, such as pediatrics or family health. After nursing school, a nurse practitioner must go through a formal education program in his or her specialty field. A pediatric nurse practitioner focuses on caring for infants, children and teens. Family nurse practitioners often see all family members, including children. Nurse practitioners typically work closely with or under the supervision of one or more physicians.

FACTORS TO CONSIDER

Before you choose a care provider for your baby, think about what you're looking for in a care provider. For example:

Training Would you prefer your baby to see the same care provider who takes care of the rest of your family's health or a care provider who specializes only in pediatrics? Would you like a care provider who is older and may have more experience or an individual who is younger and also may have young children at home?

Personal approach What kind of parenting and child rearing philosophy would you like your baby's care provider to have? Are you looking for a care provider of a particular sex or who shares your religious background?

Cost Do you need to find a care provider from among your insurance company's list of approved care providers?

Location, accessibility and hours Where would you like the care provider's office to be located? What locations would be most convenient for you? Would you prefer an office that has ex-

tended hours? Is it important for you to be able to contact the care provider at night or on the weekends or by email? Would you like your child's care provider to have privileges at a particular hospital? Would you prefer that he or she have an office that has separate waiting rooms for children who are well and those who are sick?

EVALUATING YOUR OPTIONS

Once you've thought about what you're looking for and have compiled the names of some possible care providers, call each provider's office to confirm that he or she is accepting new patients. If necessary, double-check that he or she works with your insurance company. Then, ask if you can schedule an appointment to meet or talk to the care provider. Try to schedule

the visit at a time when both you and your partner can attend, so you can both ask questions. Be sure to ask if the visit carries a charge.

If you're given a recommendation by a family member or friend, try to get some basic information from him or her before talking to the care provider. For example, you might ask about:

- *Bedside manner.* Does the care provider interact well with both adults and children? Does the friend or family member's child like the care provider?
- *Office atmosphere.* Is the office staff helpful? How do staff members manage phone calls, particularly when it comes to emergencies? Is it difficult to make an appointment when a child is sick? Is there generally a long office wait before being able to see the care provider?
- *Knowledge.* Does the care provider seem to be up to date on current medical advances, and does he or she offer helpful advice?

Issues to consider When you do sit down to talk to a potential care provider, you might bring a list of questions or just have an informal chat with the provider. Don't feel embarrassed about asking questions that might help you get to know the person and make the right decision for your family.

Training How long has the individual been caring for children? At what hospitals does the care provider have privileges? Is he or she board certified? Board certification requires the provider to undergo testing and take classes on a periodic basis after residency to maintain his or her knowledge and skills.

Accessibility and hours What are the office's hours? Is the office open at night and on weekends? Does the office have an after-hours answering service? How does the care provider handle emergencies, including those that occur after hours? When is the best time to call with nonurgent questions? Does the office have guidelines for what kind of questions can be resolved with a phone call and what requires a visit? Does the care provider communicate via email? How does the office handle billing, payment and insurance claims? Is the office a group practice? If so, will you be able to request an appointment with a specific care provider? If you choose a care provider who is part of a group practice, make sure you feel comfortable with other members of the practice who might treat your baby.

KEEP MEDICAL INFORMATION HANDY

Write down key information about your baby's care provider, such as his or her contact information, the office's hours and location, and any policies for making appointments. Keep this information in a place that will be easy for you and anyone caring for your child to access. Also, create a file or notebook or an electronic record for your baby's medical information. Include information such as his or her immunization record, measurements, and any prescriptions or lab test results.

Philosophy and style What is the care provider's philosophy when it comes to the use of certain medications, discipline or other subjects you consider important? Does the care provider listen to your questions and answer them? Does he or she appear interested in your concerns?

Making your decision After meeting with a care provider, consider his or her overall approach to health care and your interactions with the staff. Most important, would you trust this person to provide care for your child? Trust your instincts. If you don't feel comfortable, consider another care provider.

Once you've selected your baby's care provider, you may have a number of issues to discuss. You may want to get the provider's input on topics such as breastfeeding, circumcision or child care. If you feel it would be helpful, schedule an appointment to discuss these issues.

A TEAM APPROACH

If you're ever unhappy with the care your baby receives, talk to the care provider about your concerns. Chances are, once the issue is discussed, you can come to a resolution that is mutually agreeable. If you can't resolve the problem, you might consider seeking another care provider for your baby.

In the coming months, your baby's care provider will play an important role. His or her guidance can help you make healthy choices for your baby, as well as determine what to do if your son or daughter has a health problem. While you may have certain viewpoints, don't forget that your provider is trained in infant care and likely has considerable experience. It's important that the two of you work together as a team to stay on top of your baby's health.

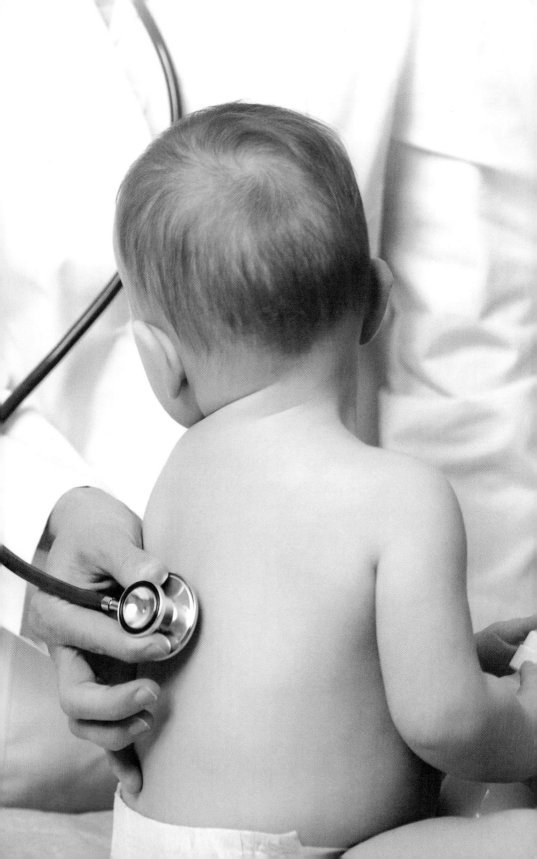

CHAPTER 11

Checkups

Frequent checkups with a care provider are an important part of your baby's first year. These checkups — often called well-baby visits — are a way for you and your baby's care provider to keep tabs on your baby's health and development, as well as spot any potential problems. Well-baby visits also give you a chance to discuss any questions or concerns you might have and get advice from a trusted source on how to provide the best possible care for your baby.

Well-baby visits sometimes aren't easy on you or your baby. Your baby might not like getting undressed and measured, and then there are vaccinations. Rest assured, however, that visiting the care provider will soon become a part of your and your baby's routine and, with time, the visits will become less stressful and more enjoyable as your baby becomes familiar with exploring the office's toy selection, and you look forward to finding out just how big your baby is getting. You'll also find the care provider's guidance invaluable in the months ahead.

CHECKUP SCHEDULE

Most newborns have their first checkups within 48 to 72 hours of being discharged from the hospital. This timeline is particularly important for breast-fed babies, who need to have their feeding, weight gain and skin color — in case of jaundice — evaluated. During your baby's first year of life, he or she should see a care provider at ages:

▶ 2 months
▶ 4 months
▶ 6 months
▶ 9 months
▶ 1 year

Your baby's care provider may also ask to see your baby more frequently. In addition, you can make an appointment for your baby to see a care provider any time your child is sick or you're concerned about his or her health and development.

If possible, both parents should try to attend baby's first few checkups. This will give both of you a chance to get to know the care provider and ask basic questions.

If only one parent can attend, ask a family member or friend to help you navigate these early visits. Remembering your questions and listening to your care provider's advice can be difficult when you're also trying to undress or calm a fussy baby. An extra set of hands also may prove useful during your first few outings.

WHAT TO EXPECT AT EACH VISIT

Each care provider does things a bit differently, but here's what's generally on the agenda during a well-baby exam.

Measuring your baby Your baby's checkup will usually begin with measurements. A nurse or your baby's care provider will measure and record your baby's length, head circumference and weight. To get accurate measurements you'll need to take off your baby's clothes and, for his or her weight, the diaper. To measure your baby's length, the nurse will lay your baby on a flat table with his or her legs stretched. The nurse will use a special tape to measure your baby's head size and an infant scale to weigh him or her. Keep a blanket, a fresh diaper and wipes handy.

Your baby's measurements will be plotted on a growth chart. This will help you and your baby's care provider see how your baby's size compares with that of other babies the same age. Try not to fixate on the percentages too much, though. All babies grow and develop at different rates. In addition, babies who are breast-fed gain weight at a different rate than do babies who are formula-fed. Keep in mind that a baby who's in the 95th percentile for height and weight isn't necessarily healthier than a baby who's in the fifth percentile. What's most important is steady growth from one visit to the next. If you have questions or concerns about your baby's growth rate, discuss them with your baby's care provider.

Head-to-toe physical exam Your child's care provider will give your baby a thorough physical exam and check his or her reflexes and muscle tone. Be sure to mention any concerns you have or specific areas you want the doctor to check

---

TIPS FOR SCHEDULING APPOINTMENTS

When scheduling appointments, think about what are the care provider's busiest times. You might have the best chance of getting in and out of the care provider's office quickly if you ask for the first appointment of the day or choose a time right after lunch. On the other hand, if you think you'd like to have extra time to speak with your baby's care provider, you might ask for an appointment at the end of the day. Also, try to avoid making appointments on Mondays and Fridays, as well as on holidays when the care provider's office is open. These days tend to be busier than others. The end of summer vacation also tends to be a busy time for care providers, since many children are required to have a physical before the start of the new school year.

out. The more information you can provide about your baby's health, the better. Here are the basics of what provider's commonly check for during an exam:

Head Your baby's care provider will likely check the soft spots (fontanels) on your baby's head. These gaps between the skull bones give your baby's brain plenty of room to grow in the coming year. They're safe to touch and typically disappear within two years, when the skull bones fuse together.

The care provider may also check baby's head for flat spots. A baby's skull is soft and made up of several movable plates. If his or her head is left in the same position for long periods of time, the skull plates might move in a way that creates a flat spot. If flat spots are a concern, continue to place your baby on his or her back to sleep. However, your baby's care provider may recommend alternating the direction your baby's head faces in the crib, giving your baby more tummy time while he or she is awake, and limiting the amount of time your baby spends in a car seat — unless he or she is actually riding in a car. If these types of changes are made, the flattening typically improves in two to three months. Occasionally, babies need to wear a positioning helmet to improve head shape.

Ears Using an instrument called an otoscope, the care provider can see in baby's ears to check for fluid or infection in the ears. The care provider may observe your baby's response to various sounds, including your voice. Be sure to tell the care provider if you have any concerns about your son's or daughter's ability to hear or if there's a history of childhood deafness in your family. Unless there's cause for concern, a formal hearing evaluation isn't usually needed at a well-baby exam.

Eyes Your baby's care provider may use a flashlight to catch your child's attention and then track his or her eye movements.

The provider may also check for blocked tear ducts and eye discharge and look inside your baby's eyes with a lighted instrument called an ophthalmoscope. Be sure to tell the care provider if you've noticed that your baby is having any unusual eye movements, especially if they continue beyond the first few months.

Mouth A look inside your baby's mouth may reveal signs of oral thrush, a common, and easily treated, yeast infection. The care provider might also check your baby's mouth for signs of tongue-tie (ankyloglossia), a condition that affects the tongue's range of motion and can interfere with a baby's oral development as well as his or her ability to breast-feed.

As your child gets older, the care provider may ask whether your baby has started to drool more than usual, become fussy or irritable, or lost his or her appetite. These are often the first signs of teething. Your baby's care provider will check for emerging teeth. After teeth erupt, he or she will likely discuss with you the importance of regularly cleaning your baby's new teeth to prevent decay.

Skin Various skin conditions may be identified during the exam, including birthmarks, rashes and jaundice, a yellowish discoloration of the skin and eyes. Mild jaundice that develops soon after birth often disappears on its own within a week or two. Cases that are more severe may need treatment. For more on jaundice, see page 378.

Heart and lungs Using a stethoscope, your baby's care provider can listen to your baby's heart and lungs to check for abnormal heart sounds or rhythms or breathing difficulties.

Abdomen, hips and legs By gently pressing a child's abdomen, a care provider can detect tenderness, enlarged organs or an umbilical hernia, which occurs when a bit of intestine or fatty tissue near the navel breaks through the muscular wall of the abdomen. Most umbilical hernias heal without intervention by the toddler years. The care provider may also move your baby's legs to check for dislocation or other problems with the hip joints, such as dysplasia of the hip joint.

Genitalia Your baby's care provider will likely inspect your son's or daughter's genitalia for tenderness, lumps or other signs of infection. The care provider may also check for an inguinal hernia, which results from a weakness in the abdominal wall. For girls, the doctor may ask about vaginal discharge. For boys, the care provider will make sure a circumcised penis is healing well during early visits. The care provider may also check to see that both testes have descended into the scrotum and that there's no fluid-filled sac around the testes, a condition called hydrocele.

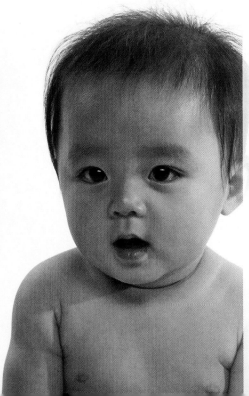

Nutrition information Your baby's care provider will likely ask you about your baby's eating habits. If you're breast-feeding, the care provider may want to know how often you're feeding your baby during the day and night and whether you're having any problems. If you're formula-feeding, the care provider will want to know how many ounces of formula your baby takes at each feeding.

In addition, the provider may also discuss with you your baby's need for vitamin D and iron supplements. He or she will likely also ask how many wet diapers and bowel movements your baby produces on a daily basis.

Although breast milk or formula will be the main part of your baby's diet throughout the first year, there will come a time when you will want to discuss introducing your baby to solid foods. A care provider can offer advice on the best foods to start with, the importance of making healthy choices and how to feed your baby. Once your baby starts eating solid foods, your child's care provider may check to see if you're having any problems feeding your baby or if your baby has had any allergic reactions. If you're concerned about your baby developing food allergies, discuss the issue with his or her care provider.

As your son or daughter gets older, discussion topics may include drinking from a sippy cup and when it's OK for your child to start to use utensils to feed himself or herself. You might also discuss weaning your baby from the bottle by age 1 and how to start giving your baby whole cow's milk after he or she turns 1.

Sleeping status Your child's care provider may ask you questions about your baby's sleep habits, such as how you put your baby to sleep and how many hours he or she is sleeping during the day and night. Don't hesitate to discuss any concerns you may have about your baby's sleep habits.

Development Your baby's development is important, too. Over the course of your baby's first year, the care provider will monitor your baby's developmental milestones in five main areas, including:

Gross motor skills These skills, such as sitting and walking, involve the movement of large muscles. Your baby's care provider may ask you how well your baby can control his or her head. Is your baby

FAILURE TO THRIVE

Failure to thrive is a term — not a disease or diagnosis — that's used to describe a baby or toddler who isn't growing or developing at an appropriate rate. The term might be used when a child's weight or height appears below the fifth percentile on a growth chart or if a child's growth rate is lower than expected. Failure to thrive can be caused by multiple issues, such as an underlying health problem or environmental problems. If your care provider is concerned about your baby's growth and development, he or she may ask you questions about your pregnancy and delivery, your baby's medical and dietary history, and your family history. With early intervention, many children respond well and catch up in their growth and development.

attempting to roll over? Is your baby trying to sit on his or her own? Is he or she trying to crawl and pull himself or herself up into a standing position?

Fine motor skills These skills involve the use of small muscles in the hand. Does your baby reach for objects and bring them to his or her mouth. Is your baby using individual fingers to pick up small objects? Can your baby transfer objects from hand to hand?

Personal and social skills These skills enable a child to interact and respond to his or her surroundings. Your baby's care provider may ask if your baby is smiling. Does your baby relate to you with real joy? Does he or she play peekaboo? Is your baby showing stranger anxiety?

Language skills These skills include hearing, understanding and use of language. The care provider may ask if your baby turns his or her head toward voices or other sounds. Does your baby laugh? Is he or she responding to his or her name? Does your baby appear to understand the word *no*? Is your baby babbling?

Cognitive skills These skills allow a child to think, reason, solve problems and understand his or her surroundings. Your baby's care provider might ask if your baby can bang together two cubes or search for a toy after seeing you hide it? Development milestones are discussed further in Part 3 of this book.

Behavior Your child's care provider may ask you questions about your child's behavior. Explain what you've noticed so far and anything that seems out of the ordinary to you or is causing you concern.

As your baby gets older and begins exploring everything in sight, you may find yourself saying no quite often. Your baby also might get frustrated as his or her growing sense of independence conflicts with his or her limited vocabulary and physical abilities. Your baby's care provider might discuss the importance of providing a predictable home environment and routine and acting calmly when handling meltdowns.

Vaccinations Your baby will need a number of vaccinations during his or her first year. The care provider or a nurse will

DEVELOPMENTAL DELAYS

If your baby doesn't reach a specific milestone by an expected age, he or she may have a developmental delay. Delays can occur in one or several areas of development. Your baby's care provider might ask you about factors that can contribute to a delay, such as a history of developmental delays in the family or stressful home conditions. If your baby has a developmental delay, the care provider can recommend a type of developmental therapy that may help your baby make progress. Most babies are eligible to receive a wide range of therapies in their homes, often at no cost. Early identification of a developmental delay is important because it will enable you to get your baby the help he or she needs as soon as possible. For more information on developmental delays, see Chapter 40.

KEEP A RECORD

Consider starting a file, notebook or electronic medical record for your baby's medical information, such as his or her vaccination record, measurements, and any prescriptions or lab test results. Taking time to organize your child's health information will give you a chance to review any information the care provider gives you. It's also a good habit to start early because when your child enters school or preschool, you will likely be required to provide certain medical information. Plus, your notes about your baby's growth make for a cherished keepsake.

explain to you how to hold your baby as he or she is given each shot or, in some cases, an oral solution. Be prepared for tears. Keep in mind, however, that the pain caused by a shot is typically short-lived and the benefits are long lasting. Chapter 12 provides more detailed information on the immunizations your son or daughter will receive during the first year.

Safety Your child's care provider may talk to you about safety issues, such as the importance of placing your baby to sleep on his or her back and using a rear-facing infant car seat. As your baby becomes more mobile, the care provider may give you tips for baby-proofing your home. He or she may discuss how to prevent falls and the importance of water safety.

QUESTIONS AND CONCERNS

During your son's or daughter's checkups, it's likely that you'll have questions, too. Ask away! Nothing is too trivial when it comes to caring for your baby. Write down questions as they arise between appointments so that you'll be less likely to forget them when you're at your baby's checkup. Feel free to ask your ba-

by's care provider for advice on topics that aren't medically related, too. For example, if you're looking for child care, ask the care provider if he or she has any advice.

Also, don't forget your own health. If you're feeling depressed, stressed out, rundown or overwhelmed, describe what's happening. Your baby's provider is there to help you, too.

Before you leave the care provider's office, make sure you know when to schedule your baby's next appointment. If possible, set the next appointment before you leave the provider's office. If you don't already know, ask how to reach your child's care provider in between appointments. You might also ask if the care provider has a 24-hour nurse information service. Knowing that help is available when you need it can offer peace of mind.

CHAPTER 12

Vaccinations

Before you met your baby, did you think about his or her health? Chances are, you did. Think back to your pregnancy — the things you did to keep yourself healthy and to prevent problems from occurring, so the baby inside you could grow and develop.

Prevention is crucial to good health. It's far better to prevent a disease than to treat it. And one of the best ways to protect your family from many diseases is to get vaccinated. Immunization is the best line of defense against diseases such as tetanus, hepatitis, influenza and many other infections.

Thanks to vaccines, many infectious diseases that were once common in the United States are now rare or nonexistent. As a parent, you no longer have to fear that your child will die of or become disabled by smallpox and tetanus. And you no longer have to keep your children away from water fountains and swimming pools to avoid getting polio.

Truth be told, vaccinations aren't exactly fun — for children and parents alike. It's hard to see your little one cry after receiving a series of shots. But as much as you want to shield your child from discomfort and tears, keep in mind that the discomfort is temporary and very minor compared with the potential discomfort of a serious disease.

Vaccinations have saved billions of lives worldwide. However, despite the availability of vaccines, many people remain underimmunized. One reason is that some people have concerns about the safety and risks of vaccines. In addition, some people feel it's dangerous to give more than one vaccine at a time, and others feel certain vaccines are no longer needed. These concerns are often the result of incorrect information.

HOW VACCINES WORK

Every day, the human body is threatened by bacteria, viruses and other germs. When a disease-causing microorganism enters your (or your child's) body, your immune system mounts a defense, producing proteins called antibodies to fight off the invader. The goal of your immune system is to neutralize or destroy the foreign invader, rendering it harmless and preventing you from getting sick.

One way the body's immune system fights off foreign invaders is through what's called post-exposure immunity. After you've been infected with a certain organism, your immune system puts into play a complex array of defenses to prevent you from getting sick again from that type of virus or bacterium.

Another way the immune system prevents disease is through vaccine immunity. With this method, a person avoids having to get infected with the organism. A vaccine — which contains a killed or weakened form or derivative of

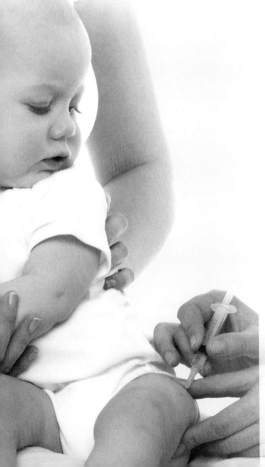

the infectious germ — triggers your immune system's infection-fighting ability without exposure to the actual disease. When given to you before you get infected, the vaccine makes your body think that it's being invaded by a specific organism, and your immune system begins building defenses against the organism's invasion to prevent the organism from infecting you again.

If you're exposed to a disease for which you've been vaccinated, the invading germs are met by antibodies prepared to defeat them. And vaccines can be given without the risk of the serious effects of disease.

Sometimes it takes several doses of a vaccine for a full immune response — this is the case for many childhood vaccines. Some people fail to build immunity to the first doses of a vaccine, but they often respond to later doses. In addition, the immunity provided by some vaccines, such as tetanus and pertussis, isn't lifelong. Because the immune response may decrease over time, you may need another dose of a vaccine (booster) to restore or increase your immunity. And for some diseases, the organism evolves, and a new vaccine is needed against the new form. This is the case with the annual flu (influenza) shot.

WHY GET VACCINATED?

Because many vaccine-preventable diseases are now uncommon in the United States, some people feel less urgency about getting themselves or their children immunized. If you wonder if it's necessary to vaccinate your family and to keep everyone up to date with vaccinations, the answer is yes. Many infectious diseases that have virtually disappeared in the United States can reappear quickly. The germs that cause the diseases still exist and can be acquired and spread by people who aren't protected by immunization.

As travelers unknowingly carry disease from one country to another, a new outbreak may be only a plane trip away. From a single entry point, an infectious disease can spread quickly among unprotected individuals. Outbreaks of mumps and measles have repeatedly occurred in just this way in the United States the past few years.

VACCINE SAFETY

As a new parent, you might be understandably leery about giving your child vaccines. You don't want to do anything to harm your child. And while you know that vaccinations are important, you've also heard that they could be harmful, too — possibly causing side effects. You may worry after hearing or seeing reports about a severe "reaction" that occurs shortly after a child's immunization visit that's said to be a side effect or complication of the vaccine. Unfounded stories such as these frequently circulate on the Internet.

The fact is, vaccines are extremely safe. Before they can be used, they must meet strict safety standards set by the Food and Drug Administration (FDA). Meeting these standards requires a lengthy development process of up to 10 years, followed by three phases of clinical trials. These studies, unlike drug studies, involve tens of thousands of individuals.

Once vaccines are licensed and made available to the general public, the FDA and the Centers for Disease Control and Prevention (CDC) continue to monitor their safety. Furthermore, vaccines are subject to ongoing research, review and refinement by doctors, scientists and public health officials. Those who provide vaccines, such as care providers and nurses, must report any side effects they observe to the FDA and CDC.

The bottom line is, your child's chances of being harmed by a disease are far greater than his or her chances of being harmed by a vaccine used to prevent disease.

Vaccine additives In addition to the killed or weakened microorganisms that make up vaccines, small amounts of other substances may be added to a vaccine to enhance the immune response, prevent contamination, and stabilize the vaccine against temperature variations and other conditions. Vaccines may also contain small amounts of materials used in the manufacturing process, such as gelatin.

One additive that has received much attention is a preservative called thimerosal, which is a derivative of mercury. Thimerosal has been used in medical products since the 1930s and in small amounts in some vaccines to prevent bacterial contamination. No evidence shows that children have been harmed by its use in vaccines. Nonetheless, childhood vaccines are now made without thimerosal or with only trace amounts.

Vaccines and autism Many parents have heard claims that vaccines cause autism. The most common and specific claims are that autism stems from the measles-mumps-rubella (MMR) vaccine or from vaccines that contain the preservative thimerosal. Many large studies have been conducted to investigate these specific concerns, but no link has ever been found between vaccines and

WELL-CHILD VACCINATION SCHEDULE

The following chart lists the recommended routine childhood vaccinations. Vaccine guidelines for children change fairly often as new vaccines are developed, recommendations on timing and dosages are revised, and more combination vaccines are created. Check with your child's care provider to make sure that your child is up to date on his or her vaccinations. You can also view current vaccination schedules from the American Academy of Pediatrics (see page 552).

Health insurance usually covers most of the cost of vaccinations. A federal program called Vaccines for Children provides free vaccines to children who lack health insurance coverage and to other specific groups of children. Ask your care provider about it.

Recommended vaccination schedule for children ages 0-18 months*

	Ages							
Vaccine	Birth	1 month	2 mos.	4 mos.	6 mos.	12 mos.	15 mos.	18 mos.
Hepatitis B	HepB	HepB †			HepB †			
Rotavirus			RV	RV	RV			
Diphtheria, tetanus, pertussis			DTaP	DTaP	DTaP		DTaP‡	
Haemophilus influenzae type b			Hib	Hib	Hib	Hib		
Pneumococcal			PCV	PCV	PCV	PCV		
Inactivated poliovirus			IPV	IPV	IPV			
Influenza					Influenza (Yearly)			
Measles-mumps-rubella (MMR)						MMR		
Varicella						Varicella		
Hepatitis A						HepA (2 doses)		

* Based on 2012 recommendations.

† If monovalent HepB is used for doses after the birth dose, a dose at 4 months is not needed.

‡ The fourth dose of DTaP may be administered as early as age 12 months, provided six months have elapsed since the third dose.

    Indicates an age-range when vaccination is recommended.

Source: Centers for Disease Control and Prevention

autism. In fact, large numbers of studies from around the world have shown, beyond a doubt, there is no association. Unfortunately, the claims persist, and they've led some parents to refuse to vaccinate their children.

The causes of autism aren't fully understood, and it's likely that many factors are involved. But scientific evidence overwhelmingly suggests that vaccines are not a possible cause.

Some people also worry that receiving too many vaccines early in life can overwhelm a baby's immune system and that this might somehow lead to autism. Such reasoning doesn't fit with what we know about the remarkable capacity of the immune system. From the moment a child is born, his or her immune system begins battling microorganisms in the form of bacteria, viruses and fungi on a daily basis. A system that copes with exposure to countless bacteria each day can easily withstand exposure to the antigens in vaccines.

CHILDHOOD VACCINATIONS

Fortunately, many of the most familiar diseases of childhood — measles, mumps, and chickenpox — can be prevented through immunization.

Chickenpox Chickenpox (varicella) is a common childhood disease. It can also affect adults who aren't immune. More children in the United States die of this disease than of any other vaccine-preventable disease.

The chickenpox virus is spread by breathing in infected droplets or by direct contact with fluid from the rash, which is the best-known sign of the disease. The rash begins as superficial spots on the face, chest, back and other areas of the body. The spots quickly fill with a clear fluid, rupture and turn crusty.

Recommendation Children should receive one dose of the chickenpox vaccine between 12 and 18 months of age.

Diphtheria Diphtheria is a bacterial infection that spreads from person to person through airborne droplets. It causes a thick covering (membrane) to develop in the back of the throat and can lead to severe breathing problems, paralysis, heart failure and death. The disease is now rare in the United States.

Recommendation The diphtheria vaccine typically is given in combination with the tetanus and pertussis vaccines (a DTaP shot). Immunization should begin when a child reaches 2 months of age. A child should receive five shots in the first six years of life and continue to receive boosters of tetanus, diphtheria and pertussis (Tdap) every 10 years, beginning at age 11 or 12. The Tdap vaccine, approved in 2005, is recommended for children 11 years and older instead of the older Td booster vaccine.

German measles German measles (rubella) is a contagious disease that spreads through the air from people sick with the infection. It's typically a mild infection that causes a rash and slight fever. However, if a woman develops rubella during pregnancy, she may have a miscarriage, or the baby could be born with birth defects.

Recommendation Usually, two doses of the combination measles-mumps-rubella (MMR) vaccine are given, the first at ages 12 to 15 months and the second at ages 4 to 6 years.

ALTERNATIVE VACCINE SCHEDULES

Some health care professionals tout what they call alternative vaccine schedules that delay shots or space them further apart. For parents who may be skittish about giving their children so many shots, the idea of the alternative schedule is to encourage vaccination by slowing the pace.

But public health officials say that these approaches leave too many kids unprotected for too long, and they aren't backed up by science. Alternative schedules are unstudied, and they can be dangerous because of the increased risks they pose. Skipping or spacing out vaccines dramatically increases a child's risk of illness.

If you're concerned, the best advice is to talk with your child's care provider to make sure you are getting the correct information.

Hib disease *Haemophilus influenzae* type b (Hib) disease is primarily a childhood illness, but it can also affect some adults. It's caused by bacteria that spread from person to person through the air. This infection can cause serious and potentially fatal problems, including meningitis, sepsis, severe swelling in the throat, and infections of the blood, joints, bones and membranes around the heart (pericarditis).

Recommendation The Hib conjugate vaccine is given to children at ages 2 months, 4 months, 6 months and 12 to 15 months. The vaccine typically is given at the same time as other vaccines.

Hepatitis A Hepatitis A is a liver disease caused by the hepatitis A virus. It's usually spread by eating or drinking contaminated food or water or by close personal contact.

Recommendation The two-dose series of hepatitis A vaccine is recommended for all children in the U.S. The first dose is generally given at 12 months and the second dose at 24 months.

Hepatitis B The hepatitis B virus can cause a short-term (acute) illness marked by loss of appetite, fatigue, diarrhea, vomiting, jaundice, and pain in muscles, joints and the abdomen. More rarely it can lead to long-term (chronic) liver damage (cirrhosis) or liver cancer.

The virus is spread through contact with the blood or other body fluids of an infected person. This can happen by having unprotected sex, sharing needles when injecting illegal drugs, or during birth, when the virus passes from an infected mother to her baby. However, over one-third of people who have hepatitis B in the U.S. don't know how they got it.

Recommendation The hepatitis B vaccine is given to children in three doses — at birth, at least one month later (1 to 4 months of age) and then at 6 to 18 months.

Flu (influenza) Influenza is a viral infection that sickens millions of people each year and can cause serious complications, especially in children and older adults. Flu vaccines are designed to protect against strains of flu virus expected to be in circulation during the fall and winter. The vaccine is generally offered between September and March, which is typically the flu season.

Recommendation The influenza vaccine is now recommended yearly for infants and children, beginning at age 6 months. Babies require two doses of the flu vaccine the first time they've been vaccinated for influenza. That's because they don't develop an adequate antibody level the first time they get the vaccine. Antibodies help fight the virus if it enters your child's system. However, if a flu vaccine shortage were to occur and your child couldn't get two doses of vaccine, one dose might still offer some protection.

Measles Measles (rubeola) is primarily a childhood illness, although adults also are susceptible. It's the most contagious human virus known. The measles virus is transmitted through the air in droplets, such as from a sneeze.

Signs and symptoms include rash, fever, cough, sneezing, runny nose, eye irritation and a sore throat. Measles can lead to an ear infection, pneumonia, seizures, brain damage and death.

Recommendation Typically, two doses of a combined measles-mumps-rubella (MMR) vaccination are given, beginning at ages 12 to 15 months and then again at 4 to 6 years.

Mumps Mumps is a childhood disease that can also occur in adults. Mumps is caused by a virus that's acquired by inhaling infected droplets. The disease causes fever, headache, fatigue, and swollen, painful salivary glands. It can lead to deafness, meningitis, and inflammation of the testicles or ovaries, with the possibility of sterility.

Recommendation Two doses of a combined measles-mumps-rubella (MMR) vaccination are given, usually beginning at ages 12 to 15 months and then again at 4 to 6 years. Use of this vaccine has markedly decreased the incidence of mumps in the United States.

Pneumococcal disease Pneumococcal disease is the leading cause of bacterial meningitis and ear infections among children younger than 5 years old. It can also cause blood infections and pneumonia. Children below the age of 2 are at greatest risk of the most serious complications of this disease.

Pneumococcal disease is caused by *Streptococcus pneumoniae* bacteria. The bacteria spread from person to person through physical contact or by inhaling droplets released into the air when a person with the infection coughs or sneezes. Because many strains of the bacterium have become resistant to antibiotics, the disease can be difficult to treat.

Recommendation Pneumococcal conjugate vaccine (PCV) can help prevent serious pneumococcal disease. It can also prevent one cause of ear infections. The vaccine is given to all children in four doses between ages 2 and 15 months.

Polio Polio is caused by a virus (poliovirus) that enters the body through the mouth. Polio affects the brain and spinal cord, often resulting in paralysis or death. Polio vaccination began in the U.S. in 1955. No polio cases have been reported in this country for many years, but the disease is still common in some parts of the world, and the virus could be brought to the United States. For that reason, getting children vaccinated against polio continues to be important.

The vaccine, called inactivated polio vaccine (IPV), contains the chemically killed virus. IPV is given by multiple injections.

Recommendation IPV is given in four doses, at ages 2 months, 4 months, 6 to 18 months and at about age 5 years. This last vaccination is a booster dose. Contrary to the fears of some people, the shots can't cause polio.

WHY SO MANY SO SOON?

Newborns need multiple vaccines because infectious diseases can cause more serious problems in infants than in older children.

While a mother's antibodies help protect newborns from many diseases, this immunity may begin to disappear as quickly as one month after birth. In addition, children don't receive maternal immunity from certain diseases, such as whooping cough. If a child isn't vaccinated quickly and is exposed to a disease, he or she may become sick and spread the illness.

Research shows that it's safe for infants and young children to receive multiple vaccines at the same time, as recommended by the Centers for Disease Control and Prevention. In addition, giving several vaccinations at once means fewer office visits, which saves time and money for parents and may be less traumatic for the child.

Remember, newborns and young children can be exposed to diseases from family members, care providers and other close contacts, as well as during routine outings — such as trips to the grocery store. Vaccines can often be given even if your child has a mild illness, such as a cold, earache or mild fever. It's important to keep your child's vaccination status up to date.

Rotavirus Rotavirus is the most common cause of severe diarrhea among infants and children, resulting in the hospitalization of approximately 55,000 children yearly in the U.S. Almost all children are infected with rotavirus before their fifth birthday. The infection is often accompanied by vomiting and fever.

Recommendation Rotavirus vaccine is an oral (swallowed) vaccine, not a shot. The vaccine won't prevent diarrhea or vomiting caused by other germs, but it's very good at preventing diarrhea and vomiting caused by rotavirus.

There are two brands of rotavirus vaccine. A baby should get either two or three doses, depending on which brand is used. The first dose is given at 2 months, the second at 4 months and the third dose, if needed, at 6 months.

Tetanus Tetanus causes painful tightening of the muscles, usually all over the body. It can be difficult to open your mouth (lockjaw) or swallow. Tetanus isn't a contagious disease. The tetanus bacteria enter the body through deep or dirty cuts or wounds.

Recommendation The tetanus vaccine typically is given in combination with those for diphtheria and pertussis

(DTaP vaccine). Vaccinations typically begin when a baby reaches 2 months of age and are given in a series of five shots in the first six years of life.

Starting at age 11, people should continue to be immunized every 10 years with the adult forms of the vaccine.

Whooping cough Whopping cough (pertussis) is a disease that causes severe coughing spells, making it hard for infants and toddlers to eat, drink or even

breathe. The word *pertussis* is from the Latin word for "cough." These coughing spells can last for weeks and can lead to pneumonia, seizures, brain damage and death. Severe whooping cough primarily occurs in children younger than 2 years and is contracted by inhaling infected droplets, often coughed into the air from an adult with a mild case of the disease.

Recommendation The DTaP vaccination combines vaccines for diphtheria, teta-nus and pertussis. It's given as a series of five shots beginning when the infant is 2 months old and continuing to between ages 4 and 6. The DTaP vaccine is a better tolerated version of an older vaccine called DTP. The "a" stands for acellular, meaning that only specific parts of the pertussis bacteria are used in the vaccine.

At age 11, a form of the vaccine for adolescents and adults, called Tdap, is recommended.

VACCINATIONS FOR PRETERM BABIES

If your baby was born early or with a low birth weight, you might be concerned about having your baby immunized at the standard schedule. However, it's recommended that even premature babies should be given the routinely recommended vaccinations at the normal times.

Keep in mind that premature babies have a greater chance of having disease-related problems, putting them at particular risk if they acquire a preventable infection. All of the vaccines that are currently available are safe for premature and low birth weight babies, and pose the same risk of side effects.

There is only one exception to this: the hepatitis B vaccine that is given soon after birth. For an infant that weighs less than 2.2 pounds at birth, your pediatrician may advise to delay the timetable for this particular vaccine until the baby is older. But stable premature babies weighing more than 2.2 pounds may be given the first hepatitis B vaccine as scheduled.

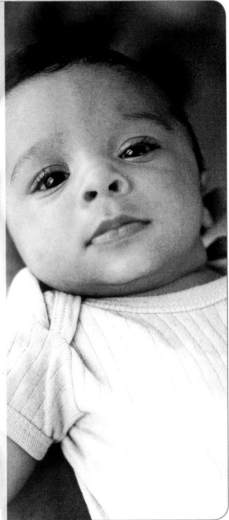

SIDE EFFECTS OF VACCINES

Although vaccines are considered very safe, like all medications they aren't completely free of side effects. Most side effects are minor and temporary. Your child might experience a sore arm, a mild fever or swelling at the injection site. Serious reactions, such as a seizure or high fever, are very rare.

According to the Centers for Disease Control and Prevention (CDC), serious side effects occur on the order of 1 per thousand to 1 per million of doses. The risk of death from a vaccine is so slight that it can't be accurately determined. When any serious reactions are reported, they receive careful scrutiny from the Food and Drug Administration and the CDC.

Some vaccines are blamed for chronic illnesses, such as autism or diabetes. (See page 161 for more on the issue of autism and vaccines.) However, decades of vaccine use in the United States provides no credible evidence that vaccines cause these illnesses. Researchers have, on occasion, reported a link between vaccine use and chronic illness. But when other researchers have tried to duplicate those results — a test of good scientific research — they haven't been able to produce the same findings.

When to avoid vaccination In a few circumstances, immunization should be postponed or avoided. Talk to your child's care provider if you question whether your baby should be vaccinated.

Immunization may be inappropriate if a child has:

▶ Had a serious or life-threatening reaction to a previous dose of that vaccine

▶ A known, significant allergy to a vaccine component, such as chicken eggs or gelatin

▶ A medical condition, such as AIDS or cancer, that's compromised the child's immune system and could allow a live virus vaccine to cause illness

Immunization may need to be delayed if a child has:

▶ A moderate to severe illness

▶ Taken steroid medications in the last three months

▶ Received a transfusion of blood or plasma or been given blood products within the past year

Immunization shouldn't be delayed because your baby has a minor illness, such as a common cold, an ear infection or mild diarrhea. The vaccine will still be effective, and it won't make your child sicker.

SIGNS OF A SEVERE REACTION

After vaccination, watch for any unusual conditions, such as a serious allergic reaction, high fever or behavior changes. Signs and symptoms of a serious allergic reaction include difficulty breathing, hoarseness or wheezing, hives, paleness, weakness, a fast heartbeat, dizziness, and swelling of the throat. Severe reactions are rare, but if you think that your baby may be experiencing one, call your child's care provider or go to an emergency department immediately.

WEIGHING THE
RISKS AND BENEFITS

The consequences of acquiring a disease that can be prevented by immunization are far greater than the extremely rare risk of a serious side effect that may result from vaccine use. For example, if your child gets mumps, the risk of him or her developing encephalitis, a brain inflammation that can cause permanent, serious brain damage, is 1 in 300. For measles, the risk is 1 in 2,000. In contrast, the risk of contracting encephalitis from the mumps and measles vaccines is less than 1 in 1 million.

If a child gets serious Hib disease, the chances of death are 1 in 20. The vaccine for Hib disease, meanwhile, hasn't been associated with any serious adverse reactions and is highly effective.

Most childhood vaccines are effective in 85 to 99 percent or more of children who receive them. For example, a full series of measles vaccine protects 99 out of 100 children from measles, and a polio vaccine series protects 99 out of 100 children from polio.

CHAPTER 13

Child care

When you first bring your baby home from the hospital, it might be hard to imagine trusting anyone else to take care of him or her. You might have a difficult time feeling comfortable taking your baby with as you run errands, let alone picturing yourself dropping him or her off at a child care center. But for many families, child care — whether in the form of a nanny, family member or a child care center — is a necessity. So how do you find child care that will promote your baby's health, safety and development but won't completely empty your bank account?

To begin with, determine how much you can afford to spend on child care, and identify your expectations — what's important to your family when it comes to child care. Then begin researching the available options in your area as soon as possible. Before your visits, make sure you know how to identify quality child care providers.

GETTING STARTED

Whether you plan to work after your baby is born or just need some help a few days a week, it's never too early to start thinking about child care arrangements. Even if you're not sure about your plans, start exploring and researching your options early. You might want to visit multiple child care centers to find the right one for your baby — and many child care centers have long waiting lists. If you're looking for in-home care, you might need time to find a child care agency, interview caregivers, and set up health insurance or workers' compensation for your child's caregiver.

Before you return to work, you might want to have your child spend time at a child care center or with a child care provider to see how your baby handles the situation and whether the arrangement works for your family.

When you begin to look for child care, start by asking your friends, neighbors and co-workers for recommendations.

You might ask your baby's care provider for advice. Child care agencies or referral services are great resources, too. Your local child care resource and referral agency can tell you about licensing requirements in your area, how to get information about complaints or licensing violations, and whether your family qualifies for financial assistance. If you're still having trouble finding information, consider contacting placement services at local colleges for the names of child development or early education students who baby-sit. You might also find the names of potential sitters in community newspapers or on church or community bulletin boards.

CHILD CARE OPTIONS

Child care options vary. Generally, though, child care options include the following settings.

In-home care Under this arrangement, a caregiver comes to your home to provide child care. The person might live with you or come to your home each day, depending on the agreement you have worked out. Some examples of in-home caregivers include relatives, nannies and au pairs. Au pairs are people who typically come to the United States on a student visa and provide child care in exchange for room and board and a small salary.

Pros One of the big advantages of this type of arrangement is that your baby can stay at home. You don't have to be bundling up your baby early in the morning to drop him or her off on your way to work. In addition, you set your own standards, and you might have more flexibility with your work hours. Other advantages of an in-home arrangement are that your child will receive individual attention, and he or she won't be exposed to other children's illnesses or bad behavior. Plus, you won't need backup care if your baby becomes ill. You won't need to worry about transportation for your baby unless you want your child care provider to take your baby somewhere. An in-home caregiver also might be able to help with light housework or preparing meals during your baby's naps.

If you use an agency to find a child care provider, you'll have the comfort of knowing that someone has already checked the backgrounds and references of potential candidates. If you have more than one child, the cost of in-home care might not be significantly more expensive than other care options.

Cons This type of care isn't well regulated and is typically more expensive than other options. If you use an agency to find a child care provider, you'll likely have to pay a hefty fee. Your caregiver might have minimal training in child development, first aid or CPR. As an employer of a child care provider, you also might have certain legal and financial obligations, such as meeting minimum wage and tax-reporting requirements or providing health insurance. Some people also feel uncomfortable having another person spending time in or living in their home. There might not be as much opportunity for your baby to socialize with other children. When your child care provider becomes sick or goes on vacation, you'll need to find back-up care. Unless you set up a home surveillance system, you won't be able to observe what happens to your baby in your absence.

Family child care Many people provide child care in their homes for small groups of children, sometimes in addition to caring for their own children. Typically, family child care centers provide care for children of mixed ages. Small programs provide care for up to six children at one time, while large programs are for seven to 12 children.

Pros One of the main attractions of family child care is that it allows your baby to be in a homelike setting with other children. In addition, family child care is often less expensive than care provided by an in-home caregiver or a child care center. Homes that offer child care usually have to meet state or local safety and cleanliness standards. Some facilities might be able to cater to your baby's and family's specific needs, providing care for children with special needs or extended hours.

Cons The quality can vary widely. While many family child care providers undergo background checks and participate in ongoing training, not all may be required to do so. Unless the facility has an online surveillance system, you won't be able to see what your baby is doing in your absence. You may have to drop off and pick up your baby at the family child care at specified times.

Child care centers Child care centers, also called day care centers, child development centers, or sometimes preschool or pre-kindergarten programs, are organized facilities with staff members who are trained to care for groups of children. In these settings, care typically is provided in a building — rather than a home — with separate classrooms for children of different ages. Programs can be large or small, based on their maximum capacity. A child care center can be part of a chain, independent for profit, nonprofit, state-funded or part of a federal program,

such as Head Start. Some child care programs also have religious affiliations or income eligibility requirements.

Pros Child care centers offer many advantages. They're generally required to meet state or local standards. Many have structured programs designed to meet the needs of children at different age levels. Child care centers often have high education requirements for staff. And because most centers have several caregivers, you likely won't need backup care if a child care provider becomes sick. In addition, child care centers provide opportunities for socialization with other children. Some centers might allow you to enroll your baby for less than a full week if you work part time or provide extended hours. Some child care centers also allow you to check in on your baby

during the day via secure online surveillance systems.

Cons Some of the drawbacks of larger facilities are that they might have long waiting lists for admission, and spending time with other children can increase your baby's risk of getting sick. Because of this, some child care centers might not let you bring your child to the center if he or she is mildly ill. Child care centers also can be expensive, depending on the services offered. Regulations also vary. If the program is large or the ratio of care providers to children is low, your child might not receive a lot of individual attention. You may have to drop off and pick up your baby at the child care center at spec-

ified times. Some centers charge fees if you don't pick up your baby on time.

Relative or friend Many people rely on relatives or friends to provide part-time or full-time care for their children. While having someone you know and trust take care of your child is comforting, there are advantages and disadvantages to this type of arrangement, too.

Pros Chances are your baby will receive plenty of individual attention. You might even be able to have your relative or friend care for your baby in your own home so you don't need to worry about transportation. Your baby won't be exposed to other children's illnesses or bad behavior, and you won't need backup care if your baby becomes ill. This type of arrangement also might give you some flexibility with your work hours. It's also possible, depending on the agreement you work out, that you might not need to pay your friend or relative for child care services, or you can pay at a discounted rate.

Cons Your friend or relative might not have any training in CPR or other emergency care. The main drawback of having a family member or friend provide care is that it can cause tension. You might not feel comfortable talking to a family member or friend if you have differing opinions about how he or she cares for your child. Your relative or friend might also offer unwanted parenting advice.

FACTORS TO CONSIDER

Before you begin looking at facilities or interviewing child care providers, take some time to think about what kind of child care might work best for your fam-

CARE FOR BABIES WITH SPECIAL NEEDS

If your baby has a developmental disability or chronic illness, finding quality child care is more important than ever. The best programs encourage normal activities and also meet each child's special needs. To find a child care program for your baby, consult your baby's care provider or your state's department of health or education. Your baby's care provider can also help you determine what kind of care will best address your baby's needs. Look for a program that meets the basic requirements you'd want in a child care program. In addition, look for:

Specialized staffing and equipment Has the program's staff been trained to meet your baby's specific needs and recognize when your baby might need medical attention? Does the program have a medical consultant who is involved in the program's development? What kind of specialized equipment does the program provide, and is it in working condition? Has the staff been trained to use it? Does the program tailor emergency plans to the needs of its children?

Confidence-building activities What kinds of activities will your baby be able to participate in? Does the program include children who don't have special needs? Programs that contain children who have different levels of ability can help encourage social confidence and sensitivity.

ily and what you can afford. Understanding your priorities will help you figure out what questions to ask as you start evaluating your options.

Expectations Think about your family's needs and what's most important to you in a child care provider. How many days and hours a week do you expect your child to need care? What kind of disciplinary techniques do you want your child care provider to use? If you're considering hiring a nanny, do you want him or her to be able to drive and do light housework? If you're considering out-of-home care, how far away from your home or place of work would you like your child to be? How will you handle transportation to and from the child care center or access to transportation your caregiver and child might need dur-

ing the day? What kind of backup arrangements can you make if your child or an at-home care provider becomes sick? Do you want your child to be exposed to a specific language?

Budget Think about how much money you can afford to spend on child care and how different types of child care will affect your budget. Are you eligible for any state subsidies or assistance from your employer, such as employer discounts or dependent care spending accounts? If you're considering in-home care, are you prepared to pay any necessary state taxes and the cost of backup care during your child care provider's vacation and sick days? If you're concerned about the expense of child care, could you or your partner adjust work hours or schedules to reduce your need for child care?

EVALUATING YOUR OPTIONS

Once you've thought about what kind of child care will work best for your family, compile a list of potential caregivers or facilities in your area. Next, call or visit the caregivers or facilities. During your visit, pay special attention to the way staff members treat the children. After the tour, be prepared with a list of questions. If you're evaluating several different settings or child care providers, consider taking notes and recording your first impressions.

In-home care When looking for someone to come into your home to care for your baby, checking references is crucial. Talk to several of the child care provider's previous employers and ask questions about his or her strengths and weaknesses, as well as any problems or concerns the employer might have had. Do a background check. Search for information about the person online via a search engine or social networking site. Ask about the child care provider's approach to child rearing. What will the care provider do if your baby won't stop crying? What kind of disciplinary techniques does he or she typically use? What kind of hours can he or she work? What kind of salary does the child care provider expect? Does he or she need health insurance? Does he or she have CPR and first-aid training?

Family child care Look for a facility that's certified, licensed and provides a safe environment for children. Ask about how many child care providers are on staff and if they have undergone background checks. Request references. Ask about the provider's training, how many children are enrolled and about the facility's hours. Discuss the facility's approach to child rearing. How many child care providers are currently certified in CPR and have first-aid training? Who lives in and visits the home? What are their backgrounds, and how might they interact with your child? How does the facility plan to deal with emergencies? What safety measures are in place? Are there daily activities for the children? Find out what happens if the care provider becomes ill and if he or she closes for vacations. How much does the program cost?

Child care center When evaluating child care centers find out about each

---

SICK CARE

When your baby becomes ill and you need backup care, you might have options beyond staying home to care for him or her. Some child care centers or family child care programs offer care for sick children in a segregated area. Your community might also have child care centers or family child care programs that specialize in providing care only for sick children. Some employers also provide sick care for their employees' children. Investigate your options before your baby becomes ill. When looking for this type of care, ask about how much individual care your baby will receive, how the facility and equipment are cleaned, and whether the facility has a care provider on call.

HANDLING THE SEPARATION

Babies up to age 7 months often adjust well to being taken care of by a new child care provider. Older babies, however, might have a harder time with the transition. Between age 7 months and one year, babies begin to develop stranger anxiety. They might need extra time and help getting used to a new child care provider and setting. If possible, arrange for an in-home care provider to spend time with your baby while you're at home. Or take your baby to visit the family child care or child care center before he or she begins attending it. Stay nearby while your child plays, and steadily increase the length of your visits. When you begin dropping your child off at the program, create a goodbye ritual, and let him or her bring a reminder of home, such as a stuffed animal or picture of you, to the program. Always say goodbye to your baby before leaving. If your baby shows persistent fear about being left alone with a caregiver, talk to your baby's care provider.

Separation is sometimes harder for the parents than the baby. Checking in regularly with your child care provider to see how your baby is doing might help reassure you. Talk to friends and family who've been through it before. Carrying a picture of your baby with you might help, too.

---

program's practices. Many child care centers provide pamphlets or have websites that will answer your questions. You can also speak to the program's director. Consider asking about:

Credentials and staff qualifications Make sure the program is licensed and has a recent health certificate. Programs that are accredited have met voluntary standards for child care that are higher than most state licensing requirements. The National Association for the Education of Young Children and the National Association for Family Child Care are the two largest organizations that accredit child care programs. Staff should have training in early child development, CPR and first aid. References should be available upon request. Ask if there are frequent staff changes, since high staff turnover might be a sign of a problem, and changing care providers can be hard on a child. Talk to at least one parent whose child was in the program in the past year. Be sure to search for information online about the program and its child care providers, too.

Adult-to-child ratios Ask about the ratio of adults to children. The fewer the children for each adult, the better the child care experience may be for your son or daughter. For infants, look for an adult-to-child ratio of 1-to-3 or 1-to-4. Also, look for a group size that's no larger than six to eight infants or six to 12 young toddlers. Keep in mind that infants and young toddlers do better in smaller groups.

Health and sanitation practices Ask whether the program requires children and staff to have standard vaccinations and regular checkups. Is the staff prohibited from smoking inside and outside of the building? What happens if your baby becomes ill during the day? Are parents notified when a child or staff member contracts a communicable disease, such as chickenpox? When should you keep your sick baby home? How are medications and first aid administered? How often are a baby's diapers changed? Are diapering areas and toys regularly cleaned and sanitized? Do staff members regularly wash their hands? How are babies put to sleep? How regularly is bedding cleaned?

Safety and security What kind of security system does the facility have to ensure that strangers don't enter the building? What happens if a child becomes injured or lost? Are outdoor play areas secured? Do outdoor play areas have sturdy structures and safe surfaces? What kind of security measures are taken during field trips? How are children transported? What is the program's emergency evacuation plan? How are other emergencies handled?

Daily activities Ask what your child's daily routine would be like. Is there a mix of group play and individual attention? Is there a balance between physical activity and quiet time? Is there time for free play? Are there activities appropriate for different age levels? Do care providers read to the children? Are meals and snacks provided? If so, what kinds? What are the program's overall goals? Is parental involvement expected or encouraged?

Additional details What is the program's admissions policy? What kind of information will you need to provide? If the program has a waiting list, how long is it, and how does it work? What are the program's hours of operation and cost? Can you pay in installments? Will you need to pay if your baby is absent for a vacation? What is the policy for withdrawing a child from the program? How

are parents notified of weather cancellations? Do parents need to provide any supplies? Can you drop in and visit your baby during the day? How can parents contact staff?

CONTACT INFORMATION

Whenever you leave your baby with a child care provider or a sitter, make sure you've provided a list of important contact information, including your phone number and how to reach you at all times. Also, provide the phone numbers of any other close family members or friends who can be contacted in the event of a problem. Explain what you want your baby's care provider to do in the case of an emergency.

If you're leaving your baby with a child care provider in your home, show the child care provider the locations of all exits, the smoke detector, fire extinguisher and the poison control telephone number. Make sure that anyone who provides care for your baby understands the importance of putting your baby to sleep on his or her back. If the child care provider will be driving your child anywhere, make sue he or she knows how to properly use car seats.

It's also a good idea to write down your address and your child's full name and birth date in the event of accident. The stress of an emergency may make it difficult for a child care provider or sitter to remember those details.

WORKING TOGETHER

In the coming weeks, carefully monitor the performance of the child care provider you hire or the child care providers at the center your baby attends. Pay close attention to your baby, his or her adjustment, and the way he or she interacts with the child care provider or providers. Establishing a good relationship with your baby's care provider benefits everyone involved. You may worry that your child will come to love his or her provider as much as you. Remember, no one can replace you in your child's heart.

Showing your baby's child care provider warmth and courtesy will make him or her, as well as your baby, comfortable. This will also make it easier for you and your baby's care provider to communicate. Be sure to set aside a few extra minutes when you leave your baby with the care provider and when you return to discuss any relevant issues. If your baby didn't sleep much the previous night, is teething or there's another matter that might affect his or her behavior that day, let your baby's care provider know. If your baby is taking any medications, explain what the medication is for and provide written instructions detailing how it needs to be stored and administered and what side effects might occur. If there are certain activities you'd like your baby's care provider to do with your baby, or if you don't want your baby to watch any TV, discuss it with the child care provider.

When you return, you'll want to find out what happened with your baby that day. How much did he or she drink and eat and at what times? How many diapers did he or she wet and soil? What activities did he or she do? How many naps did he or she have, and how long were they? Did your child achieve any new milestones or display any behavior that's of concern? Are you running low on any necessary baby supplies? Going over these topics regularly will help ensure consistency in your baby's care and might help eliminate some confusion.

For instance, if you're unaware that your baby skipped his or her afternoon snack, you might be bewildered when he or she has a total meltdown due to hunger just before dinner. Some child care centers provide daily logs with this information. You can also ask your baby's care provider to create a daily log for you.

Beyond going over your baby's daily activities, make time occasionally to have longer talks about your baby's changing needs and how to meet them. This will also give you and your baby's care provider a chance to discuss any other issues or concerns. Be sure to listen to your child care provider's thoughts on each topic and, if possible, work together to come up with solutions. If you're happy with your baby's care, don't forget to mention it, too. Showing appreciation for your baby's caregiver can help strengthen your relationship.

Finding good child care can be a stressful process. By considering your family's needs at the outset and thoroughly researching your options, you'll save time and energy. Carefully reviewing each candidate's background and evaluating different child care settings will help you feel more comfortable with your decision and ease your concerns about spending time apart from your baby.

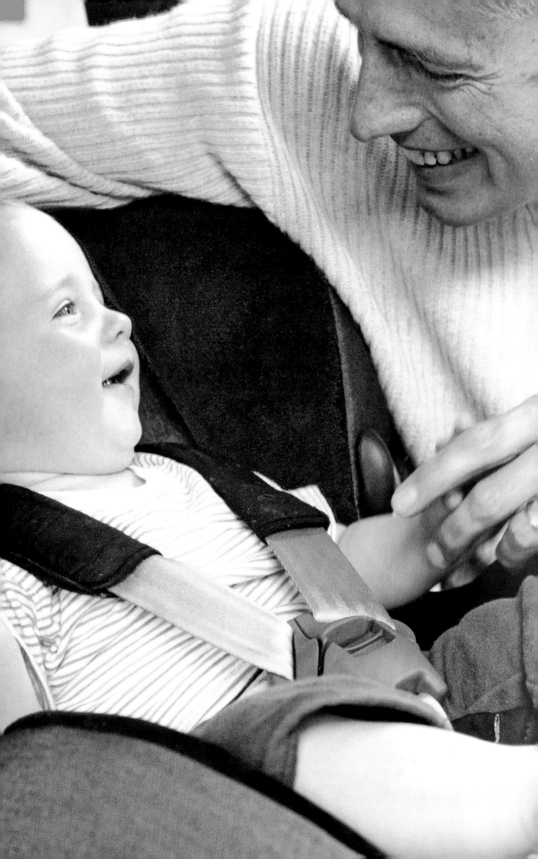

CHAPTER 14

Traveling with baby

Whether you're bringing your baby home from the hospital, taking him or her for a stroll around the block, or going on your first family flight together — you and your baby are likely to do some traveling in the months ahead.

As you might have guessed, traveling anywhere with a baby takes some planning. Your baby may never have a leaky diaper, spit up all over, or stray from his or her eating schedule when you're at home, but it always seems to happen when you're out and about.

It's a good idea to be prepared for anything when you're traveling with your child. In addition to knowing what to bring with you to meet your baby's needs while you're away from home, you'll have to figure out which modes of transportation work best and how to use them safely. You probably have more options than you might realize.

Before you hit the road, find out what you need to know about traveling with a child, and then have fun!

HEADING OUT

You and your baby are both likely to benefit from getting out of your home. As early as your baby's first month, you might consider taking him or her out for walks. While you may feel nervous about leaving the comfort of your home as you learn to care for your baby, fresh air and a change of scenery may lift your spirits. Taking small trips with your baby now will also help you gain confidence and help you prepare for bigger adventures later on.

Remember, if you've been up all night with your baby, your baby is having a fussy day or you can't face figuring out how to work the stroller yet, that outing you planned can always wait until tomorrow. There's no gold medal for the new mom who gets out of the house first. Take your time and head out with your baby when you feel ready. To help ensure a successful outing, consider the following tips.

Limit contact When you first take your newborn out, consider avoiding places where he or she will come into close contact with a lot of people and, as a result, germs. Or head to a destination when it's least likely to be crowded.

Check the weather report If possible, avoid going out with your baby in cold and rainy weather — especially early on. If you do head out, bundle your baby and cover his or her head and ears in a warm hat.

Dress for the weather Young babies have trouble regulating their body temperatures when exposed to extreme heat or cold. As a rule, dress your baby in one more layer than you're wearing. Infants should wear hats when it's cold because they can lose a large amount of heat from their exposed heads. If you're unsure about your baby's temperature, check her hands, feet and the skin on her chest while you're out. Your baby's chest should feel warm, while her hands and feet should feel slightly cooler than her body. If your baby feels cold, unwrap him or her and hold him or her close to your body. Feeding your baby something warm also might help. Dressing your baby in layers and bringing extra layers will help you adapt if the weather changes.

Provide sun protection Babies have sensitive skin. If your baby is younger than 6 months, keep him or her out of direct sunlight for long periods of time. Protect your baby from sun exposure by dressing him or her in lightweight, light-colored protective clothing and a hat with a brim. If adequate clothing and shade aren't available, apply sunscreen on exposed areas of your baby's skin. For more information on babies and sunscreen, see page 103)

Keep baby equipment cool Avoid letting your baby's car seat or stroller sit uncovered in the sun for long periods of time before using them. Plastic and metal parts may become hot enough to burn your child.

Be prepared Don't leave your home without diaper supplies, a change of clothes for your baby and, if you're bottle-feeding, food for your baby — just in case. If you're nervous, ask a family member or friend to go with you on your first few outings.

BABY CARRIERS

One of the most convenient and intimate ways to carry your baby around is in a baby carrier. If you're considering purchasing a baby carrier, you've got options, including:

▌ *Backpack or front pack.* This device allows you to carry your baby in an upright position on your back or against your chest.

▌ *Baby sling.* This is a one-shouldered baby carrier made of soft fabric.

Choosing a baby carrier Not all baby carriers are created equal. Some carriers aren't appropriate for certain babies. Others are quickly outgrown. When looking for a carrier:

▌ *Find the appropriate size for your baby.* The carrier's leg holes should be small enough so that your baby can't fall through them. Keep in mind that some models aren't appropriate for newborns.

▌ *Check the weight minimum and limit.* Different models have different weight limits. Consider how long you'd like to use it.

Look at the construction. Will the carrier provide adequate support for your baby's head and neck? Is the material sturdy? If you're looking for a backpack with an aluminum frame, is it padded to protect your baby if he or she bumps against it?

Try it out. Is the carrier comfortable for you and your baby? If you plan to use the carrier for a while, consider how the straps will feel when your baby grows, gains weight and becomes more restless.

Baby carrier risks When used incorrectly, a baby sling can pose a suffocation hazard to an infant younger than age 4 months. Babies have weak neck muscles and can't control their heads during the first few months after birth. If the baby sling's fabric presses against a baby's nose and mouth, he or she may not be able to breathe. This can quickly lead to suffocation. In addition, a baby sling can keep a baby in a curled position — bending the chin to the chest. This position can restrict the baby's airways and limit his or her oxygen supply. In turn, this can prevent a baby from being able to cry for help.

A baby is at higher risk of suffocating in a baby sling if he or she:

- Was born premature or with a low birth weight (less than 5 pounds, 8 ounces)
- Is a twin
- Has breathing problems, such as a cold

If your baby meets one of these conditions, don't use a baby sling until you talk to your baby's care provider. In addition, if your baby was born prematurely or has respiratory problems, don't use an upright positioning device until you talk to your baby's care provider.

Safety tips When using any baby carrier, take the following precautions:

Be careful when bending. Bend at the knees, rather than at the waist, when picking something up. This will help keep your baby settled securely in the carrier.

Keep up with maintenance. Keep an eye out for wear and tear. Repair any rips or tears in the carrier's seams and fasteners. Also, check the Consumer Product Safety Commission's website to make sure the carrier hasn't been recalled (see page 553).

Keep your baby's airway unobstructed. If you use a baby sling, make sure your baby's face isn't covered by the sling and is visible to you at all times. Check your baby frequently to make sure he or she is in a safe position.

Be careful after breast-feeding. If you breast-feed your baby in a baby sling,

make sure you change your baby's position afterward so his or her head is facing up and is clear of the baby sling and your body.

STROLLERS

If you're like most parents, you'll want to get at least one stroller for your baby. But what's the best stroller for your baby, family and lifestyle? When looking for a stroller for your baby, consider the following:

Where and how will you use it? If you live in or near a city, you'll need to be able to maneuver your stroller along crowded sidewalks and down narrow store aisles. You also might need to be able to collapse your stroller in a pinch to get on a bus or down stairs to the subway. Suburban parents, on the other hand, might want to look for a stroller that fits into their trunk. If you have twins or an older child, you might consider getting a double stroller or a stroller with an attachment that allows your older child to stand or sit in the rear. Frequent travelers might also want a collapsible umbrella stroller — either in addition to or as their primary stroller. Plan to take your baby along on your runs? You might look for a jogging stroller, too.

Is it appropriate for a newborn? If you plan to use a stroller while your baby is a newborn, you'll need to make sure that the stroller offers enough of a recline — since newborns can't sit up or hold up their heads. Some strollers fully recline or come with bassinet attachments. Strollers that can be used in combination with an infant-only car seat are also a good choice. However, most umbrella strollers typically don't provide adequate head and back support for young babies. In addition, most jogging strollers aren't appropriate for a baby until age 5 or 6 months.

Do you need a travel system? If so, you might look for a stroller that can hold your baby's car seat. Some car seats and strollers come in matching sets, while others require you to buy separate attachments that allow the strollers to be used with certain car seats. Once you strap your baby into his or her car seat, these kinds of strollers will allow you to easily move your baby between the stroller and car. This type of stroller can also be helpful in an airport, if you plan to take your baby's car seat on the plane.

What kinds of accessories are available? You might consider whether you'll want features or accessories for your stroller, such as a basket, rain cover, a stroller blanket, a sun shade or parasol, or a cup holder. Some accessories aren't available for certain strollers.

Other features Strollers with wide bases are less likely to tip over. Many strollers have brakes that lock two wheels — a special safety feature. If you're looking for a double stroller, choose one with one footrest that extends across both sitting areas — since small feet can get trapped in between separate footrests. Always read the stroller manufacturer's weight guidelines, especially when looking for a stroller with an area for an older child to sit or stand.

Safety tips Once you find the right stroller, follow these safety tips, and remember to never leave your child unattended in his or her stroller:

▌ *Take caution when folding.* Always make sure the stroller is locked open before you put your child in it.

▌ *Buckle up.* Always buckle your child's harness and seat belt when taking him or her for a stroller ride.

▌ *Be careful with toys.* If you hang toys from a stroller bumper bar to keep your baby entertained, make sure that the toys are securely fastened.

▌ *Properly store belongings.* Don't hang a bag from the stroller's handle bar, which can make a stroller tip over. Place items in the stroller basket.

CAR SEATS

Whenever you travel by car with your baby, a car seat is a must. Not only are car seats required by law in every state, but they're essential for your child's safety. Traveling with your baby in your lap could put him or her at risk of serious injury in case of an accident. Find out how to choose the right car seat for your child and use it safely.

The best time to get a car seat for your baby is during your pregnancy, so you'll be able to install the car seat in your car — which might be a more complicated process than you realize — and have it ready for your baby's trip home from the hospital. When choosing a car seat, you'll have lots of options. Don't assume that the pricier models are best. Instead, look for a car seat that will keep your baby safe and best serve your family's needs. First, decide if you want an infant-only car seat or a convertible car seat. You might also check with the store to see if they will let you try out the car seat before you purchase it.

If you have two cars, you might consider buying two car seats or, for an infant-only car seat, two bases. Otherwise, be sure to always move the car seat to the car in which your child will be traveling.

Infant-only car seat Infant-only car seats are for babies who weigh up to 22 to 32 pounds, depending on the model. They come with five-point or three-point harnesses and can only be used in the rear-facing position. This type of car seat typically has a handle and can be snapped in and out of a base in your car. This allows you to strap your baby into the car seat inside your home and then simply lock the car seat into the base. You can also use this type of seat without a base, which might make traveling a little easier. Some models can also be snapped in and out of a stroller base. When your baby reaches the maximum weight or height allowed for an infant-only car seat, you'll need to purchase a convertible car seat.

Convertible car seat You can also start with a convertible seat, which can be used rear-facing or forward-facing and typically has a higher rear-facing weight and height limit than an infant-only seat. This type of car seat typically has a five-point harness or an overhead shield — a padded guard that can be pulled down around the child. When your child reaches 2 years of age or the rear-facing weight or height limit of the convertible seat, you can begin to face the seat forward.

Other considerations Once you know what type of car seat you want, look for a model that will fit into your car. Also, look for a model with a cover that's easy to clean — in case your child spits up, vomits or spills food in the car seat at some point. No matter what kind of car seat you choose, make sure the label says that it meets all federal safety standards. Register your car seat online or by filling out the manufacturer's product registration card so you can be notified in the event of a recall.

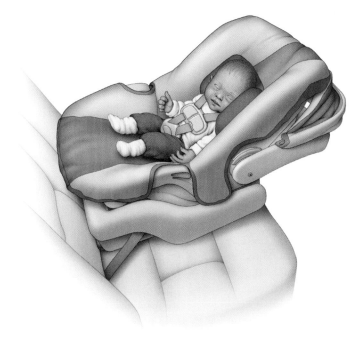

© MFMER

Infant-only seat

IS YOUR CAR SEAT TOO OLD?

Yes, car seats do expire — typically after six years. The expiration date is usually stamped in the plastic on the bottom of the seat. With time, pieces of the car seat may become worn, jeopardizing the seat's ability to keep your baby safe in a crash. As technology improves, safety recommendations may also change, but for now, the six-year time frame does matter.

Used car seats If you're considering borrowing or buying a used car seat, make sure the car seat is safe. Look for these things:

◗ Comes with instructions and a label showing the manufacture date and model number
◗ Hasn't been recalled
◗ Isn't more than six years old
◗ Has no visible damage or missing parts
◗ Has never been in a moderate or severe crash

If you don't know the car seat's history, don't use it. If the car seat has been recalled, be sure to find and follow instructions for how to fix it or get the necessary new parts.

INSTALLING A CAR SEAT

Properly installing a car seat and correctly buckling your child into it before the

Convertible seat

start of every car ride, is crucial. Before you install the car seat, read the manufacturer's instructions and the section on car seats in your vehicle's owner manual.

To install an infant-only car seat, you'll use a back seat seat belt or a car seat latch. To install a convertible car seat, you can use a back seat seat belt or, in vehicles made after 2002, a Lower Anchors and Tethers for Children (LATCH) restraint system. In the LATCH system, lower anchors secure the car seat to the vehicle. However, the tether — a strap that hooks to the top of the seat and attaches to an anchor in the vehicle to provide stability — is only used on forward-facing seats. Make sure the seat is facing the correct direction and it's tightly secured — allowing no more than one inch of movement from side to side or front to back when it's grasped at the bottom near the attachment points. If necessary, use a locking clip to secure the position of the seat belt holding the car seat in place. All new car seats come with locking clips.

If you're using an infant-only seat or a convertible seat in the rear-facing posi-tion, use the harness slots described in the instruction manual, usually those at or below the child's shoulders. Also, place the harness or chest clip even with your child's armpits — not the abdomen or neck. Make sure the straps and harness lie flat against your child's chest and over his or her hips with no slack. If your car seat has a carrying handle, position it according to the manufacturer's instructions.

After you install the car seat, consider having a certified child passenger safety technician check your handiwork at a local car seat clinic or inspection event. You can also check with the National Highway Traffic Safety Administration for help finding a car seat inspection station. Before each trip you take, check that the car seat is installed tightly.

In the rear-facing position, recline the car seat according to the manufacturer's instructions so that your child's head doesn't flop forward. Many seats include angle indicators or adjusters. You can also place a tightly rolled towel under the seat's front edge to achieve the correct angle. To prevent slouching, place tightly rolled baby blankets alongside

SLEEPING IN A CAR SEAT

A car seat is designed to protect your child during travel. It's not for use as a replacement crib in your home. Limited research suggests that sitting upright in a car seat might compress a newborn's chest and lead to lower oxygen levels. Even mild airway obstruction can impair a child's development.

Sitting or sleeping in a car seat for lengthy periods can also contribute to the development of a flat spot on the back of your baby's head and worsen reflux, a condition that causes a baby to spit up. In addition, a child can easily be injured by falling out of an improperly used car seat or while sitting in a car seat that falls from an elevated surface, such as a table or counter.

While it's essential your child be in a car seat during car travel, don't let your child sleep or relax in the car seat for long periods of time out of the car.

RENTALS, TAXIS, TRAINS AND MORE

Follow the same car safety rules, whether you're traveling in your own car, a rental car, a taxi, train or any other vehicle. Plan to bring your baby's car seat with you on any trip in which you might be riding in a vehicle or renting a car from a rental car company. If you're using an infant-only car seat that has a base, determine if you're going to bring the base with you. If not, make sure you know how to install the car seat in a vehicle without the base.

your newborn. If necessary, place a rolled washcloth between the crotch strap and your baby to prevent slouching. Don't use any additional products unless they came with the car seat or from the manufacturer.

Resist the urge to place your child's car seat in the forward-facing position just so you can see his or her smile in your rearview mirror. Riding rear facing is recommended until a child reaches age 2 or the highest weight — typically at least 35 pounds — or height allowed by the car seat manufacturer. If you want to know what's happening with your baby, have someone sit in the back seat next to your baby or pull over to check on your baby. Back seat mirrors, while helpful, can be distracting to drivers.

Remember, never leave your baby alone in a car. Babies can quickly become overheated, cold or frightened, and a baby alone in a car could easily be abducted. Even though it might be hard to imagine forgetting your child and leaving him or her in the back of the car, it can happen. To remind yourself of your precious cargo, place your purse or wallet on the floor of the back seat whenever your baby rides in the car with you so you'll have an extra reason to check the back seat before leaving the car.

As your baby gets older, he or she may not enjoy riding in a car seat. Some children may even try to climb out of a car seat. If your child begins to put up a fight about sitting in a car seat, be stern. Tell your child that he or she must stay in the car seat during travel and that you won't get going unless everyone is securely buckled up. Try to remain calm and remember that this is likely a passing phase. To keep your child entertained during travel, talk, play music or sing songs together.

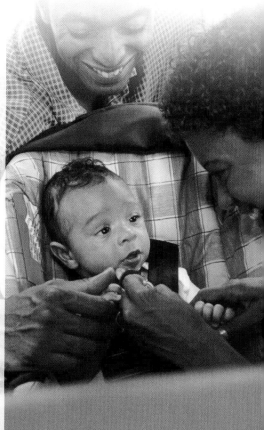

MOTION SICKNESS

Any type of transportation can cause motion sickness, a feeling of uneasiness that might cause your child to develop a cold sweat, feel dizzy or vomit. While children ages 2 to 12 are particularly susceptible to motion sickness, the problem doesn't seem to affect most infants and toddlers. If your baby experiences motion sickness, talk to your child's care provider for advice. Keep in mind that medications typically used to treat motion sickness aren't recommended for children under age 2.

Car seat and air bag safety The safest place for your child's car seat is the back seat, away from active air bags. If the car seat is placed in the front seat and an air bag inflates, it could hit the back of a rear-facing car seat — right where your child's head is — and cause a serious or fatal injury. A child who rides in a forward-facing car seat could also be harmed by an air bag.

If it's necessary for a child to travel in a vehicle with only one row of seats, deactivate the front air bags or install a power switch to prevent air bag deployment during a crash. Otherwise, air bag power switches should only be used if your child has certain health problems, his or her care provider recommends constant supervision of your child during travel, and no other adult is available to ride in the back seat with your child.

If you're placing only one car seat in the back seat, install it in the center of the seat — if possible — rather than next to a door to minimize the risk of injury in case of a crash.

PREEMIES AND SMALL BABIES

If your baby is born prematurely or at a low birth weight, he or she might need to be monitored while sitting in a car seat before he or she is discharged from the hospital. If this is the case, you'll need to bring your baby's car seat to the hospital. Your baby will be placed in it and have his or her vital signs recorded for a certain period of time. This is because sitting semireclined in a car seat can increase the risk of breathing problems or a slow heartbeat. If your baby has a health problem that requires him or her to lie flat, a vehicle bed may be recommended. Look for a vehicle bed that's been crash tested. Position the bed lengthwise in the back seat so that your baby's head will be in the center of the car. Always use the buckle and harness to secure your baby in the bed.

When you have the OK to use a car seat, you may need an infant-only car seat to accommodate your small baby. Use it only during travel, and don't let your child sleep in it outside of the car. If you use a convertible car seat for a small infant, make sure you use a model with a five-point harness, rather than an overhead shield. During an accident a baby's head could hit the shield.

If your baby needs to travel with devices such as an oxygen tank, secure them in the vehicle so they don't become flying objects in case of a sudden stop or accident. You might try placing the equipment on the floor and surrounding it with pillows or buckling it in with a seat belt.

AIR TRAVEL

Your first flight with your baby will likely be a lot different than your previous flights. Instead of worrying about whether you have enough reading material, you may now be worried that your baby will scream the entire flight. While there's no telling how your baby will react to his or her first time on an airplane, careful planning can go a long way toward calming you and your baby's nerves.

Identification Depending on your destination, your baby might need a passport. If you know you'll be traveling outside of the country with your baby in the future, consider applying as soon as possible. The application process can typically be expedited for a fee.

Seat safety Although airlines typically allow infants to ride on a caregiver's lap during flight, the Federal Aviation Administration recommends that infants ride in properly secured safety seats. Most infant car seats are certified for air travel. In order for your baby to travel in a car seat on the plane, your child will need

his or her own seat. The best way to ensure your child has a seat is to buy one. When booking your flights, check if there are any discounts for infant children. Keep in mind that car seats must be secured in a window seat so other passengers will be able to exit the row.

If you don't want to buy a seat for your baby, try to take a flight in which empty seats are likely to be available. Or, if you're traveling with another person, try booking the aisle and window seats — which might give you a better shot at an empty middle seat. You can also ask about open seats when you board the plane — in case one can be assigned to your infant.

If you don't bring a car seat for your child on the plane, ask the flight attendant for instructions on how to hold your baby during takeoff and landing. If you sit in an aisle seat with your baby, be sure to protect your baby's head, hands and feet from getting bumped by service carts or other passengers.

Many traveling families seek out the bulkhead of the plane, which offers extra space. Others prefer the back of the plane, which is typically noisy enough to

---

IS IT SAFE FOR YOUR BABY TO FLY?

Generally, age doesn't affect an infant's ability to handle air travel. While it's always a good idea to avoid enclosed, crowded spaces when you have a newborn, most healthy term babies are OK to fly at age 1 to 2 weeks. If your baby was born prematurely or has a history of lung disease, however, consider talking to your baby's care provider before flying with your baby. Because your baby's lungs might be sensitive to the effects of the changes in altitude, the care provider might recommend postponing air travel until age 1 or later. If your baby has an underlying respiratory condition, his or her care provider might recommend supplemental oxygen.

Ear infections and ear tubes aren't thought to pose problems during air travel. However, if your baby is ill you might want to consider postponing the flight.

drown out crying and may even lull a baby to sleep. Do what makes the most sense to you.

Getting through the airport If you plan to bring a car seat on the plane, a stroller that allows you to attach the car seat to it is a smart investment. You'll be able to wheel your child in his or her car seat until you board the plane, at which point you can collapse the stroller base and check it at the gate. You will, however, have to take your baby out of a car seat to go through the metal detector.

While the Transportation Security Administration limits the amount of fluids you can bring on a plane, exceptions are made for baby-related items, such as medications, formula, baby food, juice and breast milk. Be sure to notify security officials about what you're carrying and expect it to be inspected. Also, let security officials know if your baby is using or has any special medical devices.

Boarding Many airlines allow families to board the plane first. This might be a good option if you have a lot of baggage. However, some families prefer sending one parent ahead with the bags, while the other boards last with the baby to minimize the amount of time spent stuck on the plane.

Keeping baby happy Dress your baby in comfortable, easy-to-remove layers. This will help you keep him or her warm or cool enough and make diaper and clothing changes easy. Sucking on a pacifier or bottle might ease discomfort during takeoff and landing, since babies can't intentionally "pop" their ears by swallowing or yawning to relieve ear pain caused by air pressure changes. Breast-feeding your baby — when it's safe to do so — also can help.

Take occasional breaks to walk up and down the aisle — as long as the crew approves moving throughout the cabin.

Giving your baby a sedating over-the-counter medication to make him or her sleep during the flight isn't recommended. The medication could end up producing the opposite effect.

If your baby does cry during the flight, do your best to figure out what's wrong — just as you would at home — and try to stay calm. Chances are that many passengers on the plane have been in your situation before and likely sympathize.

TRIP BASICS

Taking your baby on a trip — particularly those involving flights, overnight stays and different time zones — requires some planning. When you schedule your trip, think about your baby's normal routine and what you can do during your travels and trip to accommodate his or her daily needs.

Minding your baby's internal clock
If your baby is an early riser, consider booking an early morning flight and scheduling morning activities during your trip. Think about what times your baby typically naps and eats and how you'll be able to keep his or her schedule intact while away. Keep in mind that if you cross time zones during your trip, it might take your baby a few days to adjust to new sleeping and eating schedules.

Gathering essentials Start by packing your baby's diaper bag, which you'll need to keep with you at all times. Fill it with diapers, wipes, diaper ointment and a changing pad. If you feed your baby formula, make sure you have formula, bottles and nipples. Bring enough formula to cover your travel time and well beyond, just in case you encounter delays. If

you're breast-feeding, a blanket or nursing cover might come in handy. If your baby uses a pacifier, bring at least one.

It's always smart to pack an extra change of clothes — or two — for your baby and an extra shirt for yourself in the diaper bag, just in case. You might also bring disposable bags for dirty diapers, in case you don't have immediate access to a garbage can during travel, and travel-size hand sanitizer.

When packing your baby's clothes for the trip, think about the weather you're likely to encounter, how many outfit changes your baby typically needs in a day, and whether you'll have access to a washer and dryer. You might bring along a few familiar items, such as small toys or a white noise machine, to help your child feel comfortable in the new environment. If you'll be staying at a hotel, call ahead and see if you can reserve a crib for your room. Otherwise, you'll need to bring a collapsible crib with you. In addition to the bottle supplies you bring with you on the plane, consider what kind of sterilizing or cleaning equipment you might need to bring for the rest of your trip.

Traveling with a baby takes some planning and — often — a lot of luggage. Think about what your baby might need, and do your best to prepare for the worst. And don't forget to enjoy your trip!

CHAPTER 15

Home and outdoor safety

As your baby becomes more mobile, exploration will become the name of the game. Rocking, rolling and sitting will give way to crawling, climbing and cruising along the furniture. Your baby's budding curiosity and inexperience, however, can prove to be a dangerous mix. Power cords, dresser drawers, kitchen cabinets, dish soap and the toilet are just a few household items that your baby might touch, grab or try to climb onto in the coming months. Small toys, hot drinks, slippery surfaces and furniture with sharp edges can also pose hazards for your little explorer. While trying to prevent injuries, you can take lots of steps to safeguard your home and keep your baby safe outdoors.

To get started childproofing your home, consider your family's lifestyle and the layout of your home. Think about which rooms your baby will spend time in and what dangers each room poses. Sit on the floor in each room to get an idea of what might catch your baby's attention or be within your baby's reach. If you don't childproof every room in your home, you'll need to take extra vigilance to keep your child away from those areas. Remember, however, that as your child gets older, it will become harder to exclude him or her from certain areas of the house.

NURSERY SAFETY

Your son or daughter will spend a lot of time in the nursery. To help keep him or her safe while in the room, here are some helpful tips:

Use safety straps Always use the safety strap on your baby's changing table and never leave a baby alone on the changing table. Even at young ages babies can move suddenly and flip over the edge of a high surface. Look for a changing table with a guardrail and keep diapering supplies within your reach but beyond your child's reach.

SAFE TOYS

Babies love to play with toys, but you want to make sure the toys around them don't pose any dangers.

Choose toys carefully Don't let your baby play with balloons, marbles, coins, toys that contain small parts or other small items. Balloons, in particular, pose a major choking hazard when uninflated and broken. Avoid projectile toys, extremely loud toys and toys with cords, long strings and small magnets. Remove plastic wrapping and stickers from new toys, and make sure any decorations or small parts — such as eyes, wheels or buttons — are tightly fastened to the toy. Regularly check your baby's toys for small parts that could come loose, sharp edges and mechanical parts that could trap a child's finger, hair or clothes.

Safely store toys with small pieces If you have an older child, you likely have toys in your home with small pieces that your baby could easily choke on or swallow. Gather up games and toys that have small parts, and do your best to keep them out of your baby's reach. When your older child wants to play with these kinds of toys, make sure he or she plays with them in an enclosed area and picks up all of the pieces afterward.

Take care with electronics Don't allow small children to play with toys that need to be plugged into electrical outlets. Make sure battery covers are securely fastened. If the toy contains a button battery, make sure your child cannot access the battery.

Avoid baby walkers A young child may fall out of the walker or fall down the stairs while using a walker. The American Academy of Pediatrics has called for a ban on the manufacture and sale of baby walkers with wheels.

Safely store disposable diapers If you use disposable diapers, keep them out of your baby's reach and cover them with clothing when he or she is wearing them. A child can suffocate if he or she tears off pieces of the plastic liner and eats them.

Avoid powders Baby powders containing talcum can harm your baby's lungs if they're inhaled.

Take crib precautions Keep your baby's crib free of small objects. Always put your baby to sleep on his or her back and not on a soft comforter or pillow. Don't allow your baby to sleep with loose blankets. For more information on crib safety, see page 120.

Watch toy box lids If you use a toy box, look for one with no top, a lightweight lid, or sliding doors or panels. If you have a toy box with a hinged lid, make sure it has lid support for any angle to which it's opened. In addition, look for a toy box with ventilation holes, in case your child gets trapped inside it. Don't block ventilation holes by storing the toy box against the wall. Rounded edges are also a plus.

KITCHEN SAFETY

The kitchen can be an especially dangerous place for a baby. When you need to spend time in the kitchen, consider placing your baby in a high chair with a few toys to play with. Or fill a kitchen cabinet with safe items for your baby to play with — such as plastic bowls and cups. You might place your child in a playpen in an adjoining room where you can see him or her. Also take steps to prevent accidents.

Reduce water temperature Set the thermostat on your hot water heater to below 120 F. If you bathe your baby in the kitchen sink, never run the dishwasher at the same time — in case hot water from the dishwasher backs up into the sink. Don't run the faucet while your baby is in the sink.

Safely store hazardous objects and substances Keep sharp instruments in a drawer with a latch or a locked cabinet. Make sure appliances are unplugged and out of your child's reach. Don't allow electrical cords to dangle where your child could tug on them. Keep hazardous substances out of sight, out of reach and — whenever possible — in a high cabinet that locks automatically every time you close it. Hazardous substances in the kitchen might include dishwasher soap, cleaning products, vitamins and alcohol.

Avoid hot spills Don't cook, drink or carry hot beverages or soup while holding a child. Know where your child is when you're walking with a hot liquid so you don't trip over him or her. Keep hot foods and liquids away from table and counter edges. Don't use tablecloths, placemats or runners, which young children can pull down. When you're using the stove, use the back burners and turn the handles of your pots and pans inward. Don't leave food cooking on the stove unattended.

Safeguard your oven Try to block access to the oven. Place tape on the floor around the oven and call it a "no-kid" zone. Never leave the oven door open. If you have a gas stove, turn your dials to the off positions and — if possible — remove them when you're not cooking. Otherwise, use knob covers.

Look around Watch out for other situations that could be hazardous.

▶ Put away small refrigerator magnets. A baby could choke on or swallow them.

▶ Address slippery or uneven surfaces and clean spills quickly.

▶ Keep a fire extinguisher handy.

FEEDING SAFETY

Feeding your baby is often a messy experience, but you don't want it to be a dangerous one. If you use a high chair during feedings, always use the chair's safety straps to buckle your child in. And before you feed your child, always check the

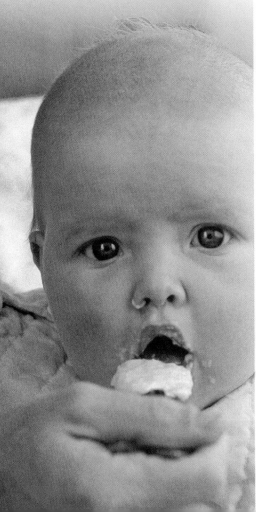

temperature of the food. Never warm your baby's formula or milk in the microwave. Food or liquids warmed in a microwave may heat unevenly. For more information about feeding your baby, see Chapter 3.

Choking prevention Choking is a common cause of injury and death among young children, primarily because their small airways are easily obstructed. It takes time for babies to master the ability to chew and swallow food, and babies may not be able to cough forcefully enough to dislodge an airway obstruction.

Sometimes health conditions increase the risk of choking as well. Children who have swallowing disorders, neuromuscular disorders, developmental delays and traumatic brain injury, for example, have a higher risk of choking than do other children. To prevent infant choking:

▶ *Don't introduce solids too soon.* Giving your baby solid foods before he or she has the motor skills to swallow them may lead to infant choking. Wait until your baby is at least 4 months old, preferably 6 months old, to introduce pureed solid foods.

▶ *Stay away from high-risk foods.* Don't give babies or young children small, slippery foods, such as whole grapes and hot dogs; dry foods that are hard to chew, such as popcorn and raw carrots; or sticky or tough foods, such as peanut butter, marshmallows and large pieces of meat.

▶ *Supervise mealtime.* Don't allow your child to play, walk, run or lie down while eating.

Keep in mind that as babies explore their environments, they also commonly put objects into their mouths — which can easily lead to infant choking. For information about how to respond if your baby chokes, see page 210.

BATHROOM SAFETY

The easiest way to avoid bathroom injuries is to make sure your baby can't access bathrooms in your home without an adult. Consider taking these precautions:

Keep the bathroom door closed Bathrooms can be dangerous for many reasons. The best way to avoid accidents is to keep young children out. Install a safety latch or doorknob cover on the outside of the door. It's also a good idea to install childproof locks on toilet lids.

Reduce water temperature Make sure the thermostat on your hot water heater is set below 120 F. Don't run the faucet while your baby is in the tub. Instead, fill it and test the water temperature before placing your baby in the water. Consider installing anti-scald devices on bathtub faucets and shower heads.

Supervise bath time Never leave a child alone or in the care of another child in the bathtub. A child can drown in just a few inches of water. Drain water from the tub immediately after use. Remember, infant bath seats or supporting rings aren't a substitute for adult supervision.

Safely store hazardous objects and substances Make sure electrical appliances, such as hair dryers, are unplugged and out of your child's reach. Don't allow electrical cords to dangle where your child could tug on them. Keep substances in a cabinet that locks automatically every time you close it. Hazardous substances in the bathroom

might include nail polish remover, mouthwash, medications and bathroom cleaners. Dispose of unused, unneeded or expired medicines.

Address slippery or uneven surfaces Use a rubber pad or slip resistant stickers in the bathtub to help prevent slipping. Place a bath mat with a non-skid bottom on the bathroom floor. Clean spills quickly.

GARAGE AND BASEMENT SAFETY

Accidents and injuries can also happen in areas where kids don't spend a lot of time. Don't forget to childproof areas of the house such as the garage and basement.

Safely store hazardous objects and substances Keep them in a cabinet that locks automatically every time you close it. Hazardous substances in the garage or basement might include cleaning products, windshield washer fluid, paint and paint thinner. Always unplug and store tools after using them. If you have an unused refrigerator or freezer, remove the door so that a child can't become trapped inside.

Don't allow your child to play near the garage It might be difficult for a driver to see a small child. Automatic garage doors can pose a danger for children. Always keep the garage opener out of reach.

Carefully store ladders Put ladders away after each use, and anything else that a young child could climb up on. Always store a ladder on its side.

FRONT YARD AND BACKYARD SAFETY

To protect children from outdoor hazards:

- *Set boundaries.* If your backyard doesn't have a fence, make sure you keep your child within the areas where he or she should play. Don't let your child play unattended.
- *Check for dangerous plants.* If you're not sure about the plants in your yard, contact your regional poison control center for advice. If you have poisonous plants in your yard, remove them.
- *Be cautious when using pesticides and herbicides.* Wait at least 48 hours before allowing your child to play in an area that's been treated.
- *Keep children away from power mowers.* Mowers may throw yard debris with enough force to injure a child. Keep your child away when mowing. Also don't allow your child to ride on a riding mower.
- *Watch grills and fire pits.* Don't allow children to play near these potential hazards. If you have a grill, screen it so your child can't touch it. Make sure charcoal is cold before you dump it.

GENERAL SAFETY TIPS

To reduce the risk of injury in other areas in and outside of your home:

Use furniture bumpers Cover sharp furniture and fireplace corners with corner or edge bumpers, just in case your child falls. Consider moving items with sharp edges out of high-traffic areas while your child is learning to walk.

Secure furniture Furniture, such as TVs, can tip over and crush a young child. Injuries typically occur when a child tries to climb onto, falls against or uses the furniture to stand up. Be sure to anchor TV stands, shelves, bookcases, dressers, desks, chests and ranges to the floor or attach them to a wall. Free-standing stoves or ranges can be installed with anti-tip devices. Move floor lamps behind other furniture.

Use door knob covers, locks and stops Door knob covers and door locks can help prevent your child from entering a room where he or she might encounter hazards. Look for a door knob cover that's sturdy but can be used easily by adults, in case of an emergency. Make sure any locks you use on a door can be unlocked from the outside. Consider temporarily removing swinging doors and folding doors or keep your child away from them.

Keep hazardous objects out of reach Common household items that may pose a choking hazard include safety pins, coins, pen or marker caps, buttons, small batteries, baby powder and bottle tops. Always safely store all potentially poisonous substances in a high, locked cabinet. Always keep products in the original containers, which might contain important safety information. Don't allow your baby to play with plastic bags or to play on waterbeds. Consider placing your trash can in a locked cabinet or getting a childproof lock for it, in case you throw out potentially hazardous items.

Address outlets and electrical cords Place plastic plugs that don't pose a choking hazard in electrical outlets, or cover them with plates. Keep electrical cords and wires out of the way so children don't chew on them or grab them.

Keep cords out of reach Keep telephone, computer and window-blind cords tied up and inaccessible — especially near your baby's crib. Safety tassels and inner cord stops for window blinds and draperies can help prevent strangulation. When buying new window coverings, be sure to ask about safety features.

Watch out for liquid containers Keep your child away from fish tanks and coolers. Empty buckets and other containers immediately after use. Don't leave them outside, where they may accumulate water.

Avoid certain houseplants Some plants can be hazardous to children. Contact your regional poison control center for information and advice.

Safely store firearms If possible, don't keep firearms in your home or in an area where your child plays. If you do keep firearms in your home, keep the unloaded gun and ammunition in separate locked cabinets.

PREVENTING BURNS

Children get burned because they don't know certain objects may be hot. To prevent burns, follow these burn-safety tips:

▶ *Establish 'no' zones.* Block access to the fireplace, fire pit or grill, so a child can't get near it.
▶ *Use space heaters with care.* Make sure a child can't get near a space heater. Also keep the heater at least three feet away from bedding, drapes, furniture and other flammable materials. Never leave a space heater on when you go to sleep or place a space heater near someone who's sleeping.

▶ *Watch where you park.* If you park in direct sunlight, cover the car seat with a towel or blanket. Before putting your child in the car seat, check the temperature of the seat and buckles.
▶ *Lock up matches and lighters.* Store matches, lighters and flammable liquids in a locked cabinet or drawer.
▶ *Choose a cool-mist humidifier.* Steam vaporizers can burn a child.
▶ *Unplug irons.* Store items designed to get hot, such as irons, blow dryers and hair straighteners, unplugged and out of reach.
▶ *Practice fire safety.* Install smoke alarms on every level of your home, and regularly maintain all alarms in your home. Keep extinguishers near places where a fire might start.

PREVENTING FALLS

There's plenty you can do to prevent falls. Follow these simple tips:

Beware of heights Never leave a baby alone on a piece of furniture. Always use the safety strap on strollers and other infant seats. Don't allow a young child to play alone on a high porch, deck or balcony.

Install safety gates Block a child's access to stairs or doorways with safety gates. Look for a safety gate that a child can't easily dislodge but that adults will be able to easily open and close. If you're putting a safety gate at the top of a staircase, attach it to the wall. Avoid accordion gates with large openings, which can trap a child's neck.

Lock windows and secure screens A young child may squeeze through a window opened as little as 5 inches. Limit window openings to 4 inches or less. Although all windows that open should have guards or screens, screens often aren't strong enough to keep a child inside. Discourage play near windows and patio doors. Don't place anything a child could climb on near a window. When opening windows for ventilation, open windows from the top.

Use night lights Consider using them in your child's bedroom, the bathroom and hallways to prevent falls at night.

AVOIDING LEAD POISONING

Lead is a metal that's found in many places — including old homes, drinking water and children's products — and it can be hard to detect. Children are at especially high risk of lead exposure because they tend to put their hands and objects in their mouths, and their growing bodies readily absorb lead. Even children who seem healthy might have high levels of lead in their bodies. If you suspect that your home contains lead hazards, you can take simple measures to minimize your child's risk of exposure.

If you think your child has been exposed to lead, ask your child's care provider about a blood test to check for lead.

Check your home Homes built before 1978 are most likely to contain lead. Professional cleaning, proper paint stabilization techniques and repairs done by a certified contractor can reduce lead exposure. Before you buy a home, have it inspected for lead.

Keep children out of potentially contaminated areas Don't allow your child near old windows, old porches or areas with chipping or peeling paint. If your home contains chipping or peeling paint, clean up chips immediately and cover peeling patches with duct tape or contact paper until the paint can be removed.

Filter your water Ion-exchange filters, reverse-osmosis filters and distillation can effectively remove lead from water. If you don't use a filter and live in an older home, run cold tap water for at least a minute before using it. Use cold, flushed tap water for cooking, drinking or making baby formula.

Avoid certain products and toys Lead may be found in children's jewelry or products made of vinyl or plastic, such as bibs, backpacks, car seats and lunch boxes. A child can absorb lead found in these products by mouthing or chewing on them or can inhale lead if the product is burned, damaged or deteriorating. Avoid buying old toys or nonbranded toys from discount shops or private vendors, unless you can be sure that the toys have been produced without lead or other harmful substances. Don't give costume jewelry to young children.

PREVENTING DROWNING

Swimming pools and hot tubs are very dangerous to young children. Multiple layers of protection can help ensure water safety and prevent drowning in a home pool or hot tub. If you have a pool or hot tub, consider these general safety tips:

Fence it in Surround your pool or hot tub with a fence that's at least 4 feet tall. Make sure slatted fences and openings under fences have no gaps wider than 4 inches, so kids can't squeeze through. Install self-closing and self-latching gates with latches that are beyond a child's reach. Make sure the gate opens away from the pool or spa. Check the gate frequently to make sure it's in working order.

Install alarms If your house serves as part of your pool or hot tub enclosure, protect any doors leading to the pool or hot tub area with an alarm. Add an underwater alarm that sounds when something hits the water. Make sure you can hear the alarm inside the house.

Block pool and hot tub access If your house serves as part of your pool enclosure, use a power safety cover to block access when the pool isn't in use. Always secure a cover on a hot tub when it isn't in use. Sliding glass doors that need to be locked after each use aren't effective pool or hot tub barriers. Remove above-ground pool steps or ladders or lock them behind a fence when the pool isn't in use. In addition, empty inflatable pools after each use.

SAFETY AROUND PETS

To prevent your child from being bitten or injured, follow some basic animal precautions.

- *Never leave your child alone with a pet.* Your child might inadvertently provoke an animal to bite him or her through roughhousing, teasing or mistreatment.
- *Teach appropriate behavior.* Don't allow your child to tease pets. Never let your child pull an animal's tail or take away its toys or food. Don't let your child put his or her face close to a pet.
- *Get your pets vaccinated.* Make sure your pets are fully immunized, including against rabies.
- *Be cautious around new animals.* Don't allow your child to approach unfamiliar animals.
- *Show your child how to greet animals.* For example, show your child how to let a dog sniff him or her and then slowly extend his or her hand to pet the dog.
- *Think twice about petting zoos.* Young children are at higher risk of contracting an infection through contact with cattle, sheep, goats and other domestic and wild animals. If you choose to take your child to a petting zoo or other venue where animals might be present, be sure to wash your child's hands if they become dirty in an animal's area and after leaving the animal's area.

Use life preservers Young children should always wear life preservers when in a watercraft. Don't use inflatable toys to keep your child afloat, since they can deflate suddenly or your child might slip out of them. Even if your child is wearing a life preserver, you always need to keep an eye on him or her while in the water.

Beware of drains Don't allow children to play near or sit on a pool or hot tub drain. Body parts and hair may become entrapped by the strong suction. Use drain covers, and consider installing multiple drains to reduce the suction.

Keep your eyes peeled Never leave children unsupervised in a pool or near a pool or hot tub. An adult — preferably one who knows cardiopulmonary resuscitation (CPR) — should always provide supervision. Don't multitask while watching children in or near water.

Keep emergency equipment handy Keep pool safety equipment beside the pool. Make sure you always have a phone in the pool area.

BE CAUTIOUS, NOT PANICKED

It might seem as if everything in your home and yard poses a potential threat to your baby. Don't panic! You can do plenty to childproof your home in a single afternoon or evening. As your baby gets older, continue to stay on the lookout for new hazards. Go through your home from top to bottom every few months to make sure you're doing everything you can to keep your child safe. Be alert when visiting new places and friends' or family members' homes. If your child is going to spend a lot of time

at his or her grandparents' homes, you might consider asking them to do some childproofing, too. The most important safeguard, though, is adult supervision.

CHAPTER 16

Emergency care

Every parent wants a healthy baby, but occasional accidents or injuries can happen. Even parents who have plenty of experience with babies can occasionally have a tough time distinguishing normal illnesses from more serious problems.

You can prepare for emergencies by asking your baby's care provider during a scheduled checkup what to do and where to go if your baby needs emergency care. It also is important to learn basic first aid, including CPR, and to keep emergency phone numbers handy.

WHEN TO SEEK EMERGENCY CARE

Seek immediate care for:
▸ Bleeding that can't be stopped
▸ Poisoning
▸ Seizures
▸ Trouble breathing
▸ Head injuries
▸ Unresponsiveness

▸ A sudden lack of energy or an inability to move
▸ Large cuts or burns
▸ Neck stiffness
▸ Blood in the urine, bloody diarrhea or persistent diarrhea
▸ Skin or lips that look blue, purple or gray

In case of an emergency, call 911 or your local emergency care number immediately. If it's not possible to call for emergency assistance, take your child to the nearest emergency facility. In case of possible poisoning, call the Poison Help hotline at 800-222-1222. Have this number by your telephone.

BLEEDING

You generally can judge the seriousness of the bleeding by the rate of blood loss. Serious bleeding comes from injured arteries. Slower bleeding — a steady, slow flow of dark red blood — generally comes from injuries to veins or the body's smaller blood vessels (capillaries). Bleeding can be the result of a cut, puncture or abrasion.

How serious is it? The rate of blood loss is a good indicator of the severity. Remember, because babies have a much smaller volume of blood, they can't afford to lose as much blood as an older child or adult. Serious injuries that result in bleeding from the arteries can cause death in minutes if untreated.

What you can do If the bleeding is serious and it doesn't stop on its own or if the cut or puncture is large or deep or has rough edges, apply pressure directly to the injury with a sterile gauze pad or clean cloth. Keep pressure on the wound until the bleeding stops. In most cases, you can stop bleeding with direct, firm pressure to the wound. Follow these steps:

1. Remain calm. This can be difficult, but it's important.

2. Immediately apply steady, firm pressure to the wound with a sterile gauze pad, clean cloth or your hand until the bleeding stops. Don't attempt to clean the wound first or remove any embedded objects.

3. When the bleeding stops, cover the wound with a tight dressing and tape the area securely. If the bleeding continues and seeps through the dressing, place more absorbent material over the first dressing.

4. If possible, elevate the bleeding area.

5. If the bleeding continues, apply pressure to the major vessel that delivers blood to the area.

6. If the bleeding doesn't stop, despite these measures, call 911 or your local emergency number. If this isn't possible, take your child immediately to the nearest emergency department.

CHOKING

Most of the time when something blocks your baby's throat, he or she will instinctively cough, gasp or gag until the object clears his or her windpipe. Usually children will breathe on their own, and you don't need to interfere. But if your baby cannot make sounds, stops breathing and turns blue, you must act immediately.

Anytime a baby inhales anything other than air, he or she will choke. Babies most commonly choke on toys with small parts or foods that "go down the wrong way." Keep from baby's reach anything that he or she can choke on, such as hot dogs, whole grapes and any small food that may obstruct his or her breathing. Coins also are commonly swallowed and can obstruct baby's airway.

How serious is it? When your baby's airway is blocked and he or she cannot clear it, the situation is life-threatening. You must deal with it immediately. The longer your baby is deprived of oxygen, the greater the risk of permanent brain damage or death. If you cannot clear the airway, ask someone to call for emergency help.

What you can do If your child is coughing, let him or her cough until the windpipe is clear. If you can see something that's blocking the throat, carefully place your fingers in the baby's mouth to remove the obstruction. You don't want to push the object farther back. If nothing is visible, don't stick your fingers in his or her throat. Again, you don't want to cause the object to become more deeply lodged. To clear the airway of a choking infant:

1. Assume a seated position. Hold the infant facedown on your forearm, which is resting on your thigh.

2. Thump the infant gently but firmly. Do this five times on the middle of the back using the heel of your hand. The combination of gravity and thumps to the back should release the blocking object.

3. Hold the infant faceup on your forearm, with the head tilted downward. Do this if the previous steps don't work. Using two fingers placed at the center of the infant's breastbone, give five quick chest compressions. If the infant is too large, lay him or her facedown on your lap with the head lower than the rest of the body.

4. Repeat the thumps to the back and the chest thrusts. Do this if the child's breathing doesn't resume. Call for emergency medical help.

5. Begin infant CPR. As soon as the obstruction is relieved, either the child will breathe spontaneously or you'll need to begin CPR.

If the child resumes breathing within a minute or two, he or she probably won't suffer any long-term ill effects. If, after the child is breathing again, he or she continues coughing or choking, it may mean that something is still interfering with his or her breathing, and you should call 911 or your local emergency number.

CARDIOPULMONARY RESUSCITATION (CPR)

It's a good idea for all parents, and for anyone who provides child care, to take a certified course in infant cardiopulmonary resuscitation (CPR). You can contact your local American Red Cross or American Heart Association chapter to sign up for a course.

You may need to give a baby CPR if he or she experiences the following:
- Has no pulse or heartbeat
- Has blue lips or skin

A gentle thump on the back can help clear the airway of a choking infant.

- Has difficulty breathing or stops breathing entirely
- Is unresponsive

Chances for saving your baby's life or avoiding permanent injury increase dramatically the sooner you start CPR.

What you can do The procedure for giving CPR to an infant is similar to the one used for adults. Loudly call out the child's name and stroke or gently tap the child's shoulder. Don't shake the child.

If you're the only rescuer and CPR is needed, do CPR for two minutes — about five cycles — before calling 911 or your local emergency number. If another person is available, have that person call for help immediately while you attend to the baby.

Circulation: Restore blood circulation

1. Place the baby on his or her back on a firm, flat surface, such as a table. The floor or ground also will do.

2. Imagine a horizontal line drawn between the baby's nipples. Place two fin-

gers of one hand just below this line, in the center of the chest.

3. Gently compress the chest about 1½ inches.

4. Count aloud as you pump at a rate of about 100 compressions a minute.

Airway: Clear the airway

1. After 30 chest compressions, gently tip baby's head back (head-tilt maneuver) by lifting the chin (chin-lift maneuver) with one hand and pushing down on the forehead with the other hand.

2. In no more than 10 seconds, put your ear near the baby's mouth and check for breathing: Look for chest motion, listen for breath sounds, and feel for breath on your cheek and ear.

Breathing: Breathe for the infant

1. Cover the baby's mouth and nose with your mouth.

2. Prepare to give the baby two rescue breaths. Use the strength of your cheeks to deliver gentle puffs of air (instead of deep breaths from your lungs) to slowly

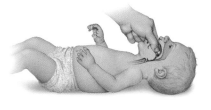

Before giving CPR to an infant, tilt the child's head back to open the airway. If you see an object in the infant's mouth, try to pick it out without pushing the object farther back in the airway.

During infant CPR, alternate compression of the infant's chest with gentle breaths from your mouth. When breathing for the infant, you want to cover the infant's mouth and nose with your mouth.

© MFMER

breathe into the baby's mouth one time, taking one second for the breath. Give a deep enough breath to cause baby's chest to rise gently. If it does, give a second rescue breath. If the chest does not rise, repeat the head-tilt and chin-lift maneuvers and then give the second breath.

3. If the baby's chest still doesn't rise, examine the mouth to make sure no foreign material is inside. If an object is seen, sweep it out with your finger. If the airway seems blocked, perform first aid for a choking baby.

4. Give two breaths after every 30 chest compressions.

5. Perform CPR for about two minutes before calling for help unless someone else can make the call while you attend to the baby.

6. Continue CPR until you see signs of life or until medical personnel arrive.

BURNS

Burns can range in severity from minor problems to life-threatening emergencies. They occur most often on a child's hands or face. Burns may result from fire, the sun (sunburn is discussed on page 388), heated objects, hot fluids, electricity or chemicals.

Common sources of burns in infants are hot liquids (such as coffee or tea), bottles that have been heated in a microwave, stoves and cigarettes. Some burns result from water heater temperatures that are excessively high (more than 120 F). You also want to be cautious about a baby's clothing catching fire from a spark or ashes.

How serious is it? Burns can range from mild to serious and are classified according to their severity:

First-degree burns They cause redness and slight swelling of the skin. These are the most mild and affect only the outer layer of skin.

Second-degree burns They generally cause blistering, intense reddening, and moderate to severe swelling and pain. The top layer of skin has been burned through, and the second layer also is damaged.

Third-degree burns They're the most severe. Third-degree burns appear white or charred and involve all the layers of the skin. There may be little pain with these burns because of substantial nerve damage.

What you can do For minor burns, take the following action:

Cool the burn Hold the burned area under cool (not cold) running water for 10 or 15 minutes or until the pain subsides. If this is impractical, immerse the burn in cool water or cool it with cold compresses. Cooling the burn reduces swelling by conducting heat away from the skin. Don't put ice on the burn.

Apply antibiotic ointment After cooling the burn for comfort and cleaning, cover the burn with antibiotic ointment. This will prevent bandages or dressings from adhering to the burn.

Cover the burn with a sterile gauze bandage Keeping the burn clean and covered provides comfort by keeping air off the injury, and it reduces the risk of infection. Don't use fluffy cotton, or other material that may get lint in the wound. Wrap the gauze loosely to avoid putting pressure on burned skin.

Give acetaminophen Talk to your baby's care provider if you have concerns about using medication. Refer to dosage instructions on the bottle.

Minor burns usually heal without further treatment, but watch for signs of infection, such as increased pain, redness, fever, swelling or oozing. If infection develops, seek medical help.

For major burns — third-degree burns or second-degree burns that involve a large area of skin — call 911 or your local emergency number. Until an emergency unit arrives, follow these steps:

- Don't immerse large severe burns in cold water. Doing so could cause a drop in body temperature (hypothermia) and deterioration of blood pressure and circulation (shock).
- Check for signs of circulation (breathing, coughing or movement). If there is no breathing or other sign of circulation, begin CPR.
- Cover the area of the burn. Use a cool, moist, sterile bandage; clean, moist cloth; or moist towels.
- Elevate the burned body part or parts. Raise the area above heart level, if possible.

ELECTRICAL SHOCK

The most common ways that infants receive electrical shocks are by biting into electrical cords or by poking metal objects or their fingers into unprotected outlets. Holiday decorations provide another source of possible injury, when electrical cords and light bulbs are often within a baby's reach.

An electrical injury often results in only minor or local injury at the point of contact, similar to a burn. An electrical shock may cause your baby to stop breathing and may stop the heart's beating. Internal organ damage may not be obvious, but it may be present. A less severe shock may burn your baby's mouth or skin.

How serious is it? Depending on the voltage and the length of the contact with electrical current, an electrical shock may range from mildly uncomfortable to causing serious injury or death.

What you can do If you see that your child is in contact with electricity, attempt first to disconnect the source. If you cannot disconnect the source, attempt to move your child away from the electricity. Don't attempt to handle a live wire with your bare hands; use an object made of plastic or wood that won't conduct electricity.

As soon as your baby is away from the source of electricity, check his or her breathing and heart rate. If either is stopped or erratic, or if your child is unconscious, begin CPR and call or have someone else call for emergency help. If your baby is conscious, look for evidence of burns and notify your child's care provider.

You can prevent accidental electrical shocks by using safety plugs in all electrical outlets. In addition, avoid stringing long extension cords where a baby can reach them.

ANIMAL OR HUMAN BITES

If your baby is bitten, try to discover the source of the bite as quickly as you can. Household pets are the cause of most animal bites. Although pet dogs are more likely to bite than are cats, cat bites are more likely to become infected. Bites from some wild animals are dangerous because of the possibility of rabies. Most human bites that children get are only bruises and not dangerous. However, human bites can lead to infection if they break the skin.

How serious is it? An animal bite can cause serious wounds — especially to the face — as well as considerable emotional trauma. You should consider any animal or human bite that breaks the skin to be a serious injury. Fortunately, cases of rabies are uncommon today; still, any animal bite caused by a dog, cat, skunk, raccoon, fox or bat should be evaluated for rabies risk. Bites by rabbits, gerbils and hamsters generally are harmless and only require local wound care.

What you can do If your child is bitten, follow these guidelines:

For minor wounds If the bite barely breaks the skin and there's no danger of rabies, treat it as a minor wound. Wash the wound thoroughly with soap and water. Apply an antibiotic cream or ointment to prevent infection and cover the bite with a clean bandage. If the bite breaks the skin, contact your child's care provider to see if your child should receive medical evaluation and treatment with antibiotics.

For deep wounds If the bite creates a deep puncture of the skin or the skin is badly torn and bleeding, apply pressure with a clean, dry cloth to stop the bleeding. See your child's care provider or go to your local emergency department. If you suspect the bite was caused by an animal that might carry rabies, seek medical assistance immediately.

Also seek medical assistance if you see any signs of infection: pus draining from the wound, increasing redness and swelling several days after the bite, or red streaks coming from the wound.

DROWNING

Infants can drown in very shallow water. Never leave your baby alone in the bathtub, even briefly. If a phone call, doorbell or something else interrupts your baby's bath, either ignore the interruption or bring the baby with you, wrapped in a towel. Keep the toilet lid and bathroom door closed. Fence swimming pools with automatic latching gates, and constantly supervise your infant when near lakes, pools or rivers. Toddlers have even drowned after falling into buckets used for cleaning.

What you can do If your child has been submerged in water long enough and isn't breathing or has breathing difficulty, has blueness of the skin, is unconscious or has a decreased level of

consciousness, call for emergency help or have someone call for you. If your baby has no pulse or isn't breathing, begin CPR immediately (see page 211). Continue CPR until medical help arrives.

INJURY FROM A FALL

Infants can fall for many reasons. Falls tend to occur when a baby is able to roll or to tip an infant seat or walker more easily than a person realizes, or when he or she begins to crawl or walk.

How serious is it? If your baby cries immediately after receiving an impact to his or her head and remains alert, chances are the fall didn't cause serious injury. Falls can be serious, but babies' soft bones don't fracture as easily as those of older children. Important factors that can affect the seriousness of a fall are the force and distance of the fall and the surface onto which your baby has fallen.

What you can do Use ice to control swelling, but be careful not to freeze the baby's skin. In case of a head injury, observe your baby carefully for 24 hours for any behavior changes. If the injured body part looks abnormal, or if your baby cannot move it, seek immediate care. Also seek immediate care if you notice any of the following signs:
- An inability to crawl or walk, if he or she was able to do so before the injury
- Persistent irritability, possibly indicating a severe headache
- Blood or watery fluid discharge from the ears or nose
- Persistent vomiting
  Call 911 if your child experiences:
- Breathing irregularity
- Lethargy or excessive sleepiness

- A seizure
- Loss of consciousness

If your baby stops breathing or if you cannot detect a heartbeat, begin CPR immediately (see page 211).

SWALLOWED POISON

Almost any nonfood substance is poisonous if taken in large doses. Babies explore by putting things in their mouths. Toxicity of substances varies greatly, and with immediate treatment most children aren't permanently harmed from poisons they swallow.

Always keep the Poison Help hotline number nearby (800-222-1222), and be sure to tell anyone who takes care of your child where the number is. If you have a cell phone, keep the Poison Help hotline number in your phone.

Some common items you keep around your house can be quite dangerous to an infant: plants, medications (including acetaminophen and aspirin), alcohol, mouthwashes that contain alcohol, automatic dishwasher detergents, pesticides, antifreeze and cleaning substances that contain lye. Personal care products, cleaning substances and plants are the cause in about one-third of poison cases.

Suspect poisoning if you find your infant with an open or empty container of a toxic substance. Look for behavior differences; burns or redness of the lips, mouth or hands; unexplained vomiting; breath that smells like chemicals; breathing difficulties or convulsions.

If you suspect that your infant has swallowed a poison, remove your baby from the source of the poison and call the Poison Help hotline immediately. Be prepared to read the labels on the container, and to describe the substance and amount ingested and any physical changes you detect.

How serious is it? Substances vary widely in the seriousness of their effects and the amount required to do harm. Remember, though, that a small amount of some products or medications can be much more damaging to an infant than it would be to an adult. If you have any questions about whether a substance may be toxic, call the Poison Help hotline for advice.

What you can do Call the Poison Help hotline (800-222-1222) if you suspect that your child has swallowed a poison. If your child is in obvious distress (unconscious, hallucinating, convulsing, experiencing breathing difficulties), call 911 or your local emergency number immediately. Have the container in front of you when you call so that you can tell emergency personnel what substance caused the problem. If you need to go to the emergency department, bring the product or container with you if possible.

Don't give anything by mouth until you've received advice from the Poison Help hotline. Depending on several factors, the medical staff might or might not want your baby to vomit. Seek advice from the Poison Help hotline or emergency personnel before you attempt to induce vomiting because doing so can cause more damage in some instances.

Prevention Any medication and many products in your house can be harmful to your child. If you don't need the medication or product in your house, remove it to avoid accidental ingestion. Be especially cautious when visiting grandparents or "nonchildproofed" homes. Be sure that all substances are in their proper, child-resistant containers and clearly la-

beled. Be sure to check the label on medicine bottles each time you give a medication, especially in the middle of the night, to confirm that it's the proper medicine and that you're giving the proper dosage.

INHALED POISON

Inhaling poisonous substances can cause various reactions, including nausea and vomiting, loss of or decreased consciousness, headache, breathing difficulties, coughing, or lethargy. Your baby's reaction will vary, depending on the amount of exposure and the substance inhaled.

Numerous substances are toxic when inhaled. They include carbon monoxide,

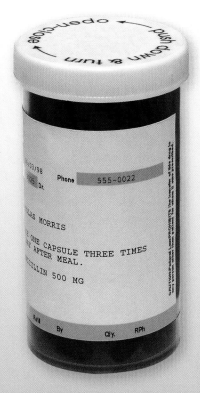

smoke and fumes from fires, propellants, gasoline, kerosene, turpentine, furniture polish, charcoal, cigarette lighter fluid, glue, paint remover, and lamp oil.

It can be dangerous for your baby to inhale toxic substances. You need to act quickly when you suspect that your baby has inhaled a dangerous substance.

What you can do It's not a good idea to use aerosol products near your baby, because babies can react more severely to a small amount of inhaled poison. Never run your car in a closed garage, and be sure to maintain coal, wood or kerosene stoves regularly. If you smell a strong gas odor, turn off the gas burner or oven, leave your house immediately and call the gas company. Avoid breathing the fumes yourself, and get your baby to a well-ventilated area. Check your baby's breathing and pulse, and if necessary begin CPR.

Call 911 or your local emergency number immediately if your baby is in obvious distress — having difficulty breathing, showing a decreased level of consciousness or lethargy, is without a heartbeat or is convulsing.

POISON ON THE SKIN

If you suspect that a poison has come into contact with your baby's skin, look around nearby your child for some evidence of the poison. Spilled household cleaners would probably leave a baby's skin looking red and irritated. The chemicals in many household cleaning substances, especially oven and drain cleaners, are caustic and can easily damage your baby's skin.

What you can do Keep all cleaning solutions in a childproof cabinet out of reach. To confirm a method of treatment, check with the Poison Help hotline (800-222-1222) if your baby comes into contact with a poison.

If your baby is experiencing obvious distress — unconsciousness, lethargy, hallucinations, convulsions, or breathing difficulties — call 911 immediately.

POISON IN THE EYE

Poison can get in a baby's eye when a liquid splashes into it. Many substances can damage your baby's eyes, but your infant will not be able to tell you about the problem. Therefore, it's important that you be alert to possible situations in which this can happen. Acting quickly could make the difference between a temporary problem and a long-term disability.

What you can do Use a large glass or pitcher filled with cool tap water to flood your baby's eye for 10 to 20 minutes. Try to get your baby to blink frequently as you flood the area. Keep the baby's hands out of his or her eyes. You may need to wrap him or her with a bed sheet to keep his or her hands out of the affected eye. Get another adult to help you, if possible.

Call the Poison Help hotline (800-222-1222) if you're unsure whether the liquid that splashed in your baby's eye is poisonous or if you are unsure whether to seek emergency treatment.

PART 3

Growth and Development Month by Month

CHAPTER 17

Month 1

The first month of your baby's life can feel like a whirlwind — coming home from the hospital, getting your baby situated in your home, becoming accustomed to the rhythms of parenting, recuperating from childbirth. There's a lot going on!

At the same time, being with a newborn can make you feel like time has slowed down to a crawl. After all, newborns spend most of their time sleeping and eating, with a diaper change and a crying spell here and there. The most exciting times may be when your child's eyes are open for a few minutes and you can interact for a short while. Even then, you may wonder, should my baby be moving more? Is he or she getting enough to eat?

But that's what the first month is all about, slowing down enough to rest, recover and get to know each other. By the end of the first month, you'll be surprised at the changes that have occurred in your little one and the jump in your own self-confidence as a parent.

BABY'S GROWTH AND APPEARANCE

During the first few days of life, your newborn loses the excess body fluid he or she was born with, which means that by the time you go home your baby will weigh slightly less than at birth. But no worries, most babies will quickly gain this weight back, and in about 10 days to two weeks, your baby will once again be at his or her birth weight. And growth certainly won't stop there. Most babies grow rapidly in their first few weeks. By the end of the first month, your baby is likely to weigh around 10 pounds. Your baby's height will also lengthen by 1½ to 2 inches.

Many people envision newborns as cute, round and smooth-skinned, but that's not always the case. If your little guy or gal doesn't look exactly like the glowing pictures you've seen of newborns — those babies are probably 2 or 3 months old already — don't be discouraged. Passing through the birth canal isn't an easy journey, and it takes a while for baby's skin to adjust to the outside world. Most newborn appearance issues pass quickly. To help you gauge what's normal, here are some brief descriptions of how a typical newborn is likely to appear.

Head Forging headfirst through the birth canal can put a lot of pressure on a baby! Literally, pressure from the tight birth canal can cause the bones in your baby's skull to shift and overlap. This can leave your newborn's head looking slightly elongated or cone shaped at birth. Don't worry though, your baby's head should round out in a few days. Babies born buttocks or feet first or by C-section are more likely to have round heads at birth. Pressure on your baby's face may leave your newborn's eyelids puffy or swollen.

The size of your baby's head is important because the growth rate of your baby's head reflects the growth of the brain.

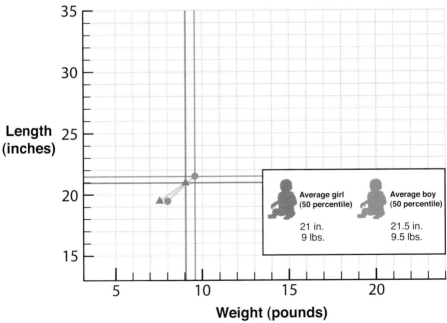

Month 1

Average girl (50 percentile)
21 in.
9 lbs.

Average boy (50 percentile)
21.5 in.
9.5 lbs.

© MFMER

Both the brain and the skull grow incredibly fast in the first few months. In the beginning, the average newborn's head measures about 13¾ inches around and grows to about 15 inches by the end of the first month. At birth, baby's brain accounts for about 20 percent of his or her body weight. By adulthood, this percentage decreases to about 2 percent.

At the top of your baby's head, you'll notice two soft areas where the skull bones haven't yet grown together (see page 27). These soft spots, called fontanels, allow a baby's relatively large head to move down the narrow birth canal. They also accommodate a baby's rapidly growing brain. You may notice slight bulging from these spots when your baby cries or strains.

Skin A newborn's skin can cause considerable distress to new parents. It's just more blotchy, flaky, pimply and wrinkled than they expected. But most of the time, this is completely normal. For example, switching from the moist environment of the womb to the relatively dry air outside of it can cause the top layer of your baby's skin to flake off shortly after birth. You may notice plenty of dry, peeling skin for the first few weeks.

Your newborn's skin may also look slightly mottled, with some patches looking paler or darker than others, especially near the hands and feet. Your baby's hands and feet may also be colder than the rest of his or her body, and may appear a little blue or purple, but if you reposition your baby or move your baby's arms and legs a little, they should regain normal color.

In some cases, your baby's complexion may remind you more of an adolescent's than a newborn's, due to the appearance of tiny white pimples. The white pimples are harmless spots known as milia (see page 100). Later, your newborn may even develop newborn acne, characterized by small red bumps on his or her face (see page 100).

Many newborns have birthmarks. You may notice reddish or pink patches above the hairline at the back of the neck, on the eyelids or between your newborn's eyes. These marks — nicknamed salmon patches or stork bites — are caused by collections of blood vessels close to the skin (see page 31). Darker skinned babies are sometimes born with a large, flat, bluish-gray mark on the buttocks or lower back. This type of mark is commonly called a mongolian spot or slate gray nevus (see page 30).

INFANT JAUNDICE

It's not uncommon for a healthy newborn to have a yellow color to his or her skin and eyes. This is called jaundice and occurs when the baby's blood contains an excess of bilirubin, a yellow-colored pigment of red blood cells.

Jaundice typically develops because a baby's liver isn't mature enough to properly get rid of bilirubin in the bloodstream. Mild infant jaundice is harmless and usually resolves on its own within a few weeks. If your baby's jaundice doesn't go away after a couple of weeks or gets worse, contact your care provider promptly. You can find out more about infant jaundice on page 378.

Umbilical cord The stump of a newborn's umbilical cord is usually yellowish green at birth. If the stump is treated with an antiseptic solution called triple dye, it may look blue. As the stump dries out and eventually falls off — usually within two to three weeks after birth — it'll change in color from yellowish green to brown to black. In the meantime, keep the stump clean and dry.

Breasts and genitalia Before birth, the mother's hormones pass through the baby's system. This may lead to swollen breasts at birth — for both boys and girls.

Newborn girls may have a swollen vulva and light mucus-like or bloody vaginal discharge. The swelling typically disappears within two to four weeks. Normal vaginal discharge may last only several days.

For some newborn boys, fluid can accumulate around a testicle. This swelling, known as a hydrocele, usually disappears within a few months. Frequent erections are common, too.

Legs and feet A newborn's legs and feet often look bowed or bent, thanks to the cramped quarters of the womb. As long as your newborn's legs and feet are flexible and can easily be moved about, there's no need for concern. These curves typically straighten on their own as your baby becomes more mobile. When a child is born, part of a newborn checkup includes an evaluation of a baby's hips, legs and feet.

Hair Don't be alarmed if that great head of hair your baby was born with falls out within the first few weeks. Almost all newborns lose at least some of their baby hair. It will grow back in a few months. Plenty of babies also develop temporary bald spots on the back of the head from regular contact with the crib mattress or other sleeping surface. Once your child starts rolling over and moving around, this won't be a problem anymore.

Some newborns are covered by fine, downy hair at birth — known as lanugo — especially on the back, shoulders, forehead and temples. Tiny hairs may also appear on your newborn's ears or in other spots. Lanugo is most common in premature babies. It typically wears off from normal friction within several weeks.

SPOT-CHECK: WHAT'S GOING ON THIS MONTH

Here's a snapshot of what your baby's basic care looks like in the first month.

Eating Baby will need breast milk or formula generally every two to three hours, although the frequency at first can be pretty variable. The goal is a minimum of eight to 12 feedings a day to make sure your newborn is getting enough to eat. (Chapter 3 discusses nutrition in more detail.)

Sleeping Expect your newborn to sleep about 16 hours a day, in one- to three-hour spurts, fairly evenly distributed throughout the day and night. Place your baby on his or her back to sleep to decrease the risk of sudden infant death syndrome (SIDS).

SOOTHING BY SUCKING

Most babies have a strong sucking reflex. Beyond nutrition, sucking often has a soothing, calming effect. That's where a pacifier can come in handy.

Some babies are interested in pacifiers; others aren't. If your baby isn't enthralled at first, you can try invoking your baby's natural sucking reflex by gently stroking the side of your baby's mouth while holding the pacifier in his or her mouth until the sucking gets going.

If a pacifier seems to help your baby, feel free to use it. The American Academy of Pediatrics gives pacifiers the go-ahead for soothing between feedings and helping baby fall asleep. Pacifiers used during sleep may even help reduce the risk of sudden infant death syndrome (SIDS). The downside is that you may be woken up more often during the night to retrieve a lost pacifier.

In the beginning, be sure that pacifier use doesn't interfere with your breast-feeding routine, especially while you and your baby are still learning the ins and outs of nursing. Also, choose a pacifier that's made of one piece to avoid any choking hazards, and that's dishwasher safe for ease of cleaning. It helps to have several identical pacifiers handy, so you're not searching for the lone favorite in a desperate time of need. Also make sure to replace pacifiers that have worn or cracked nipples, as the nipples can tear off and pose a choking hazard.

Most kids stop using pacifiers on their own between ages 2 and 4.

BABY'S MOVEMENT

In this first month, your baby doesn't have a whole lot of control over his or her movements, which are likely to be jerky and quivering. Your baby may also startle easily and even cry at sudden movements or loud noises. Holding your baby close or swaddling him or her will help bring comfort.

Because your newborn's brain and nervous system are still immature, movements are largely reflexive, or involuntary. In order to move purposefully, your baby's brain must send messages via nerve cells to his or her muscles with specific instructions for movement. In the first few weeks of life, brain and nerve cells are rapidly developing, but they haven't achieved fluid communication yet.

Over time, the maturation of your child's nervous system will allow your baby to gain control over different parts of his or her body. This follows an orderly sequence from head to toe, so your baby's first major milestone is gaining head control, followed later by sitting, crawling and walking. By the end of the first month, your baby's neck muscles will have developed considerably. When lying facedown, your baby may lift up his or her head and turn it from side to side.

In the first few weeks, your baby's hands are apt to be curled up into tight little fists much of the time. By the end of the first month, you may catch your baby trying to bring those fists toward his or her face for closer inspection. Over time, your baby's hands will relax and spread wide, allowing him or her to use them more deliberately.

Baby reflexes From birth, your baby comes hard-wired with a number of automatic responses (reflexes), some of which are focused on surviving his or her entry into the big, new world. These include:

Rooting reflex If you stroke your baby's cheek or the corner of his or her mouth, your baby will turn toward your hand and move his or her tongue in that direction. This helps your baby find the nipple of the breast or bottle and initiate feeding. This reflex usually disappears around 4 months of age.

Sucking reflex This reflex is present even in utero, and you may have even seen your baby sucking his or her thumb during an ultrasound examination. After your baby is born, placing a nipple in his or her mouth will cause your baby to automatically begin sucking. At first he or she squeezes the area around the nipple between the tongue and palate to force out the milk. Next, your baby moves his or her tongue toward the end of the nipple to move the milk into his or her mouth. The American Academy of Pediatrics reminds parents that even though this rhythmic sucking is a reflexive action, it generally takes a bit of practice for your baby to turn the reflex into an effective voluntary skill.

So don't get discouraged if you and your baby don't seem to nail breast-feeding at first pass. Give yourselves a little time to practice and adjust.

Grasp reflex Placing your finger in your newborn's palm causes your baby to grasp your finger, and you'll find that if you try to remove your finger, he or she will grasp it even tighter. A similar reaction occurs if you stroke the sole of your baby's foot. These reflexes generally disappear by 2 to 3 months of age.

Startle reflex If your newborn hears a loud noise, he or she will react by throwing out his or her arms and legs and then drawing in his or her arms. This reaction is also known as the Moro reflex. Another time it occurs is if your baby's head suddenly falls back. Doctors may check this reflex to make sure your baby's development is healthy. The startle reflex usually disappears by about 2 to 4 months of age.

Tonic neck reflex This reflex occurs when your baby turns his or her head to the side. Simultaneously, his or her arm and leg on the same side will extend out, while the opposing arm and leg flex, giving your baby the look of a fencer. It's a fairly subtle reflex though, so don't worry if you don't notice it every time. The tonic neck reflex disappears around 4 to 7 months.

Stepping reflex If you hold your newborn upright and let his or her feet touch a flat surface, your baby will pick up one foot and then the other, as if walking. Of course, your baby's not ready to walk yet, and this reflex will disappear around 2 months, but it will become a controlled skill by the time he or she is walking, usually around a year or so of age.

BABY'S SENSORY DEVELOPMENT

From the get-go, your baby arrives with all five senses intact. Not only does your baby use his or her senses to learn about the surrounding environment, he or she also uses them to form emotional attachments with you and others. By identifying your face, your smell and the sound of your voice, your baby establishes a connection with you.

In addition, your baby rapidly begins using multiple sensory skills to explore and interact with you. For example, your baby will quickly connect the sight of the breast or bottle with a particular scent, all of which equals food!

In the first month, this is how your baby is likely to perceive the world:

Sight At birth, your baby is fairly nearsighted, with the ability to focus on objects that are roughly eight to 12 inches away. Coincidentally, this is just about the distance between your baby's eyes and your face when you're nursing or holding him or her. Thus, from early on, your baby is able to gaze at your face and quickly learns to recognize it. In fact, at this stage, your baby prefers the human face to any other patterns.

Right after birth, your baby is very sensitive to bright light and is likely to close his or her eyes tightly to keep the light out. Over the next few weeks, though, your newborn's vision will develop enough so that he or she can see a widening range of lights and darks. The higher the contrast in a pattern, the more likely it is to catch your child's attention during this first month.

Sound Your baby's hearing is fully mature at birth, but it takes a little while for your baby to learn how to recognize and react to different sounds. As with your baby's visual preference for the human face, your baby favors the sound of human voices, reacting especially to high-pitched voices, such as the mother's. It's possible that your baby may even recognize your voice from having heard it in utero and will turn his or her head toward the sound of your voice from the beginning.

Some babies are more sensitive to noise than others. Too much noise, for example, and your baby may start to cry. In general, low, rhythmic tones are most likely to soothe your baby.

Smell Your baby already has a keen sense of smell and quickly becomes able to discern his or her mother's breast milk from other mothers' breast milk. Other smells new babies seem to like include sweet or fruity smells, such as vanilla, banana and sugar. Harsh or acidic smells, such as alcohol or vinegar, are likely to meet with wrinkled noses.

Taste As a newborn, your baby has more taste buds than does an adult. Therefore, your little one can be fairly picky about different taste sensations, including the temperature of his or her breast milk or formula. Most babies also prefer sweet tastes to sour ones.

Touch New babies have a fully developed sense of touch, as well. For example, they prefer soft, smooth surfaces to coarse or scratchy ones. And they can feel pain at the prick of a needle. Most importantly, they respond to the way they're touched. In essence, this is the first form of communication between you and your baby. Gentle handling, snuggling and holding are not only soothing to your baby but a sign of your love and affection, as well.

BABY'S MENTAL DEVELOPMENT

Your baby's brain has been on a development fast track — generating new brain cells (neurons) at a rate of 250,000 a minute — ever since the early days of your pregnancy. By the time your baby is born, he or she has virtually all of the brain cells that he or she will use in a lifetime.

But having all of these brain cells is just the beginning. As your baby is exposed to a whole new world, his or her brain cells rapidly start making connections called synapses. These connections create pathways between brain cells that, when reiterated through day-to-day experiences and activities, form the basis for knowledge and thought and for skills such as remembering, analyzing and problem solving. For example, repeated interaction with you as a loving and attentive caregiver will soon establish your image as a symbol of safety and security in your baby's mind. These connections

---

TOYS AND GAMES

During the first month, your baby doesn't need a lot of toys to be entertained — there are so many other things to take in. Still, you can provide different things for your baby to look at and listen to, which will help his or her brain cells develop more and better connections. Generally, the best time to play with your new baby is when he or she is quiet and alert.

Chit chat Since your face is one of your baby's favorite things to look at, why not make it available? Position yourselves face to face and have a conversation. Talk to your baby about your day and what you're planning for dinner. Make faces, smile and sing to him or her.

Listen to music Play soft music while your baby lies in a crib or swing and you fold laundry or take care of some other chore.

Provide a view During the first few weeks to months, your baby's neck muscles are still developing. But your baby can look from side to side. Securely install an unbreakable mirror on the inside of your baby's crib or hang a picture with bold, graphic lines near the changing table at baby's eye level.

Read a book Although your baby isn't old enough to understand or interact with a book yet, it's never too early to start reading together. Your baby will enjoy the rhythmic sound of your voice as you read, whether it be Dr. Seuss' *Hop on Pop* or your usual news source.

Get some tummy time Place your baby on his or her tummy for a short time while he or she is awake. This will encourage your baby to hold his or her head up and strengthen those neck muscles.

also set the foundation for communication and the interpersonal skills your child will use when relating to others.

Remember, it's never too early to set the foundation for essential skills such as language. It may still be a number of months yet before your newborn will be talking, but he or she is already forming necessary connections for language development. You can further encourage such development by speaking and reading to your child. And it doesn't have to be a children's book. Read your own pleasure book out loud, or your email or the newspaper out loud.

Your baby's environment has a tremendous impact on how his or her brain develops. While your baby's genetic makeup and physical development provide the essential "nature" ingredients, you provide the "nurture" components. You'll get lots more information in the following chapters on how you can create the best environment for your child's mental growth and development. But the one thing that is essential to know, especially now in the first month, is that all children thrive in an environment of love and attention, no matter how old they are.

Communication Of course you knew your baby wouldn't be able to talk for quite some time, but who knew it would be such an adjustment to stare at your newborn and realize you were temporarily going to have to rely on something other than words to communicate?

You'll quickly discover, however, that your baby has a few different ways of communicating during this first month.

Crying This is the only way your baby can verbalize his or her needs and feelings. All babies can and should cry, because this helps them receive the care they need. Adults, in turn, have a strong

drive to respond when a baby cries, making this form of communication between you and your baby fairly innate. Responding warmly to your baby's cries helps your baby feel safe and secure in his or her new environment.

Lots of crying can be hard to take, of course. If you've run through your mental checklist and your baby is dry, full, comfortable and snug, then maybe he or she just needs comforting for a bit. Or your baby may need some downtime without any stimulation, even if he or she does cry for a few minutes. Sometimes you may not know why your baby is crying, and that's OK, too. If your baby cries a lot, it's OK for you to take a break. Let your partner take over for a while, or lay your baby in a safe place for a few minutes of alone time. Crying usually increases over the first few weeks, peaking at about three hours a day at 6 weeks of age and gradually decreasing to about an hour a day at 3 months old. Chapter 8 discusses crying in more detail.

Body language During these first few weeks, your baby also communicates through body language. For example, when awake and alert, your baby may make eye contact with you and carefully scan your face. Or if your baby thinks there's simply too much going on at the moment, your baby may react by turning away from the source of stimulus, closing his or her eyes or becoming irritable.

Although new babies aren't capable of responding in so many vocal ways yet, they are able to receive information from you and interpret the nonverbal signals you send, such as the expression on your face and the way you hold your baby.

BABY'S SOCIAL DEVELOPMENT

The main social event on your baby's calendar this first month is getting to know you. While you're occupied trying to figure out

---

STATES OF CONSCIOUSNESS

Scientists have observed, and you will too, that new babies fluctuate between different states of consciousness throughout the day. Some of these states are during sleep, and some occur while your baby is awake. There's no need to memorize them, but understanding the different states of consciousness may help you better understand your baby's moods.

▶ *Deep sleep.* During the deep sleep state, your baby sleeps quietly and does not move.

▶ *Active or light sleep.* In this state, your baby moves while sleeping, and may be startled or wakened by loud noises.

▶ *Drowsiness.* Drowsiness may occur before or after a sleep state. You'll notice your baby's eyes become a little droopy, and he or she may yawn or stretch. Keep this one in mind for when you want to put your baby down to sleep on his or her own.

▶ *Quiet alert.* In this state, your baby looks bright-eyed and bushy-tailed, but his or her body is quiet.

▶ *Active alert.* During active alert, your baby is wide-eyed and moving actively. He or she may be busy entertaining himself or herself.

▶ *Crying.* This state of consciousness is not hard to recognize because of the wails coming from your baby's mouth. When your baby is crying, he or she also tends to flail or thrash about.

The best time to interact with your baby usually is during the quiet alert state. In this state, he or she is most likely to be receptive to play and outside stimulation. Be warned, though, that new babies tend to cycle through states of consciousness fairly quickly. So don't be surprised if a toy elicits attention for a short while and then quickly becomes a source of irritation when your baby starts crying. Just move on to what your child wants next, which is probably comforting.

your baby, your baby is busy using all his or her senses to become acquainted with you — how you smell, sound, look and feel.

Becoming attached Babies are pretty amazing self-functioning packages when they arrive, but they still depend on their environment for survival. Every time you feed your baby, change your baby's diaper, respond to your baby's cries or simply hold your baby close, you're establishing a pattern of consistent availability to your baby's needs. This creates a bond of trust and confidence between the two of you. This bond is the primary building block for your child's early social development. It's also your baby's template for later interactions with the world at large. As a primary caregiver, you become your child's "home base," to which he or she will repeatedly return over the years for comfort, help and sustenance.

For many women, breast-feeding is a natural way of bonding with a newborn because it covers many of the baby's needs at once — food, warmth, comfort and security all rolled into one. But don't worry if you're not breast-feeding. You can still connect with your baby when you're feeding your baby a bottle or doing any of the other myriad activities involved in baby care. It's your general approach of love and gentle care that communicates safety to your child.

For some people, bonding comes more easily than for others. If you don't feel immediate attachment to your baby on day one, don't worry too much. After all, this is a new person in your life, no matter how little. As you spend time together and get to know each other's traits and characteristics, you'll develop a unique relationship that will only be strengthened in the months and years ahead. In addition, many new mothers have a mild case of the blues after childbirth, not to mention fatigue and soreness. If you don't start feeling better and more involved in your parenting role after a few weeks, talk to your care provider about getting treatment.

Building up to smile Smiles actually take a while to develop, but you may notice over the course of this first month that your baby sometimes smiles during sleep or after a feeding. Around 4 weeks or so, your baby's smile may evolve a little further, involving the eyes more, and come several seconds after hearing your voice or feeling your touch. Next month, you can look forward to full-blown happy smiles involving the whole face that come in response to your own smiles.

CHAPTER 18

Month 2

By the beginning of your baby's second month, you're probably starting to get a handle on having a new baby in the house. You're more adept at basic caregiving activities, such as changing diapers or fixing bottles, and you've almost gotten your swaddle technique down. If you're breast-feeding, you've probably started ironing out some of the kinks, and you and your baby are feeling a lot more confident in your techniques.

During month two, you'll still be perfecting a lot of these activities, but you'll also see your baby's personality begin to emerge. Your diligent efforts are more apt to be noticed by your little tyke, and you'll likely be rewarded with the beginnings of true interactive smiles. What's nice about month two is that the cogs of family life are slowly sliding into place and yet the excitement of it all is still bright.

BABY'S GROWTH AND APPEARANCE

During the second month of life, your baby keeps growing at about the same rate as he or she did during the first few weeks — gaining about 5 to 7 ounces a week and growing about ½ inch a month. Your baby is starting to fill out — cheeks are getting chubbier and arms and legs fuller!

The head and brain are still growing rapidly so that head circumference increases by about ½ inch a month, as well. It's normal for your baby's head to be proportionally larger than the rest of his or her body at this point — it's still growing faster than anything else. The soft spot on your baby's head is still open, but toward the end of this month and into the third month, it should start to become more firm and closed.

Keep in mind that healthy infants come in a range of sizes. Although it's easy to cite generalizations, such as the figures just listed, it's difficult to predict your baby's exact growth. Your care provider will monitor your son's or daughter's growth at each well-child visit. Where your child's numbers fall on the growth chart or how they compare with other babies' numbers isn't nearly as important as whether your baby is maintaining his or her own steady growth curve.

Baby skin issues start looking a little better. Any jaundice should be mostly gone by the second month. If not, contact your care provider. Other newborn skin conditions, such as the little white pimples known as milia, are largely disappearing, although newborn acne may stick around for another month or two. If your baby has acne, gently cleanse your baby's face with baby soap several times a week, and stay away from lotions and oils.

Fits and stops Just when your baby is finally sleeping for several nighttime hours at a stretch, he or she seems to revert to waking up every two hours again. What's going on? Nothing out of the ordinary, probably. The fact is that infant growth and development occurs in fits and stops. Sometimes it may even seem that your baby is forgetting recently learned behaviors. Usually this pause precedes a new leap forward. For example, your baby may be subtly working out the maneuvering necessary to roll over, but until he or she masters the right techniques, your infant may not fall or stay asleep as he or she once did.

BABY'S MOVEMENT

Most of your baby's movements are still jerky and involuntary (reflexive) at this

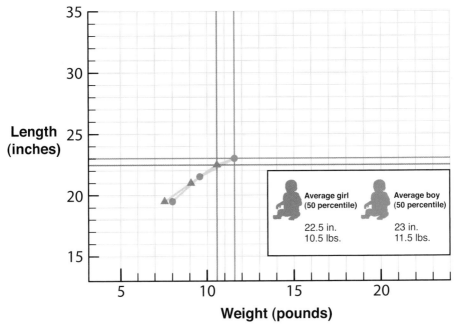

Month 2

Length (inches)

Weight (pounds)

Average girl (50 percentile)
22.5 in.
10.5 lbs.

Average boy (50 percentile)
23 in.
11.5 lbs.

© MFMER

point. But as the month progresses, these newborn reflexes will begin to give way to more purposeful movements. While this is occurring, your baby may seem less active for a short period until he or she begins to get the hang of major muscle coordination. Your little son or daughter is practicing new positions by stretching, moving and watching.

Your baby's neck muscles are getting stronger, too. When pulling your baby gently to a sitting position, you'll notice that his or her head still lags behind a bit. But when upright, your baby can probably hold his or head steady for a few seconds, although not much longer. Continue to support your baby's head when holding or carrying your baby. When lying belly-side down, your baby may raise his or head to look straight ahead for a few moments, rather than just side to side. Lying on his or her back, your baby can keep his or her head centered and look straight up — a handy skill for watching mobiles!

At this age, most babies aren't ready to roll from front or side to back yet — that generally happens around 3 to 4 months of age. But you cannot be certain that your baby will stay in one place either. Babies this young can use their feet to push off surfaces and scoot around. And even though they're just learning controlled maneuvers, they can unexpectedly flip themselves over by sudden, startled movements. Don't leave your baby unattended on the changing table or other elevated surface, and take proper precautions to securely strap your baby in while on a changing table.

Toward the end of the second month, your baby may also start to become aware of his or her hands and fingers and try to bring them together to play with them.

TOYS AND GAMES

During the second month, your baby will gradually be awake for longer periods of time and have more quiet alert times. You can take advantage of these times by providing stimuli that encourage your child's development.

But let your baby guide playtime. Watch for clues that he or she is tired or overstimulated, such as turning away, closing his or her eyes, or becoming irritable. Also, keep in mind your baby's physical limitations. During physical play, be gentle and careful not to shake your baby or toss him or her in the air. These activities can cause severe injury to your baby's eyes, neck and brain.

Here are a few suggestions for playtime with your 1- to 2-month-old.

Keep up tummy time Regularly placing your baby on his or her belly for a short time while he or she is awake helps develop neck muscles and increase head control. You can share in tummy-time fun by lying on the floor facing your baby and talking to him or her. Your baby will work neck and arm muscles to lift up and be face to face with you. You can also encourage your child to work those muscles by putting toys just within his or her reach.

Set up a mobile Your baby is better able to hold his or her head steady enough to look straight up while lying on his or her back. Mobiles can become particularly fascinating. When choosing a mobile, look at it from your baby's perspective. Keep in mind a child's preference for simple shapes, high contrast and bright objects. Some models will even twirl around to music, engaging both your baby's eyes and ears. Be sure all items are secured completely and placed out of baby's reach.

Introduce color As your child's vision improves, he or she will become more appreciative of bold, vivid colors in addition to high-contrast patterns. Visit your local library to borrow books containing brightly colored art or photographs. Or arrange a still life of bright oranges, tomatoes and asparagus for your baby to contemplate.

Encourage familiarity Try reading the same story several nights in a row to your baby, and see if he or she starts to show signs of recognition. Or play a favorite song several times during the week and see how your baby reacts after hearing it multiple times.

BABY'S SENSORY DEVELOPMENT

During the second month, your baby's eyes are getting better at moving and focusing on objects at the same time, making it easier for your child to visually track moving objects. Your baby's brain isn't mature enough to speedily process visual information, but he or she can track a toy moving in front of him or her if it's moving very slowly. Although your baby is still likely to prefer the sight of human faces, he or she will also enjoy patterns that are more complex and colorful than simple black-and-white checkerboard images.

When you talk to your baby, you'll find that he or she is actively listening and watching the movements of your lips with interest as you speak. In return, your baby may move arms and legs excitedly or try to make his or her own vocalizations.

BABY'S MENTAL DEVELOPMENT

So far, your baby has been taking in a lot of information, but by now he or she may be ready for some outward expression, as well. Child psychologists refer to incoming language as "receptive" and outgoing speech as "expressive" language. Receptive language, where your baby listens and absorbs speech and sounds around him or her, almost always precedes expressive language, which is when your baby starts to vocalize his or her own thoughts. In general, children understand language much earlier than they are able to clearly use it themselves. For example, your baby will understand the meaning of the words "Come to mama" months before he or she can articulate them.

Cooing and gurgling One of the most gratifying developments for parents this month — generally around 6 to 8 weeks of age — is their babies' first attempts at expressive language. These are typically soft, single-vowel sounds that sound like "ooohs" and "aaahs," or like cooing. As opposed to crying and grunting, which emanate from the chest, cooing and gurgling sounds come from your baby's larynx. Cooing also involves using different mouth muscles than does crying. Eventually your baby will begin to use his or her tongue and then lips to make more precise vocalizations. This pattern of language development — starting from the center and moving outward — mirrors your

---

OUT OF SIGHT, OUT OF MIND

At this age, your baby's young mind has yet to grasp the concept that things continue to exist even if they're out of sight. For example, if a dog wanders into your 2-month-old's field of vision and then out again, your baby may stare for a few seconds at the spot where the dog was, not understanding that although the dog isn't visible it still exists. In other words, once something is out of sight, it's also out of your baby's mind. It isn't until later during the first year — around 8 months or so — that your baby will understand that even if you hide your face behind a blanket, you are still there. Up until that point, peek-a-boo games can be pretty exciting!

baby's motor development (fine-tuning movement from arms to hands to fingers).

Cooing is a way for your baby to express happiness and contentment. Your baby may coo and gurgle for self-entertainment, but he or she may also do it to attract your attention. If your baby coos at you and you talk back, your baby quickly discovers that this is a two-way game. By talking back, you reinforce the notion that communication is important and, furthermore, that it can be a source of great delight.

Crying at its peak Your baby still relies heavily on crying to convey his or her needs and moods. In fact — brace yourself — crying tends to reach a peak of about three hours a day right around 6 to 8 weeks of age. This is normal. A lot of babies develop a period of fussiness and prolonged crying at the end of the day, perhaps as a way of releasing pent-up stress (not unlike adults, if you think about it).

If you've already accounted for all of your baby's needs, listening to your baby cry can be difficult. A parent often feels frustrated with his or her parenting skills at this point. But it's not always possible to calm a crying baby, especially if your baby is just letting off steam. Avoid the temptation to perceive your baby's crying as a rejection of your efforts or to feel as if you're a failure at this parenting business. Babies cry; that's what they do. And eventually, your baby will fall asleep or his or her mood will change. By the time your baby is 3 or 4 months old, the amount of time he or she spends crying will have decreased substantially.

If your baby's crying is accompanied by other symptoms, or you feel the length or intensity of your baby's crying is unusual, trust your intuition and call your care provider. For more on how to comfort a crying infant, read Chapter 8.

BABY'S SOCIAL DEVELOPMENT

During the second month, your baby still spends a lot of time sleeping and the interaction you experience with your baby is still fairly limited. But at the same time, your baby is making definite strides in his or her social graces. By the age of 1 month, your baby is learning to recognize you,

SPOIL AWAY

Don't worry about spoiling your baby during the early months of his or her life. Addressing your child's physical needs and desire for attention helps establish a pattern of consistent and predictable loving care in your son's or daughter's mind. If your baby knows that he or she can expect physical and emotional comfort from you, this allows your baby to establish his or her own emotional comfort level. In other words, your baby is learning to feel safe and secure and to trust you and him- or herself. In addition, when you soothe your baby during a crying spell, you're teaching your child how to regulate his or her emotions even in times of intense emotion or stress.

So pick your baby up as often as you like, and hold your baby as much as you want. It's good for both of you!

BIG SISTERS AND BROTHERS

Having a new baby in the house brings a special excitement for families that already have kids. Although caring for other children as well as a newborn can be challenging, you'll also have the rich experience of watching the relationships of your children grow as brothers and sisters.

Generally, children are quite excited at the prospect of having a real, live baby in the house. But what they may not realize is that they'll need to share you, their parent, with another person. Sometimes this can lead to older children acting out in order to garner more attention, or even lashing out at the baby. With time, though, most children learn to adjust to the household reorganization and find their own special niche. You can help them with this by doing the following:

Postpone major changes During the weeks following your baby's arrival, try to avoid any drastic changes in older children's routines. This may mean waiting a while to potty train, switch from a crib to a bed or move to another home.

Let each child set the pace Despite being raised in the same family, each child can react differently to a new baby. Responses may vary from excited giggles to hyperactivity to lack of interest. Sometimes a child's reaction is delayed for weeks. Allow your children to become accustomed to the baby in their own time.

Set clear expectations Let your older children know what is appropriate behavior around the baby. For example, let your child know it's never OK to pick up the baby without permission, but that it is OK to sit next to the baby and talk nicely to him or her.

Offer sincere praise When you find your older child behaving well, be sure to acknowledge it. Commend your child for speaking gently to the baby or playing nicely. This kind of positive reinforcement shows your child that you still value his or her presence, and you appreciate his or her contributions to the family.

Make time for older kids Sisters and brothers of babies need lots of personal attention, too. Make plans to leave the baby with your partner or a reliable sitter, and spend some undivided time with your older children.

Be patient and positive Some children start to regress after a new baby arrives, going back to trying on diapers, sucking a thumb or talking baby talk. This isn't uncommon. Be patient during this period of adjustment. Treat regression in a matter-of-fact way. For example, "I see you wet your bed this morning. I'll change the sheets as soon as I can." These simple sentences state the problem and offer a ready solution.

✔️ 2ND MONTH MILESTONES

During the second month, your baby is busy:
- Working on lifting up shoulders while lying on belly
- Holding head steady while sitting
- Becoming aware of own fingers
- Relinquishing grasp reflex
- Straightening out legs and strengthening kicks
- Focusing on objects moving across field of vision
- Cooing and making sounds
- Recognizing parents' faces, being reassured by parents' touch
- Learning to smile in response to parents' smiles
- Learning to smile spontaneously to express happiness or contentment

perhaps reacting with a jerky arm wave or a few bobs of the head at the sight of you. By six weeks, many babies start to smile in response to a parent's smile. After weeks revolving around feeding, diaper-changing and trying to catch some sleep, seeing your baby smile back at you can be very rewarding.

By reacting to your baby's smiles with your own show of delight, your baby learns that his or her actions have an impact, and that he or she has a certain amount of control over what's happening. This initial awareness is the beginning of your baby's ability to distinguish between him- or herself and others.

Baby smiles can also be spontaneous expressions of happiness or contentment even at this stage. For example, your son or daughter is starting to recognize certain objects by sight, such as a bottle or bathtub, and he or she may smile or coo excitedly in anticipation of what's to come.

CHAPTER 19

Month 3

While a solid block of sleep may still seem elusive at your house by the third month, your son's or daughter's range of motor control, mental engagement and social interaction is widening dramatically. The confluence of a number of factors affecting your baby's growth and development — maturation of the nervous system, development of the senses, reinforcement of the memory pathways in the brain, increase in the range of emotions — all contribute to your baby's burgeoning interest in his or her family and the world around him or her.

BABY'S GROWTH AND APPEARANCE

In the third month, the rate at which your baby gains weight and grows in length should continue at a good clip and roughly match last month's rate. Most babies gain between 1 and 1¾ pounds and lengthen by about ½ inch a month during the first six months of life. Head circumference increases by about ½ inch a month during this time, as well.

If you're worried that your baby seems too thin or too chubby, be careful not to judge by appearance alone. Since infants tend to carry different amounts of weight at different stages of development, making judgments about baby fat on the basis of appearance alone isn't reliable or effective. Instead, talk to your baby's care provider about your concerns. He or she will plot your baby's growth on charts that show measurements for height, weight and head circumference. You can use the charts yourself to compare your baby's growth with that of other infants of the same sex and age. What really matters, however, is the trend revealed on growth charts — not any particular percentile. Your baby's care provider will look mainly for predictable changes in weight over time.

If you're following your baby's hunger cues for feeding and his or her growth is progressing steadily, there's generally no reason to worry about your baby's size.

Is my baby too fat? Babies need a diet high in fat to support growth during infancy. In addition, a diet high in fat helps to build a thick casing (myelin sheath) around nerve fibers in the brain and spinal cord. This sheath offers "insulation" for nerve fibers and helps ensure that nerve impulses are sent efficiently.

Even if you think your baby is a little too chubby, bear in mind that most kids grow out of their baby fat in a few quick years as their bodies start to stretch out. In a few cases, it's possible that too much baby fat might be problematic. If you're concerned about your child's weight, talk with your infant's care provider. He or she can best determine whether your baby's growth poses any problems.

Many health care providers and medical researchers are concerned about the rise in childhood obesity. Some evidence suggests that this problem may arise earlier than previously believed. For example, some studies have linked rapid weight gain in the first year of life to obesity later on in life. Excess baby fat may also have more immediate consequences, such as delaying the development of crawling and walking.

The first year of life is no time to put your baby on a diet or restrict calories, unless your baby's care provider has given you specific feeding instructions. Your baby needs adequate nutrition to develop properly. Steps that may help prevent excess baby fat include:

Breast-feed for as long as possible
Several studies have shown a connection between breast-feeding and reduced childhood obesity. The mechanisms for this link aren't clear, but it may have to do with the ability of breast-fed babies to self-regulate their intake of milk. In other words, baby decides when to stop eating. If you're bottle-feeding, try to follow your

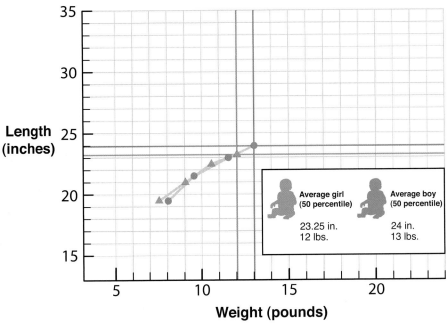

Month 3

Length (inches)

Weight (pounds)

Average girl
(50 percentile)

23.25 in.
12 lbs.

Average boy
(50 percentile)

24 in.
13 lbs.

© MFMER

Here's a snapshot of what your baby's basic care looks like in the third month.

Eating Breast milk or formula exclusively. Longer stretches of sleep at night may mean more frequent feedings during the day. But through this month and the next, you can expect your baby to gradually take in more milk at a single feeding, perhaps resulting in fewer feedings throughout the day. Between 2 and 4 months of age, the average baby eats around 2 ounces per pound of body weight every 24 hours.

Sleeping About 15 hours a day. By about 3 months old, many babies sleep for a solid six to eight hours during the night. Still, this doesn't always coincide with your own block of six to eight hours of sleep. Expect to be up once or twice during the night, especially if your baby has a growth spurt and needs more frequent feedings.

baby's cues that he or she is full. Don't make your baby finish a bottle just because the milk is there.

Avoid juice Don't give your child juice until he or she is older than 6 months (and even then, you don't have to). Offering juice before this age may displace regular breast milk or formula feeding, which can leave your baby deprived of necessary nutrients. If you choose to offer juice after your baby is 6 months old, serve it in a cup rather than a bottle, and limit it to no more than 4 ounces a day.

Don't use food as a pacifier If you've just fed your baby and he or she still seems fussy, try other methods of distracting him or her before resorting to another feeding to quiet baby down.

BABY'S MOVEMENT

By the third month, most babies are beginning to move around to explore the world. Added muscle strength gives your baby new vantage points from which to peer at the world. As your baby becomes more and more purposeful in his or her movements, you'll notice those newborn reflexes fade.

Head and neck Lying belly-side down, babies this age can usually lift up head and shoulders. Some infants may even extend their arms and rest on their elbows. This gives them even more support for looking around. In turn, looking upward and sideways while on his or her tummy further increases your baby's neck strength and head control.

Increased head control means that your baby's head lags less when you pull him or her into a sitting position. Also, when you support your baby seated on your lap, your baby can hold his or her head up for longer periods of time instead of just a few seconds. In the third month, you'll notice your baby's back still rounds forward. But as your child's movement (motor) skills develop, the muscles in the upper and then lower back will strengthen, as well. Strong back muscles act as a balance and brace for your baby's body so that he or she can eventually sit straight unsupported, crawl, stand and then walk.

Hands and arms Around this time, babies often become fascinated with their hands. In fact, a favorite pastime for your baby this month is likely to be watching his or her hands, bringing them together at eye level and trying to bring them to his or her mouth.

You may also notice your child's hands begin to uncurl from their previous clenched fist position. At this age, babies begin to experiment with opening and shutting their hands and spreading their fingers wide to test and inspect them. Your son or daughter may also start to grip objects intentionally rather than reflexively, but then have a hard time letting go. The next step will be to gain enough finger dexterity to hold on to a toy, and then transfer it from one hand to the other. Eventually, he or she will be able to pick a toy up and set it down again, solidifying basic fine motor skills.

At the same time, your child may start reaching for objects by swiping or batting at them with broad arm movements and clenched fists. As your child's hands become more open, he or she will have better luck hitting the intended target.

Legs Your baby's legs are becoming impressively strong, and he or she is likely to experiment with flexing his or her legs and knees at will. Some babies, especially when they're excited, may even kick hard enough to flip themselves over. In preparation for purposely rolling over, your baby may start rocking back and forth. In fact, by 3 months of age, many babies start to roll from their backs onto their sides and then onto their backs again.

Because your baby is more mobile, always take proper precautions to prevent him or her from wiggling off of a changing table or flipping out of a car seat. Strap your baby in and stay nearby to avoid any accidents.

HOLD OFF ON THE SOLIDS

For the first six months, breast milk or formula is generally the only food your baby needs. Its liquid form perfectly matches your baby's eating skills, habits and digestive abilities.

Before age 4 to 6 months, your baby isn't developmentally ready for solid foods. At this stage, your baby still manages milk or formula by moving it from the front to the back of the mouth by sucking, then swallowing. This sucking reflex is aided by the tongue-protrusion reflex, in which the tongue pushes forward to help the baby suck. This reflex is still strong during this month and next, which means that it's difficult for a baby to manage solid foods. Babies at this age tend to push out cereals or solid foods rather than swallow them, which can make spoon-feeding a frustrating experience for you and baby.

Signs that your baby may be ready for solid foods include good head and neck control and being able to sit supported, skills that usually come a bit later. Chapter 3 discusses the introduction of solid foods in detail.

BABY'S SENSORY DEVELOPMENT

Although the development of your baby's senses isn't as easy to observe as the development of motor skills and coordination, one is essential for the other. Even though your baby can't tell you what he or she is experiencing, playing with and watching your baby will help you know how well your child sees and hears.

Vision Your son's or daughter's sight is maturing rapidly. In the next few months, he or she will begin to view the world in much the same way as you do. By 2 or 3 months, your baby's ability to simultaneously turn both eyes inward to focus on a close object (convergence) is developing steadily. Convergence allows the baby to focus on and play with his or her hands. At the same time, your baby is learning to focus on distant objects by simultaneously turning both eyes outward (divergence).

As your child's vision matures and focus improves, he or she will be able to notice details of a pattern and to tell whether there is more than one object in a picture. As distance vision improves, you may catch your baby studying you across the room or gazing intently at a ceiling fan. Your baby is also getting better at distinguishing between colors and may be particularly attracted to primary colors.

Around this time, your baby also learns a skill that encompasses both sensory and social development. Your baby will look at your eyes and then turn to discover what it is that you're looking at. This is called shared attention.

During the third month, if you still see your baby's eyes crossing or you notice there seems to be a lag in one eye, let your baby's care provider know. If it happens consistently, the care provider may refer your child to an eye specialist to assure that, if needed, steps are taken to correct the vision problem.

Hearing Your baby's hearing contributes to a growing sense of familiarity and comfort with the world around him or her. Around the third month, your baby may quiet when he or she hears your voice or get excited when he or she hears siblings or a favorite song.

Taste and smell Toward the end of this month, your baby is starting to distinguish between different tastes, such as breast milk versus formula or a new brand of formula. Your baby also is likely to favor certain smells or be turned off by other smells. These factors can sometimes affect feeding preferences, depending on your baby's temperament. For example, if your baby is very sensitive to odors and finds a smell unpleasant, he or she may not want to eat while the smell is present.

TOYS AND GAMES

As your baby becomes more interactive, it becomes even more fun to play together, especially when your baby discovers the ability to laugh sometime during this month or next.

Around this time, your baby may also become more interested in objects or toys that he or she can touch or hold. Choose ones that are lightweight, easy to grasp, drool-resistant, too big to swallow and that don't have sharp edges. Some examples include board books, soft blocks, wooden and plastic spoons, measuring cups, empty containers, rattles, balls and squeeze toys. As long as the toys are safe, let your creativity flow. (Avoid shiny plastic wrap or plastic bags, though, which can easily cover your baby's mouth and nose and cause suffocation.)

Here are some other ideas for fun and games in the third month:

Get rolling To help your baby practice his or her rolling skills, lie side by side with your baby and encourage him or her to roll toward you. Your baby will try to do this with his or her whole body, which essentially means rolling over. In the beginning, babies usually find it easier to roll from back to side and then back again. Congratulate your child when he or she manages a roll. There's no need to push or pull, though, as your child will perfect this skill in his or her own good time.

Touch and feel As your baby's hands gradually open up, try placing different textures in his or her palm — soft, smooth, fuzzy, bumpy. See what textures your baby likes most.

Get a grip Place a toy or object in your son's or daughter's hand. Let him or her hold it, feel it and move it. Also, try this with objects that rattle, squeak or make noise. Share in your baby's surprise when he or she succeeds in producing sound.

Set up batting practice Place your baby on an infant floor gym or play mat — the kind that usually has brightly colored, different-shaped objects dangling from it. Your baby can practice reaching and batting at the toys, as well as discover different shapes and textures. Another way to encourage reaching and grasping is to place your baby in an infant seat and offer items that are in front, just above or below, or just to the side of your baby's eye level. These games also help your baby develop depth perception and hand-eye coordination.

Get giggling Almost all little tykes love gentle tickling, especially if you deliver it with laughter and exaggerated facial expressions. Or try blowing a raspberry on your baby's belly. Your baby may register surprise at first, but eventually these activities are sure to generate not just chuckles but deep-down belly laughs.

BABY'S MENTAL DEVELOPMENT

As the nerve cells in your baby's brain mature, connect with other brain cells and become insulated with fatty myelin, your baby's brain is able to assert greater control over the rest of his or her body. You can see this when you observe your baby making purposeful movements, such as bringing a hand up for inspection or reaching out for a toy.

To execute these intentional motor skills requires subtle complexities in thinking, reasoning and planning skills:

▶ *Interest.* What is that thing mom is dangling in front of me?
▶ *Speculation.* What happens if I try to touch it?
▶ *Trial and error.* Moving my arm this way seems to work better than moving it that way.

If your baby succeeds in making the toy rattle or make noise, for example, further information processing and analysis is required. What was that noise? How did it happen? Can I make it happen again?

Laying down tracks Repetition of experience is how memories are created in an infant's brain. Over time, your consistent response to your baby's needs — feeding, cuddling, bathing, soothing, carrying — lays down pathways among your baby's brain cells that become reinforced and streamlined every time you respond in a similar manner.

By the third month, these memory pathways are becoming more clearly defined, and your baby is starting to have a better understanding of the connection between his or her behavior and your reactions. For example, your baby has figured out that by crying, he or she can get your attention fairly quickly, or that by smiling he or she is likely to get a smile in response.

Expanding communication At the same time, your baby is building an increasing repertoire of sounds and gestures as means of communication — squealing, growling, blowing raspberries, and experimenting with consonant sounds.

As your baby approaches 3 and 4 months of age, he or she may initiate "conversations" with you by smiling, cooing or squealing. Acknowledging your baby's overtures is sure to delight. Repeat the sounds your baby makes so he or she knows you're listening. Also, talk back to your baby in "parentese" — use real words pronounced correctly and clearly but at a high pitch and with exaggerated tones. This helps your baby learn

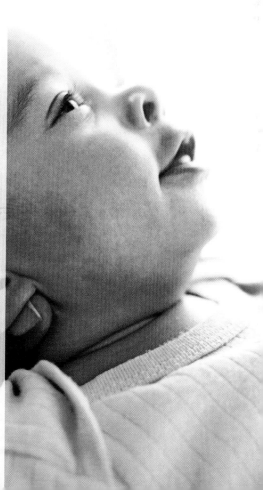

RETURNING TO WORK

Around this time, many working mothers are preparing to end their maternity leave and return to work. It's certainly not easy to leave a new little one in the care of someone else, even if temporarily, and especially after spending so much time together.

In the meantime, though, nothing can change the fact that you are now a mom and you have a baby who thinks the world of you. To make the transition to a new schedule and routine a little smoother, try some of these suggestions:

Let go of the guilt Returning to work after having a baby leaves many new mothers feeling particularly torn. But working outside the home doesn't make you a bad mother — and it's OK to look forward to the challenges and interactions of your job.

Talk to your boss If you're interested, you might ask about flexible hours, telecommuting or working part time.

Plan for feeding changes If you're breast-feeding and plan to continue doing so after returning to work, ask your employer about a clean, private room for breast pumping. About two weeks before returning to work, change your nursing schedule at home so you're pumping during the day and nursing before and after your upcoming work hours. Have someone else feed your baby a bottle of stored breast milk to help your baby adapt.

Start short If you can, go back to work late in the week. That'll make your first week back to work go by more quickly.

Get organized Sketch out a daily to-do list. Identify what you need to do, what can wait — and what you can skip entirely.

Stay connected Call your baby's caregiver to find out how your baby is doing. Some caregivers may be willing to email you a photo of your baby during the day. Place a favorite picture of your child on your desk or in your work area.

Make backup plans Know what you'll do if your baby is sick or your baby's caregiver is unavailable on a workday — whether it's taking the day off yourself or calling a friend or loved one to care for your baby.

Above all, maintain a positive attitude. Tell your baby how excited you are to see him or her at the end of the day. He or she may not understand your words but will pick up on your emotions.

(If you're not entirely sure you want to go back to work or are still looking for appropriate child care, turn to Chapters 13 and 35, which have more information about child care and balancing work and parenting.)

the sounds of your language. Most parents naturally use parentese when they talk to babies. So don't be embarrassed; go ahead! Your baby will love it.

Once you've said your piece, pause to allow your baby to respond with a look, wiggle or sound. This will help him or her learn the rhythm and timing of effective communication.

vigorously with those around him or her. Some babies even start to giggle or laugh in response to facial and vocal expressions or in response to touch. In general, laughter usually comes about a month after social smiling and is a great addition to your relationship!

BABY'S SOCIAL DEVELOPMENT

It doesn't take long for parents and family to become the most important people in an infant's life. Your baby's world is centered entirely around you. He or she is involved in your everyday lives, watching, listening and picking up clues on how humans interact. And your family will be the first people with whom your baby interacts.

A real charmer Around this time, your baby is not only pleased with your attention but is starting to discover his or her own powers of attraction. With a smile or a squeal of excitement, your baby knows he or she can draw you out to respond in kind. Your baby is able to make and maintain eye contact, and interact more

At this stage, your baby has yet to develop anxiety about meeting strangers and may even be fairly outgoing and happy to meet other people. This may be an opportune time to introduce your baby to the concept of staying with grandparents or a trusted baby sitter for a few hours while you are gone. In a few months, your baby may not be so keen to be separated from you. But if he or she has been accustomed to the idea that although you may go away for a short while, you always come back, this may make it a little easier when it is necessary for you to temporarily leave your child in the care of another.

Wanting attention During this month, you may also notice that your child cries not just to express a need or feeling, but in order to get your attention. In the coming weeks, crying in general will decrease (thankfully), but it's likely to become more purposeful and directed at bringing you back to your baby's side. Continuing to respond quickly (or, as quickly as possible) and warmly, even if just by calling out to your child, will help reassure him or her that you're still there. This continued responsiveness helps to cement the trust and sense of security your baby feels in you.

✅ 3RD MONTH MILESTONES

During the third month, your baby is busy:
- Raising head and chest to look around while lying on belly
- Working on supporting upper body with arms while lying on belly
- Holding head steady for longer periods while sitting
- Playing with hands at eye level
- Trying to bring hands to mouth
- Swiping at dangling objects
- Opening and closing hands, stretching fingers wide
- Holding toys briefly
- Stretching and kicking legs
- Developing distance vision
- Recognizing familiar people and objects from a distance
- Using eyes and hands in coordination
- Distinguishing between different colors, tastes and smells
- Increasing repertoire of sounds to include squealing, growling, consonant sounds and maybe even giggling
- Turning head toward sound
- Making eye contact
- Enjoying family and familiar faces, maybe even new people
- Using expanding communication skills to express emerging emotions
- Imitating some sounds, movements and facial expressions
- Learning to self-entertain

CHAPTER 20

Month 4

Before you delve into month four, pat yourself on the back. You've made it through the first few months of parenthood, quite possibly one of the biggest transitions of your adult life. At this age, most babies have begun to adjust to life in this brave new world. They've also become much more secure in their relationship with their parents and their own abilities to adapt and react to their environment.

New families often find the next few months to be a joyous time. You've probably settled into a familiar routine and eating and sleeping schedules have become fairly regular. The amount of time your baby spends fussing is probably on the decline. Your baby's brain and nervous system have matured enough that he or she is ready to become much more interactive with family and friends, while continuing to explore new sights and sounds. Newborn reflexes are fading and your little one is starting to move and do things by design now. In addition, your infant is getting much better at conveying emotions and desires, and you're getting much better at understanding him or her. In other words, the bond between the two of you is truly blossoming!

Take advantage of this time to enjoy each other's company and revel in the little things — a giggle and a smile, a splash in the tub, or a bug on a window. Who knew life could be so exciting?

BABY'S GROWTH AND APPEARANCE

Between 3 and 4 months your baby's growth rate is likely to slow a little, although you can still expect your baby to gain between ¾ and 1½ pounds over the course of the month and grow about ½ inch in length. Some babies may have doubled their weight by the end of the fourth month. Head circumference increases by about ½ inch, as well. You'll be able to compare notes with your baby's care provider at the 4-month well-child visit. Keep in mind your baby's individual growth rate.

Skin rashes You're getting ready to change your baby's diaper, and there, right there, under your baby's Onesie is a bright red rash. Alarm bells go off and you rush to the phone to call your care provider. This happens to just about every parent. And while you should always call your baby's care provider if you notice something unusual or are concerned about your baby's health, you should also know that most skin rashes in infants are common and usually not serious. If the rash occurs along with a fever, call your care provider promptly.

Rashes in babies often result from skin irritants, such as soap or scratchy fabric, or an underlying viral infection, such as a parvovirus infection or roseola. Because rashes are so visible, they're a common cause of concern for new parents. Most of the time, though, rashes aren't a sign of a serious problem and may not even require treatment other than proper skin care and perhaps a mild cortisone cream, as indicated by your child's care provider.

Some general rules of thumb for baby skin include avoiding long, hot baths and staying away from any substances or textiles that seem to cause a reaction. Using gentle moisturizers can help soothe the skin. You can read more about common skin rashes in Chapter 5.

Bedtime routine It's probably a safe bet that almost all new parents are hoping to find somewhere — in the pages of a book, in advice from a friend or on a website — the simple secret to getting their kids to sleep. Alas, there is no silver bullet. Your child's sleeping habits depend on a number of factors, including his or her age, the length of time he or she can go without feeding, and his or her personality. Some babies snuggle down without a peep and waken briefly

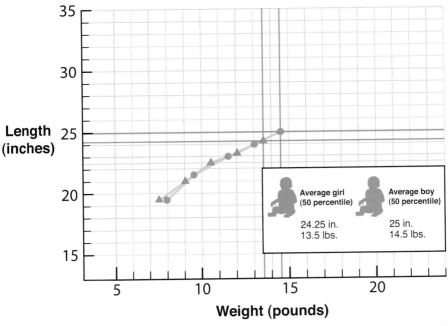

Month 4

Length (inches) — vertical axis: 15, 20, 25, 30, 35
Weight (pounds) — horizontal axis: 5, 10, 15, 20

Average girl (50 percentile)
24.25 in.
13.5 lbs.

Average boy (50 percentile)
25 in.
14.5 lbs.

© MFMER

SPOT-CHECK: WHAT'S GOING ON THIS MONTH

Here's a snapshot of what your baby's basic care looks like in the fourth month.

Eating Feed breast milk or formula exclusively. During this month, the number of daytime feedings generally decreases to about four or five, but a midmonth growth spurt may lead to more frequent feedings for a few days. Although it may be tempting to get your baby started on cereal or other solid foods during this month — especially if you've heard the rumor that it might help your baby sleep better (a theory that has yet to be proved) — hold off a little bit longer until your baby shows clear signs that he or she is physically ready for solids.

Sleeping Expect your child to sleep about 15 hours a day, including more predictable nighttime hours of sleep — generally six to eight hours, although every baby is different. By 4 months old, your baby may awaken only once or twice during the night. Around this age, babies become more active sleepers, making noise, scooting around and often waking their parents. If your baby has been sharing your room, this may be a time to consider moving him or her to his or her own room.

By this time, your baby may also have settled into two to three daytime naps, lasting about an hour or two each (hopefully, long enough to give you some time to yourself!).

---

for feedings. Others cry every time you put them in the crib and have a hard time lulling themselves to sleep.

During the first few months of your baby's life, it's important to respond to your baby's cries and provide enough soothing to optimize sleep. But around the third and fourth month, you can start taking steps to help your child fall asleep on his or her own, an important skill that every child must eventually learn.

Parents at this stage often worry about letting their babies "cry it out." There is plenty of advice out there on the "best" way to get your baby to sleep. See what method works best for you. In the meantime, there are a couple of things to keep in mind. One, a little bit of crying won't harm your baby, and it won't affect his or her attachment to you. Your overall approach of loving care is what bonds

the two of you together. Two, if your son or daughter isn't keen on self-soothing at first, hang in there. It can be tough initially, but one thing is for sure: This phase won't last forever, and if you establish consistent bedtime practices, your child eventually will be "sleeping like a baby." (Oh, the irony.)

For tips on how to help your little one sleep well, see Chapter 7.

BABY'S MOVEMENT

Around the fourth or fifth month, the newborn reflex that makes your child look like a baby fencer — when your baby's head turns in one direction, the arm on that side straightens and the other arm bends over the head (tonic neck reflex) — begins to fade. This clears the way for further development of your baby's gross motor skills — skills that involve his or her large muscles. At this stage, babies often seem "fidgety," but they're really exploring purposeful coordination of their large muscle groups to move around.

At 4 months, most babies are exercising their arm muscles by pushing up with their elbows or hands when on their tummies. These mini-pushups give your baby a new vantage point and help strengthen muscles necessary for rolling. Some babies may even use this new-found arm power to scoot around in a circle or even move a few inches forward or backward.

At the same time, your baby's fine motor skills — skills that generally involve the hands and fingers — are being refined.

Head and back control As your baby's 4-month birthday approaches, he or she is achieving good control of the head and neck. Full head control is an important milestone that's essential for other motor skills, including sitting, crawling and walking.

While lying down, your baby is apt to lift the head and shoulders to look straight ahead while resting on his or her hands and arms (a favorite portrait pose of photographers, and who can blame them? It's downright cute).

When pulled up to a sitting position, about half of 4-month-old babies are able to keep their heads in line with their bodies. In fact, your baby may even lift his or her head to try to "help" him- or herself sit up. By the middle of this month, most babies can keep their heads steady when held in a sitting position.

While sitting, your baby's back muscles are working on keeping the spine straight, reducing the hunched appearance.

Rolling over On average, this is the month that babies really get rolling. Some may have started rolling even earlier. But don't worry if your baby isn't there yet by age 4 months. You'll probably notice some rolling attempts in the near future. A few babies even skip this milestone altogether.

Rolling from front to back, which requires only a shift in gravity, is generally easier than rolling from back to front. This is why many babies roll from front to back first. Giving your baby a little floor space and plenty of tummy time while he or she is awake will provide him or her with opportunities for practice.

Rolling from back to front, which tends to occur a little later, requires more complex maneuvering, such as rocking, arching the back, and twisting the legs to flip over. Each baby is different, though.

Some roll one way; others another. Whether your baby is rolling or not, and which way, isn't as important as whether he or she shows interest in moving from one spot to another.

Don't wait to discover your baby's ability to roll when he or she ends up on the floor from having rolled off the couch or bed. Take precautions not to leave your baby unprotected on elevated surfaces.

Standing By the end of the fourth month, most babies can, with a little help, bear their own weight on their legs. If you hold your baby upright, he or she will likely push down with his or her feet. In fact, you may start to feel as if your lap is an infant trampoline as your baby learns to bounce vigorously in that position. Standing and bouncing while well supported won't hurt your baby's legs or hips, but will give them (and you) a good workout. Just make sure you're not trying to hold a hot cup of coffee or tea at the same time.

If your baby doesn't push off with his or her feet right away at age 4 months, don't fret. If your child still doesn't do this at 6 months, you might mention it to your child's care provider, so that he or she can determine if further investigation is necessary.

Reaching and grasping During this month, your baby is likely to be busy

---

KEEPING PLAYTIME SAFE

Your baby might not be crawling yet, but it's around this time that babies start putting whatever (literally) they can in their mouths. Take advantage of this limited period of immobility to make sure the spaces you use to play with your baby are free of any potential hazards. Get into the habit of doing a "baby-level" safety check each time you put your baby down on the floor to play. Get down on your hands and knees, at your baby's level, and look for these items:

- Small objects your baby could accidentally swallow, such as coins, button batteries, magnets, paper clips, or small pieces of food or candy
- Toys with small parts
- Balloons
- Uncovered electrical outlets
- Pulls for window blinds, in which your baby could get entangled
- Electrical cords to irons, lamps or other appliances that could fall if the baby tugs on the cord
- Plastic bags or wrappings that could suffocate your baby
- Newspapers and magazines
- A pet's toys or treats
- Houseplants

These safety searches also can become fun and helpful activities for older siblings to get involved in. Help them understand the things that can be harmful to a baby. This will increase their awareness about the hazards of leaving toys and objects around the play area.

waving his or her arms about, batting at nearby objects and trying to reach them. If you present your baby with a rattle or similar toy, he or she is likely to grasp it, shake it and maybe even bring it to his or her mouth.

You may notice that sometimes your baby intentionally looks at and reaches for an object. Other times, your baby's hand may touch something and instinctively grab it, and your baby may seem surprised or intrigued by what has unexpectedly appeared in his or her hand. This change from grasping as a reflex to reaching for things voluntarily is gradual.

BABY'S SENSORY DEVELOPMENT

Throughout these months and until your baby's sixth month, your child will do a lot of exploring by touching, feeling and mouthing whatever comes across his or her grasp. Combined with hearing and seeing, these sensory skills promote the development of your child's motor, mental and social skills.

Seeing an object encourages your baby to reach for it. Grasping and touching the object helps your infant become familiar with it. Shaking it and hearing it make noise helps your child learn about cause and effect. Listening to you respond to his or her accomplishment aids in his or her language development and social interaction. You can see how various aspects of development form a complex interplay that contributes to your child's overall growth as a person.

Mouthing At this stage, your baby's mouth is more sensitive to an object's characteristics than are his or her fingers. Your baby also lacks the dexterity to manually investigate an object, but tongue and lips are perfect! And if your baby can't bring the object of interest to his or her mouth, he or she will likely bring mouth to object by bending down to suck on it.

You can spend a lot of time discouraging your son or daughter from putting things in his or her mouth, or you can stockpile a variety of safe toys with interesting textures that will further pique your child's curiosity and encourage oral exploration.

If your baby reaches for something dangerous, your best bet is to quickly remove it from sight and distract your baby with a more appropriate toy. At this age, your baby doesn't understand that something may be harmful and is only interested in its appearance. This is why it's especially important to safeguard your baby's play area and remove any potential hazards.

Hearing Listening is another way of exploring an environment. By the fourth month, your baby may not only quiet at the sound of your voice but turn his or her head toward you, as well. He or she may also turn his or her eyes toward a specific sound, for example, a rattling sound or the sudden onset of music, to find out where the sound is coming from.

Vision By 4 months, many babies have improved visual tracking abilities and can watch a brightly colored object as it moves in a slow arc overhead. You might also notice your baby focusing on very small objects, such as a piece of yarn or a crumb, and regarding things in the distance with great interest, such as a tree outside the window. Improving hand-eye coordination — being able to both see and reach for an object — further encourages his or her exploration instincts.

BABY'S MENTAL DEVELOPMENT

Brain activity during these early months is at one of the highest peaks in a person's lifetime. And as your baby becomes more mobile, you can really observe his or her curiosity begin to emerge. Everything is an object of interest, and your baby uses all of his or her powers — looking, touching, smelling, chewing — to discover and explore whatever's nearby, including his or her own hands, cheeks, legs and other body parts.

Language skills Since birth, your baby has been building language skills by listening to others and by picking up communication clues from the inflection and tone of their voices. Although words are still a jumble by 4 months, your baby is familiar with many of the sounds you make and may begin to experiment with making some of these sounds on his or her own.

Laughter During this month, your baby probably laughs out loud frequently. Laughter evolves out of cooing and gurgling and usually comes about a month after your baby's first real smile.

At first, the laugh tends to come in response to something — a laugh from you, a funny face or a tickle of the belly. Your baby may also laugh to get your attention or just for the experience of making noise. In the coming months, though,

---

LAUGHTER AS A LIFE SKILL

Encouraging laughter and humor in your household can have benefits for both you and your family. Laughter can be a:

Bonding agent When people laugh together, they bond together over the shared experience and emotion. Laughing with your baby helps you become closer.

Stress reliever When the house is a mess, your clothes smell like spit-up and dinner is mediocre at best, balancing it all with a good laugh can diffuse the stress you might be feeling and unconsciously passing on to your children. Even babies sense when their caregivers are stressed and tend to reflect these emotions. So instead of rushing to load the dishwasher or check your work email, take a few minutes to giggle and laugh with your baby after a long day. It'll make you and your child feel better.

Immune system booster Evidence suggests that a good belly laugh can actually increase immune system cells that fight viral illnesses and various cancers.

Resilience maker If you habitually show your children that you can still laugh, despite life's curveballs and momentary imperfections, you're ultimately teaching them about resilience and the ability to withstand distress, a skill that will serve them well throughout life.

you'll notice the beginnings of a sense of humor. For example, something out of the ordinary or unusual may strike your baby's funny bone. Older siblings especially are likely to induce laughter from a baby.

BABY'S SOCIAL DEVELOPMENT

During the fourth month, your child's social world is continuing to broaden, as is his or her ability to function within it and relate to you and others. By now, your

---

 TOYS AND GAMES

Promote your baby's motor development, pique his or her curiosity, and encourage exploration of the world around him or her with some of these activities and toys:

Practice sitting Once your baby can hold his or her head up fairly well, try sitting your infant up in a baby seat or against cushions for support. This will improve your baby's sense of balance and help strengthen back muscles. Sit face to face and play singing and clapping games together. You can also set him or her up against the curve of your own body while you lie on the floor. Don't expect the sitting to last too long at this point, though. After your baby topples over a few times or tires of sitting, switch to a different activity, such as belly play or reading a book together.

Choose toys that stimulate the senses Keeping in mind your baby's penchant for mouthing at this age, choose toys that won't be harmed by a little dampness or chewing. Soft books with textured corners and squeaky pages are both fun and practical. Other ideas include a bumpy teething ring, a ring of big plastic keys, measuring cups or soft blocks. Also, look for toys or everyday objects that your baby can practice holding on to, shaking and manipulating. Make sure the toys you choose have no small parts that can come off and pose a choking hazard to your baby.

Play mimicking games Starting around this age, your baby is becoming intent on studying the sounds you make and trying to produce his or her own versions. Take the time to listen to your baby's vocalizations, then try to imitate his or her sounds. Talk back to your baby, enunciating slowly and clearly, and allow him or her time to try to make the same sounds. If you speak a second language, use it with your child. Mimic facial expressions and laughter, too. This encourages your baby's language skills and social interactions.

Enjoy bath time As it becomes easier for babies to sit when supported, parents often turn bath time into playtime, sometimes even getting into the tub with their babies. The weightlessness of the warm water and the freedom from restrictive diapers and clothing all make for a great sensory experience. However, remember that bubble bath and soap can be irritating to a baby's eyes, skin and genitals. And keep a close eye and good grip on your baby. The water makes your wiggly, active baby extra slippery.

During the fourth month, your baby is busy:
- Pushing up on elbows and hands to look around when lying on belly
- Sitting supported with head steady
- Practicing moves that enable rolling over
- Bearing weight on legs, bouncing with arms supported
- Grasping and shaking toys, practicing letting go
- Bringing hands to mouth, exploring items with mouth
- Studying small items
- Gazing at things in the distance
- Looking for the source of a sound
- Becoming more communicative with body language and vocalizations
- Laughing
- Imitating language sounds
- Engaging in back-and-forth "conversations" with you
- Enjoying playing with others, capturing attention

baby likely is starting to show clear signs of recognizing you and other members of your family. He or she will love spending time with you and others. If you have another child, that older brother or sister may be your baby's most popular playtime friend. Children can easily make a baby smile and laugh.

For siblings, this is a "honeymoon" time. By 3 or 4 months, the baby is old enough to thrill an older brother or sister with smiles and giggles but still too young to be "trouble," getting into toys and interrupting playtimes.

At this age, your baby has yet to develop stranger anxiety and is likely to enjoy meeting new people, smiling, wriggling and laughing with anyone who will respond. This is a comfortable time for most parents. The baby is big enough that you're not overly concerned about safe handling, and you know the baby is comfortable with someone else. At this age, you can easily share the fun of your baby with others.

Distractions As your baby nears 4 months old, feeding times become less frequent, and his or her attention is drawn to other people and activities during feeding. Your baby may move around or stop feeding to play or "talk" to you. This distraction isn't a sign that your baby is rejecting breast-feeding or is bored with formula. An easily distracted baby is normal as the baby discovers and explores the world. Your baby may discover that feeding time can be more than a time to eat; it's also a time to socialize, experiment and assert a little independence.

As much as you want your child to learn through exploration and interaction, it can be frustrating to try to feed a distracted baby. You might want to try a quiet, uninterrupted feeding place, but acknowledge that everything is new and worthy of exploration to your baby. You may find that your baby's early morning feeding — when your baby is still sleepy and the room is dark — may be the best feeding of the day.

CHAPTER 21

Month 5

Many parents eagerly look forward to this month because it means you can finally start introducing your baby to foods other than breast milk or formula. Food is a big part of human culture, and it plays a role not only in survival, but also in societal traditions and pastimes. So it's natural for parents to want to share the joy of eating favorite foods with their children. It's also another step toward integration into the family when baby gets to join the others at the dining table.

As much as you may be excited to embark on culinary adventures with your baby, keep in mind your baby's stage of growth and development. In this chapter you'll read about signs that indicate that your baby is ready for solid foods, as well as tips on a successful introduction. You can read a more in-depth discussion of infant nutrition in Chapter 3.

During the fifth month your baby gains increasing control over his or her body, enthusiastically exploring each newfound function. He or she also is continuing to discover new emotions, ranging from happy to grumpy, and solidly establishing his or her place in the family.

BABY'S GROWTH AND APPEARANCE

Between 4 and 5 months old your baby's growth rate is likely to match last month's, which is a little slower than the first three months, but not by much. Most babies gain anywhere from just shy of 1 pound to 1½ pounds or more. Length and head circumference both increase by about ½ inch during this month.

Introducing solid foods Between this month and next, your baby will begin to develop the coordination to move solid food from the front of the mouth to the back for swallowing. At the same time, your baby's head control will improve, and he or she will learn to sit with support — essential skills for eating solid foods.

Breast milk or formula is all your little tyke needs in the first four to six months of life to grow and develop properly. But eventually additional nutrition is necessary so that your baby can continue to thrive. After 6 months of age, for example, breast milk alone generally isn't enough to provide your baby with the amount of energy, protein, iron, zinc and other vitamins he or she requires.

Is your baby ready? Sometime between ages 4 and 6 months, most babies are ready to begin eating solid foods as a complement to breast-feeding or formula-feeding. But age should not be the only determining factor. You want to make sure your child is both physically and socially ready. And you shouldn't feel pressured to begin solids. The American Academy of Pediatrics prefers that parents wait until a child is 6 months old to introduce solids, if possible. If you're not sure whether your baby is ready for solids, ask yourself these questions:

▶ Can your baby hold his or her head in a steady, upright position?
▶ Can your baby sit well with support?
▶ Is your baby interested in what you're eating, perhaps eyeing your breakfast toast or opening his or her mouth if you offer a spoon?

If you answer yes to these questions and you have the OK from your child's doctor or dietitian, you can begin supplementing your baby's liquid diet. Read more about what to serve when and which foods to avoid in Chapter 3.

Tips for a successful meal Once your baby starts eating foods besides breast milk or formula, feedings are likely to become a lot more interactive, and most probably, a lot messier! But that's OK. It's all part of the process of exploring new things. Here are some sugges-

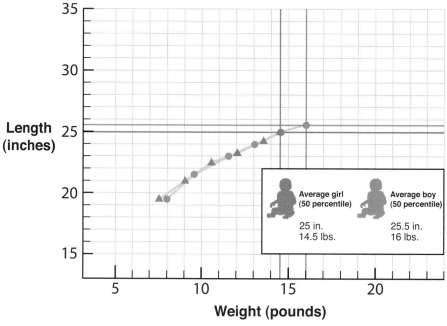

Month 5

Length (inches)

Weight (pounds)

Average girl (50 percentile)
25 in.
14.5 lbs.

Average boy (50 percentile)
25.5 in.
16 lbs.

© MFMER

tions for when your little one reaches that point that he or she is ready to try solids:

Pick a happy time For your first try, choose a time when your baby's most likely to be open to adventure, such as when he or she is alert, dry, comfortable and not starving. If your baby's very hungry, you might want to start off with a little breast milk or formula first and then switch to solids.

Set your expectations Remind yourself that the goal of these first meals is to introduce your baby to the experience of food, rather than meeting your child's nutritional needs. In fact, it will likely be several weeks before the amount of food that actually gets into your baby's belly is contributing to his or her overall nutritional requirements.

Sit up At first, try feeding your baby propped up in your lap or in an infant car seat. When your baby can sit without support, you can move him or her to a highchair.

Use a spoon The American Academy of Pediatrics recommends always using a spoon when feeding your baby complementary foods. A small espresso spoon or a rubber-coated baby spoon usually works well. Eating off a spoon helps your baby learn to swallow without sucking, and allows your baby to learn the process of eating in the same way the rest of the family does. Avoid giving your child cereal in a bottle, which may encourage excessive calorie intake.

Start small For your baby's first meal, start out with just a couple of spoonfuls of food in a bowl. Thin the complementary food with breast milk or formula until it's the consistency of heavy cream, to help ease the transition from bottle to spoon. Over the next few meals, you can gradually make the consistency thicker as your baby becomes accustomed to swallowing solid foods.

Be patient Although some babies seem thrilled with their first bowl of cereal, others may not be convinced of its joys the first time around. If your baby flat out

GETTING YOUR KIDS TO LIKE FRUITS AND VEGETABLES

A common battle parents face as their kids begin to eat solid foods is getting them to eat their fruits and vegetables! Scientists are finding that part of the solution to this dilemma may very well go back to the mother's own eating habits, perhaps even before your baby is born.

Since a number of food flavors are transmitted via amniotic fluid or breast milk to a baby, what the mom eats affects the baby's early experiences with flavor. Some evidence suggests that the more often a baby experiences a particular flavor — such as carrots, for example — during pregnancy or breast-feeding, the more accepting the baby is likely to be of that taste when he or she begins eating solid foods. And because breast-feeding offers a child a greater variety of flavor experiences due to a mother's varying diet, breast-fed infants seem less picky and more willing to try new foods.

Another finding suggests that flavor learning after the introduction of solid foods is based on repeated exposure to new foods. One study, for example, found that the first time a group of babies tasted green beans, many squinted, raised brows or upper lips, or wrinkled noses. But after repeated offerings of green beans, expressions of surprise or distaste were fewer, and willingness to eat the vegetables was greater, especially if the green beans were followed by a sweet-tasting fruit, such as peaches.

This type of research is ongoing, but in the meantime, it doesn't hurt to eat well yourself and keep setting the good stuff out there. Chances are good that eventually your kids will enjoy it for themselves, and not just because you said so.

refuses the first feeding, don't give up hope. Put the box of cereal away for a couple of weeks and then try again. Focus on enjoying the meal rather than getting your baby to eat solid foods by a certain date. He or she will have plenty of time to warm up to the spoon as another vehicle for gastronomic delights.

The scoop on poop Once you start feeding your baby solid foods, you'll likely notice a difference in the texture, color and smell of your baby's stools. Solid foods make for more solid stools. Foods such as peas, blueberries and beets can make noticeable differences in the color of stool, as well. Last but not least, get ready for stinky stools. The added sugars and fats in solid foods can lead to a stronger odor.

BABY'S MOVEMENT

Between 4 and 5 months old, most babies achieve the first big milestone — good head control. By the end of this month, your baby is likely able to hold his or her head up steadily while sitting. He or she is also learning to turn the head from side to side, making it easier to track moving objects and place different sounds and voices.

Once your baby has full head control, he or she has the skills necessary to move on to sitting. And just in time, too. As your baby gets older, he or she may become increasingly less satisfied with lying either faceup or facedown and will probably want to spend more time upright. During this month and next, your baby is working toward sitting up without help. Playing facedown on the floor and lifting the head and chest to see toys are good exercises to help your baby strengthen neck muscles and develop the head control necessary for sitting up.

Rolling over At this point, most babies are making progress in their attempts to roll over, too. By the end of this month, some babies can even roll both ways without help. Once babies learn to roll from front to back and back to front again, they may start out sleeping on their backs just the way you laid them, but then flip over in the middle of the night. If this happens, don't feel compelled to flip him or her back again. The risk of SIDS begins to decrease once your baby gains head and neck control and is able to roll over.

Reaching and grasping During the fifth month, you may notice your baby start working for a toy or other object. At first, this may mean that he or she reaches out for a toy but may not be able to grasp it at first try. At 4 months of age, your baby still manipulates objects by batting at them. But eventually he or she may try to pick up a larger object by pressing it with the palm of the hand and curling the fingers around the object. When your baby does get a hold of a toy, he or she may grasp it with both hands and have fun shaking it around. Dangling toys are still a source of entertainment at this age and help your child further develop his or her hand-eye coordination.

Bouncing Your 4-month-old most likely gets great joy out of being upright and "standing" on your lap, and perhaps bouncing. All the bouncing your baby does is a part of normal development and isn't harmful to the baby's hips, legs or feet. By about 5 months, you will notice your baby can probably bear full body weight on his or her legs. Standing alone and walking are still a long way off, but you can see how the small stages of development are preparing your baby for greater mobility.

Encouraging physical activity Take a look around your local baby supply store, and you'll see an amazing range of infant equipment — swings, playpens, infant seats, stationary activity centers, walkers, baby gyms, bouncy chairs — oh my! And with your baby learning so many new skills, it's tempting to try to physically help him or her along with the latest gadget. Quite a lot of infant equipment is marketed with the idea of helping your baby reach a new milestone, such as sitting or walking.

Truth? What infants need more than anything to develop their motor skills is freedom of movement in a safe space that allows them to explore their surroundings and to practice their budding skills under the watchful eye of a nearby caregiver. Warm interaction with a supportive caregiver during playtime also is important.

Does that mean you have to be constantly down on the floor with baby? Not always. Certain pieces of baby gear can definitely come in handy, such as a stationary activity center where your baby can sit and bounce or play with attached toys, or a molded seat that helps your baby sit up. Swings and playpens also can be essential, at times. But keep in mind that these items are mostly for your convenience, allowing time for you to move about unrestricted, to do some chores, say, or eat breakfast. Try to limit the amount of time your child spends in these devices, as extended movement restriction in turn may limit your child. Be sure to supervise older siblings around these devices, too, as they may become overenthusiastic in "helping" the baby

use them, potentially causing injuries or unintentional harm (think "Mom, look how fast Sammy can go in the swing!").

The American Academy of Pediatrics (AAP) advises specifically against using mobile walkers. These devices generally have a cloth seat set in a frame with wheels that allows the baby to move around the room even though he or she might not be able to crawl or walk yet. A number of studies have shown that these devices can make a baby more prone to injury, such as falling down steps or reaching for dangerous objects. Even under supervision, the AAP contends that walkers are simply too fast for a parent to reach before an accident happens. Other experts have cautioned against the use of door jumpers — seats that hang from a door frame — as well. If you need a place for your baby to safely amuse himself or herself for a few minutes, consider a stationary activity center or playpen instead. A highchair also can serve this function, once your baby is able to sit in it safely.

Keep in mind that if your baby has a developmental disability, his or her care provider may in fact recommend certain pieces of equipment to help your baby sit with support or move with help.

BABY'S SENSORY DEVELOPMENT

During this month, mouthing becomes an even more important avenue of exploration for your young child. Keep offering him or her safe toys and everyday objects to practice the art of picking things up and bringing them to the mouth. This helps your baby develop sensory and motor skills. At the same time, keep a sharp eye out for anything that might be a choking or poison hazard for your baby.

Vision Earlier, your baby was learning to distinguish between similar bold colors. Improved visual awareness during this month and the next helps your baby discern more subtle shades of color, such as soft pastels, although bold colors may still be favorites. Improved visual tracking and coordination also helps your baby become more adept at reaching and grabbing larger objects and toys. Small objects are definitely catching his or her attention at this point, but he or she doesn't yet have the dexterity to pick these up.

Babies at this age are also starting to discriminate between the different emotions they see in others — such as joy, fear or sadness — and to make similar responses.

Hearing Between 4 and 5 months, about half of all babies turn their heads toward a voice. Most babies at this age will turn toward a rattling sound to investigate its source. At this age, babies also learn to distinguish emotions by tone of voice.

If by this month your baby doesn't respond to sounds, talk to his or her care provider. Although newborns are generally checked right after birth for hearing loss, your observations at home are key to identifying the need for further testing.

BABY'S MENTAL DEVELOPMENT

As the brain develops, and more and more connections are made between brain nerve cells, your baby's memory of faces, sounds, places and event patterns increases. Although your baby has been absorbing information about the surrounding world since birth, he or she has had only limited ability to respond to this new knowledge. But as his or her motor skills increase, you can observe your infant begin to apply the knowledge stored in his or her memory.

This is evident in the way your baby reacts to seeing you or to certain daily routines, such as a feeding or a bath. If you sit in your favorite chair for breast-feeding or a bottle, you may notice your baby quickly settles in with you and may make noises or kick in anticipation of what he or she knows is coming. And if for some reason, what's expected isn't forthcoming, you may hear a squawk or two of displeasure.

Learning how things work At the same time, your baby's curiosity and attention span are increasing. This allows him or her to spend more time examining things and observing how things work. This natural curiosity also drives your baby to start to work for objects that are out of reach. Even if he or she can't quite get to a toy yet, you can see the focus and concentration in your child's eyes.

During this month, your baby is also learning more about cause and effect. When he or she cries, you come. When he or she bangs a toy on the table, it makes noise. When he or she giggles, siblings giggle, too. Like a scientist, your baby may test different actions over and over to see if they always get the same effect. And, like a successful scientist, your baby will be proud every time the response is the one expected. You'll appreciate your baby's smiles and squeals of accomplishment and self-confidence.

Language skills Your 5-month-old may have already started imitating some of the speech sounds you make, even though it will be a few more months before he or she understands how these sounds work together to communicate. During this month and the next, your baby is likely to pick up on a single sound — such as "ah" or "oh" — and repeat it over and over, and then a few days later discover a new sound and practice it repeatedly. Babies seem to enjoy playing with a new sound as much as they delight in playing with a favorite toy. Pretty soon, he or she will be babbling away at you, excited to hear sounds emanating not just from others, but from his or her own mouth.

BABY'S SOCIAL DEVELOPMENT

At this age, your baby is quickly figuring out how to express a variety of emotions through facial expression, vocalizations and body language. For example, he or she now uses laughter to express happiness and excitement. At the same time, your baby may start to show dislikes, making a face or turning away from things he or she doesn't care for. You may notice this latter type of reaction more as you introduce new foods to your child or you start to set limits to your child's actions for safety's sake.

TOYS AND GAMES

At this young age, babies are interested in very simple objects and toys. They also don't need a heap of toys to stay occupied. In fact, too many toys or too much activity can overwhelm your baby and lead to tears. Limit toys to just a few at a time. That way your baby can take the time to study each one and see what it can do. Toys and games your baby may enjoy during this month include:

Toys that make noise By now, your baby is starting to play purposefully with rattles and toys that squeak or make noise. Offer him or her toys that make noise to enhance his or her discovery of cause and effect as he or she bangs and rattles about. Infants also seem to derive great joy from pressing buttons that make things happen, such as on a pop-up toy or a baby phone.

Music to bounce, sway or swing to Music can help express emotions and thoughts when the words aren't quite there yet. Most babies love music and will move along to a rhythm they find catchy. Make a playlist of your favorite kid-friendly (but not necessarily "kiddy") songs, and play them for your baby. Better yet, pick your baby up and sing and dance around the room together in accompaniment to the music.

The company of a mirror Place an unbreakable mirror in front of your baby and watch as he or she and "the other baby" get acquainted. At this age, your baby probably won't know that it's his or her own reflection, but will have fun watching his or her antics, regardless of perception.

Stuff to reach for While your son or daughter is lying prone on the floor or sitting upright, place a couple of bright toys or objects just out of his or her reach. This will encourage your child to practice reaching skills and improve his or her hand-eye coordination.

Growing attachment By the fifth month, your baby is establishing a solid place in the family structure and clearly knows who his or her loved ones are. Your baby feels comfortable with the family routine and indeed expects it. Spending time with you is still his or her favorite activity. In fact, this closer sense of attachment to you and other family members may lead your baby to feel upset and display unhappiness when you stop playing a game or leave the room. He or she may even need a little extra reassurance that you're still available — perhaps by talking to him or her or singing a song — and will return as soon as possible.

This narrowing focus of attachment goes hand in hand with a gradual realization that some people are strangers. Although your baby likely still has an accepting, welcoming response to unfamiliar people, in the months ahead, you'll notice that he or she is becoming increasingly picky about the company he or she keeps.

Emerging personality As your baby matures, his or her personality traits will rapidly become more apparent. Is your baby bouncy and full of energy? Or perhaps more quiet and cautious? Is he or she easily frustrated when a goal can't be obtained? Or is your infant persistent to the point where you might call it stubbornness? Does your baby adjust easily to new environments, or does he or she take a while to warm up?

Everyone is born with certain behavioral characteristics that form his or her basic temperament. Depending on the situation, a temperamental trait can be pleasing or frustrating to you as a parent. For example, the same high energy that makes your baby so fun to play with — pleasing — can also make for difficult

During the fifth month, your baby is busy:
- Perfecting mini-pushups while lying on belly
- Sitting balanced by hands on floor in front (tripod style)
- Bearing weight on legs
- Rolling over from front to back, maybe even back to front
- Working to get to a toy
- Grasping with both hands
- Exploring with mouth
- Studying small objects
- Locating sounds and voices by turning head
- Imitating speech sounds
- Repeating single sounds
- Laughing, squealing
- Expressing dislikes, making faces
- Enjoying playing with others, crying when playing stops

diaper changes or wriggly feedings — frustrating!

Generally, your baby's natural traits can't be changed — it would be like trying to change his or her personality. But by learning your baby's normal behaviors and understanding his or her temperament, you can better appreciate your infant and adjust your parenting style to bring out the best in him or her. How you interact with your baby now can set the stage for your relationship throughout childhood, adolescence and even adulthood. You can read more about temperament in Chapter 9.

CHAPTER 22

Month 6

As you approach your baby's half-year mark, think about how far you've both come. By now, that little person in the nursery is no longer a baby, but a world-class explorer. And you have become an ever-more-confident parent, familiar with the rhythms of baby care and more secure in your ability to meet upcoming challenges.

During this month, your baby is becoming more adept with his or her hands and may even start to sit unsupported by the end of the month. Each aspect of your baby's motor and sensory development gives your baby new tools to explore the world and expand his or her mental and social development. This is a fun time as your baby babbles and laughs, excited to be part of his or her family.

BABY'S GROWTH AND APPEARANCE

By the time the sixth month rolls around, many babies have doubled their birth weight. Your baby's growth rate this month is likely to be similar to last month's — weight gain of 1 to 1½ pounds or more and an increase in length and head circumference by about ½ inch. But don't be surprised if the growth rate starts to slow down in a few weeks. Most babies grow a little more slowly during months seven through 12 than they did in the first six months.

Teeth! Drooling, crankiness and tears — could it be baby teeth coming in? Although timing varies widely, most babies begin teething by about age 6 months. The two bottom front teeth (lower central incisors) are usually the first to appear, followed by the two top front teeth (upper central incisors).

Classic signs and symptoms of teething often include:

- Drooling, which may begin about two months before the first tooth appears
- Irritability or crankiness
- Swollen gums
- Chewing on solid objects

Many parents suspect that teething causes fever and diarrhea, but researchers say this isn't true. Teething may cause signs and symptoms in the mouth and gums, but it doesn't cause problems elsewhere in the body. If your baby develops a fever, seems particularly uncomfortable, or has other signs or symptoms of illness, contact your child's provider. Otherwise, teething can usually be handled at home.

If your teething baby seems uncomfortable, consider these simple tips:

Rub your baby's gums Use a clean finger, moistened gauze pad or damp washcloth to massage your baby's gums. The pressure can ease your baby's discomfort.

Offer a teething ring Try one made of firm rubber. The liquid-filled variety may break under the pressure of your baby's chewing. If a bottle seems to do the trick,

fill it with water. Prolonged contact with sugar from formula, milk or juice may cause tooth decay.

Keep it cool A cold washcloth or chilled teething ring can be soothing. Don't give your baby a frozen teething ring, however. Contact with extreme cold may hurt, doing your baby more harm than good. If your baby's eating solid foods, offer cold items such as applesauce or yogurt.

Dry the drool Excessive drooling is part of the teething process. To prevent skin irritation, keep a clean cloth handy to dry your baby's chin. Saliva is used in the digestion of food, so isn't it interesting that the body knows to produce more saliva at the time when infants begin solid foods.

Try an over-the-counter remedy If your baby is especially cranky, acetaminophen (Tylenol, others) or ibuprofen (Advil,

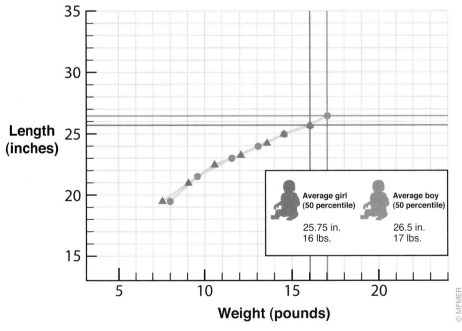

Month 6

Average girl
(50 percentile)

25.75 in.
16 lbs.

Average boy
(50 percentile)

26.5 in.
17 lbs.

Length (inches)

Weight (pounds)

© MFMER

Motrin, others) may help. Don't give your baby products that contain aspirin, however, and be cautious about teething medications that can be rubbed directly on a baby's gums. The medication may be washed away by your baby's saliva before it has the chance to do any good — and too much of the medication may numb your baby's throat, which may interfere with his or her normal gag reflex.

Caring for new teeth Ideally, you've been running a clean, damp washcloth over your baby's gums every day. If not, now's a great time to start. The washcloth can keep bacteria from building up in your baby's mouth. When your baby's first teeth appear, switch to a small, soft-bristled toothbrush. There's no need to use toothpaste. Water is all you need until your child learns to spit — about age 2. If you have well water or you use bottled water in your home, your baby may not be getting necessary fluoride for healthy tooth development. Discuss this issue with your child's care provider.

It's also time to think about regular dental checkups. The American Dental Association and the American Academy of Pediatric Dentistry recommend scheduling a child's first dental visit after the first tooth erupts and no later than his or her first birthday. Your baby's teeth and gums will also be examined at well-baby checkups. Regular childhood dental care helps set the stage for a lifetime of healthy teeth and gums.

BABY'S MOVEMENT

By 5 or 6 months old, most babies have achieved pretty good head control and are rolling over both ways. By now, they may be ready to move on to learning how to sit without help. By 7 months or so, most babies have learned to sit independently, but some may wait until 9 months to do so, which is within the range of normal.

At the same time, baby's hand control skills are rapidly improving, allowing your child even more flexibility in exploring his or her surroundings, and even other parts of his or her body.

Tripod sitting Your baby's first attempts at sitting will probably be very entertaining. At first, he or she will sit hunched over, balancing on arms extended to the front. Experts call this the "tripod sitting" stage. Almost anything will topple a baby in this position — leaning a little to one side, a distraction that makes the baby look in another direction or any attempt to shift weight.

This hunched-over sitting takes all of your baby's energy. He or she probably can't do much else but hold his or her head up without falling over. In a few weeks, his or her balance will improve.

Toes, toes, toes! If your baby hasn't discovered his or her toes yet, he or she is likely to do so this month. When fingers don't seem so novel any more, baby may catch sight of those wiggly things at the end of his or her feet and bring them up for investigation. At first, your baby may explore those little toes just by grabbing and feeling them. But sooner or later —

with the help of incredibly flexible limbs — your baby is likely to bring toes to mouth for a good sucking.

Picking up and letting go By age 5 or 6 months, your baby's hand control is good enough that he or she can reach for a desired object using a rake-like motion and grasp it. After learning to grab a toy, your baby will practice moving things from hand to mouth, using both touching and tasting to explore the toy. You may even see your baby repeating the hand to mouth to hand movement, taking the object out of his or her mouth with alternating hands. By 6 months, your baby may learn to move something directly from one hand to the other.

Your baby will soon discover that letting go of something is as much fun as picking it up. At first, letting go is almost accidental. As soon as your baby learns to hold something, he or she will also drop it. But over the next few months, he or she will begin to let go more purposefully. By the end of your baby's first year, he or she will have acquired other means of getting rid of unwanted objects, such as throwing them or pressing them down on a surface.

At this age, babies still use their whole hands to pick things up. When babies are relaxed, their hands are open; by now, they've outgrown the closed-fist pose of younger babies. You can see the slow progression from that tight-fisted infant to a more mobile and coordinated baby. Right now, your baby is just beginning to use hands for small tasks. And it's hard work! Watching your baby, you can probably see the amount of effort that goes into this kind of "play." When your baby reaches for an object, his or her other hand may mirror the movement of the reaching hand. Both hands may close as one hand reaches for and grasps a toy.

A LEFTY OR A RIGHTY?

At this age, it's too early to tell whether your baby is left-handed or right-handed. For now, babies may seem to favor one hand for a while, then switch and use the other hand more often. A 1-year-old may use both hands equally. By 18 months to 2 years, toddlers start to show a preference for which hand they use. Still, true handedness isn't usually determined until a child is about 3 years old.

Handedness develops naturally, although scientists still aren't sure what role genes play in it. Children with left-handed parents have an increased chance of being left-handed, but the inheritance pattern isn't clear-cut.

If you do notice when your child is an infant that he or she favors one hand over the other, let your care provider know. Sometimes, further investigation is necessary to make sure that both hands do, in fact, work equally well.

BABY'S SENSORY DEVELOPMENT

Although your baby's senses will continue to mature throughout early childhood, they're now almost as fully developed as those of an adult. Your baby sees and hears the world almost as clearly as you do, and this ability allows the two of you to understand and share many of the same experiences.

Vision By 6 months of age, your baby has more clearly focused vision and can probably track the course of a falling toy or other object quite smoothly. Ongoing development of your baby's visual system allows for greater depth perception. And now that your baby is sitting upright more often, he or she can gaze across at you and at other things, rather than just look up. Both of these skills — increased depth perception and the ability to look across — come in handy, such as when baby is learning to eat solid foods, and you're aiming a spoon full of cereal at his or her mouth.

During this month, your baby is also able to take in more complex visual im-ages and observe them studiously. You might notice this increased visual curiosity when your baby picks up a toy and examines it, although eventually it's likely to end up in his or her mouth for a truly thorough examination. Looking at picture books together is great fun at this age, as are sturdy board books that provide visual interest as well as something for your baby to practice manipulating with his or her hands.

Hearing By the end of this month, most babies respond readily to sound and turn their heads quickly toward the direction of a voice or other noise. With improving memory and increasing exposure, they may even be able to distinguish between male and female voices.

Touch In addition to exploring his or her environment, your baby is discovering all sorts of new things about himself or herself. By touching his or her cheeks, nose, toes and genitals, your baby is becoming familiar with the shapes and contours of his or her body. Baby also continues to explore new textures and shapes.

BABY'S MENTAL DEVELOPMENT

Between 5 and 6 months, your baby is working out some of the first inklings of his or her own identity, what it feels like to be a separate person with individual powers of action and reaction. In parallel with these discoveries, your baby is uncovering the possibilities that exist for interaction with others.

As your baby's memory expands, he or she can start to roughly catalogue his or her experiences — the kitchen floor is hard, daddy's beard is prickly, this toy is fun to gum, the music comes from there, and so forth.

Me, myself and I Combining sensory, motor and mental skills, your baby begins to realize that moving certain muscles always produces physical sensations that correspond with specific visual results. For example, baby's effort to kick his or her legs is always accompanied by the sight of these legs moving.

Sensations associated with self are easier to reproduce with regularity than sensations associated with others. Every time your baby kicks, he or she can see his or her legs move. But every time he or she cries, the sight of you may or may not appear immediately.

Playing becomes serious business
At the same time, playing rises to a new level. Toys that stimulate the senses and simple games, such as peek-a-boo or mimicking games, become the tools and experiments of your small scientist. Even the process of getting your attention requires a certain amount of strategy and can become a game for baby.

Again, you don't need expensive toys to stimulate your child's mind and senses. Common household items with different shapes and textures — such as cardboard boxes, egg cartons, lids, paper towel rolls, spoons, tea towels, nesting bowls, home-made noisemakers (think tightly capped clear containers filled with

TOYS AND GAMES

Now that your baby is becoming more comfortable sitting upright, he or she has a whole new vantage point from which to watch, play and interact with the world. And as baby's sensory and motor skills continue to develop, he or she will become much more interested in anything that provides additional opportunities for adventure and discovery.

Colorful books and magazines Your baby's vision is such that now he or she is able to focus on an entire pattern and distinguish a range of colors. Reading colorful board books together becomes especially fun at this age. Simple texts allow you to repeat sounds that your baby can try to repeat. Don't be offended if baby decides to take over, though, turning the pages or flipping back to the cover every time you try to read the next page. At this age, the main idea isn't to understand the story line but to make sounds, look at pictures and chew on the covers. Old magazines that you don't mind being torn up can also be fun to look at; just make sure the baby doesn't eat the pages.

Short trips Once your baby is able to sit up in a stroller, walks around the neighborhood or the park take on a whole new dimension. Now your baby can see most of the things you see and will enjoy the sight of a passing dog or a squirrel hopping to the nearest tree. With a turn of the head, your baby can locate different sounds, too, such as the honk of a goose or the sounds of children playing. If it's nice out, place your baby on a patch of grass and let him or her feel the differing textures. Trips to the zoo or your local library also become more entertaining at this age, but don't expect them to last too long — it's probably best to keep them to under an hour or two to match your baby's finite stamina and short attention span.

Bouncy lap games Good head control also allows for slightly more physical games. Almost all babies seem to love bouncing around on a grown-up's lap. Have your baby sit on your lap facing you, hold his or her hands, and bounce him or her gently on your knees while singing a song. If you don't know any such songs, ask your parents or grandparents. They'll probably remember some, and it will be fun to hear what they sang to you at one point. Or try looking up nursery songs and rhymes. Here's a classic to get you started:

Pat-a-cake, pat-a-cake, baker's man,
Bake me a cake as fast as you can.
Roll it, and prick it, and mark it with a B
And put it in the oven for Baby and me!

Reach! Once baby is able to raise his or her body up on straight arms while lying belly down on the floor, you can start encouraging him or her to reach out with one arm for a toy just ahead. Eventually, your baby will lean on one arm and reach for toys with other. This act of reaching forward is generally the first step toward crawling. Rolling balls or other toys also provide an incentive for chasing.

rice) — offer plenty of opportunities for sensory exploration and discovery.

Peekaboo is still fairly magical because your 5- to 6-month-old hasn't quite grasped the concept that you're still there behind the blanket even though he or she can't see you (object permanence). Your little one may, however, look for a dropped toy but give up quickly if it's not in sight. Mimicking games become more important as your baby strives to match your facial expressions and imitate the sounds and cadences of your voice.

Babbling Babbling usually begins with babies trying out vowel sounds, something you may have already noticed your baby doing. A few weeks later, baby may start to add in consonant sounds. By 6 months, about half of all babies babble by repeating one syllable over and over, such as *mah* or *bah*. Some babies may even have started adding more than one syllable to their babbling. You may hear your baby practice one kind of sound, then move on to something else and not repeat the sound for several days.

Much of your baby's "talking" may seem more like sound effects than babbling. Squeals, sliding pitches and bubbling sounds are all common for babies at this age. Giggles and laughter are favorite sounds for both babies and parents.

BABY'S SOCIAL DEVELOPMENT

This is a fun age to socialize and play with your baby. Adults have the remarkable ability to express almost any emotion through facial expression, and babies love to watch and try to imitate these expressions. Sharing emotional states with someone else is vital for social development and is one of the basic foundations for communication.

Don't be discouraged if playing with your baby seems uncomfortable at first. Remember, it's been a few years since you spent your evenings on the floor with rattles and a box of blocks. Watch the "expert," observing which toys your baby is drawn to and what he or she does

PLAYING WITH SIBLINGS

An older brother or sister can get a lot of enjoyment out of a 5- to 6-month-old baby. By six months, the baby has moved beyond face-to-face interaction and may even play with toys offered by an older child. Your baby can probably entice a bigger brother or sister into picking up dropped toys or playing passing games.

At this age, it's important that your baby have personal toys separate from an older sibling's toys. Illnesses can be easily spread from one child to another through shared toys. Keep the baby's toys clean. Plastic toys should be washed often, and fuzzy toys that aren't as easily washed should be reserved just for the baby's play.

Babies love older kids mostly because they're fun to watch. Although babies will play some turn-taking games, they delight in being an audience and responding to what older children do. For safety reasons, always supervise playtime between your baby and an older child.

with them. Then join in. Soon you'll know what games and toys make playtime fun for your baby. Your baby will give you the kind of immediate response — giggles, turn-taking, smiles — that make playtime rewarding for both of you.

Your baby will let you know if playtime is too intense or has gone on too long. Watch for clues that he or she is overstimulated, such as turning away or becoming grouchy or tense.

Don't be surprised if you feel your baby needs even more attention now than in the newborn days. Your baby wants and needs stimulation, especially from you. Left alone in a playpen, crib or infant seat, he or she is apt to become bored. But life doesn't have to be all games and playtime. You can meet many of your baby's social needs by including him or her in your daily tasks or just by positioning baby where he or she can watch you at work.

CHAPTER 23

Month 7

The next few months are a time of growing independence for your little one. This can be both exhilarating and frightening for an infant. You may find your baby vigorously venturing into new things, but afraid to be too far away from the security of what he or she already knows — you. By sharing in your child's curiosity while still providing lots of affection and comfort, you can help your baby become more confident and competent in his or her evolving skills.

From month seven on, mobility starts to take off. Day by day, your baby will build on existing motor skills, such as reaching, rolling over and sitting, and move on to new ones, such as crawling and standing (some faster than others).

Since you can't predict when your baby will make his or her first move across the floor, now is a good time to review your home safety. (See Chapter 15 for more information on childproofing your house.) Keep an eye out for dangling cords and unsteady furniture. As your baby's mobility progresses, he or she will latch on to nearby items to help himself or herself along or even up. Removing treasured or breakable items and creating a safe environment will give your baby the freedom and confidence to explore and learn. At this age, it's generally easier to modify the environment than to teach a child not to touch.

BABY'S GROWTH AND APPEARANCE

During these past months, your baby's growth rate was on fast forward. Once your baby reaches 6 months, though, you'll find that growth tends to slow a bit. Previously, your baby was likely to gain over a pound a month. Now, his or her weight increase is more likely to be just under a pound each month, and his or her increase in length around ⅜ inch or less. You can also expect the growth of your son's or daughter's head to begin to slow, too.

From here on out, your child will continue to grow steadily, with additional growth spurts here and there. But he or she will never grow quite as fast as in those first six months.

BABY'S MOVEMENT

When your baby was younger, indications of developing motor skills were subtle, with some so basic as to go almost unnoticed. Fidgeting, for example, is a normal phase of growth and development, but it isn't nearly as exciting as the motor skills that are now blossoming. Between now and baby's first birthday, noticeable changes take place that transform your son or daughter from a totally dependent infant to a trundling independent toddler.

Sitting At 6 months, many babies sit up with help or sit alone by leaning forward, hands to the floor. Over the next few weeks, your baby is perfecting the art of sitting — keeping the head steady and back straight to maintain balance. By 7 months, your baby may be sitting alone with no support, even working to put arms to the side to keep from toppling over. By his or her ninth month, your baby may be steady and strong enough to play for longer periods while seated on the floor, even pivoting and reaching to get to different toys.

Hand and finger coordination At 6 months, babies have very clumsy hand movements and pick up objects by pressing all their fingers against their thumbs ("mitten grasp"). But between now and the ninth month, most babies will learn to use a more refined "pincer" grasp, us-

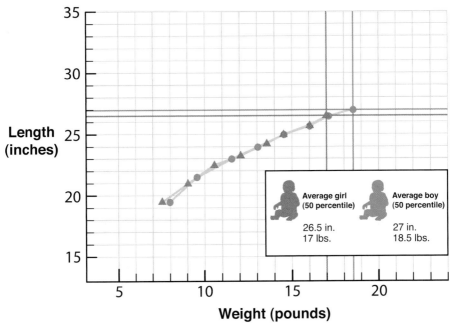

Month 7

Length (inches) / Weight (pounds)

Average girl (50 percentile)
26.5 in.
17 lbs.

Average boy (50 percentile)
27 in.
18.5 lbs.

© MFMER

Here's a snapshot of what your baby's basic care looks like in the seventh month.

Eating Breast milk or formula is still part of your baby's diet, but by this time you may be introducing additional foods. If you introduce one new food at a time at first, you'll have the advantage of knowing whether a particular food is likely to cause a reaction of some sort, such as diarrhea, rash or vomiting. If your baby does have such a response to a food, avoid it until you talk to your baby's care provider about it. See Chapter 3 for more on introducing new foods.

Sleeping Baby is more likely to sleep six to eight hours at night with no interruption. Some babies still wake up once or twice during the night for a feeding, although they're unlikely to need middle-of-the-night feedings by this age. Total sleep may add up to between 14 and 15 hours in a 24-hour period, including a couple of daytime naps, usually one in the morning and one in the afternoon. Some babies may need a third nap late in the afternoon. As your baby becomes more curious and mobile, it may be harder to settle down to sleep at night. Establishing and maintaining a consistent, relaxing bedtime routine — such as having a bath, reading books together or singing a quiet song — can be a great help in getting your child used to the idea of going to sleep at nighttime.

ing the thumb and index finger to pick up small objects.

The graduation from a mitten grasp to a pincer grasp is gradual. First, you may notice your child using a cross between the two, picking up objects with the thumb, index and middle fingers. You may also see baby resting his or her arm and hand on a surface to steady the hand and pick up a small object.

At the same time, your baby is also getting better at transferring an object from one hand to the other, turning it around and upside down, holding it this way and that, and getting to know how it feels. About half of babies this age gain the ability to hold an object in each hand. Eventually, they'll delight in banging objects against each other, but for now your baby may simply enjoy banging objects against a leg or table.

BABY'S SENSORY DEVELOPMENT

By 7 months, your baby's eyesight is nearly mature. His or her distance vision is continuing to improve so that faraway people and objects appear clearer and more distinct. Your baby is also able to track faster movements with his or her eyes and follow moving objects closely. In fact, if you roll a ball to your baby, he or she can monitor its path and probably put a hand out to it as it gets near.

By age 6 or 7 months, your baby's hearing is almost fully developed. He or she also is becoming more selective about the sounds he or she reacts to. For example, your baby at this age can quickly and accurately locate you when you speak. He or she also may stop to listen to quieter sounds.

ENTER FLUFFY

One thing that might help your baby negotiate transitions, such as going to bed or to child care, is to carry along a favorite stuffed animal, blanket or even book. Having a loved object to hang on to while venturing into uncharted territory can make your little one feel more secure and confident, and help him or her become more independent.

Watch to see if your baby turns toward a sound, even if the sound comes from outside his or her line of vision. If you notice that he or she doesn't respond to surrounding sounds, talk to your baby's care provider. If there's a problem with your baby's hearing, it's better to identify it sooner rather than later. Untreated, hearing loss can interfere with other aspects of development, such as language and social development.

BABY'S MENTAL DEVELOPMENT

During month seven, your baby continues to pick up on language skills from listening to you and others speak. Before, your son or daughter may have focused on imitating specific sounds, such as *mmm* or *bbbb*. In these next few weeks, you may notice him or her start to combine different sounds together, such as consonants and vowels. Around 6 or 7 months, your baby may make sounds such as *dadada* and *mamama*. As tempting as it may be to think your baby is referring to you when saying these sounds, it will likely be several weeks still before he or she is able to attach names to people.

The art of conversation In addition to imitating sounds and even combinations of sounds, your baby may also begin to follow your pattern of speech — pausing between "sentences" or ending a string of sounds with an upward inflection, as if posing a question. You can help your baby practice the art of conversation by talking to him or her and acknowledging his or her efforts with your own warm responses.

An infant's understanding of words is far ahead of his or her ability to use them. At this age, your baby understands the meaning of what you say by listening to your tone of voice. Even the word no (which you may find yourself using more and more often as your baby starts to push against the limits you've established) is understood by your inflection and tone and not necessarily by the word itself.

The more you talk to your son or daughter — whether it's while you're driving around town, doing chores around the house, or changing or feeding him or her — the more your little one learns about all facets of communication, including sounds, inflections, tone of voice, as well as facial expression and body language.

TOYS AND GAMES

As your baby becomes more interested in interacting with the outside world, give him or her new opportunities to do so.

Introduce the high chair By this month, your baby is likely to sit well supported. Putting him or her in a high chair can be a great way to include baby in family mealtimes. It can also be an interesting new vantage point for your baby to sit and watch daily household activities and play with small toys on the high chair tray (he or she can start working on thumb-finger coordination). Choose a high chair that has a comfortable seat and straps to keep your baby safely positioned. A detachable tray that you can take to the sink to wash is convenient. Experienced parents may advise removable washable parts in general, as high chairs invariably become a backdrop for bits of cereal, splattered applesauce and mashed up yams. Hosing off the entire apparatus in the backyard or shower isn't unheard of.

Provide warm-up time If baby is shy or cautious, offer him or her plenty of time to warm up to a new situation or activity. Allow your child to sit and observe on the sidelines for a while. This will give him or her time to assess the situation and approach it on his or her own terms. Once your baby feels secure, he or she will become more involved in what's going on.

Make new friends If you haven't already done so, now might be a good time to introduce your baby to other children. Although they likely won't play together for some time yet, at this age, babies will play side by side. Also, they're intrigued by others who are similar in size and deed. Exposure to other children can help expand your baby's social horizon. But be sensitive to when your baby has had enough "socializing."

Check out activities at your local library Libraries often have special activities for infants, such as story time. Often a staff member will read a book aloud and include activities, such as singing silly songs and interacting with puppet shows. Many libraries also have play areas designed especially for younger children. This may also be a good place to meet other parents and children. Plus, having all those books to look at can't hurt, right?

The art of empowerment As your baby's understanding of his or her own power to make things happen grows, you can see how he or she begins to test the limits of what he or she can achieve. How far can I push this train over the edge of my tray before it falls out of sight? Does mommy bring it back intact every time? How much can I kick during a diaper change before I receive a frown?

Amid all of this experimentation, you will find that your son or daughter is likely to waver between feeling confident and exuberant, and needy and cautious.

By helping him or her feel secure — creating a safe environment to explore and practice, offering warm praise and support, setting firm yet practical limits — you can encourage experimentation and promote competence. In this type of setting, your baby learns to tackle challenges with enthusiasm, adding skill upon skill.

While finding the energy to repeat the same game or story over and over again may drive you crazy at times, remember the process of repetition is key to your baby's learning.

BABY EINSTEIN: HELP OR HYPE?

Chances are if you're an American parent of a young child, at some point you've found yourself holding a DVD intended to improve your baby's intelligence and wondered if it could help promote junior's brain cell connections.

Turns out human interaction still is likely to trump anything on a screen. While such DVDs might catch your baby's attention, the screen time probably won't contribute to his or her development. In fact, an infant can learn just as much — if not more — by interacting with you or other caregivers.

Research examining the specific effects of baby DVDs and other infant programming is limited. In a 2007 study, children ages 8 months to 16 months who were exposed to baby DVDs scored lower on a language development test than did babies who had no screen time. A 2009 study of children ages 2 months to 4 years showed that turning on the television reduced verbal interaction between parents and children — which may delay language development. In addition, a 2010 study found no evidence that children ages 1 to 2 learned words highlighted in a Baby Einstein DVD. In contrast, research has shown that regularly reading to young children boosts language ability for both babies and toddlers.

Many pediatricians discourage screen time for children younger than age 2. Instead of relying on Baby Einstein DVDs, concentrate on proven ways to promote infant development — such as talking, playing, singing and reading to your baby. Even if your baby doesn't understand what you're saying, or grasp the plot of a story, he or she will soak in your words and revel in your attention. These simple activities form the foundation for speech and thought.

That being said, all DVDs aren't necessarily off-limits. If your family enjoys this kind of programming, make conscious decisions about how to use it. Turn it on only occasionally — and encourage interaction by watching the programming together.

BABY'S SOCIAL DEVELOPMENT

Between 6 and 7 months old, your baby is becoming quite the expert at nonverbal communication, expressing his or her emotions through laughing, crying, shrieking, squealing and cooing.

Stranger anxiety Even as your infant becomes more expressive around you, he or she may begin to show the first signs of reticence around strangers. Your child has come to associate you with his or her own well-being and is increasingly reluctant to let you go. He or she is also becoming keenly aware of who is familiar and who isn't. By 8 or 9 months, your baby may openly reject strangers, clinging to you and even crying if unknown people come too close.

This is a normal phase of development and is a sign of the strong bond your baby has developed with you. Shyness toward strangers can last months and even years, depending on your child's temperament. Some children are naturally more shy than are others.

Discipline in infancy Discipline is a concern that arises in every parent's mind at some point, perhaps even before a baby is born. You may have definite ideas about guiding your child's behavior, or you may not. It can be a fuzzy topic, especially if you have little previous experience. During the first six months, distracting your baby from unwanted behavior is usually enough to stop it. But by the time your baby reaches the seventh month, you may need to start setting additional limits.

Keep in mind that true discipline — throughout the childhood years — is positive in its approach, with the ultimate goal of teaching rather than simply punishing. Your goal as a parent is to help your child become a secure, independent and well-adjusted adult who is able to successfully navigate almost any social environment. You can start this process early on by establishing a trusting relationship between you and your child and setting simple, consistent limits.

Create a foundation of trust During your baby's first year, you can set the foundation for a pattern of parent-child interaction that will serve you well in later, potentially more trying times. This is done in the way you nurture and react to your infant, including simple things such as following a consistent schedule, attending to your baby's needs promptly and spending time bonding as a family.

As your baby gets a little older and more independent, he or she will likely start testing the boundaries you've carefully created. This is not "misbehaving" — it's how a baby explores the world. If you manage that exploration safely, you can prepare the way for your child to become a happy, competent and confident member of your family and, ultimately, of society at large.

Be gentle yet firm By this time, your child's needs and wants have already started to separate. For example, your son or daughter might prefer to fall asleep in your arms, but he or she doesn't need to sleep in your arms. Now or even earlier, start teaching your baby to fall asleep on his or her own, in his or her own crib. Helping your baby learn to self-soothe is a first step toward independence and will make bedtime much easier in the future. In addition, it's likely that your baby will get better rest this way, and so will you.

Likewise, at this age your baby's sense of curiosity and touch has kicked into a higher gear. As your baby discovers the use of his or her hands, those hands will grab keys, hair, earrings, a nose — anything within reach. He or she will judge what's OK by your reaction. Use your tone of voice and facial expressions to express disapproval. If baby pinches your nose and it hurts, make a funny face or set your baby down and say "No," or "Ouch." Your baby can't control the impulse to touch and grab, so gently guide him or her to what is acceptable.

Being consistent and firm in your limits will make it easier for your child to remember what's OK and what's not. Establishing your authority now — showing that you have the final say — will make your life and your baby's life easier as he or she grows up.

☑️ 7TH MONTH MILESTONES

During the seventh month, your baby is busy:
- Learning to sit unsupported
- Sitting and looking around
- Perhaps supporting self in a crawling position, while reaching out with one hand
- Using hands to rake up small objects
- Getting better use of thumb and fingers
- Transferring objects from one hand to the other
- Visually tracking rapid movements
- Readily responding to sounds
- Looking for sounds outside of field of vision
- Starting to look for dropped toys
- Combining different sounds together
- Imitating patterns of speech
- Distinguishing strangers from loved ones
- Starting to test limits and boundaries

Be proactive Once your baby is crawling — then walking — your baby thinks everything in the house is there for him or her to touch, pull, mouth, open and, in general, spread around the room. This is normal and expected behavior. Take a proactive approach and prevent problems before they happen. Set up boundaries by childproofing your house. Gates, cabinet locks and outlet covers can help you establish a positive learning environment for your baby and you won't have to constantly say "No."

What to avoid Day-to-day management of an active, curious child can be frustrating at times. If you lose your patience with your infant, give the baby to a partner or set the baby in his or her crib and take a break to cool off. Never shake your baby. If you're struggling with your child's behavior or how to handle your frustrations, talk to your child's care provider. If your child has a physical or developmental disability, managing behavior can be even more challenging. You may need more intense strategies, so don't be afraid to ask for help.

CHAPTER 24

Month 8

By month eight, most of your baby's newborn reflexes have faded away and are now replaced by intentional, purposeful movements. This is a result of your baby's maturing nervous system. As more and more nerve endings become encased in protective sheaths (myelin sheaths), the nerves become more efficient at carrying messages from the brain to muscles, making your baby's movements increasingly "smarter" and more refined.

At the same time, your 7- to 8-month-old's brain is developing the ability to attach meaning to different sounds and gestures. For example, he or she may quiet at the sound of his or her own name. Or if you have a dog in the house and the dog's name is often repeated in conjunction with its appearance on the scene, your baby may begin to associate the dog with the dog's name.

Your child's thinking processes are becoming ever more complex, and you can see this by the way he or she begins to indicate likes and dislikes, and be fairly emphatic about them. This may be es-

pecially apparent in your infant's social preferences, as he or she becomes increasingly aware of the difference between familiar and unfamiliar people.

Your child's conceptualization of object permanence is setting in, as well. He or she is starting to realize that although people and things may temporarily disappear from his or her line of vision, that doesn't mean they're gone forever. This realization tends to coincide with a reluctance to be separated from you, making transitions to child care and baby sitters a little more challenging for a while.

BABY'S GROWTH AND APPEARANCE

During this time, your baby is growing steadily but probably at a slightly slower rate than in previous months. The average baby at this age tends to gain just under a pound over the course of the month and grow about ⅜ of an inch in length.

Your baby's head circumference is still increasing but only slightly compared with early months.

As long as your baby is following a steady growth curve based on measurements by your baby's care provider, there's no need to be overly concerned about specific numbers. At this stage, your baby's nutritional intake is starting to become a little more varied. But keep in mind that he or she still needs a proper balance of fats, carbohydrates and protein. Be sure to discuss your baby's diet with his or her care provider, who can help you decide how to best meet your child's nutritional needs.

Establishing good eating habits As you introduce new foods to your son or daughter, take the opportunity to establish good eating habits right away. Here are some tips to help your baby develop healthy eating patterns:

Offer a wide variety of foods You still want to introduce new foods one at a time, but that doesn't mean you have to stick to a single food for weeks on end. If your baby does well with pureed yams, try some ground chicken after a few days. Or after a successful course of mashed peas, provide a dessert of mashed bananas.

Include a good balance of foods Prioritize fruits, vegetables, lean meats and healthy carbohydrates over processed foods and baked goods. Instead of a cut-up hot dog, for example, offer bits of turkey. Or instead of a soft cookie, offer pureed peaches. Minimize salt and offer sweets in moderation. Examples of not-so-obvious salt-rich foods include processed cheese, cottage cheese, canned vegetables and soups, and instant puddings.

Avoid overfeeding Watch your baby for cues to know when he or she is full.

Month 8

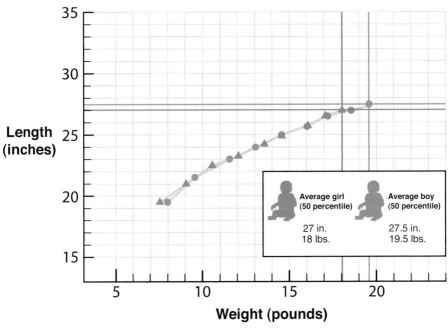

Average girl (50 percentile): 27 in. 18 lbs.

Average boy (50 percentile): 27.5 in. 19.5 lbs.

While you control what your baby eats, let your baby determine how much.

Enjoy food for its nutrition But avoid using it as a reward or as a comfort item. Instead, reward and comfort your baby with hugs, kisses and attention.

Introducing a cup You can give your baby a cup as soon as he or she starts eating solid foods. A two-handled cup is usually easy for baby to grasp. This will help your child become familiar with the idea of using a cup. But at this age, your baby will probably bang, drop and dump the cup more than drink from it. It will probably be another few months before he or she is using it properly.

Even if your baby uses a cup at mealtimes, you may decide to continue breastfeeding or using a bottle for supplemental feedings, simply because baby can't get much out of the cup just yet. Feeding your baby breast milk or formula from a cup at mealtime may help pave the way for weaning when you're ready.

BABY'S MOVEMENT

Your child's rapid development during these months can be astonishing. In just a few weeks, he or she may go from barely sitting up without your help to bustling around the room by scooting, crawling and cruising.

Sitting up By 8 months, your baby is literally sitting pretty and is steadier than ever on his or her bottom. His or her sense of balance is improving, and he or she will be able to sit up unsupported for longer periods of time without falling over. Your baby may even start to reach with his or her arms while sitting to try to grasp nearby toys. These exercises will help further strengthen your baby's core muscles, which are important for standing, walking and any kind of forward-propelling movement.

Getting around After your baby learns to sit up without much effort, you'll notice other movements that are predecessors to crawling — rolling, twisting, crouching, and rocking back and forth on the knees. In fact, it will be hard for your baby to be still for long. If lying tummy-down, he or she will push up on hands and arms to look around. Lying faceup is an incentive to kick and grab for toes. Your baby can now also flip around at will. Some babies even roll repeatedly as a means of getting from one place to another.

Because your youngster is getting so mobile, it's important to take appropriate safety precautions, such as swapping the changing table for the floor or bed to change diapers and installing safety gates at the top and bottom of stairs to avoid an accidental, and potentially serious, tumble. (See more about making your home safe in Chapter 15.)

Hand and finger coordination Once your baby is able to sit well, he or she is also able to maintain upper torso balance while coordinating simultaneous movements of arms and hands. Most babies this age are able to hold a toy in each hand. Eventually they'll develop enough coordination to bring both hands inward and bang the toys against each other.

During this month, your baby probably still uses a raking motion to bring small objects closer. But he or she is also working on coordinating the thumb and first or second finger to pick up small objects (pincer grasp). Baby will practice this technique until he or she achieves such a grasp. This usually happens by his or her first birthday.

Your baby is also learning to let go of items at will. This is evident by his or her enthusiasm for dropping and throwing things.

BABY'S SENSORY DEVELOPMENT

During this month, your baby's senses continue to contribute lots of information to his or her brain. This stimulates the development of other skills, such as reaching and crawling, and drawing conclusions about spatial relationships.

Vision Your son's or daughter's vision is now almost adult-like in clarity and depth perception. By 8 months, most babies' vision is 20/40. Although he or she still sees things close up better than far away, your baby's vision should be clear enough to recognize people and objects across the room. Increased depth perception helps your baby accurately reach for objects and judge distances correctly when moving forward.

Touch Between 7 and 8 months old, your budding physicist is learning rapidly about the way matter takes up space, how different surfaces feel and how they're related. For example, he or she may start to realize that balls are round and roll, boxes have flat surfaces, and some toys have a top and a bottom part. Objects with tags, handles and parts that can be manipulated are especially intriguing at this point.

BABY'S MENTAL DEVELOPMENT

Around this time, your son or daughter is beginning to understand that certain things have meaning beyond the immediate sensory experience. For example, words and gestures, besides being seen and heard, can convey messages. And things your baby once thought were there and then gone when out of sight are actually still there even if hidden from view. Your child's brain is starting to make connections between what is seen and unseen and draw conclusions from repeated experiences. Although it will be awhile before your child can actively formulate and express symbolic thought — such as pretend play, which usually develops in the second year — the very first formations of abstract thought are emerging.

Attaching meaning By 8 months or so, you may notice your child quiet or perk up at the sound of his or her name, or even turn toward you when you say it. He or she doesn't fully understand at this point that this word refers to himself or herself, but your baby is becoming familiar with hearing that word when you actively seek a face-to-face connection with him or her.

Other words are starting to become significant, too. You'll probably notice that your baby is gaining a better understanding of the word no. He or she may hesitate when he or she hears the word, especially when it's delivered with a sharp inflection. At this age, baby begins to associate words with specific objects and actions, including gestures (see "Baby sign language" on page 296). About half the babies at this age begin to wave bye-bye.

Object permanence Previously, if your baby dropped something, he or she likely thought it was gone entirely and made no effort to look for it. Now he or she is starting to realize that, in fact, it may still be there and will look for a hidden toy. Games of peekaboo take on a new significance as your baby realizes that if he or she pulls the blanket away — Aha! Mom is still there! And now that baby knows you're still around even if you leave the room, he or she may make more of a fuss to get you to come back.

Language skills By this time, your baby is likely becoming a proficient babbler, repeating not just single sounds but combining syllables, such as *bah-dah.* Some babies are very expressive and jabber away like an excited squirrel. Others are a little quieter and may listen more than chatter. But this doesn't mean they're not absorbing what's being said around them. Be sure to talk to your little shy guy as much as you might to a little jabberwocky, encouraging him or her to communicate verbally as well as non-verbally.

BABY'S SOCIAL DEVELOPMENT

As your baby learns new skills and becomes more mobile, he or she is torn between two desires: to be with you and to experience some independence. You may notice this struggle surface in many situations as your baby searches for both

---

BABY SIGN LANGUAGE

By age 8 months or so, many infants begin to know what they want, need and feel, but they don't necessarily have the verbal skills to express themselves. Baby sign language allows children to use their hands to bridge the communication gap. Slightly older children who have developmental delays may benefit, too. Limited research suggests that using baby sign language may improve a child's ability to communicate and ease frustration, particularly between ages 8 months and 2 years. Teaching and practicing baby sign language also can be fun and give you and your child an opportunity to bond.

At the same time, don't neglect your baby's verbal skills. Continue to talk to your child, and encourage him or her to use spoken words (or what may only sound like words in the beginning) to express himself or herself.

A variety of books, websites, community classes and other sources are available to help you learn baby sign language. You can also use variations of American Sign Language. Start with signs to describe routine requests, activities and objects in your child's life — such as more, drink, eat, mother and father.

To get the most out of your baby sign language experience, keep these tips in mind:

▶ *Set realistic expectations.* Feel free to start signing with your child at any age — but remember that most children aren't able to communicate with baby sign language until about 8 or 9 months.

▶ *Stay patient.* Don't get upset if your child uses signs incorrectly or doesn't start using them right away. The goal is improved communication and reduced frustration — not perfection.

▶ *Be consistent.* Repetition is the best way to ensure your child's success in using baby sign language. Encourage your child's other caregivers to use the same signs, too.

 **TOYS AND GAMES**

Around this age, most babies enjoy toys they can bang, poke, twist, squeeze, drop, shake, open, close, empty and fill. Toys should be lightweight with no sharp edges. Remember that all toys will end up in your baby's mouth, so don't give your baby toys with small parts.

For the most part, your child's playtime will center around playing on the floor, working on crawling, sitting and standing. You can encourage these skills by putting a toy just beyond your baby's reach and encouraging the baby to move toward it. Other playtime ideas include:

Peekaboo As mentioned previously, games of peekaboo take on a new dimension around the time your baby develops a sense of object permanence. He or she will enjoy games in which objects and people "disappear" and your baby finds them again. Use a small blanket to cover toys, and let your baby uncover and discover them. Your baby may even cover them up again only to rediscover them.

Mirror games Your little one is starting to learn the concept of three-dimensional space. Contrast two-dimensional images with three-dimensional ones by playing games in the mirror. If your son or daughter is looking in a mirror and you suddenly appear in the mirror too, he or she is likely to turn around and look for you instead of believing you're in the mirror itself.

Buckets of stuff Your baby is also learning how things relate to one another. Infants at this age start to understand that smaller objects fit inside bigger ones. Stacking toys starts to appeal at this age. Games in which toys can be put into a container and dumped back out again are popular, as well. For a quick and easy version, fill a plastic mixing bowl with odds and ends from the kitchen — measuring spoons, plastic lids, small containers, empty baby bottles — and let your baby sort through it, dump it out and put it all back in again.

Book of animals As your baby begins to understand that things have names and labels attached to them, introduce him or her to a book with simple pictures of various animals and their names. You can read it together. As you point to the picture and name the animal, your baby will eventually start to associate the name with the animal. In time, you can introduce animal sounds, too. For a more lyrical version, read *Brown Bear, Brown Bear, What Do You See?*, by Bill Martin Jr., and Eric Carle, which contains rhythmic prose and colorful illustrations that are a favorite of children and parents alike.

predictability and adventure. Living with this new assertiveness may take a bit of adjustment for all parties involved. But understanding it as a normal phase of development helps most parents take the new challenges in stride.

Separation anxiety At 8 months, most babies are clearly attached to the parent providing most of his or her care. Your baby may seem most assertive when you make any attempt to separate from the baby, whether it be for a few hours or a few minutes. He or she may become more clingy — not wanting to let you out of sight — and may grasp or cry if you manage to break away. Your baby may even begin to prefer the parent he or she spends the most time with. Both parents should understand that this situation is normal and will diminish with time.

Every baby goes through a stage of "separation anxiety," which often begins around this age, peaks between 10 and

ENJOYING A RELAXING NIGHT OUT

Because babies react so strongly to separation from their parents, parents are often reluctant to leave their babies with baby sitters. You might even wonder if a night out is worth the heartbreak your baby seems to endure when left with a sitter. You can help yourself and your baby through this stage by taking these steps:

Practice Take advantage of occasions at home to leave your baby alone for a few minutes (in a safe zone, of course) while he or she plays. If your baby becomes upset at your absence, call out to him or her, but wait a few seconds before coming back. Eventually, your baby will learn that it's OK to be away from you and that you always do come back.

Get acquainted If a baby sitter is new, take some time to let your baby become acquainted with him or her. Hold your baby on your lap while you and the baby sitter talk, and then gradually engage the baby in the conversation. Once your baby seems comfortable with the sitter's presence, put your baby on the floor with a favorite toy and the baby sitter, and let them get to know each other. Once you're comfortable with your baby sitter and you feel assured your baby is getting loving, qualified and competent care, you will be less bothered if your baby should cry when you leave.

Say goodbye When you're ready to leave, tell your baby goodbye and provide reassurance of your eventual return. Although it's tempting to just sneak out when baby is preoccupied with something else, this approach won't help your baby overcome this anxiety (instead, he or she may become more clingy, never sure when you might leave). At the same time, there's no need to prolong the farewell. Have a distraction ready to go — a bath or new toy — and a few minutes after your departure, your baby's short attention span will be directed elsewhere.

18 months, and gradually fades as the second birthday approaches. Some babies pass through this phase fairly quickly, but others remain reluctant to part for quite some time.

Part of your baby's frustration stems from not having the motor skills to follow you or keep up with you, coupled with the budding realization that you're still there even if baby can't see you. The positive side of this development is that your baby has clearly established a strong bond with you and wants to make sure you stick around for the long haul. Eventually, as your baby realizes that you're a permanent part of his or her life, despite temporary separations, this anxiety will ease.

Smoothing the way This strong attachment to the primary caregiver can result in a seeming dislike for everyone else, which can be crushing to grandparents, other relatives and friends who feel close to the baby. You can ease feelings of rejection by explaining separation anxiety as a normal phase and helping to create a time of adjustment and transition.

If someone approaches your baby quickly, eagerly trying to engage the baby, the baby will probably cling to you even more tightly. Encourage others to spend some time just talking with you while you let your baby watch and listen. Your baby may eventually open up and jabber or want to play.

Peekaboo can be an icebreaker at this age because this game is so tempting for most babies. But don't be surprised if your baby will play this game only when you're close by. Assure others that your baby will outgrow this exclusivity.

CHAPTER 25

Month 9

Your baby has a lot going on these days. And get ready for a big change! During the ninth month is when most babies learn to crawl, and once your baby is on the move, life changes forever. No longer is your baby content to stay in one spot. There are so many places to go, so many things to see, so much stuff to get into! Daily life with an emerging toddler can be a challenge. But it's also a happy time of having fun and discovering new skills. With a little bit of prep work, you and baby will be all set to enjoy life on the go.

BABY'S GROWTH AND APPEARANCE

During this month, your baby is growing steadily at about the same rate as the previous month. The average baby at this age tends to gain just under a pound a month, and grow about ⅜ of an inch in length. Your baby's head circumference is still increasing slightly every month.

By now, your baby may have a nice head of hair. And now that he or she can flip and turn at will, bald patches are a thing of the past. At 9 months old, most babies still look like pudgy little butterballs. But within a few short months of growing, walking and running, your baby will stretch out into a full-blown toddler.

BABY'S MOVEMENT

It's around this time that many babies catapult forward to a new level of mobility and independence. All that wiggling and fidgeting, rocking and rolling is paying off. Your baby is up and moving!

Crawling Crawling uses the complex give-and-take movements of all four limbs that are necessary for walking later. It takes some time to understand how to make those little arms and legs work together. The average age an infant starts to crawl is 9 months.

At first, a baby's arms are stronger than the legs, which makes for some funny crawling variations. Many babies begin crawling by using just their arms, scooting across the floor like a soldier in training. Others may find themselves up on their knees, give their arms a good push and begin moving backward.

Eventually, most babies will become experts at using their legs and arms simultaneously when they crawl. You might look away for a minute, then look back and wonder, "Where did my baby go?"

If your baby isn't interested in crawling, or crawls just for a short time before moving on to something else, remember that moving is the goal. How your baby moves isn't as important as the fact that he or she is interested in getting around.

Standing At 8 or 9 months, if you stand your baby up next to the sofa, baby will probably be able to stand there, using the furniture for support. When your child realizes how much fun standing is, he or she will probably start figuring out how to pull up to a standing position without your help.

By 8 months, most babies can stand up with support. At 9 months, more than half of all babies can pull themselves into a standing position, and some may even begin "cruising" around the room, holding on to furniture for support.

At first, your baby may not know how to sit down from a standing position and, instead, may just fall on his or her bottom. Soon he or she will learn how to lower himself or herself down without falling. You can show your baby how to do this by gently helping him or her bend at the knees and then squat down to a sitting position.

Sitting By now your son or daughter is likely a proficient sitter. Indeed, at this

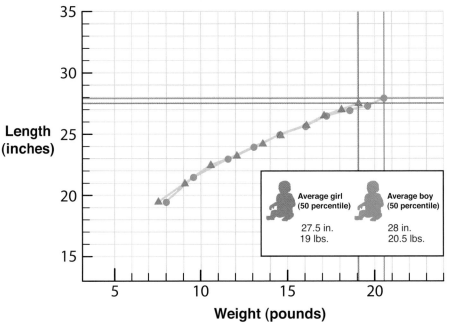

Month 9

Length (inches) / Weight (pounds)

Average girl (50 percentile)
27.5 in.
19 lbs.

Average boy (50 percentile)
28 in.
20.5 lbs.

© MFMER

age, babies love to sit and play and may do so for extended periods of time. From a seated position, your baby has a wider vantage point from which to observe and interact with the world and delights in taking full control of his or her view. Between ages 8 and 9 months, your child is learning to point to desired objects and lean forward while sitting to reach toward you or an interesting toy.

As a result of your child's improved stability and balance, he or she can now sit unsupported and turn his or her head to look at things. He or she may even twist his or her torso to peer around — although leaning sideways may not be possible quite yet.

Hand skills Baby is working steadily on his or her thumb-finger (pincer) grasp.

With the pincer grasp, your baby can — and probably will — pick up objects as small as a piece of lint. Self-feeding also is likely to become a popular activity during this month, if it hasn't already. And by now, your baby may have learned to hold a cup or bottle and drink independently. Because almost everything your baby touches goes directly into the mouth for further exploration, be sure to remove anything from baby's reach that could cause choking.

Your baby is also learning to move his or her fingers individually, so that he or she can soon hold a string between finger and thumb and pull a toy along. Letting go voluntarily is becoming easier, allowing baby to set one thing down in order to pick up another. Other impressive hand skills your child may develop during this month include pointing toward things he or she wants, clapping, and waving goodbye. These are also forms of communication. Encourage your child's development in this area by using these skills yourself, such as pointing at different objects and naming them, or playing clapping games.

A common milestone achieved during this month is the ability to bang toys together. This is no mean feat, as working both arms simultaneously in this fashion requires an infant to sit upright steadily without support and display a fair amount of balance.

BABY'S SENSORY DEVELOPMENT

By 8 to 9 months, your child's sensory skills are fairly evolved and a great help in practicing his or her new motor, mental and social skills. Combined with your child's expanding memory skills and understanding of object permanence, his or her sensory abilities make for easy recognition of recurring sights, sounds and patterns. They're helping your young one in gaining knowledge of the general order of things.

BATTLE OF THE SPOONS

Some babies are determined to eat without help — or at least play with eating utensils without your interference. Every time you try to slide that spoon in with some food, up comes the little hand to grab it, and splat goes the food. How to get your baby to eat?

If this is the case, provide different ways for your baby to get food and entertain himself or herself at the same time. Put some finger foods on the baby's tray. Give baby his or her own spoon and use a spoon yourself. You may need to be persistent in finding opportunities to get some food into the baby's mouth.

You can try to teach your baby to eat with a spoon, but if you're not successful, let your baby eat with hands and fingers. For now, these handy utensils are generally faster.

If your baby truly isn't doing any eating, only playing, he or she probably isn't hungry at the moment. You can call it quits for this particular meal and try again later.

Vision Your baby's visual acuity is constantly improving, and he or she can see things clearly from across the room. At this age, your baby is quick to recognize familiar faces and objects. He or she may adjust his or her position to get a better look at something and is more likely to look for a hidden toy.

Crawling and moving about helps develop your baby's depth perception, as he or she studies one hand moving forward and then the next, over the varying ground beneath. Better depth perception leads to an increased awareness of heights and a well-timed, more cautious approach to obstacles.

Hearing Your son or daughter now recognizes sound without difficulty and probably responds to his or her own name. He or she may respond to other familiar words, as well, such as bottle, mama, dada and no.

Touch Baby is learning how to wrap his or her hands around a cup or bottle, how to pick up a spoon and how to handle different toys appropriately.

FINGER FOODS FOR LITTLE ONES

As your baby develops a better pincer grasp and more advanced chewing skills, you can start offering finger foods. Self-feeding can be great entertainment. What could be more fun than exploring things that actually are supposed to go in the mouth (although they often end up on the floor)? And it helps foster your child's sense of independence and ability to accomplish a task on his or her own.

Parents were once told to avoid feeding young children eggs, fish and peanut butter. Today, however, researchers say there's no convincing evidence that avoiding these foods during early childhood will help prevent food allergies. Do keep in mind, however, your baby's ability to handle textures and foods of various sizes. Soft and mushy is the way to go. Small, hard, round or chewy bits of food can be choking hazards. Here are some suggestions for finger foods to get you started:

- Well-cooked diced vegetables (yams, potatoes, carrots, green beans)
- Soft ripe fruits, cut up into small pieces (berries, mangos, peaches, bananas)
- Whole-grain breakfast cereals (without nuts or chunks)
- Teething biscuits or crackers
- Cut-up, well-cooked pasta

BABY'S MENTAL DEVELOPMENT

By 9 months, your infant is sophisticated enough to be bored. (So quickly does it set in!) This is because his or her memory is developing and what was once new and interesting isn't so much anymore. Baby is on the hunt for new stimulation and is gung-ho to try out new games and skills.

This is certainly a fun age, but it can also be frustrating for baby and parents alike if baby moves quickly from one thing to the next, leaving little time for mom or dad to get other things done. Don't fret too much, though. As your child develops further and becomes more mobile and independent, he or she will be more capable of creating his or her own fun. In the meantime, swap out some of your child's simpler toys for more complex ones (but still age-appropriate), or fill a basket with board books that your child can easily access on his or her own. For the time being, you might also spend a little extra time on the floor each day with your youngster to bridge the gap until he or she is better able to self-entertain.

Language and understanding About 3 out of 4 infants are jabbering away by age 8 months or so. Most are starting to combine syllables and vocalize in strings of sounds pulled together. By 9 months, you may even notice your baby start to use the words *mama* and *dada* to refer specifically to you.

Your child's understanding of language is increasing, as well, even more rapidly than his or her vocal expressions. By now, baby likely understands the meaning of a number of words, including his or her own name, as mentioned previously. He or she is also starting to understand simple games and rhymes and will laugh and giggle at appropriate parts. For example, about half of babies can

---

GET READY

It's tempting to think that as your baby gets older, he or she will require less time and attention. But once your son or daughter is on the move, he or she actually requires more supervision. Before, your baby would wait for you to come. Now that he or she is mobile, he or she can come to you. You are still your child's primary object of love and favorite companion, and there is so much your baby wants to share as he or she scoots around and explores.

Very active or very curious babies may need especially careful supervision. Once they discover their ability to move, they are off and into everything, touching, pulling, tasting, testing. Babies on the go need your presence to ensure that heads don't get bonked, fingers don't get pinched, small objects don't get swallowed and prized possessions remain intact.

This period of intense supervision generally lasts until about 3 years of age, when children are more accustomed to limits and spend more time playing alone or with friends. If you think you'll never make it to 3 years, take heart, you will. This is a time-intensive period of parenting, but it's also one of great joy as you watch your child grow and develop into a walking, talking toddler with some very definite opinions of his or her own.

TOYS AND GAMES

Physical games are fun at this stage of your baby's development and can help him or her hone new motor skills. At the same time, your child's communication and language skills are rapidly progressing, so include games that stimulate his or her mind, too. Try some of these.

Indoor gym Once your baby learns to crawl, getting through, in and around things is a great source of entertainment. Create your own gym with stuff you already have on hand:

- Drape a blanket or a sheet over a table to make a tunnel. Place an unbreakable mirror inside for a visual surprise.
- Create an obstacle course with pillows, laundry baskets and rolled-up towels.
- Use yourself. Lie down with an interesting toy in front of you and baby behind you. Encourage your baby to climb over your legs to get it.

Walk together Your baby may not be walking independently just yet. But you can get him or her acquainted with the necessary leg movements by holding his or her hands and helping your child take small steps forward.

Clapping games To help your baby practice arm coordination and build balance skills, teach him or her clapping games, such as patty-cake or Miss Mary Mack.

Nursery rhymes Never underestimate the power of a few silly rhymes to make your child laugh. There are plenty of old-

ies but goodies, such as "Old McDonald" and "Little Miss Muffet." If you find yourself a little rusty on some of these, you can look them up on the Internet or borrow a book from the library. In fact, chances are, there's a mobile app out there to help you learn some rhymes on the go, whether in a crowded restaurant or on a long drive home.

play clapping games, such as patty-cake, by 9 months.

As the understanding of object permanence becomes more established in your baby's mind, he or she will persist longer in searching for something he or she knows is there, such as a key you've folded in your hand. Object permanence also helps your baby understand the physical nature of the world, such as the ability of balls to roll, and its social nature. When your baby waves bye-bye as you walk out the door, he or she acknowledges you're leaving but also is coming to expect that you'll be back.

BABY'S SOCIAL DEVELOPMENT

Once your baby starts to crawl and move around, limits begin to play a larger role in both baby's life and yours. Before, there wasn't much your baby could do without your help. Now that he or she can crawl and climb and discover without you, there are bound to be necessary limits — "No, you can't climb the bookshelf," or "No, don't pull the cat's tail."

Oh, the frustration This can be an adjustment for children and parents alike. Not having been stopped from doing much before, a 9-month-old is understandably confused and frustrated when all of a sudden Mom and Dad are shouting "No!" when he or she reaches for an interesting electric cord, or they make unhappy faces when an innocent roll of toilet paper is torn apart. Your child has no way to differentiate between what's safe and what's not, and won't really understand the reasons behind your rules until much later, around age 4 or 5 years.

With his or her increased capability for expression, your infant is likely to let

you know just how he or she feels about these new restrictions, too. At this point, your child has clear likes and dislikes and will communicate them through body language — pointing, clapping, making faces, stiffening or arching his or her back — and vocalizations such as squealing, howling and jabbering.

To a parent, this period can be frustrating, as well. The orderly routine you finally seemed able to carve out is now being completely turned on its head. Turn your back for a moment, and the basket of folded laundry that you had set on the floor (in blissful ignorance) is now strewn around the dining area. The mail littering the coffee table and living room floor is a shocking discovery that your child can now pull to stand.

Also, it can be difficult to move from being the nurturing parent to being the limit setter, as well, and having to deny some of your child's wishes.

Making life easier Neither you nor your baby will be happy in a home in which you must constantly keep a close watch and remind baby to keep away from dangerous situations and objects. So many things around the house are tempting, and it's unreasonable to expect much self-control from your child at this age. Instead, try these strategies:

Childproof regularly Maintaining a safe space for your child to explore on his or her own will make things easier for all parties involved. Soon after babies learn to crawl, they can also climb stairs. Keep gates at the top and bottom of stairs and use them properly. Make sure heavy bookcases and TV stands are securely anchored to the wall so that curious climbers can't pull them down. Pad coffee table corners, and remove dangerous items from the reach of little fingers.

Offer safe opportunities for exploration Think about ways you can let your child explore without getting into trouble. Some parents reserve a low kitchen cabinet for items the baby can safely get into. Or set up an "activity center" with pillows to climb and empty boxes to investigate. If the weather is nice, a small pop up tent in the yard can provide lots of fun.

Provide comfort but stay firm When your child is frustrated, provide some help and comfort but realize that overcoming frustration is a skill he or she will need to develop. Distraction or redirection from a forbidden object or activity usually works well. Kids need consistency, however, so stay firm with the safety limits you've set.

Keep your baby busy Most 9-month-olds are active and need a lot of stimulation, but they don't like to be apart from Mom or Dad. It's difficult to give your baby that attention and get anything else accomplished. Fill a small basket with toys for each room of the house; then take the baby with you as you go from room to room, and let your baby play while you work.

Family life Although your baby may not feel comfortable around strangers, he or she loves to be around you and the rest of the family. Your baby may show affection by patting you on the back or even start imitating fond gestures such as hugs and kisses. He or she definitely wants to be a part of the family commotion.

Big brothers and sisters still love the baby and want to play, but the initial enchantment may largely be over, especially once baby can scoot around and get into a sibling's toys. Try to encourage a spirit of cooperation with an older child.

CHAPTER 26

Month 10

Many of the motor skills your baby has been working on since birth are starting to come together this month. These basic skills enable his or her transition from infancy into toddlerhood. From this point forward, your child is moving steadily toward an upright view of the world. And even though he or she may still only see knees and legs and the lower half of the world for a while, his or her ability to maneuver about is a very exciting development.

During month 10, many babies practice pulling themselves up to stand with the help of furniture or a parent's leg. By the end of the month, some babies are even able to stand on their own for a few seconds.

Babies also start to be big copycats around this time, which can provide for some enjoyable and laughable moments. Copying the facial expressions, gestures and vocalizations of adults and older children is one of the primary ways a baby learns how to fit into the family and society at large.

BABY'S GROWTH AND APPEARANCE

Baby is growing at much the same rate as last month — gaining just under a pound a month, and growing about ⅜ of an inch in length. Your baby's head circumference is still increasing slightly every month.

When your baby first starts to stand and then walk, you might notice that his or her legs appear slightly bowed. This is normal. In most babies, legs become straighter within the next year or so.

BABY'S MOVEMENT

By month 10, you can really start to see how your baby's early motor accomplishments are building on each other. Good head control, along with strong muscles conditioned by months of pushing up, looking around, wriggling and rolling, allow your baby to become proficient at more advanced motor skills, such as crawling, standing and walking.

Most babies can now sit unsupported with a straight back for an indefinite period. For baby, this is a comfortable position from which to play and engage the world. In a matter of weeks, your baby is becoming an efficient crawler, moving with singular ambition from one place to another. And he or she can bear weight on his or her legs, holding on to something to stand upright. Refinements of these basic skills accumulate this month.

Pulling to sit By the end of month 10, most babies have learned how to pull themselves into a sitting position — bringing the torso up from lying down, flopping over from crawling, or squatting down from a supported standing position. Being able to switch positions at will gives your child a little taste of the mobile freedom and independence ahead.

Pulling to stand Although baby probably still needs support while standing, he or she is working steadily at pulling himself or herself up to stand. He or she might do this by grasping whatever support is handy, such as the rails of the crib, your pant leg or even a patient dog's tail. Since your baby doesn't know the difference between what's safe to climb and what's not, it's important to keep safety a priority. Empty the crib of things your baby might use to climb too high and unintentionally pitch forward out of the crib. Also, keep heavy bookshelves and cabinets anchored to the wall so that baby doesn't accidentally pull down an unsteady structure.

Picking up, pointing and poking By month 10, most babies are refining their heavy-handed grasp of small objects and graduating to a more delicate thumb-finger grasp. As well as manipulating

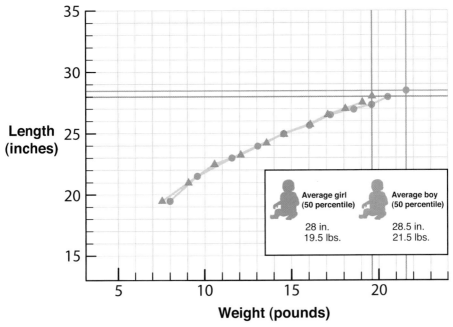

Month 10

Length (inches)

Weight (pounds)

Average girl (50 percentile)
28 in.
19.5 lbs.

Average boy (50 percentile)
28.5 in.
21.5 lbs.

© MFMER

items with a greater degree of accuracy, babies are also getting better at releasing things at will. Letting go at this age (and for a while to come), however, tends to mean throwing a toy aside rather than gently laying it down.

Your little one has also discovered the power of the index finger, using it to point, prod and poke at items of interest (yourself included). Picture books are great for practicing pointing and learning the names of things. Use the same words each time for each picture, and your son or daughter will soon start helping you out. Some books feature different textures, such as furry or rough patches, or foldout flaps, which make them doubly interesting for baby.

BABY'S SENSORY DEVELOPMENT

As your child approaches the end of his or her first year, he or she is becoming skilled at using his or her senses to learn and explore.

Hearing By 10 months, your baby recognizes sounds without difficulty, such as the sound of his or her name, familiar songs and words, and even the doorbell.

Your son or daughter is also becoming more selective as to what sounds he or she listens to. For example, he or she can listen to other people talking and pay attention to conversations without being distracted by other noises.

PREPARE FOR SOME BUMPS

As your baby starts to stand and move around on two feet, falls and short tumbles naturally become more frequent. This isn't really a big deal, as your baby doesn't have very far to fall and is unlikely to get hurt landing on his or her bottom.

Often, when your baby falls, he or she will look at you first to gauge your reaction before committing to his or her own. Among childhood experts, this is called social referencing. Babies will look to trusted adults for emotional guidance before proceeding with a novel experience.

You can help your child understand that a minor tumble is no obstacle to getting back up by treating it matter-of-factly and offering cheerful reassurance. Some babies will cry no matter what. But if you offer loving encouragement accompanied by positive facial expressions, your baby will quickly learn to shrug off such small setbacks.

At the same time, be sure to provide a forgiving environment for your baby to knock about in. For example, pad sharp coffee table corners and keep loose cords out of sight and reach to avoid accidents.

Touch With the expansion of your baby's mental and fine motor skills — such as increased memory and individual finger skills — he or she now enjoys more control over his or her exploratory activities. Some things are even starting to become routine. By now, for example, your child knows that a maraca is to be shaken, a cup goes to the mouth, buttons are pushed and a favorite doll is gently patted (just like Mommy does it).

Your baby also enjoys self-feeding. And even though it's bound to be messy, it's important to let him or her practice, as this is the only way your baby will get better at it. To make cleanup a little easier, consider spreading a splat mat or newspapers under your baby's highchair.

BABY'S MENTAL DEVELOPMENT

It's during the last quarter of your baby's first year that his or her language skills really start to blossom. Not only is your baby's comprehension of what's being said expanding, he or she may also be on the way to saying his or her first words. First words are cause for excitement, and deservedly so. There's so much to say!

Your child's ability to think as a separate individual is becoming more sophisticated, and you may see clues of this expressed through your baby's nonverbal communication, as well.

First words During this month, many new parents start to hear baby sounds bound to warm their hearts. About half of babies use *dada* and *mama* to refer specifically to father and mother at this point. A few babies even start to use one other word in addition to *dada* and *mama*, such as *baba* for bottle or *mok* for milk. These words are often hard to understand at first, and it may be a while before you figure out your son or daughter is saying something meaningful. In general, a word at this age is any sound used

TOYS AND GAMES

Go for toys and games that help enrich your child's growing awareness of the way things work, from toys that stimulate exploration of different functions to ones that allow baby to mimic grown-up behaviors. Games made up of simple actions can be fun, and silly songs with accompanying gestures are sure to be a hit.

Busy toys With your child's growing dexterity, he or she may enjoy toys that feature multiple functions, such as pushing buttons, opening drawers, making noises and lifting lids. Stacking toys and nesting toys are fun for baby to assemble and disassemble.

Mimic Offer your child toys that resemble adult accessories, such as a toy phone, plastic keys, a comb, toothbrush or teacup. See what your child does with them. Or make a silly face or gesture and encourage your child to imitate you. Wait to see if he or she makes a funny face or odd gesture at you. Return the favor and imitate him or her.

Give and take Nine- to 10-month-olds often enjoy simple games that involve passing an object or toy back-and-forth between you and him or her. Offer your child a ball. Once he or she grasps it, ask for it back. This may sound a bit tedious to an adult, but your baby loves it, and it helps him or her learn the concept of game play and following simple instructions.

Silly songs Babies at this age delight in silly songs that have accompanying hand gestures. These help stimulate not only the funny bone, but hand-eye coordination and fine motor skills, as well. "Itsy, Bitsy Spider," "I'm a Little Teapot" and "This Little Piggy" will never go out of style with this crowd.

A TWO-WAY STREET

Multiple studies have shown that a child's mental development and grasp of language, specifically, are strongly associated with the amount of language a child is exposed to in the first three years of life. The greater variety of adult words an infant or toddler hears early on, the greater his or her language skills tend to be in the preschool years.

Because of this strong association, parents are often encouraged to expose their children to as much language as possible, through reading, storytelling or even just narrating the day's activities.

One study in particular, published in the journal *Pediatrics*, sought to expand on the kind of adult language exposure that might be most beneficial to a young child. If simply hearing adult vocabulary is the only requirement for child language acquisition, then you could reasonably assume that turning on the TV would help your baby develop his or her language skills. But evidence indicates that heavy TV exposure tends to have a negative impact on a child's language, reading and math skills.

To conduct their research, the authors of the *Pediatrics* study fitted each participant in the study, ranging in age from 2 to 48 months, with a digital recorder worn throughout the day. Using special software, the investigators differentiated between three types of speech that a child might hear: adult speech, television and adult-child conversations. During the study, the children's language development was assessed several times by a speech-language pathologist.

When evaluated alone, adult speech had a positive impact on language development and TV had a negative impact, as you might expect. But when all three types of verbal input were evaluated simultaneously, only adult-child conversations continued to have a significant effect on a child's language skills.

This suggests that more important than merely hearing adult vocabulary is hearing adult speech that elicits a child's response. More conversations with you, for example, means more opportunities for your child to practice verbalizing and conversing. It also means more chances for your child to learn as you correct his or her mistakes. From a parent's perspective, frequent back-and-forths with your child helps keep you in tune with your child's evolving abilities. This awareness helps you calibrate your speech so that it's neither too simplistic nor too difficult for your child.

Granted, when your child's vocabulary consists of one word, having a full-blown conversation may seem a little hard. But as you've probably noticed, communicating with your child need not always involve words. Teaching your child that conversation is a two-way street can be done with facial expressions, sounds and gestures. Doing this will set the foundation for further language skills as your child's vocabulary expands.

Bottom line: Keep on reading and talking to your child, but be sure to include some "conversation" time, as well!

consistently to refer to the same person, object or event.

When opportunity presents itself, you can reinforce the correct way to say the words your baby is learning. For example, readily acknowledge your child's request for a *baba*, and then say the correct word, *bottle*, when offering it back to him or her. Eventually, your child's language skills will develop enough for him or her to use the correct version.

Conversation As a result of listening to you talk, your child's own babbling will start to sound more like the ups and downs of a real conversation. Even if most of it makes no sense, join in the conversation and repeat your baby's sounds back to him or her. Try to discern any words that might be popping up in the middle of all the jabbering. Respond positively to your baby's talking, and pause at times to encourage a rhythm like that of real conversation. Your baby will be delighted that you're interested and paying attention.

Nonverbal communication Although your baby still has few words with which to express himself or herself, this won't stop him or her from communicating with you. Now that your baby is starting to discover personal likes or dislikes, he or she will communicate wants and desires through pointing, shaking his or her head no, reaching and making sounds, and pulling or holding arms out to be picked up.

Not only does this nonverbal communication show that your child is trying to relay ideas to you, but also indicates an increase in your child's self-perception. He or she is now able to formulate thoughts related distinctly to himself or herself, apart from others, and to his or her own personal desires. Your child is also developing thinking skills sophisticated enough to communicate those wants and devise ways to achieve them.

Simon says Along with simple expressions of his or her own thoughts, your son or daughter is beginning to understand brief requests of action from you. He or she may do what you ask if you use hand gestures with your request, and it involves some sort of interaction with you. If you ask your child for one of his or her crackers and hold out your hand, indicating what you want, he or she may comply.

BABY'S SOCIAL DEVELOPMENT

As your child's skills and independence increase, he or she will still look to you for safety and security. Even if you have officially "bonded" at this point, hugs, kisses and warm affection are still vital to expanding on the trust your baby has placed in you. Giggles and laughter and quiet times together deepen your relationship and further cement the bond you have.

Since birth, your baby has been learning through listening to and watching you. In earlier months, it may have felt like your baby wasn't paying much attention to your day-to-day activities. But soon you'll notice you have a "mini-me" at your heels, imitating many of the activities you thought had gone unnoticed.

Mimicking Around this age, babies like to mimic the gestures, facial expressions and some of the sounds made by adults and older kids. If your baby gets ahold of the remote control, for example, you might find him or her pointing it at the TV. Or if baby's older brother blows a raspberry, the baby will try to do it, too (a scenario that all too often unfolds at the dinner table when you're engaged in the serious business of trying to eat a meal). After a meal, your baby may try to wipe your hands and face.

Babies also like to initiate copycat games, making a sound or gesture and looking to see whether you will do the same thing back.

Mimicking is an important way of learning essential skills. Even adults make use of this form of social learning when they are confronted with new cultural situations. Your actions and behaviors as a parent can be powerful teaching tools for your child. For example, if you consistently use the words "please" and "thank you," and you always treat your spouse or partner with kindness and respect, you'll find your child eventually doing the same.

SHARING

Between months 10 and 12, babies love to be with other babies and watch them play. But they're still not capable of playing with each other. Interactive play usually doesn't take place until around 2 to 3 years of age.

What babies are capable of right now is taking an interest in another child's toy. This can lead to some tussles over toys and other playthings. It would be nice if babies had an innate ability to share and be polite, but at this stage it's all about them and what they want. In general, kids don't understand the concept of sharing or taking turns until the age of 3 or so. And even when they do understand the concept, they may not always put it into practice.

If conflict arises around a toy or other object, your best bet is to distract your baby with something else. Aided by his or her short attention span, it's fairly easy to engage your baby in a different activity, making the sharing issue a moot point. Eventually, you can start showing your child how to share with someone else. For now, though, the lesson is likely to be lost on your baby (especially if it's a long-winded one).

During the tenth month, your baby is busy:
- Mastering crawling
- Standing with support
- Pulling up to stand
- Maybe standing alone for a few seconds
- Using thumb and first finger together (pincer grasp)
- Manipulating toys appropriately
- Learning to let go voluntarily
- Using gestures to communicate, such as shaking his or her head for no
- Feeding self
- Recognizing and responding to familiar words
- Babbling, stringing syllables together
- Saying *mama* and *dada*
- Verbalizing other familiar words
- Looking for hidden toys
- Imitating the activities of adults and older kids
- Testing limits and observing parental reactions
- Avoiding strangers yet interacting more with family

Eyeing mom and dad By 9 to 10 months, your child's awareness of strangers is obvious. Although he or she may be affectionate and playful around you, the same is generally not true for strangers and even relatives or baby sitters. In addition, separation anxiety tends to peak sometime between 10 and 18 months. While playing, your baby may repeatedly look for you in a room to make sure you're still there. This makes it hard to leave your baby with other caregivers without some emotional stress.

As you probably realize, this is a sign that your child is strongly attached to you. It can be amazing to realize how much this little one loves and depends on you, but at times your baby's neediness can make you feel suffocated and guilty when you need to leave. This is normal. Bear with your tiny guy or gal for a little while, and try to make him or her feel as loved as possible. Take breaks when you need to. As your child becomes more secure in his or her independence, emotions will become more stable.

CHAPTER 27

Month 11

Wow. It may seem like just yesterday that you brought your baby home from the hospital. But here he or she is, fast closing in on the end of his or her first year. So much has happened since birth that those early months may now start to seem like a blur. And in the eagerness to celebrate your baby's first birthday, month 11 might feel like it gets a little lost in the shuffle.

But there's plenty going on. Your little tyke is headed toward an upright view of the world, which allows him or her to see so much more. This vantage point also places more toys and other objects within easy reach. Your baby will start inching, or cruising, along furniture to get to things and places. These are the first steps toward walking without help.

Your son or daughter can also see clearly and is learning to listen and look at the same time — a big step forward in the ability to focus and concentrate. His or her language skills are building as understanding increases, and he or she starts using meaningful "words" to indicate people, places and things.

BABY'S GROWTH AND APPEARANCE

As your child heads into toddlerhood, you can expect his or her growth rate to begin to slow down quite a bit compared with the first year, which is the period of most rapid growth a person experiences in a lifetime.

For example, during baby's second year, he or she is likely to gain about half the amount in a month that he or she gained in months six through 12. Growth in height slows down considerably, too, from about a 10-inch growth spurt in the first year to about 5 inches in the second year. Head growth also is much slower in the second year, totaling about 1 inch for the whole year.

For month 11, however, your son's or daughter's growth rate will likely be the same as last month's. Keep in mind, though, that babies tend to grow in fits and starts, so don't be surprised if a period of very little growth is followed by a big growth spurt.

BABY'S MOVEMENT

On average, month 11 is when many babies start "cruising," shuffling alongside furniture, going from one piece to another as they make their way around the room. It doesn't take long for a baby to become quite good at this method of traveling. Although walking without help is just a few steps away, crawling still rules for most babies, affording the most efficient way of getting from point A to point B.

Crawling With added experience, your baby is getting faster and more confident at crawling (whatever his or her technique might be). Crawling around helps develop your child's ability to absorb slightly differing views from both eyes, so that his or her brain can see with three-dimensional capability. This ability provides new depth perception. As your baby's depth judgment improves, his or her movements become more controlled, and he or she may become more cautious about heading down a slight slope or up a gradual incline.

If your baby has started cruising, he or she will drop down to crawl if there's nothing to hold on to. And many babies continue to crawl even after they start walking. Kids are fairly efficient creatures, though. Once walking becomes the fastest way to get around, they'll stick mostly to walking.

Standing Your baby is getting pretty good at standing, too. Most babies this age can stand with support, such as while holding your hand, for at least a couple of seconds. Some babies even start to stand alone for a brief second or two.

Around 11 months, the average baby is also able to maneuver himself or herself into a sitting position from a stand-

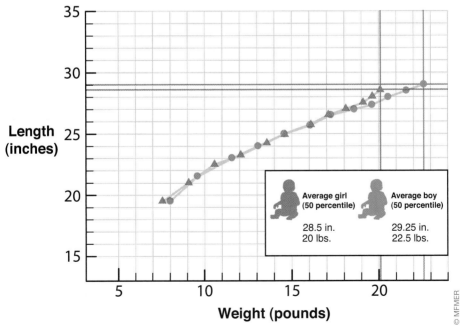

Month 11

Length (inches)

Weight (pounds)

Average girl (50 percentile)
28.5 in.
20 lbs.

Average boy (50 percentile)
29.25 in.
22.5 lbs.

© MFMER

Here's a snapshot of what your baby's basic care looks like in the eleventh month.

Eating During this month, your baby is probably eating many of the same foods that the rest of the family is eating. Be sure the food you give to your baby is of the size and texture that he or she can handle. Overcooked or finely chopped foods are still appropriate, as are small chunks of foods that are easy to chew and swallow. Breast milk and formula take on a more supplemental role, but are still necessary sources of nutrition.

Sleeping Most 10- to 11-month-olds sleep as long as 10 to 12 hours at night and take a couple of naps during the day. A few babies may start giving up their morning naps during this month. If that's the case for your baby, try starting the afternoon nap a little earlier and make bedtime a little earlier, as well. This will help avoid overtiredness. Pay attention to your child's cues, too, and adjust his or her sleeping schedule to accommodate his or her need for sleep.

ing position without just falling on his or her bottom. He or she will probably need to hold on to furniture or your leg, for example, for support while doing this.

Cruising Some babies walk sooner than do others, and a few babies will start to take their first independent steps during this month. However, most continue to rely on nearby furniture to support their movements. You'll see your baby slide his or her hands along a piece of furniture, taking small sideways steps to get around. Every so often, he or she may pause to examine a toy or a scratch in the wood, or to bang vigorously and happily on the coffee table.

At first, your son or daughter will likely keep one arm on one piece of furniture and reach out with the other arm to secure himself or herself to the next piece — from couch to coffee table to chair, for example. Gradually, he or she will become confident enough to move between pieces that are farther and farther away, such as from couch directly to chair if it's close enough. You might even catch your son or daughter taking a few quick steps unaided.

Finger skills Passing objects back-and-forth is a fun game for baby, giving him or her lots of practice in using the thumb-finger grasp and in deliberately letting go. Your baby also enjoys pointing at things he or she finds interesting.

Your child's improved depth perception helps him or her realize that an empty cup has space inside of it and that, amazingly enough, things can be put into the cup. By the end of month 11, about half of babies are adept at putting things in a container. The new big attraction will be dumping everything out of a basket or a bucket and then putting the things back in again.

Having greater depth perception also makes it possible for your son or daughter to take part in simple ball games, such as rolling a ball back-and-forth.

BABY'S SENSORY DEVELOPMENT

By month 11, your child's sensory abilities are running in practically full gear.

Vision Although your baby is still nearsighted, he or she can see as clearly as you can, recognizing familiar faces from 20 feet away. Your little tyke has become a keen observer, watching the movements of others with interest. He or she can visually track moving objects with no problems. And now that your baby knows that things continue to exist even when out of sight, he or she is able to look in the right places for playthings and objects that have dropped or rolled out of sight.

Hearing and listening Your baby's hearing and listening abilities — along with an increasing ability to focus his or her attention — are improving to the point where he or she is starting to listen and look at the same time. These skills help your child pull in valuable information about the surrounding world.

Touch During this month, your child is learning about concepts such as behind and inside, which is one of the reasons why taking inventory of a purse or bag becomes so much fun at this point. Your child will probably also delight in poking his or her fingers into holes, tearing up paper, or putting his or her fingers into something wet or gooey.

SHOES: DOES YOUR BABY NEED THEM?

When their babies start standing and cruising, many parents wonder whether shoes are necessary. At this age, your baby doesn't need shoes for standing or walking. You might put shoes on your baby because they look cute, to keep the baby's feet warm or to protect the bottoms of the feet. But your baby doesn't need shoes for any other reason and is probably growing so fast that buying shoes seems impractical.

You may think your baby's feet look flat and seem to be supported by unstable ankles. This is normal. All babies have chubby, thick feet with a fat pad that hides their arches. And they are generally unsteady on their feet. They are just learning to walk, after all. But putting your baby in shoes with special arches, inserts, high backs or reinforced heels won't change your baby's feet or help baby walk more easily. On the contrary, your baby may benefit from being barefoot to get a "feel for the road" when learning to walk.

If you do buy shoes for your baby, make sure they're comfortable and have nonskid soles to avoid slips. You should be able to feel a space as wide as your index finger between your baby's big toes and the tips of the shoes. Shoes should also be wide enough across the front to allow your baby's toes to wiggle.

GETTING YOUR CHILD TO LISTEN

During this past year, you've had the luxury of being the center of your baby's universe. It's likely that every time your little guy or gal hears your voice, his or her ears perk right up, and he or she turns to you with full attention.

But as your child gets older and interested in more and more things, you might find that it gets a little harder to capture and keep his or her attention (see your older kids, or consult any parent of an older child for expert testimony). To get good at commanding your child's attention in the face of outside forces — such as TV, candy aisles, warring siblings, and other various and sundry onslaughts — requires a bit of practice. If you start working on your skills now, you'll be one step ahead in helping your child become a better listener, and in making yourself heard:

- *Eliminate background noise.* It's hard for your little one to concentrate if there are a lot of other sounds swirling around.
- *Go to your child.* Don't shout from across the room. Stop what you're doing and go directly to your child. Your child is more likely to hear, understand and respond if you are right in front of him.
- *Get down to his or her level.* Being face to face helps your child focus his or her attention on you.
- *Say his or her name.* Do this clearly and loudly. Then pause before continuing to allow your son or daughter time to shift his or her attention away from current activities to you.
- *Maintain eye contact.* This helps your child stay focused and increases his or her concentration on what you're saying.

BABY'S MENTAL DEVELOPMENT

Your little one's receptive language skills, what he or she understands, are still way ahead of his or her expressive language skills, what he or she can say. Around this age, your baby is becoming adept at using body signals to communicate, such as nodding, waving goodbye, pointing, and shaking his or her head for no. But if you pay careful attention, you may notice that amid all of the babbling, your baby constantly uses particular sounds ("words") for certain things.

Capitalizing on body language If you say, "It's time for breakfast!" your son or daughter may smile and nod enthusiastically in response. While the two of you are communicating, use signs or hand motions. Doing so will help your youngster communicate his or her immediate needs (and minimize frustration) while learning verbal expression.

Increasing vocabulary About half of infants have learned their first words by the end of their first year, but it's not unusual for some to wait until their second birthday to really start talking. Boys usually say their first words later than do girls. Other factors affect language development, such as whether your child has a cautious temperament or is the youngest child in a large family. If there's no need for your baby to talk, he or she may not view it as a necessary skill just yet. Also, babies tend to work separately on different skill sets. If your toddler is working hard at walking, he or she may not have any energy left to work on talking. Once an active toddler is walking well, he or she is more likely to devote attention to learning words.

Once first words arrive, vocabulary can increase fairly rapidly in the months following. The best way to help your child increase his or her vocabulary is to talk with him or her. You want your child to not only hear words, but hear them as part of an interaction with others. Once you hear your child working on a new word, incorporate it into your conversations. Use it in ways that are easy for your child to understand. Take the words *mama* and *dada,* for example, which are typically some of the first words a child learns. Hang around parents of young children for any length of time and you'll hear them frequently referring to themselves in the third person. "Do you want mama to help you?" "Can dada put you in the swing?" Doing this accomplishes several things: It reinforces who mama and dada are, places the words in a context that's easy for the child to understand and helps the child learn to vocalize them.

BILINGUAL BABIES

If you speak a second (or third) language, feel free to use it with your baby. The rule of thumb is that the younger a person is when exposed to a different language, the less difficulty he or she will have in acquiring it. Giving your child the gift of a second language is a gift he or she can use throughout life.

Some parents are concerned that their child will become confused if presented with two languages at the same time. But there is little evidence to support this concern. In fact, research suggests that the human brain is adaptable enough to learn two languages simultaneously just as well as one. Consider also the millions of families around the world who speak more than one language at home and in their communities.

Although bilingual kids may mix words from different languages or attach verb endings from one language to words in another, research shows that eventually they sort it out. If they consistently use one language over another, that language may become the dominant one — for example, if English and French are both spoken at home but English is used everywhere else, English is likely to become the dominant language. Nonetheless, the child can still become proficient in French if he or she uses it often enough.

Even if your partner doesn't share your second language, you can still expose your baby to it by using it to narrate your day, read books in that language or have the same kinds of "conversations" with your baby that you would have in your family's primary language. You might feel funny at first, but it will be worth it when you hear your child say his or her first words in English and in Vietnamese or Spanish or Russian.

TOYS AND GAMES

This is often a good month to introduce toys that complement your toddler's growing skills, such as cruising, walking or sorting through objects.

Push toys These are toys your child can push around while standing upright, such as a toy grocery cart or stroller. Such a toy can help your child practice walking while still offering some support. Stay close, though, to offer a hand when your child gets tired of pushing.

Fill a basket Place a variety of small, nonhazardous objects in a basket or plastic bowl. Let your child sort through the items, dump them out and put them back in again. You'll be surprised at how entertaining this can be for your little one.

Play catch Although your son or daughter can't catch a ball in midair yet, he or she will have fun corralling a ball that's rolled in his or her direction.

Godzilla Give your child a chance to unleash some energy and laugh in the process by building a tower of soft blocks for your child to knock down. In a few months, he or she will have the skills to build a tower himself or herself, just to knock it down again, of course.

Create an exploration zone To build on your child's ability to pull up to stand and cruise, place some interesting objects on a low table that will attract his or her attention. This will give your child extra motivation to stand and move around while holding on to the table.

BABY'S SOCIAL DEVELOPMENT

When your baby was born, he or she had no sense of himself or herself as a separate entity from you or the rest of the world. But from about 8 months or so, your child starts to figure out that, "Hey, I'm Sam. I have my own face, hands, fingers and toes. I can wiggle my body when I want, and when my dad makes a funny face, I can make it myself!"

You might notice this when you and your child are in front of a mirror. Before, your baby may have thought the image in the mirror was a different baby altogether. Now your child is starting to recognize that it's his or her own image and may touch his or her nose or pull a strand of hair to confirm the physical feeling with the actions in the mirror. When you make a face in the mirror, your baby may try to copy you while watching his or her own reflection.

As your child's self-concept grows, it affects the way he or she interacts with the world. You may notice a growing self-confidence, as well as a newfound wariness of things that may previously have had little to no effect on your child.

Increased assertiveness The more practiced your son or daughter becomes at new skills, the more assertive he or she is likely to become. This growing independence is good and a sign of healthy development, but it raises the potential

✅ 11TH MONTH MILESTONES

During the eleventh month, your baby is busy:

- Mastering crawling
- Standing with support
- Pulling up to stand
- Maybe standing alone for a few seconds or even taking a few steps
- Holding on to furniture to walk around (cruising)
- Using thumb and first finger together (pincer grasp)
- Manipulating toys appropriately
- Learning to let go voluntarily
- Using gestures to communicate
- Feeding self
- Recognizing and responding to familiar words
- Babbling, stringing syllables together
- Saying *mama* and *dada*
- Verbalizing other familiar words
- Looking for hidden toys
- Imitating the activities of adults and older kids
- Testing limits and observing parental reactions
- Becoming more assertive
- Avoiding strangers yet interacting more with family

for the first power struggles between you and your child (see Chapter 26). Your child's discovery of his or her own will may make him or her more likely to refuse certain foods, demand more privileges or protest your restrictions more loudly.

Your baby's personality starts to shine through more clearly when he or she can assert both likes and dislikes. For example, you can now see evidence of your child's amazing persistence when he or she insists on finding that hidden object. Or when your son or daughter crawls off to play alone for a while after being surrounded by other people, you realize that he or she may need some downtime to recharge his or her batteries before interacting with people again.

Newfound fears As your baby's brain continues to develop, so does his or her perception of danger and sense of fear. This is a primal step in the development of a child's judgment and ability to recognize unsafe situations. Things that may not have bothered your child before, such as the dark, thunder or loud noises, may now become scary and provoke intense feelings of fear. At this point, it's easier to remove or minimize the sources of fear than to attempt to rationalize them. For example, you might install a night light in your child's room or leave a closet light on at night. If a scary something is impossible to avoid, stay close and calm. Eventually, based on your reaction and comfort, he or she will learn there's nothing to be afraid of in these situations.

CHAPTER 28

Month 12

This month marks the end of your baby's first year. Your son or daughter has changed dramatically the past 12 months. During those first days and weeks, you may have wondered if you would ever understand each other and work as a team. Now you can read your baby's moods and cues and respond with exactly what he or she needs. Your baby also understands you and your partner and knows how to thrill you, make you smile and even exasperate you.

You've changed, too. While your baby has become more independent and communicative, you've become a more confident and interactive parent. Congratulations! It's not easy becoming a parent, but it's definitely doable. And although this is the last month of year one, it's really only the beginning of many adventures to come.

The confidence you've developed and your ability to understand and communicate with your baby are your best tools in the months ahead. No one knows your son or daughter as well as you do. As your little one makes the transition from infant to toddler, your in-depth knowledge of your child will help you provide the challenges, support and assurance he or she needs.

BABY'S GROWTH AND APPEARANCE

What a difference 12 months can make! For most babies, their birth weight has tripled by the end of their first year. So if your baby weighed 7.5 pounds at birth, he or she is likely to be between 21 and 23 pounds now.

During the first year, most babies grow about 10 inches from birth. The average baby is now between 28 and 32 inches tall. The typical head size at 12 months is about 18 inches, up 4 inches from a newborn size of approximately 14 inches. Some babies may have only one tooth at this stage; others may have up to 12 or more.

Childhood experts and care providers use a baby's first birthday as a natural benchmark for many milestones, but keep in mind that all babies will continue to grow and develop at their own unique rates. What's important is not that your baby's height and weight numbers match up with national averages, but that he or she is following his or her own steady growth curve.

In the same way, the normal range for many developmental milestones is quite wide, so don't be concerned if your baby isn't walking or talking yet, or is still very leery of strangers. The first birthday is magical only in the sense that loved ones make it so in celebration of reaching that one-year milestone. However, in terms of measuring development, it's much less significant. Your baby will begin doing all of the things he or she is supposed to, whether it be a few months before or a few months after the big birthday bash.

BABY'S MOVEMENT

Your son or daughter has learned so much in the past year. In a matter of months, he or she has gone from struggling to hold up his or her head to learning how to sit, crawl, cruise and maybe even walk, all on his or her own. Where once your child was able only to bat at large objects with closed fists, he or she can now pick up an item as small as a crumb. This is all a result of the rapid development of your baby's nervous system, which is now a much more efficient conductor of messages from brain to muscles and vice versa.

Sitting Not only can your baby sit for indefinite periods of time without toppling over, he or she can pivot while seated to reach a toy or to turn toward you. He or she can also easily get in and out of a sitting position at will.

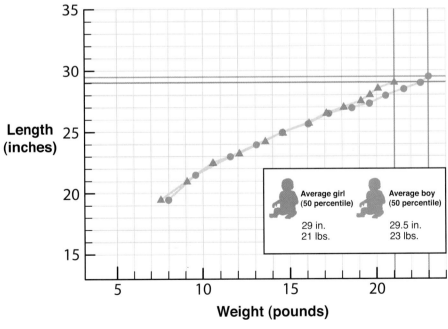

Month 12

Length (inches)

Weight (pounds)

Average girl (50 percentile)
29 in.
21 lbs.

Average boy (50 percentile)
29.5 in.
23 lbs.

© MFMER

SPOT-CHECK: WHAT'S GOING ON THIS MONTH

Here's a snapshot of what your baby's basic care looks like in the twelfth month.

Eating By now, your baby's diet probably includes foods with various textures and flavors. But the amount your baby eats at a meal may seem very small. Many parents become concerned that their babies aren't getting enough. Keep in mind that portions for an 11- to 12-month-old are pretty small compared with an adult's, perhaps ¼ cup from each food group. And as babies transition into the second year, their appetite tends to drop and becomes more erratic. Altogether, this might translate into a meal of a few tablespoons of cooked carrots, two bites of rice, a taste of meat and several bites of pears. Focus on your baby's signs of hunger and thirst rather than how much is left on the plate. Allow him or her to stop eating when he or she is full, rather than coaxing or playing tricks to get more food in. If you make a healthy selection of foods available, your child won't starve or lose significant weight.

Keep giving your baby breast milk or formula. Both are important sources of nutrition. If you've decided to wean your baby from breast-feeding, replace the breast milk with iron-fortified formula. After the first birthday, you can gradually transition your baby to drinking whole milk.

Sleeping Most 11- to 12-month-olds sleep as long as 10 to 12 hours at night and take a couple of naps during the day. Most babies still need two naps a day, but some start giving up their morning naps around this time. If that's the case for your baby, try starting the afternoon nap a little earlier and make bedtime a little earlier, as well. This will help avoid overtiredness. Pay attention to your child's cues, too, and adjust his or her sleeping schedule to accommodate his or her need for sleep.

By 11 to 12 months, most babies don't need nighttime feedings anymore. Nursing or taking a bottle is likely to be for reasons of comfort, not calories. If your baby is still waking up for feedings and you want to work toward sleeping through the night, try gradually shorter nursing sessions or smaller bottles. Eventually you can cut down to none at all. Also look at your child's bedtime routine. Place your child in bed while tired but still awake so that he or she learns how to put himself or herself to sleep.

Standing and bending During this month, about half of babies gain enough balance to stand alone for a few seconds or even longer. This opens up a whole new level of vision and reach for your baby, as he or she can now play with toys above ground. At the same time, about 25 percent of infants are learning to stoop down while standing to recover an item from the floor.

Walking Between months 11 and 12, about 1 out of 4 babies learns to walk well. Walking is a complex activity that requires coordination, balance and a good dose of confidence. A key stage in learning how to walk independently is learning to lift first one foot and then the other so that the baby is briefly standing on one leg. Your baby practices doing this while cruising around holding on to furniture for support.

When your baby first shows an interest in taking steps, walk with your baby, holding his or her hands, praising his or her efforts to move forward. Once baby signals that he or she is ready to walk alone, crouch down a short distance away with your arms out, and encourage him or her to walk toward you. Pretty soon, look out — there goes your toddler! First steps are always exciting. It's good to stand back and let your baby practice, but continue to stay close, as it takes awhile to get the hang of walking without help.

Don't fret if your baby doesn't seem to be interested in walking just yet. A few babies start walking as early as 9 months, but others wait until 17 months to take the plunge. Both are perfectly normal.

Getting up and down stairs Even before a baby starts walking well, he or she will likely figure out how to get up a set of stairs, which involves a mix of crawling and walking maneuvers. In a few weeks, usually sometime between 12 and 15 months, children learn to go down the stairs, too, most often by sliding down feet first on his or her tummy.

Getting up and down stairs is an important skill to learn, but you'll want to be close by whenever your child is working on them, to catch any slips and avoid tumbles that are bound to happen.

IT'S A PARTY!

At the end of this year, the whole family deserves a party — perhaps for the family more so than baby, who likely won't grasp the significance of the event until around age 3. In any case, it's a traditional time to celebrate, and why not? For many families, the baby's first birthday marks the end of a period of labor-intensive parenting. There's more to come, sure, but colicky evenings, breast-feeding struggles and chronic sleep deprivation are now largely behind you. It's time for cake!

While it's tempting to invite everyone you know to such a grand occasion, for baby's sake you might consider having a small party with immediate family. At 1 year of age, your baby may not enjoy a large, noisy gathering of friends and neighbors. Even if your little one is the gregarious type, you might still want to limit the duration of the party to an hour or so, to avoid any baby-related meltdowns.

Hand and finger skills Your son's or daughter's refined pincer grasp at 12 months allows him or her to pick objects up with ease. When reading a book together, your child can turn the pages with a little bit of help. Later, he or she will use these same skills to learn to draw, paint, write, and work buttons and zippers.

Most babies can hold an object in each hand by this age and enjoy banging them together. Your baby may even have figured out how to hold two objects in one hand and how to put them into a container. He or she may also throw toys to the side when they lose appeal or to pick up something more interesting. But your fickle juggler won't have much control over where he or she can throw.

Between 11 and 12 months old, many infants are getting a better grasp of their eating and drinking utensils, both literally and figuratively. Your baby may know how to pick up a cup and drink from it but may not be able to set it down just yet, and will probably drop it if you don't take it. He or she is also getting better at using a spoon and has probably discovered that spoons make good toys (especially if they're filled with food).

BABY'S SENSORY DEVELOPMENT

By the end of the first year, your child's senses are working together in a coordinated fashion to make your child aware of the outside world. And as he or she becomes used to routine sights and sounds around the house, your son or daughter learns to filter out distractions and better focus on things of interest, such as eating a meal or listening to a favorite story.

Looking and listening Your baby's hearing is sharper now, and he or she listens with greater attention. In fact, he or she can look and listen at the same time, making reading books together that much more enjoyable. If you think your baby isn't hearing well, talk to your baby's care provider about a hearing assessment.

Touch Even though your little guy or gal is benefiting from integrated sensory input, he or she still enjoys singular sensations, such as feeling different textures or pouring water from one container into another. For some adventure as your baby learns to walk, let him or her tread barefoot on different surfaces, such as on soft grass or in a puddle of water. Your baby also enjoys human touch and loves to return hugs and kisses, although not always on demand.

Even at 1 year, your baby still explores using fingers and mouth together. Anything your baby picks up will be taste tested.

BABY'S MENTAL DEVELOPMENT

Brain imaging studies of sleeping infants between 0 and 2 years of age reveal that the total volume of a baby's brain increases by over 100 percent during the first year of life. Pretty amazing, isn't it? No wonder their head size grows so much — it has to accommodate all of that growth in gray and white matter.

The older your baby gets, the greater the myelinization of your baby's nerves — the process whereby nerves become encased in a fatty sheath called myelin, which makes them stronger and more efficient messengers. This myelinization helps to bring more and more areas of the brain into use.

Some areas of the brain don't mature until much later, such as a part known as the reticular formation, which helps you maintain attention. This area doesn't become fully myelinated until puberty or later. The frontal lobes, responsible for executive thinking and judgment, don't become fully myelinated until adulthood (and you thought impulsive teenagers were just out to give a parent gray hair).

Increasingly complex thinking By age 1, your baby is starting to gain control of the limbic system — the area of the brain responsible for emotions, appetites and basic urges, but also information processing and directing incoming information from the outside world to the appropriate areas of the brain. Thus, a 1-year-old's thinking gains in complexity and starts to contain longer chains of thoughts. If you offer two toys to a 1-year-old, for example, he or she will likely make a choice between the two rather than trying to grab both. Or if your baby sees a toy with a blanket on it, he or she may employ knowledge of cause and effect to pull the blanket to get to the toy.

TOYS AND GAMES

Through the end of the first year and beyond, your baby will still enjoy toys and games that use and build new motor skills. Games that involve picking up and dropping objects will likely be entertaining. At 12 months, your baby's play may range from exercising large muscles to working and mastering fine motor skills. He or she will likely think it's fun to push, throw and knock down everything.

When walking down the toy aisle of your local retail store, it may be easy to get carried away because there's so much to choose from. When purchasing a toy for your child, keep in mind the fun factor. Toys can certainly be educational, but try to stick with something appropriate for your child's level of development. If a toy or game is too difficult for your child to comprehend, he or she will quickly lose interest. And while toy manufacturers may think of their products as the perfect development aid, there's nothing that beats interaction with you when it comes to helping your baby grow and learn.

A 1-year-old is still entertained by simple things. Here are some ideas to get you started.

Find open space Often the best thing you can do for your baby when he or she is learning how to crawl and walk is to give him or her plenty of space to move around in. This could be at a park if the weather is nice or at a community recreation center or kids' gym. If you have older children who are taking a class in a gym or other open area, such as ballet or karate, take your baby along so that he or she can benefit from the space, too.

Walk together Practice walking together with your baby by holding hands. Gradually, he or she will move to holding one hand only and then just a finger. Soon, you'll be able to take a step back and let your baby walk toward you. Let your baby try out different surfaces, too, such as warm sand, soft grass or a wet puddle.

Crayons Some babies start to scribble around 12 months or so. Give your child a crayon and a piece of paper and see what happens. Show him or her how it works and see what your child does. He or she may be delighted at the results, and so will you.

Pull toys With your son's or daughter's increased dexterity, he or she can pull a toy along if it has a string or ribbon attached. Pulling a toy can be just as fun as pushing one around.

Water toys A book in the bath? Little ones love sitting in the tub and flipping through a waterproof picture book. Your little guy or gal might also enjoy bathtub paints and crayons that rinse right off with the bath water. Water is fascinating to kids, and many will be content to simply pour it from one cup to another. Just be sure to always supervise your child around water to avoid any possibility of drowning. Remember, if the phone rings or the doorbell sounds, don't leave your baby in the bathtub alone.

Understanding The part of the brain involved with understanding is maturing as well. By the end of the first year, babies are beginning to respond to one-step commands. For example, your child may hold on to you on request when you pull his or her pants up to get dressed. Or your baby may give you a kiss when you ask.

Your son or daughter may also show understanding of simple questions, such as "Where's daddy?" or "Is that a puppy?" when pointing at a picture of a puppy in a familiar book.

Language Speaking comes slower than understanding, and it won't be until the second or third year that your child's vocabulary begins to expand dramatically. And it may take even longer for people outside of the family to understand what your child is saying.

Still, the beginnings of speech are at hand. More than half of babies know at least one word by the age of 1 in addition to *mama* and *dada*, such as *uh-oh*. Some may even know two or three words. Continue to encourage your baby's exploration of words by listening intently and responding to the baby's jabbering. Repeat new words your baby is learning, and verbally name gestures that he or she already uses for communication.

If you're concerned about your child's speech development, try to discover what he or she is channeling his or her energies toward. Perhaps your son or daughter is spending more time standing, cruising and walking. Eventually, once these skills are mastered, speaking will become a priority. Allow your baby to learn these skills within his or her own time frame.

You should also know that how well your baby understands language is a better measure of language development than are the words he or she is able to say.

BABY'S SOCIAL DEVELOPMENT

Your baby may be on the road toward independence but still has lots to learn. Some of the fear that accompanies that early independence is starting to fade as your baby becomes more sure of his or her place in the family. However, you and other family members will be the ones your baby relies on for safety and security.

Veni, vidi, vici Your baby is starting to take up Julius Caesar's famous motto, "I came, I saw, I conquered." Everything is up for mastery. Early signs of your baby's drive for independence include self-feeding, drinking from a cup and being able to move about on his or her own. For most youngsters, the thrilling part of learning to walk is gaining more control over the world. The world is no longer limited to what comes to them; now they can go out and conquer it. This independence can be both exciting and intimidating.

Tantrums Although tantrums become more common during a child's second year, you may be noticing the first signs of your baby's temper. Your 1-year-old may get upset when something is taken away or when he or she doesn't get what he or she wants. As your baby's drive for independence and mastery run up against his or her still-limited abilities and your parental limits, he or she may feel frustrated and mad. Some babies express these feelings more loudly and intensely than do others, depending on their personalities (see Chapter 9 for more on a baby's temperament).

When you see your child becoming irritable, more often than not it's a sign that he or she is tired or hungry. This is true even for older children and adults. If your baby is out of sorts or seems increasingly resistant to your efforts at

✔️ 12TH MONTH MILESTONES

During the twelfth month, your baby is busy:

- ◗ Standing alone
- ◗ Cruising
- ◗ Maybe taking first steps
- ◗ Using pincer grasp accurately
- ◗ Manipulating toys appropriately
- ◗ Feeding self
- ◗ Learning to let go voluntarily
- ◗ Looking and listening simultaneously
- ◗ Increasing attention span
- ◗ Using gestures to communicate
- ◗ Recognizing and responding to familiar words
- ◗ Increasing vocabulary
- ◗ Responding to one-step commands and simple questions
- ◗ Imitating the activities of adults and older kids
- ◗ Testing limits and expressing frustration
- ◗ Still being wary of strangers but very affectionate with family

soothing, your best bet may be to head for a nap rather than repeated attempts at discipline. Your baby may need to "vent" a little before actually falling asleep.

Saying no By now, your son or daughter understands what you mean when you say the word no. It's just that everything in your home is so fascinating — including pot handles, fireplaces, holiday decorations, the way the water swirls in the toilet and your pet's whiskers, tail and food. His or her desire to explore is stronger than the desire to listen to your warnings. This isn't a sign of defiance, just your baby's natural, irrepressible craving to explore.

As much as possible, remove valuable or dangerous objects that tempt your baby. For the remaining objects, keep a close watch and be prepared to move your persistent baby away from dangerous objects or offer a distraction. If the object remains in the room, expect that your child will likely go right back to what you just said no to. Try hard to reserve no for those things that can harm your baby. (Easier said than done!) You can also teach your baby the meanings of "be gentle" and "be soft" for situations that require caution, such as playing with a friend or the family pet.

Relating to others Most babies this age are very affectionate with family members and enjoy snuggling and cuddling up for lap time. But don't be surprised if your baby's wariness of strangers continues through these months. Many babies have a fear of strangers past their first birthdays. Others have shorter stages, and many even have on-and-off periods of stranger anxiety.

PART 4

Common Illnesses and Concerns

Among the many challenges you face as a parent is caring for your baby during illnesses or medical emergencies. This can be scary, but thank goodness true medical emergencies in infants are fairly rare. And because your son or daughter can't verbally tell you when something hurts, it's sometimes difficult to sort out more serious illnesses from those that are common and easily managed at home.

Illnesses in general are more frequent in the first year of life, simply because your new baby is small and still developing in many ways. He or she also is confronting a whole new environment filled with all kinds of elements that weren't present in the uterus, including people, pets and germs. But as your baby matures and his or her immune system becomes stronger and better adapted to the environment, illnesses will become less frequent.

As you get to know your son or daughter better, it will become easier for you to know when your child has a minor illness and when you need medical help. You know your child better than anyone else — including details about his or her current and previous illnesses. You will notice, for example, if your little one is suddenly more fussy than usual, or has changed eating or sleeping patterns. You'll also be able to tell if your baby is less active or clinging to you more.

You are an important member of the team that cares for your sick child. In most cases, you will determine when you can handle an illness at home or when it's time to call your baby's care provider or visit an emergency department. You can help your care provider determine if a problem is present when things just don't seem right with your son or daughter. You also play a key role in caring for your sick infant: knowing when to give medication, understanding what changes to watch for and foods to avoid, and determining when your baby can return to child care. Remember, parents' instincts about sick children are usually very good — trust yours.

INFANTS AND MEDICATIONS

A question new parents often have when faced with a sick baby is whether it's OK to give medication. When you have a headache, for example, the easiest and most effective solution is to take a pain reliever. But what about for a baby?

When it comes to medications, whether for adults or children, the benefits of the medication must always be weighed against the risks. While some medications certainly can play a role in helping infants and children get better, many others do not. Plus, almost all drugs have potential side effects. So it's important to choose wisely when and what type of medication to give.

The general approach to over-the-counter medications in an otherwise healthy baby is that they're rarely needed. If you do use nonprescription medications, use only those that are designed for infants. Use them only when necessary and as indicated by your baby's care provider.

Fever and pain Call your baby's care provider right away if your baby is under 3 months of age and has a rectal temperature of 100.4 F or higher. If your child has a fever and isn't uncomfortable, medication isn't necessary. If your child has a fever and is uncomfortable, acetaminophen (Tylenol, others) is generally considered safe for babies under 6 months of age. In addition to helping with fever discomfort, acetaminophen can help relieve pain, such as soreness after shots and painful earaches. Ibuprofen (Advil, Motrin, others), another pain reliever, is safe for babies older than 6 months, although it can aggravate illnesses affecting the digestive tract. Ask a care provider before giving medication to a child with a chronic illness, such as kidney disease or asthma.

Cough and congestion When your baby is coughing or congested, it's tempting to pick up one of the many cough and cold medications available at your local drugstore, but research indicates that these aren't very effective in curing infants' and toddlers' colds. The Food and Drug Administration also warns that they can have rare but serious side effects (see "Cough and cold medications" on page 361). A safer and more effective alternative for a stuffy nose may be to use saline nasal drops to thin the mucus (see "Cold" on page 359) or a suction bulb to remove secretions from your baby's nose.

Precautions When giving your baby medicine, follow these precautions:

Give the right dose Infant medicines usually come in liquid form but in different strengths based on the individual medicine. Use only the dispenser that came with the medication, and follow the directions on the label carefully so that you give your baby the right dose. Often, for children under 2, the medicine label will tell you to ask your care provider for instructions on dosing (see also the dosage charts for acetaminophen and ibuprofen on page 370). If you know your child's weight, use that as a guide.

Avoid overdosing Avoid giving your baby multiple medicines with the same active ingredient at the same time, such as a pain reliever and a decongestant, which can lead to an accidental overdose. Some parents alternate between pain relievers such as acetaminophen and ibuprofen, but be cautious about doing this. Each medicine requires a specific interval between doses (see the dosage charts on page 370). Trying to keep the two straight may become confusing, and you may unintentionally overdose your baby.

Avoid aspirin Aspirin is not approved for children under 2. And it's generally not recommended for children under age 18 because of its association with a serious illness called Reye's syndrome, which can damage the brain and liver. The risk is mostly associated with using aspirin to treat symptoms of a viral illness, such as the flu or chickenpox. But since it's not always easy to accurately distinguish between a viral and a nonviral type of illness, experts recommend avoiding aspirin altogether in children under 18, unless specifically prescribed by a care provider.

If you have any questions about giving your baby a medication, call your baby's care provider. This will help you avoid unnecessary risks. If your baby vomits or develops a rash after taking a medicine, call the care provider promptly.

How to give medicine When your child does need to take a medicine, here are some tips to make the job easier:

- A baby is usually more willing to take medicine by mouth before a feeding.
- Place a small amount of medicine inside the baby's cheek, where it's not as easy to spit out.
- Don't refill bottles or use measured droppers for anything other than the original medicine.
- Avoid chewable medications in babies younger than age 2.
- Follow the directions of your baby's care provider for continuing to use a medication, even if it doesn't taste good or your baby's symptoms are getting better. A course of antibiotics, for example, needs to be taken in full for it to work as it should.

TAKING BABY'S TEMPERATURE

If your child feels warm or seems under the weather, it's probably time to take his or her temperature. Sounds simple enough — but if you're new to it, you may have questions. Which type of thermometer is best? Are thermometer guidelines different for babies and older children? Here's what you need to know to take your child's temperature.

Thermometer options A glass mercury thermometer was once a staple in most medicine cabinets. Today, digital thermometers are recommended instead of mercury thermometers, which can break and allow mercury to vaporize and be inhaled.

Regular digital thermometers, which use electronic heat sensors to record body temperature, can be used in the mouth, armpit or rectum. Digital ear thermometers, also called tympanic thermometers, use infrared energy detection to measure the temperature inside the ear canal. Other options include a digital pacifier thermometer and temporal artery thermometer — which uses an infrared scanner to measure the temperature of the temporal artery in the forehead.

If you want to get a single thermometer for the entire family, a regular digital thermometer is probably best. However, if you plan to use the digital thermometer to take a rectal temperature, get two digital thermometers and label one for oral use and one for rectal use. Don't use the same thermometer in both places.

Accounting for accuracy The most accurate way to take a child's temperature is to use a digital thermometer rectally or orally. Rectal temperatures provide the best readings for infants. Ear thermometers are another option for older babies and children. However, earwax or a small, curved ear canal can interfere with the accuracy of a temperature taken with an ear thermometer.

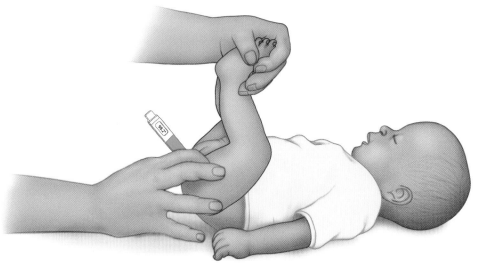

Taking a baby's temperature rectally

© MFMER

With armpit (axillary) temperatures, it can sometimes be difficult to get an accurate reading. Temperatures measured with a pacifier thermometer are considered the least accurate. The reliability of temporal artery thermometers hasn't yet been verified.

Whatever the method, make sure you carefully read the instructions that came with your thermometer. After each use, clean the tip of the thermometer with rubbing alcohol or soap and lukewarm water. For safety — and to make sure the thermometer stays in place — never leave your child unattended while you're taking his or her temperature.

Age matters The best type of thermometer — or the best place to insert the thermometer, in some cases — depends on your child's age.

Birth to 3 months For newborns, use a regular digital thermometer to take a rectal temperature. Turn on the digital thermometer and lubricate the tip of the thermometer with petroleum jelly. Lay your baby on his or her back, lift your baby's thighs, and gently insert the lubricated thermometer half an inch into your baby's rectum. Insert the thermometer slowly, and stop if you feel any resistance. Hold the thermometer in place for about 30 seconds or until the thermometer signals that it's done. Remove the thermometer and read the number. Call your baby's care provider right away if your child is under 3 months of age and has a temperature of 100.4 F or higher.

3 months to 4 years For older infants and toddlers, continue to use a rectal thermometer as long as you are able to. Ear thermometers are often too big for an older baby's small ear canals and are likely to be inaccurate. For toddlers, you can more easily use a digital ear thermometer, since a toddler's ears are usually large enough. Plus, it's more difficult to obtain a rectal temperature at this age. Carefully follow the instructions that came with your thermometer. You can also use a regular digital thermometer to take a rectal temperature or an armpit temperature. To take an armpit temperature, first turn on the digital thermometer. When you place the thermometer under your child's armpit, make sure it touches skin — not clothing. Hold the thermometer tightly in place for about a minute or until the thermometer signals that it's done. Remove the thermometer and read the number.

4 years and older By age 4, most kids can hold a digital thermometer under the tongue for the short time it takes to get a temperature reading. Turn on the digital thermometer. Place the tip of the thermometer under your child's tongue, and ask your child to keep his or her lips closed. Remove the thermometer when it signals that it's done and read the number. If your child has been eating or drinking, wait at least 15 minutes to take his or her temperature by mouth. If your child is too congested to breathe through his or her nose, you may need to take an armpit or rectal temperature — or use a digital ear thermometer.

CARING FOR A SICK BABY

Many common childhood illnesses can be treated at home. If you have any questions, seek the help and advice of your baby's care provider. When you have a sick baby at home, a little extra loving care is always in order. To help your child recover quickly and fully, there are some simple steps you can follow.

Encourage rest Make sure your baby has plenty of opportunity to rest. Getting enough sleep will help ease crankiness and smooth over irritability and discomfort. Take the opportunity to snuggle up and relax together. A mild illness is often just the excuse you need to pause the family's hectic schedule and spend quality time with your baby.

Offer plenty of fluids One of the biggest risks associated with infections and other common childhood illnesses is dehydration. Dehydration occurs when your baby loses more fluids than he or she is taking in — because of vomiting, diarrhea, difficulty feeding, or just the increased demands on your baby's metabolism. If your baby is having difficulty eating or keeping fluids down, offer small, frequent sips of breast milk, formula, water or oral rehydration solution (see "Vomiting" on page 395 for more details on getting your baby to take in enough fluids). Older babies may enjoy sucking on an ice pop or crushed ice.

Make your baby comfortable If your baby is congested, adding extra moisture to the air by running a humidifier or vaporizer may help soothe your baby's nose. Or have your child breathe the warm, moist air in a steamy bathroom. Saline drops into the nose can help with congestion. If your baby's room feels hot and stuffy, circulate the air with a fan. Also make sure your child isn't dressed too warmly.

Use medications wisely If your baby is more than 3 months old and has a fever but is eating and sleeping well and playing normally, medication may not be necessary. But if your son or daughter is fussy and uncomfortable, it's fine to give him or her acetaminophen (Tylenol, others) to relieve the discomfort. Ibuprofen (Advil, Motrin, others) should only be given to babies older than 6 months. Follow the directions on the label, the dosage charts on page 370, or the advice of your child's care provider. Be sure to wait for the appropriate amount of time before giving your baby another dose. If your child's care provider has prescribed antibiotics or another medication, follow the instructions exactly to maximize the drug's benefits and reduce possible risks.

Contact your baby's care provider When dealing with a sick child, trust your intuition as a parent. If you feel like you should call your baby's care provider — call. Describe what's worrying you and what you've tried so far. A phone call to a care provider often can solve a lot of problems and give you reassurance that the steps you've already taken are the right ones. If you feel like you should have your child seen in either the doctor's office or the emergency department — go in.

Prevent the spread of germs Young babies are especially vulnerable to viruses and bacteria. Take common sense steps to keep germs from spreading. Sneeze or cough into a clean tissue or into your elbow if tissues are unavailable. Toss used tissues promptly. Don't share eating and drinking utensils. Keep surfaces clean, including pacifiers and toys that your baby likes to chew on. Avoid people who are sick, and stay away from crowded areas in the fall and winter, when more people are indoors and the chances of infection are higher. Above all, wash your hands frequently and thoroughly and make sure other family members do the same. You may want to keep bottles of hand sanitizer in various places around the house.

A TO Z ILLNESS GUIDE

Following are some illnesses most common to newborns and young children and tips on how to treat them.

ALLERGIES

Allergies occur when your body's natural defense system incorrectly identifies a harmless substance as harmful. The body then overreacts in an attempt to protect itself, and the result is an allergic reaction. A tendency to develop allergies is usually inherited.

As with adults, infants can develop an allergic reaction when they eat, breathe in or touch something that offends their immune systems. Certain drugs (most commonly penicillin) and stings and bites from insects and other animals also can cause an allergic reaction.

How to recognize it Allergies often cause signs and symptoms such as:

▶ Runny nose with a thin, clear discharge
▶ Itchy, watery or swollen eyes
▶ Sneezing
▶ Itchy skin
▶ Rash
▶ Hives
▶ Swelling
▶ Cough, wheezing or shortness of breath

Food allergies can create the above symptoms, as well as diarrhea and vomiting. Almost any food can cause an allergic reaction, but most reactions are caused by only a few foods: cow's milk, egg whites, nuts, fish and shellfish, wheat, soy and corn.

Food allergies are sometimes confused with an intolerance or sensitivity to certain foods. Intolerance of a certain food can cause digestive problems — such as stomachache, gas and diarrhea — but isn't related to the immune system. For example, some babies don't have enough of the enzyme required to digest milk sugar (lactose), making them lactose intolerant. Also, sometimes the acid found in certain foods, such as tomatoes or oranges, can cause a red rash around the mouth that parents mistake for allergies.

How serious is it? Most of the time, allergies are annoying but not serious. In a few cases, though, an allergic reaction can be life-threatening and require emergency treatment (anaphylaxis). Signs and symptoms to watch out for include:

▶ Difficulty breathing
▶ Facial swelling
▶ Bluish skin color
▶ Loss of consciousness

When to call If your baby has symptoms of anaphylaxis, call 911 or your local emergency number. After emergency treatment, see your child's care provider to determine what caused the reaction and to figure out how to avoid another one. Doctors will often prescribe an emergency injectable medication (EpiPen or Twinject) that you can keep with you at all times. This medication provides your child relief until you are able to reach the emergency department.

If your baby has allergy signs or symptoms such as a constant runny nose, chronic cough or dry, itchy skin, make an appointment with his or her care provider to discuss what's causing it and to learn how to treat it.

What you can do The best way to prevent any allergy is to avoid the substance that's triggering the reaction. If you're in the midst of introducing new foods to your child, and he or she shows signs of a possible food allergy, your child's care provider may advise going back to foods you know are safe and holding off on new foods for a week or two. Then introduce new foods one at a time, so you can monitor which food might be causing problems. If necessary, your child's care provider may refer you to an allergy specialist who can conduct special tests to identify potential allergens.

If your baby has irritated skin, use lukewarm water and gentle, fragrance-free soaps for baths. Apply fragrance-free skin moisturizer frequently, especially right after a bath to lock in moisture. Avoid clothing that's rough, scratchy, woolen or too tight. To relieve severe itching or oozing, apply a wet, lukewarm washcloth or compress to the irritated skin. Your child's care provider may also recommend using an over-the-counter hydrocortisone cream or prescription ointment to treat dry, itchy skin.

Respiratory allergies — to dust, pollen, mold or other allergens in the environment — are fairly uncommon under the age of 2. But if you think your baby is allergic to any of these substances, try to keep your home environment as free from them as possible. You can purchase dust mite-proof covers for mattresses and pillows. Washing sheets and blankets in hot water every week or two helps, too.

ANEMIA

Anemia is a condition in which blood lacks a sufficient number of healthy red blood cells. Red blood cells carry oxygen to the brain and other organs and tissues, providing energy and giving skin a healthy color. They're also essential to a child's growth and development.

The most common cause of anemia in infants is a lack of iron (iron deficiency). Iron is necessary for the creation of hemoglobin, the substance that enables red blood cells to deliver oxygen to the body. In full-term infants, iron deficiency usually results from a lack of iron in the baby's diet. Babies who drink cow's milk too early, for instance, miss out on iron because cow's milk is a poor source of iron. Iron deficiency can also occur as a result of premature birth or excessive blood loss.

Most full-term babies are born with a supply of iron that lasts about four months. After that, the supply diminishes and needs to be supplemented with other sources of iron, such as food, infant formula or an iron supplement.

How to recognize it Signs and symptoms of anemia aren't always easy to recognize. Often, babies are diagnosed with anemia as a result of a blood test done for a separate reason. In general, though, a baby with iron deficiency anemia may:

▶ Appear pale or ashen
▶ Tire easily
▶ Be persistently irritable
▶ Have a poor appetite

How serious is it? If untreated, iron deficiency in children can cause delays in normal growth and development. Some studies show a long-term association between iron deficiency anemia in infancy and later deficits in intellectual capacity.

Don't try to treat your child on your own. Always talk to your child's care provider before giving your baby any type of vitamins or supplements.

When to call If your baby seems unusually pale, tired, irritable or uninterested in eating, or if you're concerned about the amount of iron in your baby's diet, talk to your baby's care provider. In most cases, a simple blood test is all that's needed to diagnose anemia.

If your baby has iron deficiency anemia, his or her care provider will likely recommend iron supplements, usually in a liquid form for infants. Generally, you administer the supplements for about seven to nine weeks until your baby's iron supply is at a healthy level. Iron medications can change your baby's stool to a dark color, so don't be concerned if this happens. Once your child's iron levels are back to normal, you'll want to make sure he or she continues to get enough dietary iron, through food or supplements.

It's possible to overdose on iron supplements — too much iron is poisonous — so be sure to give any supplements to your child exactly as the care provider recommends. Also, keep this and any other medications away from small children.

What you can do Iron deficiency anemia can be prevented by making sure your baby gets an adequate supply of iron in his or her diet. Here are some simple steps you can take:

Wait on cow's milk Don't give your baby cow's milk until he or she is at least 1 year old. Until then, give your baby breast milk or formula.

Introduce iron at the right time If you're breast-feeding, give your baby iron-fortified cereal when you start to introduce solid foods. If you're breast-feeding exclusively beyond age 4 months, talk to your child's care provider about giving your baby an iron supplement.

Use iron-fortified formula If your baby drinks formula, make sure it has iron added (4 to 12 milligrams of iron per liter). Most standard formulas on the U.S. market contain iron.

Offer a balanced diet As your son or daughter gets older, you can include iron-rich foods in his or her diet, such as pureed meat, egg yolks, green beans, peas, squash, spinach, sweet potatoes, tuna, ripe apricots and stewed prunes.

Enhance iron absorption Offer your baby foods rich in vitamin C, which helps the body to absorb iron. Examples of vitamin C-rich foods include strawberries, cantaloupe, kiwi, raspberries, broccoli, tomatoes, potatoes and cauliflower.

ASTHMA

In some people, the lungs and airways become easily inflamed — more easily than in other people — when exposed to certain conditions called triggers. The inflammation constricts the airways and leads to difficulty breathing. This is referred to as asthma, or an older term, reactive airway disease. In young children, the first sign of asthma may be wheezing that's triggered by a cold, goes away and then recurs with the next cold.

Asthma can be difficult to diagnose, especially in younger kids because it's hard to get accurate results on lung function tests. Also, a number of childhood conditions — bronchiolitis and pneumonia as examples — can have symptoms similar to those caused by asthma. If your child has repeated episodes of wheezing, your care provider is likely to consider asthma as a possible underlying problem.

Asthma is more common in children who have a family history of asthma, allergies or eczema.

How to recognize it Wheezing — a high-pitched whistling sound produced when your child breathes out (exhales) — is generally the first sign to raise a parent's suspicion of asthma. Other signs and symptoms include a cough that gets worse at night, tightness in the chest and shortness of breath. With asthma, wheezing or coughing episodes tend to recur.

While wheezing is most commonly associated with asthma, not all children with asthma wheeze. Some kids may have only one sign or symptom, such as a lingering cough or chest congestion.

How serious is it? Asthma signs and symptoms vary from child to child and may get worse or better over time. Some kids outgrow recurrent wheezing when they reach 5 or 6 years old. For others, wheezing episodes may stop and then recur again later in life. Still others have chronic, persistent wheezing that requires daily management.

When to call Seek immediate medical care if your baby has severe trouble breathing, or his or her mouth or fingertips are turning dusky or blue.

Make an appointment right away with your child's care provider if you notice a fever with persistent coughing or wheezing, or if your child has difficulty sleeping or eating because of wheezing, coughing or troubled breathing.

Asthma is treated with prescription medications. Quick-relief medications work by opening up the airways and making breathing easier right away. Controller medications are used everyday by children who have been diagnosed with asthma and have regular symptoms.

If your baby has symptoms of asthma, your child's care provider may use a wait-and-see approach before prescribing medications, depending on the severity of symptoms. If your baby has severe wheezing episodes, a care provider may prescribe a quick-relief medication to help ease your baby's symptoms. This medication comes in the form of an inhaler. Medical staff can show you how to use a spacer, a plastic tube — usually with a mask attached — that makes it easier to deliver the medication to your baby. You may also use a nebulizer, a machine that turns liquid medication into fine droplets, to deliver the medication to your infant's lungs. Sometimes, an oral medication may be prescribed. Asthma medications are very safe. All medications carry risks if used inappropriately, but when asthma medications are used correctly, their benefits far outweigh the small risks.

Asthma medications can sometimes be difficult to remember to use because when your child's asthma is well controlled, he or she has no symptoms. As a parent, it may not seem necessary to give your child a medication if he or she isn't ill. But it's very important not to stop the medication. Left untreated or undertreated, childhood asthma can lead to permanent lung changes that can result in poor lung function in adulthood.

If your son's or daughter's wheezing persists over time, his or her care provider will likely recommend a full evaluation for asthma. If your child does have asthma, you and the care provider can create a comprehensive treatment plan that best controls your child's symptoms and helps to prevent severe attacks.

What you can do Keep track of your child's wheezing episodes, preferably in a journal if you can, and don't be afraid to call your care provider when symptoms warrant it. If you're not sure when you should call, ask your child's care provider to tell you.

If you notice that certain things tend to trigger your baby's wheezing, such as dust or pollen, try your best to avoid them. Clean regularly to eliminate dust, and use air conditioning during pollen season to keep out airborne allergens. If your baby's wheezing is worsened by cold air, bundle your baby in a blanket to keep the air around his or her face warm and moist. Not all studies show that allergen-avoidance measures are effective in controlling asthma, though, so don't feel like you need to surround your baby in a protective bubble at all times.

BRONCHIOLITIS

Bronchiolitis is a common lung infection in babies. It's caused by a virus, often the respiratory syncytial virus (RSV). In adults, RSV infection typically causes only mild upper respiratory tract symptoms. In infants, however, the infection sometimes spreads to the smallest of the lungs' airways (bronchioles), leading to inflamed, narrowed airways (bronchiolitis). RSV infection is very contagious and is most common during the winter months. Other less common viral causes of bronchiolitis include influenza, parainfluenza, measles and adenovirus.

How to recognize it Bronchiolitis typically starts out like the common cold with a runny nose, mild fever and a cough. Over several days, the cough becomes more pronounced and you may hear your baby wheezing. Babies are nose breathers, and when too much mucus is stuffing a baby's nose or trickling down his or her throat, sucking and swallowing become more difficult. Because of this, he or she may not be interested in eating.

How serious is it? Even if your baby is otherwise healthy, symptoms of bronchiolitis may range from mild to severe. Wheezing typically lasts for a week to a month or more and then goes away on its own.

In some cases, especially if your child has an underlying health problem or is a significantly premature newborn, bronchiolitis can become very severe and require hospitalization.

During the illness, it's important to encourage babies to drink frequently. Those who don't get enough fluids become at risk of dehydration, which itself can be serious.

When to call If your baby's symptoms are severe — such as marked difficulty breathing or skin that's turning blue from lack of oxygen (especially around the mouth and fingertips)— call 911 or your local emergency number .

Call your child's care provider right away (or seek urgent care if after office hours) if your baby:

- Is making a high-pitched, whistling sound (wheezing) each time he or she breathes out
- Is having difficulty sucking or swallowing
- Develops signs of dehydration (infrequent urination, dry mouth, crying without tears, taking less fluid)
- Is under 3 months old and has a fever, or has a fever that lasts more than three days

Also, call your child's care provider without delay if you suspect bronchiolitis and your baby was born prematurely or has an underlying health problem.

If the severity of your child's symptoms require a hospital stay, your child will likely receive humidified oxygen to maintain sufficient oxygen in the blood, and perhaps fluids through a vein (intravenously) to prevent dehydration.

What you can do You can treat most cases of mild bronchiolitis at home with self-care steps. Treat the cold symptoms with a humidifier and perhaps saline nasal drops if your baby is very congested (see more tips on relieving cold symptoms under "Cold"). Encourage plenty of fluids; breathing difficulties often cause your baby to eat or drink less and more slowly.

Wash your hands frequently to prevent the spread of viruses. When your baby is a newborn, avoid this and other infections as you much as you can by avoiding close contact with children or adults who have any type of respiratory infections — even if the symptoms seem mild.

COLD

Babies are especially susceptible to the common cold — a viral infection of the nose and throat — in part because they're often around other children with colds. In fact, within the first year of life, most babies have seven to 12 colds. Colds generally last a week or two, but occasionally they persist longer. Sometimes it may seem as if your baby has a runny nose all winter! This is especially true if a child has older siblings or he or she attends child care.

Colds are most commonly spread when someone who is sick coughs, sneezes or talks, spraying virus-carrying droplets into the air that others inhale. Colds can also be spread through hand-to-hand contact. Some viruses can live on surfaces for a few hours, so contaminated toys may be another source of infection.

Once your baby has been infected by a virus, he or she generally becomes immune to that specific virus. But because there are so many viruses that cause colds, your baby may experience several colds a year and many throughout his or her lifetime.

How to recognize it When your baby has a cold, he or she will likely develop a congested or runny nose. Nasal discharge is typically clear at first, then turns yellow, thicker and even green. After a few days, the discharge again becomes clear and runny.

Colds may produce a low fever — around 100 F — in your baby for the first few days. Your baby may also sneeze and have a cough, a hoarse voice or red eyes.

Some colds seem to settle mainly in a baby's nose, and others settle in the chest. If your infant seems to have a lot of sneezing or snorting and is frequently congested, he or she may not always have a cold. Because babies' nasal passages are quite small, it doesn't take much mucus to cause congestion. Congestion may also result from dry air or from irritants such as cigarette smoke.

How serious is it? Colds are mostly a nuisance and usually don't require a visit to a care provider. If your baby has a cold with no complications, it should resolve within about 10 to 14 days.

Keep an eye on your baby's symptoms, though, because sometimes colds can progress into more serious problems, especially in smaller or younger infants. If your baby's symptoms seem to be worsening, call your child's care provider promptly.

When to call If your baby is younger than 2 to 3 months of age, call the care provider early in the illness. For newborns, a common cold can quickly develop into croup, pneumonia or another more serious illness. Even without such complications, a stuffy nose can make it difficult for your baby to nurse or drink from a bottle. This can lead to dehydration. As your baby gets older, his or her care provider can guide you on when your baby needs to be seen by a doctor and when you can treat a cold at home.

If your baby is under 3 months and has a temperature of 100.4 F or higher, contact your child's care provider right away. If your baby is 3 months or older, call your care provider if he or she:

▶ Has a temperature that lasts more than three days
▶ Seems to have ear pain
▶ Has red eyes or develops yellow eye discharge
▶ Has a cough for longer than three weeks
▶ Has thick, green nasal discharge for more than two weeks
▶ Experiences signs or symptoms that worry you

Seek medical help immediately if your baby:

▶ Refuses to nurse or accept fluids
▶ Coughs hard enough to cause persistent vomiting or changes in skin color
▶ Coughs up blood-tinged sputum
▶ Has difficulty breathing or is bluish around the lips and mouth

What you can do Unfortunately, there's no cure for the common cold. Antibiotics kill bacteria but don't work against viruses. Over-the-counter medications should generally be avoided in infants. However, fever-reducing medications may be used — provided you carefully follow dosing directions — if fever is making your child uncomfortable (see "Fever" on page 369). Ibuprofen (Advil, Motrin, others) is OK, but only if your child is age 6 months or older. Cough and cold medications are not safe for infants and young children.

In the meantime, consider these suggestions for easing your baby's symptoms and making him or her more comfortable:

Offer plenty of fluids Liquids are important to avoid dehydration. Encourage your baby to take in his or her normal amount of fluids. Extra fluids aren't necessary. If you're breast-feeding your baby, keep it up.

Thin the mucus If your baby's nasal discharge is thick, saline nose drops or saltwater nasal sprays may help loosen the mucus. Saline nose drops and sprays are made with the optimal amount of salt and water. They're inexpensive and available without a prescription. To help your son or daughter eat better, place a couple of drops in each nostril 15 to 20 minutes before a feeding. This can be followed by suction with a nose bulb, if desired.

Suction your baby's nose You can use a rubber-bulb syringe to suction mucus from your baby's nasal passages, but sometimes it's more trouble than it's worth. Suctioning usually works best in infants under 6 months of age or babies who don't mind it. Squeeze the bulb syringe to expel the air. Then gently insert the tip of the bulb into your baby's nostril, pointing toward the back and side of

COUGH AND COLD MEDICATIONS

The Food and Drug Administration (FDA) strongly recommends against giving over-the-counter (OTC) cough and cold medicines to children younger than age 2. Over-the-counter cough and cold medicines don't effectively treat the underlying cause of a child's cold and won't cure a child's cold or make it go away any sooner. These medications also have potential side effects, including rapid heart rate and convulsions.

In June 2008, the Consumer Healthcare Products Association voluntarily modified consumer product labels on OTC cough and cold medicines to state "do not use" in children under 4 years of age. Many companies have stopped manufacturing these products for young children.

FDA experts are studying the safety of cough and cold medicines for children older than age 2. In the meantime, remember that cough and cold medicines won't make a cold go away any sooner — and side effects are still possible. If you give cough or cold medicines to an older child, carefully follow the label directions. Don't give your child two medicines with the same active ingredient, such as an antihistamine, decongestant or pain reliever. Too much of a single ingredient could lead to an accidental overdose.

the nose. Slowly release the bulb, holding it in place while it suctions the mucus from your baby's nose. Remove the syringe from your baby's nostril, and empty the contents onto a tissue by squeezing the bulb rapidly while holding the tip down. Repeat as often as needed for each nostril. Clean the bulb syringe with soap and water.

Moisten the air Running a cool-mist humidifier in your baby's room can help improve a runny nose and nasal congestion. Aim the mist away from your baby's crib to keep the bedding from becoming damp. To prevent mold growth, change the water daily and follow the manufacturer's instructions for cleaning the unit. It might also help to sit with your baby in a steamy bathroom for a few minutes before bedtime. We do not recommend the use of hot steam vaporizers because there have been reports of burns to infants and children from their use.

To prevent colds in the first place, use common sense and plenty of soap and water.

Avoid sick people Keep your baby away from anyone who's sick, especially during the first few days of an illness. Remind family and friends that the most loving thing they can do when sick is to stay away from a new baby. If possible, avoid public transportation and public gatherings with your newborn.

Keep hands clean Wash your hands before feeding or caring for your baby. Use hand gels, wipes or soap and water.

Don't share Don't share bottles, utensils or sippy cups. If your baby attends a child care facility, make sure his or her items are clearly labeled. Clean your baby's toys and pacifiers often.

Use tissues Teach everyone in the household to cough or sneeze into a tissue — and then toss it. If you can't reach a tissue in time, cough or sneeze into the crook of your arm.

COUGH

Cough is common in infants and toddlers. It's also a common cause of anxiety in parents. Your baby usually coughs because something is irritating his or her air passages. A baby's cough most often is caused by a cold or other upper respiratory tract illness. But it can also result from the irritation caused by an aspirated chunk of food, a toy or other small object that has "gone down the wrong pipe" and settled in an airway. A chronic cough that's triggered by exercise, cold air, sleep or allergens may be a sign of asthma.

How to recognize it Coughs may vary according to the part of the respiratory tract affected. An irritation near the vocal cords may cause a barking, croupy cough, and an irritation of your baby's trachea may cause a raspy cough. Allergies or asthma may cause a dry, unproductive cough that often occurs during the night. Pneumonia may cause your baby to have a deep chest cough that occurs both day and night. Babies with pneumonia usually have a fever and look sick.

How serious is it? Your baby's cough, by itself, is usually bothersome but not serious. The seriousness of the cough depends on the condition that causes it. Treating the underlying problem usually helps the cough.

When to call Contact your child's care provider promptly if your baby:

- Is younger than 2 months and develops a cough
- Is younger than 3 months and has a rectal temperature of 100.4 F or higher
- Develops a cough with fever
- Has a cough that lasts longer than one week
- Seems to be in pain

Call 911 or your local emergency number if your baby:
- Begins turning blue
- Has problems swallowing or difficulty making sounds
- Stops breathing

What you can do You may be able to ease your baby's cough by providing extra fluids and adding moisture to the air with a humidifier. If your baby's cough is interfering considerably with eating and sleeping, check with your baby's care provider. Cough medicines aren't recommended for children under age 2 because of potential side effects and because they're generally not very effective in this age group (see "Cough and cold medications" on page 361).

CONSTIPATION

Parents sometimes worry that their child is constipated because several days go by without a bowel movement. But it's not unusual for an infant who is exclusively breast-fed to go for several days — even up to a week — without a bowel movement. Constipation refers to dry, hard stools that are difficult to pass. As long as the stool is soft and easily passed, constipation likely isn't a problem.

Constipation tends to be more common in toddlers who are potty training than in infants.

How to recognize it Constipation may be a problem if your baby:
- Is a newborn and hasn't passed his or her first meconium stool one to two days after birth
- Has painful bowel movements (baby grunts and grimaces or shows discomfort, fussiness) with stools that are hard and dry
- Has streaks of blood in or on his or her stools
- Appears to have abdominal pain that seems to be relieved after a large bowel movement

How serious is it? Most infant constipation is mild, a result of a change in the baby's diet, and resolves within a short time. Constipation often causes more distress for the parents than the child. It can usually be managed by providing extra fluids and more high-fiber foods.

When to call Call your baby's care provider if your baby seems chronically constipated or if your efforts at home aren't providing any relief. Don't give laxatives, enemas or medication without consulting your care provider first.

What you can do Although many cases of constipation can be traced to diet, breast-fed babies are seldom constipated

from changes in the mother's diet. If a change of diet seemed to start the problem, it will likely improve with time. Offer plenty of fluids. Ask your child's care provider about giving your baby small amounts of prune juice. If your baby is eating solid foods, add high-fiber foods — such as prunes, apricots, plums, peas and beans — to his or her diet.

CROSSED EYES

Crossed eyes (strabismus) is one of the most common eye problems in babies. It occurs as a result of an imbalance in the muscles controlling the eye.

It's normal for a newborn's eyes to wander or appear cross-eyed because his or her brain cells haven't yet learned how to control eye movements. But by 4 months of age your baby's nervous system should be developed enough that his or her eyes work together to focus on the same point at the same time. If they continue to cross or wander, then it's time to see your baby's care provider.

How to recognize it You may notice one of your baby's eyes turns in, out, up or down. This misalignment of the eyes may be present all the time, or it may come and go.

Some babies have what's referred to as false strabismus (pseudostrabismus). Although their eyes are perfectly aligned, they appear cross-eyed because of the way their face is shaped. They might have extra skin around the inner folds of the eyes or a wide bridge of the nose. As your child gets older, the appearance of being cross-eyed should fade.

How serious is it? A child can't outgrow true strabismus, and the condition typically gets worse if left untreated. At first, a misaligned eye can lead to double vision. But eventually the brain will learn to ignore the image from the turned eye, and the eye may become "lazy" (amblyopic). This may result in permanently reduced vision.

When to call If by 4 months of age your baby's eyes appear crossed, even if only sometimes, make an appointment with your baby's care provider. He or she may refer you to a pediatric eye doctor for an evaluation. It's important to get an accurate diagnosis as soon as possible. The earlier treatment is started, the better the outcome for your child.

Rarely, a baby's eyes may suddenly become misaligned after having been straight. If this happens, call your child's care provider right away, as it may signal a more serious problem.

To treat strabismus, your child's eye doctor may recommend prescription eyeglasses, eyedrops or surgery on the eye muscle. Surgery is usually reserved for when other treatments aren't working. It's safe and effective, but a second procedure is sometimes required to get the eyes exactly aligned.

What you can do You can't treat strabismus at home, but you can monitor your child's eyes during the early months. Request an evaluation as soon you suspect any problems with the alignment of your son's or daughter's eyes. If your child requires treatment, do your best to make sure your child complies by wearing his or her glasses or by administering eye- drops exactly as your doctor recommends. If necessary, surgery is usually performed between 6 and 18 months of age. An eye surgeon will help you learn exactly what you need to know about the procedure.

CROUP

The most common characteristic of croup, a viral infection of the upper respiratory tract, is a harsh, repetitive cough that's often likened to a seal barking. Because the cough is so harsh, it can be scary for children and their parents. But croup usually isn't serious, and most cases can be treated at home.

The barking cough of croup is the result of inflammation around the vocal cords and windpipe. When the cough reflex forces air through this narrowed passage, the vocal cords vibrate with a barking noise. Because young children have small airways to begin with, they tend to have more marked symptoms.

As with a cold, croup is contagious until the fever is gone, or a few days into the illness. The virus is passed by respiratory secretions or droplets in the air.

How to recognize it The classic sign of croup is a loud, harsh, barking cough — which often comes in bursts at night. Your child's breathing may be labored or noisy. Other cold-like symptoms — such as a runny nose, fever and a hoarse voice — are common, too.

How serious is it? Most cases of croup are mild, and your baby likely won't need to see a care provider unless symptoms are severe. Croup generally lasts three to seven days (plan on at least a couple of "bad" nights) and then resolves on its own.

Rarely, the airway swells enough to interfere with breathing, warranting a trip to an urgent care clinic or emergency department. Pneumonia is a rare but potentially serious complication.

When to call If your baby's skin is turning blue or grayish around the nose, mouth or fingernails, or he or she is struggling to breathe, dial 911 or your local emergency number.

Call immediately or seek medical care if your baby:
- Makes noisy, high-pitched breathing sounds when inhaling (stridor)
- Begins drooling or has difficulty swallowing
- Seems agitated or extremely irritable
- Becomes unusually sleepy or lethargic
- Has a fever of 103.5 F or higher

Call as soon as you're able if you're concerned that your baby:
- Can't sleep, and your efforts won't settle him or her
- Is getting worse night after night, despite home treatment
- Isn't taking fluids well for 24 hours

What you can do While your baby's sick, try to keep him or her as comfortable as possible:

Stay calm Comfort or distract your child — cuddle him or her, read a book, or play a quiet game. Crying makes breathing more difficult.

Moisten the air Use a cool-air humidifier in your child's bedroom or have your child breathe the warm, moist air in a steamy bathroom. Although researchers have questioned the benefits of humidity as part of emergency treatment for croup, moist air seems to help children breathe easier — especially when croup is mild.

Get cool Sometimes breathing fresh, cool air helps (although if your child is wheezing, cold air may make the wheezing worse). If it's cool outdoors, wrap your child in a blanket and walk outside for a few minutes.

Hold your child in an upright position Sitting upright can help make breathing easier. Hold your child on your lap, or place your child in a favorite chair or infant seat.

Offer fluids For babies, breast milk or formula is fine. For older children, soup or frozen ice pops may be soothing.

Encourage rest Sleep can help your child fight the infection.

DIARRHEA

Diarrhea is a common concern for new parents. Since bowel movement patterns can vary widely among young infants — from a single bowel movement once a week or so to over 10 a day, especially in breast-fed babies — it can be tricky to tell when diarrhea is a problem. A "blowout" every so often is nothing to worry about, but if you notice stools that are more frequent than usual and have a watery consistency, your baby may have diarrhea.

Diarrhea is most often caused by an infection of your baby's stomach and intestines (gastroenteritis), usually by a virus. Sometimes bacteria or parasites may cause diarrhea. Although your baby will seldom have diarrhea from a specific food allergy, it can be caused by certain dietary factors, such as increased juice intake, lactose intolerance or the addition of new foods. Antibiotics also may cause diarrhea.

How to recognize it If you're changing more dirty diapers than usual and the contents are consistently thin and watery, your baby likely has diarrhea. Diarrhea caused by an infection may also be accompanied by vomiting and fever. Bacterial infections may cause blood in the stool and abdominal pain, as well. Occasionally, babies have small streaks of blood in their stool, caused by skin irritation from frequent passing of stool or by irritation of the intestinal lining.

How serious is it? Dehydration is the main complication that can result from your baby's diarrhea, especially if your baby has also been vomiting. Your baby has a much smaller reserve of fluids than you do because his or her body's volume is much less. Milk or lactose intolerance can cause explosive diarrhea that persists for more than two weeks.

When to call Contact your child's care provider immediately if your child:
- Passes more than eight diarrheal stools in eight hours or has blood in the stool
- Seems to have abdominal pain, a fever of more than 102 F (a fever of more than 100.4 F for a child less than 3 months old) or other obvious signs of illness
- Can't keep any fluids down
- Shows signs of dehydration — reduced urination, no tears when crying, dry mouth, or sunken eyes or fontanels (the soft spots in the head)
- Seems unusually sleepy or noticeably less active than usual

If your baby has mild diarrhea for more than a week and you're concerned, you might also contact your child's care provider.

What you can do To avoid dehydration, offer your baby liquid that's easily absorbed. For moderate to severe diarrhea, your baby's care provider may suggest an oral rehydration solution (Pedialyte, others) to replace fluid lost in the baby's stool. For severe diarrhea, don't give your baby liquids high in sugar, such as fruit juice, or salty broths or liquids very low in salt, such as water or tea;

these drinks don't have the proper amounts of sodium and other electrolytes to replace those lost in stool.

If your baby has mild diarrhea and is hungry, there's no need to restrict his or her diet. Continue breast-feeding normally and give a rehydration solution only if your child's care provider recommends it.

When the diarrhea improves, if your baby is eating solid foods, offer bland foods such as rice cereal, oatmeal, bananas, potatoes, applesauce and carrots. Offer frequent, small feedings rather than large feedings. Aim to get your baby back to his or her normal diet within a few days to ensure adequate nutrition.

If diarrhea is persistent, your child's care provider may recommend a lactose-free diet to see if it helps improve symptoms.

EAR INFECTION

An ear infection (acute otitis media) is a common reason children visit their care providers. An ear infection is caused by a bacteria or virus that affects the middle ear, the air-filled space behind the eardrum that contains the tiny vibrating bones of the ear. Children are more likely than are adults to get ear infections.

Ear infections often occur after a cold or other respiratory infection. These illnesses set the stage for inflammation and buildup of fluids in the middle ear.

Ear infections often clear up on their own. For infants, or in severe cases, however, your child's care provider may recommend antibiotic medications.

How to recognize it Infants with an ear infection usually develop the infection after an upper respiratory tract infection. Signs and symptoms may include:

▶ Ear pain, especially when lying down
▶ Difficulty sleeping
▶ Unusual crying or fussiness
▶ Difficulty hearing or responding to sounds
▶ Drainage of fluid from the ear
▶ Loss of appetite
▶ Tugging or pulling at an ear

How serious is it? Symptoms of ear infections usually improve within the first couple of days, and most infections clear up on their own within one to two weeks without any treatment.

Long-term problems related to chronic ear infections — persistent fluids in the middle ear, persistent infections or frequent infections — can cause hearing problems and other serious complications. So it's important to bring ear infections, especially recurring ones, to the attention of your child's care provider.

When to call Contact your baby's care provider if:

▹ Symptoms last for more than a day
▹ Ear pain is severe
▹ Your infant or toddler is sleepless or irritable after a cold or other upper respiratory infection
▹ You observe a discharge of fluid, pus or bloody discharge from the ear

In babies, most ear infections are treated with antibiotics. Among older children, a doctor may wait to see if the condition improves on its own before prescribing antibiotics. Your child's care provider may also recommend numbing drops or an infant pain reliever to ease your baby's ear pain.

Ear tubes — tiny tubes that are surgically placed in a hole through the eardrum to help ventilate the middle ear and prevent the accumulation of more fluids — are usually reserved for children who have recurrent ear infections and persistent fluid behind the eardrum, along with hearing problems.

What you can do Placing a warm (not hot), moist washcloth over the affected ear may lessen pain. If your child's care provider recommends a pain reliever or numbing drops, use them exactly as the care provider instructs. To administer the drops, warm the bottle first in warm water, then put the recommended dose in your baby's ear while he or she lies flat with the infected ear facing up.

To reduce your baby's risk of ear infections, practice good infection prevention skills by washing hands frequently, not sharing eating and drinking utensils, and avoiding contact with others who are sick. Secondhand smoke also can contribute to frequent ear infections. In addition, hold your baby upright when feeding him or her a bottle, to avoid blocking the passage between the middle ear and throat (eustachian tube).

EARWAX BLOCKAGE

Earwax blockage occurs when earwax (cerumen) accumulates in the ear or becomes too hard to wash away naturally.

Earwax is a helpful and natural part of the body's defenses. It protects the ear canal by trapping dirt and slowing the growth of bacteria. Normally, it will dry up and tumble out of the ear on its own. But occasionally, wax buildup occurs, perhaps because of a narrower than usual ear canal, an excess production of earwax or even well-meaning attempts to clean out the ear, which can push the wax further into the ear and cause a blockage.

How to recognize it Although it may not be easy to identify in your child, signs and symptoms of earwax blockage are likely to resemble some of those related to an ear infection. Your baby may pull or tug at his or her ear, cough, or be unusually fussy or irritable. You may also notice that your baby doesn't hear quite as well or doesn't respond to sounds.

How serious is it? A buildup of earwax is unlikely to cause serious problems, unless you try to dig it out yourself. Trying to remove earwax with a cotton swab or other instrument may push the wax further into your baby's ear and cause serious damage to the lining of the ear canal or eardrum.

When to call Make an appointment to have your baby's ears checked out if he or she is tugging at his or her ears, you notice hearing problems, or you see a lot of waxy discharge coming out of your child's ears.

Your child's care provider can determine if there's an excess of earwax by looking in your child's ear with an otoscope, a special instrument that lights and magnifies the eardrum. A care provider can often remove excess wax using a small instrument called a curet or by using suction while inspecting the ear. He or she may also flush out the wax using a water pick or a rubber-bulb syringe filled with warm water.

What you can do Avoid cleaning your baby's ears with cotton swabs, your finger or anything else. If your child doesn't have any tubes or holes in his or her eardrum, his or her care provider may recommend eardrops to soften the wax. Ask the provider to show you how to gently irrigate the outer ear with warm water and a rubber-bulb syringe to wash out the softened wax.

FEVER

Normal temperatures vary for different people. Your newborn's temperature will change up and down by about 1 degree throughout the day. It's usually lowest in the morning and highest late in the afternoon. In general, infants and young children have a higher normal body temperature than do older children and adults.

When faced with an infection or other illness, however, your baby's central nervous system cranks up his or her internal "thermostat" to help fight the infection. This results in a fever. In newborns and infants less than 3 months of age, a fever warrants an immediate call to your baby's care provider. In older infants and children, the need for medical evaluation of a fever depends more on how your child is behaving and whether there are other accompanying signs or symptoms of illness.

How to recognize it If your baby feels unusually warm to you, take his or her temperature with a thermometer (see "Taking baby's temperature" on page 350). Although laying your hand or your cheek on your baby's forehead may give you a suspicion of fever, it won't tell you the difference between 99 F and 101 F.

A rectal temperature of 100.4 F is generally considered the upper range of normal. Anything higher constitutes a fever.

How serious is it? A fever itself isn't harmful. Any potential harm would come from the infection that's causing the fever. Usually, when a baby has a fever, he or she is fighting an infection; fever is a sign of the immune system at work.

In young infants, however, an infection signaled by a fever can quickly become serious. Their immune systems are not yet up to the task of fighting off bacteria and other germs, making them particularly vulnerable to infection that can easily spread throughout the body.

When to call Call your baby's care provider right away if your baby is under 3 months of age and has a rectal temperature of 100.4 F or higher. This is important because your baby's immune system is still developing and may not be able to fight off an infection as well as an older baby. So call, even if you're feeling reluctant to bother your baby's care provider.

Call if your baby is between 3 and 12 months old and doesn't respond to acetaminophen or shows other signs of illness, such as:

▶ An unexplained rash
▶ Repeated vomiting or diarrhea
▶ Unusual fussiness or irritability
▶ Coughing
▶ Refusal to eat or drink
▶ Dehydration — reduced urination, dry mouth, crying without tears, sunken eyes and fontanels (the soft spots in the head)
▶ Lethargy and unresponsiveness

If your baby seems feverish after spending time in an overheated area, such as on a hot beach or in a hot car, seek medical help immediately. Overheating (heatstroke) is an emergency and needs to be treated quickly.

What you can do If your baby has a fever, monitor his or her behavior closely. Look for other signs or symptoms of illness, such as loss of appetite, vomiting, irritability or unusual sleepiness. Call your baby's care provider if you have any concerns.

Most of the time, mild fevers don't need treatment and resolve along with the associated cold or other infection that brought it on. In the meantime, you can:

Provide plenty of fluids Continue breastfeeding or formula-feeding as usual. Frozen ice pops work well in older infants. If your baby is eating solid foods, let him or her decide whether and how much to eat. If you're concerned that your baby is getting dehydrated, offer a commercially prepared oral rehydrating solution (Pedialyte, others).

FEVER AND PAIN RELIEVERS: RECOMMENDED DOSAGES

Acetaminophen dosages (every 4 hours)*

Child's weight: 6 to 11 lbs. Dose: 40 mg Infant drops: ½ dropper (0.4 mL) Infant liquid: 1.25 mL in syringe	**Child's weight: 12 to 17 lbs.** Dose: 80 mg Infant drops: 1 dropper (0.8 mL) Infant liquid: 2.5 mL in syringe Children's liquid: ½ tsp. (2.5 mL in cup)
Child's weight: 18 to 23 lbs. Dose: 120 mg Infant drops: 1½ droppers (1.2 mL) Infant liquid: 3.75 mL in syringe Children's liquid: ¾ tsp. (3.75 mL in cup)	**Child's weight: 24 to 35 lbs.** Dose: 160 mg Infant drops: 2 droppers (1.6 mL) Infant liquid: 5 mL in syringe Children's liquid: 1 tsp. (5 mL in cup)

Ibuprofen dosages (every 6-8 hours)

Child's weight: 12 to 17 lbs.† Dose: 50 mg Infant drops: 1 dropper (1.25 mL)	**Child's weight: 18 to 23 lbs.** Dose: 75 mg Infant drops: 1½ dropper (1.875 mL)
Child's weight: 24 to 35 lbs. Children's liquid: 1 tsp. (100 mg per tsp. dose/5 mL in cup) Chewable tablets: 2 tablets (50 mg per tablet/100 mg total) Junior strength caplet or chewable tablet: 1 tablet (100 mg per tablet)	

*The U.S. Food and Drug Administration was expected to publish updated guidelines in 2012 on acetaminophen use in children, which could change these recommended dosages. Check with your child's care provider for the latest information.

†For a child younger than 6 months, ask his or her care provider before giving ibuprofen.

FEBRILE SEIZURES

Some babies experience convulsions as a result of a rapid rise or fall in body temperature, often from an infection. Watching your baby have a febrile seizure can be alarming, but the good news is that it's usually harmless and typically doesn't indicate a long-term or ongoing problem. Studies suggest there also isn't much that can be done to prevent a febrile seizure.

You can tell your baby is having a febrile seizure if he or she has repeated rhythmic jerking of both arms and legs and is not responsive to you or aware of his or her surroundings. (Occasional odd twitchy or jerky movements are common, especially in sleepy infants — these are not seizures.)

Most of the time, a febrile seizure occurs the first day of an illness, sometimes even before parents realize that their child is ill.

If your child has a febrile seizure, stay calm and follow these tips to help your child during the seizure:

- Place your child on his or her side, somewhere where he or she won't fall.
- Stay close to watch and comfort your child.
- Remove any hard or sharp objects near your child.
- Loosen any tight or restrictive clothing.
- Don't restrain your child or interfere with your child's movements.
- Don't attempt to put anything in your child's mouth.

Have a first-time febrile seizure evaluated by your child's care provider as soon as possible, even if it lasts only a few seconds. If the seizure ends quickly, call the care provider as soon as it's over and ask when and where your child can be examined. If the seizure lasts longer than five minutes or is accompanied by vomiting, a stiff neck, problems with breathing or extreme sleepiness, call for an ambulance to take your child to the emergency department.

By staying calm, observing your child and knowing when to call for medical help, you're doing everything that's needed to take care of your child.

Encourage adequate rest Provide extra opportunities for rest and quiet play until the fever is improved or over.

Keep cool If your baby seems hot, keep his or her room comfortably cool and dress him or her lightly.

Try a sponge bath Your son or daughter may enjoy a sponge bath with lukewarm (not cold) water. Don't put rubbing alcohol in the bath or rub your baby with it — doing so is not safe.

Use medication for discomfort If your baby seems uncomfortable and weighs 6 pounds or more, you can give him or her acetaminophen (Tylenol, others). If your child is 6 months or older, ibuprofen (Advil, Motrin, others) is OK. Read the label carefully for proper dosage (or see the opposite page). Don't use aspirin to treat a fever in anyone age 18 years or younger, as it can cause a rare but serious disorder called Reye's syndrome. Keep in mind that it's generally not a good idea to give fever-reducing medication for more than three days without consulting your child's care provider.

FIFTH DISEASE

Fifth disease is a highly contagious and common childhood ailment caused by the parvovirus — you may also hear it referred to as parvovirus infection or slapped-cheek disease because of the rosy rash that appears on the cheeks. In most children, the infection is mild and requires little treatment.

How to recognize it You may suspect that your baby has fifth disease if he or she develops bright red, warm, raised patches on both cheeks. During the next few days, a baby with fifth disease will develop a pink, lacy, slightly raised rash on the arms, trunk, thighs and buttocks.

Generally, the rash occurs near the end of the illness when the child is no longer contagious. Some children develop mild cold-like symptoms before the rash, such as sore throat, mild fever, headache and fatigue. Itchiness also may be an early symptom.

It's possible to mistake the rash for other viral rashes or a medicine-related rash. The rash may come and go for up to three weeks, becoming more visible when your baby is exposed to extreme temperatures or spends time in the sun.

How serious is it? Generally, infants feel fairly well when they have fifth disease. For most, it's a mild illness unless your baby has sickle cell anemia or a weak immune system, in which case it may cause more serious problems.

Parvovirus can be a concern for pregnant women, though, so keep a sick baby away from anyone who's pregnant, par-

ticularly in the first trimester. If a woman develops a parvovirus infection during pregnancy, her baby may be affected.

When to call Rashes aren't always easy to diagnose at home, so if you suspect fifth disease in your child, it's best to call your baby's care provider to make sure it's not a sign of a different illness that may require treatment. Also, call the care provider if your baby has a fifth disease-like rash and another condition such as sickle cell anemia or a weak immune system.

What you can do Make sure you or your child gets plenty of rest and drinks lots of fluids. You can use acetaminophen (Tylenol, others) to relieve fever or minor aches and pains (see "Fever" on page 369).

It's not always practical or necessary to isolate a child with fifth disease. You won't know your son or daughter has parvovirus infection until the rash appears, and by that time, he or she is no longer contagious.

FLU (INFLUENZA)

Influenza, routinely known as the flu, is a common fall and wintertime viral illness that affects the upper respiratory system. It's often confused with the common cold, although the flu usually leaves your child feeling more achy and miserable than does a cold.

Several types of viruses can cause influenza (A and B are the most common), with each type having several strains. Influenza viruses are constantly changing, with new strains appearing regularly. This is why it's important to receive an annual flu vaccine — each year's vaccine is developed to prevent the three most likely strains to appear that year. The Centers for Disease Control and Prevention now recommend annual flu vaccination for all Americans over the age of 6 months. It's typically available as an injection or as a nasal spray. However, at this time, the nasal spray is only available for children who are at least 2 years old.

How to recognize it Having the flu usually causes:

- A sudden onset of fever, typically more than 101 F, although not everyone gets a fever
- Chills
- Achy muscles
- Extreme tiredness
- Dry cough

How serious is it? Influenza can be a serious illness for your otherwise healthy baby, although most babies recover without major problems. The main complications of influenza are ear infections and pneumonia; both require treatment from your baby's care provider. Children with underlying health problems are at greater risk of complications.

Influenza infections are contagious a day or so before your child becomes sick and while he or she is sick.

When to call Children under age 2 are at higher risk for complications from the flu. Call your baby's care provider for advice if you notice flu-like symptoms. Call right away if you suspect your baby is developing complications or if coughing or fever persists. If your baby has flu-like symptoms and trouble breathing, seek medical care immediately. If you know your infant has been exposed to influenza, contact your child's care provider.

What you can do The best way to prevent the flu is to receive the flu vaccine, available to everyone 6 months of age or older. If your whole family receives the vaccine, you're less likely to get the flu and pass it to each other. If your baby is under 6 months of age, it's especially important to take common-sense precautions against infections:

- Wash your hands frequently.
- Keep heavily-used surfaces clean.
- Cough or sneeze into a tissue or the crook of your elbow (discard used tissues promptly).
- Don't share eating or drinking utensils or toothbrushes.
- Avoid cross-contamination between sick family members by not kissing each other on the hands or mouth.
- Avoid people who have the flu.
- Avoid crowds at peak flu season, where the chances of coming into contact with influenza viruses are greater.

If your child does develop influenza, encourage plenty of rest, fluids and hugs. If your baby seems fussy and uncomfortable, acetaminophen can help ease aches and pains, as well as reduce fever (see the medication chart on page 370). Don't give aspirin, which can cause serious side effects in young people who have a viral infection.

Sometimes adding extra moisture to the air makes it easier for your baby to breathe. Keep your baby home from his or her child care center at least 24 hours after the fever has passed.

HAND-FOOT-AND-MOUTH DISEASE

Hand-foot-and-mouth disease — a mild, contagious viral infection common in young children — is characterized by sores in the mouth and a rash on the hands and feet. Hand-foot-and-mouth disease is most commonly caused by a coxsackievirus.

Hand-foot-and-mouth disease isn't related to foot-and-mouth disease (sometimes called hoof-and-mouth disease), which is an infectious viral disease found in farm animals. You can't contract hand-foot-and-mouth disease from pets or other animals, and you can't transmit it to them.

Once your child is exposed to the virus that caused the hand-foot-and-mouth disease, he or she will build up immunity to it in the future.

How to recognize it A fever is often the first sign of hand-foot-and-mouth disease, followed by a sore throat, irritability and sometimes a poor appetite. One or two days after the fever begins, painful sores may develop in the mouth or throat. A rash on the hands and feet and possibly on the buttocks can follow within one or two days.

How serious is it? Hand-foot-and-mouth disease is usually a minor illness causing only a few days of fever and relatively mild signs and symptoms.

The sores in the mouth and throat can make swallowing painful and difficult for your baby, however, increasing his or her risk of dehydration. Watch closely to make sure your child frequently sips fluid during the course of the illness.

Infected people are most contagious during the first week of illness.

When to call Contact your baby's care provider if mouth sores or a sore throat keep your child from drinking fluids. Call also if after a few days, your child's signs and symptoms worsen.

What you can do As with most viral illnesses, there's not much you can do but encourage plenty of fluids and plenty of rest. Acetaminophen can help relieve dis-

comfort from fever or aches and pains (see "Infants and medications" on page 348).

If your baby is eating solid foods, keep in mind that certain foods may irritate blisters on the tongue or in the mouth or throat. You can help make blister soreness less bothersome and eating more tolerable by:

▶ Offering frequent feedings of breast milk or formula. Drinking is more important than eating solids.
▶ Offering a small amount of sherbet to soothe the throat.
▶ Avoiding acidic foods and beverages, such as citrus fruits and fruit drinks
▶ Offering soft foods that don't require much chewing

HIVES

Hives is the name for an allergic reaction that produces patches of red, raised, itchy skin. Often there's no clear explanation for what triggers hives, but viral infections are a common cause. Hives can also occur as an allergic reaction to a food, drug or insect bite.

How to recognize it Hives is characterized by splotchy, red, raised areas of skin, often with pale centers. The rash itches and can become uncomfortable. Hives can appear all over your baby's body or be concentrated in one area. The rash is irregularly shaped and may change locations. Some areas may enlarge and merge into each other. Hives may come and go for a few days or a few weeks.

How serious is it? Hives usually isn't serious unless your child also develops difficulty breathing or swallowing, a sign of swelling around the throat area and windpipe.

When to call If your baby develops hives, ask his or her care provider about the proper treatment. Call your baby's care provider right away if your infant:

▶ Has difficulty breathing or swallowing or develops a swollen tongue
▶ Develops hives while taking medication (discontinue the medication until you've talked with your child's care provider)
▶ Seems to have soreness in his or her joints
▶ Has hives for more than a few days

What you can do Babies with hives often look much worse than they feel. To keep your baby as comfortable as possible, administer an antihistamine as indicated by your baby's care provider. Keep your baby dressed in light clothing and avoid bathing him or her in hot water. Lukewarm water is less likely to exacerbate itching. Trim your baby's fingernails to avoid scratching.

If you notice a pattern to the appearance of hives on your baby, try to determine what may be triggering it. Avoiding the trigger will help prevent a recurrence of hives.

IMPETIGO

Impetigo usually appears as red sores on the face, especially around a child's nose and mouth (see the photo on page 101). It's a highly contagious skin infection that's more common in infants and children than in adults. Although it commonly occurs when bacteria enter the skin through cuts or insect bites, it can also develop in skin that's perfectly healthy.

Keeping the skin clean is the best way to prevent infection. Treat cuts, scrapes, insect bites and other wounds right away by washing the affected areas and applying antibiotic ointment to prevent infection.

How to recognize it Your child might have impetigo if you notice:

▶ Red sores that quickly rupture, ooze for a few days and then form a yellowish-brown crust
▶ Itching
▶ Painless, fluid-filled blisters, usually on the trunk, arms and legs (These are more common in children under 2.)
▶ Painful fluid- or pus-filled sores that turn into deep ulcers (This is the more serious form.)

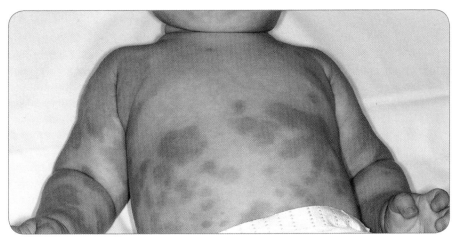

This photo shows an infant with hives, characterized by patches of red, raised skin.

How serious is it? Impetigo is seldom serious and usually clears on its own in two to three weeks. But because impetigo can sometimes lead to more severe infection, your child's doctor may choose to treat impetigo with an antibiotic ointment or oral antibiotics.

When to call If you suspect that you or your child has impetigo, ask your child's care provider for advice on treatment. Sometimes he or she may choose to treat minor cases of impetigo with only hygienic measures. Keeping the skin clean can help mild infections heal on their own.

In other cases, your child's care provider may recommend an antibiotic ointment to apply to the affected areas.

If your child is uncomfortable, or the sores are oozing or widespread, make an appointment to have the sores examined. Severe or widespread cases may be treated with oral antibiotics taken by mouth. Be sure you child finishes the entire course of medication, even if the sores are healed. This helps prevent the infection from recurring and makes antibiotic resistance less likely.

What you can do For minor infections that haven't spread to other areas, try the following:
- Soak the affected areas of skin with a vinegar solution — 1 tablespoon (½ ounce) of white vinegar to 1 pint (16 ounces) of water — for 20 minutes. This makes it easier to gently remove the scabs.
- After washing the area, apply an over-the-counter antibiotic ointment three times daily. Wash the skin before each application, and pat it dry.

To help keep the infection from spreading to others:
- Wash your hands frequently.

- Cut an infected child's nails short to prevent scratching and spreading the infection. Applying a nonstick dressing to the infected area can help, too.
- Avoid touching the sores as much as possible until they heal.
- Wash your baby's clothes, blankets, washcloths and towels every day, and don't share them with anyone else in your family.
- Wear gloves when applying any antibiotic ointment and wash your hands thoroughly afterward.

Your son or daughter can usually return to child care after his or her care provider says he or she is no longer contagious — often within 48 to 72 hours of starting antibiotic therapy.

INSECT BITES AND STINGS

Bites from bees, wasps, hornets, yellow jackets and fire ants are typically the most troublesome. Bites from mosquitoes, ticks, biting flies and some spiders also can cause reactions, but these are generally milder.

How to recognize it Bites and stings may come from:
- *Bees, yellow jackets and hornets.* In most children, stings cause initial pain and become red and swollen within the first several hours. But in a few kids, stings can cause severe symptoms, including vomiting, diarrhea, dizziness and sometimes trouble breathing.
- *Mosquitoes.* Usually the site simply itches and swells.
- *Deerflies, horseflies, fire ants, harvester ants, beetles and centipedes.* These may cause painful red bumps that may blister.

How serious is it? Most children will have only a mild reaction to bites and stings. But a few children are more sensitive than are others to insect venom, especially from stinging insects, and can have a severe allergic reaction (anaphylaxis) that requires emergency treatment.

When to call Call your baby's care provider immediately if your child:

- Has difficulty breathing
- Vomits
- Shows signs of shock (rapid breathing, dizziness, clammy skin)
- Has received multiple stings
- Develops extreme facial swelling, or hives all over the body or in an area separate from the sting itself
- Has increased swelling and redness around the sting or bite after the first six to eight hours

What you can do If a stinger is noticeable, remove it from your baby's skin as soon as possible. Use a fingernail, credit card or other thin dull edge to scrape the stinger away. Avoid pinching or squeezing the stinger, as this may release more venom into the skin.

Once the stinger is gone, apply a cool washcloth or ice pack to relieve pain and swelling. Cool compresses can also help relieve itching associated with mosquitoes, flies, ants and other insect bites.

Ask your baby's care provider about applying ointments or creams to relieve itching, such as calamine lotion, hydrocortisone cream or baking soda paste. If itching is severe, your child's care provider may recommend giving your baby an oral antihistamine.

To decrease the likelihood of experiencing insect bites:

- Cover your baby's skin with lightweight clothing when you take him or her outdoors.

- Avoid areas where insects are commonly found, such as garbage cans, stagnant water (breeding ground for mosquitoes) and blooming flowers.
- Don't use strong perfumes or scented soaps and lotions on yourself or your baby.
- Cover all picnic food, and seal picnic garbage in plastic bags.
- Keep garbage cans securely covered.
- Don't allow pools of stagnant water in your backyard.

DEET is the most widely used chemical found in insect repellents. Products that contain DEET are not recommended for babies under 2 months old. In older infants, the maximum concentration of DEET in the product should not exceed 30 percent.

The American Academy of Pediatrics (AAP) recommends applying DEET only once a day and washing it off at the end of the day to avoid toxicity. The higher the concentration of DEET in a product, the longer the protective time it supplies. The AAP recommends using the lowest effective concentration for the amount of

time your child spends outside. Products with 4.75 percent DEET afford about an hour and a half of protection. A 20 percent DEET product provides about four hours of protection.

To apply repellent to your baby, put it on your hands first and then rub it on your baby's skin. Avoid your baby's hands, which he or she is likely to put in his or her mouth.

There are alternatives to DEET products. Picaridin in 5 to 10 percent concentrations is safe for young children. Oil of lemon eucalyptus is a plant-based repellent, but it's not recommended for children under 3 years of age.

JAUNDICE

Jaundice is a yellow discoloration of a newborn baby's skin and eyes. Newborn jaundice is a common condition, particularly in babies born before 38 weeks gestation (preterm babies) and breast-fed babies. It develops when a baby's liver

isn't mature enough to filter out bilirubin, a yellow-colored pigment of red blood cells, from the bloodstream.

How to recognize it The main signs of newborn jaundice are yellowing of the skin and eyes. These usually appear between the second and fourth day after birth. You'll usually notice jaundice first in your baby's face. If the condition progresses, you may notice the yellow color in his or her eyes and on the chest, abdomen, arms and legs.

The best way to check for newborn jaundice is to press your finger gently on your baby's forehead or nose. If the skin looks yellow where you pressed, it's likely your baby has jaundice. If your baby doesn't have jaundice, the skin color should simply look slightly lighter than its normal color for a moment.

It's best to examine your baby in good lighting conditions, preferably in natural daylight.

How serious is it? Mild newborn jaundice often disappears on its own within two or three weeks. If your baby has moderate or severe jaundice, he or she may need to stay longer in the newborn nursery or be readmitted to the hospital for phototherapy. This is a special blue light that helps the body clear the bilirubin.

Although complications are rare, severe infant jaundice can lead to cerebral palsy, deafness and brain damage.

When to call Most hospitals have a policy of checking babies regularly for jaundice while they are hospitalized and before they're discharged. The American Academy of Pediatrics recommends that your newborn be examined for jaundice whenever a routine medical check is done.

Your baby should be checked for jaundice when he or she is between 3 and 7 days old, when bilirubin levels usually peak. If your baby is discharged earlier than 72 hours following birth, schedule a follow-up appointment with your baby's care provider to check for jaundice within two days of discharge.

The following signs or symptoms may indicate severe jaundice or complications from jaundice. Call your doctor if:

▶ Your baby's skin looks yellow on the chest, abdomen, arms or legs.
▶ The whites of your baby's eyes look yellow.
▶ Your baby seems listless, sick or difficult to wake.
▶ Your baby isn't gaining weight or is feeding poorly.
▶ Your baby makes high-pitched cries.
▶ Your baby develops any other signs or symptoms that concern you.
▶ Diagnosed jaundice lasts more than three weeks.

What you can do Feeding more frequently will provide your baby with more milk and cause more bowel movements, increasing the amount of bilirubin eliminated in your baby's stool. Breast-fed infants should have eight to 12 feedings a day for the first several days of life. Formula-fed infants usually should have 1 to 2 ounces of formula every two to three hours for the first week.

If your baby is having trouble breast-feeding, is losing weight or is dehydrated, your baby's care provider may suggest giving your baby infant formula or expressed milk in addition to his or her breast-feedings. In some cases, a care provider may recommend only infant formula for a couple of days and then resuming breast-feeding.

Ask your baby's care provider what feeding options are right for your baby.

LAZY EYE

Lazy eye (amblyopia) develops when nerve pathways between the brain and the eye aren't properly stimulated. This can lead to a condition in which the brain favors one eye, usually due to poor vision in the other eye. The weaker eye tends not to track with the stronger eye, commonly referred to as "wandering." Eventually, the brain may ignore the signals received from the weaker — or lazy — eye.

Treatments such as corrective eyewear or eye patches can often correct lazy eye. Sometimes, lazy eye requires surgical treatment.

How to recognize it Lazy eye usually affects just one eye, but it may affect both eyes. With lazy eye, there's no apparent damage or abnormality to the eye. Signs and symptoms to look for include:

▶ An eye that wanders inward or outward
▶ Eyes that may not appear to work together
▶ Poor depth perception

How serious is it? Left untreated, lazy eye can cause permanent vision loss. In fact, lazy eye is the most common cause of single-eye vision impairment in young and middle-aged adults, according to the National Eye Institute.

Depending on the cause and the degree to which your child's vision is affected, treatment options may include:

Corrective eyewear If a condition such as nearsightedness, farsightedness or astigmatism is contributing to lazy eye, an eye doctor will likely prescribe corrective glasses or contact lenses. Sometimes corrective eyewear is all that's needed.

Eye patches To stimulate vision in the weaker eye, a doctor may recommend that your child wear an eye patch over the stronger eye — possibly for two or more hours a day, depending on the severity of the condition. This helps the part of the brain that manages vision develop more completely.

Eyedrops A daily or twice-weekly drop of a medication that temporarily blurs vision in the stronger eye is used to encourage use of the weaker eye. It offers an alternative to wearing a patch.

Surgery If your child has crossed or outwardly deviating eyes (strabismus), the eye muscles may benefit from surgical repair. Droopy eyelids or cataracts also may need surgical intervention.

For most children with lazy eye, proper treatment improves vision within weeks to several months — and the earlier treatment begins, the better. Although research suggests that the treatment window extends through at least age 17, results are better when treatment begins in early childhood.

When to call If you notice your child's eye wandering at any time beyond the first few weeks of life, consult your child's care provider for an evaluation. Depending on the circumstances, he or she may refer your child to a doctor who specializes in eye conditions (ophthalmologist or optometrist).

What you can do There's really nothing you can do at home to treat lazy eye. However, you can monitor your child's eyes closely in the first few months of life to make sure they are in proper alignment and to make sure your baby's vision seems to be consistently improving. The sooner treatment for lazy eye begins, generally the better the outcome for your child.

PINK EYE (CONJUNCTIVITIS)

Pink eye is an inflammation or infection of the transparent membrane (conjunctiva) that lines your eyelid and part of your eyeball. It's frequently caused by a bacterial or viral infection (usually the same virus that causes the common cold), but it can also result from allergies.

How to recognize it You might suspect that your baby has pink eye if you notice that the white part of the eye and the eyelid are reddened in one or both eyes. Pink eye can also cause mucus, or "matter," to form in your baby's eye, varying from thin and watery to thick and yellowish green. Bacterial infections are more likely to cause thick, green discharge.

If your baby has pink eye, you may find his or her eyelids stuck together on awakening, requiring you to wash them clean. Also suspect pink eye if your baby experiences discomfort with exposure to bright lights, or if he or she does a lot of blinking.

How serious is it? Pink eye generally lasts about as long as a cold, usually a week or so, but sometimes up to two or three weeks. If infectious, pink eye is contagious by contact.

Viral infections just need time to run their course; bacterial infections may be treated with antibiotic drops. If pink eye is due to allergies, your care provider may recommend specific eyedrops for people with allergies.

When to call Make a call if your baby:
◗ Develops a red and swollen eyelid
◗ Develops a fever or starts acting ill
◗ Has the symptoms of an ear infection
◗ Doesn't seem to improve after starting treatment

What you can do Wash the outside of your baby's eyelid, using clean cotton balls (a new one for each eye) and warm water. Or you can use a washcloth and warm water. Wipe from the inner to the outer part of eye to prevent spreading infection to the uninfected eye. Because pink eye is usually contagious, you and others who care for your child should take precautions to avoid spreading it. A baby with pink eye should have his or her own towel and washcloth, both at home and away. Wash your hands carefully after you come into contact with secretions from your child's eyes.

In case of a bacterial infection, your child's care provider may recommend antibiotic drops or ointment. Some parents find ointment easier to use than eyedrops, although ointment can blur your child's vision for up to 20 minutes or so after application. In either case, the discharge should improve within the first two days or so, although the redness may persist a few days more. Follow the instructions of your child's care provider and use the antibiotics until the prescription runs out to prevent recurrence of the infection.

Applying the drops or ointment in your baby's eye is sometimes easier with two people. Wash your hands before applying ointment or drops. (The other person should do the same.) To prevent contamination of the medication, don't let the applicator tip touch any surface, including the baby's eye. When you finish, wipe the tip of the tube with a clean tissue and tightly close it. Wash your hands after touching your baby's eyes.

To administer medication, follow these tips:

Eyedrops Lay your baby on his or her back. Gently pull the lower eyelid down to form a little pouch, and place the drops in the pouch. The drops will disperse over the eye as your baby blinks.

Ointment Pull your baby's lower eyelid away from the affected eye to form a pouch. Unless your child's care provider tells you otherwise, squeeze a thin strip of ointment into the pouch. Release your child's lower eyelid, and then ease the upper eyelid down to cover your baby's eye. Hold the lid closed for just a moment or two.

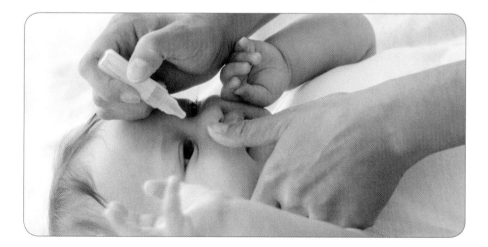

PNEUMONIA

Babies who get pneumonia are usually ill first with a viral upper respiratory tract infection, such as a cold. Some viral infections can the affect the lungs, resulting in viral pneumonia. Pneumonia can also stem from a bacterial infection, perhaps after a cold. In children under 2 years of age, bacterial pneumonia is less common than the viral kind. Bacterial pneumonia may be helped by antibiotics.

How to recognize it Pneumonia is usually worse than a bad cold. A baby with pneumonia may cough and have difficulty breathing. Breathing may become fast and labored. You might notice that your baby's lips or nails have a bluish tint. Your baby may also appear pale, develop a fever, lose his or her appetite, and become either more listless or fussier than usual.

How serious is it? In the past, pneumonia could be a dangerous illness. Now, most babies recover well if they receive prompt medical attention.

When to call Call immediately if you suspect that your baby may have pneumonia or your baby is less than 3 months old and has a rectal temperature of 100.4 F or higher. Be sure to check back with your care provider if:

▶ Your baby's fever continues more than two or three days, despite taking an antibiotic
▶ Your baby has difficulty breathing

What you can do If your child's care provider suspects bacterial pneumonia, he or she may prescribe a course of antibiotics for your baby. Antibiotics don't help viral infections, but sometimes it's difficult to distinguish between viral and bacterial pneumonia. Be sure to give your baby the full course of medication prescribed, even if he or she starts to feel better. This helps reduce recurrence of the infection and minimizes the chances that the bacteria will become resistant to the drug.

Viral pneumonia typically doesn't require anything other than home treatment. Encourage quiet activities so that your baby gets plenty of rest. Your baby may need extra holding and cuddling. He or she also needs plenty of fluids. Coughing is usually beneficial for babies with pneumonia because it helps to clear the mucus and secretions associated with the infection.

You can help prevent your baby from developing pneumonia in many cases by making sure your son or daughter is up to date with his or her immunizations — especially against pneumococcal infections (pneumococcal conjugate, or PCV13), a bacterial cause of pneumonia, *Haemophilus influenzae* type b (Hib), varicella and the seasonal flu.

REFLUX

Spitting up is common in new babies, occurring in about half of newborns under age 3 months. Normally, the condition goes away after the first few months. But in some babies, spitting up continues throughout the first year or so. The medical term for this condition is gastroesophageal reflux, or GER.

The causes of infant GER are generally simple. Normally, the ring of muscle between the esophagus and the stomach (lower esophageal sphincter) relaxes and opens only when you swallow. Otherwise, it's tightly closed — keeping stomach contents where they belong. Until this muscle matures, stomach contents may sometimes flow up the esophagus and out of your baby's mouth. Sometimes air bubbles in the esophagus may push liquid out of your baby's mouth. In other cases, your baby may simply drink too much, too fast.

How to recognize it Although infant GER most often occurs after a feeding, your baby also may spit up when he or she coughs, cries or strains. You may also notice your baby becomes more irritable during or after feedings, or coughs, wheezes or cries when you lay him or her on his or her back, especially after feeding.

How serious is it? Infant GER typically resolves on its own when your baby is around 12 to 18 months old. Unless severe — gastroesophageal reflux disease (GERD) is a severe version of reflux that can cause pain, vomiting and poor weight gain — infant GER doesn't interfere with a baby's growth or well-being.

When to call Call your child's care provider if your baby:
- Isn't gaining weight
- Spits up forcefully, causing stomach contents to shoot out of his or her mouth
- Spits up green fluid (Call immediately if this happens.)
- Spits up blood or a material that looks like coffee grounds
- Resists feedings
- Has blood in his or her stool
- Has other signs of illness, such as fever, diarrhea or difficulty breathing
- Begins persistent vomiting at age 6 months or older

What you can do Infant GER is usually little cause for concern, but you may have to keep an extra supply of spit-up cloths on hand until your baby outgrows the condition. To minimize reflux in the meantime:

Try smaller, more frequent feedings Feed your baby slightly less than usual if you're bottle-feeding, or cut back a little on the amount of time you breast-feed.

Take time to burp your baby Frequent burps during and after each feeding can keep air from building up in your baby's stomach. Sit your baby upright, supporting his or her head with your hand, and rub his or her back. Avoid burping your baby over your shoulder, which puts pressure on your baby's abdomen.

Check the nipple If you're using a bottle, make sure the hole in the nipple is the right size. If it's too large, the milk will flow too fast. If it's too small, your baby may get frustrated and gulp air. A nipple hole that's the right size will allow a few drops of milk to fall out when you hold the bottle upside down.

Thicken the formula or breast milk If your baby's care provider approves, add a small amount of rice cereal to your baby's formula or expressed breast milk. You may need to enlarge the hole in the nipple to make sure your baby can drink the thickened liquid.

Make a change Occasionally, some babies develop an allergy to cow's milk protein. If you are breast-feeding, that means you may have to eliminate milk products from your diet. If you are formula-feeding your baby, your child's care provider may suggest switching to a different formula that doesn't contain cow's milk.

RSV

Respiratory syncytial virus (RSV) is a virus that can cause infections of the upper respiratory tract, such as a cold, or the lower respiratory tract, such as bronchiolitis and pneumonia. It's so common that most children get RSV before age 2. Reinfections with RSV are common, but a child gets older, symptoms usually become less severe.

In many cases, the symptoms of an RSV infection resolve on their own. Self-care measures are usually all that's needed to relieve any discomfort.

But in a few cases, the infection can be severe enough to require a stay at the hospital. Premature babies and infants with underlying health conditions are at greater risk of severe illness.

How to recognize it Initially, infection with RSV may cause a runny nose, decrease in appetite and perhaps a fever. Over the next few days, the infection may spread to the lower airways and lungs and your baby may start coughing,

wheezing and breathing fast. Ear infections are occasionally associated with RSV infections.

In babies who are only a few weeks old, infection with RSV may cause more general symptoms, such as coughing, wheezing, extreme tiredness, irritability and poor feeding.

How serious is it? RSV can be very serious. However, babies who are otherwise healthy generally recover from the illness in one to two weeks without the need for medical treatment.

Babies who are finding it difficult to breathe may need to stay at a hospital to receive supportive care, such as supplemental oxygen and suctioning of mucus from their airways. Even among babies who need to be hospitalized, most have a full recovery within a few weeks.

When to call Call your baby's care provider right away if your child:
▶ Is less than 2 months old and you suspect an infection
▶ Is struggling to breathe
▶ Runs a high fever, or a fever of 100.4 or above if your baby is less than 3 months old
▶ Turns blue, particularly on the lips and in the nail beds
▶ Shows signs of dehydration (dry mouth, reduced urination, sunken eyes and fontenels, extreme fussiness or sleepiness)
▶ Breathing or poor eating seems to be getting worse

What you can do Mild symptoms can be treated at home, although you should be ready to call your child's care provider promptly if symptoms worsen. If your child is more than 3 months old and has a fever and is uncomfortable, you can give him or her acetaminophen (Tylenol, others). Keeping your child upright and the air moist with a humidifier also may help ease congestion. Have your child drink plenty of fluids to prevent dehydration. Continue breast-feeding or bottle-feeding your infant as you would normally. Wash hands frequently and avoid sharing eating and drinking utensils to prevent spreading the infection.

The medication palivizumab (Synagis) can help protect children under age 2 who are at high risk of serious complications from RSV, such as premature babies or those who have an underlying lung or heart problem. The medicine is started prior to the RSV peak season. If you think your baby may qualify for this treatment, talk to your child's care provider. The medication isn't helpful in treating RSV infection once it has developed.

ROSEOLA

Roseola is a generally mild infection that typically affects children by age 2. It's extremely common — most children have been infected with roseola by the time they enter kindergarten.

Two common strains of herpes viruses cause roseola (but not the same ones that cause sexually transmitted herpes). The condition typically causes several days of fever, followed by a rash.

How to recognize it Roseola typically starts with a sudden, high fever — often greater than 103 F. Some children have a slightly sore throat, runny nose or cough along with or preceding the fever. Your child may also develop swollen lymph nodes in his or her neck along with the fever. The fever lasts for three to five days.

Once the fever subsides, a rash typically appears — but not always. The rash consists of many small pink spots or patches, mainly on the baby's trunk. Although not itchy or uncomfortable, the rash can last from several hours to several days before fading.

How serious is it? Roseola typically isn't serious. If your baby is otherwise healthy, he or she will most likely recover quickly and completely. Treatment includes rest, fluids and, if your child is uncomfortable, medications to reduce fever.

When to call Call your child's care provider if your baby is under 3 months old and has a rectal temperature of 100.4 F or higher. The care provider may want to examine your child to rule out more serious causes of fever. Also call if the fever lasts more than seven days, or if the rash doesn't improve after three days.

What you can do Like most viral illnesses, roseola needs to run its course. Encourage plenty of rest and plenty of fluids. A lukewarm sponge bath or a cool

washcloth applied to your child's head can soothe the discomfort of a fever. Once the fever subsides, your child should feel better soon. Most children recover fully from roseola within a week of the onset of the fever. The rash should fade on its own in a short time.

If the fever is making your baby uncomfortable, you can give him or her acetaminophen (Tylenol, others). Once your child is older than 6 months, you can give him or her ibuprofen (Advil, Motrin, others). See page 370 for more on fever medications. However, don't give aspirin to a child who has a viral illness because aspirin has been associated with the development of Reye's syndrome, which can be serious.

If your child is sick with roseola, keep him or her home and away from other children until the fever has broken.

STOMACH FLU (GASTROENTERITIS)

Although it's commonly called stomach flu, gastroenteritis isn't the same as influenza. Influenza affects your baby's respiratory system — nose, throat and lungs. Gastroenteritis, on the other hand, attacks the intestines.

The rotavirus and noroviruses are two common causes of gastroenteritis. Babies usually become infected when they put their fingers or other objects contaminated with a virus into their mouths.

A vaccine against rotaviral gastroenteritis is available in some countries, including the United States, and appears to be effective in preventing severe symptoms.

How to recognize it Gastroenteritis typically causes signs and symptoms such as:

▸ Watery, usually nonbloody diarrhea — bloody diarrhea usually means a different, more severe infection
▸ Abdominal cramps and pain
▸ Vomiting
▸ Loss of appetite
▸ Irritability
▸ Low-grade fever

Depending on the cause, viral gastroenteritis symptoms may appear within one to three days after your baby is infected and can range from mild to severe. Symptoms usually last just a day or two, but occasionally they may persist as long as 10 days.

How serious is it? A bout of viral gastroenteritis usually resolves on its own within a week or two (although it can often include a miserable few days). Antibiotics offer no help for viral infections.

The main complication of viral gastroenteritis is dehydration. If your baby can't take in enough fluids — through breast milk, formula or an oral rehydration solution — to replace the fluids being lost through diarrhea or vomiting, he or she will become dehydrated and may need to go to a hospital to receive fluids through a vein (intravenously).

If your baby has severe or prolonged diarrhea, especially if accompanied by vomiting, watch carefully for signs of dehydration — extreme thirst, dry mouth, crying without tears and reduced urination compared to your baby's usual output. Babies who are dehydrated usually will change from fussy to quiet to lethargic. Call your care provider promptly if you notice signs of dehydration.

When to call Call your child's care provider right away if your child:
▸ Has a fever that is high for his or her age
▸ Seems lethargic or very irritable
▸ Is in a lot of discomfort or pain

- Has bloody diarrhea
- Has vomiting that lasts more than several hours
- Hasn't had a wet diaper in six to 12 hours and can't keep fluids down
- Has a sunken fontanel — the soft spot on the top of your baby's head
- Has a dry mouth or cries without tears
- Is unusually sleepy, drowsy or unresponsive

What you can do When your baby has an intestinal infection, the most important goal is to replace lost fluids and salts. After vomiting or a bout of diarrhea, let your baby's stomach rest for 30 to 60 minutes, then offer small amounts of liquid, 1 to 2 teaspoonfuls at a time. If you're breast-feeding, offer just one breast and let your baby nurse for five minutes. If you're bottle-feeding, offer small amounts of regular formula. Don't dilute your baby's already-prepared formula. After 15 to 30 minutes, if the liquid stays down, offer it again. If you're concerned about possible dehydration, ask your child's care provider about giving your baby a small amount of an oral rehydration solution.

If your baby is eating solids, these suggestions may help ease your baby's discomfort and avoid complications:

Help your child rehydrate Give your child an oral rehydration solution (Pedialyte, others). Don't give him or her only water. In children with gastroenteritis, water isn't absorbed well and it won't adequately replace lost electrolytes. You can find oral rehydration solutions in most grocery stores. Talk to your care provider if you have questions about how to use them. Avoid giving your child apple juice for rehydration because it can make diarrhea worse.

Return to a normal diet slowly Drinking is more important than eating. When your child seems ready to eat, there's generally no need to restrict his or her diet, but bland foods — such as toast, rice, bananas and potatoes — are usually easier to digest.

Avoid certain foods Don't give your child dairy products and sugary foods. These can make diarrhea worse.

Make sure your child rests The illness and dehydration may have made your child weak and tired.

Don't give children aspirin It may cause Reye's syndrome, a rare, potentially fatal disease. Also don't give your child over-the-counter anti-diarrheal medications such as Imodium, unless advised to do so by your child's care provider. They can make it more difficult for your child's body to eliminate the virus.

STY

If you notice a red, painful-looking lump appear fairly rapidly near the edge of your baby's eyelid, he or she may have a bacterial eyelid infection called a sty. A sty may develop when your baby rubs or scratches his or her eyes with dirty hands or fingernails, transferring bacteria to the eyelids.

In most cases, a sty will disappear on its own in a few days to a week. In the meantime, you may be able to relieve the pain or discomfort of a sty by applying a warm washcloth to the eyelid.

How to recognize it A red lump on your baby's eyelid that looks similar to a boil or a pimple is usually an indication of a sty. A sty often contains pus. Your baby's eyelid may also be swollen and the eye may be teary.

How serious is it Most sties are harmless and don't require treatment. A sty typically resolves on its own in a few days to a week.

When to call Contact your baby's care provider if the sty doesn't go away in a week, or the redness and swelling extend beyond your baby's eyelid, involving his or her cheek or other parts of the face.

For a sty that persists, your care provider may recommend antibiotic ointment or drops to help clear the infection.

What you can do Don't try to pop the sty or squeeze the pus from a sty, and keep your baby's face and hands clean. To relieve discomfort, apply warm compresses to your baby's eyelid. Run warm water over a clean washcloth. Wring out the washcloth and place it over the closed eye. Re-wet the washcloth when it loses heat. Continue this for five or 10 minutes. Applying a warm compress several times each day may encourage the sty to drain more quickly.

SUNBURN

Your baby's skin is quite thin and susceptible to sunburn, even with only 10 to 15 minutes of exposure, and even on a cloudy or cool day. It's not the visible light or the heat from the sun that burns but the invisible ultraviolet (UV) light. The lighter the color of your baby's skin, the more sensitive it is to UV rays, but that doesn't mean darker skin is immune from sun damage.

Most sun damage occurs in the childhood years. While you certainly don't want to minimize the fun your child has outdoors, it's important to be sun smart. You can help prevent sun damage by setting up in shady areas (or using an umbrella), using sunscreen appropriately, and dressing your child in hats and light, protective clothing.

How to recognize it You may not realize that your baby has sunburn because the pain and redness may not appear for several hours. Sunburn may cause red, tender, swollen or blistered skin that is usually hot to the touch.

How serious is it? It's a good idea to be cautious about the possibility of your baby sunburning. Babies can develop blisters, fever, chills and nausea with sun exposure that may not affect an older person.

When to call Contact your baby's care provider if the sunburn blisters or if your baby begins vomiting or acts ill.

What you can do Treat sunburn by gently applying cool compresses every few hours, taking care not to allow your baby to become chilled. Encourage plenty of fluids. Give your baby acetaminophen (Tylenol, others) to relieve the pain. Avoid using anesthetic lotions or sprays on a baby's skin. Some sting, and a baby's skin may react to anesthetic sprays. Benzocaine in particular can have rare but serious side effects in children under age 2. Don't use it without the advice of your baby's care provider.

It's also important that you take steps to prevent sunburn:

In babies under 6 months Keep your baby out of direct sunlight as much as possible, especially between 10 a.m. and 3 p.m., when the sun's rays are strongest.

This precaution includes cloudy days, when the clouds don't block but simply scatter UV rays. You can also protect your baby by routinely dressing him or her in a hat for outings during the middle of the day. If you can't avoid sun exposure, use sunscreen just on areas of the body that will be exposed, such as the face and backs of the hands.

In babies older than 6 months Apply a broad-spectrum sunscreen, which protects against UVA and UVB rays, 30 minutes before going outside. Use a sunscreen with a sun protection factor (SPF) of at least 30. Don't forget the back of the neck, ears, nose, lips and tops of the feet. Reapply it every two hours or after the baby has played in the water, even if the sunscreen is waterproof. If you think your baby might have sensitive skin, do a patch test. Apply a small amount of sunscreen to your baby's forearm and watch for the next 48 hours for any reaction. If your baby is sensitive to one sunscreen, try a sunscreen without chemical sunblock components — one with only zinc oxide or titanium dioxide.

If at any time you notice your baby turning pink, take him or her out of the sun. Pink now can mean red and sunburned later.

SWOLLEN SCROTUM (FROM A HYDROCELE)

A hydrocele is an accumulation of fluid in the pouch that holds the testicles (scrotum), making the scrotum look swollen and large on one side. This condition is not uncommon in newborn boys. Before birth, your baby's testicles develop in his abdomen and move through a passage into the scrotum. When the opening to the abdomen doesn't fully close, fluid that is normally in the abdomen can pass into the scrotum and cause swelling.

A hydrocele is usually painless. By the time a baby is a year old, the fluid typically has been absorbed and the hydrocele goes away on its own.

How to recognize it You may notice that your baby boy's scrotum seems swollen on one side. It may seem more swollen when he is crying or active and less when he is lying down.

How serious is it? Generally, a hydrocele isn't serious and doesn't cause your baby any discomfort. It usually goes away without treatment by the time your baby is a year old. However, if the area becomes very large and tender, part of the intestine may have moved into the scrotum, causing an inguinal hernia. In this case, surgery may be required to move the intestine back into the abdominal cavity and close the opening between the abdomen and the scrotum.

When to call If your baby develops a sudden, painful swelling of the scrotum, call your child's care provider immediately. Most causes of such symptoms are benign, but if the testicle twists on the cord (testicular torsion) the blood supply to the testis can be cut off. This requires immediate surgery. If your baby's care provider did not notice your baby's hydrocele when your baby was born, mention it at your baby's next well-child visit. Your child's care provider will likely continue to examine it regularly for changes.

In the meantime, call your care provider promptly if your baby shows marked tenderness in the scrotum, or starts vomiting or showing signs of nausea for no apparent reason.

What you can do If you suspect that your baby has a hydrocele, share your concerns with your baby's care provider and watch for any change in your baby's condition.

TEARY EYES

Teary, or watery, eyes in a newborn are usually caused by a blocked tear duct. Normally, tear fluid flows down the surface of the eye to lubricate and protect the eye. It then drains through a system of holes and canals into the nose, where the fluid evaporates or is reabsorbed. This system typically takes time to fully develop. Babies under 8 months of age produce enough tear fluid to coat the eye, but not necessarily to cry "real tears."

Quite a few babies have a blocked tear duct at birth. Often, a thin tissue membrane remains over the opening (duct) that empties into the nose. This blockage causes tear fluid to well up in your baby's eyes, leaving them watery.

How to recognize it One or both of your baby's eyes may appear to be continuously watery, with tears occasionally running down the cheeks, even though he or she isn't crying. Usually, the eye isn't red or swollen, unless it becomes infected.

How serious is it? A blocked tear duct generally isn't serious, and most of the time resolves by about 6 to 9 months of age. Because the tear fluid isn't draining as it should, however, infections (pink eye, or conjunctivitis) are slightly more common when a tear duct is blocked. In the morning, your baby's eyes may be crusted over with dried up discharge.

When to call Call your baby's care provider if your baby's eye is red or swollen or looks infected.

What you can do Your child's care provider may show you how to massage the lower inner corner of your baby's eye, where the tears collect (lacrimal sac). Use a cotton-tipped swab or clean finger to gently press upward from the inner corner. This may or may not help open the duct, but it can help empty out the lacrimal sac of stagnant fluid.

Use moist compresses to wipe away the fluids from your baby's eyes. Keeping your baby's face and hands clean will help prevent infections.

TEETHING

Your baby may have a first tooth by 6 months or may not begin teething until much later. Often the two bottom center teeth (incisors) appear first, but not always. When they've both come in, a tooth may appear on the top. Your baby will probably get four top teeth before a matching set of four is completed on the bottom.

Your infant's baby (deciduous) teeth were formed during pregnancy. As these teeth come in, your baby's body will begin preparing adult teeth to take their place in a few years.

How to recognize it Drooling is a classic sign of teething. However, it may take about two months after the drooling starts before the first tooth pops up. For some babies, teething causes pain or discomfort. So your baby might be more irritable or crankier than usual. You might also notice swollen gums and a drive to chew on solid objects.

Many parents suspect that teething causes fever and diarrhea, but researchers say this isn't true. Teething may cause signs and symptoms in the mouth and gums, but it doesn't cause problems elsewhere in the body.

How serious is it? Teething is a normal and healthy process in your baby's development. But where there are teeth, there's the possibility for tooth decay. When your baby's first teeth appear, brush them with a small, soft-bristled toothbrush and some water, or wipe them with a cloth. Some parents find it easier to use a soft finger toothbrush that fits over the parent's finger. There's no need to use toothpaste until your child learns to spit — about age 2.

The American Dental Association and the American Academy of Pediatric Dentistry recommend scheduling a child's first dental visit after the first tooth erupts, and no later than his or her first birthday. Your baby's teeth and gums will also be examined at well-baby checkups. Getting in the habit of good dental care now will serve your child's teeth and mouth well in later years.

When to call Contact your baby's care provider if your baby develops a fever, seems particularly uncomfortable, or has other signs or symptoms of illness — including fever or diarrhea.

What you can do Sometimes you may not even notice your baby is teething until you see the new tooth! But if teething is making your baby uncomfortable:

Rub your baby's gums Use a clean finger, moistened gauze pad or damp washcloth to gently massage your baby's gums. The pressure may help ease your baby's discomfort.

Offer something to chew on Try a teething ring. Some are made from firm rubber and others plastic with liquid inside. Keep in mind the liquid-filled variety may break under the pressure of your baby's chewing. If your baby is eating solid foods, you can try a homemade teething ring such as a frozen bagel. (Make sure you offer a frozen food that will turn soft so that baby can swallow any pieces that might break loose.) A pacifier may help. If a bottle seems to do the trick, fill it with water. Prolonged contact with sugar from formula, milk or juice may cause tooth decay.

Keep it cool A cold washcloth or chilled teething ring can be soothing. Be careful when giving your baby something frozen, however. Contact with extreme cold may hurt the gums. If your baby's eating solid foods, offer cold items such as applesauce or yogurt.

Dry the drool Excessive drooling is part of the teething process. To prevent skin irritation, keep a clean cloth handy to dry your baby's chin. You might also make sure your baby sleeps on an absorbent sheet.

Try an over-the-counter remedy If your baby is especially cranky, acetaminophen (Tylenol, others), or ibuprofen (Advil, Motrin, others) if your baby is more than 6 months old, may help reduce gum irritation and discomfort. Don't give your baby products that contain aspirin, however, and be cautious about teething medications that can be rubbed directly on a baby's gums. Avoid teething medications that contain benzocaine. Benzocaine has been linked to a rare but serious and sometimes deadly condition that decreases the amount of oxygen that the blood can carry, especially in children under 2 years of age.

THRUSH

Thrush is the name for a fungal infection that can occur in your baby's mouth. It's caused by the same fungus that causes yeast infections, *Candida albicans*. This fungus is normally found in the mouth, skin and other mucous membranes. If the mouth's natural bacterial balance is upset — typically by medications or an illness — an overgrowth of candida may result, producing thrush.

How to recognize it When your baby has thrush, it looks like he or she has patches of milk on the inside of the cheeks and on the tongue that won't wash off (see the photo on page 101). Occasionally, thrush causes discomfort and your baby may have trouble feeding or be fussy and irritable.

If your baby's tongue looks white all over but there are no white patches inside the lips or cheeks, this is probably not thrush. Milk can make your baby's tongue have a white coating.

How serious is it? Thrush can be painful in severe cases, but it doesn't generally cause discomfort or serious problems. It can lead to a diaper rash in your baby as the yeast travels through the baby's gastrointestinal tract.

Infants can pass the infection to their mothers during breast-feeding. The infection may then pass back and forth between mother's breasts and baby's mouth. Women whose breasts are infected with candida may experience the following signs and symptoms:

- Unusually red, sensitive or itchy nipples
- Shiny or flaky skin on the darker, circular area around the nipple (areola)
- Unusual pain during nursing or painful nipples between feedings
- Stabbing pains deep within the breast

When to call If you notice white patches inside your baby's mouth, call your baby's care provider during office hours. Check back with the care provider if your baby's mouth becomes increasingly coated and causes discomfort, or if your baby has difficulty swallowing.

What you can do Your child's care provider may prescribe a liquid antifungal medication for your baby, which you apply to the patches of thrush in the mouth. If your baby is having recurring infections, it's probably a good idea to replace your baby's pacifiers and bottle nipples, which could be harboring the fungus.

If you're breast-feeding an infant who has oral thrush, you and your baby will do best if you're both treated. Otherwise, you're likely to pass the infection back and forth.

▶ Your doctor may prescribe a mild antifungal medication for your baby and an antifungal cream for your breasts. You can also use a nonprescription antifungal cream, such as clotrimazole (Lotrimin). Apply it four times a day after feedings.

▶ If you use a breast pump, rinse all the detachable parts in a vinegar and water solution.

▶ If you develop a fungal infection on your breasts, using pads will help prevent the fungus from spreading to your clothes. Look for pads that don't have a plastic barrier, which can encourage the growth of candida. If you're not using disposable pads, wash the nursing pads and your bras in hot water with bleach.

URINARY TRACT INFECTION

Urinary tract infections are fairly common in young children, especially girls.

The urethra, the tube that carries urine out of the bladder, is shorter in girls than in boys, making it easier for bacteria to travel to the bladder. When bacteria enter the bladder or kidneys, an infection may result. Most often, the bacteria come from stool and the anal area.

How to recognize it In babies younger than 2 years old, a urinary tract infection can be hard to discern. Often the only sign is a fever with no apparent cause, one that's not explained by an upper respiratory infection or diarrhea. Less common signs and symptoms of a urinary tract infection are irritability, poor feeding and not gaining weight properly.

How serious is it? Urinary tract infections require prompt treatment. Left untreated, the infection can cause permanent damage to the kidneys.

When to call Call anytime your baby has an unexplained fever that persists for more than 24 hours, especially when the temperature is greater than 102.2 F. Call your child's care provider right away if your child is under 3 months of age and has a rectal temperature of 100.4 or higher.

What you can do? Be alert to unexplained, persistent fevers in your child, and don't be afraid to call you child's care provider when necessary. A care provider can diagnose a urinary tract infection with a urine sample. In infants, a urine sample is usually obtained by briefly inserting a catheter into the urethra to withdraw a small amount of urine.

If your baby has a urinary tract infection, his or her care provider will prescribe a course of antibiotics, which may last up to two weeks. Make sure to give your child the whole prescription, even after the fever goes away. This will keep the infection from coming back. After treatment is over, the care provider may request another urine sample to make sure the bacteria have been eliminated. An ultrasound of the kidneys may be performed if the care provider wants to rule out a urinary system abnormality.

VOMITING

In the first few months of life, it's common for babies to spit up or easily regurgitate their food from time to time. Vomiting is different. It's the forceful ejection of a large portion of the stomach's contents through the mouth and sometimes even the nose. Because your baby won't understand what is happening, vomiting can be a frightening experience for him or her. And as a parent, it can be very stressful when your baby begins to vomit without warning.

Most vomiting in infancy is caused by viral infections that affect the stomach and intestines (gastroenteritis). Your baby also may have fever and diarrhea.

How to recognize it Normal infant spit-up seems to dribble out of your baby's mouth without much ado. Vomit, on the other hand, comes out like a projectile, fast and furious. Generally, there's more of it, too, compared with spit-up.

How serious is it? Most of the time, vomiting is due to a viral infection and stops on its own within 12 to 24 hours. The greatest risk your baby faces from vomiting is dehydration from losing too many bodily fluids.

In a few cases, vomiting can be a symptom of a more serious problem, such as an intestinal obstruction, stomach disorder or infection.

When to call If your baby is very young — between 2 and 6 weeks — and vomits forcefully within 30 minutes after every feeding for six to 12 hours, call your baby's care provider right away. This may be a sign of a stomach disorder called pyloric stenosis, a narrowing of the stomach's outlet into the intestines that prevents food from passing (see page 543). This requires prompt attention (occasionally surgery) so that your baby can get the nutrition he or she needs to grow.

Also, call immediately if your baby seems to be getting more ill, you're concerned about possible poisoning, or he or she experiences any of these signs or symptoms:

◗ Blood or green matter (bile) in the vomit
◗ Vomiting for more than 12 hours in newborns, 24 hours in older infants
◗ Forceful, repeated vomiting
◗ Dehydration — no wet diapers in eight hours, dry mouth, no tears (although newborns don't usually show tears), sunken soft spots (fontanels) in the head
◗ Unusually sleepy or unresponsive
◗ Inability to keep liquids down
◗ Seems to have persistent abdominal pain

What you can do To prevent dehydration in your baby:

Wait a little after a vomiting episode After your baby vomits, let the stomach settle for a while. Wait 30 to 60 minutes before offering more fluids. Sleep may help ease your baby's nausea.

Offer small amounts of liquid Start out with a teaspoon or two. Breast-fed babies usually tolerate breast milk fairly well and digest it quickly. Offer just one breast and nurse for only five minutes. Small amounts of regular formula for bottle-fed babies are OK, too. After 15 to 30 minutes, if the liquid stays down, offer it again.

Offer an oral rehydration solution If your baby continues to vomit, switch to feeding a teaspoon or two of oral rehydration solution (Pedialyte, others). Gradually increase the volume as your baby tolerates it. If your baby can't keep anything down, call your child's care provider.

Gradually return to normal diet After eight hours without vomiting, gradually return to normal breast- or formula-feeding amounts. If your baby is eating solids, you might want to start out with easily digested foods, such as baby cereal, bananas, crackers, toast or plain pasta.

WHOOPING COUGH

Whooping cough (pertussis) is a highly contagious bacterial infection of the respiratory tract. It's transmitted from person to person through airborne droplets from coughing or sneezing.

A vaccine against whooping cough is part of your baby's recommended immunizations, usually given as a series of five injections at 2 months, 4 months, 6 months, 12 to 18 months and 4 to 6 years. Because babies under 6 months haven't been fully vaccinated, they're at greater risk of getting the infection and of developing significant complications. However, being up to date on vaccinations usually makes symptoms less likely to be severe.

The protection offered by the vaccine wears off after several years, meaning that teens and adults who haven't updated their vaccinations may become infected and pass it on to infants and young children. Because of this, it's now recommended that adolescents and adults receive a vaccine booster shot for whooping cough.

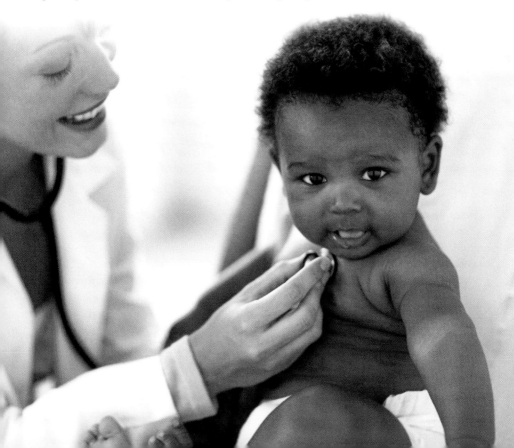

How to recognize it At first, it may seem as if your baby has a mild upper respiratory tract infection — a runny nose, congestion and cough, but no fever. Only the cough worsens throughout the first week, until he or she experiences exhausting coughing fits consisting of 10 to 30 forceful, abrupt coughs, sometimes followed by a "whoop" sound as your baby inhales forcefully. Many babies don't develop the whoop sound. Some vomit after a coughing fit.

In infants under 3 months of age, the initial phase of mild symptoms may not always be obvious. The first sign of whooping cough may be a sudden fit of coughing or difficulty breathing. In between episodes of coughing or trouble breathing, the baby may appear well.

How serious is it? In infants — especially those under 6 months of age — complications from whooping cough are more severe than in older children and adults, and may include ear infections, pneumonia, respiratory failure and seizures. Complications such as pneumonia can be life-threatening in new babies.

Young infants diagnosed with whooping cough are often kept at a hospital to receive supportive care and to be closely monitored for potentially serious complications. If your baby is older and has mild symptoms, hospitalization may not be necessary. Antibiotics, when given early in the illness, may help shorten the duration of symptoms and can decrease the chances of transmitting the infection to others.

When to call Contact your child's care provider right away if your baby:
- Is under 6 months old or hasn't been fully immunized, and has been exposed to someone with a chronic cough or whooping cough
- Has severe coughing fits
- Has spells of difficulty breathing, turning blue or gagging
- Has had a bad cough for more than five to seven days
- Vomits after a coughing fit, eats poorly or seems ill

What you can do If you're caring for your baby at home, these steps may help your son or daughter feel better while recovering:

Encourage plenty of rest A cool, quiet and dark bedroom may help your child relax and rest better.

Offer plenty of fluids Water, juice and soups are good choices. If your baby is having trouble consuming enough fluids, offer small amounts of an oral rehydrating solution (Pedialyte, others).

Offer smaller meals To avoid vomiting after coughing, give your baby smaller, more-frequent feedings.

Vaporize the room Use a mist vaporizer to help soothe irritated lungs and to help loosen respiratory secretions. If you use a vaporizer, follow directions for keeping it clean. If you don't have a vaporizer, sitting in a warm bathroom with the shower turned on can also temporarily help clear the lungs and ease breathing.

Clean the air Keep your home free of irritants that can trigger coughing spells, such as tobacco smoke and fumes from fireplaces.

Prevent transmission Cover your cough and wash your hands often; keep your baby away from others. Ask your family's care provider about getting your whole family's immunizations up to date.

PART 5

Managing and Enjoying Parenthood

CHAPTER 29

Adapting to your new lifestyle

It's not just baby's first year — it's also mommy's and daddy's first year with this new little person. Adding a baby to your family brings some of the most profound changes you'll ever experience, from the mundane (diapers) to the magical (the first smile). No matter how many baby-care websites or books you've perused, or how meticulous you've been in getting everything in place, nothing can fully prepare you for the first weeks and months after your baby's birth.

This time can be exciting — and over-whelming. You're dealing with many different physical, social and emotional issues all at once. You're recovering from pregnancy and childbirth, trying to get a handle on your baby's needs and habits, and adjusting to a new role and identity. Relationships with your partner, family and friends are shifting. And round-the-clock newborn care can turn your life upside down, making even simple tasks such as showering a challenge.

The first few weeks after you bring your baby home are likely to be some of the most challenging times of your life. The changes in the daily rhythms of your life may feel chaotic and foreign. A few practical strategies can help you adapt. It may take months or even a year, but you'll get there.

LIVING ON LESS SLEEP

If there's any issue to which all parents can nod their heads and say, "I've been there," it's the fatigue that comes with having a baby. You're up at all hours feeding, diapering and otherwise tending to your newborn, who needs time to develop regular sleep-wake cycles. Parents' sleep is often disturbed for weeks, if not years, after a baby's birth. Lack of sleep not only can leave you exhausted, but also can make you irritable and less able to focus, remember details and solve problems.

But seasoned parents will also tell you that it gets better. By age 3 months, many babies can sleep at least five hours at a stretch. By 6 months, many infants sleep through the night, and 70 to 80 percent of babies are doing so by 9 months. In the meantime, hang in there — and try to sneak in as much sleep as possible.

While there's no magical formula for getting enough sleep, here are some tips that may help.

Sleep when your baby sleeps While this is one of the common pieces of advice, it's not always so easy to follow. Some babies doze off for just 15 or 20 minutes at a time, and you may need to seize that time to shower, eat a meal or just go to the bathroom.

Still, even an hour or two of extra sleep can make a big difference, so make it a priority. Turn off the ringer on your cellphone and your house phone, hide the laundry basket, and ignore the dishes in the kitchen sink. Your chores can wait.

Set aside your social graces When close friends and loved ones visit, don't worry about entertaining them. Let them care for the baby while you excuse yourself for some much needed rest. Allow them to help with cooking and cleaning.

Avoid bed sharing during sleep It's OK to bring your baby into your bed for nursing or comforting, but return your baby to the crib or bassinet when you and your baby are ready to go back to sleep.

Share nighttime duties Work out a schedule with your partner that allows both of you to rest and care for the baby. If you're breast-feeding, perhaps your partner can bring you the baby and handle nighttime diaper changes. If you're using a bottle, take turns feeding the baby. You could also split the night into two shifts or trade nights to be on duty.

Wait a few minutes Sometimes middle-of-the-night fussing or crying is simply a sign that your baby is settling down. Unless you suspect that your baby is hungry or uncomfortable, wait a few minutes before responding.

WHEN SLEEP BECOMES A STRUGGLE

The rigors of caring for a newborn may leave you so exhausted that you feel you could fall asleep anytime, anywhere — but that's not always the case. Some new parents experience insomnia.

Prolonged sleep deprivation can set the stage for depression and other health problems. If you're having problems sleeping even when you have the opportunity, try these suggestions.

▶ Make sure your environment is suited for sleep. Turn off the TV and keep the room cool and dark.

▶ Avoid nicotine, caffeine and alcohol late in the day or at night.

▶ If you don't nod off within 30 minutes, get up and do something else. When you begin to feel drowsy, try going back to bed.

If you think you have a sleep problem, consult your care provider. Identifying and treating any underlying conditions can help you get the rest you need.

A HOUSE BECOMES A HOME

Children's book writer Christopher Harder describes the way his house changed after he and his wife had a child:

We had renovated the house by getting rid of our dining room, living room and den and replacing them with one, house-sized playroom. We had scarred the new furniture, stained baseboards and repainted walls. ... Half our books were in the attic. The hardwood floors had skid marks. ... And it felt like home.

Go easy on yourself If you're not getting enough sleep, you may feel cranky and in a fog. Try not to beat yourself up about it. Set aside complicated tasks, such as preparing elaborate meals, balancing your budget and operating heavy machinery, for a time when you're feeling more rested.

GETTING COMFORTABLE WITH CHAOS

In the first weeks after you bring home your baby, you might feel like you're in a fog. With the baby's constant need for care and attention, your day-to-day routine goes out the window. On top of feedings, diaper changes and crying spells, parents must find time to do household chores and other daily activities.

Although your days will likely include moments of awe and enjoyment, you still might miss your former carefree life, a predictable schedule and control over your time. Maybe you long for the comfort of your old routines, like a quiet morning cup of coffee, a structured workday, weekly get-togethers with friends or movie night with your partner.

Over time, you'll adjust to the new normal, revive old routines and create new ones. In the meantime, you can bring some order to the chaos — and learn to embrace it.

Check your expectations Many new parents start out with unrealistic expectations — that life won't be much different from before. The gap between expectations and reality can lead to stress and disappointment, or even a feeling that something's wrong with you. Throw out any preconceived notions about what life with a new baby should be like, and be realistic about the increased demands you face.

Go with the flow It's never too early to establish a routine — but let your newborn set the pace. Allow plenty of time each day for nursing sessions, naps and crying spells. Keep scheduled activities to a minimum. When you need to head out, give yourself extra time to pack your supplies and change the inevitable out-the-door dirty diaper.

Relax your standards Learn to live with a messier house. Every room doesn't have to be perfect. Hide the broom and vacuum and leave dust bunnies where they lie. Store clean clothes in the laundry basket until you need them — or in stacks on the floor, for that matter. Clean the bathroom with a fresh diaper wipe.

Simplify and streamline Find ways to make life easier by cutting back on cooking, cleaning and other household routines:

- Serve cold cereal and peanut butter toast for dinner when you're too tired to prepare a more traditional meal.
- Get takeout food when your budget allows it.

- Use disposable plates and utensils when you don't have time to do dishes.
- Pare down your baby equipment. You don't need every gadget on the market.
- Set up a baby-care station with everything you need in one place.
- Keep cleaning supplies where you use them, such as in the bathroom.
- Get a new haircut if your hair routine takes too much time.

Stock up Buy a month's supply of toilet paper, diapers and other essential household items. Accept pre-made meals from friends and family. Prepare double dinner portions and freeze the leftovers, or buy healthy heat-and-serve options.

Establish visiting rules Friends and loved ones may seem to come out of the woodwork to admire your newborn. Let them know which days work best and how much time you have for a visit. Insist that visitors wash their hands before holding the baby, and ask anyone who's ill to stay home.

Accept help When people ask if there's anything they can do, give them a job. It can be as simple as watching the baby while you take an unhurried shower and wash your hair. If you have other children, let someone take them for a few hours or the whole day so you can have some alone time with the new baby. And never refuse a meal you don't have to cook. If someone is staying with you, let that person wait on you. You deserve it and need it, and it will probably make your guest feel special as well.

Keep your perspective The newborn days won't last long. Before you know it, your infant will be a toddler, walking and talking. Try to step back and appreciate the moment, even amid the chaos.

ADJUSTING TO YOUR NEW ROLE

Taking care of a new baby is an awesome responsibility — both in the sense of "amazing" and of "what am I doing?" Infants depend utterly on their parents to meet all their physical and emotional needs. Even if you've dreamed about being a parent since you were a kid, the realities of dressing, feeding, bathing and performing the many other child care routines take time to learn. Along with the joy, excitement and fulfillment parenthood brings, don't be surprised to experience doubts and uncertainties in your new role.

Feelings of incompetence are normal. Like many new parents, you may be going from a working life where you feel confident and successful to a job for which you lack experience and won't get instructions or feedback from your new "boss." You're acquiring a whole new skill set at a rapid pace. Although the "maternal instinct" is supposed to kick in, new mothers (and fathers) don't automatically know exactly what their babies need. You may feel anxious, helpless or powerless as you try to figure out why your baby is crying or not sleeping. Should you feed her, entertain her, or just let her take in the new surroundings?

If you're wondering how you'll handle one of life's biggest responsibilities, take a deep breath and relax. Becoming a parent is a process. It doesn't happen overnight. As you gain experience, you'll learn to read your baby's cues and begin to master the tasks of baby care. In turn, your sense of competence and satisfaction will increase. As one mom remarked six weeks after giving birth, "I know how to put him back down to sleep. And I can tell if he's hungry when he's crying or he's just tired. ... I have my little tricks now that I feel like I know him a little more."

Believe in yourself Parenting brings a seemingly endless array of decisions. Where will baby sleep? Cloth or disposable diapers? Should you circumcise your son? Ultimately, you'll have to trust that you do know what's best for you and your family. Each parent and each baby is an individual, so there's no one right answer for every situation. Your parenting is now and always will be a work in progress. You'll learn as you go, and you'll learn from your inevitable mistakes.

Let go of being perfect These days, moms and dads experience a new level of anxiety as parenting has become a verb and often feels like a competition. You may find yourself seeking the "best" way to care for your child or painstakingly following a nurse's or doctor's example. This can be frustrating and overwhelming. Instead, remember that you know your baby better than anyone else, and you and your partner love your baby like no one else can. Because of this, you will always have your child's best interests at heart. In the end, that's what matters the most.

Tune in to your baby Your baby will also help build your confidence. As you respond to his needs, you receive in return a response — a contented gaze, a grasp of your finger or a fleeting smile. Spending time alone with your baby, away from distractions, can be ideal for fostering this relationship. Bonding with your baby and learning his or her habits and rhythms takes time.

Take advice with a grain of salt Chances are, you're sure to face an onslaught of often-conflicting advice from friends, family and even strangers on the street. You'll hear about the "right" way to do everything, from feeding and clothing your baby to burping and diapering. And if your mother, mother-in-law or another experienced adult is on hand, you may feel as if you're constantly being evaluated on your baby-care skills. Such advice and help from others may heighten your feelings of inadequacy or undermine your confidence. Support from others can be wonderful, but be specific about what you want, such as reassurance or suggestions for a particular question you have. Learn to take advice with a grain of salt — you're the expert on your baby.

Seek out other new parents Talking with other new parents can help you realize you're not alone — they're in the same boat and can offer support and empathy rather than advice. Consider joining a new moms or new parents group, which may be organized by a hospital, place of worship, community center or school district. You can also reach out to other new moms or dads through online support groups or at the neighborhood park. By sharing honest stories, laughing and maybe even crying together, you'll not only realize that you're all dealing with similar issues, but you might also form strong, lasting friendships.

Over time, you'll become confident of your abilities to recognize and meet your baby's needs. As your doubts diminish and your confidence grows, you'll carry your new responsibility with grace and ease.

HANDLING NEW-BABY STRESS

Your bundle of joy also brings a bundle of stress, which goes hand in hand with a major life change. Besides the disrupted sleep, new responsibilities and changes in your lifestyle, other sources of stress include financial strain, hormonal fluctuations, changes in your identity, less time with your partner and for yourself, and (at least a temporary) loss of sexual activity.

Realistically, you won't be able to avoid stress altogether during your baby's first year. But you may be able to keep from becoming overwhelmed by taking steps to minimize it.

Drink fluids and eat well Keep a bottle or glass of water and nutritious snacks handy. If you can afford it, buy prepared foods or takeout, but try to avoid fried fast foods. Spend some time each evening stocking your refrigerator with individual servings of healthy foods and cold drinks. Sandwiches make an easy one-handed meal. Do whatever you can to make mealtime easier, including accepting people's offers of meals and cooking.

Get some exercise Exercise is a great stressbuster. Walk your baby in the stroller outside or at the mall or a gym. Join a parent-baby exercise class. Carry baby while you garden or hike. See Chapter 30 for more on exercise.

Build a network of social support Social support is one of the most important buffers against stress. Both women and men need a support network during their baby's first year. Seek out friends and family who can give you encouragement and practical help. Your support network may include your partner, friends, parents, siblings, a lactation consultant, doula, co-workers, neighbors or visiting nurses. Find ways to connect with other parents in your neighborhood or community. Having friends who can really relate makes your journey easier and more fun.

Get out of the house The change in routine during maternity leave can be especially hard on women who are used to going to work. If you're going stir-crazy with a fussy newborn, take the baby out for a walk. Bring your baby to the office for a meet and greet. If you can, have your partner, a friend or someone else you trust stay with the baby so that you can get out by yourself.

Nurture your other relationships
Your newborn needs your love and attention, but you won't let your baby down by spending time with others. If you have other children, set aside one-on-one time with each of them. Schedule dates with your partner. Meet a friend for lunch or a movie.

Know when to seek additional help
Parenting is a challenge, even on a good day. If you're depressed or having trouble adjusting to life with a newborn, consult your care provider or a mental health professional. (See Chapter 30 for more information about postpartum depression.) Feeling overwhelmed or stressed doesn't make you a bad parent. Learning to handle the new stress in your life can help you enjoy the riches parenting has to offer.

LONG DAYS, SHORT YEARS

Despite the ups and downs of the first year, chances are your sense of accomplishment and joy will make up for the long days and nights, the fatigue and the worries. As your baby grows and changes, you'll grow and change, too. You'll create new routines, discover your parenting quirks and learn from missteps. You may even discover a new sense of meaning in life, greater self-esteem and a deeper connection to your family and community.

CHAPTER 30

Taking care of yourself

After months of anticipation and the rigors of labor and delivery, your attention shifts to caring for your new baby — but you also need to take care of yourself. In many cultures throughout the world, postpartum customs hold that new mothers recuperate by resting — often for a month or longer — eating (or not eating) certain foods and being pampered by family members. You probably won't have someone bringing you chicken soup while you lounge around for 40 days, but it's important to restore your strength and nurture yourself.

Personal care after labor and delivery may involve managing a C-section wound or vaginal tear, sore breasts, urination problems, hair loss, and more. But recovery extends beyond your physical health. It also includes your mental well-being — dealing with mood swings, irritability, sadness and anxiety. And it encompasses your emotional health, from your need for personal time and interests to shifting friendships and the gradual return of romance.

RECOVERING FROM LABOR AND CHILDBIRTH

The early weeks after labor and delivery can be exhausting, and you may experience a wide range of aches and pains. Will your body ever get back to normal?

Realistically, you're not going to bounce back right away. It takes time to recover from the dramatic changes that took place over the previous nine months. Gradually, however, you'll start to feel better and get back in shape. If you had a cesarean delivery, you can expect a few additional discomforts and precautions during the postpartum period.

Pain and fatigue are the most common complaints after delivery, whether vaginal or cesarean. After your baby's birth, your uterus begins shrinking back to its normal size. You may feel contractions — called afterpains — for a few days after delivery. During the first weeks of caring for your newborn, you may also feel profoundly tired. After the demands of labor, you're hit with round-the-clock infant care and night after night of interrupted sleep. The energy required for breast-feeding and carrying around a baby can add to your exhaustion. Over time, your fatigue should lessen as your body adjusts to the rhythms of motherhood, you gain experience in dealing with your baby and the baby sleeps through the night.

Beyond the first few weeks of physical recovery, you may continue to experience various changes. While not always discussed openly, these issues are common.

All about the breasts Your breasts may remain enlarged for a while after your baby's birth. If you're not nursing, they may be engorged — heavy, swollen and tender — and hard until you're no longer producing milk. Even if you're breast-feeding, your breasts may at times overfill and become engorged. Engorgement usually lasts less than three days, but it can be uncomfortable.

When you begin breast-feeding, your nipples may feel sore or tender. In the early weeks of breast-feeding, a milk duct may become blocked. Your breast may feel tender and lumpy, and the skin may be red. Leaky breasts are another common problem. You might find yourself leaking when you think or talk about your baby, hear a baby cry, or go for a long stretch between feedings.

To keep your breasts comfortable:

▶ *Seek support.* Wear a good-quality, well-fitting bra.

▶ *Keep your breasts clean and dry.* Let your nipples air-dry between feedings, and go topless occasionally, especially when resting.

▶ *Wear nursing pads.* You can't do anything to stop your breasts from leaking, but wearing nursing pads inside your bra can help keep your shirt dry. Avoid pads that are lined or backed with plastic, which can irritate your nipples. Change wet pads.

▶ *Don't pump to prevent leaking.* This may prompt more milk production.

▶ *Help ease engorged breasts.* Express a little milk, either manually or by feeding your baby. If you're not breast-feeding, avoid pumping or massaging your breasts, as this encourages milk production.

▶ *Soothe sore or engorged breasts.* Apply cold washcloths or ice packs to the breasts, or take a warm bath or shower. Over-the-counter pain relievers may help, too.

▶ *Take a break.* If a nipple becomes cracked, you may need to keep your baby off that breast for a few days and express milk to avoid engorgement.

▶ *Try to clear a blocked duct.* Start feedings with the affected breast and gently massage it while feeding.

Healing down under You'll have vaginal discharge (lochia) for up to six weeks after delivery. Expect a bright red, heavy flow of blood for the first few days. The discharge will gradually taper off, changing from pink or brown to yellow or white. To reduce the risk of infection or injury, use sanitary pads rather than tampons.

If you had an episiotomy or vaginal tear during delivery, the wound may hurt for a few weeks — especially when you walk or sit. Extensive tears may take longer to heal. In the meantime, to help promote healing:

▶ *Soothe the wound.* Use an ice pack, or wrap ice in a washcloth. Chilled witch hazel pads — available in most pharmacies — may help, too.

▶ *Keep the wound clean.* Use a squirt bottle filled with water to rinse the tissue between the vaginal opening and anus (perineum) after using the toilet. Soak in a warm tub.

- *Take the sting out of urination.* Squat rather than sit to use the toilet. Pour warm water over your vulva as you're urinating.
- *Prevent pain and stretching during bowel movements.* Hold a clean pad firmly against the wound and press upward while you bear down. This will help relieve pressure on the wound.
- *Sit down carefully.* To keep your bottom from stretching, squeeze your buttocks together as you sit down. If sitting is uncomfortable, use a doughnut-shaped pillow to ease the pressure.
- *Do your Kegels.* These exercises help tone the pelvic floor muscles. (See page 418 for instructions.)
- *Look for signs of infection.* If the pain intensifies, or the wound becomes hot, swollen and painful or produces a pus-like discharge, contact your care provider.

Return of your period (maybe) Women who aren't breast-feeding can expect their menstrual cycle to start up again six to eight weeks after the birth, or sooner. If you're breast-feeding, your periods may not start again for months, or even until your baby is fully weaned.

Before your first period returns, your ovaries may release an egg. That means you could get pregnant again, even if you're breast-feeding. Unless you want another baby right away, use birth control as soon as you resume having sex.

Bathroom woes A leak when you cough or laugh. Hemorrhoids. Bowel troubles. After you give birth, you may find that going to the bathroom isn't the simple act it once was.

Urination problems Soon after delivery, the tissues surrounding your bladder and

---

PREVENTING BACK PAIN

Back pain is common during pregnancy. It typically gets better within a few weeks of delivery, but lifting and carrying a growing baby all day can bring back your backaches.

To help prevent back pain or injury, try these tips:
- Begin exercising soon after delivery to restore muscle tone to your abdomen and back. Do stretching exercises on the floor to restore hip and back flexibility.
- Practice good posture. Stand up straight when holding your baby. While nursing, sit in an upright chair and bring baby to your breast, rather than bending over.
- Carry your baby in a front pack when you're walking. Don't carry a child on your hip, as this overloads your back muscles.
- Try not to lift anything heavier than your baby for a while.
- When you pick up your baby, keep him or her close to your chest. Avoid twisting your body or stretching out your arms to lift him.
- When picking up baby from the floor, bend at your knees, squat down and lift with your legs.
- Be careful when bending over the crib side and lifting your baby out. If it is safe for baby, raise the crib mattress so you don't have to reach down so far.

urethra are swollen and bruised, which can lead to difficulty urinating. Fearing the sting of urine on the tender perineal area can produce the same effect. Difficulty urinating usually resolves on its own within about a week. To encourage urination:

▶ Contract and release your pelvic muscles while sitting on the toilet.
▶ Drink plenty of fluids.
▶ Try taking a warm bath.
▶ Soak your hands in cold running water, or run the tap while you're in the bathroom.
▶ Spray warm water across your vulva with a squeeze bottle.

A potentially longer term issue is leaking urine (urinary incontinence). Pregnancy and birth stretch the connective tissue at the base of the bladder, which can damage nerves and muscles in the bladder or urethra. As a result, you may leak urine when you cough, strain or laugh. This problem usually improves within three months, but for some women, incontinence persists. In the mean-

time, wear sanitary pads and do frequent Kegel exercises. If urinary problems don't go away, talk to your care provider.

Bowel movements You may not have a bowel movement for a few days after delivery. Your abdominal muscles are relaxed and stretched, which can slow the passage of feces through your bowels. This slowing can lead to constipation. In addition, you may find yourself avoiding bowel movements out of fear of hurting your perineum or aggravating the pain of hemorrhoids.

Some new moms have trouble controlling bowel movements (fecal incontinence) — especially if they had an unusually long labor. Frequent Kegel exercises can help. If you have persistent trouble controlling bowel movements, consult your care provider.

Hemorrhoids Pain during a bowel movement and swelling near your anus may indicate hemorrhoids — stretched and

WHEN TO CALL YOUR CARE PROVIDER

If you have concerns about your postpartum recovery, talk with your care provider. Also call your provider if you:

▶ Have a fever or your abdomen is tender to the touch
▶ Are soaking a sanitary pad every hour for more than a few hours
▶ Feel dizzy
▶ Have a foul-smelling vaginal discharge
▶ Notice your blood flow suddenly becomes bright red again after fading in color
▶ Experience new or worsening perineal pain
▶ Have symptoms of a urinary tract infection, such as pain or burning when urinating, a feeling of being unable to empty your bladder completely, or an unusually frequent urge to urinate
▶ Have breast pain and feel sick or have a fever
▶ Notice your legs become swollen or painful
▶ Feel hopeless or sad much of the time

swollen veins in the anus or lower rectum. You may develop hemorrhoids during pregnancy or discover them after giving birth.

To ease discomfort while hemorrhoids heal, soak in a warm tub and apply chilled witch hazel pads to the affected area. Your care provider may recommend a topical hemorrhoid medication as well.

Avoiding constipation and straining can help prevent hemorrhoids. To keep your stools soft and regular:

- Eat foods high in fiber, including fruits, vegetables and whole grains.
- Drink plenty of water.
- Remain as physically active as possible.
- If your stools remain hard, ask your care provider about a stool softener or fiber laxative.

Hair and skin changes During pregnancy, elevated hormone levels put normal hair loss on hold. The result is often an extra-lush head of hair — but now it's payback time. After delivery, your body sheds the excess hair all at once. Don't worry — the hair loss is temporary, and by the time your baby is 6 months old, your hair will probably be back to normal. In the meantime, shampoo only when necessary, use a conditioner and find a hairstyle that's easy to maintain.

As for your skin, you may see small red spots on your face after giving birth, caused by small blood vessels breaking during the pushing stage of labor. The spots usually disappear in about a week. Most women get some degree of the dreaded stretch marks, especially on the abdomen, breasts, buttocks and thighs. Unfortunately, the marks won't disappear after delivery, but eventually they'll fade from reddish purple to silver or white. Any skin that darkened during pregnancy — such as the line down your abdomen (linea nigra) — may slowly fade as well.

BABY BLUES AND DEPRESSION

You're marveling at the miracle of the newborn in your arms and falling in love with this new person in your life. At the same time, you might find yourself sitting on the couch in the middle of the afternoon, still in your pajamas and needing a shampoo. You see dishes in the sink, dirty laundry overflowing the hampers and dust bunnies lurking under the furniture. The tears flow as you wonder when you'll get more than an hour and a half of sleep at a time. Perhaps you're resentful of your partner, who's out in the world with other adults.

Childbirth triggers a jumble of powerful emotions, from excitement and joy to fear and anxiety. Mood swings, irritability and sadness are common. Most new moms experience what's called the baby blues — feeling stressed, anxious or upset, angry with their partner, the new baby or their other children. You may cry for no clear reason, have trouble eating, sleeping and making decisions, and question whether you can handle caring for your baby. The baby blues usually set in two or three days after the birth and last from a few hours to a week or so.

You can beat the blues more quickly if you get as much rest as you can, even if that means asking for more help with the baby. Eat a healthy diet and get some exercise. And try to talk openly about your feelings, particularly with your partner. If these measures don't help, you may have a more severe form of depression.

About 10 to 20 percent of new mothers experience a more serious, long-lasting depression, called postpartum depression (PPD). Postpartum depression may appear to be the baby blues at first, because they share some of the same symptoms. How do you know if it's PPD? One clue is the length of time you've been feeling down. The mood swings, anxiety and irritability of baby blues tend to last a few days to a week or two. Postpartum depression is more severe and long lasting. Symptoms may begin at any time during your baby's first year, and they tend to get worse, rather than better. PPD may eventually interfere with your ability to care for and enjoy your baby and handle other daily tasks.

The abrupt drop in levels of estrogen and progesterone after childbirth, compounded by lack of sleep, may trigger the baby blues and contribute to postpartum depression. Other factors that may play a role include:

- Stress from changes in your work and home routines
- Poor emotional and social support
- Physical changes after pregnancy
- Financial or work problems
- Unrealistic expectations about parenting
- Doubts about your ability to be a good parent
- Changes in your identity and relationships
- Letdown after the excitement of giving birth

SIGNS OF POSTPARTUM DEPRESSION

If you experience any of these signs or symptoms, make an appointment with your care provider right away. Don't wait until your next postpartum visit.

- Baby blues that last more than about a week
- Changes in appetite or sleep
- Intense irritability and anger, or severe mood swings
- Overwhelming fatigue
- Persistent sadness, depression and crying
- Headaches, chest pains, heart palpitations (the heart beats fast and feels like it's skipping beats) numbness, or fast, shallow breathing
- Trouble focusing, remembering or making decisions
- Excessive worry about the baby
- Difficulty bonding with the baby
- Overwhelming feelings of hopelessness, worthlessness, shame or guilt
- Lack of joy in life
- Withdrawal from family and friends
- Thoughts of harming yourself or the baby
  Call for immediate help if you have thoughts of harming yourself or your baby.

- Having a challenging baby or a baby with special needs
- Other major stresses in life, such as the death of a loved one

Some men also experience symptoms of depression after their babies are born. Men whose partners have postpartum depression may be more likely to have depression themselves.

Don't feel ashamed or guilty if you experience postpartum depression. It can happen to anyone — it doesn't mean you're a bad mother or father. One mother recalls, "After I had my daughter, I felt miserable. It started when she was a week old and all I could do was cry. I felt like a horrible mom and wife but was ashamed to be put on any medicine. It took me eight weeks of crying before I asked for help."

Some people don't tell anyone about their symptoms because they feel embarrassed or guilty about feeling depressed at a time when they're supposed to be happy. But prompt treatment is important. Left untreated, postpartum depression can last for months and make it hard for you to take care of your baby and bond with him or her. A number of effective treatments can help you cope and find the joy in life again.

GETTING BACK INTO SHAPE

There's nothing like looking in the mirror after you give birth and realizing you still look like you're pregnant. Don't worry. This is perfectly normal. Unless you're a Hollywood celebrity, you're not going to slip back into your skinny jeans two weeks after having a baby.

Most women lose more than 10 pounds during birth, including the weight of the baby, placenta and amniotic fluid. Within the next few weeks, you'll likely also drop additional pounds as you shed retained fluids. After that, weight loss is likely to slow down — and the fat stored during pregnancy won't disappear on its own.

To return to your pre-pregnancy weight, you'll need a commitment to eating healthy foods and fitting in physical activity — as well as plenty of patience. By maintaining a healthy-eating plan and exercising regularly, you can expect to gradually lose weight. Sleep counts in your weight-loss plan, too. When you're exhausted, it's harder to make smart choices about food and exercise.

This effort is worth more than fitting into your favorite pants again. The excess pounds you shed now can help promote

a lifetime of good health. Keep in mind that women who haven't lost their pregnancy weight by six months after the birth usually end up heavier for the long term. In one study, they were 13 pounds heavier eight to 10 years later. By 15 years, these moms faced a high risk of developing heart disease and other obesity-related health problems. Women who exercised during those first six months were less likely to be obese 15 years later compared with women who weren't active.

A healthy diet It might seem counterintuitive, but to take off those excess pounds, it's important to eat regular meals after your baby is born. Even though you might be busier and more tired than you bargained for, be careful to eat healthy meals and snacks. It's also important to make conscious choices about what — and how much — you eat. Compared with women without children, mothers consume more sugar-sweetened beverages, calories and saturated fat.

Good nutrition not only is important to your well-being, but also benefits your baby if you're breast-feeding. Instead of cutting back significantly on how much you eat, skipping meals or going on a fad diet, choose healthy foods. Making wise choices can promote weight loss while keeping you and your baby in good health.

Focus on fruits, vegetables, whole grains Foods high in fiber — such as fruits, vegetables and whole grains — provide you with many important nutrients while helping you feel full longer. Other nutrient-rich choices include low-fat dairy products, such as skim milk, yogurt and low-fat cheeses. Skinless poultry, most fish, beans, and lean cuts of beef and pork are good sources of protein.

Avoid temptation Surround yourself with healthy foods. If junk food poses too much temptation, don't buy it. Keep it out of the house.

Eat smaller portions You may want to trade the traditional three meals for smaller, more frequent meals. But don't skip meals or limit the amount of fruits and vegetables in your diet. You'll miss vital nutrients.

Eat only when you're hungry If you're anxious or nervous, or if you simply think it's time to eat, find a way to distract yourself. Take your baby for a walk, call a friend or read a favorite magazine. Also keep in mind that fatigue can masquerade as hunger.

Exercise Daily exercise can help you recover from labor and delivery, restore your strength and get your body back to its pre-pregnancy shape. It can boost your energy level and cardiovascular fitness and help prevent backaches. Physical activity also brings important psychological benefits. It improves your sense of well-being and your ability to cope with the stresses of being a new parent. It also helps prevent and promote recovery from postpartum depression.

If you exercised during pregnancy and had an uncomplicated vaginal delivery, it's generally safe to begin exercising within days of delivery — or as soon as you feel ready. If you had a C-section or a complicated birth, talk to your care provider about when to start an exercise program.

It might seem crazy to expect to fit in exercise when you can't even find time for sleep — but every bit helps. You might be surprised by how much better you feel after a 10-minute walk. Here are some tips to get you started.

Get comfortable If you're breast-feeding, feed your baby right before you exercise. Wear a supportive bra and comfortable clothing.

Go for a walk Walking is a great way to get back in shape. You can walk almost anywhere at any time, and the only equipment you need is a pair of comfortable shoes. You can go by yourself, with your baby, and with your partner or a friend. Brisk walks will prepare you for more vigorous activities when you're ready for them.

Start slowly and build up Begin with light aerobic activity, such as walking, stationary cycling or swimming. Exercise a few times a day in brief sessions rather than for one long period. As your stamina improves, gradually increase the length and intensity of your workouts.

Include your baby If you have trouble finding time to exercise, include your baby in your routine. Take your baby for a daily walk in a stroller or baby carrier. If you prefer to jog, use a jogging stroller designed for infants. Lay your baby next to you while you stretch on the floor.

Target your abs Losing abdominal fat takes dietary changes and aerobic exercise, but abdominal crunches and other ab exercises can help tone your abdominal muscles (see "Strengthening your core" on page 416).

Make it social Invite other new moms to join you for a daily walk, or join a postpartum exercise class at a local fitness club, community center or hospital.

Breast-feed or pump before a vigorous workout High-intensity physical activity may cause lactic acid to accumulate in breast milk, producing a sour taste baby might not like. If you're breast-feeding, you can prevent this potential problem by sticking to moderate physical activity and drinking plenty of fluids during and after your workout. If vigorous activity is a priority during the first few months of breast-feeding, consider feeding your baby or pumping before your workout — which can also help you stay comfortable while you're exercising. Another option is to discard milk produced 30 minutes after vigorous exercise.

Exercise safely Remember to drink plenty of water before, during and after each workout. Stop exercising immediately if you experience pain, dizziness, shortness of breath or a sudden increase in vaginal bleeding. These may be signs that you're overdoing it.

Stick with it Even after you lose your pregnancy weight, exercise brings many physical and mental health benefits.

STRENGTHENING YOUR CORE

Exercises to tone and strengthen your abdominal and pelvic floor muscles can be beneficial after giving birth. They restore abdominal strength, tone and flatten the abdomen and help you maintain good posture. It's also important to strengthen your back. If you have the time and with your care provider's OK, try these exercises.

Exercises printed with permission. © 2009 The American College of Obstetricians and Gynecologists.

Leg Slides They tone the abdomen and legs. This exercise does not put much strain on your incision if you've had a cesarean birth.
1. Lie flat on your back and bend your knees slightly.
2. Inhale. Slide your right leg from a bent to a straight position. Exhale, and bend it back again.
3. Keep both feet relaxed on the floor.
4. Repeat with left leg.

Kneeling Pelvic Tilt This exercise also strengthens your abdominal muscles.
1. Kneel on your hands and knees with your back straight. Inhale.
2. Exhale and pull your buttocks forward, rotating the pubic bone upward.
3. Hold for 3 seconds. Repeat five times.

© MFMER

Head Lifts Head lifts can progress to shoulder lifts and curl-ups, all of which strengthen the abdomen. When you can do 10 head lifts at a time, proceed to shoulder lifts.

1. Lie on your back with your knees bent, your feet flat on the floor, and your arms along your sides. Inhale.
2. Exhale slowly as you lift your head off the floor.
3. Inhale as you lower your head.

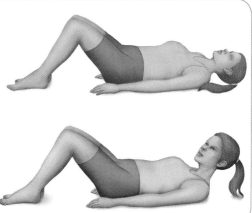

Shoulder Lifts When you can do 10 shoulder lifts at a time, proceed to curl-ups.

1. Lie on your back with your knees bent, feet flat on the floor, and arms along your sides. Inhale.
2. Exhale slowly and lift your head and shoulders off the floor. Reach with your arms so you do not use them for support.
3. Inhale as you lower your shoulders to the floor.

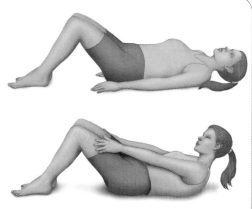

Curl-ups

1. Lie on your back with your knees bent and your feet flat on the floor.
2. Exhale. Reach with your arms, and slowly raise up halfway between your knees and the floor.
3. Inhale as you lower yourself to the floor.

© MFMER

Kegel exercises These exercises also tone your pelvic floor muscles and can help control bladder leaks, heal your perineum and tighten your vagina. Tighten (contract) the muscle that you use to stop your urine flow. Hold the contracted muscle for up to 10 seconds and then release. Repeat the exercise 10 times. Do Kegels at least three times a day. You can do them while standing, sitting or lying down — even while breast-feeding.

Keep it real(istic) Through diet and exercise, you can lose up to 1 pound a week. It may take six months or longer to return to your pre-pregnancy weight — and even then, your weight may be distributed differently from how it was before you became pregnant. Be gentle with yourself as you accept the changes in your body. Above all, take pride in your healthy lifestyle. Being physically active will help you set a positive example for your child in the years to come.

MOM AND DAD BREAKS

During the first weeks at home with a newborn, simply finding a few minutes a day to attend to basic hygiene — bathing, showering, getting dressed — can be challenge enough. Part of the stress of early parenting comes from the nearly constant demands on your energy and resources. But burning yourself out won't help you or your baby. You'll be better able to meet these demands if you arrange to have at least a few hours to yourself every week. Taking occasional breaks from your parenting role is good. Doing so can reduce stress, help you feel more in control and give you a sense of return to your normal self.

Look good, feel good Yes, there will be days when you're still not showered or dressed at 3 o'clock in the afternoon, and that's OK. But getting dressed and cleaned up will make you feel like a regular adult again. Figure out which grooming routines make you feel good and which are too time-consuming. If drying your hair takes half an hour, consider a shorter cut. Keep the routines you prize most, such as putting on lipstick. Keep your beauty and grooming supplies in one convenient place.

Get out of the house Being housebound with a crying newborn day after day can make anyone stir-crazy. A little fresh air or a change of scenery can go a long way in renewing your energy. As parenting columnist Lisa Belkin writes, "The lightness. The freedom. The awe that the world is still here, just the way you left it. The return of a previous version of yourself. It's the way I felt when each of my boys were newborns, and I left the house alone for the first few times."

Take your son or daughter out for a walk, or find someone to watch the baby for a few hours while you get out. Consider swapping child care with other new moms or joining a child care cooperative. If possible, plan a regular activity outside the house, such as a yoga class or book group.

Pamper yourself Make an arrangement with your partner, a friend or a relative to watch the baby while you have lunch with a friend or go on a special outing. Schedule a manicure, massage or facial, or take advantage of a free makeover at a local department store. If you can't get away, treat yourself to a soothing, scented bath, or shut the door to your bedroom, light a candle and listen to some music.

Hang on to your own interests Of course, your baby may be your No. 1 interest right now, but try to find time to pursue other activities or hobbies you enjoy. Go for a walk, read a book, write, draw or listen to music.

Share your feelings Talk about your feelings with someone you trust. Be open about your feelings of anger, frustration and sadness. Be sure to keep communicating with your partner.

Let go of guilt Many moms say they feel guilty about taking a time-out from baby and household duties. By nurturing yourself, however, you're helping yourself be a better parent.

Cut yourself some slack If you haven't checked off everything on your to-do list, be realistic about what you can accomplish in one day. Cut down on some of the less important "shoulds" to make time for some wants.

SHIFTING FRIENDSHIPS

Along with all the other changes in your life, expect some transformations in your friendships after you have a baby. You might miss your friends and still need them as much as ever, but you won't have as much time and energy to devote to them. You can't pop out for coffee or a walk without some planning, and concerts or movies, parties, and late dinners may be a thing of the past (at least for now). The baby's wail can bring phone conversations to an abrupt end.

As you're adapting to your new identity and lifestyle, it might take a while to sort out how your friendships fit in. Staying connected to friends who don't have kids requires patience and understanding on both sides. Some friendships may drift or fall away, while others form new patterns.

This is also a time when you'll make new friends with other parents who can relate to the sleepless nights, spit-up and diapers. "Truly, there was no comfort to me like fearfully asking, 'Does your baby do this?' and getting knowing nods in response," says one mom. Another mom appreciated connecting with other women in a lactation group: "It was just nice to get advice from other moms, or just to say, 'Oh yeah. I've been there.' … Sometimes you'd hear a worse story than yours, like, 'Oh, your child got up nine times last night! Mine got up only three times. That makes me feel better!'"

The support of friends can help you avoid isolation and help beat the blues. To help keep friendships strong through this time of transition, try these tips.

Let your friends know you care You might not be able to go out for a weekly dinner like you used to, but reassure your friend you still want her to be part of your life. Even if you have just five minutes, call or text a friend to say hello.

Connect with other parents Make friends with other parents. Keep in touch with the people you met at prenatal class, take a parenting class or join a parenting group. You may find parenting resources and groups at local schools, child care centers, community centers, health clinics, hospitals or houses of worship.

Avoid the 'child vs. childless' battle Many people without kids say their parent friends treat them like they just don't get it. While your friends might not know exactly what you're going through, that doesn't mean they can't empathize with you or don't care about your baby.

Spend time together in ways that work for everyone Explain your new realities to your friends — you need to be home by 6:30, for example, or might have to cancel at the last minute. Maybe you can put your baby in a backpack and go hiking, or walk together while you push the stroller. (Your baby is more portable now than he or she ever will be again!) If you're craving some one-on-one time to catch up, find a time when you can get out by yourself.

Be a friend as well as a mom Your focus these days might be almost exclusively on your little one, but friendship is built on mutual empathy, listening, laughing together and sharing interests. Even other moms might want to talk about something other than parenting. Take an interest in your friend's life, and make sure you're listening and giving to her.

Talk it out If you're feeling tension in a friendship after bringing baby into the picture, have an honest conversation about the changes you perceive.

REKINDLING ROMANCE

Sex after pregnancy happens. Honestly. But it might not happen very soon, or very often — romance usually isn't a priority for new parents. Many factors contribute to a decrease in sexual activity in the first year after childbirth. These include vaginal soreness, exhaustion, postpartum blues, an unpredictable schedule, changes in libido and body image, and the adjustment of going from partners to parents. Your bedroom may have turned into a nursery, pumping station and diaper storage center — not exactly conducive to romance.

Some women feel ready to resume sex within a few weeks of giving birth, while others need a few months or longer. In surveys of new parents, most say they're having sex by six weeks after the baby is born — and most also say that sleep is more important than sex, and they're not having sex as often as they did before.

Whether you give birth vaginally or by C-section, your body will need time to heal. Many care providers recommend waiting six weeks before having sex. This allows time for the cervix to close, postpartum bleeding to stop and any tears or repaired lacerations to heal. After a vaginal delivery, decreased muscle tone in the vagina may reduce pleasurable friction during sex — which can influence arousal. This is usually temporary. Due to hormonal changes, your vagina may be dry and tender, especially if you're breastfeeding. If this is bothersome, talk to your care provider about estrogen cream to alleviate some of the dryness.

Until you're ready to have sex, you can maintain intimacy in other ways. Spend time together without the baby, even if it's just a few minutes in the morning and after the baby goes to sleep at night. Share short phone calls throughout the day or occasional soaks in the tub. Rekindle the spark that brought you together in the first place. (For more ideas on nurturing your relationship, see Chapter 32.)

Most sexual problems that women experience after pregnancy resolve within a year. In the meantime, concentrate on promoting your physical and mental health, be patient and ease back into intimacy and sex.

Take it slow Start with cuddling, kissing or massage. Gradually build the intensity of stimulation. If vaginal dryness is a problem, use a lubricating cream or gel. Try different positions to take pressure off any sore areas and control penetration. Tell your partner what feels good — and what doesn't.

Share your feelings If you're not feeling sexy or you're afraid sex will hurt, share your concerns with your partner. Also talk about your feelings about your new roles as parents.

Focus on the moment For most women, sexual response requires the entire brain. Keep your mind on yourself and your partner — not the diapers, laundry and other household chores.

Make love when you have the energy If you're too tired to have sex at bedtime, say so. Consider making love early in the morning or while your baby naps.

Get help if problems persist If months go by and you're still not interested in sex, your mood is consistently low or you find little joy in life, contact your care provider. Postpartum depression can sap your sexuality. Also consult your provider if sex continues to be painful.

CHAPTER 31

Dads and partners

Nature consigns dads and partners to a supporting role during pregnancy and labor. Not so after the baby arrives. Then parenting becomes a gender-neutral activity — dads and partners can (and do) take on just about any baby-care task except breast-feeding. These days, fathers spend twice as much time performing child care each day compared with dads in 1985 and nearly three times as much as dads did in 1965.

Still, many dads and partners feel uncertain about their new roles and responsibilities. Becoming a parent is a momentous transition for both parents. While you didn't go through the physical changes of pregnancy and labor, you may be experiencing your own dizzying mix of feelings, from doubts about whether you can diaper a baby to a surge of love and pride. You're trying to be supportive of your partner while figuring out who you're going to be as a dad. Work and financial pressures also may loom large. This can be a rewarding, yet stressful, time.

Few first-time parents — men or women — feel fully prepared for the mixture of emotions ahead. Sometimes new parents are amazed at the intensity of their feelings for their new son or daughter and the extraordinary sense of closeness they feel to their partner and the baby. Such feelings are important buffers in the hectic days ahead, when infants cry frequently and fatigued mothers may have trouble coping.

Later, perhaps on your child's first birthday, you may look back and realize that, for all the strain associated with pregnancy and that first year, parenthood brings an incredible richness to daily living — a bond that's so unique and rewarding.

Nothing can quite compare to the joy of seeing a newborn's smile or to the excitement of watching the wobbly first steps of a toddler. "You know those moments of him giggling and falling asleep on your shoulder," says one new father. "Those things are just priceless."

SHIFTING ROLES

Just a few decades ago, fathers were not expected to play much of a role in family life. Dads were viewed mainly as breadwinners. That meant long hours at work, which was a man's first priority. Moms, as "homemakers," assumed most or all of the responsibility of raising the children.

Today, the traditional family structure — where one parent works and the other stays home to care for the kids and do the housework — is the exception. It's been replaced largely by dual-earner couples and single-parent households. As women spend more time at work, they expect more help at home, and men and women are increasingly sharing child-raising responsibilities.

It's not just external influences leading men to be more involved with their families. Most dads today want to fully embrace their roles as fathers — being a "good father" means caregiving as much as being a breadwinner. Dads want to be there for their kids physically and emotionally. One new father explains: "I'd like to be close to our son. … and I'd like to do the things that maybe weren't typical of a father before — feedings, changing diapers, holding him, getting him to relax before bed, walking with him in the middle of the night."

Men's shifting roles have led to new options and opportunities, as well as conflicts and challenges. For some men, shared parenting is better than "allowing work to take over every nook and cranny of your life," as one dad puts it. For others, taking care of the children provides a sense of purpose and structure during times of unemployment. Many dads are working to find a balance between their breadwinner and caregiver roles. "Manliness means facing the challenges and fears of parenting, acquiring the skills, taking responsibility, having fun, learning to love and be loved," says one father. "It's about being your own man, instead of just being your job."

DECIDING TO STAY HOME

If you're a stay-at-home dad, you're in the minority — just 3 percent of parents who care for their kids full-time are dads. You might also be the envy of other dads. Although very few fathers stay home full time to raise children, more than half said they would consider this option if they could, according to one study.

For most parents, regardless of gender, staying home with the baby isn't an option, since both incomes are needed. Even if it's financially feasible, other barriers might keep a man from staying at home. Deeply rooted cultural beliefs can make men uncomfortable with the role of primary caregiver. You may feel less "manly" or tough if you stay home with the kids.

Stay-at-home dads may also face criticism from family members. One father notes, "I am copping a lot of flak for choosing to be a stay-at-home dad. Especially from my own parents. … They feel that (my wife) needs to bond with the baby more than I do, and they think the baby will get confused."

At the other extreme, some stay-at-home dads find themselves the subject of too much attention — almost glorified — when they're out and about with baby. Notes one such dad, "We don't need special treatment and certainly don't want it. We're parents, just like all of those moms. All we care about is doing what's best for our kids."

If you do decide to become a pioneer and stay home with your baby, consider the trade-offs you'll face. You need to balance your parenting goals with your career goals, taking into account what you might be giving up in terms of retirement benefits and possible promotions, skills or opportunities related to work.

HANDLING COMMON CONCERNS

For both dads and moms, the first weeks home with baby can be overwhelming, especially if being at home is new to you. On top of feedings, diaper changes and crying spells, you must find time to do household chores and other daily activities. If you're used to a carefree, independent lifestyle, you may have trouble accepting your new responsibilities. Sleep deprivation can take a toll on your ability to cope. During this time of transition, you may feel surprised, amazed, confused, stressed — or all of the above.

Many dads and partners experience some common challenges and concerns.

Uncertainty about baby care The ability to care for children may seem to come naturally to some people, but most parents learn on the job. Feeling unsure or anxious about how to handle a baby, especially in the first weeks, is normal. Women don't know instinctively what to do either, but they often spend more time with the baby in the first months. If you have to go back to work while your partner stays home, you miss out on that full-immersion experience of caring for your infant.

The best way to master the tasks of caring for a baby is to jump in and do them. Get involved — do whatever you can, whenever you can. With time and practice, you'll recognize your baby's needs and

WHAT DADS DO

As a father, or a partner, you play a key role in your baby's healthy development. Positive interactions and shared activities between infants and dads enhance children's mental development and improve their social and emotional outcomes. Even when mothers and fathers share equally in the parenting duties, dads bring their own style to the venture. While mothers often can calm an upset baby more easily, fathers tend to play with their children more. The games men traditionally play — vigorous, active games — help babies develop physically as well as intellectually. Fathers do well in a teaching or coaching role, setting goal-oriented tasks for their children.

Being actively involved with your infant not only benefits your baby, but also enhances your own well-being. Dads who spend time with their infants and children report an increased sense of competence, greater satisfaction with parenting, and a newfound sense of maturity, personal growth and responsibility. As one dad reflects, "Taking care of my children is the toughest challenge I ever faced, but facing it strengthened me and enlarged my life."

acquire the skills to feed, diaper, hold, dress, bathe and soothe him or her.

Consider taking parental leave The more time you can spend with your baby, the more competent and effective you'll feel (and be) as a caregiver. If your company doesn't offer paid parental leave, find out if you can take some time off without pay.

Take turns caring for the baby Switch off with your partner in feeding and changing duties and putting your baby to sleep. If your partner is breast-feeding and planning to return to work, she may want to pump and store her breast milk. You can help out by bottle-feeding the stored milk. When your baby cries at night, take turns responding to baby.

Go along to doctor's appointments You'll learn more about how your baby is doing and will hear firsthand suggestions from the doctor.

Get information If you don't know something, ask questions or learn from other parents, books, websites and professionals.

Trust your instincts You'll get to know your baby and learn what's normal for him or her and what's not.

Increased financial responsibility The cost of your baby's delivery, health care, diapers, clothing and furniture can add up quickly. Moving to a bigger home or paying someone to take care of your baby while the both of you work can increase the financial strain. Finances also can become an increased concern if one of you takes unpaid leave or quits work to take care of the baby.

If you're the family's main financial provider, you're probably nervous about the bump in expenses. But burying yourself in work can keep you from providing the physical and emotional support your partner and baby need. While there are no easy answers, talk together about family finances. Work out a plan you and your partner both feel good about. Talking with other couples facing similar issues or meeting with a financial adviser may also be useful.

Reduced attention Some dads fear that their partners will focus all of their attention and affection on the baby now. The fear has roots in reality. After the birth, babies and moms usually do get most of the attention from family and friends — and you will have to share your partner's affections and attention with this new member of the family. Try not to take feelings of exclusion personally. Talk with your partner about how you feel, and spend some time alone with her.

Support and resources Some new fathers have dads who weren't around during their growing-up years or who weren't the best role models. In this case, you may have to sort through conflicting feelings about fatherhood and find other models of a "good father." Some men say they're motivated to be a different kind of father than they had: "I wish that he could have been a listener, instead of a lecturer," says one new dad. "I want to be able to understand my child's experience."

While many new moms rely on their own mothers for support, men don't often turn to their fathers for support. In general, new fathers often lack support networks, and they have access to fewer parenting resources, including education, discussion groups and play groups. For suggestions on how to build or boost your support network, see page 404.

Work-family balance This is no longer just a women's issue. After decades of social and demographic changes, mothers can choose to stay at home or work out-side the home. Both roles are seen as legitimate. But workplaces tend to be less accepting of men who make family a top priority, and many dads face challenges in balancing the competing demands of work and family.

While many men say they'd like to spend more time at home after the baby's birth, few actually take significant time off, perhaps because of limited paternity leave. It can be difficult to return to work so soon, however. You may feel like you're missing out, feel bad about leaving your partner on her own and feel squeezed for time to spend with your newborn.

Many dads and partners say that while their responsibilities at home have increased, their job expectations and hours stay the same. Other challenges include demanding workloads, long workdays and lack of flexibility. Some dads say they welcome a more balanced approach to life — that they don't want to think about work 24/7. Others worry

about losing ground or status at work because they're less able to dedicate time to their jobs.

Like women, men are realizing it's difficult if not impossible to have it all — to be an ideal worker and parent at the same time. Combining work and family requires some flexibility, as well as a supportive boss and work culture. It might also mean redefining what "success" looks like and making tough choices.

BONDING WITH YOUR BABY

The powerful and personal experience of pregnancy, labor and birth gives a woman a head start on intimacy with her baby. Fathers and partners have to get to know this tiny new person.

For some, the emotional attachment starts directly after the birth. Many dads and partners find that bonding happens gradually and may begin with a mix of positive and negative feelings. After you've changed a few diapers and hummed and rocked your child to sleep a few times, you may sense a warmth of feeling you didn't notice in the delivery room. A smile, a tiny hand grasping your fingers, the first unsteady steps and the first *da da* can work wonders.

Take time to connect physically and emotionally with your baby. It will happen naturally as you're doing the many baby-care tasks. Here are some other techniques to promote bonding:

- Hold your baby close and gaze into his or her eyes.
- Talk or coo to your baby, stroke his or her skin, and rock your child.
- Sing or hum a favorite song or lullaby at bedtime.
- Lie on your side with your baby next to you, facing you.

- Snuggle baby under your chin.
- Lay your naked or diapered baby on your bare chest for skin-to-skin contact. Turn your baby's head to the side so he or she can hear your heartbeat.
- Wear your baby in a carrier, and keep him or her close to you all day.
- Give your baby a bath.
- As your baby grows, keep holding and hugging him or her.
- Play with the baby. Face-to-face play helps focus your baby's attention and provides the first lessons in the sharing of expression and emotions.
- Don't expect to feel like a dad from the moment your child is born. Allow your love and commitment to grow over time.

UNDERSTANDING YOUR PARTNER'S MOODS

After childbirth, along with the physical changes your partner is experiencing, she may seem to be on an emotional roller coaster — and taking you along for the ride. One minute she's beaming with joy, and the next she's crying. Mood swings are common, and most new moms experience the baby blues, triggered in part by major hormonal shifts after birth. Symptoms include tearfulness, anxiety and irritability. Your partner may have trouble eating or sleeping, and she might become angry or upset with you or the new baby. The baby blues usually pass within a week or two.

A more serious issue is postpartum depression, which lasts longer and includes more severe symptoms. Because you know your partner better than anyone else, you're in the best position to notice changes in mood and behavior that might indicate a problem.

Be patient It takes time for your partner to recover physically and emotionally from pregnancy while caring for an infant. Be patient with her, and ask for her patience with you, too. This is a new experience for both of you.

One of your most important jobs is to provide support and help create a nurturing environment for her. Here are some ideas about how to do that.

Don't wait for requests or orders Look for household and baby-care tasks you can help with without your partner having to tell you.

Let your partner sleep Arrange for a block of time for her to sleep. Let her take a nap during the day or cover the night feedings.

Give her time to herself This is especially important if she's home all day with the baby. Allow and encourage her to take quiet breaks by herself, get out with a friend, exercise or just run errands by herself.

Give her time to exercise Support your partner in getting some form of exercise most days and in getting out of the house.

Expect times when she's moody It can be upsetting or frustrating to deal with your partner's emotional swings, but remember that the baby blues are temporary. Try not to take it personally. At the same time, you can set limits — it's not fair for her to use you as an emotional punching bag.

Watch for postpartum depression Signs and symptoms include anxiety, lack of confidence and frequent crying spells (see page 411 for a list of symptoms). If you believe your partner may have a mood disorder, make an appointment to see your care provider together.

Be a good listener Whether your partner just wants to talk about how she's feeling or needs to vent, give her your undivided attention. If she's experiencing the blues or depression, avoid giving advice, such as, "Just think positive" or "You can snap out of it."

Pamper your partner Serve her breakfast in bed on occasion or give her a massage. Make time for her to enjoy a long soak in the bath.

Let her know it's OK not to be perfect Encourage her to lower her expectations about keeping up the house and other daily responsibilities. If she's bothered by a messy house, if you are able to, hire someone to come in and clean.

FINDING TIME FOR YOURSELF

During this time of transition — when you're embarking on a great new journey and your life is turned upside down — you also need support and time for yourself. But those are just the things many dads and partners say they lack. In studies of new fathers, many report having few support systems beyond their partners. Parenting resources, such as classes, play groups and support or discussion groups, are often more geared to moms than dads, especially for those who can't take time off during the day. Men may also perceive a lack of support at work. You may not be able to take time off or work a more flexible schedule.

Finding time for yourself can also be very challenging. As fathers are spending more time with their children and on housework, they're sacrificing their personal time, interests and hobbies. It's im-

portant to take care of yourself so you have the reserves you need to be there for your partner and baby. Try these tips to cultivate support and carve out time for yourself:

Take some time for yourself Even if it's just a couple of hours a week, doing something you enjoy — watching a game on TV, running or biking, playing golf, or getting together with a friend — will help you deal with the new stresses in your life. Don't cut yourself off from your friends and family or adult activities and fun.

Ask for help and encouragement Let your partner know if you need some time for yourself or you could use some reassurance that you're doing OK as a dad.

Get guidance, if you need it No one is born an expert on bringing up a baby. Read books and websites about parenting and infant development, and don't be afraid to ask your care provider, family members or other parents for tips.

Reach out to other parents, especially other partners Support, information and encouragement from others who are going through the same experience can help you with practical issues and build your confidence. In turn, this strengthens your bond with your baby. Consider joining a parent-child class or a dad-baby play group. If you can't find one in your area, you could form a group yourself or join an online community. Many websites by and for dads offer support, a sense of community and resources.

Eat well and try to get enough sleep While you may not be getting seven or eight hours of uninterrupted sleep, you can make up some of the deficit by taking naps or going to bed earlier than usual.

REKINDLING ROMANCE

While resuming your sex life might be your No. 1 priority, your partner needs time to rest, recover and get used to the new normal before she'll be ready. Your sex life might disappear for a time. How long? On average, six weeks.

Just because sex is off-limits temporarily doesn't mean you and your partner can't be affectionate — and yes, romantic. Schedule private times together, perhaps a weekly lunch or dinner date. If your budget doesn't allow dining out, do something special at home — have dinner by candlelight, or enjoy breakfast in bed. Cuddle and kiss. Let your partner know you find her as attractive as ever.

Instead of pressing your partner to have sexual intercourse, let her decide when the time is right. Go slowly, and encourage your partner to share her feelings and concerns with you. When you begin having intercourse, make sure to use birth control if you don't want another pregnancy right away.

Eventually you'll settle into a new routine, and you'll have some time for yourselves again. But even then, most couples don't have sex as often as they did before baby. Many factors can affect your partner's (and your) desire for sex, including fatigue, stress, lack of time for yourselves and emotional swings. Make an effort to stay connected as a couple, which will help your romantic and sexual life. (See Chapter 32 for more ideas about maintaining a healthy relationship with your partner.)

Parenting as a team

As new parents, you're busy keeping baby fed, diapered, clean, safe, loved and nurtured. But parenting also entails getting dinner on the table, doing laundry, keeping up with housework and earning money to support the family. Along with sharing the joys and pleasures of parenthood, you and your partner must also juggle a never-ending, round-the-clock set of tasks and responsibilities. The stepped-up demands of life with a baby require you to negotiate new arrangements for dividing up duties. At the same time, your relationship as a couple is changing as your focus shifts to the baby and you have less time and energy for each other.

These stresses can set the stage for strife and ambivalence. About half of couples say they're less satisfied in their relationship after having a baby. That's a discouraging statistic — but the arrival of your baby doesn't have to lead to a decline in the quality of your relationship. Many new parents adapt to family life while maintaining a positive view of their relationship. What makes the difference? Creating practical strategies to share decisions, responsibilities and rewards. Staying alert to potential pitfalls. Remaining committed to preserving a deep connection with your partner. The goal is to work as a team.

As you and your partner develop complementary roles and support, you may be surprised at the strengths you uncover. And the stronger your bond is, the more effective you'll be as parents. A supportive, mutually satisfying relationship serves as the foundation for a healthy, happy family.

A NEW BOND

Many couples say that having a child brought them closer than ever, and it gave them a new and powerful point of connection. Watching your partner cuddle with the baby, lying next to one another with the baby nestled between you, joining hands with your baby as he or she takes those first wobbly steps — sharing moments such as these bonds you and your partner in new ways.

Many people also appreciate feeling like a family or a "complete package." You and your partner may feel a sense of achievement and fulfillment, especially if you've both longed for a baby or your journey to parenthood included a few bumps in the road. A baby can be a powerful symbol of your love and commitment. And then there's the fun and humor you enjoy together, from the silly stuff you do to entertain your baby to the sight of him or her covered in peas or carrots as you start solid foods. You can even bond over your tales from the trenches, such as surviving a week of the flu.

NEW CHALLENGES

The rewarding moments are interspersed with the day-to-day stresses of child care and housework. The first year or so of parenthood is especially hard on a couple's relationship. No matter how well you got along before the baby arrived, you may find yourselves disagreeing and becoming annoyed with each other now. As one new mom says, "We bickered. We said crazy things to each other that we never did before."

Part of the problem in the first year is the unique demands of caring for an infant, including the lack of a regular schedule, the crying and the nighttime feedings. Infant care adds an estimated 35 to 40 hours of work each week to the average couple's household. Many couples say they didn't realize how difficult and time-consuming caring for a baby would be. In addition, disagreements that might have lived in the background — about life goals, for example, or how to handle finances — may be brought to the forefront.

Other issues also may put a strain on your relationship.

Division of labor Along with sex and money, the issue of "who does what" is one of the most common arguments among couples. How partners divide their responsibilities both inside and outside the home is an ongoing source of discussion and debate, not only in individual couples but also in books, blogs and articles about parenting.

Less time as a couple After your baby arrives, your couple time may seem to vanish overnight. Gone are the leisurely meals, evenings snuggling in front of the TV and impromptu nights out. Now that you're a family, you have less

time, energy and attention to devote to your partner. Even your identity as a couple may seem threatened at first. "It was always about the baby," notes one mom. You may feel less like a couple and more like business partners checking items off your endless to-do list.

Fatigue and exhaustion Lack of sleep adds to couples' stress. Sleep deprivation can make you irritable toward your partner while dampening positive feelings. You might find it harder to convey your needs and goals and to consider your partner's point of view, two skills needed for healthy communication.

Decline in disposable income The financial squeeze of increased costs, along with a possible dip in income if one parent reduces work hours, can leave you with little money to spend on a baby sitter or outings as a couple.

Changing roles Most parents struggle with the competing demands of work, parenting and their relationship. In dual-earner couples, balancing the competing demands can cause confusion and conflict. Even when men and women aspire to share equally in caring for their children and their home, women often spend more time with the household chores and men put in more hours at their jobs.

SHARING THE LOAD

Who will do the baby's bath? Who's responsible for planning meals, buying the groceries and cooking? Will you or your partner be the one to work more hours or spend more time at home with the baby?

As the saying goes, "The devil is in the details." Working out the nitty-gritty of the day-to-day duties causes many of the conflicts among parents. Before childbirth, most parents-to-be share the ideal of participating equally in family life, household management and child rearing. After childbirth, traditional gender patterns often assert themselves. Although men and women have similar workloads overall, fathers spend more time doing paid work, while mothers put in more hours on the home front. The difference between expectations and reality can come as a surprise and disappointment to both partners.

To avoid this scenario, jointly work out a division of labor that distributes the stresses — and the rewards — of parenthood. It's not that you have to split all the responsibilities of life 50-50, but you want to come up with a plan that you can both embrace — one that allows you to work as a team in caring for your baby and sharing decisions and tasks.

How much responsibility should you each take on? Negotiate. Make a list and talk about what you can do, want to do and are good at. Structure the arrangement as an experiment, and tweak it as you go. Keep communicating about what's working and what's not. One dad comments, "It's a lot of give and take. In the morning I wake (the baby) up, get her dressed, and I get her out the door. (My wife) picks her up, she takes care of her while she's cooking, And when I get home we feed her together. ... Then my wife takes care of her while I do the dishes and then we play for a while. I put her to bed."

Acknowledge you may have different priorities Discuss what matters most to each of you in terms of your baby, your career, your free time and the household chores. You and your partner aren't going to agree on everything — and you probably won't find a perfect balance. Be willing to negotiate some compromises. When you're dividing up household chores, take into account your preferences and strengths and the most efficient use of your time.

Check your assumptions Sometimes what seems like a choice is actually influenced by social or gender norms. For example, many people (and employers) assume that a woman will take more time off work after the baby's birth than a man will. In one study, both spouses viewed the wife's job as more flexible than the man's, even if they had the same job!

Stay flexible about how things get done Your partner won't do chores and baby care the same way you do. Agree that it's OK for each of you to have different ways of doing things, as long as you're providing consistency for your baby.

Avoid scorekeeping You and your partner are on the same team — you don't need to keep score. Instead of taking a tedious inventory of everything your partner is (or isn't) doing, trust that you're both committed to your family's success. Work together to solve problems, and don't complain about who has the short end of the stick. Pitting yourselves against each other — or men vs. women — shortchanges everyone.

Watch out for gatekeeping Does this sound familiar? Dad dresses the kids wrong, leaves the house a mess or can't soothe a crying baby. You may be falling into the trap of thinking only mom knows how to do things the "right" way. This phenomenon, known as "gatekeeping," happens when a mother assumes the major responsibility for child rearing or criticizes a father's parenting efforts. Moms can positively influence their partners' involvement by encouraging their efforts and ensuring they have opportunities to gain experience.

Consider alternatives to dividing the work If you can afford it, think about hiring someone to help with the housework or yardwork. But be clear whose responsibility it is to make those arrangements. Join a baby-sitting co-op, if one exists in your area, or start one yourself.

NURTURING YOUR TEAM

To parent together as a team, you have to nurture your couple relationship as well as your baby. You and your partner depend on each other for support, both physically and emotionally. By tending to your relationship, you'll feel more satisfied as a couple. In turn, this improves your parenting ability. Studies show that couples who experience ongoing conflict are less responsive and sensitive to their infants in their first year of life. Negativity in a couple's relationship expands to family interactions.

On the other hand, supportive, mutually satisfying couple relationships enhance the well-being of the whole family. Making a special effort to see yourself not just as a mother or father, but as a partner, is good for both of you — and your baby. Here are some other ways you can nurture your team:

Communicate openly Discuss issues and difficult situations as they arise. Express your feelings, and be specific and honest about your concerns. Don't use this as an opportunity to blame or criticize your partner. Make sure you both have time to talk.

Set realistic expectations Couples do better when they share realistic expectations about their relationship and parenting. Discuss what you expect of each other and your family life. Acknowledge that the first years of parenting are

challenging and your relationship requires maintenance.

Encourage each other Both of you need support and encouragement during this stressful year. Be sure to talk about what's positive as well as what's more difficult. Tell your partner what you need to feel supported, and do the same for him or her. Discuss how well your needs are being met.

Be courteous and considerate When you're feeling depleted or overwhelmed, you're more prone to lash out at your partner and to be less forgiving. Try not to let courtesy and caring go by the wayside. Cut yourself and your partner some slack by not overreacting if one of you is irritable. Try to see situations from your partner's point of view.

Be adventurous Plan something small but special for your family each month, and look forward to it together.

AGREEING ON CHILD REARING

From infancy on, child rearing brings countless decisions about a range of issues — rules and expectations, discipline, structure and routines, time with grandparents, and exposure to TV and other media, to name a few. Granted, during baby's first year, discipline won't be a major issue, but by the time he or she is a toddler, you'll be dealing with misbehavior as your child tests the limits. Will you and your partner agree on what those limits are and how to enforce them?

New parents tend to emulate their own parents in their child-raising beliefs and behavior — though some people make a point of doing the opposite of what their parents did. What's important is for you and your partner to discuss your parenting beliefs and come to agreement on the strategies you'll use. For example, what type of consequences will you set when your toddler breaks a rule? How will you handle tantrums or requests to sleep in your bed? How will you encourage cooperation?

You and your partner may not agree on everything. Acknowledge any differences, and develop compromises that allow you to maintain a united front. Make sure you and your partner (and other adults who care for your child) observe the same rules and discipline guidelines. This reduces your child's confusion and need to test you. Work together to provide love, attention, praise, encouragement and a degree of routine.

Both you and your partner come to parenthood with inner visions of what you hope it will be. To build a life that satisfies both of you and nurtures your child, share your core values and choose goals that matter to both of you. Some partners don't want to discuss their hopes and anxieties because they're afraid that they'll reveal unbridgeable differences or start major conflicts. But confiding what you hope will happen and what you're concerned about strengthens the bond between you.

A FIRM FOUNDATION

Your relationship with your partner serves as the foundation for your family. You make your foundation stronger by engaging with each other with respect and mutual appreciation, sharing tasks and responsibilities, and regularly tending to your relationship. Parents in satisfying relationships report feeling more confident in their parenting and more resilient in the face of challenges. They're less worried and stressed.

Your parenting patterns are the least stable during your baby's first year. Over time, you'll establish patterns that work for you, and the stress on your relationship will ease. Practice does makes perfect — handling the challenges of this year together will help you and your partner weather future stresses better.

By approaching parenting as a unified team, you create an optimal environment for your baby to grow up in and form a secure attachment to you. You'll set the tone for an affectionate, communicative family life. For all the challenges raising your child brings, you and your partner are also in for a lot of fun, love, surprises and deep satisfaction.

CHAPTER 33

Single parenting

If you're raising your baby on your own, you're not alone. Single-parent families are more common than ever — more than one-fourth of children in the United States live with one parent, according to the U. S. Census Bureau.

The pathways to becoming a single parent range from divorce or the breakup of a relationship to unplanned pregnancy to the choice to go it alone. Despite the large number and variety of one-parent families, stereotypes persist — such as the struggling "welfare mom." Today's reality, however, is far more complex. For one thing, about 1 in 5 single parents is a father.

Parenting without a partner brings special challenges. The responsibility for all aspects of day-to-day child care may fall squarely on your shoulders. Juggling work and child care can be financially difficult and socially isolating. But single parenting can also be rewarding, and it can result in an especially strong bond between you and your child. Yes, you can raise a healthy, happy child while tending to your own needs and happiness as well.

One of the keys to raising a baby on your own is to develop a solid support network. Other strategies also can help you manage the challenges that come with the territory.

HARD WORK, ADDED PRESSURE

All new parents face many of the same challenges in taking care of a baby and raising a child. But parenting without a partner puts more pressure on you. Along with handling the day-to-day duties and decisions, it's up to you to support your family. One woman who chose to become a single parent felt panicked after she came down with a severe bout of flu: "What if anything happens to me?" Another single mom worried, "What happens if (my baby) gets sick, and I have to go to work? Will I lose my job because I'm on my own?"

Many single parents can relate to these fears. You may face several specific challenges as you adjust to your new role and raise your baby.

Financial and work issues Single parents often are the sole provider for their families. This makes it harder to earn enough money to meet your basic needs, and you may lack a safety net for emergencies. As a result, single parents — especially mothers — tend to have fewer financial resources. Compared with single mothers, single fathers do better financially, but they earn less money on average than do married fathers.

Single mothers also confront more challenges in finding and keeping jobs. To juggle their work and caregiving roles, single parents may have to reduce their work hours, turn down promotions or take less demanding jobs. Single parents in rural areas may lack public transportation, employment opportunities, family support programs and subsidized child care centers.

As a single parent, you may have to find ways to do more with less and become a careful planner. These suggestions may help.

Assess your financial situation Figure out your income and expenses so that you can budget your money. Will you receive child support? Pay for child care? How many hours will you work? Now that you have a baby, your expenses will likely increase, and your income may decrease if you've reduced your work hours. You may need to adjust your budget.

Cut down on spending Figure out where you can make cuts. Decide which items are most important. Take advantage of free or low-cost activities, and eat out less often.

Prepare for emergencies Even if money is tight, try to build up an emergency fund. Ideally, you'd have enough to cover several months' expenses.

Find out if you qualify for assistance Public programs such as food stamps and subsidized child care and housing can help you stay afloat if you're having trouble making ends meet. In addition to federal benefits, state governments, private foundations and faith-based organizations also offer grants, scholarships and other assistance.

Check into employment resources If you need help with finding a job (or getting a better job), contact your state employment office.

Consider getting more education or training Getting a high school diploma, college education or special training can boost your chances of finding a job.

Getting it all done As described in Chapter 32, one of the biggest issues new parents must contend with is how to divide the endless tasks and responsibilities of life with a baby. If you're flying solo, you don't have the luxury of this debate. You bear the burden of child care and housework, including the logistics, organizing and planning. As one single mother writes, "There is a constancy of parenting on your own that you don't understand until you've had to do it. Nothing ever stops. The minute you wake up in the morning, you hit the ground running, and needs don't stop until you pass out. That's when things go right."

On the other hand, since division of labor is a main source of conflict among couples with children, you don't have to worry about fighting over who will take out the garbage or change a diaper!

Support issues In the first weeks and months after having a baby, you're likely feeling more physically and emotionally vulnerable.

As a single parent, it's important to reach out for support — see the suggestions on page 444. Being a single parent in itself doesn't increase your risk of depression or other mental health problems, but single parents are more likely to have other risk factors for depression, such as financial hardship and unemployment. Keep in mind that having a partner doesn't help much if your partner isn't supportive. A relationship with an unsupportive partner may be worse for your mental health than is single parenting.

Emotional struggles Many single parents say that the emotional challenges of single parenting can be as difficult as the practical ones. You may feel different from traditional families or be envious of the support couples get from each other. You might feel guilty about raising a child without another parent. If your relationship with the other parent has ended, you may be grieving the loss of your partner, as well as your dreams and visions of how your life would be as you raised your child together.

Acknowledge your feelings and mourn the losses. Recognize that it can take months or even years to resolve the emotional fallout of separation or divorce. The first two years after the breakup are generally the hardest. As you accept your new reality and your feelings, you can begin to move on and create new dreams.

SINGLE DADS

One of the first hurdles single fathers must face is their invisibility in society. When people hear "single parent," they usually think of a mother. But in the United States, more than 2 million fathers are raising kids on their own. Most became single parents as a result of divorce, separation or out-of-wedlock birth.

In general, single fathers have higher economic status, work satisfaction and level of education compared with single mothers. Perhaps because of this, single dads' overall well-being tends to be higher as well.

But single dads face other issues. Finding support and a peer group for single dads can be more difficult . Many parenting classes, support groups, play groups and books are geared toward women. As a single father, you might feel like you stick out at the playground. You might not appreciate the unsolicited advice you get. Eventually you're likely to meet other men in the same situation. And if you don't, make an effort to seek out — or create — a support group in your community.

FROM SURVIVING TO THRIVING

As a single parent, some days it may feel like you're doing all you can just to survive. It will get better. As one mother says, "I learned that regardless of whether or not this is the life I planned, this is my life and I need to embrace it. I love being a mom and wouldn't trade it for the world. My son makes all of the difficult times worthwhile."

Several strategies have been shown to improve outcomes for single-parent families. With these in mind, you can create an environment that helps you and your baby thrive and grow.

Seek and accept support Probably the most important thing you can do as a single parent is to develop a strong support network. Practical and emotional support from others not only can help you handle your responsibilities but also boost your well-being. Asking for help can be hard on your pride, since many people are brought up to believe they should and must do everything by themselves. But it's better to lean on others a little than to become so overwhelmed, depressed or stressed that you can't parent effectively.

Many single moms say their own mothers are their best source of both practical and emotional support. You can also turn to other trusted family members, friends or co-workers. Ask for what you need, whether it's someone to babysit while you run errands, a friend to call when you need to talk or someone who's willing to provide backup child care if your baby is sick or your regular arrangement falls through.

If you don't have family members or friends who can help, look for a support group for single parents, or seek social services. Faith communities can be helpful resources, too. A support group, whether in person or online, offers a great opportunity to share feelings and get advice.

Find quality child care Good child care is crucial for your baby's well-being and your peace of mind. If you need regular child care, look for a qualified caregiver who can provide stimulation in a safe environment. (See Chapter 13 for more information.) Many single parents say they view their child care provider as a valued partner in raising their child.

Be careful about asking a new friend or partner to watch your baby. Anyone who cares for your baby should be someone you know and trust and who has some experience with babies.

To learn about financial assistance for child care in your area, contact your local child care resource and referral (CCR&R) agency. The agency can help you find out if you qualify for free or subsidized child care. Links to state CCR&R agencies are available through the National Child Care Information and Technical Assistance Center or Child Care Aware (see "Additional Resources," beginning on page 552). The federally funded Early Head Start serves infants and toddlers in low-income families. Local government, United Way agencies and other community or faith-based organizations sometimes provide child care scholarships. Some employers may provide scholarships or discounts.

Aim for a stable family life Changes in family structure, such as one parent leaving or a new adult entering the family, can be hard on kids. Try to ensure consistency in your family and your baby's caretakers and, if possible, keep moves and major changes to a minimum.

Create routines Family routines — such as regular bedtimes, mealtimes, naps and reading — promote good health and cognitive development in children. A lack of bedtime and mealtime routines, for example, increases the risk that children will have sleep problems, eat a less healthy diet and become overweight.

Single-parent families are less likely to keep daily routines for young children than are two-parent families. Some of the reasons include time constraints, financial pressure, fatigue and lack of support. Do the best you can to establish routines.

During your baby's first months, you're still helping him or her develop regular sleep habits, and the feeding schedule might vary from one day to the next. As your baby gets older, create a regular schedule for meals, naps and bedtime. If you're having trouble establishing daily routines, figure out what's in your way and brainstorm solutions. You can also seek assistance from your child's care provider.

Take care of yourself To help keep stress at bay, include physical activity in your daily routine, eat a healthy diet and get plenty of sleep. Make sure you get some "me time" regularly. Time away from your baby will help replenish your energy and spirit, helping you to be a better parent. Even taking 15 or 20 minutes to relax can be helpful.

Of course, this is all easier said than done. Here are some tips:

◗ Arrange for a baby sitter for a few hours once a week so you can get out of the house and do something you like, either by yourself or with friends.
◗ Find a gym with free child care.
◗ Take naps when you can.
◗ Read or walk on your lunch break.
◗ Take a bath or read a magazine after baby is in bed.
◗ Get up a little early to enjoy a quiet cup of coffee, write in a journal or do some yoga stretches.
◗ Reduce stress with relaxation techniques.
◗ Let go of guilt about taking time for yourself.
◗ Accept your limits, and don't be too hard on yourself.

Prioritize family time Throughout your child's life, and particularly in the early years, time with parents is important to health and development. Single parenting can put the squeeze on your time with your baby. Make it a priority —

even if it means having a messier house or not getting something else done that day. Set aside time each day to cuddle, play with or simply hold your baby. Find out if you can modify your work schedule to have more time with your baby.

Get organized Being organized can help reduce stress. Try these tips:
- Stock up on basic household supplies, such as toilet paper and diapers, as well as easy-to-prepare foods and meals that can be frozen and reheated.
- Eliminate clutter.
- Plan your week on a calendar.
- Develop a list of timesavers.
- Keep a list of baby sitters.
- Set goals. Figure out what's most important for your baby's needs and your needs, and focus on those.

Provide opposite-sex role models Children benefit from interactions with both women and men. If your baby's other parent isn't involved, create opportunities for the baby to interact with an opposite-sex adult who can be a positive role model. It doesn't have to be a romantic partner. If you're a single mother, spend time with a responsible, positive male family member or trusted friend. Involve the men in your life in family rituals, such as holidays and birthdays.

Stay positive Make a conscious decision to focus on the positive and not dwell on the negative aspects of single parenthood. Try to keep your sense of humor when dealing with everyday challenges, and don't forget to have fun. Take a break from the routine and plan a fun activity you can do with your baby, such as a hike in the park, trip to the zoo or picnic with friends.

One single mother advises recognizing your accomplishments and blessings:

"Give yourself a pat on the back daily. What worked out well and what made you smile today? There is no question that being a new single mom is one of the hardest challenges life will throw your way, but you will get through it and it will get better."

If you're feeling down much of the time or find yourself stuck in a pattern of negative thinking, talk to your doctor or consult a counselor or psychologist.

REWARDS AND STRENGTHS

Despite the difficulties, being a single parent also brings rewards, including a strong parent-child bond. In this relationship, the parent and child depend on each other, and they may become more communicative and supportive. Over time, you may create special routines and rituals together or discover places you like to go and things you like to do.

Children growing up in single-parent families often learn to take on more responsibility at home and develop self-reliance. As for the parents, many say they find a strength they never knew they had. Some also appreciate the freedom to make child-rearing decisions on their own, without constant negotiation and compromise. You may find yourself with a welcome clarity about what's important and learn to let go of what's not. As a single parent, you can take pride in your accomplishments and feel good about what you're giving your baby.

At first, you might feel overwhelmed and sad about being a single parent. Overcoming such feelings can foster a sense of inner strength. As one mom comments, "I have done things I never thought I was capable of all by myself. I am in control of my own happiness."

CHAPTER 34

Siblings and grandparents

Bringing home a new baby can be an exciting experience for your family. If you already have a child or children, your baby is a new sibling. He or she will likely become someone your older child or children will play with, laugh with and share a lifelong relationship with. If this is your first baby, your parents might be more eager than you expected to dote on and help care for your newborn. You and your partner might also begin to view your parents and your relationships with them differently.

Bringing a newborn home can also require some adjustments within a family. Babies need a lot of attention — which can cut into the amount of time you spend with your older child or children and cause jealousy. Grandparents, on the other hand, may be so excited about your new baby that they unknowingly overstep certain boundaries, such as by giving unwanted parenting advice.

Don't underestimate the impact your tiny newborn might have on your family. Consider your personal family dynamics, and understand how you can help your older child or children, as well as your parents, adjust to their new roles.

SIBLINGS

The experience of bringing a newborn home is a little different the second time around. With your first child, you were probably focused on recovering from childbirth and figuring out how to care for a baby. With the second — or third or fourth — baby, you're more likely wondering how your older child or children are going to react to having a new sibling and how you're going to juggle and meet all of their needs. Help set the tone for your children's early interactions by preparing your older child or children for what's ahead.

Introducing your new baby You've probably been talking to your older child for a while now about the arrival of your new baby. Perhaps your child has asked questions about your growing stomach, gone with you to prenatal checkups or helped you set up the nursery. Or maybe your child attended a sibling preparation class at your hospital. But it may still be difficult to know how your child will react to an addition to the family and the changes a new baby will bring.

While older children are typically eager to meet a new sibling, young children may be confused or upset and have a hard time adjusting — especially as the new baby sleeps less and begins to demand more of your attention. Explain to your older child that your newborn will probably cry, sleep and eat most of the time. The baby won't be a playmate right away.

To minimize the stress your child might experience once the new baby comes, think ahead. If your child will need to change rooms or move out of the crib so that your new baby can use it, do this before the new baby is born. It will give your older child a chance to get used to the new setup before dealing with the other changes associated with the new baby's arrival. Arrange for your child's care during your time in the hospital, and explain the details to him or her.

When the new baby arrives, have your partner or a family member bring your child to the hospital for a brief visit to meet your newborn. This is a great way for your child to meet the new baby and spend some time with you. Be sure to allow another family member to hold the baby for a while, so that you can give your older child plenty of cuddles. Consider giving your older child a gift that's from the baby — such as a T-shirt that says big brother or big sister — or taking your child someplace new or special to celebrate the new baby's arrival.

SIBLING REACTIONS

Your older child's age and development will affect how he or she reacts to having a new sibling.

Children under age 2 Young children likely won't understand yet what it means to have a new sibling. Try talking to your child about the new addition to

---

WHEN YOUR NEWBORN IS SICK

If your new baby has health problems, try to answer your older children's questions about the new baby simply. You might explain that their baby sister or brother is sick, and you're worried. Reassure your children that the baby's illness isn't their fault. If your baby needs to stay in the hospital after he or she is born, ask about the sibling visitation policy. You might also take pictures of the baby and show them to your older children.

Keep in mind that even if you don't talk to your older children about the baby's illness, they will sense that something is wrong and may act out to get your attention. Rather than keeping them in the dark, give your older children some basic information about the situation, and do your best to show that you are there for them.

your family and looking at picture books about babies and families.

Children ages 2 to 4 Children at this age may feel uncomfortable sharing your attention with a newborn. Explain to your child that the baby will need lots of attention. And encourage your child's involvement by taking him or her shopping for baby items. Read to your child about babies, brothers and sisters. Give your child a doll so that he or she can practice taking care of it. Look at your child's baby pictures together. Tell him or her the story of his or her birth.

If possible, complete your child's toilet training before the baby is born. Otherwise, wait until a few months after you bring your baby home to start the process. Keep in mind that siblings sometimes regress after the arrival of a new baby — such as by having toilet training accidents, drinking from a bottle or asking to be carried to bed — to get your attention. There's no need to punish this type of behavior. Instead, give your child plenty of love and assurance. Don't forget to praise your child when he or she demonstrates good behavior.

School-age children Children ages 5 and older may feel jealous of how much attention the new baby gets. Try talking to your child about your newborn's needs. Encourage your child to get involved by helping to decorate the baby's room with handmade artwork and participate in taking care of the baby. Be sure to explain the importance of being gentle with the new baby. Point out to your child the advantages of being older, such as being able to go to bed later or play with certain toys.

All children Regardless of your older child's age, make sure that he or she gets plenty of individual attention from you and other family members once your baby arrives. Grandparents can be particularly helpful during this time. Watching mom and dad coo over a new baby can be difficult for an older child to watch. If you're taking lots of pictures or videos, be sure to include your older child, too. Take some pictures or videos of him or her alone, as well as with the new baby. Consider having a few small gifts on hand to give to your older child, in case friends visit with gifts for the new baby. During your newborn's feedings, try to make your older child feel included by reading stories together. Reassure your older child that you love him or her and your new baby. And remind your older child that he or she has an important role to play now, too — that of big brother or big sister.

SIBLING RIVALRY

Right now, sibling rivalry may not be a concern, but it can become an issue as your child gets older and competes with other children for parents' love and respect. Signs of sibling rivalry might include hitting, name-calling, bickering and regressive behavior. This kind of behavior is common after the birth of a new baby — but it can also happen anytime one child in the family receives extra attention.

While sibling rivalry is a natural part of growing up, many factors can affect how well your children might get along with each other, including their sex, ages and personalities, as well as the size of your family and each child's position in it.

For example, younger children might be more likely to fight physically, while older children might argue instead.

Children who have less than a two-year age difference might battle each other more than children who have bigger age gaps between them. Although children of the same sex might share more of the same interests, they might also be more likely to compete against each other. Middle children might feel less secure and be more likely to seek affection because they may believe they don't get the same privileges or attention as the oldest or youngest child in the family.

Although all siblings are bound to fight, tease and tattle on one another at some point, there are things you can do

SIBLING SAFETY HAZARDS

If you have an older child, you probably have toys in your home with small pieces that an exploring baby could easily choke on or swallow. Be sure to round up games and toys that have small parts, and keep them out of your baby's reach. When your older child wants to play with these kinds of toys, keep the toys in an enclosed area. This will give your older child a chance to play without fearing the intrusion of little hands. Encouraging your children to play separately with their own toys may also help you sidestep a few battles — especially if your older child is younger than age 3 and isn't eager to share his or her things. For more information on child-proofing your home, see Chapter 15.

as a parent to encourage healthy sibling relationships now and as your children get older. Consider these tips:

Respect each child's unique needs Treating your children uniformly isn't always practical — and the harder you try, the more your children may look for signs of unfairness. Instead, focus on trying to meet each child's unique needs.

Avoid comparisons Comparing your children's abilities can cause them to feel hurt and insecure. While it's natural to notice your children's differences, try to avoid discussing them out loud in front of your children. When praising one of your children, stick to describing his or her action or accomplishment — rather than comparing it with how his or her sibling does it.

Set the ground rules Make sure your children understand what you consider acceptable and unacceptable behavior when it comes to interacting with each other, as well as the consequences of their misbehavior. Consistently follow through with discipline, such as a time-out or loss of certain privileges, when your children break the rules.

Listen to your children Being a sibling can be frustrating. Let your children vent their negative feelings about each other, and listen. Respond by showing your child that you understand what he or she is feeling. If your child is old enough, you can ask him or her to help in devising an acceptable solution to whatever is bothering him or her. If you have siblings, share stories of conflicts you had with your brother or sister when you were a child. Holding regular family meetings can give your children a chance to talk about and work out sibling issues, too.

Don't take sides Try to avoid being drawn into your children's battles, unless violence is involved or one of your children could get injured. Encourage your children to settle their own differences. While you may need to help younger children resolve disputes, you can still refrain from taking sides. In addition, avoid using derogatory nicknames for your children that might perpetuate sibling rivalry.

Give praise When you see your children playing well together or working as a team, compliment them. A little praise and encouragement can go a long way.

MANAGING SIBLINGS DURING BREAST-FEEDING

If you're breast-feeding your newborn, you may wonder how your older child will react to your nursing sessions — or how to keep your older child busy while you nurse. Try not to worry. Your child will likely express curiosity and may hover upon first seeing you breast-feed. Simply explain what you're doing, and try to answer any questions your child might have. If you breast-fed your older child, explain that you did the same thing for him or her when he or she was a baby. To keep your child entertained while you nurse, consider setting out a couple of toys or a workbook nearby beforehand. You might also play music or audio versions of children's books.

IF YOU HAVE MULTIPLES

Sibling rivalry often isn't an issue for multiples. While the children may compete against each other, multiples typically also depend on each other and develop close relationships early on. However, they may have problems maintaining their individuality. For example, twins are often treated as a unit, rather than two children with unique personalities. As a result, twins are often dressed alike and given the same toys. If you have multiples, pay attention to their different needs and try to foster individuality.

Multiples can also cause other children in the family to feel left out or jealous — since they are not part of this unique relationship. If you have multiple babies and an older child, be sure to spend plenty of special one-on-one time with your older child. Also, encourage your multiples to play separately with other children. For example, arrange a play date for one of your twins while the other twin plays with a sibling. Your multiples may resist separation, but being able to be apart is a skill your children will benefit from as they get older. For more information on multiples, see Chapter 38.

GRANDPARENTS

Grandparents can play a major role in your newly expanded family. Your parents (yours and your partner's) will likely give you and your partner emotional support and encouragement, and calm your nerves as you figure out life with a newborn. They may share their experiences as well as helpful tips. They'll likely be great baby sitters and helpful in a pinch. Grandparents can serve as role models for the kinds of parents you want to become. And, best of all, they can provide your child with a special kind of love and affection.

Changing relationships Pregnancy and the birth of a baby often cause new parents to re-examine their relationships with their own parents. As you prepare for your future as parents, it's only natural that you and your partner think about the ways in which you were raised and what you would like to carry forward from the past or would like to change. In the process, you might find that you have questions for your parents about how they handled becoming a mom or dad and why they made certain decisions. Your parents will likely be able to share advice, discuss some of the ups and downs they experienced as new parents and reassure you that you'll be able to handle your new role.

Typically, the birth of a new baby brings families closer together, giving new parents and their parents a chance to renew and strengthen their bonds. But the shift in your role and your parents' roles may not always go as smoothly as you might hope. You and your parents might unknowingly have different understandings and expectations of your new roles. Make an effort to talk to your parents about how you feel about becoming a parent and your parents becoming grandparents — and be sure to listen to their feelings on the subject, too.

Receiving help As you navigate the early stages of parenthood, your parents will likely want to provide help and support. Sometimes, however, the support you get isn't the support you need. For example, excited new grandparents might want to come to stay for a few days once the baby is born. While some new moms and dads might find this helpful, others — as they learn the ropes of caring for a new baby — might find the presence of relatives stressful.

Think about what might work best for you and your family, and discuss your needs with your parents before the baby is born. Would you and your partner like to spend a few days on your own with your new baby before relatives visit? Or would you prefer to have relatives come to help you early on, go with you to your baby's first doctor's appointment or assist with caring for your other children? Would you like to have your parents and in-laws visit at different times so that each set of grandparents can have time with the baby?

Tell your parents what they can do to be most helpful — household chores included. This may help prevent misunderstandings and tension, as well as help you make the most of your parents' desire to be there for you.

Like it or not, your parents might go a little overboard on the baby gifts. While you might not be able to stop your eager parents from buying the baby gifts, be sure to tell your parents what the baby needs. Also, remind your parents that what your baby really needs isn't a toy or treat, but to spend quality time with his or her grandparents. Doing an activity together, such as taking a walk in the park, can be a fun way for grandparents and new babies to begin bonding.

And don't forget that as much as your parents want to help you during this time, they likely also want to spend some

---

GIVING GRANDPARENTS TIME

Sometimes, new grandparents aren't quite ready for their new role. They may still have career aspirations and life plans, and the idea of being grandparents may make them feel old. If your parents are struggling with becoming grandparents, give them an honorable "out." Don't bathe them with all of the grandparent language or expect them to perform the traditional grandparent duties or tasks. With time, things may change, but until your parents are ready, take it slow.

LETTING GO OF THE PAST

If you and your parents aren't close or have a difficult relationship, the birth of your baby might serve as motivation to work through your problems — especially if you want your parents and your child to have a strong connection. During your pregnancy or after your baby is born, consider making an effort to work on your relationship with your parents. In addition, remember that your child will have a separate and different relationship with your parents than you do. When couples divorce, the grandparents on both sides of the family will still want to spend time with him or her.

time cuddling with your baby and getting to know him or her. This is especially important if your parents don't live nearby or won't be able to visit your baby frequently. Offer your parents as much time with the baby as you're comfortable giving them. If you're bottle-feeding or you're breast-feeding and already pumping, consider letting your parents feed the baby. Remember, this is a precious and exciting time for your parents, too.

Conflicting opinions You and your partner likely have some ideas about how you plan to care for your baby — and they might be different from your parents' ideas. For example, while your parents might have fed you formula, you might plan to breast-feed. One of your parents might have stayed home to take care of you, while you and your partner both plan to continue working. As your baby gets older, you and your parents may also have different opinions about the toys your child should play with — wood or plastic? — or the amount of television he or she should be allowed to watch. This can be tricky territory.

If your and your parents' parenting styles differ, it might be difficult for your parents to keep their opinions to themselves. Consider telling your parents or in-laws that what you could really use is support or help around the house, not unsolicited advice. You and your partner have the final say over the way your child is raised and the rules in your house. However, try not to dwell on these issues. Keep in mind that your parents are probably trying to help and may be struggling with the transition from being your parent to being a parent and a new grandparent. And expect that if your parents baby-sit your child, they will likely handle things slightly differently than you would. These little differences may even help your child learn how to be flexible.

In addition, just as you and your partner have your own thoughts about what kinds of parents you'd like to be, your parents might have thoughts about what kinds of grandparents they'd like to be. Some grandparents aren't comfortable baby-sitting and prefer a formal relationship with their grandchildren. Others are playful and enjoy engaging their grandchildren in activities. And still others want to be a part of their grandchildren's daily lives, serving as surrogate parents. Consider talking to your parents about what kinds of roles they'd like to play in your child's life. Do they want to baby-sit? How available do they plan to be? Are they willing to help out in case of a crisis?

When making requests for help in taking care of your child, be sure to keep in mind your parents' ages, abilities and any other limitations. To avoid unnecessary misunderstandings or resentment, ask your parents what they can handle and if you're expecting too much from them.

The holidays Your baby's first holidays and birthdays will likely be important events that his or her grandparents will want to help celebrate. But while big family parties can be fun, they're not always possible. Chances are that you'll end up alternating holidays with different grandparents. Or perhaps you'll have two celebrations, one with each set of grandparents, on different days.

Either way, if holidays are particularly important to your parents, talk to them ahead of time about your plans and your desire to make sure everyone feels included in your child's big days. If your parents are having a hard time understanding the situation, explain that alternating holidays will allow each set of grandparents to spend more quality time with your child in a more relaxed setting. You might also encourage your parents to focus on new or different traditions, such as taking your child out for his or her half-birthday.

GRANDPARENTS AS CHILD CARE PROVIDERS

Some couples rely on grandparents to provide part-time or full-time care for their children. Having someone you know and trust take care of your child can be comforting. Grandparents are often flexible with their hours, may be able to watch your child in your home and

GRANDPARENTING FROM A DISTANCE

If your parents don't live nearby, they might miss out on your baby's first smile, giggle or attempts at rolling over. Consider helping your parents keep in touch with your baby through regular phone calls, video phone chats — perhaps at the same time each week — or by frequently sending videos or pictures. While it might still be awhile before your baby can talk much, he or she will likely enjoy listening to your parents' voices and grabbing the phone or computer. If your parents aren't up on current technology, regularly mailing printed pictures might be your best option. To help your baby get to know your parents and other family members, make a photo album with their pictures, and look at it with your baby during playtime or before bed. Be sure to tell your baby the names of the people in the photos.

may not ask for payment. However, grandparents might not have any training in car seat use, CPR or other emergency care. These types of arrangements can also cause tension, especially if you don't feel comfortable telling your parents how you want your child cared for or if you don't want unsolicited parenting advice.

Think about the pros and cons before asking your parents to provide regular child care. If you decide to go that route, ask them to take a CPR class. Be sure to discuss the details, and come to an agreement beforehand about how the arrangement will work. For more information on child care, see Chapter 13.

If your parents will be watching your child in their home, consider asking them to purchase their own crib or highchair — or offer to get one for them. This will make meals and naps easier on your baby, as well as your parents. You might also consider asking your parents to buy their own stroller, car seat and basic medications, such as for a fever or diaper rash.

If it's been awhile since your parents took care of a baby, they might need a refresher on the basics — especially in areas where the rules have changed over the years, such as in car seat safety and baby-sleeping positions. Before you leave your child in your parents' care, discuss safety topics. Make sure your parents are aware of all safety precautions discussed in Chapters 14-16. If your baby is going to be at their house, the house needs to be childproofed. It's also important that they not leave medications and other dangerous items within a child's reach, and that they take precautions around hot liquids and other items that could lead to a burn. These are just some of the safety issues that need to be addressed.

Car seats Make sure your parents purchase a reliable car seat and know how to use it properly when transporting your baby. Explain the importance of having your baby ride rear-facing until he or she reaches age 2 or the highest weight — typically at least 35 pounds — or height allowed by the car seat manufacturer. For more information about car seat safety, see Chapter 14.

Sleep positions Insist that your parents put your baby to sleep resting on his or her back, rather than on the stomach or side, until your baby can roll over both ways without help. Make sure your baby is put to sleep on a firm mattress in a crib. Remind your parents that adult beds aren't safe for infants. For more information about sleep safety, see Chapter 7.

EDUCATION CLASSES

Many hospitals, birth centers, senior centers, churches and community colleges offer classes for grandparents. These classes may serve as refreshers on baby care and changes in maternity care. They might also touch on how to deal with role changes, parents' goals and expectations, what it's like to grow up today, and any other concerns new grandparents might have. If your parents or in-laws are interested in taking a class, start by inquiring at your hospital or birthing center. If they live far away, suggest that they contact a local hospital for information.

CHAPTER 35

Finding contentment: Home or job?

It is perhaps one of the most difficult decisions new parents face — staying at home with a newborn or returning to a job. For many couples, juggling parenthood and a job has become the norm. More than half of U.S. mothers with infants under a year old work outside the home, most of them in full-time jobs. And as their children get older, the majority of moms hold a paying job.

Almost all parents try to balance their family and career roles. Women with children may move in and out of the paid workforce at different points, shift careers or start their own business. They may work part-time or work from home. Sometimes dad chooses to stay home or change careers to help with child care.

It's up to you to decide if, when and how you go back to work after having a baby. And it may take some time to make this decision. You may appreciate the sense of identity and accomplishment you get from work, but at the same time you feel a strong emotional pull to be with your baby. You might feel torn between competing roles, expectations and responsibilities. The bottom line is, whatever choice you make, it will be the right one for you and your family. There's no right or wrong decision, but there's probably one that's best for you. And what works now might not be the best solution later.

If you decide to return to your job, know that quality child care is available for your son or daughter, and there are steps you can take to make the transition back to work easier for you and everyone involved.

ISSUES TO CONSIDER

As you navigate the work-life balance of a new parent, there are a number of issues to weigh. If you are struggling over whether to stay home with your child or return to your job, consider your personal needs as well as those of your baby and family.

Career consequences If you've worked hard to attain a certain position, or your occupation is very meaningful to you, you may not want to give it up. In fact, having a career that you genuinely love can be a positive influence and inspiration for your children. Other reasons you may want to keep working include the intellectual challenge, adult interaction and sense of accomplishment you may get from working outside the home.

Your decision about whether to return to your job may be influenced by your employer's policies and culture. Family-friendly benefits may include flexible work schedules, part-time work, child care referrals or on-site child care, and parental leave. Practical matters, such as your commute, also can be a deal breaker.

Nevertheless, many working parents, especially moms, also contend with feelings of guilt. You may feel guilty about leaving your baby in someone else's care or not spending enough time with him or her. You may feel guilty for wanting to keep your career.

To the contrary, some stay-at-home parents struggle with feeling lonely and isolated. An infant doesn't provide the kind of companionship they may have expected. Some parents who leave a job to stay at home with a child also experience a mini identity crisis — feelings of personal loss. This can come as a surprise to a parent who was looking forward to a new stay-at-home routine.

None of this is out of the ordinary. These are all normal feelings.

Finances If you're the sole provider for your family, or your partner's income doesn't cover your expenses, you may not have the option of staying at home. Although money isn't everything, you do need enough to provide basic care for your family.

If, on the other hand, you or your partner makes enough income to sustain the family, you may choose to stay at home or take on a part-time job or a job that you can do from home.

Carefully review your finances before making a decision. Consider not only your and your partner's salaries but also the cost of having two people working — including child care, commuting, parking and clothing. For some parents, child care would cost more than they could earn by working. On the other hand, some couples are nervous about living on a single paycheck in tough economic times. If you prefer to stay home, can you cut enough expenses to make up for your lost income and still have a cushion?

Another financial issue to consider is the longer term impact of staying at home. Will you be able to save money for your child's college education or your retirement?

Child care Another important factor that can influence the decision of whether to remain at home or return to a job is child care. Many options are available, each with pros and cons.

You want your baby to be cared for in a safe, healthy environment by supportive, affectionate adults who help your child learn and interact. The more reliable, dependable and attentive to your child's needs your care provider is, the more you'll be able to focus on work. As one new mother says, "If you find a good place where you know the child is well looked after, then you are comfortable at work. If not, it's unbearable, and you can't concentrate on anything." For more information on child care and issues to consider as you look for child care, see Chapter 13.

Once you've found child care you feel comfortable with, you can return to work with confidence, knowing that your child is in good hands. By building a good relationship and communicating effectively with your baby's caregivers, you may come to view them as valued partners in helping your baby thrive.

Stresses and rewards No matter what choice you make, you can be sure it will bring some stresses — and its own rewards. Juggling parenting and working outside the home takes a lot of energy and can lead to burnout, especially if you work long hours, spend time commuting, work nights or weekends, or travel a lot for work. Among two-career couples, parents need to share household and child care responsibilities, which can lead to resentment and conflicts.

Staying at home comes with its own stresses. Taking care of a baby 24/7 is exhausting, especially if you don't get many breaks away from your baby to do some of the things you enjoy. Some parents also experience stress because they no longer feel the sense of accomplishment they used to get from earning money or performing well at their job. The job of parenting doesn't come with objective measures of success. However, many parents will say it is the most rewarding job of all!

LIVING WITH YOUR DECISION

Remember, the decision you make now doesn't have to last until the day your child enters kindergarten. Many parents make adjustments to their work or child care arrangements during their baby's first few years.

You may not know how you're going to feel about your decision until you've

EFFECTS ON YOUR CHILD

Opinions on whether child care is good for kids can run strong. Some people insist that to be a good parent, you have to be home with your child. Research doesn't bear this out, however. There's no evidence children are harmed when their parents work, and good-quality, stimulating and nurturing child care offers some benefits. Spending time in child care can improve school readiness, language development, independence, social competence and peer interaction skills.

The most influential factor in parenting is not the sheer quantity of time you spend with your child but that you have a loving, nurturing relationship. Studies have found no difference between working mothers and stay-at-home mothers in the quality of mother-child interactions or their influence on children. And on average, working moms spend only about 10 hours a week less caring for their children compared with at-home moms. What's important is that when you're with your child — whether you're a stay-at-home parent or you work outside the home — the time you spend together is quality time.

Whatever your choice, if you feel happy and fulfilled, your child will enjoy the happiness as well. If you resent your current arrangement or feel cheated by it, you'll likely pass on these feelings to your child.

lived with it for a while. If you go back to your full-time job and find yourself miserable, you could cut back on your hours, take an extended leave or step away for a while. If you decide to stay home and find the financial strain too stressful, or miss the camaraderie or your career, you may choose to go back to work. One mom who cut her maternity leave short notes, "I was getting bored at home and needed the structure in my life of returning to work. I wasn't happy and was driving my husband crazy." Another mom had the opposite experience: "I thought I'll just take 2 months off and I'll go back to work. But having my daughter totally changed me."

MAKING THE TRANSITION BACK

If you've decided to return to your job, take some time and consider when would be the best time to go back. Although there's no perfect time frame, experts suggest spending three to four months at home with your baby, if you are able to do so. That gives you time to settle into a schedule, bond emotionally and learn to care for your child. Fatigue is a big factor for both parents during those first few months. Three to four months at home gives you plenty of time to rest and recover.

The standard 12-week maternity leave passes quickly, and many women dread the day it will end. You may not feel ready. With some planning, you can ease your transition back to work — and stay connected to your baby.

While you're still on leave You can help your return to work be successful by following these basic steps:

Talk to your employer Clarify your job duties and schedule so that you'll know what's expected of you after your maternity leave. You might ask about flexible hours, telework or working part-time.

Set a return-to-work date Try to avoid going back to work at a time when you're going through other stressful life events or major changes, such as moving or an illness or death in the family. If you can, go back to work later in the week. This will make your first week back to work a short one.

Try a trial run with child care Consider having your baby stay with his or her caregiver for part of the day just before the end of your maternity leave. You can stay there awhile to help the baby adjust, then take some time to run errands or have a little time to yourself.

Prepare to continue breast-feeding If you plan to continue breast-feeding after returning to work, tell your employer that you'll need to take breaks throughout the day to pump. Ask about a clean, private room with an outlet for breast pumping. Consider buying or renting an electric pump that allows you to pump both breasts at once.

About two weeks before returning to work, adjust your breast-feeding schedule so that you're pumping two or three times during the day and nursing before and after your upcoming work hours. Have someone else feed your baby a bottle of stored breast milk to help your baby adapt. If you're lucky enough to have onsite or nearby child care, consider breastfeeding your baby during the workday.

Plan ahead Write a list of everything you'll need to pack for your new routine — such as a breast pump, diaper bag, extra diapers — and figure out how much time you'll need to get ready in the morning.

When you go back to work Expect ups and downs as you become more adept at managing multiple demands. The first day can be especially emotional. One mom recalls, "I'll never forget the first day we picked (our baby) up from her baby sitter's house, and I got her home and changed her little diaper and started crying because she was wearing a diaper that I didn't put on her! But it gets easier." Allow for some tears that first day! Here are some other tips to help smooth the transition:

Let go of the guilt Often when mothers first return to work after their baby is born, they feel guilty for leaving the child

with someone else. You may be anxious that the baby will bond more with the caregiver than with you, or that you'll miss an important milestone. But don't worry, you'll still have time to spend with your child. Working outside the home doesn't make you a bad mother — and it's OK to look forward to the challenges and interactions of your job. Remind yourself that you're doing what's best for you and your family.

Provide continuity of care Develop a good relationship with your baby's caregiver. Spend time talking to him or her when you drop off or pick up your baby. Share family stresses — both good and bad — that might affect your baby. Before you take your baby home, ask about any important events that occurred in your absence, such as a change in bowel movements or eating patterns or a new way of playing. Take time to periodically discuss your baby's progress and any problems or concerns.

Stay connected Consider a daily phone call or text message to your baby's caregiver to find out how he or she is doing. Place a favorite photo of your baby on your desk or in your work area. Set aside time after work to reconnect with your baby.

Make backup plans Know what you'll do if your baby is sick or your baby's caregiver is unavailable on a workday. Options might include taking the day off yourself, asking your partner to take the day off, or calling a friend or loved one to care for your baby.

Get plenty of rest The first few weeks back will no doubt be emotionally and physically draining. Go to bed as early as you can, and ask your partner to help with night feedings.

Continue to breast-feed If you're breast-feeding, bring your breast pump, containers for expressed milk, an insulated bag and ice packs to work. Keep a stash of breast pads and extra blouses handy, in case your breasts leak. If finding time to pump is a concern, consider alternatives — pumping during your breaks or working from home to make up for the lost hours, for example. If you can't express milk at work, breast-feed your baby or pump just before you go to work and as soon as you return home. You could also pump between feedings on your days off for extra breast milk to be used while you're working.

Network with other working parents Even if it feels like you have no spare moment in the day, reach out to other moms in the same position. You can trade tips and gain support. Have lunch with a co-worker who's also a parent, or organize a moms' night out.

Re-evaluate your decision if you need to If your transition is much tougher than you expected, or you're experiencing severe anxiety, consider talking to a counselor or joining a support group. Give yourself a time frame for re-evaluating your decision, such as two months.

Give yourself some time to adjust to your new circumstances, and maintain a positive attitude. Being separated from your baby all day is probably harder on you than on your baby. Tell your baby how excited you are to see him or her at the end of the day. Your baby might not understand your words, but will pick up on your emotions.

BALANCING WORK AND HOME LIFE

Achieving balance between work and home is the holy grail for working parents. Difficulty finding this balance is a perennial topic of discussion in the media and one of the top reasons people seek counseling or psychotherapy.

Both moms and dads struggle with work-life balance, but mothers tend to identify much more with their family

---

STAYING CONNECTED AT HOME

Women who leave the paid workforce to care for children often find re-entry challenging, as office technology, jobs and workplace norms change. If you're staying home for an extended time, you can take steps to stay connected to the work world and avoid the insecurity that can follow the post-Mommy years.

- *Keep up your networks.* Maintain personal and business contacts. Have lunch with former colleagues, keep in touch through social media or email, or attend networking events.
- *Stay abreast of industry trends.* Read trade magazines, check out industry websites or subscribe to e-newsletters in your field.
- *Consider doing some work on the side.* If you can take on an occasional project or even some part-time work, you can keep your foot in the door.

role. They take on the bulk of the responsibility for running the household, raising children and having careers. They're more likely to be the ones to get the baby ready in the morning, pick him or her up at the end of the day and stay home if the baby is sick or child care isn't available.

Working moms soon realize that they can't do everything perfectly — and that "having it all" often means sacrificing something. As one mom says, "I've opted not to take promotions because they would have involved more time commitment than I felt comfortable giving while being a mother to my children." In some cases, working moms feel like they're not doing very well in either role. Others follow the mantra that you can have it all, just not all at once.

Despite the challenges, it is possible to manage and even thrive with the juggling routine. Here are some suggestions for creating balance.

Embrace 'good enough' If you've always set high standards for yourself, this is the time to let go of perfectionism. Balance requires being good enough rather than perfect. Your home might not be as tidy and organized as it was before you had a child. You might not have time to cook meals from scratch anymore. Maybe you can't work the long days as you used to — and get as much done. Focus on the positive aspects of your situation, and let go of guilt about what you're doing or not doing.

Find the right fit for work You're more likely to create work-life balance if you work for an organization that's supportive of parents. Flexibility is on top of women's wish lists when choosing an organization. Control over your schedule can buffer work-life conflicts and reduce the chance of negative health outcomes.

Just as important as a company with family-friendly policies is having a supportive boss. One mom notes that her supervisor at the time of the birth of her first child was a woman who'd raised two children by herself: "She was supportive in allowing me to work part time and sometimes from home. This made breast-feeding and logistics much easier."

If your work setting doesn't give you time to be a parent, consider working less — or somewhere else.

Get organized Make a daily to-do list. Divide the list into tasks for work and tasks for home, or tasks for you and tasks for your partner. Identify what you need to do, what can wait — and what you can skip entirely. Organization can help you get more work done in less time.

Seek support Don't try to do everything yourself. Accept help from your partner, loved ones, friends and co-workers. Speak up if you're feeling guilty, sad or overwhelmed. If you can afford it, consider paying for weekly or biweekly housekeeping to buy yourself extra time for your family or yourself. Keep up your friendships, whether it's for a girls' night out or someone you can call to talk with or to ask for baby-sitting help.

Share more of the load with your partner Ask your partner to split more of the responsibilities with you. Maybe you can work different schedules so that you can have your baby in child care for fewer hours. (See Chapter 32 for more on this topic.)

Recognize the issue is bigger than you It can be helpful to put your struggles into context. You're not alone in finding it tough to balance work and family, and if you sometimes feel like you're losing the battle, it's not because you're inefficient or unmotivated. The traditional model of career success in the United States poses challenges for working families, and the global economic downturn has increased the pressures to perform. Media messages that pit working moms against stay-at-home-moms add to the problem.

Keep your career options open Creating a sense of independence from a specific employer or career can give you the freedom to move between positions and companies, and possibly take some time off or consider starting your own business. Maintain your personal and professional networks and contacts, and build a strong reputation in your field.

Nurture your own well-being Cut down on unnecessary commitments. Exercise and move your body. If you feel as if going to the gym takes away from time with your baby, go for a walk with your baby in the stroller, or try for some active play together. Relax in the tub after you put baby to bed, or unwind with a book or some favorite music. Pick a reasonable bedtime and stick with it. On your days off, sleep when your baby sleeps.

CHAPTER 36

When to have another child

As your baby approaches toddlerhood, family, friends and perfect strangers start asking the inevitable question — are you going to have another child? (Often it's "when" and not "if.") And the question may be foremost on your mind as well.

Like other parenting decisions, figuring out how many children you want is a personal process, though you may receive plenty of advice and opinions. Deciding whether or not to have another child is one of the most important decisions you'll make for your family, and it may be even harder than deciding to have the first one. It's normal to worry about how another child will affect your family, relationships, lifestyle, finances and work and to wonder if you're making the right choice.

If you think you want another child, when might be the best time? Again, only you and your partner can answer that question. Pregnancy spacing affects how close your children are in age and may have an impact on your health and your baby's health. There are many factors to weigh when planning your next pregnancy.

As you and your partner consider the possibility of having another child, approach each other with compassion, respect and a willingness to listen. Talk about the issues with an eye toward strengthening your relationship and your family.

DECIDING ON ANOTHER CHILD

Maybe you've always dreamed of having three kids, each spaced three years apart. Or you're agonizing over whether you can really handle another baby. Whatever your hopes, fears and dreams, there are a number of issues to consider as you think about expanding your family.

Added responsibilities Caring for a growing family can be physically, mentally and emotionally taxing, despite its many rewards. Most parents say that adding a second child more than doubles the work. You need plenty of time and energy to care for an infant, while your older child also needs your attention. With two kids, your life will be more hectic — and your house will no doubt be messier. But you'll also find that you grow to meet the challenges.

"I felt like my life as a parent finally had a rhythm to it (he finally slept at night, I didn't need to lug around all the baby paraphernalia anymore, etc.) and I wasn't sure how I'd do once a second child came along," writes one mom. "Taking care of the needs of two little people can definitely be more stressful, but you get progressively more creative to get everything done." With a second baby, you'll realize how much you learned the first time around. You'll have increased confidence in your abilities and knowledge, and you'll find it easier to handle things that might have seemed daunting the first time around, such as breastfeeding and taking care of a sick baby.

Your partner's preferences Sometimes one partner is ready for another baby and the other isn't. It's important to understand each other's concerns. Sit down together and talk about your points of view and your differences. What does having a second child mean for each of you? What are your goals and dreams? Explore ways to resolve concerns and conflicts. If your partner is worried that your relationship will suffer, make specific plans for keeping date night alive. Work together to come up with ways to lessen the financial burden.

Both of you need to be on board with the decision. If you remain at odds, perhaps you can agree to revisit the issue in a year or two. It might also be helpful to talk to other couples who've been in the same position or to consult a marriage and family therapist.

Family finances A new child adds to your family's expenses. You'll want some

extra money in the budget before you conceive another child. Think about what your financial picture will look like with a new baby. Will you or your partner need to reduce your work hours or stay home to care for your children? Can you afford to pay for the new baby's child care if you keep your job? Are you willing to sacrifice certain things in order to cover baby costs? Will you have enough money to save for college tuition? If you're living paycheck to paycheck or fear a layoff, you may decide to hold off on having the next baby.

In the longer term, having babies close together frees you from child care costs sooner. On the flip side, spacing children further apart can give you more time to recover from the financial impact of pregnancy and early child care.

Impact on your career It might be harder to juggle your job and child care responsibilities when you add another baby to the mix. Will you be able to keep up with your job after the next baby? Is it important for you to reach another level in your career path before you take on pregnancy, childbirth and caring for an infant again? Then again, it might be easier to focus on your career later if your kids are in school at the same time.

Family dynamics Many people have more than one child because they don't want their firstborn to be an only child. Providing a sibling for your child may be part of your motivation, but it's important to want to raise another baby just for him- or herself. You can't predict how well siblings will get along, and there are pros and cons to having siblings or not. (See "Deciding one is enough," page 474.)

Another common concern is that you'll disrupt the smoothly functioning, happy family you've created. Change of any sort can bring up fears, and a second

child will change the dynamic and logistics of your family life. However, most parents say that soon after the arrival of the second baby, they can't imagine life without him or her.

Sharing the love Probably most parents have wondered how they could possibly love the second child as much as they love their first. You may worry that you'll lose your special relationship with your first child and shortchange the second child by having to share your attention and time. It's common to worry that the second child will feel less wanted and loved and that the first one will feel resentful. Rest assured that your relationship with each child will be unique, like the children themselves, and that you'll have plenty of love to go around.

As writer Lisa Belkin notes, "I remember, with Polaroid clarity, the moment I said goodbye to Evan as I left for the hospital to deliver Alex. I had the overwhelming feeling that I was about to ruin his life. I tried to remember what I try to remember in all tough parenting situations — that I am giving them something, not taking it away. … And when I brought home a baby brother, I gave each of them proof that neither of them was alone in the world, and that neither was the center of the universe."

Social pressures Although one-child families are increasingly common, couples still face cultural and family pressure to have a second child. If your friends are all having a second or third child, you may feel left out. You may feel the pressure from your partner or feel guilty if he or she wants another baby and you don't. Be honest with yourself about what's right for you. Parenting another child is a big responsibility to take on because someone else thinks it's a good idea.

Having more children than you want or can manage can increase the risk of poor parenting.

Thinking in reverse If you're having trouble making a decision about having another child, you might try turning the question on its head. How would you feel if you were told you couldn't have another child? Your sadness or your relief may give you insight into what you really want.

Until you make a decision about when to have another child, be sure to use a reliable method of birth control — even if you're breast-feeding. If you and your partner agree that your family is complete, you can stick with your present form of birth control or switch to something long lasting, such as an IUD or implantable rod. You might also opt for something permanent, such as a vasectomy or tubal ligation. Remember that a decision as big as this one takes time and thought. Do your research and discuss any concerns with your health care provider. Make sure you have the information you need — and the time you need to process it — before going through with a permanent plan.

DECIDING ONE IS ENOUGH

The number of families with one child has nearly doubled since the 1960s, as more people are starting families later in life and facing financial pressures. But negative stereotypes about only children — that they're spoiled, selfish, lonely and bossy — still persist. Such beliefs may prompt couples to have more than one child.

Years of studies in several countries have found no evidence to support these stereotypes. Only children are no different from their peers in terms of character, sociability, adjustment or personal control. One way they are different is that they score consistently higher in intelligence and motivation compared with children with siblings. Interestingly, some research suggests that parents of only children are happier than are parents with more than one child. When you have just one child, you spend a lot of time with that child, which can make for a close relationship. However, parents with multiple children also are close to their children.

If you're struggling with the idea that a childhood without siblings will damage or shortchange your child, you can let go of that fear. Yes, having brothers and sisters can be a positive experience and help kids learn skills such as dealing with conflict. As a parent of a singleton, you'll want to make an effort to give your child opportunities to interact with other children.

What's most important is to know what's right for you and your partner. "I am being honest with myself when I admit that I will be a much happier and better parent to one child than more," says one mother. "Some people thrive in busy, spirited environment. ... I fall apart. I think the worst thing about deciding to have an only child is dealing with my own feelings of needing validation." Another says, "By having a second child, we would stretch ourselves way too thin mentally, emotionally, financially, physically, and we know we would end up in pure misery."

SECOND PREGNANCY TIMING

Once you've said yes to another baby, the next decision is when to start trying. There's no perfect time to have another baby, and if you wait until the circumstances are just right, you might never do it. Even with careful planning, you can't always control when conception happens. You might get pregnant sooner than you thought or long after you hoped you would. In the end, pregnancy spacing is often based on a combination of personal preference and luck.

You can make an informed decision about when to grow your family by understanding the health issues associated with timing your pregnancies too close together or too far apart, as well as the advantages and disadvantages of different pregnancy intervals for parents and children.

Health issues Some studies show that spacing pregnancies too close together or too far apart can pose health risks for both mother and baby.

Short interval between pregnancies

Closely spaced pregnancies may not give a mother enough time to recover from the physical stress of one pregnancy before moving on to the next. It can take a year or longer to develop stores of essential nutrients that may have been depleted during pregnancy and breast-feeding. If you become pregnant before replacing those stores, it could affect your health or your baby's health.

Getting pregnant within 18 months of giving birth may slightly increase the risk of low birth weight, small size for gestational age and preterm birth. If you had a cesarean birth and allow for less than an 18-month interval before your next child is born, you may increase your

risk of uterine rupture if you decide to try a vaginal birth.

Limited research suggests that a pregnancy within 12 months of giving birth is also associated with an increased risk of placental problems. One study reported a link between pregnancy intervals of less than 12 months and an increased risk of autism in second-born children.

It's possible that behavioral risk factors, such as smoking, substance abuse or lack of prenatal care, as well as stress and poverty, are more common in women who have closely spaced pregnancies. These risk factors — rather than the short interval itself — might explain the link between closely spaced pregnancies and health problems for mothers and babies.

Long interval between pregnancies

Spacing pregnancies many years apart also may pose some health concerns for mothers and babies. A pregnancy five years or more after giving birth is associated with an increased risk of:

▶ High blood pressure and excess protein in your urine after 20 weeks of pregnancy (preeclampsia)
▶ Slow or difficult labor or delivery
▶ Preterm birth
▶ Low birth weight
▶ Small size for gestational age

It's not clear why long pregnancy intervals are linked to these potential problems. Researchers speculate that women who wait five years or more to have another baby may lose some of the protective effects generated by the first pregnancy. Maternal age or factors such as maternal illnesses also may play a role.

To reduce the risk of pregnancy complications and other health problems, wait at least 12 months before getting pregnant again. An ideal interval might be to wait at least 18 to 24 months but no more than five years before attempting your next pregnancy.

If you do get pregnant while breast-feeding and decide not to wean your baby, you'll need to take extra care with your diet. You may want to meet with a dietitian to be sure you're meeting your nutritional needs.

Family issues As a child, Mary M. Murry, a certified nurse-midwife at Mayo Clinic, pictured herself married to a handsome pop singer: "We'd have four children, two boys and two girls with two years between each child. ... I'm not sure why two years between children seemed like the perfect pregnancy spacing in my 9-year-old imagination. As an adult who started having children a little later in life, two years seemed too long between babies — yet my second and third children are two and a half years apart."

You might have a similar fantasy of how far apart in age you'd like your children to be. Is there an ideal spacing between children for their sake and yours? Probably not. Many families settle on an interval of two to three years, but various types of spacing all have advantages and disadvantages.

1 to 2 years apart Having children one to two years apart can be the ultimate test of your endurance. But that doesn't mean it can't work.

Advantages Some of the benefits are:
▶ Your children will be close in age as they grow up. They may share many of the same interests and activities, making it easier to juggle family schedules. Parents often hope that siblings close in age will be close companions and play together.

You condense the time when you're dealing with carrying, feeding, diaper changing, sleep deprivation and toilet teaching. Also, you may not need to childproof your home as many times as you would if you had your children further apart.

You can double up on some tasks, such as reading to your older child while nursing the baby or having them nap at the same time.

Your first child may have an easier time adjusting to a sibling and will barely remember what life was like without him or her.

Disadvantages Some of the possible drawbacks are:

Caring for two in diapers is likely to leave you exhausted much of the time and with little personal space for a few years. Tantrums, dirty diapers and potty accidents times two can feel like constant chaos.

Stress and fatigue can take their toll on your marriage. You and your partner will need to work as a team to meet the challenges ahead. And you'll need to set aside some quality time for each other.

Supplies for two infants can be costly.

Sibling rivalry may be a problem as your children grow up.

2 to 5 years apart A spacing of two to five years is what most experts recommend. Your first child is a little more independent, and you and your partner have had some time to regain strength and energy.

Advantages Some of the benefits are:

During the interval between pregnancies, you'll have time to bond with your first child and give him or her your undivided attention.

Your first child will have the opportunity to be the baby of the family without any competition.

When the new baby arrives, the older sibling will be more likely to play on his or her own at times, giving you some one-on-one time with the baby.

Your children will still be close enough in age to bond easily.

You're only paying for diapers for one. Some baby supplies, such as a crib or stroller, can be recycled.

Your body has time to restore its nutritional supply to prepare for the next pregnancy.

You've fine-tuned your parenting skills, but it hasn't been so long that they're rusty.

Disadvantages Some of the possible drawbacks are:

Your first child may feel jealous of the new baby. It's not uncommon for 3- and 4-year-olds to revert to baby-like behavior when faced with having to compete for a parent's attention. This usually goes away with time, though.

Rivalry issues regarding toys and activities may occur as the baby gets older and starts getting around on his or her own.

Your older child may be outgrowing his or her naps just as your baby is settling into a regular nap schedule.

The further apart your children are, the more different each child's activities are. Coordinating schedules may require considerable organization and planning and can be stressful.

5 years or more apart Some parents liken having kids who are five years or more apart to having an only child twice.

Advantages Some of the benefits are:

You get a big break between babies.

This may give you some time to go back to doing things you enjoyed before having an infant, such as going out for dinner or a movie or taking adventurous vacations. It may also give you a chance to refocus on your career or your marriage. Waiting five years or more can also give you a financial break and allow you to save money for the next baby.

- Each child gets plenty of individual attention in infancy and beyond.
- You get to enjoy and focus on specific stages of growth and development with each child.
- Because of the difference in age, sibling rivalry tends to be less intense. Instead, your younger child may regard his or her older sibling as more of a hero, while the older child may assume a more protective or guardian-like role. Depending on the age of your first child, you may even have a built-in baby sitter.

Disadvantages Some of the possible drawbacks are:

- After several years of being out of baby mode, you may have a hard time getting back into it. You tend to forget how much work caring for an infant can be and how exhausted you become at the end of the day.
- It may be a challenge to keep up with your older children while caring for a baby.
- You'll probably need new baby gear, because your car seat and stroller will likely be out of date.
- Schedules in your household may vary widely. It can be stressful to keep them all coordinated.
- Due to the age difference, your children may not share many of the same interests. They may not be as close as children who are more similar in age.

Other issues Other factors also can influence the time of a second baby.

- *Your age.* Couples who start a family when they are older sometimes must race against the biological clock. If you're a woman in your late 30s and you would like two more kids, you may not have the luxury of spacing your children three years apart.
- *Your fertility.* If it took you a long time to conceive the first time, or you used fertility procedures, you may not want to wait long before trying to conceive again.
- *How many children you want.* If you would like to have a large family, you may need to space your children closer together.

Most important, listen to what your heart says. Whatever the pros and cons of various pregnancy intervals, if you and your partner both want another baby, this might be just the right time.

PART 6

Special Circumstances

CHAPTER 37

Adoption

One of the most deliberate ways of becoming a parent is through adoption. Adoption is an active process, often involving a great deal of paperwork to be filled out, personal information to be shared, home studies to complete and agency fees to work into the budget. And unlike a nine-month pregnancy, adopting a child can take anywhere from several months to several years. The wait can be difficult, and adoptions can sometimes fall through.

Prospective parents, whether through adoption or surrogacy, are often required to undergo a level of introspection and outside scrutiny that can be considerably greater than for others making the transition into parenting. In short, those who undertake adoption are some of the best prepared parents around! This can be a great strength when it comes to facing the challenges and opportunities ahead.

Most of what you need to know about caring for a baby is already in this book: All babies require love, nurturing, guidance and medical care. But because you

may have no control over the prenatal and postnatal care of the child you adopt, you may have some unique concerns. This chapter offers basic advice on adoption and addresses medical and emotional issues that may be on your mind.

SUPPORTING YOUR CHILD'S HEALTH

Like any parent, one of your jobs is to keep your child as healthy as possible. Since you may not know ahead of time what your child's health status or medical history is, you may need to take a few extra steps to ensure your child gets on the right track.

Find a care provider The best time to choose a care provider is before your child arrives, if at all possible. Although many professionals who care for children's health have experience with adoption, you may need to shop around a bit before you find one that suits your needs. Talk to other parents who have adopted and ask for recommendations. Call a few of those care providers to say you're planning to adopt, and ask if there's any specific medical information you should request from the agency concerning your child. If you'll be adopting internationally, ask care providers if they've had experience with international adoptions.

If possible, schedule a pre-adoption visit with the care provider you prefer. Most providers appreciate the opportunity to meet parents before the child arrives so that they can discuss issues such as sleeping, eating, making the house childproof, immunizations and any pertinent medical concerns. They can also discuss with you general developmental expectations based on the age your child will be on arrival.

Some international adoption clinics offer physician services, such as reviewing a child's medical information before a prospective parent accepts a referral, travel consultations for parents traveling abroad to pick up their child, and post-adoption checkups.

Update family immunizations Adults and children who will be in close contact with the child being adopted may need to catch up on immunizations, including vaccines against measles, hepatitis A and B, tetanus, diphtheria, and pertussis. If you're traveling to a different country to receive your child, your care provider can also give you advice on travel safety and any necessary vaccines or medications you'll need to receive before or during your trip, depending on your child's country of origin.

Try to track down a medical history If possible, try to acquire any medical, genetic and social records of your child's history in writing from the birth parents or adoption agency. There might not be much information, but it will be easier to track down now rather than years later.

It's especially important to gain full disclosure from the agency before you adopt, to have a more accurate representation of any medical conditions your child may have. This is where having a care provider for your child already selected may come in handy. He or she may be able to help you make sense of medical reports you obtain, explain the implications of a medical condition, or alert you to what might be missing from the records.

Get post-adoptive care If your baby has a known medical condition or arrives ill, you may need to visit your child's care provider soon after arrival. But if your baby appears healthy when he or she joins your family, you might wait a couple of weeks or even a month. This gives the child a chance to adjust and the parents a chance to get to know the new arrival so they can better answer a care provider's questions about their child's "usual" behavior. If your baby is an open-adoption newborn, you may just need to follow the same well-child schedule as any new baby. (For more information on routine medical care, see Chapters 11 and 12.) First-time parents, especially if they did not have a pre-placement visit, may want to consult their child's care provider sooner if they need information and support.

For children arriving from overseas, the Centers for Disease Control and Prevention recommends a medical examination within two weeks of arrival in the United States, or sooner if your child has a fever, anorexia, vomiting or diarrhea. In addition to a comprehensive exam, your child's care provider may also recom-

INTERNATIONAL ADOPTIONS

Immigration laws in the United States require that all immigrants seeking permanent residence in the U.S. show proof of having received the vaccines recommended by the Advisory Committee on Immunization Practices (ACIP). Internationally adopted children under 10 years of age are exempted from this law, however, as long as the parents sign a waiver declaring their intention to comply with immunization requirements within 30 days of the child's arrival in the U.S. Over 90 percent of children adopted from abroad need catch-up immunizations when they arrive.

Certain countries also have high rates of infectious diseases or parasites that prompt testing and treatment, if necessary, both for the care of the child and protection of the rest of the family. In addition to a complete physical examination (including vision and hearing screenings), your child's care provider may recommend screening for the following:

- Hepatitis B
- Syphilis
- HIV
- Intestinal parasites
- Tuberculosis
- Anemia and blood disorders
- Vitamin and mineral deficiencies
- Thyroid disorders

- High lead levels in the blood

  Depending on your child's country of origin, the care provider may also recommend testing for:
- Hepatitis A
- Hepatitis C
- Chagas' disease
- Malaria

Treatment exists for many of these conditions. The sooner a health concern is detected, the more effectively it can be treated.

---

mend certain screening tests and immunizations, depending on your child's country of origin.

At the first appointment, your son's or daughter's care provider will review the child's immunizations and perform any age-appropriate screening tests, as well as any further tests indicated by the examination. If your child has no written record of immunizations or has missing or ineffective vaccines, the care provider may recommend starting a new schedule. The risk of side effects from repeating a vaccine is lower than the risk of getting an infection. If your child is older than 6 months, his or her care provider may recommend checking antibody levels in

your child's blood before recommending certain vaccines to see if he or she has already had certain infections.

A few children have no official birth date. Determining their age can be difficult if their growth is delayed because of prematurity, problems at birth, malnutrition or neglect. Your doctor will try to make an educated guess based on the information available.

After your child's first medical examination, it's important to follow the schedule of examinations and immunizations recommended by your care provider.

Give it time It's not uncommon for children adopted internationally to show delays in development when they arrive. But most are able to catch up within the first 12 months of arrival, after being on a nutritious diet coupled with a stimulating, nurturing environment. For example, a baby who may not have had the opportunity to learn to crawl because of his or her previous conditions may quickly learn to do so by being placed on a blanket on the floor and given the incentive of a toy just out of reach.

Get support If you're adopting an older child, especially one who has had a difficult past, or a child with special needs, your child's care provider may refer you to a counselor or mental health care provider who has experience with adoption. Such a therapist can help ease the transition for the whole family and provide help in working through issues of loss and change. Support groups for families created through adoption also can be helpful.

BONDING

Some parents bond immediately with their baby the first time they meet their son or daughter. It seems as if the family they've established was always meant to be. But for others it takes a little longer. Don't fret too much if the first time you meet your baby, both you and your child feel more bewildered than besotted. As with any relationship, it takes time and commitment to establish a deep, solid connection.

The longer you're there to provide consistent, loving care, the more your son or daughter will realize that you're in this for the long haul and that he or she is safe and secure. With time and consistent effort, you both will become more confi-

dent and comfortable with each other and in the way you interact.

The same activities can foster the attachment process for both biological and adoptive parents: holding your baby close, cuddling, feeding, laughing, serenading, playing games, going through the daily activities of living.

Allow time for adjustment Parents who adopt have sometimes waited so very long for a baby that they cannot wait to smother the child with love and attention. Depending on your child's age, he or she may have just been separated from everything that was familiar and needs time to warm up to you and take in a new environment.

Holding children close is important because it helps them get accustomed to your scent, to hear your heartbeat and to feel your body warmth. But pay attention to their signals. Some children prefer to be held more than others do.

In general, the best way to nurture a healthy attachment to your child is by observing closely what he or she needs and determining how best to make your son or daughter feel supported, safe and loved in any situation. This may call for different strategies in a young infant when compared with an older child. Older children are more likely to have difficulties with attachment, and parents of these children may wish to connect with specialists in post-adoption services either through their adoption agency or through their primary care provider.

Talk, sing and read to your baby These activities allow the child to get used to the sound of your voice. This is especially important for children who come from another country because it helps them get acquainted with the natural rhythms of a new language.

Respond to your baby's needs Be quick to find out why he or she is crying. Tending promptly to your child in the first few months won't spoil the child but will provide reassurance and comfort. Eventually, your son or daughter will become more secure in his or her role in the family and less clingy or demanding. In fact, this is common advice for every parent.

Also investigate if your child doesn't yet signal his or her discomfort. Children who have spent time in an institution or have been neglected may internalize feelings of abandonment and insecurity by withdrawing from others and failing to make their needs known. Keeping a quiet eye on your child and maintaining a regular schedule for meals, naps and bedtime will help promote health and provide a sense of security and well-being.

Learn about your child Inquire about the child's environment and routine before he or she enters your family so you can help smooth the transition. For instance:

▶ A child who shared a crib or a mat with other children or family members may be frightened at night in a room by him- or herself. You may want to bring the child into your bedroom and keep his or her crib in your room for a while until he or she gets used to her new environment and has had time to adjust. After a while, the child likely will establish more independence and be able to sleep on his or her own. You might also consider giving your child a soft blanket or stuffed animal. Having a loved object to hang on to while everything seems to be in transition may help your son or daughter feel more secure and eventually, more independent.

▶ A child who was carried everywhere on the back of his or her caregiver, as is the custom in some countries, may feel right at home if you put him or her in a back carrier. Even a child who isn't used to it may enjoy the security of being carried close to you in a front or back baby carrier.

▶ A baby who is used to falling asleep with the room light on may be extremely attached to that simple routine. Be sensitive to any behaviors that seem important to your child, and allow some time before gradually trying to change habits.

▶ A child who comes from little means may experience sensory overload with a nursery full of toys, unable to decide what to play with first. Introduce one toy at a time, as the child is ready.

Identify baby's developmental stage
On joining your family, your child's developmental stage can affect how he or she interacts with you. For instance, in the first four months, babies cry mostly when they need something and they'll bond most easily with the person who responds to their cries. Later, they begin learning cause and effect and may cry just to see what happens. This behavior could frustrate parents meeting their child for the first time at this stage. At around nine months, separation anxiety can be very intense for a child who's been attached to another caregiver.

Read through the chapters in Part 3 of this book that correspond to your baby's developmental stage. You'll find that some of your child's behavior is indicative of the developmental phase he or she is in rather than of his or her personality.

If you're adopting a child who's 6 months or older, keep in mind that he or she may have already learned certain cultural behaviors. For instance, a child from a country where passivity is encouraged may appear unresponsive.

If you're adopting a child of 12 months or older, it may take more time and understanding to get acquainted and develop mutual trust. You may find reassurance in reading about parenting, talking to someone from the adoption agency or a counselor familiar with the adoption process, and in doing what you can to help your child feel loved, secure and wanted. Eventually, the majority of children — especially those who arrive most needy — make great gains in their social and behavioral skills, a testament to the resilience of human nature.

Take care of yourself It's tempting to let everything else fall by the wayside — including yourself — when focusing on your newest family member. But allowing yourself to become sleep deprived, worn down and stressed out isn't helpful to anyone and may in fact undermine the attachment process.

Like any new parent, it's not uncommon to feel overwhelmed when faced with the intense demands of parenting. Accept help from family members and friends with housecleaning and other chores, spend some time on your own, get some exercise (even if it is just a walk around the block) and eat regular, healthy meals. If you take care of yourself, you'll be better equipped to care for your new son or daughter and your family.

Get help when needed All children are individuals with definite likes, dislikes and inborn personality traits. Some adjust quickly and respond with joy to their new families, but others might have a difficult adjustment period. Many families benefit from talking to an outside

BREAST-FEEDING AN ADOPTED BABY

Many adoptive mothers are surprised to learn that nursing their babies may be an option for them. Because lactation, or the production of breast milk, can sometimes be induced (with a combination of pumping and nipple stimulation), a woman might be able to breast-feed without ever having been pregnant.

Adoptive mothers who seek to nurse young infants usually do so to enhance their relationships with their children. Although most adoptive mothers can't produce all the milk their infants need, even limited breast-feeding allows them the opportunity for physical and emotional attachment with their babies.

When the baby's arrival can be anticipated, some women try to establish a milk supply in advance by using an electric breast pump at regular intervals.

Others wait until the baby arrives, because the baby's sucking will stimulate lactation better than any pump on the market. These mothers use a supplemental nursing device that allows infants to receive formula through a soft tube inserted in their mouths while nursing. Even after their milk comes in, many mothers continue to use supplemental nursing devices if they need to increase their breast milk volume.

Babies are usually more willing to breast-feed if they are younger than 8 weeks of age, but some adoptive mothers have reported success with older infants, too.

If you try breast-feeding but aren't able to produce milk, don't be anxious. There are plenty of other ways to foster attachment with your baby, including holding your baby close with skin-to-skin contact during feedings, and at other times, too.

If you think you might like to nurse your adopted infant, discuss the advantages, disadvantages and techniques with your doctor or a lactation consultant weeks or even months before you anticipate your child's arrival. There may be a lactation consultant on staff at your hospital, or you may contact the International Lactation Consultant Association or La Leche League International. See page 552 for contact information.

party who has seen and talked to other adoptive families, and can help them work through the necessary steps to achieve mental and emotional wellness and to bond as a family.

If you're feeling discouraged or lost, or if your child exhibits behavior problems or doesn't seem to be building a relationship with you, seek professional help. Your child's care provider, adoption agency, a social worker or mental health professional may be able to help you understand and resolve the challenges you're facing.

SHARING YOUR FAMILY STORY

A renewed focus on an adoptive child's well-being has paved the way for increased openness when it comes to telling the adoption story. More adoptions are now carried through as open adoptions, where the birth parents are in contact with the adoptive family during the adoption process and possibly beyond. This avoids the scenario of previous generations when parents didn't always tell their children they were adopted. The news might be revealed by a relative or come as a surprise later on, leaving the children feeling puzzled, angry or betrayed.

But even with open adoptions, it's not always easy for a child to understand the relationship between the two sets of parents. While it's best not to keep the adoption a secret, you also don't want to overwhelm your child with information. Right now your adoptive son or daughter may be too little to understand, but when he or she is older and the time is right, look for natural opportunities to weave your family's story into your daily life. If you start early and simply, the transition to more complex discussions down the road may be that much smoother. Keep in mind that this is your own family story; how you share it with others outside of your immediate family is up to you.

Be positive Start by making sure your own attitude toward adoption is positive.

Experts agree that if parents demonstrate they are comfortable talking about adoption as a positive, normal experience, their children will be much more likely to feel comfortable with it themselves. They will also be more willing to share their questions and concerns about adoption as issues arise.

Use books Even before your child is old enough to ask questions, you can begin to introduce age-appropriate books that explain adoption through simple concepts and words.

Tell your story Many experts recommend that parents develop their own story of how their family was created and tell it to children from the very beginning. Children won't understand everything at first, but the words and phrases will become a natural part of their vocabulary.

ONE MOM'S STORY

We have a fairly open relationship with my 4-year-old daughter's birth mother. My daughter knows her birth mother's name and a picture of the two of them hangs above her bed. Her birth mother and I exchange emails and pictures, and we all talk on the phone on holidays and birthdays. When my daughter and I discuss our family story, it goes something like this.

"I feel so lucky that your birth mom (we use her first name) chose me to be your mommy! I remember the day that you were born ... when I first held you, I couldn't believe how small you were! I'd been waiting for you and seeing you made me smile so big. You had tiny little fingers, and you wrapped them around my little finger right away — I think maybe that's why we like to hold hands today. Your birth mom and I took turns holding you and feeding you. We talked about how cute you were and about what we hoped you'd do when you got older. We both want you to be happy and to do good in school and be nice to your friends. We want you to have lots of adventures and to go to college when you're bigger. Most importantly, we want you to know that you're loved. You grew in your birth mom's tummy and you grew in my heart and that means that you get two people to love you."

SIBLINGS AND ADOPTED CHILDREN

If you have other children in addition to your adopted child, you'll probably face some of the same issues as any parent has when introducing a sibling to brothers and sisters (see Chapter 34).

Help your other children with the transition by including them in plans for the new baby's arrival, welcoming him or her home and in daily caregiving activities. Children typically love babies and will be thrilled to help out. Even after the novelty wears off, big brothers and sisters still continue to bond with the baby, even when conflicts arise. Also, try to find some time to spend with each child individually, even if it means running a quick errand together or snuggling for a few minutes before bedtime.

The younger the siblings and the adopted child, the more likely they are to bond with little trouble. Most children under the age of 4 generally don't notice differences among themselves and like to hear the adoption story. Older children are more likely to ask questions and feel some differences.

In some cases, an older adopted child may have developed certain behaviors before joining a permanent family that persist for weeks or months after adoption. This might include sur-vival behaviors, such as hoarding food or sleeping with the back against a wall. Other siblings may perceive this as "weird." But it's important to realize that these behaviors are likely there for a reason. Over time, as your new child continues to receive consistent, loving care, these behaviors are likely to fade. In the meantime, encourage your children to focus on the positive aspects of their relationship with the new brother or sister. Younger children, for example, are usually easily distracted by a new topic of conversation or by the suggestion of a game. Older children may be able to better understand the possible reasons for unusual behaviors and may be able to help you in providing consistent support to their sibling.

Sibling relationships can be a lifelong gift, continuing to be a source of strength even after parents are gone. Look for opportunities to promote bonding between all of your children. If you have doubts or questions, or you feel your family needs help in bonding together, talk to someone who is knowledgeable in the matter. This may be someone from your adoption agency, your primary care provider, a social worker, or a family counselor or therapist.

And all children love hearing stories about themselves.

Use the story to introduce your child's birth parents in an understanding way, explain why you chose adoption to build your family, and give your child a sense of personal history and belonging. Any details you can add to such a story about the joy of your first encounter will make it more delightful to your child.

Creating a "life book" for your child is another way to celebrate the unique way he or she joined your family. Save any mementos such as letters, toys, hospital name tags or documents that came with your child at the time of placement; they can serve as a source of "roots" later. Include pictures, too. Save any information or mementos that are directly from your child's birth parents, no matter how small they may appear to be. Even a slip of paper with the birth parent's handwriting may ultimately become a treasured possession for your child. If your child is from another country, pictures, trinkets and other mementos from your trip there can provide a sense of background.

Tell the truth Be factual about your child's story, while keeping in mind what's age appropriate. It's important not to embellish or add details that you don't know to be true. You may be uncomfortable with the fact that there are holes in the story, and you may wish you knew all of the answers. Your child may ultimately grieve the loss of those details, too. However, it's healthier to acknowledge the missing information and deal with the ramifications of not knowing than it is to make up details that you don't know to be true. And don't feel the need to share all of the information with your child right away; there may be some details that are better saved until your child is mature enough to handle them.

Use positive language Let your language reflect your own positive values toward adoption. Be open and honest about the adoption, but don't use it as a label. Say my child and not my adopted child. Phrases such as "given up for adoption" may leave children feeling there was something wrong with them that made their parents give them away. Instead, talk about the decision made by the birth parents to "make an adoption plan" or "arrange for an adoption" so that their child could be well cared for.

Celebrate your family Some families make a tradition of doing something special on the day their family was created, such as having a family anniversary party or doing something special for the birth parents. This is a great way to get your other children involved, as well.

Seek out other families like yours Look to make connections with other families that have been touched by adoption — both the children and the parents will find this type of peer group helpful. Transracially adopted children will get the added benefit of spending time with children — and other families — who resemble them.

HANDLING DIFFICULT REMARKS

At one time or another, parents and children may be faced with ignorant or even hurtful remarks from others. It isn't always easy to speak up when someone says something naive or offensive, but it is important to keep your child's well-being in mind. You don't have to answer every question, and you don't have to let everyone know you adopted your child. Instead, your response may be more for your child's benefit than to educate the person asking the question or making the comment.

Here are some responses suggested by adoptive parents to frequently asked questions:

- *Who are his real parents?* We are — we're not imaginary. We are the ones who do the parenting. (Information about the birth parents is the child's to give.)
- *Are they really brother and sister?* Yes, they have the same parents. (Whether or not they are biologically related is also the child's information.)
- *I don't know how any mother could give up her child.* The decision to place a child for adoption is a painful, difficult decision for any woman, but it's always made in the best interests of the child. It's not because a birth mother doesn't care, but because she and the birth father could not care for any child at that time in their lives.
- *Too bad you couldn't experience pregnancy.* You don't get to experience everything in life. I may never get to Africa either. But my adoption experience has been wonderful, and I wouldn't trade it for anything.

PARENTING IS PARENTING

Becoming a parent opens up opportunities for amazing fulfillment and incredible challenges, no matter how you come into that role.

In the end, parenting is parenting. In order to move successfully from dependent infant to independent adult, every child requires consistent, loving care in a warm and nurturing environment. Providing this to your child makes you a parent, and research indicates that parents through adoption are keenly aware of their parental responsibilities. Together, you and your child make a family, a family that more often than not is abundantly prepared for the adventures ahead.

CHAPTER 38

Caring for multiples

Congratulations on not one but two (or more) babies! Your first year together will likely be a busy one, filled with chaos and, yes, delight. Like any new parent, there may be times when you wonder if you'll ever make it through and times when you feel that it's all more than worth the effort.

Raising multiples, especially in the early months, can seem truly overwhelming, simply because of the extra logistical and physical demands involved. Daily parenting tasks may be doubled or tripled, and the amount of time left to yourself may very well be miniscule. But most parents of multiples are able to rise to the occasion and find inner reserves of energy and strength they never imagined they had.

You already have plenty of helpful information in other sections of this book. This chapter aims to give you some practical tips on caring for multiple infants and finding time to care for yourself. If your babies were born prematurely, you may also find Chapter 39 to be helpful.

FEEDING

Mothers of multiples report that one of the most stressful aspects of being a new mom involves feeding their children. Newborns and young infants need to eat frequently — generally between eight and 12 times a day. When you're feeding more than one child that many times, you may feel as if all you do is sleep, eat and feed your babies. Even bottle-feeding, which many assume would be the most efficient method, takes a surprising amount of time and technique — not to mention a lot of bottles that require washing and storing!

Feeding your infants may seem to be an insurmountable task at times but there are a couple things to keep in mind:

Regardless of which method you choose to feed your babies — breast-feeding or formula-feeding — a source of support and help is invaluable. This may come through your partner, grandparents, support groups or a hired caregiver. No one says you must do this alone.

This stage doesn't last forever (even though it may feel that way). As one experienced mother said, "The days are long but the years are short." In a few months, as your children begin eating other foods and become more independent, the demands placed on you will become less intense.

A quick note: Don't let others pressure you into one form of feeding or another. This is a personal decision between you and your partner, based on sound advice from your children's care provider or another specialist. The most important thing is that your children grow and thrive, and that you and your partner are able to enjoy the process (at least some of the time).

Breast-feeding Most experts agree that breast milk is the ideal source of nutrition for infants. Breast milk's nutritional value is also one of the biggest reasons that mothers of multiples seek to breast-feed. While it takes a certain amount of dedication, it is possible to do, as shown by so many mothers who have successfully breast-fed multiples. Some mothers even say that breast-feeding is easier and less time-consuming, once lactation is established, than is bottle-feeding. And research studies indicate that most women will generally produce as much milk as is demanded, so it's possible to produce enough milk for multiple children.

If you decide to breast-feed, it's helpful to find a mentor who can give you insights and tips. This may be an experienced mother of multiples, care provider or lactation consultant. Support groups for parents of multiples, such as the Mothers of Twins Clubs (see page 553), are another way to meet experienced mothers and fathers of multiples.

At first, most women breast-feed one infant at a time. This allows you time to recover from childbirth, get the hang of breast-feeding and spend time with each infant. You can find out more about breast-feeding basics in Chapter 3.

Simultaneous breast-feeding Many mothers find that once their milk supply is established and breast-feeding is going well for all involved, they're able to feed their babies simultaneously. This may or may not be for you, but it's worth a try because it can save time and energy. As with feeding one baby, be sure to get comfortable. Use pillows to support yourself and your infants. Some manufacturers make breast-feeding pillows designed specifically for multiples.

Here are some commonly used positions for breast-feeding twins:

- *Double clutch or double football hold.* In this position, you hold each baby in a clutch or football hold. Place a pillow on each side of your body. You might also want to place another pillow on your lap. Place each baby on a pillow beside your body — almost under your arm — so that the babies' legs point toward the back of your chair. Make sure each baby lies on his or her back with his or her head at the level of your nipple. Place the palm of one hand at the base of each baby's head to provide support. Alternatively, you can place both babies — head to head — on pillows directly in front of you. Be sure to keep your babies' bodies turned toward you, rather than facing up. Use the palms of your hands to provide support for each baby's head.
- *Cradle-clutch combination.* In this position, you hold one baby in the cradle position — with his or her head on your forearm and his or her whole body facing yours — and the other baby in the clutch position. If

one of your babies has an easier time latching onto your breast or staying latched, place him or her in the cradle position. To use the double cradle position, you place both of your babies in the cradle position in front of you. Position your babies so that their legs overlap and make an X across your lap.

Rather than assign one baby to each breast, try to alternate them. This way, if one infant sucks less vigorously, the other may make up the demand and balance out the supply in each breast. If you have three or more babies, use a rotation system so that each one gets milk from both breasts. For example, if you have triplets, you might breast-feed one on each breast simultaneously and then the third on both breasts. At the next feeding, rotate their positions.

Combined breast- and bottle-feeding

Breast-feeding doesn't have to be all or nothing. While frequent breast-feeding helps establish and maintain your milk supply, any amount of breast milk you can give to your children is beneficial.

Many moms find that a combination of breast- and bottle-feeding works well because it allows them to breast-feed their babies but also share the job of feeding with a partner or other caregivers. For example, you might breast-feed one baby while your partner bottle-feeds the other one, then swap at the next feeding. Or your partner might take over a double bottle-feeding session while you get some rest. Ideally, you want to establish a milk supply before supplementing regularly with formula.

Some mothers of triplets prefer to set up a rotation where they breast-feed two infants supported by pillows while bottle-feeding the third sitting in an elevated infant seat. This is usually easier when babies are a little older and can hold up their heads well.

If you give your babies formula, keep in mind that your milk production might

To breast-feed two babies at once you might use the double clutch or double football hold position. In this position, you hold each baby in a clutch or football hold under your arms. Make sure each baby lies on his or her back with his or her head at the level of your nipple. Place the palm of one hand at the base of each baby's head to provide support.

© MFMER

begin to decrease if you breast-feed or pump less than eight to 10 times within 24 hours.

Pumping If one or both of your babies are preemies or require an extended stay at the hospital, you can still establish a milk supply by renting a hospital-grade breast pump and pumping milk until you're able to nurse. A breast pump may also be beneficial if you have one baby at home and one at the hospital, or one or both babies have difficulty latching on or sucking. Pumping is also helpful if you need to return to work but would like to continue feeding your babies breast milk. See Chapter 3 for how-to's on pumping.

Bottle-feeding Parents decide to feed their babies formula for a variety of reasons — illness on the part of the mother or one of the babies, difficulty sustaining an adequate milk supply, the ability of both parents to feed rather than just the mother, or simply the convenience of having as much as you need whenever you need it. Ultimately, it comes down to the babies' needs — getting adequate nutrition and avoiding dehydration are the ultimate goals.

As with breast-feeding, it may be best to start out feeding one infant at a time. Chapter 3 will tell you what you need to know about bottle-feeding basics. Once your babies are feeding well, you can save time and bottle-feed simultaneously with the right techniques. One thing to avoid is propping up bottles and leaving a baby unattended, as this can increase the risk of aspiration and choking.

Two pediatricians who are also mothers of twins offer some different ways to bottle-feed twins simultaneously:

▶ Sit on the floor with your legs extended in a V shape. Place the babies between your knees with their feet toward you and heads propped on a pillow. Hold a bottle in each hand and use your thighs as armrests.

▶ Sit in a comfortable armchair with your left elbow propped on the armrest. Hold both babies with their heads resting against your left arm and their bodies supported in your

---

TIPS TO OPTIMIZE MILK PRODUCTION

Taking care of your body will help you make the most of breast-feeding:

▶ *Rest when you can.* Although a solid night's sleep may be a thing of the past, take every chance you get to rest. Extreme fatigue can interfere with breast milk production.

▶ *Eat a healthy and adequate diet.* Avoid dieting while breast-feeding, which in itself burns calories. Eat a well-balanced diet with plenty of liquids.

▶ *Continue taking prenatal vitamins.* Your prenatal vitamins provide nutrients that may be missing from your daily diet.

▶ *Drink plenty of fluids.* Although extra intake of fluids hasn't been proved to increase milk production, nursing does tend to make you thirsty. Have a glass of water or juice before you sit down to nurse and keep water handy while nursing. Some nursing pillows even have pockets for just such a purpose.

lap. Hold one bottle with your right hand and lean the other bottle against your chest.

- Cradle one infant in your left arm and curl your left wrist and hand around the baby to offer this baby's bottle. Support the other baby's head in your lap with his or her feet extended away from you and offer this baby's bottle with your right hand.
- Lean back in an armchair or against pillows and put both babies on your lap facing away from you with their heads supported against your chest. Offer a bottle from each hand.
- Place one baby in an elevated infant seat next to you on the floor and hold the other baby in your lap. Offer a bottle from each hand.
- Use two infant seats and sit between them on the floor. Offer a bottle from each hand.

Are my babies getting enough? If your babies are growing adequately, then they're getting enough milk. Your babies' care provider may recommend some extra office visits to make sure each is gaining weight properly. You may also consider renting a scale, such as a baby scale, for the first month to monitor each baby's weight gain. Knowing your babies are getting enough to eat and they're gaining weight properly may help you feel more confident in breast-feeding. As a general rule, after the first week of life, weight gain should be ½ to 1 ounce a day.

During the first few weeks, you might find it helpful to maintain a daily chart to record feedings, wet diapers and bowel movements. In general, a baby who's getting adequate nutrition will eat eight to 12 times a day, produce at least four to six wet diapers (and at least one that's really soaked) and one bowel movement a day. There may be slight differences between babies that are breast-fed or bottle-fed. If you have any questions or concerns, don't hesitate to ask your babies' care provider.

RAISING STRONG INDIVIDUALS

Multiples are born with a strong connection with each other. They have similar genetic material, they're usually delivered within minutes of each other, and they go through each phase of development around the same time. They come into the world with a ready-made companion and playmate at hand. They're likely to share bedrooms, toys and even attention from others.

When you have twins or other sets of multiples, it can be easy to slide into a mode where you treat them as a pair or a set. For example, you may dress them alike or others may refer to them as "the twins." This isn't necessarily harmful but it can sometimes get in the way of each child's ability to develop separately. Also, if you treat your multiples as alike in every way, you may be missing out on some effective parenting strategies.

One-on-one time Research shows that, overall, multiples grow and develop in much the same way as single-born children — unless they were born prematurely, in which case prematurity may impact growth and development.

Some studies indicate that children who are multiples tend to display a slight delay in language development compared to singletons. This delay can be a common concern among parents. One study attempting to find out why concluded that one of the reasons for this delay may have to do with the level of parent-child interaction. Mothers of twins were less likely to engage each child in back-and-forth "conversations" and less likely to report regular book sharing — looking at books together and talking about pictures or pointing at them and investigating the story further.

This seems fairly natural, as mothers of twins tend to have more demands placed on them on a day-to-day basis than do mothers of singletons, who may have more time to actively engage with their child. Although the study was limited to studying mother-child interaction, in real life fathers and other caregivers can also play major roles in a child's daily care. In the long run, being a twin doesn't appear to affect academic performance once children reach school age. So while studies like these don't mean that multi-

ples are permanently disadvantaged, they do illustrate the value of spending interactive one-on-one time with each child when possible.

Parenting strategies Another reason to look at each child as an individual — one who just happened to be born at the same time as his or her sibling — is that you can learn to recognize different temperamental qualities in each one. Especially as your children get older, you can use your understanding of their different temperaments to target your parenting strategies more effectively.

For example, you may notice that one child is more flexible when it comes to transitioning from one activity to another, but the other may need ample warning that a change is coming. Knowing this difference between the two may help you smooth your day and avoid meltdowns. (See Chapter 9 for a more in-depth discussion of temperament.) However, as you come to recognize their differences, try to avoid labeling your twins, such as referring to one of them as the "quiet one" and the other as the "outgoing one."

LOGISTICS

In addition to the physical demands of raising multiples, there are logistical challenges, as well. You don't just need one crib, stroller, highchair and car seat. You need two or more. Here are some practical tips that may help you save money and get the job done.

Buy in bulk If you're near a warehouse club that sells items in bulk, such as a Costco, BJ's or Sam's Club, it may be worth considering a membership. These places offer formula, baby food, diapers and wipes in large volumes and at a discount. Another option is to purchase bulk items online and have them delivered right to your door. Some retail websites have special membership programs for parents, such as Amazon Mom, that allow parents to access baby and toddler items at a discount.

Check out supply stores Preschool and child care supply stores carry equipment that's specifically designed for handling multiple children of the same age at once. Some examples include feeding tables with multiple seats built in, diaper storage units, activity tables built to accommodate multiple children and stackable toddler chairs. Plus, these items are generally built to withstand a fair amount of use.

Join a parent group Groups for parents of multiples not only provide regular gatherings and emotional support, members of the group also may hold resale events where families can buy and sell gently used baby equipment.

Explore different options Assessing your needs and knowing what's available is helpful when it comes to equipment:

Gates and locks Thoroughly childproofing your home — placing gates in bathroom and kitchen doorways and in front of stairs, putting childproof locks on cabinet doors — allows you to rest more easily when you're busy with one toddler and don't have a hand on the other.

Strollers Double strollers for twins come in a few variations. Side-by-side ones are nice for walks in the park and jogging with your infants. Front-to-back models are easier to navigate in and out of doorways and in tight spaces. You can also clamp two lightweight umbrella strollers together to make a double stroller.

Harnesses Once your children start walking, you might consider purchasing child harnesses. These devices allow a child to walk independently and still be within reach. Harnesses can be especially helpful in crowded areas.

All the equipment and supplies you acquire may seem to overwhelm your house, car and everything else in the first year. But as your children get older, you'll find that some things are no longer necessary, such as infant swings, playpens and eventually highchairs and cribs. Hang in there!

TAKING CARE OF YOURSELF

During your first year together with your little ones, you're likely to find yourself so immersed in caring for them that a life apart may seem almost surreal. Although this may come as small comfort, rest assured that your parenting job will become less labor intensive and easier to manage as time goes by.

In the meantime, it's important to carve out time for yourself. Extreme fatigue and lack of personal time can understandably lead to depression and isolation. If you feel overwhelmed or unable to enjoy your babies, it's important to seek professional help from your children's care provider, a counselor, therapist or other mental health professional — someone who can help you get back on track.

Taking care of yourself may seem like it should come last on your to-do list, but in fact it is the first step toward taking care of your family. If your energy supply is depleted, it will be much harder for you to accomplish the daily tasks required to care for your children.

Keeping in mind that the demands of early parenthood are exponentially increased for parents of multiples and the fact that real life rarely falls together as neatly as advice found in a book, here are some suggestions that might help make life a little easier:

Get enough rest When others tell you to get more sleep, it may feel like a joke at times. How, you ask? Two nurses conducted a survey of mothers and fathers of twins, published in *Applied Nursing Research*, to see if they could find any consistent answers to this dilemma. Their question was simple: What strategies did parents of twins employ to obtain sleep in the first six months after taking their babies home?

Although no single answer emerged as completely effective, common strategies employed by the parents included:

- Assigning shifts or taking turns with nighttime caregiving
- Getting help from relatives
- Sleeping while the babies slept, although some parents reported taking advantage of this time to complete other tasks
- Getting the twins on the same sleeping and eating schedules
- Using white noise and dimming the lights to help the babies sleep

During the first few weeks, it will likely be difficult to get enough sleep as everyone adjusts to the transition. But eventually, you'll develop a routine and your days and nights will even out a bit. If you have difficulties or concerns about getting enough sleep or getting your children to sleep, talk to your children's care provider. He or she may be better situated to assess your needs and give you specific advice.

Get help and support Getting help can make a big difference. Some families hire help, some rely on extended family, and some get help from friends, neighbors, their church or other organizations.

Also consider attending a local support group for parents of twins or other multiples. You'll likely get many invaluable ideas and practical suggestions from other parents. Online communities dedicated to supporting parents of multiples are another option.

Let go of guilt After experiencing infertility and then having multiples, some parents feel guilty when they become stressed or exhausted by the demands of caregiving. They may believe that they should only have feelings of happiness and joy after finally achieving their wish for children.

This is a false and unrealistic proposition. There's no doubt that having children when you may have felt you couldn't is a great source of pleasure. But this doesn't mean you won't feel tired, out of sorts and wondering at times what you've gotten yourself into. These are normal feelings for any parent.

Parents of multiples sometimes feel as if they should be able to bear the full load of caregiving because "they got what they were asking for." This is an emotional trap to avoid. Accepting help doesn't make you a bad parent. In fact, as demonstrated earlier, it can help you be a better one.

Take outside attention in stride Twins, triplets and greater numbers of multiples frequently attract attention in public, which can be positive or negative. Regardless of what others say about you or your family, remember to keep your eye on the prize — raising happy, healthy and well-adjusted children who will eventually contribute to society in their own right.

Take time for yourself The stresses and demands of early parenting can take a toll on marriage and relationships. It's important to remain flexible about your changing roles in the family and maintain open communication so that each knows what the other is thinking.

In addition to taking time for yourself, take periodic breaks with your partner to nurture and sustain your relationship. This doesn't have to be anything complicated — it might be as simple as watching a favorite TV show together or making a decent dinner for yourselves after the kids are in bed. Look for ways to support each other as new parents and compliment one another on a job well done. Read Part 5 of this book, if you haven't already, which has several chapters on managing and enjoying parenthood.

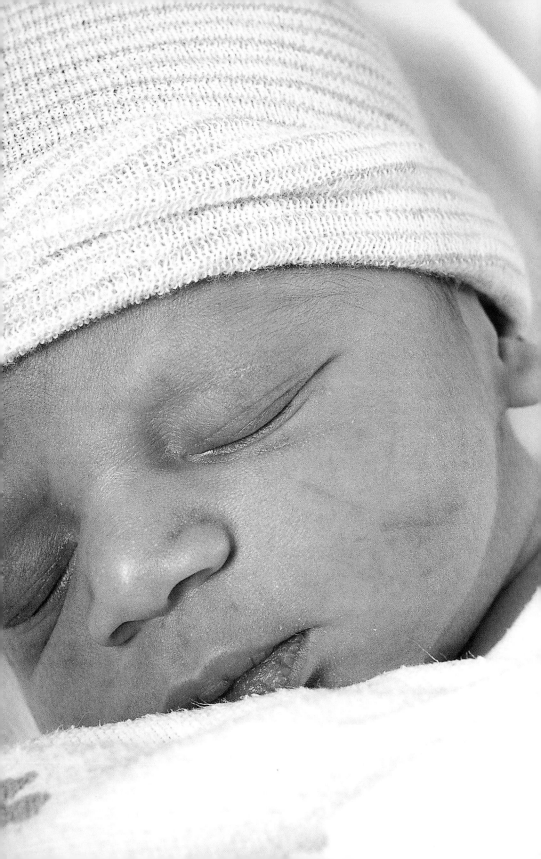

CHAPTER 39

Premature baby

Every parent dreams of having a healthy, full-term baby. Unfortunately, that dream isn't always the reality. Although most babies are born full term and free of medical problems, some are born too early. A premature (preterm) birth — a birth that occurs before 37 weeks of pregnancy — gives a baby less time to develop and mature in the womb. As a result, premature babies may need specialized treatment in the neonatal intensive care unit (NICU). Sometimes, even after a premature baby leaves the hospital, he or she may continue to need medical care.

If your baby was born prematurely, the miracle of birth might be overshadowed by concern about his or her health and the possible long-term effects. However, there's much you can do to take care of your premature baby — and yourself — as you look toward the future. Understand what to expect after your premature baby is born, the health problems that premature babies sometimes face, and how to cope and care for your premature baby.

WHY PREMATURE BIRTH HAPPENS

Many factors can increase the risk of premature birth. A multiple pregnancy is one cause. Chronic conditions experienced by a pregnant mother, such as diabetes, high blood pressure, and heart and kidney disease, also can lead to premature birth. However, the specific cause of a premature birth often isn't clear. And a premature birth can happen to anyone, including women who have no risk factors.

As the parent of a premature newborn, you might feel that you did something to cause the preterm birth or that you could have done more to prevent it. Mothers especially might think about how they might have changed the outcome by making different decisions during pregnancy. Try to let go of any feelings of guilt about your baby's premature birth by talking about them with your baby's care providers and your partner, who might be able to provide comfort. Focus your energy on caring for and getting to know your child.

Definitions If your baby was born prematurely, you're not alone. It's estimated that premature births occur in about 13 percent of pregnancies in the United States and that nearly 60 percent of multiple deliveries result in premature births. While all babies born before 37 weeks' gestation are considered preterm, there are a few specific types of preterm birth, including:

- *Late preterm.* A baby who is born at 34 through 36 weeks of pregnancy
- *Moderately preterm.* A baby who is born at 32 to 34 weeks of pregnancy
- *Very preterm.* A baby who is born at less than 32 weeks of pregnancy
- *Extremely preterm.* A baby who is born at or before 25 weeks of pregnancy
- *Low birth weight.* A baby who is born weighing less than 5 pounds, 8 ounces
- *Very low birth weight.* A baby who is born weighing less than 3 pounds, 5 ounces

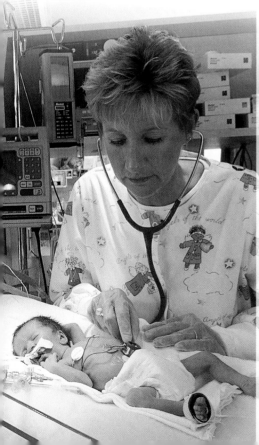

- *Extremely low birth weight.* A baby who is born weighing less than 2 pounds, 3 ounces

The NICU Your first close-up look at your premature baby might be in the hospital neonatal intensive care unit (NICU), which is designed to provide round-the-clock care for premature babies as well as full-term babies who develop problems after birth. You'll probably be amazed, overwhelmed — and perhaps a little shocked — by this first look at your newborn.

Your son or daughter may be in an enclosed incubator. An incubator provides warmth, which is important because premature babies have less protective body fat than do full-term babies and may get cold in normal room temperatures. The unit may have a round porthole through which you and the NICU staff can reach in and touch your little one. You may also notice an array of tubes, catheters and electrical leads taped to your baby. For example, he or she may be placed on a cardiorespiratory monitor, which tracks his or her heart rate and rate of breathing. Seeing this equipment may be intimidating. It's important to remember that these are tools to help keep your baby healthy and inform the medical staff about your baby's condition.

In the NICU, your baby will receive specialized care, including a feeding plan tailored to his or her needs. Some premature babies may initially need to have fluids given to them intravenously or through a feeding tube that passes through the mouth or nose into the stomach. If you plan to breast-feed but your baby is unable to nurse at first, you can pump your breast milk. Your milk can then be given to your baby via a feeding tube or bottle. The antibodies in breast milk are especially important for preemies.

THE NICU TEAM

In the NICU, your baby may be cared for by many specialists and other health care professionals. The team attending your baby may include:

▶ *Neonatal nurse.* A neonatal nurse is a registered nurse who has special training in caring for premature and high-risk newborns.

▶ *Neonatal nurse practitioner.* An experienced neonatal nurse who has completed additional training in the treatment of newborns, particularly babies in NICU.

▶ *Neonatologist.* A neonatologist is a pediatrician who specializes in the diagnosis and treatment of newborn health problems.

▶ *Pediatrician.* A pediatrician is a doctor who specializes in treating children from birth through adolescence.

▶ *Pediatric resident.* A pediatric resident is a doctor who is receiving specialized training in treating children.

▶ *Respiratory therapist.* A respiratory therapist or respiratory care practitioner assesses respiratory problems in newborns and manages respiratory equipment.

▶ *Pediatric surgeon.* A pediatric surgeon specializes in performing surgery for newborns and children.

Keep in mind that your baby's medical team may also call on other specialists for help in providing care for your child.

CARING FOR A PREMATURE NEWBORN

A premature newborn may require some special care. The medical team caring for your baby will do everything they can to help your baby thrive. Keep in mind that your role as a parent is essential, too. Consider ways to get involved in your baby's care and begin bonding with your newborn.

Appearance A premature baby may look a little different than a full-term baby. The earlier a baby is born, the smaller he or she may be and the larger his or her head will be in relation to the rest of the body. Your baby's features may appear sharper and less rounded than do a full-term baby's.

A preemie's skin may be covered with more fine body hair (lanugo) than is common in full-term babies, and his or her skin may look thin, fragile and transparent. These characteristics will be easy to see because most premature babies aren't dressed or wrapped in blankets. This is so nursery staff can closely observe a preemie's breathing and general appearance. The medical team will likely treat your baby's skin with care, avoiding lotions and ointments and using special tape that's gentle to the skin.

Your son or daughter has a lot of growing to do in the coming weeks. In time, he or she will begin to look more like a full-term baby.

Condition and care Uncertainty can be frightening — as can seeing and hearing monitors, respirators and other types of equipment in the NICU. Ask questions about your baby's condition and care or write them down and seek answers when you're ready. Read material provided by the hospital, or do your own research. If you would prefer to be present during a procedure, let the NICU team know. If necessary, make an appointment to discuss your baby's progress. The more you know, the better you'll be able to handle the situation. In addition, if you're concerned about changes in your preemie's condition, talk to your child's caregivers.

Medical team You may see a dizzying number of medical professionals providing care for your baby. Until you become familiar with staff rotations, introduce yourself every time you see a new face and ask what his or her role is in caring for your son or daughter.

Nutrition Breast milk contains proteins that help fight infection and promote growth. Although your preemie might not be able to feed from your breast or a bottle at first, breast milk can be given in other ways — or frozen for later use. Begin pumping as soon after birth as possible. Aim to pump at least six to eight times a day, round-the-clock. Keep in mind that it will take time to establish your milk supply but that every drop of breast milk is precious to your baby, whose first feedings will be small anyway. Give the milk in a container — clearly labeled with your baby's name and the date and time you pumped — to one of your baby's nurses, who can refrigerate or freeze it and use it as your baby needs it.

When your baby is able to nurse, keep in mind that he or she might need more time getting used to the process than does a full-term baby. Give yourself and your baby time to learn and ask for help from the NICU team when you need it.

DONOR BREAST MILK

For premature babies whose mothers are unable to provide breast milk, it may be possible for the NICU to arrange for donated breast milk as a source of nutrition. The source of donated breast milk in a NICU is taken very seriously, with the milk generally coming from established milk banks. Donor breast milk is not always feasible, partly due to the expense of ensuring a safe supply.

Growth and development Become physically involved with your baby as early as possible. Loving care is important to your baby's growth and development. Gentle contact with your premature baby can help him or her thrive.

For extremely premature babies, ask the NICU nurses for the most helpful ways to comfort your baby. Even before a baby is healthy enough to be held, you may be able to comfort him or her with a steady, calm touch. For the youngest babies, patting or stroking may be overwhelming at first. Speak to your baby in loving tones or quietly hum a lullaby. Reading to your baby also can help you feel closer to him or her.

NICU nurses can help you hold your baby to allow skin-to-skin contact by placing the baby on your bare chest, covered loosely with a blanket. This type of contact, sometimes called kangaroo care, can be a powerful way for you to bond with your baby. Eventually, you'll become very comfortable in feeding, changing, bathing and soothing your little one. A NICU nurse can help with these activities and teach you how to deal with equipment such as breathing tubes, intravenous tubes or monitor wiring.

Don't hesitate to ask the NICU staff how you can become more involved in your baby's care. Being hands-on with your baby can give you confidence as a new parent, as well as make the transition home a little easier when your child is ready to leave the hospital. While this may not be the way you imagined your baby's first days or weeks, your time with him or her is special. Focus on enjoying your firsts together, such as the first time you feed your baby or bathe him or her, and your baby's progress.

HEALTH ISSUES

Due to medical progress, the outlook for premature newborns is much more hopeful than it was years ago. In fact, infants born at 24 weeks currently have a survival rate of 40 to 60 percent. A premature baby who is born after 28 weeks of pregnancy and weighs more than 2 pounds, 3 ounces has nearly a full chance of survival.

While not all premature babies experience complications, being born too early can cause short-term and long-term health problems for babies. Generally, the earlier a baby is born, the higher the risk. Birth weight plays an important role, too. Some problems may be apparent at birth, while others may not develop for weeks or months. Complications of premature birth may include the following.

Breathing concerns A premature baby may have trouble breathing due to an immature respiratory system. In some cases, breathing difficulties can prevent other immature organs in the body from receiving enough oxygen. If the baby's lungs lack surfactant — a substance that allows the lungs to remain expanded — he or she may develop respiratory distress syndrome, or RDS, (see page 538). This condition primarily affects infants born before 35 weeks. Preemies, especially those born between 23 and 32 weeks, may also develop chronic lung disease known as bronchopulmonary dysplasia, or BPD, (see page 537). In addition, most preemies younger than 34 weeks experience prolonged pauses in their breathing, known as apnea.

To detect and treat breathing problems, your baby's medical team may monitor your preemie's breathing and heart rate. If your baby has breathing problems, he or she may be given oxygen or support through a ventilator or a breathing assistance technique called continuous positive airway pressure (CPAP).

Heart concerns The most common heart problems premature babies experience are patent ductus arteriosus (PDA) and low blood pressure (hypotension). PDA, which tends to affect babies born before 30 weeks or weighing less than 2 pounds, 3 ounces, is a passage between two major blood vessels leading from the heart (see page 548). While this passage often closes on its own, left untreated it can cause too much blood to flow through the lungs and cause heart failure as well as other complications. Small premature babies who have a PDA may need to have their fluids limited and be given intravenous medication. In some cases, surgery is needed to close the passage. If your baby needs treatment for low blood pressure, he or she may be given additional fluid or intravenous medication.

Brain concerns Babies born before 28 weeks or weighing less than 2 pounds, 10 ounces are at risk of bleeding inside the brain, known as a germinal matrix or an intraventricular hemorrhage. Most hemorrhages are mild and resolve with little short-term impact. Some babies may eventually develop fluid accumulation in the brain (hydrocephalus) or neurological problems, such as cerebral palsy — a disorder of movement, muscle tone or posture — or learning disabilities. Preemies who develop hydrocephalus may need surgery. If your baby has abnormal muscle tone, he or she may need to work with a physical therapist.

Gastrointestinal concerns Preemies are likely to have immature gastrointestinal systems. The earlier a baby is born, the greater his or her risk is of developing necrotizing enterocolitis (NEC). This condition, in which the cells lining the bowel wall are injured, primarily occurs in premature babies after they start feeding. Premature babies who receive only breast milk have a much lower risk of developing NEC. Antibiotics, intravenous feedings and resting the intestine by withholding feedings for a short period helps most babies recover from NEC, although surgery is sometimes needed.

Infant gastroesophageal reflux (GER), a condition that occurs when stomach acid or bile flows back into the food pipe (esophagus), also is common in premature babies. It can cause a baby to vomit multiple times a day and disrupt weight gain. Most babies outgrow the condition as they reach their original due date. Frequent feedings in small amounts can help alleviate the condition. For more information on reflux, see page 382.

Preemies are also at risk of hernias, when a loop of intestine pushes through a weakened muscle or an unusual opening inside the body. While most umbilical hernias heal without intervention by the toddler years, inguinal hernias may require surgery. For more information on hernias, see page 35.

Blood concerns Preemies are at risk of blood problems such as anemia and jaundice. Anemia is a common condition in which the body doesn't make enough red blood cells. While all newborns experience a slow drop in red blood cell count during the first months of life, the decrease may be greater in preemies. More severe anemia may occur if your baby has a lot of blood taken for lab tests. Infants who have no symptoms may not need treatment. However, babies who experience symptoms — such as low blood pressure, a fast heart rate, weak pulse, pale color and breathing problems — may need blood transfusions. For more information on anemia, see page 535.

Neonatal jaundice is a yellow discoloration in a newborn baby's skin and eyes that occurs because the baby's blood contains an excess of bilirubin, a yellow-colored pigment of red blood cells. Jaundice is common in babies born before 38 weeks. Most babies who need treatment respond well to light therapy (phototherapy). Although complications are rare, all newborns are assessed for jaundice during the first weeks of life. This is because severe infant jaundice can cause permanent deafness and brain damage. For more information on jaundice, see page 378.

Metabolic concerns Premature babies often have problems with their metabolism. Some preemies may develop a low level of blood sugar (glucose), called hypoglycemia (see page 536). This can happen because preemies typically have smaller stores of glycogen (stored glucose) than do full-term babies and because preemies' immature livers have trouble producing glucose. Medications given during pregnancy to help control a mother's high blood pressure can sometimes contribute to hypoglycemia in a preemie. If your baby is at risk of hypoglycemia, he or she may have a drop of blood drawn from his or her finger, heel or toe and tested. Treatment usually consists of feeding the baby breast milk or formula, or giving the baby dextrose (sugar) intravenously.

Vision concerns Preemies born before 30 weeks may develop retinopathy of prematurity (ROP), a condition that develops when blood vessels swell and overgrow in the light-sensitive layer of nerves at the back of the eye (retina). Sometimes the abnormal retinal vessels leak, eventually scarring the retina and pulling it out of position. When the retina is pulled away from the back of the eye it's called retinal detachment, a condition that can impair vision and cause blindness. In most cases, retinopathy of prematurity resolves by itself with no permanent damage. If the disease is severe, laser treatment may be needed.

Premature babies are also at risk of developing other vision problems, such as misalignment of the eyes (strabismus) or nearsightedness (myopia).

If your baby is born before 30 weeks or weighs less than 3 pounds, 5 ounces, an ophthalmologist will likely examine your baby's eyes, beginning when he or she is about 4 to 6 weeks old. Generally, preemies need eye exams every couple of weeks or so until the retina has fully developed. Regardless of whether your child has ROP, your baby's care provider may recommend that your son or daughter be periodically examined by an ophthalmologist during the preschool years.

Hearing concerns Premature babies are at increased risk of some degree of hearing loss. Your baby will likely be given a newborn hearing screening before he or she reaches a corrected age of 1 month (see "Corrected age" below) or before being discharged from the NICU. If your preemie has abnormal screening results, he or she will likely have follow-up testing with a specialist. Early diagnosis is crucial. The sooner treatment begins the better your child's chances are of developing age-appropriate language and communication skills.

Dental concerns Preemies who have been critically ill are at increased risk of developing dental problems, such as delayed tooth eruption, tooth discoloration and improperly aligned teeth.

SIDS Premature babies are at increased risk of sudden infant death syndrome (SIDS). When your baby is home from the hospital, always place your baby on his or her back to sleep. In the NICU, babies may be placed on their stomachs if they have respiratory problems or on their sides if they have infant gastroesophageal reflux (GER). In these cases, the medical team will begin placing the baby on his or her back prior to discharge. For more information on SIDS, see page 118.

Future issues For some premature babies, difficulties may not appear until later in childhood or even adulthood. Children who were born premature ex-

CORRECTED AGE

A premature child's growth and development is typically measured using his or her "corrected age" — your baby's age in weeks (chronological age) minus the number of weeks he or she was premature.

For example, if your baby was born eight weeks early (at 32 weeks), when your child is 6 months old, his or her corrected age is actually 4 months (6 months minus eight weeks). For a baby born at 24 weeks (16 weeks or 4 months early), when the child is 6 months old, the baby's corrected age is 2 months (6 months minus 4 months early). This adjustment is helpful to have the fairest comparison of a premature baby's development, until the child reaches about 2½ years old.

perience developmental delays, learning disabilities, difficulty smoothly controlling their muscles, and behavioral, psychological or other chronic health problems. Preterm babies who have a very low birth weight also may be at increased risk of autism. Research suggests that some premature babies, especially those with severe intrauterine growth restriction (IUGR), may face an increased risk of type 2 diabetes and high blood pressure as adults.

Take heart. It's normal to be concerned about your baby's health, especially if he or she has spent time in the NICU. But most babies who spend time in the NICU don't have significant disabilities. And many premature babies catch up and develop into normal healthy children. Keep in mind that the way you and your family care for, interact with and stimulate your baby in the coming months also can have a major impact on his or her development.

TAKING CARE OF YOURSELF

At this point in time, all of your attention may be concentrated on your child, and helping him or her to thrive. But remember that you have special needs, too. Taking good care of yourself will help you take the best care of your new son or daughter.

Allow time to heal You might need more time to recover from the rigors of childbirth than you imagined. Be sure to eat a healthy diet and get as much rest as you can. When your care provider gives you the OK, you can start exercising.

Acknowledge your emotions Expect to feel joy, anger, fear, powerlessness and a sense of loss. Some parents report feeling strange about getting to know their newborns in the busy NICU. You might celebrate successes one day, only to experience setbacks the next. Give yourself permission to take it one day at a time. Remember that you and your partner might react to stress and anxiety differently, but you both want what's best for your baby. Keep talking and supporting each other during this stressful time.

Take a break If you leave the hospital before your baby, use your time at home to prepare for his or her arrival and get some rest. Your baby needs you, but it's important to balance time at the hospital with time for yourself and your family.

Be honest with siblings If you have other children, try to answer their questions about the new baby simply. You might explain that their baby sister or brother is sick and you're worried. Reassure your children that the baby's illness isn't their fault. Ask if you can bring your other children to the NICU to visit your baby. If your children aren't able to see the baby in the NICU, show them pictures.

Seek and accept help Allow friends and loved ones to care for older children, prepare food, clean the house or run errands. Let them know what would be most helpful. Surround yourself with understanding friends and loved ones. Talk with other NICU parents. Consider joining a local support group for parents of preemies, or check out online communities. Seek professional help if you're feeling depressed or you're struggling to cope with your new responsibilities.

BRINGING BABY HOME

As your son's or daughter's condition begins to improve, you may wonder when you finally can bring him or her home. The criteria vary, but generally hospital staff will consider allowing you to take your baby home when he or she:

▶ Can breathe without support
▶ Has a stable heart rate
▶ Is able to maintain a stable body temperature
▶ Can breast- or bottle-feed
▶ Is gaining weight steadily

In some cases, a child may be allowed to go home before meeting one of these requirements — as long as the baby's medical team and family create and agree on a plan for home care and monitoring.

When it's time to bring your baby home, you might feel relieved, excited — and anxious. After days, weeks or months in the hospital, it can be daunting to leave the support of the medical team behind. As you spend more time with your baby, you'll better understand how to meet his or her needs and your relationship will grow stronger. In the meantime, consider ways to prepare for your child's hospital discharge.

Understand care requirements Before you leave the hospital, take a course in infant CPR. Ask your baby's medical team any questions you might have and take notes. Make sure you're comfortable caring for your baby, especially if you'll need to administer medications, use special equipment, or give your baby supplemental oxygen or other treatments. Ask if any members of the hospital medical team do home visits, which can be helpful during your baby's first week home. You'll likely be asked to provide contact information for your baby's care provider so that a member of the hospital medical

REHOSPITALIZATION

Premature babies' health problems can sometimes make it necessary for them to be readmitted to the hospital. Research suggests that 15 percent of babies who are born before 36 weeks and go home need to be rehospitalized at least once during their first year. Common causes of rehospitalization include infections, respiratory problems, feeding problems and surgical complications.

If your preemie needs to go back to the hospital for treatment, try not to get discouraged or blame yourself. You may want to reconnect with some of the support personnel who helped you through the last hospital stay. For longer hospital stays or more frequent rehospitalizations, some families find it helpful to blog their baby's progress online so that they don't have to continuously call family members and well-wishers with updates. Ask the hospital medical team any questions you might have about your baby's condition and find out what you need to know to care for him or her in the future.

team can inform him or her about your baby's medical condition. Discuss symptoms — such as infant breathing or feeding problems — that might necessitate a call to your baby's care provider. Note your baby's need for follow-up visits or referrals, and find out whom to call if you have questions or concerns.

Discuss feedings Ask the medical team about your baby's need for supplementation in the form of breast milk fortifiers or preterm infant formula. Keep in mind that premature babies usually eat smaller amounts and may need to be fed more often than full-term babies. Preemies also tend to be sleepier than full-term babies and sleep through feedings. Find out how much and how often your baby should be eating.

Make travel arrangements Because sitting semireclined in a car seat can increase the risk of breathing problems or a slow heartbeat, your baby might need to be monitored in his or her car seat before hospital discharge. When you have the

OK to use a car seat, use it only during travel. If your baby has a health problem that requires him or her to lie flat, a car bed may be recommended. Talk with your baby's care providers if you may need to take an airplane flight with your newborn. Your son's or daughter's lungs may be sensitive to the effects of altitude changes during flight. Also don't place your preemie in an infant sling, backpack or other upright positioning devices until you talk to your baby's care provider. These devices may make it harder for him or her to breathe. For more information on traveling with your baby, see Chapter 14.

Protect against illness Premature babies are more susceptible than are other newborns to serious infections. Try to minimize your preemie's exposure to crowded places and make sure people who come into contact with your child washes their hands first. Babies at high risk of developing respiratory complications, such as babies who require oxygen at home, should minimize the number of

VULNERABLE CHILD SYNDROME

When a premature baby requires intensive care in the hospital, it can be a traumatic experience. As a result, parents may become excessively concerned about their child's health and development or become excessively overprotective, a condition called vulnerable child syndrome. Signs of vulnerable child syndrome might include repeatedly taking a child to the care provider for treatment of minor symptoms, underestimating a child's abilities or having trouble setting appropriate limits for a child. Overprotective behavior can affect a child's development, prolong separation anxiety and cause behavioral problems.

If you're feeling overwhelmed by your baby's premature birth, talk to your care provider or lean on family and friends for support. Finding ways to process your baby's premature birth and deal with your stress now might have a positive impact on your relationship with your child down the road.

young children they encounter. During the child's first year, or at least first winter, it may be best to avoid child care centers.

BABY'S CHECKUPS

Depending on your baby's age, weight and health, you'll likely need to schedule his or her first visit to the care provider within several days after his or her hospital discharge. The care provider may review your baby's treatment in the NICU, current medications and treatments. In addition, the care provider will likely discuss your son's or daughter's growth, nutrition, immunizations and specific medical problems and evaluate your baby's progress since leaving the hospital. Be sure to tell the care provider about any concerns you might have. In addition, discuss your baby's need for future appointments with the care provider and any specialists. Your preemie may initially need to see his or her care provider every week or two to have his or her growth and care monitored.

It's recommended that immunizations be given to medically stable premature babies according to their chronological age. Work with your baby's care provider to stay on top of your baby's need for immunizations. Your care provider may also monitor your baby for developmental delays and disabilities in the coming months. Babies who are identified as at risk may receive further evaluation and be referred to early intervention services, such as physical therapy therapy for infants.

Work with your baby's care providers to understand any health problems your baby might experience and what you can do to promote your preemie's health and well-being.

CHAPTER 40

Delayed development

Throughout the first year, your baby's care provider will monitor your son's or daughter's growth and development to make sure it's progressing steadily and it falls within the range of normal development. At each well-child visit, the care provider will likely ask you questions about your child, based on his or her age. They may include questions such as whether your baby is learning to hold up his or her head, grasp toys, roll over, coo, laugh, walk or say *mama* or *dada*.

Sometimes, a child's abilities will fall below the range of milestones achieved by his or her peers. This isn't always a cause for alarm because children tend to develop at highly individual rates. They may fall behind in one area, such as language, while focusing intently on mastering another area, such as crawling or walking. Soon after they acquire the skill they're pursuing, they move on to achieve other milestones that have been lagging.

But if your child is slower to achieve certain milestones or if you're concerned about his or her development, you and your child's care provider can take steps to detect any possible developmental problems. The earlier a problem is identified, the sooner you can take additional measures to help your child achieve his or her maximum developmental potential. If an underlying condition or disease is present, treatment may help prevent further problems.

WHAT IS DELAYED DEVELOPMENT?

A developmental delay is when your child doesn't reach developmental milestones within the same timeframe as other children of the same age. When a child is delayed in two or more important areas of development, medical experts refer to this as global developmental delay. Milestones are usually grouped into these categories:

▶ Motor skills — rolling over, sitting, picking up small objects, walking

	Typical Speech Development*	Typical Play Development*	Typical Physical Development*
BY 3 MONTHS	Sucks and swallows well during feeding Quiets or smiles in response to sound or voice Coos or vocalizes other than crying Turns head toward direction of sound	*While lying on their back…* Visually tracks a moving toy from side to side Attempts to reach for a rattle held above their chest Keeps head in the middle to watch faces or toys	 *While lying on their tummy…* Pushes up on arms Lifts and holds head up
BY 6 MONTHS	Begins to use consonant sounds in babbling, e.g. "dada" Uses babbling to get attention Begins to eat cereals and pureed foods	Reaches for a nearby toy while on their tummy *While lying on their back…* Transfers a toy from one hand to the other Reaches both hands to play with feet	Uses hands to support self in sitting Rolls from back to tummy While standing with support, accepts entire weight with legs
BY 9 MONTHS	Increases variety of sounds and syllable combinations in babbling Looks at familiar objects and people when named Begins to eat junior and mashed table foods	In a high chair, holds and drinks from a bottle Explores and examines an object using both hands Turns several pages of a chunky (board) book at once In simple play imitates others	Sits and reaches for toys without falling Moves from tummy or back into sitting Creeps on hands and knees with alternate arm and leg movement
BY 12 MONTHS	Meaningfully uses "mama" or "dada" Responds to simple comands, e.g. "come here" Produces long strings of gibberish jargoning) in social communication Begins to use an open cup	Finger feeds self Releases objects into a container with a large opening Uses thumb and pointer finger to pick up tiny objects	Pulls to stand and cruises along furniture Stands alone and takes several independent steps
BY 15 MONTHS	Vocabulary consists of 5-10 words Imitates new less familiar words Understands 50 words Increases variety of coarsely chopped table foods	Stacks two objects or blocks Helps with getting undressed Holds and drinks from a cup	Walks independently and seldom falls Squats to pick up toy

*Remember to correct your child's age for prematurity.

Signs to Watch for in Physical Development*

Difficulty lifting head

Stiff legs with little or no movement

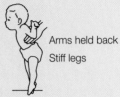

Pushes back with head

Keeps hands fisted and lacks arm movement

Rounded back

Unable to lift head up

Poor head control

Difficult to bring arms forward to reach out

Arches back and stiffens legs

Arms held back

Stiff legs

Uses one hand predominately

Rounded back

Poor use of arms in sitting

Difficulty crawling

Uses only one side of body to move

Inability to straighten back

Cannot take weight on legs

Difficulty getting to stand because of stiff legs and pointed toes

Only uses arms to pull up to standing

Sits with weight to one side

Strongly flexed or stiffly extended arms

Needs to use hand to maintain sitting

Unable to take steps independently

Poor standing balance, falls frequently

Walks on toes

Adapted with permission from Pathways.org, 2011. See page 553 for more information.

WILL MY CHILD GROW OUT OF A DEVELOPMENTAL DELAY?

Some premature infants appear delayed, based on their chronological age. However, the apparent delay may disappear when the baby's corrected age is taken into account. Of the children, preterm or term, who have true developmental delays in the preschool years — meaning they consistently lag behind in screening tests — most continue to be delayed even as they grow older. This is why early identification is so important. If you're waiting for your son or daughter to grow out of a development delay, you may be missing out on early opportunities to optimize his or her potential.

- Language and communication — recognizing sounds, imitating speech, babbling, pointing
- Thinking and reasoning — beginning to understand cause and effect, object permanence
- Personal and social skills — exploring, smiling, laughing, interacting with others
- Daily activities — eating, dressing

Part 3 of this book contains chapters for each month of the first year of your son's or daughter's life that help you understand the normal range of growth and development. If you're concerned that your child isn't developing as he or she should, talk to your child's care provider. He or she can reassure you about what's considered normal and offer advice on further testing.

HOW IS A DELAY IDENTIFIED?

Usually, a developmental problem is identified over time rather than at a single visit. If you or your child's care provider have concerns about your child's development, the care provider may conduct a developmental screening test to see if your child may be at risk for a developmental disorder.

The screening tests are usually brief and inexpensive. Your child's care provider may ask your child to play a game or perform certain activities, such as playing with a doll or picking up a small object. You may be asked to fill out a questionnaire. Based on the screening test's results, the care provider may recommend a wait-and-see approach to give your child a little more time to develop, or he or she may refer you to a childhood development expert for further evaluation.

A developmental evaluation is a more complex procedure carried out by a professional who is specially trained to administer these tests. The evaluation is designed to identify specific developmental disorders that may be affecting the child. Along with the developmental evaluation, a medical diagnostic evaluation is conducted to identify any possible underlying conditions that may be affecting development.

If it's determined that your child may be at high risk for a developmental disorder, even before a disorder is diagnosed, your child's care provider or a specialist may refer you to early intervention services. These services generally provide evaluations and other services that may be helpful during the diagnosis process.

POSSIBLE CAUSES

There are many conditions that can lead to delayed development, ranging from genetic disorders to infections to toxin exposure. But in many cases, the cause is hard to identify.

Genetic disorders In some cases, the cause is a chromosomal abnormality or an inherited disorder that interferes with normal growth and development.

One of the most common inherited disorders that causes delayed development is fragile X syndrome. This disorder is passed from parents to children and results from an altered gene that under-produces a protein vital to brain development. Because the alteration often increases in severity during transmission from parent to child, the parent of an affected child may have no symptoms of the disease.

Rett syndrome is another cause of delayed development that occurs more commonly in girls. Children with Rett syndrome appear to develop normally until 6 to 18 months of age, when they gradually begin to lose acquired speech and fine motor skills.

Problems during labor and delivery Being born prematurely or difficulties during labor that impair circulation may lead to developmental problems. More often, though, delayed development is associated with events that occur prior to labor.

Problems in utero Sometimes during a pregnancy, a fever or infection in the mother will create immune reactions that can harm the development of the baby's brain. Fetal exposure to alcohol or drugs during pregnancy can also damage a baby's developing nervous system.

Metabolic disorders Disorders of the body's chemistry, such as an underactive thyroid, can result in impaired growth and development and slower intellectual function. In most inherited metabolic disorders, a single enzyme is either not produced by the body or is produced in a nonworking form. Examples of inherited metabolic disorders include galactosemia, maple syrup urine disease and phenylketonuria (PKU). In many states, a newborn screening will identify these conditions (see pages 39 and 41).

Environmental toxins Excessive exposure to lead can harm the body's nervous system. Very high levels of lead in the body can lead to mental deficits. However, lead poisoning is not a common cause of delayed development.

Neglect or deprivation A baby's brain continues to develop even after birth. In cases of severe neglect or deprivation, where the brain isn't being appropriately stimulated or nourished, delayed development can result.

DIAGNOSING A DEVELOPMENTAL DELAY

To try to determine what may be causing your child to lag behind in achieving developmental milestones, your child's care provider or another specialist, such as a developmental pediatrician or a child neurologist or geneticist, will likely do a comprehensive physical exam. He or she may also conduct a variety of tests. The tests may include vision and hearing exams, genetic tests to look for a possible genetic abnormality, imaging tests of the brain to look for an abnormality or injury, and metabolic and thyroid tests.

Usually, the tests aren't all done at once but in a stepwise fashion. Depending on the results of one test or examination, the care provider will make recommendations about additional testing.

WHAT CAN BE DONE?

A few causes of developmental delay are treatable. These include certain metabolic disorders that may be treated by avoiding certain foods or substances or with vitamin or hormone supplementation. Lead poisoning can be treated with medications and by removing the child from further lead exposure. Removal from adverse home environments and placement in permanent, loving care can greatly stimulate development in an abused or neglected child.

More often, the condition causing developmental delay isn't curable or even known. But early identification of a problem — whether an underlying cause is discovered or not — allows therapies to be provided at a time when they may be most helpful.

If your child is identified as having special needs, he or she has access to early intervention services. You may already have been referred by your child's care provider to your local early intervention office for an evaluation of developmental concerns. A referral can be made at any time. Once a referral is submitted, your child is assessed and a caseworker is assigned to your family to coordinate the services that meet your child's specific needs. Together with the caseworker and therapists, you create a written plan called the Individualized Family Service Plan (IFSP). This plan outlines the services your child needs and how they will be provided.

The earlier these services are started, the better it is for your child. Therapists may come directly to your home to work

with you and your child, but you may also visit a center or clinic for some parts of your plan. Common services offered by an early intervention program include:

- Physical therapy to work on gross and fine motor skills
- Speech therapy to work on language and communication skills
- Occupational therapy to work on personal and social skills
- Family training and counseling to help you work with your child at home
- Transportation and assistive technology services if your child needs special equipment to get around
- Nutrition counseling if your child has trouble feeding
- Coordination of services from physicians and other agencies

Early intervention programs are funded primarily by each state but also receive help from the federal government and local resources. In a few cases, a state program will charge a small family fee. Your caseworker can discuss the cost of these services with you and may coordinate with your health insurance provider, but your ability to pay is not a prerequisite for eligibility. In general, families incur little to no out-of-pocket costs for these services.

Once your child reaches 3 years of age, your son or daughter may be eligible for services available through the public school system. Most kids with special needs start kindergarten on time or the following year. The vast majority attends schools that serve a variety of students, not just children with disabilities. Your child will continue to receive special services as needed throughout kindergarten, elementary and high school. Different states have different policies regarding when state-sponsored programs end. Your local resources can help you find out what applies in your state.

GET SUPPORT

Determining whether your child has a developmental disability, and if so, what can be done to help your child, can take time. It may require trips to various specialists, watching your child undergo different tests and waiting for results in between tests. It's not always easy dealing with the uncertainty and anxiety that often accompany this process. Your care provider or caseworker, if you've been assigned one by an early intervention program, may be able to help you navigate the various procedures and coordinate the services you need.

In the meantime, it's important to get support — not only through meeting with specialists and reading information but also through meeting other parents in similar circumstances. These are the people most likely to know what you're going through, and they may be able to offer valuable information you can't get elsewhere, such as a great dentist for kids with special needs or which kind of sippy cup works best for infants with challenges learning how to use a cup. And sometimes a friendly chat with another parent about the ups and downs of your day is just what you need to feel a little more ready to face the next day.

Here again, your care provider or caseworker may be able to connect you to a local parent group that fits your needs. Or you can check online for local chapters or online communities of national organizations for specific disabilities. For information on resources, including websites, books, videos and other sources that may be useful to you, see the Additional Resources section, beginning on page 552.

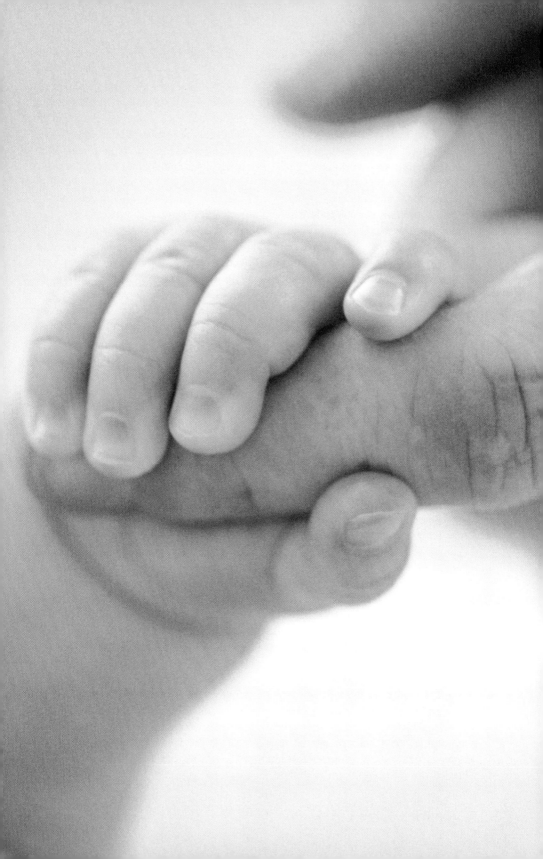

CHAPTER 41

Down syndrome

Learning that your baby has Down syndrome, whether before birth or after, can be a defining moment in your life. Within that moment, your expectations for your child — of identity, achievement, even your basic relationship together — can be shattered. It's not uncommon to react with shock, anger, fear and disappointment. Yet some parents report these feelings being dramatically softened the first time they hold their baby in their arms and gaze into their child's eyes.

Many parents wonder whether life will be more difficult having a child with Down syndrome. Certainly, it can be, especially if related medical conditions become prominent or when issues of behavior and independence come up. But where some expectations fail, other realities open up, often filled with surprising richness. Anecdotally and in surveys, parents of a child with Down syndrome frequently say they now have a better sense of how limitless life can be, how it can extend beyond previously conceived boundaries of what is and isn't possible and valuable. Many also express a greater understanding of love and tolerance, even in the midst of frustration.

This chapter will help you understand some of the basic issues you'll face in the first year of your baby's life, including some that may affect your baby in the long term. There are many resources available for children with Down syndrome and their families.

You may want to start with your baby's care provider, who may be able to refer you to helpful local resources. You can also check online for teaching hospitals or children's hospitals that have a Down syndrome clinic or center. These centers typically work closely with your baby's care provider and serve as a link to medical, educational, social and financial support systems in your community. Parent support groups and Down syndrome associations are other great resources.

GETTING TO KNOW YOUR CHILD

Babies with Down syndrome carry extra genetic material from chromosome 21 — in most cases three copies of the chromosome rather than the usual two copies. This is referred to as trisomy 21. This extra genetic material directly affects your baby's mental and physical development. It causes some common signs and symptoms, including:

▶ Decreased muscle tone (hypotonia)
▶ Small stature
▶ Characteristic facial features such as a flat nasal bridge and an upward slant to the eyes
▶ Single crease in the palm
▶ Mild to moderate intellectual impairment
▶ Slower rate of development than babies without Down syndrome
▶ Cardiac abnormalities

These effects can vary widely, so no two individuals with Down syndrome are exactly alike. As with any child, your son or daughter will have characteristics that are all his or her own, as well as characteristics that remind you of yourself or your partner.

As your child gets older, you'll get to know his or her unique temperament and likes and dislikes. You'll also become more familiar with the different aspects of your baby's development. It's likely to be slower in some areas, such as motor skills, and may be advanced in others, such as social skills. Babies with Down syndrome progress through the same developmental milestones, but generally at a different pace (see opposite page).

DEVELOPING A ROUTINE

During the early months, your baby may behave like any newborn, alternating between sleeping and eating and looking around. In fact, your daily routine is likely to be similar to any other new parent, filled with feedings, naps, cuddling and diapering.

But there are some aspects unique to Down syndrome. One of the most visible of these is hypotonia. This refers to the decreased muscle tone that most babies with Down syndrome have. Hypotonia can create a number of caregiving challenges, particularly when it comes to feedings. Other medical conditions your baby may have also can have an impact on daily activities.

Feeding Because of decreased muscle tone in the mouth and throat area, newborns with Down syndrome can have difficulty sucking and may be slow in learning to breast-feed. They also tend to have a nonrhythmic suck and may choke or gag easily. They may arch their bodies and be oversensitive to stimulation, which can distract them from feeding. If your baby also has a heart defect, he or she may become worn out before taking in enough milk.

This doesn't mean it isn't possible to breast-feed. With time and patience, you and your baby can successfully breast-feed. In fact, breast-feeding can be beneficial because breast milk is easy on your baby's digestive system. By passing on your antibodies to your baby through breast milk, breast-feeding can help decrease the number of upper and lower respiratory infections your baby gets, as well as the number of ear infections, all of which tend to be more common in babies with Down syndrome. Breast-feeding also helps develop your baby's mouth and tongue coordination, which is helpful for language and speech skills later on. And the time you spend together may help you bond as parent and child.

DEVELOPMENTAL MILESTONES

	Range for children with Down syndrome	Typical range for most children
Gross motor		
Sits alone	6-30 months	5-9 months
Crawls	8-22 months	6-12 months
Stands	1-3¼ years	8-17 months
Walks alone	1-4 years	9-18 months
Language		
First word	1-4 years	1-3 years
Two-word phrases	2-7½ years	15-36 months
Personal and social		
Responsive smile	1½-5 months	1-3 months
Finger feeds	10-24 months	7-14 months
Drinks from cup unassisted	12-32 months	9-17 months
Uses spoon	13-39 months	12-20 months
Bowel control	2-7 years	16-42 months
Dresses self unassisted	3½ -8½ years	3¼-5 years

Source: National Down Syndrome Society

In some cases, it may be necessary to supplement your baby's nutrition with formula feedings. This is nothing to feel guilty about. Breast-feeding can cause anxiety in any mother, but it can be especially stressful if your baby is having difficulty with it. If anxiety over breast-feeding is causing you to feel overwhelmed or neglect other aspects of parenting, talk to your baby's care provider. Some parents prefer to feed formula exclusively because it frees up energy for other things and allows both parents to participate in the act of feeding their child. Your child's care provider or a member of his or her health care team may have recommendations on the best nipples or bottles to use to help ensure feedings go well. The most important thing is that your baby is thriving and growing.

Sleeping New babies with Down syndrome tend to be good sleepers. This can make things a bit easier for parents, but letting your baby sleep for extended periods can interfere with your baby getting enough to eat. If your baby sleeps a lot, you might need to wake him or her every two to three hours for a feeding to make sure he or she is getting adequate nutrition. Watch for slight movements of your baby's eyes or hands, which indicate he or she is in a lighter phase of sleep and may be easier to wake. You can also try undressing your baby for a diaper change or holding him or her cheek to cheek. Ask your baby's care provider for advice if you have any questions about how long it's OK to let your baby sleep.

Carrying your baby When carrying or holding your baby, you may need to pay extra attention to giving him or her proper support. Decreased muscle tone makes a baby "floppy" so that the limbs and head fall sideways if not supported. It's also easier for a baby with hypotonia to slip out of your grasp if you're not watchful.

YOUR CHILD'S HEALTH

Babies with Down syndrome are at increased risk for certain health conditions. The list of health risks may seem long, but keep in mind that most babies with Down syndrome have only a few health issues; some have none. Occasionally, a baby with Down syndrome may have severe health problems.

A thorough assessment of your baby's health is vital to optimizing his or her growth and development. Any existing health problems can and should be diagnosed and treated promptly — they're not just "part of Down syndrome" and they can greatly affect quality of life. Your child's health should be monitored regularly throughout his or her life to address any health concerns that may arise later.

Your baby's care provider, along with the help of other specialists, plays an important role in keeping your baby as healthy as possible. It may seem at first as if you're spending most of your time making trips between your home and various medical offices. But it's important to establish your baby's health status as early as possible to enable timely and effective treatment where necessary.

Checkups and vaccinations In addition to paying special attention to health concerns associated with Down syndrome, your baby's care provider will conduct regular checkups and administer vaccinations in much the same way as with any other child. Keeping vaccinations up to date is especially important since children with Down syndrome are more prone to infectious illnesses.

Growth There are special growth charts for children with Down syndrome, which your baby's care provider will use to track your son's or daughter's growth compared with his or her peers with Down syndrome. In general, children with Down syndrome have a smaller stature than children without Down syndrome. Impaired growth rate may be especially noticeable between 6 months and 3 years of age and during puberty.

Monitoring your child's growth on these charts will also alert your doctor to potential problems associated with Down syndrome, such as thyroid disease or celiac disease, which may further impair a child's growth.

Hearing problems Up to 75 percent of babies with Down syndrome have some degree of hearing loss. In many cases, the hearing loss is due to the accumulation of fluid in the ear canal. Babies with Down syndrome often have narrow ear canals, which facilitate the buildup of fluid. Insertion of ear tubes to ventilate the ear canal can help restore hearing. Hearing loss can also be due to problems with the nerves that travel between the ear and the brain (sensorineural hearing loss). This type of hearing loss can be treated with hearing aids. Your baby's hearing will likely be evaluated at birth, as is done with almost all newborns.

Because of the often-narrow ear canal, and because of certain immune deficiencies that make babies with Down syndrome more prone to respiratory illnesses, ear infections are common and can result in hearing loss. Your son or daughter's care provider will continue to monitor your baby's ear health and hearing regularly. It's important to get ear infections treated promptly so that they don't lead to hearing loss, even if your baby passed the newborn hearing screen. Hearing loss in any baby can lead to a delay in language and communication skills, and experts suspect that hearing loss in children with Down syndrome can contribute to an even greater disadvantage in language development.

Vision problems Another aspect of your baby's health that his or her care provider will want to monitor beginning at birth is vision. About 60 percent of children with Down syndrome have eye problems, such as crossed eyes (strabismus), rapid involuntary eye movement (nystagmus) or cataracts. These vision problems are treated no differently from that of other children. Refractive problems, such as nearsightedness or farsightedness, also are common in children with Down syndrome. About half require eyeglasses between 3 and 5 years of age.

Heart problems Congenital heart defects affect about 40 to 50 percent of babies with Down syndrome. The most common defects result from heart tissue not being fully formed, leaving a hole in the heart that causes problems with blood flow. Experts recommend that all newborns with Down syndrome be evaluated by a pediatric cardiologist. Surgery, usually performed in the first year of life, may be necessary to repair a defect.

Thyroid problems Babies with Down syndrome are also at risk of thyroid problems, most commonly hypothyroidism. Hypothyroidism is a condition in which the thyroid gland doesn't produce enough of certain hormones that help

TEETHING

If you're wondering when your baby's teeth will finally come in, don't worry. They'll come, but probably a bit later than is normally expected and perhaps not in the same pattern as in the average infant. In some cases, a tooth may be unusually shaped or missing. Since dental problems, such as enamel defects and gum disease, tend to be more common with Down syndrome, it's important to practice good dental hygiene with your child as soon as teeth do appear. Establish a relationship with a dentist as soon as possible, preferably one that has experience treating kids with Down syndrome.

control metabolism. Signs and symptoms of hypothyroidism — such as decreased growth rate, increase in weight, dry skin, constipation and lethargy — can overlap with and even be masked by those of Down syndrome. But hypothyroidism is treatable. Hormone supplements can minimize or eliminate the effects of an underactive thyroid. Screening for thyroid problems is recommended at birth, 6 and 12 months, and then annually thereafter, as the risk of thyroid problems increases with age.

Gastrointestinal problems Some babies with Down syndrome are born with a gastrointestinal blockage called a duodenal atresia. This occurs when the first part of the small intestine (duodenum) doesn't develop properly, remaining closed off from the stomach and blocking the passage of food. Often this condition is diagnosed before birth during an ultrasound. Babies born with duodenal atresia have difficulty feeding, persistent vomiting, and a distended abdomen. The condition is corrected with surgery.

Down syndrome also increases a person's susceptibility to gluten allergy (celiac disease). Between 5 and 15 percent of people with Down syndrome have celiac disease. This allergic reaction to gluten damages the absorbing function of the small intestine. The body's resultant inability to absorb nutrients from food leads to bloating, diarrhea and growth problems. If your child begins showing signs of abdominal pain after starting solid foods, talk to your son's or daughter's care provider about the need to check for celiac disease. A gluten-free diet is key to treating celiac disease.

A small number of babies with Down syndrome are born with Hirschsprung's disease, a nerve cell malformation in the colon that causes problems with passing stool (see page 542). Your child's care provider might suspect the condition if your baby fails to pass stool within the first or second day of life. Chronic constipation is another clue. Hirschsprung's disease is often treated with surgery to remove the abnormal portion of the colon.

Joint problems Down syndrome is associated with a certain amount of looseness in the joints and ligaments. In most cases, this isn't a problem. But about 15 percent of people with Down syndrome develop a misalignment of the first and second vertebrae in the upper spinal column due to loose ligaments. You may hear medical care providers refer to this condition as atlantoaxial instability. This instability in the upper spinal cord poses a very small but serious increased risk of spinal cord compression that could potentially result in paralysis and loss of bodily functions. Signs and symptoms of atlantoaxial instability include neck pain, twisting of the neck to one side, changes in walking pattern, loss of bladder and bowel function, muscle weakness, and loss of muscle function.

Many parents become especially concerned about this risk when their children become older and more physically active or begin participating in sports. The American Academy of Pediatrics recommends using X-ray examination of the cervical spine to screen for atlantoaxial instability between 3 and 5 years of age, especially if your child is planning on participating in sports.

If your child has atlantoaxial instability, this doesn't mean it will inevitably progress to spinal cord compression — only that the risk of such an injury is increased. Treatment for atlantoaxial instability may consist of a neck brace to protect the spine or surgery to stabilize the affected vertebrae.

Blood cell problems Your baby's care provider will likely obtain a complete blood count sometime in your baby's first month to check for blood cell abnormalities associated with Down syndrome. Abnormalities may include too many or too few white blood cells (which help fight infection) or platelets (involved with clotting), or elevated or enlarged red blood cells. Some of these problems are temporary and resolve on their own. Others require treatment.

Obstructive sleep apnea Alterations in the shape and structure of the head and neck area and decreased muscle tone in children with Down syndrome contribute to a greater risk of obstructive sleep apnea. This breathing disorder occurs when throat muscles intermittently relax and block the airway during sleep. It's usually a more significant issue after age 1.

Signs and symptoms of sleep apnea include snoring, restless sleep, and re-peated stops and starts in breathing during sleep. Lack of adequate rest at night can lead to daytime tiredness, excessive crankiness and disruptive behavior. Obstructive sleep apnea has also been associated with intellectual deficits, decreased visual perception skills, high blood pressure and other cardiovascular problems. Treatment may consist of having your child wear a device at night that helps him or her breathe properly. Other options include various surgical procedures that change the structure of your child's nose, mouth or throat.

Behavior problems Discuss with your child's care provider at every visit your child's behavioral and social progress. Autism and other behavioral problems occur with increased frequency in children with Down syndrome. Symptoms may first become noticeable as early as 2 or 3 years of age.

EARLY INTERVENTION

In addition to monitoring and managing any health concerns your child may have, you can also help optimize his or her growth and development by becoming involved in an early intervention program.

These therapy and counseling services, which are available through state programs, are designed to promote optimal development in your son or daughter and help you as a family learn how to understand and meet your child's needs during the first three years of life.

The hospital where your baby was born or your baby's care provider can give you a referral to your local state agency. Once a referral is submitted, your child is assessed and a caseworker assigned to your family to coordinate the services that meet your baby's specific needs. Together with the caseworker and therapists, your family creates a written plan called the Individualized Family Service Plan (IFSP) — usually within 45 days of referral.

Early intervention programs are funded primarily by each state, but also receive help from the federal government and local resources. In a few cases, a state program will charge a small family fee. Your caseworker can discuss the cost of these services with you and may coordinate with your health insurance provider, but your ability to pay is not a prerequisite for eligibility. In general, families incur little to no out-of-pocket costs for these services.

The earlier these services are started, the better it is for your child. Frequently, therapists come directly to your home to work with you and your child, but you may also visit a center for some services. The most common services provided in an early intervention program for Down syndrome are as follows.

Physical therapy A big part of every child's development in the first year is learning to explore and interact with his or her environment. This early exploration depends heavily on your baby's motor skills but can be impaired by decreased muscle tone. A physical therapist can show you exercises and movements that help strengthen your baby's muscles so that he or she can achieve milestones such as holding up his or her head to look around, pulling up to sit, rolling over, and sitting up. You can read more details about growth and development in Part 3. (Don't think these chapters aren't for you just because your baby's development is likely to be delayed. The information still applies even if the timetable doesn't.)

A physical therapist can also help prevent your baby from learning inappropriate movement patterns. For example, your baby may compensate for certain deficits now by moving in a way that can lead to orthopedic and functional problems later on.

Speech and language therapy A big challenge for any baby is learning to communicate needs and wants. But it can be even more of a challenge for babies with Down syndrome. Speech and language therapy during the first years of life can help establish a stable foundation upon which your baby can learn to communicate effectively through nonverbal and verbal means. Just as with any infant, a baby with Down syndrome understands language much sooner than he or she can express it. But it may be several years before a child with Down syndrome can learn to use expressive language.

Speech skills build on the same muscles and body systems used for breathing, swallowing and eating. To prepare your baby for speech, a speech and language therapist may help you and your baby work on breast-feeding or sucking skills, which can strengthen your baby's jaw and facial muscles. The therapist may also help you and your baby work on pre-speech skills such as:

▶ Imitating sounds
▶ Using social and facial cues to communicate (you talk and then wait while your baby reacts)
▶ Learning to listen, through music and conversation
▶ Learning through touch and exploring objects with the mouth
▶ Understanding object permanence (an object under a blanket is still there even if out of sight)
▶ Understanding cause and effect ("If I smile, Daddy smiles back")

As your baby gets older, sign language and picture systems may serve as important tools of communication.

Occupational therapy An occupational therapist can help you and your baby work on personal and social skills that will help your child operate independently. Such skills are often learned through play, such as holding toys, manipulating knobs and buttons, building towers, and moving objects in and out of a basket. An occupational therapist also can help your child master progressive fine-motor skills such as self-feeding, scribbling and getting dressed.

Other services Depending on your needs, your IFSP also may include services such as nutrition counseling, locating medical and dental services for your child, getting transportation or special equipment for your child, and helping you find child care, among others. The IFSP is designed to be tailored to your family, so take the time to think about what you need and be sure to communicate this to your caseworker and medical team.

DEVELOPING A SUPPORT SYSTEM

You may spend much of your baby's first year mentally organizing all of the varying issues affecting your child, sorting out what your child does and doesn't need and generally acclimating to living a life closely connected to Down syndrome.

During this time, it's important to care for yourself, as well. The challenges of raising a child with Down syndrome may seem insurmountable at times, but you don't have to do it all by yourself. If you have a partner, develop a plan where both of you can take regular breaks to recharge your batteries. Find a trusted sitter so that you can take breaks together, too (see Part 5 of this book). If you have other children, involve them in caring for the baby and understanding the condition, but spend time alone with older children, as well.

Seek out positive reinforcement. Support groups for parents of children with Down syndrome may be invaluable. Not only will group members know what you're going through, but also may be able to offer advice, recommend helpful resources, give you a shoulder to cry on and laugh with you when others may fail to find the humor in a situation.

Unfortunately, society can still be fairly obtuse when it comes to recognizing talents and abilities hidden beneath a label such as Down syndrome. It may not always be easy to brush off insensitive comments or ill-informed reactions to your child. But if you can be straightforward and honest about your child's abilities and disabilities, you may be able to educate those around you and offer them a whole new perspective on what it means to have Down syndrome in the family. And you may even be surprised at the kindnesses of others. If you have any questions or doubts about your child's legal rights and protections, be sure to ask your caseworker, who can guide you to the right answers.

For information on resources that may be useful to you, see the Additional Resources section, beginning on page 552.

CHAPTER 42

Other newborn conditions

Even if you do everything right during your pregnancy, sometimes complications can occur during pregnancy and childbirth or shortly thereafter. If your child faces an unexpected problem, you may be concerned, confused and even frightened.

This section describes some of the conditions that can occur in newborn children and how they may be treated. Listen to the advice of your child's care provider and ask questions until you feel you understand the complication and the possible courses of action. Also trust that your child's care provider and the medical team will do the best for your son or daughter. Keep in mind that many conditions that develop in infants can be successfully managed.

If your child is healthy, there's no need to read this chapter. Reading about things that don't affect your child or that could go wrong may worry you unnecessarily. However, this chapter may be helpful if a friend or relative has a newborn with a health concern.

BLOOD DISORDERS

It's not uncommon for infants to experience blood-related conditions or illnesses. Jaundice is a very common blood-related condition, which you can read about on page 378. Following are other blood disorders that can affect children under a year of age.

Anemia Anemia is a common blood disorder in infants that can affect normal growth and development. Anemia occurs when red blood cells are broken down too rapidly, too much blood is lost or a child's bone marrow doesn't produce enough red blood cells.

The most common type of anemia in children under 2 years of age is iron deficiency anemia. It results when a child doesn't get enough iron in his or her diet or cannot absorb iron properly. Lack of iron lowers the number of healthy red blood cells needed for growth and development. Red blood cells contain hemoglobin, which carries oxygen to growing organs and tissues. Signs of infant anemia can be difficult to detect until the condition becomes more severe. They include paleness in your baby's skin, lips or nail beds. Your child may also become irritable and fatigued and experience a loss of appetite.

Babies born prematurely are at risk of iron deficiency anemia, since babies get the majority of their iron stores from their mothers during the last trimester of pregnancy. Infants who drink cow's milk in the first year of life (instead of breast milk or iron-fortified formula) also are at risk of iron deficiency anemia. Cow's milk is low in the iron necessary for infant growth. That's why it's recommended that you don't give cow's milk to your child until he or she is at least a year of age.

Iron deficiency anemia may also occur in breast-fed infants who don't eat iron-rich foods after age 6 months. Healthy newborns generally have enough iron stores in their bodies to last for at least six months. After that, more significant amounts of iron are often required.

Treatment Anemia is diagnosed with a blood test. Treatment involves supplemental iron. Common sources of dietary iron for infants are iron-fortified formulas and cereals. Iron may also be added to an infant's diet in the form of supplemental drops or powders.

Don't give your child iron supplements, without first consulting with his or her care provider. Too much iron can be dangerous.

Low blood sugar The human brain depends on blood sugar (glucose) as its main source of fuel, so it needs a steady supply. Throughout pregnancy, a baby's blood sugar stays at a fairly even level because he or she continuously receives nutrition from the mother's placenta.

After birth, a baby must quickly develop the ability to regulate his or her own blood sugar level. Most healthy babies are able to do this because they have a stored form of sugar, called glycogen, in their livers. Babies also develop the capability to generate sugar from other food reserves in their bodies. These abilities are important because a baby needs to adapt from a continuous supply of blood sugar to periodic supplies that come during feedings.

Fortunately, most babies handle the transition well. When the changeover doesn't go so well, hypoglycemia may occur. Hypoglycemia is a condition in which a person's blood sugar is lower than normal. Babies more likely to develop hypoglycemia include those born to mothers with diabetes, full-term babies who are large for their gestational age, full-term babies who are small for their gestational age (intrauterine growth restriction), and premature babies.

Too little blood sugar is a problem because it can impair the brain's ability to function. Severe or prolonged hypoglycemia may result in seizures and serious brain injury.

Some babies with hypoglycemia don't experience signs and symptoms or they may be mild. In other instances, signs and symptoms may be more severe. Some of the more common indications of hypoglycemia are jitteriness, bluish coloring (cyanosis), breathing problems, low body temperature, poor appetite and lethargy.

A simple blood test to check blood sugar levels can diagnose hypoglycemia. A newborn's blood sugar level is commonly measured within the first several hours after birth to be reassured that it's in the normal range.

Treatment When a baby's blood sugar is below normal levels, feeding him or her breast milk, formula or glucose water will usually cause the level to return to normal. If a baby isn't able to feed well the first few hours after birth — perhaps because baby is too sleepy from low blood sugar — he or she may be given some glucose via a small feeding tube directly into the stomach. Boosting the sugar level to a normal range with tube feedings can be very helpful.

If a newborn's blood glucose tests continue to be repeatedly low, prompt treatment is necessary. An intravenous (IV) tube is often started to infuse glucose directly into the baby's circulation. This will quickly correct the low glucose while the potential causes for the hypoglycemia are investigated.

Polycythemia Polycythemia is a blood disorder in which your bone marrow makes too many red blood cells — the opposite of anemia. Polycythemia also may result in production of too many of the other types of blood cells — white blood cells and platelets. But it's the excess red blood cells that thicken your blood and cause most of the concerns associated with the condition.

Infants at higher risk of the condition are those who are born past term ("overdue"), are small for their gestational age, are born to mothers with diabetes, have chromosomal abnormalities, have continually decreased oxygen levels, or are the recipient twin in a condition called twin-to-twin transfusion syndrome.

Often, there are no symptoms, but when they do occur they may include a reddish-purple coloring, lethargy, a poor appetite and breathing problems.

Treatment In newborns, the condition may resolve on its own within a few days. If treatment is required, blood may be withdrawn to reduce the number of blood cells and decrease blood volume, making it easier for baby's blood to function properly. Blood that's been withdrawn may be replaced with fluids.

BREATHING DISORDERS

The lungs are one of the last organs to fully develop during pregnancy. Most newborns have no difficulty breathing, but occasionally breathing problems can occur, especially if an infant is born prematurely. Following are some breathing disorders that can affect infants.

Bronchopulmonary dysplasia Breathing difficulties associated with premature birth generally improve within several days to weeks. Premature infants who still require assistance with ventilation or supplemental oxygen after a month are often described as having brochnopulmonary dysplasia.

Bronchopulmonary dysplasia is most common in infants born early (prematurely) whose lungs were not fully developed at birth and in infants who have been on a breathing machine (ventilator) or who need supplemental oxygen for an extended period.

Signs and symptoms of bronchopulmonary dysplasia include rapid breathing, wheezing, coughing, and bluish lips and fingernails (cyanosis). Brochnopulmonary dysplasia is often suspected in infants with respiratory distress syndrome who don't recover within the first several weeks.

Treatment Babies with bronchopulmonary dysplasia need supplemental oxygen for an extended period and may also need medication. Most get better with time; however, they may need to continue treatment for months or even years.

Some continue to have lung problems, such as asthma, throughout childhood and even into adulthood.

Meconium aspiration Meconium aspiration syndrome is a condition in which a newborn breathes (aspirates) a mixture of meconium and amniotic fluid into the lungs during labor.

Meconium is the first feces, or stool, of a newborn. Normally, meconium isn't passed until after an infant is born. In some cases, though, a baby will pass stool (meconium) while still inside the uterus. Once the meconium has passed into the surrounding amniotic fluid, the baby may inhale it into the lungs, called meconium aspiration. The meconium can potentially obstruct the infant's airways and can cause breathing difficulties due to inflammation of the baby's lungs.

Symptoms of meconium aspiration generally include breathing difficulty — the infant has to work hard to breathe — and a bluish skin color (cyanosis).

Treatment When a baby is born with meconium in the amniotic fluid, the first step is to suction the newborn's mouth after birth. Further treatment is only necessary if the baby isn't active and crying immediately after delivery. A tube may be placed in the infant's trachea and suction applied to remove the meconium.

In most cases, the outlook is excellent and there are no long-term health effects. In more severe cases, a baby may need antibiotics to treat possible infection, specialized ventilators and other technologies to keep the lungs inflated, and oxygen to keep blood levels normal.

Pneumothorax One of the miracles of birth is that within a few breaths a newborn's lungs inflate with air and the baby begins breathing. Initially, considerable pressure changes may be needed to inflate the lungs.

Occasionally, the lungs don't inflate evenly, and the pressure differences can cause a condition called collapsed lung, or pneumothorax. In this condition, the small air sacs within a baby's tiny lungs rupture and allow air to leak out into the spaces between the thin membranes lining the lungs and the inner wall of the chest. Pneumothorax may also cause babies to have other respiratory conditions.

If a small amount of air leaks, the infant may have shortness of breath, rapid breathing or grunting, and perhaps bluish lips and fingernail beds (cyanosis). If a large amount of air leaks, the infant may develop more severe breathing difficulty.

Treatment Pneumothorax can be very serious if a lung collapses suddenly, but in most cases the leakage is small and the air is reabsorbed on its own. Sometimes, no treatment is necessary. In other cases, the infant may be given extra oxygen to breathe for a period of time. In the case of severe pneumothorax, air that has leaked into the chest may need to be removed by inserting a tube into the chest wall beside the lung.

Respiratory distress syndrome Respiratory distress syndrome (RDS) is characterized by rapid, difficult breathing and perhaps a bluish skin color (cyanosis). The breathing sound made by a baby with RDS, commonly referred to as "grunting," is often very distinctive. As the child breathes out, he or she may make a noise that sounds like a lamb or a soft cry. Babies with RDS also have to work harder to move air into their lungs.

RDS is caused by lack of a slippery, protective substance called surfactant, which helps the lungs inflate with air and keeps air sacs from collapsing. It's most commonly seen in premature infants whose lungs haven't fully developed and is rarely found in full-term infants. The severity of RDS often correlates with the infant's gestational age and weight. The smaller and more premature the infant, the greater the chance he or she will have RDS. Other factors that may increase the risk are an older sibling who had RDS, a mother with diabetes, a cesarean delivery and a multiple pregnancy (twins or more).

Most infants who develop RDS show signs of breathing problems and the need for more oxygen at birth, or within the first few hours that follow. Blood tests and an X-ray of the lungs can establish the diagnosis. A child with RDS may be placed in a neonatal intensive care unit (NICU), where his or her vital signs can be constantly monitored.

Treatment Many infants with RDS require help with their breathing. A breathing tube attached to a ventilator may be inserted through the mouth into the baby's trachea to assist with breathing. Some babies are helped with a tube in the nose or a mask on the face to provide continuous positive airway pressure. Infants with severe RDS may be given surfactant directly into their lungs. Other medications may also be given to help improve breathing.

Transient tachypnea Transient tachypnea of a newborn (TTNB) is a form of respiratory distress that can occur after an uneventful vaginal delivery or cesarean birth in both premature and full-term infants. TTNB is more likely to occur after a rapid vaginal birth or among babies born by cesarean birth without labor.

Infants with this form of respiratory distress often have no signs of trouble other than rapid, shallow breathing.

Among some babies, their skin may have a bluish tinge (cyanosis).

Unlike infants with RDS, these infants rarely appear severely ill and most recover within a couple of days. However, rapid breathing makes it more difficult for the babies to eat. Once their breathing becomes more comfortable, babies with TTNB are more willing to nurse or take a bottle.

Treatment Treatment may include giving the baby oxygen until breathing improves. If the baby is breathing too fast to be fed via breast or bottle, the baby might be given intravenous (IV) fluids or milk via a feeding tube passed through the nose and into the stomach. Usually, no other treatment is necessary.

CENTRAL NERVOUS SYSTEM DISORDERS

The central nervous system consists of the brain and spinal cord. Three of the more common central nervous system disorders seen in infants may occur during early fetal development or shortly after birth.

Cerebral palsy Cerebral palsy is a disorder of movement, muscle tone or posture that's caused by infection, injury or abnormal development in the immature brain, most often before birth. Most children born with cerebral palsy had a seemingly uncomplicated course of pregnancy, labor and birth.

In general, cerebral palsy causes impaired movement associated with exaggerated reflexes or rigidity of the limbs and trunk, abnormal posture, involuntary movements, unsteadiness of walking, or some combination of these. These problems often aren't evident until an infant is 6 to 12 months old or older. Other conditions related to abnormal brain development also may occur, including intellectual disabilities, vision and hearing problems, or seizures.

There are many possible causes of cerebral palsy. One possible cause is inadequate circulation of blood in brain tissue. Abnormal brain growth and development early in pregnancy is increasingly recognized as a cause of cerebral palsy. Injury to the brain during labor and delivery can also be a cause, as well as infection or bleeding in or around the brain of the developing fetus. Other factors related to pregnancy or birth associated with an increased risk of cerebral palsy include premature birth, low birth weight, breech birth and multiple births (twins or more).

Treatment There's no cure for cerebral palsy, but in some cases surgery may help reduce muscle spasticity and resulting deformities. Physical therapy is a common component of treatment. Muscle training and strengthening exercises may help your child's strength, flexibility, balance, motor development and mobility. Occupational and speech therapy also may be part of the treatment program. As a child becomes older, medication may also be used to help lessen muscle tightness and manage complications.

Hydrocephalus Hydrocephalus is an excessive accumulation of water in the brain due to an imbalance between the brain's production of cerebrospinal fluid and its ability to absorb it. Untreated hydrocephalus in a young infant can eventually result in an extremely large head.

The outlook for a child with hydrocephalus depends on the severity of the condition and whether any underlying disorders are present. If the condition is severe at birth, major brain damage and physical disabilities are likely. In less severe cases, with proper treatment, it's possible to have a nearly normal life span and intelligence.

Premature infants are at increased risk of the condition because they're at higher risk of severe bleeding within the brain, which can eventually lead to hydrocephalus. Certain problems during pregnancy also may increase an infant's risk of developing hydrocephalus, including an infection within the uterus or problems during fetal development, such as spina bifida. In some cases, a genetic abnormality may be responsible.

Congenital or developmental defects not apparent at birth may increase an older child's risk of hydrocephalus. Other factors that increase risk include meningitis or bleeding in the brain.

Treatment Hydrocephalus is often treated with surgery. The most common treatment is the surgical insertion of a drainage system, called a shunt. It consists of a long flexible tube with a valve that keeps fluid from the brain flowing in the right direction and at the proper rate. One end of the tubing is usually placed in a fluid-filled chamber in the brain, and the tubing is then tunneled under the skin to the abdomen where the excess cerebrospinal fluid can be more easily absorbed.

If your child has hydrocephalus, his or her doctor may recommend working with specialists who can evaluate your child's developmental progress on a regular basis in order to detect any delays in social, intellectual, emotional or physical development. Effective interventions are available to help your child, if needed.

Spina bifida Spina bifida (myelomeningocele) is part of a group of birth defects called neural tube defects. The neural tube is the embryonic structure that eventually develops into the baby's brain and spinal cord and the tissues that enclose them.

Normally, the neural tube forms early in a pregnancy and it closes by the 28th day after conception. In babies with spina bifida, a portion of the neural tube fails to develop or close properly, causing defects in the spinal cord and in the bones of the backbone.

Spina bifida may occasionally cause no symptoms or only minor physical disabilities. More frequently, it leads to serious physical, and sometimes mental, disabilities. Often, the condition causes loss of neurological control of the legs, bladder and bowel. Some infants also experience accumulation of fluid in the brain (hydrocephalus) or an infection in the tissues surrounding the brain (meningitis).

Doctors aren't certain what causes spina bifida. As with many other nervous system disorders, it appears to result from a combination of genetic and environmental risk factors, such as a family history of neural tube defects or folic acid deficiency. Folate (vitamin B-9) is important to the healthy development of a fetus and can help prevent spina bifida. The synthetic form of the vitamin, found in supplements and fortified foods, is called folic acid. A folic acid deficiency before or in early pregnancy increases the risk of neural tube defects.

Treatment Treatment of spina bifida depends on the severity of the condition. It usually requires surgery to put the spinal cord and exposed tissue back in place and close the opening in the vertebrae. Rarely, this surgery may be done before a child is born while he or she is still in the womb, but it carries many risks. More surgeries and other forms of treatment may also be necessary.

DIGESTIVE DISORDERS

Disorders of the digestive tract can cause a variety of problems, including poor eating and excessive spitting up. In other chapters in this book we discuss conditions such as reflux (see page 382) and milk allergy (see page 61), which can affect newborns. Following are some less common digestive disorders that can cause complete or partial obstruction of the passage of food or stool.

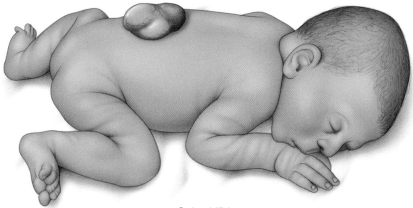

Spina bifida

Esophageal atresia In an infant born with esophageal atresia, the tube leading from the throat to the stomach (esophagus) isn't properly connected. The condition may be accompanied by other disorders. It may occur with certain genetic disorders, including Down syndrome.

Signs and symptoms of esophageal atresia are typically detected soon after birth. The infant may have an unusually large amount of secretions coming from the mouth, or may cough, choke or turn blue when attempting to feed.

Treatment Infants with this condition require surgery. If the underdeveloped segment is short, repair may be attempted immediately. If the segment is long, further growth of the esophagus may be necessary before doing surgery. Until surgery is performed, a tube is temporarily placed through the abdominal wall into the stomach for feeding.

Hirschsprung's disease An infant with Hirschsprung's disease gradually develops an abnormally large (dilated) colon. The condition is due to a failure of the muscles of the colon to propel stool through the anus.

Muscle contractions in the gut help digested materials move through the intestines. Nerves in between the muscle layers synchronize the contractions. In Hirschsprung's disease, these key nerves are missing from a part of the bowel. Areas without such nerves cannot push material through. This causes a blockage of intestinal contents.

Early signs may include a delay of or failure to pass baby's first stool (meconium). Baby may also experience vomiting and abdominal distention. Dehydration and weight loss are also common. Many infants with Hirschsprung's disease have alternating constipation and diarrhea.

Treatment Treatment generally involves surgery to remove the abnormal portion of the intestines. In cases where surgery can't be performed right away, an opening on the outside of the abdomen (stoma) is created so that stool can pass into a disposable pouch. After surgery, most children pass stool normally, but they may need long-term follow-up for constipation and other problems.

Imperforate anus An infant with imperforate anus has not formed an anal opening, preventing passage of stool. The condition may be noticeable during a physical examination, or it may be suspected when a baby fails to pass his or her first stool (meconium) a few hours to days after birth. A child with imperforate anus may have other birth abnormalities.

Treatment Treatment depends on the location of the obstruction. If the anal opening is simply narrowed, an instrument can be used to widen (dilate) the opening. More typically, surgery is necessary. Children with a less complicated obstruction generally do well after surgery and develop normal bowel control. If the obstruction is more complicated, the child may require a series of operations and have long-term challenges with passage of stool.

Intestinal blockage Intestinal atresia is the medical term for an obstruction anywhere in the intestines. The obstruction may be complete — blocking all passage of fluid and intestinal content — or it may be partial.

A high obstruction just beyond the outlet of the stomach or in the upper small intestine can cause persistent vomiting. An obstruction in the lower small intestine or the colon may cause a swollen (distended) abdomen. Vomiting may also occur with a lower obstruction, but it may come later. If a baby has a partial obstruction, symptoms may not be immediately apparent.

An infant with an intestinal obstruction generally doesn't have a bowel movement, although baby's first (meconium) stool may pass if the obstruction is high in the small intestine.

The condition is sometimes associated with certain genetic disorders, including Down syndrome.

Treatment Treatment depends on the type of obstruction. A complete obstruction generally requires immediate surgery. A partial obstruction may also require surgery. Recovery depends on the severity and location of the blockage.

Pyloric stenosis Pyloric stenosis is a condition that affects the muscles of the pylorus, which is at the lower end of the stomach. The muscles of the pylorus (pyloric sphincter) connect the stomach and small intestine.

In pyloric stenosis, the pyloric sphincter becomes abnormally large, causing the lower stomach to narrow. The enlarged muscles block food from entering the baby's small intestine, typically resulting in excessive spitting up or forceful (projectile) vomiting.

Signs of pyloric stenosis usually appear within three to five weeks after birth. The condition is rare in babies older than age 3 months.

In addition to spitting up and vomiting, other signs and symptoms may include persistent hunger — baby always wants to eat, even after vomiting — wave-like stomach contractions, dehydration, constipation or very small stools, and no weight gain or weight loss. Repeated vomiting may irritate baby's stomach and cause mild bleeding. The wave-like contractions are caused by stomach muscles trying to force food past the outlet of the pylorus.

Treatment Pyloric stenosis is generally treated with surgery. During the procedure, the surgeon cuts and spreads apart the outside layer of the thickened pylorus muscles to widen the lower stomach. For a few hours to days after surgery, intravenous (IV) fluids are given until the child can eat. The surgery doesn't increase the risk of future stomach or intestinal problems.

FACIAL AND EXTREMITY DISORDERS

A child is sometimes born with a disorder that's physically apparent. On occa-

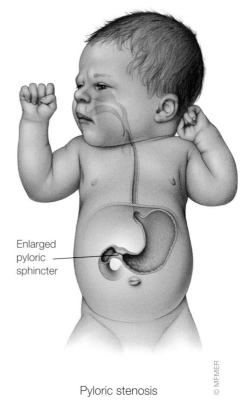

Enlarged pyloric sphincter

© MFMER

Pyloric stenosis

sion, these disorders may involve the face and the hands and feet.

Cleft lip and cleft palate Cleft lip and cleft palate are among the most common birth defects. A cleft is an opening or split in the upper lip, the roof of the mouth (palate) or both. Cleft lip and cleft palate result when developing facial structures in an unborn baby don't completely grow together.

Often, a cleft — or split — in the lip or palate is diagnosed during a prenatal ultrasound exam. Otherwise, it is identifiable immediately at birth. Cleft lip and palate can affect one or both sides of the face. Clefts can appear as only a small notch in the lip or can extend from the lip through the upper gum and palate into the bottom of the nose. Less commonly, a cleft occurs only in the muscles of the soft palate (submucous cleft palate), which are at the back of the mouth and covered by the mouth's lining. Because it's hidden, this type of cleft may not be diagnosed until later.

Researchers believe that most cases of cleft lip and cleft palate are caused by an interaction of genetic and environmental factors. Fetal exposure to cigarette smoke, alcohol, certain medications, illicit drugs and certain viruses have been linked to the development of a cleft. In many babies, however, a definite cause isn't discovered.

Treatment Surgery to correct cleft lip and palate is based on your child's particular defect. Following the initial cleft repair, your doctor may recommend follow-up surgeries to improve speech or improve the appearance of the lip and nose. Surgeries typically are performed in this order:
- *Cleft lip repair.* Between 10 weeks and 3 months of age
- *Cleft palate repair.* Between 6 and 18 months of age
- *Follow-up surgeries.* Between age 2 and late teen years

For children with cleft palate, ear tubes also may be placed during the first surgery to ventilate the middle ear and prevent hearing loss. Your child's surgeon will determine the optimal timing for all needed surgeries.

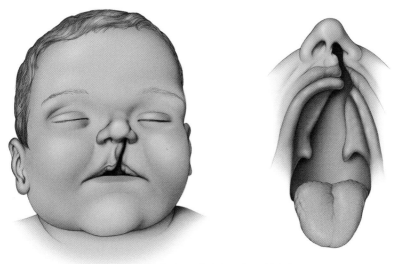

© MFMER

Cleft lip (left) and cleft palate (right)

Clubfoot Clubfoot describes a range of foot abnormalities usually present at birth in which your baby's foot is twisted out of shape or position. The term refers to the way the foot is positioned at a sharp angle to the ankle, like the head of a golf club. Also, the calf muscles in the affected leg are usually underdeveloped, and the affected foot may be slightly shorter than the other foot.

Clubfoot is a relatively common birth defect and is usually an isolated problem for an otherwise healthy newborn. The disorder can be mild or severe, affecting one or both feet. Clubfoot will hinder your child's development once it's time for your child to walk, so treating clubfoot soon after birth, when your newborn's bones and joints are extremely flexible, is generally recommended.

The cause of clubfoot isn't known; however, environmental factors may play a role in causing clubfoot. Studies have strongly linked clubfoot to cigarette smoking during pregnancy, especially when a family history of clubfoot is already present.

Treatment The goal of treatment is to restore the look and function of the foot before your child learns to walk, in hopes of preventing long-term disabilities. Treatment options include stretching and casting or taping the foot. When clubfoot is severe or it doesn't respond to nonsurgical treatments, surgery may be necessary.

Even with treatment, clubfoot may not be totally correctable, but most babies who are treated early grow up to lead normal, active lives.

Finger and toe deformities One of the first things parents often do after a child is born is to count the fingers and toes to make sure they are all there. On rare occasions, the number of fingers — or the number of toes — doesn't add up to 10.

Extra fingers or toes A child may be born with one or more extra digits, such as an extra finger or extra thumb on the hand or extra toes. Often, the extra digit consists only of skin and soft tissue and can easily be removed. If the extra digit contains bone or cartilage, surgery may

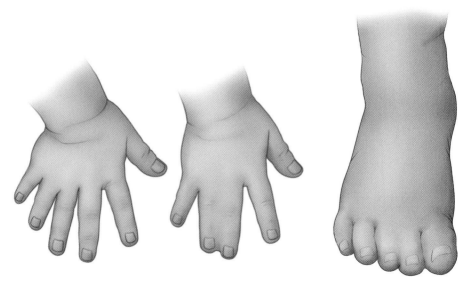

Finger and toe deformities

be necessary. This may be done after the infant is a few months old.

Webbed fingers or toes A child may be born with one or more fingers or toes that are joined ("webbed") together. Simple webbing of fingers or toes involves only the skin and other soft tissues. Occasionally, webbing may involve fused bones, nerves, blood vessels, and tendons. Surgery is advised if the webbing causes problems with appearance, or it impairs use of the fingers or toes.

Hip dysplasia This condition results from abnormal development of the hip joint. The hip is a ball-and-socket joint. In some newborns, the socket is too shallow and the ball (thighbone) may slip out of the socket, either part of the way or completely. Left untreated, the affected leg may turn outward or be shorter than the other leg. Occasionally, both hips are involved.

Hip dysplasia is often detected during an initial examination at birth or in the first weeks to months of life. Girls born breech are at greater risk of hip dysplasia and may require an ultrasound of the hips at about 6 weeks of age.

Treatment Hip dysplasia can be successfully treated. When the condition is diagnosed early, a device or harness is used to keep the legs apart and turned outward (frog-leg position). This device will usually hold the hip joint in place while the child grows. Children who are diagnosed after 6 months of age may need surgery.

GENITAL DISORDERS

Some birth conditions affect the genitals. These conditions are typically diagnosed on physical examination at birth.

Ambiguous genitalia This term refers to the uncertain appearance of a baby's external sexual features. Sometimes, a female with normal ovaries who's been exposed to an excess of male hormones in the womb is born with male-like genitals. Conversely, a male may be born with testicles but with ambiguous or completely female genitals. Some newborns have both ovaries and testicles and ambiguous genitals.

Ambiguous genitals can result from tumors, chromosome abnormalities, other genetic problems, and hormone excesses or deficiencies.

When a newborn's sex is in question, only thorough testing and evaluation can establish a correct diagnosis. Because ambiguous genitalia is an uncommon and complex condition, the baby may be referred to a medical center with doctors who have expertise in disorders of sex development.

Treatment Treatment depends on a variety of factors. It may include hormone therapy or reconstructive surgery.

Hydrocele A hydrocele is a fluid-filled sac surrounding a testicle that results in swelling of the scrotum, the loose bag of skin underneath the penis. Up to 10 percent of male infants have a hydrocele at birth, but most hydroceles disappear without treatment within the first year of life.

Treatment If the testicle can be easily examined and the amount of fluid remains constant, treatment is generally unnecessary. Usually the fluid gets absorbed within a year. If a hydrocele doesn't disappear after a year or if it continues to enlarge, it may need to be surgically removed. Sometimes, a hydrocele may recur.

Hypospadias Hypospadias is a condition in which the opening of the urethra is on the underside of the penis, instead of at the tip. The urethra is the tube through which urine drains from the bladder and exits the body. The severity of the condition varies. In most cases, the opening of the urethra is near the head of the penis. Less often, the opening is at midshaft or at the base of the penis.

You may feel distressed if your son is born with hypospadias. However, the condition is common and it doesn't cause difficulty in caring for your infant.

Treatment Treatment involves surgery to reposition the urethral opening and, if necessary, straighten the shaft of the penis. Rarely, the repair may require two or more surgeries. With successful treatment, most male infants will have normal adult sexual function.

Undescended testicle An undescended testicle is a testicle that hasn't moved into its proper position in the bag of skin hanging beneath the penis (scrotum) prior to the birth of a baby boy. Usually just one testicle is affected, but in some cases both testicles may be undescended. The condition is more common among baby boys born prematurely or before 37 weeks.

Testicles form in the abdomen during fetal development. During the last couple of months of normal fetal development, the testicles gradually leave the abdomen, pass through a tube-like passageway in the groin (inguinal canal) and descend into the scrotum.

If your son has an undescended testicle, that process was stopped or delayed at some stage of development, and the testicle is not where you would expect it to be — it may still be in the abdomen. The disorder is typically detected when your baby is examined shortly after birth.

Treatment The goal of treatment is to move the undescended testicle to its proper location in the scrotum. Early treatment may lower the risk of complications of an undescended testicle, such as the risk of infertility and testicular cancer.

The condition is usually corrected with surgery. The surgeon carefully manipulates the testicle into the scrotum and stitches it into place. When your son has surgery will depend on a number of factors, such as his health and how difficult the procedure might be. Generally, this type of surgery is performed after a child is 3 to 6 months old and before the child is 15 months old.

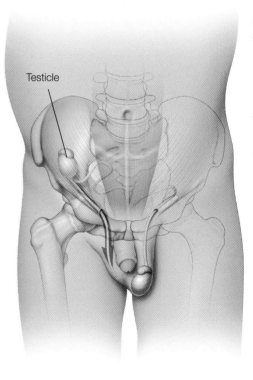

Testicle

Undescended testicle

© MFMER

HEART DISORDERS

Some infants are born with a heart defect — a problem in the heart's structure. These defects range from mild to severe, with most cases being mild. The risk of having a baby with a heart condition may be higher if you have an older child who was born with a heart defect or if other family members have had a baby with a heart defect.

The precise cause of a congenital heart defect is often unknown. Genetic defects and certain viral infections obtained during pregnancy may be possible causes.

Fortunately, with continued advances in heart surgery, many heart disorders can be successfully treated. Some may even heal on their own, without surgery.

Aortic stenosis Aortic stenosis is a narrowing of the valve through which blood leaves the heart to enter the aorta, the main artery carrying blood away from the heart. Because the valve does not fully open, blood flow from the heart is decreased.

Severe stenosis, which may be accompanied by breathing difficulties, is usually detected in early infancy. Mild or moderate stenosis may not produce any noticeable symptoms, but during a physical examination your baby's care provider may detect a distinctive heart murmur.

Treatment Surgery may be needed to treat severe stenosis. It may not be necessary for mild to moderate disease, but your baby should have periodic examinations to monitor the condition to make sure it doesn't worsen.

Atrial septal defect Atrial septal defect is an opening high in the heart between the heart's upper chambers. The opening produces abnormal blood flow and allows oxygen-rich and oxygen-poor blood to mix. If the hole is large and a lot of blood is mixed, the blood that ends up being circulated through your child's body is not carrying as much oxygen as normal. The condition may also cause increased fluid in the lungs. Children with the condition often don't experience any signs or symptoms.

Treatment If the hole is small, no treatment may be necessary. In more severe cases, surgery may be needed to close the hole.

Coarctation of the aorta In this condition, there's a narrowing (constriction) in the main artery carrying blood away from the heart to the rest of the body. The heart may have to pump harder to force blood through the narrowed area and blood pressure above the constricted area may be increased.

Initially, no symptoms may be evident. If the constriction is significantly interfering with blood flow, it may result in pale skin and breathing difficulties.

Treatment In more severe cases, immediate surgery may be necessary to fix the narrowing to increase blood flow. In less severe cases, surgery is still likely, but doesn't need to be done immediately.

Patent ductus arteriosus The ductus arteriosus is a vessel that leads from the pulmonary artery to the aorta while an infant is in the womb. It allows blood to bypass the baby's lungs by connecting the pulmonary arteries (which supply blood to the lungs) with the aorta (which supplies blood to the body). Soon after an infant is born and the lungs fill with air, this blood vessel is no longer needed. It will usually close within a couple of days.

When the ductus arteriosus doesn't close, it causes abnormal blood circulation between the heart and lungs. Babies born prematurely are more at risk of patent ductus arteriosus (PDA) than are those born at term.

When the opening is small, often there are no symptoms. A large opening will produce a heart murmur and may cause pulmonary hypertension and poor growth.

Treatment Often, especially in premature infants, the ductus will close on its own within weeks. If it doesn't, medication or surgery may be used to close the opening. In older infants with a ductus that remains open, surgery or procedures done by cardiac catheterization are used to close the opening.

Pulmonary stenosis Pulmonary stenosis is a condition in which the flow of blood from the heart to the lungs is slowed by a deformed pulmonary valve, or a narrowing above or below the valve. Mild or moderate obstruction may cause no symptoms. A newborn with a severe obstruction may have a bluish skin color (cyanosis) and show signs of heart failure.

Pulmonary stenosis is often diagnosed in childhood, sometimes soon after birth. Your baby's care provider may suspect pulmonary stenosis if he or she hears a heart murmur in the upper left area of the chest during a routine checkup.

Treatment Mild pulmonary stenosis usually doesn't worsen over time, but moderate and severe cases may get worse and require surgery. Fortunately, treatment is highly successful, and most infants with pulmonary stenosis can expect to lead normal lives.

Tetralogy of Fallot Tetralogy of Fallot is the name for a combination of four heart defects that are present at birth. These defects, which affect the structure of the heart, cause oxygen-poor blood to flow out of the heart and into the rest of the body.

Infants and children with tetralogy of Fallot usually have bluish skin color (cyanosis) because their blood doesn't carry enough oxygen. Sometimes, infants with tetralogy of Fallot will suddenly develop deep blue skin color after crying, feeding, having a bowel movement, or kicking his or her legs upon awakening. These episodes are called tet spells and are caused by a rapid drop in the amount of oxygen in the blood.

Tetralogy of Fallot is often diagnosed during infancy or soon after. However, it may not be detected until later in life, depending on the severity of the defects and symptoms.

Treatment All babies with tetralogy of Fallot need corrective surgery. Without treatment, your baby may not grow and develop properly. He or she is also at increased risk of serious complications, such as infective endocarditis, an inflammation of the inner lining of the heart caused by a bacterial infection.

With early diagnosis followed by appropriate treatment, most children with tetralogy of Fallot live relatively normal lives, though they'll need regular medical care and may have restrictions on exercise.

Transposition of the great vessels This is a complex condition in which the two arteries rising from the heart — the aorta and the pulmonary artery — are reversed. Because of this, blood returning to the heart from the body is pumped back to the body without ever going through the lungs to pick up oxygen. Newborns with this condition are often very dusky blue in color and require intensive immediate medical care within the first hours to days after birth.

Treatment A surgery called an arterial switch procedure is used to permanently correct the problem; however, not all babies have anatomy suitable for this procedure. The surgery switches the great arteries back to the normal position. Most infants who undergo arterial switch don't have symptoms after surgery and live normal lives. A medical team will determine the best approach for surgery.

Ventricular septal defect A ventricular septal defect (VSD), also called a hole in the heart, is a common heart defect that's present at birth. It occurs when the septum, the muscular wall separating the heart into left and right sides, fails to form fully between the lower chambers of the heart during fetal development. This leaves an opening that allows mixing of "red" (oxygenated) blood and "blue" (deoxygenated) blood. As a result, blood may overfill the lungs and overwork the heart.

A baby with a small ventricular septal defect may have no problems. A baby with a larger ventricular septal defect may have a bluish skin color — due to oxygen-poor blood — often most visible in the lips and fingernails. Other signs and symptoms may include rapid breathing, a poor appetite and failure to gain weight.

A ventricular septal defect at birth typically doesn't cause problems in early infancy. If the defect is small, symptoms may not appear until later in childhood — if ever. Signs and symptoms vary depending on the size of the hole. The condition may be diagnosed during a regular checkup. While listening to your baby's heart with a stethoscope, a care provider may detect a distinctive heart murmur.

Treatment Many babies born with a small ventricular septal defect don't ever need surgery to close the defect. After birth, your doctor may want to observe your baby and treat any symptoms while waiting to see if the defect closes on its own. Infants who have a ventricular septal defect that's large or is causing significant symptoms usually require surgery. Surgical treatment generally produces excellent long-term results.

OTHER DISORDERS

Two other disorders that can affect a newborn include cystic fibrosis and intrauterine growth restiction.

Cystic fibrosis Cystic fibrosis is an inherited condition that affects the cells that produce mucus, sweat and digestive juices. Normally, these secretions are thin and slippery, but in cystic fibrosis, a defective gene causes the secretions to become thick and sticky. Instead of acting as a lubricant, the secretions plug up tubes, ducts and passageways, especially in the pancreas and lungs.

Signs and symptoms can vary from child to child, depending on the severity of the disease. Even in the same child, symptoms may worsen or improve as time passes. In some children, symptoms begin during infancy. Other children may not experience symptoms until adolescence or adulthood.

One of the first signs of cystic fibrosis is an excessively salty taste to the skin. People with cystic fibrosis tend to have higher than normal amounts of salt in their sweat. Parents often can taste the salt when they kiss their child.

Most of the other signs and symptoms of cystic fibrosis affect the respiratory system or the digestive system. The thick and sticky mucus associated with cystic fibrosis clogs the tubes that carry air in and out of the lungs. This can cause a persistent cough, wheezing, and repeated lung and sinus infections. The thick mucus can also block tubes that carry digestive enzymes from the pancreas to the small intestine. Without these digestive enzymes, the intestines can't fully absorb the nutrients in the food. The result is foul-smelling and greasy stools, poor weight gain and growth, a distended abdomen from constipation, and intestinal blockage, particularly in newborns.

Within the past decade, most states have begun to routinely screen newborns for cystic fibrosis. This test checks a blood sample for a particular component that's commonly elevated in babies who have cystic fibrosis. Other tests are needed to confirm the diagnosis.

Treatment There's no cure for cystic fibrosis, but treatments can ease symptoms and reduce complications. Treatment generally includes medications and therapy.

Infants with cystic fibrosis may be given medications to treat infection, break up mucus in the lungs, and reduce lung inflammation. A child may also receive enzyme supplements with each meal to help his or her body absorb food.

To help loosen mucus in the lungs, a parent or caregiver may need to thump the baby's chest with a cupped hand. This often needs to be done a couple of times each day for about 30 minutes each time. There are also electronic devices that can perform this task.

In the past, most children with cystic fibrosis died in their teens. Improved screening and treatments now allow many children with cystic fibrosis to live into their 50s or even longer.

Intrauterine growth restriction A baby who is born full term but weighs less than 5 pounds, 8 ounces is often referred to as being at a low birth weight. The medical term for this condition is intrauterine growth restriction, or IUGR.

Intrauterine growth restriction refers to the poor growth of a baby while in the mother's womb during pregnancy. Specifically, it means the developing baby weighs less than 90 percent of other babies at the same gestational age.

Intrauterine growth restriction can result from a variety of genetic, metabolic and environmental influences. Congenital or chromosomal abnormalities are often associated with below-normal weight. Infections during pregnancy may affect the weight of the developing baby. A placenta that's particularly small or isn't functioning normally also can result in a growth-restricted baby.

After birth, the growth and development of a low birth weight baby is generally influenced by the severity and cause of the condition. Many IUGR babies see improvement in growth during the first months after birth. However, some babies continue to experience slow growth despite ample nutrition.

Treatment A baby born at a low birth weight may have to stay in the hospital longer than normal, until he or she gains sufficient weight and other problems are resolved, such as jaundice or maintenance of normal body temperature. Babies with IUGR may need specific nutritional supplements and assistance with feeding until they are growing well.

A baby with IUGR may have trouble fitting safely in a car seat. Some infants need to be transported in a crash-safe car bed until they grow large enough for a regular infant car seat.

Additional Resources

If you're looking for additional information on a particular topic, you may find the following resources helpful.

AMERICAN ACADEMY OF PEDIATRICS
847-434-4000
www.aap.org

CENTERS FOR DISEASE CONTROL AND PREVENTION
800-232-4636
www.cdc.gov

CHILD CARE AWARE
800-424-2246
www.childcareaware.org

INTERNATIONAL LACTATION CONSULTANT ASSOCIATION
919-861-5577
www.ilca.org

LA LECHE LEAGUE INTERNATIONAL
800-525-3243
www.llli.org

MAYO CLINIC HEALTH INFORMATION
www.MayoClinic.com

NATIONAL CAPITAL POISON CENTER
Poison Help hotline: 800-222-1222
www.poison.org

NATIONAL CENTER FOR FATHERING
800-593-3237
www.fathers.com

NATIONAL CENTER ON BIRTH DEFECTS AND DEVELOPMENTAL DISABILITIES
800-232-4636
www.cdc.gov/ncbddd

NATIONAL DISSEMINATION CENTER FOR CHILDREN WITH DISABILITIES
800-695-0285
nichcy.org/families-community/new-to-disability

NATIONAL DOWN SYNDROME SOCIETY
800-221-4602
www.ndss.org

NATIONAL FATHERHOOD INITIATIVE
301-948-0599
www.fatherhood.org

**NATIONAL INSTITUTE OF CHILD HEALTH
& HUMAN DEVELOPMENT**
800-370-2943
www.nichd.nih.gov

**NATIONAL ORGANIZATION OF MOTHERS
OF TWINS CLUBS INC.**
248-231-4480
www.nomotc.org

**NATIONAL WOMEN'S HEALTH INFORMATION
CENTER BREASTFEEDING HELPLINE**
800-994-9662
www.womenshealth.gov/breastfeeding

PATHWAYS.ORG
800-955-2445
www.pathways.org
friends@pathways.org

**U.S. CONSUMER PRODUCT SAFETY
COMMISSION**
800-638-2772
www.cpsc.gov

U.S. FOOD AND DRUG ADMINISTRATION
888-463-6332
www.fda.gov

Index

not introducing too soon, 200
off-limits, 71–72
pureed meat, vegetables and fruits, 70
stools and, 269
taste and texture, 70–71
soy-based formulas, 61
speech development, typical, 518
spina bifida, 540–541
spitting up, 67–69
spoiling, 26, 238
sponge baths, 89–90
spoons, 267, 310
stairs, getting up/down, 340
standing, 259, 308, 318, 328–329, 340
startle reflex, 226
states of consciousness, 230
stay-at-home dads (SAHDs), 425
stepping reflex, 226
sties, 388
stimulation, 285, 315
stomach flu (gastroenteritis), 386–388
stools, 82–84, 269
stranger anxiety, 263, 293
stress, handling, 404–405
strollers, 187
accessories, 187
double, 499–500
newborns and, 186–187
safety tips, 187
short trips, 283
in travel system, 187
use of, 186
stuffed animals, 290
suckling, 225, 226
sudden infant death syndrome (SIDS),
117–119, 510
sun, 103, 184
sunburn, 388–389
sunscreen, 103
supervision, 312
support
adopted baby, 481–484
breast-feeding, 52
dads/partners, 427, 444
delayed development baby, 523
Down syndrome baby, 533
multiples, 501
parenting, 404, 405
work and, 469
swallowed poison, 216–217
swim diapers, 76

T

tantrums, 344–345
taste, 227, 247
teary eyes, 390–391
teeth
caring for, 279
first, 391
formation, 391
month 6, 277–279
teething
recognizing, 391
seriousness of, 391
signs and symptoms, 277–278
tips for soothing, 278–279, 391–392
See also illnesses/conditions
temperament
activity, 136, 139
adaptability, 137, 140
as colic cause, 129
curiosity, 139
distractibility, 138, 141
frustration, 140
inborn traits, 136–138
initial approach, 137
intensity, 137, 140
interaction with, 143
irregular body rhythms, 140
mood, 137
in newborns, 138
parenting and, 141–143
persistence, 138, 139
quiet, 140
regularity, 136–137
sensitivity, 137, 141
surroundings and, 135–136
understanding, 135–143
working with, 138–141
temperature, taking, 350–351
tetanus vaccination, 167
tetralogy of Fallot, 549
thermometers, 350
thrush, 101, 105, 392–394
time, relishing, 22
timetables, caution, 251
toes
deformities, 545–546
discovery of, 280
tonic neck reflex, 226
touch
month 1, 227
month 6, 281

HOUSECALL

What our readers are saying ...

"I depend on Mayo Clinic Housecall more than any other medical info that shows up on my computer. Thank you so very much."

"Excellent newsletter. I always find something interesting to read and learn something new."

"Housecall is a must read - keep up the good work!"

"I love Housecall. It is one of the most useful, trusted and beneficial things that comes from the Internet."

"The Housecall is timely, interesting and invaluable in its information. Thanks much to Mayo Clinic for this resource!"

"I enjoy getting the weekly newsletters. They provide me with friendly reminders, as well as information/conditions I was not aware of."

Get the latest health information direct from Mayo Clinic. Sign up today ... it's FREE!

Mayo Clinic Housecall is a FREE weekly e-newsletter that offers the latest health information from the experts at Mayo Clinic. Stay up to date on topics that are current, interesting, and most of all important to your health and the health of your family.

What you get
- Weekly featured topics
- Answers from the experts
- Quick access to our Symptom Checker
- Healthy recipes with nutritional values listed
- Videos and slide shows
- Health Tip of the Week
- And much more!

Don't Wait ... Join Today!

http://www.mayoclinic.com/health/housecall/housecall

MAYO
CLINIC

If one doctor can light the way,

imagine the power of an entire team.

At Mayo Clinic, a team of experts works together for you. No wonder Mayo Clinic's collective knowledge and innovative treatments have been a shining light to millions around the world. Visit mayoclinic.org/connect to learn from others who've been there.

MAYO
CLINIC

PHOENIX/SCOTTSDALE, ARIZONA | ROCHESTER, MINNESOTA | JACKSONVILLE, FLORIDA

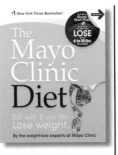

FEVER
AT DAWN

PÉTER GÁRDOS

Translated from the Hungarian
by Elizabeth Szász

BLACK SWAN

TRANSWORLD PUBLISHERS
61–63 Uxbridge Road, London W5 5SA
www.penguin.co.uk

Transworld is part of the Penguin Random House group of companies
whose addresses can be found at global.penguinrandomhouse.com

Penguin
Random House
UK

Originally published in Hungary by Libri Kiado in 2015
First English-language edition published in Australia by Text Publishing in 2016

First published in Great Britain in 2016 by Doubleday
an imprint of Transworld Publishers
Black Swan edition published 2017

Fever at Dawn is a work of fiction. In some cases true life figures appear but their
actions and conversations are largely fictitious. All other characters, and all names
of places and descriptions of events, are the products of the author's imagination
and any resemblance to actual persons or places is entirely coincidental.

Every effort has been made to obtain the necessary permissions with
reference to copyright material, both illustrative and quoted. We apologize
for any omissions in this respect and will be pleased to make the
appropriate acknowledgements in any future edition.

A CIP catalogue record for this book
is available from the British Library.

ISBN
9781784161408

Typeset in Electra
Printed and bound by Clays Ltd, Bungay, Suffolk.

Penguin Random House is committed to a sustainable
future for our business, our readers and our planet. This book
is made from Forest Stewardship Council® certified paper.

1 3 5 7 9 10 8 6 4 2

FEVER AT DAWN

One

MY FATHER, Miklós, sailed to Sweden on a rainy summer's day three weeks after the Second World War ended. He was twenty-five years old. An angry north wind lashed the Baltic Sea into a three-metre swell, and he lay on the lower deck while the ship plunged and bucked. Around him, passengers clung desperately to their straw mattresses.

They had been at sea for less than an hour when Miklós was taken ill. He began to cough up bloody foam, and then he started to wheeze so loudly that he almost drowned out the waves pounding the hull. He was one of the more serious cases, parked in the first row right next to the swing door. Two sailors picked up his skeletal body and carried him into a nearby cabin.

The doctor didn't hesitate. There was no time for pain-killers. Relying on luck to hit the right spot between two ribs, he stuck a large needle into my father's chest. Half a litre of fluid drained from his lungs. When the aspirator arrived, the doctor swapped the needle for a plastic tube and siphoned off another litre and a half of mucus.

Miklós felt better.

When the captain learned that the doctor had saved a passenger's life, he granted the sick man a special favour: he had him wrapped in a thick blanket and taken out to sit on the deck. Heavy clouds were gathering over the granite water. The captain, impeccable in his uniform, stood beside Miklós's deckchair.

'Do you speak German?' he asked.

'Yes.'

'Congratulations on your survival.'

In different circumstances, this conversation might have led somewhere. But Miklós was in no state to chat. It was all he could do to acknowledge the situation.

'I'm alive.'

The captain looked him up and down. My father's ashen skin was stretched over his skull, and there were ugly warts on his face. His pupils were magnified by his glasses, and his mouth was a dark yawning void. He virtually hadn't a tooth to call his own. I'm not quite sure why. Maybe three burly louts had beaten his scrawny frame to a pulp in an air-raid shelter lit by a naked bulb swinging from the ceiling. Maybe one of these thugs had grabbed a flat iron and used it over and over to bash Miklós in the face. According to the official version, which was rather short on detail, most of his teeth had been knocked out in the prison on Margit Street in Budapest in 1944, when he was arrested as a deserter from a Jewish forced-labour unit.

But now he was alive. And despite the slight whistle when he took a breath his lungs were dutifully processing the crisp salty air.

The captain peered through his telescope. 'We're docking in Malmö for five minutes.'

This didn't really mean anything to Miklós. He was one of 224 concentration-camp survivors who were being shipped from Lübeck in Germany to Stockholm. Some of them were in such bad shape that they wanted nothing more than to survive the journey. A few minutes in Malmö was neither here nor there.

The captain, however, continued to explain the decision, as if to a superior. 'The order came over the radio. This stop wasn't part of my itinerary.'

The ship's horn sounded as the docks of Malmö harbour became visible in the mist. A flock of seagulls circled.

The ship moored at the end of the pier. Two sailors disembarked and started jogging along the pier. Between them they carried a big empty basket—the kind washerwomen use to haul wet laundry up to the attic to hang out.

A crowd of women on bicycles was waiting at the approach to the pier. There must have been fifty of them, motionless and silent, gripping their handlebars. Many wore black headscarves.

They looked like ravens perched on a branch. It was only when the sailors reached the barrier that Miklós noticed the parcels and baskets hanging from the handlebars.

He felt the captain's hand on his shoulder. 'Some mad rabbi by the name of Kronheim dreamed this up,' the captain explained. 'He placed an ad in the papers saying that you people were arriving on this ship. He even managed to arrange for us to dock here.'

Each of the women dropped her parcel into the big laundry basket. One standing slightly back let go of her handlebars and her bicycle fell over. From where he sat on deck, Miklós heard the clang of the metal on the cobblestones. Given the length of the pier, this is quite inconceivable, yet whenever my father told this story he always included the clang.

Once they had collected all the packages, the sailors jogged back to the ship. This scene remained fixed in Miklós's mind: an improbably empty pier, the sailors running with the basket, and in the background the strange motionless army of women and their bicycles.

The parcels contained biscuits that these nameless women had baked to celebrate the arrival of the survivors in Sweden. As my father tasted the soft, buttery pastry in his toothless mouth, he could detect vanilla and raspberry, flavours so unfamiliar after years of camp food that he almost had to relearn them.

'Sweden welcomes you,' grunted the captain, as he turned away to give orders. The ship was already heading out to sea.

Miklós sat savouring his biscuits. High among the clouds, a

biplane drew away, dipping its wings in salute. When he saw it, my father began to feel he was truly alive.

~

By the end of the first week in July 1945, Miklós was in a crowded sixteen-bed hospital ward, a barracks-like wooden hut in a remote village called Lärbro on the island of Gotland. Propped up against a pillow, he was writing a letter. Sunlight poured through the window and nurses in crisply starched blouses, white bonnets and long linen skirts darted between the beds.

He had beautiful handwriting: shapely letters, elegant loops and just a hair's breadth between each word. When he finished his letter he put it in an envelope, sealed it and leaned it against the jug of water on his bedside table. Two hours later a nurse called Katrin picked it up and dropped it in the postbox with the other patients' mail.

Miklós rarely got out of his hospital bed, but two weeks after writing his letter he was allowed to sit out in the corridor. Each morning the post was handed out, and one day a letter came for him—straight from the Swedish Office for Refugees. It contained the names and addresses of 117 women, all of them young Hungarians whom nurses and doctors were trying to bring back to life in various temporary hospitals across Sweden. Miklós transcribed their details into a thin exercise book with square-ruled paper he had found somewhere.

By this time he had recovered from the dramatic pronouncement he had received a few days earlier.

~

Pressed against the X-ray machine, Miklós had done his best not to move. Dr Lindholm shouted at him from the other room. The doctor was a gangling figure, at least six foot six tall, and he spoke a funny sort of Hungarian. All his long vowels sounded the same, as if he were blowing up a balloon. He had run the Lärbro hospital—now temporarily enlarged to accommodate the intake of camp survivors—for the last dozen years. His wife, Márta, a tiny woman whom Miklós reckoned couldn't be more than four foot six, was a nurse and worked in the hospital too; she was Hungarian, which explained why the doctor tackled the language with such bravado.

'You hold breath! No frisking!' he bellowed.

A click and a hum—the X-ray was ready. Miklós relaxed his shoulders.

Dr Lindholm walked over and stood beside him, gazing with compassion at a point slightly above his head. Miklós was slumped, his sunken chest naked against the machine, as if he never wanted to get dressed again. His glasses had steamed up.

'What you say you occupied with, Miklós?' the doctor asked.

'I was a journalist. And poet.'

'Ah! Engineer of the soul. Very good.'

Miklós shifted from one foot to the other. He was cold.

'Dress. Why you stand around?'

Miklós shuffled over to the corner of the room and pulled on his pyjama jacket. 'Is there a problem?' he asked the doctor.

Lindholm still didn't look at him. He started walking towards his office, waving at Miklós to follow him. He was muttering, almost to himself, 'Is a problem.'

Erik Lindholm's office looked onto the garden. On these warm midsummer evenings the island glittered in a bronze light that bathed the countryside. The dark furniture radiated comfort and safety.

Miklós sat in a leather armchair. Opposite him, on the other side of the desk, sat Dr Lindholm. He had changed into a smart waistcoat. He was flicking anxiously through Miklós's medical reports. He switched on the sea-green glass desk lamp, though there was no real need for it.

'How much you weigh now, Miklós?'

'Forty-seven kilos.'

'You see. It works like a clock.'

As a result of Dr Lindholm's strict diet, Miklós had gained eighteen kilos in only a few weeks. My father kept buttoning and unbuttoning his pyjama jacket, which was far too big for him.

'What temperature you have this morning?'

'Thirty-eight point two.'

Dr Lindholm put the reports down on his desk. 'I won't beat away the bush any longer. Is that what they say? You are quite strong now to face facts.'

Miklós smiled. Almost all his teeth were made of a

7

palladium-based metal alloy that was acid-resistant, cheap and ugly. The day after he'd arrived in Lärbro, a dentist had come to see him. He took moulds of his mouth and warned him that the temporary plate he was getting would be more practical than aesthetic. In a trice the dentist had fitted the metal into his mouth.

Although Miklós's smile was anything but heart-warming, Dr Lindholm forced himself to look directly at him.

'I come straight at the point,' he said. 'It is easier. Six months. You have six months to live, Miklós.' He picked up an X-ray and held it to the light. 'Look. Come closer.'

Miklós obligingly stood up and hunched over the desk. Dr Lindholm's slender fingers roamed over the contoured landscape of the X-ray.

'Here, here, here and here. You see, Miklós? See these patches? This is your tuberculosis. Permanent damage. Nothing to be done about them, I'm afraid. Terrible thing, I have to say. In everyday words, the illness…gobbles the lungs. Can one say "gobble" in Hungarian?'

They stared at the X-ray. Miklós held himself up against the desk. He wasn't feeling very strong, but he managed a nod, thus confirming that the doctor had found a way through the tangle of his language. 'Gobble' was accurate enough to show what the future had in store for him; he didn't need technical terminology. After all, his father had owned a bookshop in Debrecen before the war. It was housed in Gambrinus Court in the Bishop's Palace, under the arcades, a few minutes' walk from the main square. The shop was named Gambrinus Booksellers and consisted of three narrow, high-ceilinged rooms. In one room you could also buy stationery, and there was a lending library too. As a teenager Miklós would perch on top of the high wooden ladder and read books from all over the world—so he could certainly appreciate Lindholm's poetic turn of phrase.

Dr Lindholm continued to stare into my father's eyes. 'As matters stand,' he explained, 'medical science says that you are too gone to come back. There will be good days. And bad ones. I will always be next to you. But I don't want to lead you up the path. You have six months. Seven at most. My heart is heavy, but that is the truth.'

Miklós straightened up, smiling, and then flopped back into the roomy armchair. He seemed almost cheerful. The doctor wasn't quite sure that he had understood or even heard the diagnosis. But Miklós was thinking of things far more important than his health.

Two

TWO DAYS after this conversation Miklós was allowed out for
short walks in the beautiful hospital garden. He sat on one of
the benches in the shade of a big tree with spreading branches.
He rarely looked up. He wrote letter after letter, in pencil, in
that attractive looping hand of his, using the hardcover Swedish
edition of a novel by Martin Andersen Nexø as a desk. Miklós
admired Nexø's political views and the silent courage of the
workers in his books. Perhaps he remembered that the famous
Danish author had also suffered from tuberculosis. Miklós wrote
swiftly, placing a stone on the finished letters to stop the wind
blowing them away.

The next day he knocked on Dr Lindholm's door. He was determined to charm the good doctor with his frankness. He needed his help.

At this time of day it was Dr Lindholm's custom to talk to his patients while seated on his sofa. He sat at one end in his white coat, while Miklós sat at the other end in his pyjamas.

The doctor fingered the stack of envelopes with surprise. 'Is not in tradition to ask patients who they write to and why. And not curiosity now that…' he mumbled.

'I know,' said Miklós. 'But I definitely want to let you in on this.'

'And there are 117 envelopes here? I congratulate you for diligence.' Dr Lindholm raised his arm as if he were gauging the weight of the letters. 'I ask the nurse to buy stamps for them,' he said obligingly. 'Always feel free to apply me for help in any financial matter.'

Miklós nonchalantly crossed his pyjama-clad legs, and grinned. 'All women.'

Dr Lindholm raised an eyebrow. 'Is that so?'

'Or rather, young women,' my father corrected. 'Hungarian girls. From the Debrecen region. That's where I was born.'

'I see,' said the doctor.

But he didn't. He hadn't a clue what Miklós intended with that pile of letters. He gave my father a sympathetic look—after all, this was a man who had been sentenced to death.

'A few weeks ago,' Miklós went on eagerly, 'I made an enquiry about women survivors convalescing in Sweden who were born in or near Debrecen. Only those under thirty!'

'In hospitals? My God!'

They both knew that in addition to Lärbro there were a number of rehabilitation centres operating in Sweden. Miklós sat up straight. He was proud of his strategy. 'And there are loads of girls in them,' he went on excitedly. 'Here's the list of names.'

He took the sheet of paper out of his pocket and, blushing, handed it to Dr Lindholm. The names had been carefully assessed. He'd put a cross, a tick or a small triangle beside each one.

'Aha! You look for acquaintances,' exclaimed Dr Lindholm. 'I'm in favour of that.'

'You're mistaken,' said Miklós with a wink and a smile. 'I'm looking for a wife. I'd like to get married!'

At last it was out.

Dr Lindholm frowned. 'It seems, my dear Miklós, that I did not speak myself clearly the other day.'

'You did, you did,' Miklós reassured him.

'The language is against me! Six months. Is all you have left. You know, when a doctor must say something like this, is dreadful.'

'I understood you perfectly, Dr Lindholm,' said Miklós.

They sat in uncomfortable silence, each on his end of the sofa. Dr Lindholm was trying to work out whether he should lecture someone who had been sentenced to death. Was it his job to beg his patient to think sensibly? Miklós was wondering whether it was worth trying to persuade Dr Lindholm, with all his experience, to look on the bright side of things. The upshot was they left each other in peace.

That afternoon Miklós got into bed as prescribed and lay back on his pillows. It was four o'clock—nap time. Some of the patients in his hut were asleep, and others were playing cards. His friend Harry was practising the trickiest part of the last movement of a romantic sonata on his violin, over and over, with aggravating zeal.

Miklós was sticking stamps on his 117 envelopes. He licked and stuck, licked and stuck. When his mouth became dry he took a sip from the glass of water on his bedside table. He must have felt that Harry's violin was an appropriate accompaniment to this activity. The 117 letters could have been written with carbon paper. They were identical except for one thing—the name of the addressee.

~

Did Miklós ever wonder what these girls might feel when they opened the envelopes addressed to them? What did they think when they took out the letters and began to read his neat, swirling handwriting?

Oh, those girls! Sitting on the edges of their beds, on garden benches, in the corners of disinfected corridors, in front of thickened glass windows, stopping for a moment on worn staircases, under spreading lime trees, on the banks of minia-ture lakes, leaning against cold yellow tiles. Did my father see them in his mind's eye as they unfolded the letters in their nightdresses or in the pale grey uniforms they wore in the rehabilitation centres? Confused at first, later smiling perhaps, heartbeat accelerating, skimming the lines over and over in astonishment.

> Dear Nora, Dear Erzsébet, Dear Lili, Dear Zsuzsa, Dear Sára, Dear Seréna, Dear Ágnes, Dear Giza, Dear Baba, Dear Katalin, Dear Judit, Dear Gabriella…
>
> You are probably used to strangers chatting you up when you speak Hungarian, for no better reason than they are Hungarian too. We men can be so bad-mannered. For example, I addressed you by your first name on the pretext that we grew up in the same town. I don't know whether you already know me from Debrecen. Until my homeland ordered me to 'volunteer' for forced labour, I worked for the *Independent* newspaper, and my father owned a bookshop in Gambrinus Court.
>
> Judging by your name and age, I have a feeling that I might know you. Did you by any chance ever live in Gambrinus Court?
>
> Excuse me for writing in pencil, but I'm confined to bed for a few days on doctor's orders, and we're not allowed to use ink in bed.

~

Lili Reich was one of the 117 women who received a letter. She was an eighteen-year-old patient at the Smålandsstenar rehabilitation hospital. It was early September. She opened the envelope and scanned its contents. The young man from distant Lärbro did have lovely handwriting. But he must have mixed her up with someone else. She promptly forgot the whole thing.

Besides, she was terribly excited about her own plans. A few days earlier she and her two new girlfriends, Sára Stern and Judit Gold, had decided to put an end to the grey days of slow recuperation and set their hearts on staging an evening of Hungarian music in the hospital hall.

Lili had studied piano for eight years, Sára had sung in a choir and Judit had taken dance lessons. Judit had a large, pale face with fine dark hairs above her thin, rather severe lips. Quite the opposite of Sára, who was blonde and light boned with narrow shoulders and shapely legs. Two other girls, Erika Friedmann and Gitta Pláner, joined in just for fun. They banged out three copies of the thirty-minute program on the typewriter in the doctors' room and pinned them up around the hospital. On the night of the performance, the creaky wooden chairs in the hall filled with patients and curious visitors from the nearby village of Smålandsstenar.

The concert was a resounding success. After the last piece, a lively Hungarian dance, the *csárdás*, the audience gave the five blushing girls a standing ovation.

As she ran offstage, Lili felt a sudden unbearable pain in her stomach. She hunched over, pressing her hand to her belly, moaning. And then she lay down; her forehead was bathed in sweat.

'What's the matter, Lili?' asked Sára, who had become her closest friend, crouching down beside her.

'It hurts dreadfully,' she said, and passed out.

Lili couldn't remember being put in the ambulance. She could only recall Sára's blurry face saying something she couldn't hear.

Later, she would often think that without this pain, which had something to do with her kidneys, she might never have met Miklós. If that hulking white ambulance hadn't taken her to the military hospital more than a hundred kilometres away in Eksjö; if, when she came to visit, Judit hadn't brought Miklós's letter, along with her toothbrush and diary; if, on that visit, Judit hadn't persuaded her, against all common sense, to write a few words to the nice young man (for the sake of humanity if nothing else); that's where the story would have ended.

But as it happened, on one of those interminable hospital evenings, once the noise filtering in from the corridor and the clanging of the old-fashioned lift with its grating doors had ebbed away and the bulb above her bed was casting a pale light onto her blanket, Lili took a sheet of paper and, after a bit of thought, started to write.

> Dear Miklós,
>   I'm unlikely to be the person you were thinking of, because, though I was born in Debrecen, I lived in Budapest from the age of one. Nonetheless, I've

> thought a lot about you. Your friendly letter was so
> comforting that I would be happy for you to write
> again.

That was a half-truth, of course. Confined to bed with a strange new illness, out of fear, by way of escape or just to stave off boredom, Lili allowed herself to daydream.

> As for myself, neatly ironed trousers or a smart haircut
> don't do anything. What touches me is the value
> inside someone.

~

Miklós had grown a little stronger. He could now walk into town with Harry. Each of the patients received five kronor a week pocket money. There were two cake shops in Lärbro. One of them had small round marble tables just like a café in Hungary. On the way there, Miklós and Harry ran into Kristin, a plump Swedish hairdresser, and Harry urged her to join them. So now the three of them were sitting at a marble table in a corner of the cake shop. Kristin was politely eating apple pie with a fork. The men each had a glass of soda water. They were speaking German, because the Hungarians were only just getting used to the melodic Swedish language.

'You are two very nice guys,' declared Kristin, the sugar from the icing trembling on her pale moustache. 'Where were you born exactly?'

Miklós sat up. 'In Hajdúnánás,' he boasted, as if he had uttered a magic word.

'And I was born in Sajószentpéter,' said Harry.

Kristin naturally attempted the impossible—to repeat what she'd heard. It sounded as if she were gargling. 'Haydu…nana… Sayu…sent…peter…'

They laughed. Kristin nibbled her apple pie. This gave Harry time to think up a joke. He was good at jokes.

'What did Adam say to Eve when they first met?' he asked.

So keen was Kristin to work out the answer that she forgot to chew. Harry waited a bit, then stood up, miming that he was now stark naked.

'Please, my lady, stand aside, because I'm not sure how much this thingamajig will grow!' he declared, pointing down towards his fly.

Kristin didn't understand at first, but then she blushed.

Miklós felt ashamed and took a sip of his soda. Harry, though, was just getting started.

'Here's another one,' he blurted. 'The lady of the house asked the new chambermaid if her references were good. The chambermaid nodded. "Yes, madam, they were satisfied with me everywhere." "Can you cook?" The chambermaid nodded. "Do you like children?" The chambermaid nodded. "Yes, I do, but it's better when the master of the house is careful."'

Kristin giggled. Harry grabbed her hand and kissed it fervently. Kristin was about to remove her hand, but Harry had a tight grip and she decided not to resist for a moment or two.

Miklós took another sip of soda and looked away.

Then Kristin freed herself and got up, smoothing her skirt. 'I'm off to the ladies' room,' she announced, walking demurely across the café.

Harry switched to Hungarian right away. 'She only lives two blocks away.'

'How d'you know?'

'She said so. Don't you listen?'

'She likes you.'

'You, too.'

'For all I care,' replied Miklós, giving Harry a stern look.

'You haven't been in a café for years. You haven't seen a naked woman for years.'

'What's that got to do with it?' asked Miklós.

'At last we can get out of the hospital. We should start living!'

Kristin was now sashaying back to the table.

'What do you say to a sandwich?' whispered Harry, still in Hungarian.

'What sort of sandwich?'

'The two of us and her. Kristin in the middle.'

'Leave me out of it.'

Harry switched to German, almost in the same breath, and began to stroke Kristin's ankle under the table. 'I've been telling Miklós that I've fallen head over heels for you, dear Kristin. Do I have any chance?'

Kristin put a warning finger coquettishly on Harry's mouth.

~

Kristin rented a tiny flat on the third floor of a building in Nysvägen Street. The low rumble of traffic filtered in through the open window. She sat on the bed so that Harry could get to her more easily. The first test she set him was to mend a tear in the strap of her bra. 'Are you finished yet?' she asked, monitoring the process in the mirror.

'Not quite. It'd be easier if you took it off.'

'I wouldn't dream of it.'

'You're torturing me.'

'That's the point. You should suffer. Restrain yourself. Do a bit of housework,' replied Kristin, giggling.

Harry finished at last, breaking the thread off with his teeth. Kristin went over to the mirror, turning around and fingering the mended strap.

Harry grew redder and redder. Then he hugged her and clumsily tried to undo the bra. 'I can cook, do the washing, scrub. I am a workhorse,' he whispered.

By way of an answer Kristin kissed him.

~

When Harry came back an hour later, he found Miklós at the same marble table in the corner of the café. He was writing a letter and didn't even look up when Harry flopped down beside him. The tip of his pencil seemed to glide over the white paper. Harry gave a deep dejected sigh.

When at last Miklós raised his head, he showed no surprise

at Harry's dismal expression.

'Aren't you in love any more?'

Harry swigged the remains of the soda in Miklós's glass. 'In love? I'm a wreck.'

'What happened?'

'She made me mend her bra. Then I undressed her. Her skin was so silky and firm!'

'Good. Now don't interrupt me, I've got to finish this,' said Miklós, returning to his letter.

Harry envied the way that Miklós could cut himself off from everything with the merest flick of his finger. 'But *I* wasn't firm. It doesn't work,' he muttered. 'It simply doesn't work.'

Miklós kept writing. 'What doesn't work?'

'I don't. And I used to do it five times a day. I could walk up and down with a bucket of water hanging from it.'

'Hanging from what?' Miklós enquired, biting the end of his pencil.

'Right now…a slug hangs between my legs. Soft, white and useless.'

Miklós found the right word. He smiled to himself and wrote it down, satisfied. Now he could comfort Harry.

'That's quite normal. Without feelings it doesn't work.'

Harry was chewing the side of his mouth in irritation. He slid the letter across the table and started to read. '"Dear Lili, I am twenty-five—"'

Miklós snatched at the letter. There was a brief tug of war, which Miklós won. He thrust the letter into his pocket.

Dear Lili,

I am twenty-five. I used to be a journalist until the First Jewish Law got me thrown out of my job.

Miklós had a special gift for poetic licence. The truth was that he had been a journalist for exactly eight and a half days. He was taken on at the Debrecen *Independent* on a Monday, more as messenger boy on the police rounds than an actual journalist. It was the worst possible moment. The following week a law banning Jews from certain professions came into force. His newspaper career was over. But he kept that brief apprenticeship on his CV for the rest of his life. It can't have been easy for a nineteen-year-old to get over such a setback. One day he had a pencil behind his ear; the next he was shouting, 'Soda! Come and get your soda water!' as he leaned out from a horse-drawn cart and a bitter wind whistled around his ears.

After that I worked in a textile factory, then as a bloodhound in a credit agency; I had a job as a clerk, an advertising salesman and other similar excellent posts until 1941, when I was called up for forced labour. At the first opportunity, I escaped to the Russians. I spent a month washing dishes in a big restaurant in Csernovic before I joined a partisan group in Bukovina.

There were eight Hungarian deserters. The Red Army gave them a crash course in spying and dropped them behind

German lines. Looking back, it's obvious that the Russians didn't trust them. The lessons of history teach us that the Soviets didn't trust anybody. But when those Hungarian deserters turned up, they decided to enlist them.

I can imagine my father wearing a quilted jacket and a knapsack, clinging to the open door of an aeroplane. He looks down. Below him there's vertical space, clouds, and spreading countryside. He suffers from vertigo, feels dizzy, turns away and starts to vomit. Rough hands grab him from behind and shove him into the void.

On that dawn morning, somewhere in the vicinity of Nagyvárad, Hungarian soldiers with submachine guns were waiting in open woodland. When the parachute team floated just a few metres above the ground, the soldiers casually fired off a few rounds for target practice. Miklós was lucky. He was the only one they didn't hit. But as soon as he landed, they pounced on him and put him in handcuffs. That night he was transported to a prison in Budapest where, in the space of barely half an hour, he was relieved of most of his teeth.

~

In the café in Lärbro, Harry looked at Miklós with admiration. 'How many have replied?'

'Eighteen.'

'Are you going to write back to all of them?'

'Some of them, but she's the one,' Miklós answered, patting the pocket where he had hidden the letter.

> I've introduced myself, now it's your turn, Lili. First of all, please send a photo! Then tell me everything about yourself.

'How do you know?'
'I just do.'

Three

LILI BLEW her nose and wiped away her tears. It was the end of September. She was in a four-bed ward on the third floor of the Eksjö hospital. Outside the window stood a lonely birch tree that had already shed its leaves for winter.

Dr Svensson had started going bald early. He wasn't yet forty, but pink skin, reminiscent of a baby's bottom, was already shining through his colourless hair. He was short and stocky, and his hands were like a child's. His thumbnails were the size of cherry-blossom petals.

He removed his protective apron of leather and wire mesh, and wandered into the bleak X-ray room. Beside the ugly apparatus there was a single chair on which Lili was sitting. She looked pale and scared in her washed-out striped hospital overall.

Dr Svensson squatted down beside her and touched her hand. It was encouraging that the Hungarian girl spoke excellent German. Nuances counted a lot in this context.

'I've assessed your last X-ray. This new one will be ready tomorrow. We suspected scarlet fever at first, but we've excluded that now.'

'Something worse?' whispered Lili, as if they were in the audience at the theatre.

'Worse in some ways. It's not an infection. But there's no need to worry.'

'What's the matter with me?'

'That kidney of yours is behaving badly. But I'll cure you, I promise.'

Lili started to cry.

Dr Svensson took her hand. 'Please don't cry! You'll have to stay in bed again. This time we'll have to be stricter.'

'How long?'

'Two weeks to start with. Or three. Then we'll see,' he said, taking out his handkerchief.

> I haven't got a photo of myself. I've been back in
> hospital again for the past few days.

~

I hate dancing, but I love having fun — and eating
stuffed peppers (in thick tomato sauce, of course).

The story goes that Miklós wasn't even nine years old when,
with his hair dampened down and wearing a suit that felt like
armour, he was dragged along to a dance at the Golden Bull
Hotel. He was already having trouble with his eyes, and due to
some sort of refraction error he had to wear glasses with thick,
ugly lenses that did nothing for his looks.

At an energetic moment in the dance, the young Miklós
and a little girl named Melinda were shoved into the middle
of a circle of girls. The crowd of dancers clapped wildly and
urged the pair to start spinning. Melinda came to life. Swept
up by the wave of good cheer, she grabbed Miklós's hands and
swirled round with him, until he slipped on the waxed parquet
floor. And from this ignominious position he watched Melinda
become the belle of the ball.

Now Miklós and Harry hurried back to the hospital. A
strong wind was blowing. Miklós turned up the collar of his thin
spring coat.

Harry stopped and took Miklós's arm. 'Ask her if she's got a
girlfriend.'

'Not so fast. We're only at the beginning.'

That day the men had a party. They turned the barracks
upside down, pushing the beds into the corners. They borrowed
a guitar from somewhere, and it turned out that Jenö Grieger
could at least strum the latest hits.

The dancing began. At first they just threw themselves around with abandon, then the urge to play different characters took over. They didn't discuss parts or assign roles, but began to act out dashing hussars and flirtatious girls. They clicked their heels. They curtsied; they whispered sweet nothings. They fawned over each other, swirling and spinning. Instincts that had been buried for months erupted.

Miklós didn't take part in this childish game. In silent lonely protest, he settled himself on his barricaded bed. He leaned his back against the wall, put his favourite book by Nexø across his knees, and began to write.

> You didn't say anything about your appearance!
> Now you're probably thinking that I'm some shallow
> Budapest type who only cares about that sort of thing.
> I'll let you in on a secret: I'm not.

~

Someone was knocking. Lili didn't even look up. She was reading a dog-eared German edition of *Dick Sand: A Captain at Fifteen* by Jules Verne, which Dr Svensson had given her the day before.

Sára Stern was standing in the doorway. Lili stared in shock. Sára rushed over to the bed, kneeled down and gave her a hug. The novel slipped to the floor.

'Dr Svensson gave me a referral. Right here, to this ward. Though there's nothing wrong with me.' Sára swirled round like a ballroom dancer. She undressed quickly, pulled on her night-dress and got into the bed next to Lili's.

Lili laughed and laughed as if she'd gone mad.

> Now I'll try to describe myself, since I don't have a photo. As far as my figure goes, I'd say I was plumpish (thanks to the Swedes), medium tall, with dark brown hair. My eyes are greyish-blue, my lips are thin, and my complexion is dark. You can imagine me as pretty or ugly, as you like. For my part, I make no comment. I have a picture of you in my mind. I wonder how close to reality it is.

~

On Sunday Dr Lindholm organised three buses to take his patients to the Gotland coast twenty kilometres away. Miklós and Harry wandered off from the others and found a deserted, sandy bay where they could be on their own. The radiant after-noon was a gift from heaven. The sky was like a stretched cobalt canvas. They took their shoes off and paddled in the shallows.

Later, Harry, who had taken to putting his virility to the test at every opportunity, disappeared behind a rock. Miklós pretended not to notice. The late afternoon cast long shadows. The silhouette of the invisible man, doggedly trying to satisfy himself, was projected onto the sand like a drawing by Egon Schiele. Miklós, meanwhile, tried to concentrate on the waves and the endless blue horizon.

I'd be interested to know what your views are about socialism. I gather from what you write about your family that you are middle class, just as I was until I became acquainted with Marxism—which the middle class tend to have very strange notions about.

~

Autumn came early in Eksjö. It came at night with unexpected swiftness, bringing with it sleet and a howling wind. The two girls watched in alarm as the lone birch tree swayed in the storm. The two beds were close enough for them to hold hands.

'If only I had twelve kronor!' whispered Lili.

'What would you do with it?'

Lili closed her eyes. 'There used to be a greengrocer on the corner of Nefelejts Street. My mother always sent me there to buy fruit.'

'I know the one. He was called Mr Teddy!'

'I don't remember that.'

'I do. His name was Mr Teddy. Though I called him Bear. What made you think of him?'

'Nothing really. Last month, before I got sick, I saw a dish of green peppers in a shop window in Smålandsstenar.'

'Really? I didn't think they had green peppers here.'

'Nor did I. They were twelve kronor—for a kilo, I suppose. Or was it half a kilo?'

'You had a craving for one?'

'I know it's silly, but I dreamed about those peppers yesterday. I bit into one. It was crisp. Fancy dreaming such a crazy thing.'

The sleet kept beating against the window. The two girls looked on wistfully.

> My friend Sára has been telling me a lot about socialism. I must admit I haven't taken much notice of politics so far. I'm reading a book about the show trials in Moscow in the 1930s. You probably know all about them.

~

A week or two later, in the middle of October, Miklós again felt he was going to suffocate. He didn't have time to shout out. He stood in the middle of the barracks, his body rigid, his mouth open, trying to suck in some oxygen. Then he collapsed.

This time they drained two litres of fluid from his lungs. He spent the rest of the night in a tiny room beside the surgery. Harry lay on the cold pinewood floor beside the bed so that he could let Dr Lindholm know right away if Miklós suffered another attack—though the doctor had tried to reassure him that another emergency was unlikely for a while now.

'What happened?' My father's voice fluttered in the air like a bird with a hurt wing.

'You fainted,' replied Harry. 'They siphoned off the fluid. You're in the room next to the operating theatre.'

The wooden floor was hurting Harry's side, so he sat up

cross-legged. Miklós lay in silence for a long time. Then he mumbled, 'You know what, Harry? I'll develop gills. They won't get the better of me.'

'Who won't?'

'No one will. No one knows just how stubborn I can be.'

'I envy you. You're so strong.'

'You'll be all right too. I know it. Your slug will turn into a pine tree rising to the sky. And then there'll be no stopping you.'

Harry was rocking back and forth, thinking about what Miklós had said. 'Are you sure?'

'Test my sword, ladies!' said my father, trying to smile, and remembering what he had written to Lili.

> Now for a strange question. How are you placed in the
> love department? Is that irritatingly indiscreet of me?

~

One afternoon, having asked a nurse where to find the best greengrocer in Eksjö, Sára took the lift to the ground floor and escaped from the hospital. In the persistent drizzle she made a dash for the old town, which still had its charms. Fate rewarded her: the only thing in the grocer's window was a wicker basket, and in the basket were several fleshy green peppers. Sára stared at them in amazement while she got her breath back. Then, fishing her small change from her pocket, she sauntered in.

> The answer to your 'strange' question is simple: I've
> had a few boyfriends. Does that mean I've had a lot or
> just one special one? You'll have to guess!

~

Harry was the dandy of the barracks. He loved swaggering around like some grand seducer, and his enigmatic smile suggested that he'd already broken the hearts of umpteen women. Naturally, Miklós was the only one who knew about his little 'problem'.

Then someone discovered that Harry kept a precious, shapely bottle of cologne hidden under his mattress. No one knew where he'd got it from but sometimes, before he walked into town, the whole barracks was filled with the pungent scent of lavender. One evening, when Harry was about to set out on one of his jaunts, he discovered the bottle was missing.

Soon it was flying through the air and, desperate to get it back, Harry was rushing in every direction. The men would wait for him to come close, and then throw the bottle to each other over his head. Tiring of that game, they unscrewed the top and splashed each other with the scent. Harry, tears in his eyes, pleaded with them. 'I bought it on borrowed money,' he shouted.

> My fellow patients are horrible. That's why this letter
> is such a mess. Hungarians, the lot of them! And
> there's such chaos in here that I can't even write.
> They've drenched the place in the cologne belonging

to our resident Don Juan. Some of it even landed on
my writing paper. We're in such high spirits it's almost
dangerous. Harry and I may have to break out and
trek across the country to see you and your friends.

~

When Sára got back from her expedition to the old town Lili
was asleep. This was a stroke of luck. She delicately laid the two
peppers on the pillow next to Lili's cheek.

How thrilling, dear Miklós, that you and your friend
may come and visit us.

~

Miklós and Harry often exercised by striding around the hospital
grounds. Now that a trip to Eksjö might be on the cards—Miklós
was cooking up some story about a family reunion—Harry was
full of curiosity. He was determined to get his own penfriend, or
at least to make certain of going on the visit with Miklós. 'How
many kilometres is it exactly?' he enquired.

'Almost three hundred.'

'Two days there, two days back. We won't get permission.'

Miklós led the way, keeping his eyes on the path.

'Yes, we will.'

Harry felt this was the time to banish all doubt about his
virility. 'I'm in much better shape. Every morning I wake up with

a stiff, like this!' he said, showing the length with his hands.

But Miklós didn't react.

> Whatever happens, don't forget that I'm your cousin
> and Harry is Sára's uncle. I have to warn you, though,
> that at the station, yes, right there at the station, you'll
> be getting a kiss from your cousin. We must keep up
> appearances!
>
> I send you a friendly handshake plus a kiss from
> your cousin, Miklós.

~

One rare sunny morning in Eksjö, the door swung open and there stood a grinning, chubby Judit Gold! She dropped her belongings and threw her arms out wide. 'Dr Svensson gave me a referral too. Severe anaemia. We can all be together!'

Sára flew over to Judit and they hugged each other. Lili clambered out of bed, though it was strictly forbidden, and, linking arms, the three of them danced in front of the window. Then they sat on Lili's bed.

'Does he still write to you?' asked Judit, taking Lili's hand in hers.

Lili waited a moment. She had recently learned the subtle advantage of pausing for effect. She stood up and in a dramatic gesture pulled open the drawer of her bedside table. She took out a sheaf of letters and held it high.

'Eight!'

Judit applauded. 'How industrious of him.'

Sára patted Judit on the knee. 'You should see how clever he is! And a socialist, too.'

That was a little too much for Judit, who pulled a face. 'Ugh, I hate socialists.'

'Lili doesn't.'

Judit took the letters out of Lili's hands and smelled them. 'Are you sure he's not married?'

Lili was taken aback. Why did she have to smell them? 'Dead sure.'

'We ought to check him out somehow. You know, I've been burnt so many times.'

Judit was at least ten years older than the other two, and she knew more about men. Lili took the letters from her, slipped off the rubber band and picked up the top one.

'Listen to what he says: "I've got good news for you. We can send cables to Hungary now. But you have to use special forms. You can get them either from the consulate or from the Red Cross in Stockholm. Each form can fit twenty-five words." How about that?'

This was wonderful to hear. They thought about it for a while. Lili lay back in her bed, put the letters on her stomach and stared at the ceiling. 'I haven't heard anything from Mama. Or Papa. I can't bear it. Aren't you worried too?'

The girls avoided each other's eyes.

~

Autumn had by now slunk across the island of Gotland too. It was a bleak overcast day when Dr Lindholm summoned the inhabitants of the barracks together at noon. He briskly gave them the good news that none of them remained infectious. And that early the following morning the Hungarian patients were being transferred to a temporary hospital in Avesta, north of Stockholm. Dr Lindholm would be travelling with them.

~

Avesta was a few hundred kilometres away. After a day and a half of chugging along on steam trains they arrived. At first sight, their new rehabilitation camp was a shock. Situated in the middle of thick forest, seven kilometres from the town, it was surrounded by a wire fence and, worst of all, a tall chimney rose from its centre.

They were housed in brick barracks. They might have settled in better if the weather had not been so terrible. The wind always blew in Avesta. Everything was covered in frost, and the sun, the colour of an overripe orange, never peeped out for more than a few minutes.

Outside their window was a small concrete courtyard full of weeds. Its long wooden table and benches gave it a certain spartan charm. The convalescents sat here in the evenings wrapped up in blankets.

Dr Lindholm had arranged for a Hungarian newspaper to be delivered every few days, even if it was three weeks old. The men instantly tore the shoddily printed paper into four parts. Huddled in groups, they devoured every word. A single light bulb swung overhead. Then they swapped pages in the pale light, their mouths moving soundlessly. In spirit they were far away.

THE REBUILT 250-HORSEPOWER SCREW STEAMER SETS OUT ON ITS MAIDEN VOYAGE

SOVIET PAINTER ALEXANDR GERASIMOV IS CELEBRATED IN THE HOTEL GELLÉRT

THE TOWN OF KECSKEMÉT RECEIVES A GIFT OF 300 PAIRS OF OXEN FROM THE OCCUPYING RUSSIAN FORCES

BICYCLE RACE IN SZEGED

SHOOTING STARTS ON THE FILM *THE TEACHER*

Just imagine! We got hold of an August edition of
Kossuth's People. We even read all the ads. The
theatres back home are full. A four-page newspaper
costs two pengö, a kilo of flour fourteen. The people's
court is sentencing members of the Arrow Cross
Party one after the other. There are lots of new street
names. Mussolini Square is now Marx Square. The
whole country is full of hope. People want to work.
Teachers have to attend re-education courses. The
first lecture was given by party boss Mátyás Rákosi.
But I'm sure you're sick of politics.

~

The tiny X-ray room in Avesta was no different from the one in Lärbro. Except perhaps for the hairline crack that ran the length of the ceiling. It was a symbol of something and it gave Miklós a feeling of hope. In this room he once again pressed his sunken chest and narrow shoulders up against the machine. And once again it gave out a high thin beep when the X-ray was done. Miklós always covered his eyes when the door opened and light streamed into the darkness. And it was always Dr Lindholm who stood in the doorway in his radiation-proof leather apron.

The X-rays were read the following day. Miklós entered Dr Lindholm's office and sat down in front of the desk. He leaned back until the front legs of his chair rose into the air. It was to become an annoying habit in Avesta. He had made a bet with himself. If something of vital importance was being discussed, he would pivot on his chair like a naughty child—all the while concentrating like mad.

'The X-rays came out well. Sharp, easy to read,' Dr Lindholm said, looking into my father's eyes.

'Any change?'

'I can give no encouraging.'

Miklós let the chair drop back on all four legs.

'And forget about going to Eksjö. Is too far away from Avesta. God knows how long to get there.'

'I only want three days.'

'You have always fever at dawn. There are no miracles.'

Miklós had his own thermometer. Each morning, at half past four on the dot, an inner alarm clock woke him up. The mercury always reached the same point. Thirty-eight point two. No more, no less.

'This is not about me. My cousin is lonely and depressed. It would mean the world to her.'

Dr Lindholm gave him a thoughtful glance. He and Márta, who was now head nurse in their section in Avesta, had settled into their new home. He decided to invite Miklós, who got on well with his wife, for supper. Perhaps over a family meal he could dissuade this charming and stubborn young man from his crazy scheme.

~

The Lindholms' house was next to the railway line. Trains regularly shrieked past the window. Miklós dressed for the occasion, having borrowed a jacket and tie, but he felt ill at ease. At the beginning, conversation was awkward. Márta dished out the stuffed cabbage. Dr Lindholm tucked his napkin into his shirt.

'Márta cook this dish especially for you. Hungarian, she tell me.'

There was the banshee noise of a passing train.

'It's one of my favourites,' replied Miklós when it was quiet again. He broke a crust of bread and carefully gathered up the crumbs.

Márta smacked his hand. 'If you don't stop cleaning up, I'll send you out to wash the dishes.'

He blushed. For a while they blew on the hot cabbage in silence.

Miklós started to cough. After he caught his breath, he said, 'Dr Lindholm speaks beautiful Hungarian.'

'I won on that score. In everything else Erik is the boss,' said Márta, smiling at her husband.

They continued to eat in silence. Fatty cabbage juice started to trickle down Miklós's chin. Márta handed him a napkin. He wiped his mouth in embarrassment.

'Can I ask you how you two met?'

Márta, who could barely reach the table from her chair, stretched her hand out between the glasses and laid it on Lindholm's arm. 'Can I tell him?'

Dr Lindholm nodded.

'It was ten years ago. A delegation of Swedish doctors came to visit the Rókus Hospital in Budapest. None of them was tall. I was the head nurse there,' Márta said, then stopped.

Dr Lindholm sipped his wine. He was not going to help her out.

'Since I was a teenager people have always teased me. Look at me, Miklós, you can see why, can't you? If I was asked to open a window, I had to get someone in the class to do it for me. When I was sixteen I told my mother that, as soon as I could, I would move to Sweden and find a husband. So I started learning Swedish.'

A passenger train clattered past. It felt as if it had passed between them and the plates.

'Why Sweden?'

'Is common knowledge that very short men live here,' Dr Lindholm retorted.

It was five seconds before Miklós dared to laugh. It was as if a plug had been pulled out: now the conversation flowed.

'By 1935 I could speak Swedish fluently. By coincidence Dr Lindholm had had enough of his previous wife. She was a giant—six foot. That's right, isn't it, Erik?'

Dr Lindholm nodded gravely.

'What was I to do? One evening I seduced him. In the hospital. Next to the operating theatre. I haven't left anything out, have I, Erik? Now it's your turn, Miklós. Did you tell the girl in Eksjö about your condition?'

My father, who until now had been preoccupied with his napkin, picked up his knife and fork and started to wolf down the cabbage. 'More or less.'

'Erik and I differ on this. I think you should go. To cheer up your…cousin. And yourself.'

Dr Lindholm sighed and poured more wine into everybody's glasses. 'Last week I receive letter from my colleague who work in Ädelfors,' he said. He jumped up and hurried into the other room. A moment later he returned clutching a sheet of paper.

'I read you parts, Miklós. There is women's hospital in Ädelfors, a rehabilitation centre for four hundred inmates. Well, about fifty girls were transferred to different hospital with stricter regime. What you think reason?' he asked, brandishing the letter.

Miklós shrugged. Lindholm didn't wait for the answer.

'Their loose life. I read it to you. Listen. "The girls received men in their bedrooms and in clearings in the nearby forest."'

No one had anything to say.

After a while the tiny Márta asked, 'Were they Hungarian girls?'

'I don't know.'

But Miklós knew the answer. 'They were spoilt upper-class girls!' he announced triumphantly.

Márta put down her fork in alarm. 'What's that supposed to mean, Miklós?'

My father was at last on familiar ground. He intended to enjoy himself. The dusty world of the past had been blown away by the fresh wind of socialism.

'Women like that adhere to a certain type of morality. They smoke, wear nylon stockings and chatter away about superficial things. *While from the depths not a word.*' Miklós couldn't resist quoting the poetry of Attila József.

'I'm not sure about that,' said Dr Lindholm. 'All I know, opportunity makes a thief.'

But Miklós was not so easily deterred. 'There's only one way to cure those bourgeois morals.'

'And that is?'

'By building a new world! From the foundations.'

From that point on, the supper was overwhelmed by my father's rousing manifesto in praise of the redeeming trinity of *liberté, égalité, fraternité*. He didn't even notice that they had polished off the dessert.

After midnight Dr Lindholm's car swung into the entrance of the hospital. Miklós clambered out and waved goodbye. He was buoyant, full of hope that he would soon be off to Eksjö. As soon as he got back to his barracks, he lit a candle, crouched down at his bed and excitedly condensed his world-saving ideology into a four-page letter.

> It will make me happy if you write and tell me what
> you think about all this. I'm especially interested
> because you are middle class, and probably look
> at this question from the point of view of the
> bourgeoisie.

Four

IN THE third week of October, Dr Svensson allowed Lili to get up. She forlornly roamed the tiled corridors of the hospital. The acrid smell of disinfectant mingled with the stench of gutted fish. The women's section was on the third floor, but otherwise the place seemed to be full of surly Swedish soldiers.

Lili was about to spend her first Sunday with the Björkmans. Two months earlier, at Smålandsstenar, each of the Hungarian girls had been introduced to a Swedish family who would help them find their feet. Sven Björkman ran a small stationery shop. He and his family were practising Catholics.

Lili wasn't assigned to the Björkmans by chance. It was five months since her 'betrayal'. In May, just after the war ended, when she regained consciousness in a hospital in the town of Belsen after being rescued from the concentration camp, she immediately renounced her Jewish faith. The truth is that she chose Catholicism quite randomly. But it meant that later, thanks to the thoroughness and the sensitivity of the Swedish authorities, the Björkman family was chosen to support her.

Björkman, his wife and their two sons made the long drive to Eksjö at dawn the next Sunday. They waited for Lili at the hospital entrance, hugged her joyfully on seeing her again, and then took her straight to mass in Smålandsstenar.

The Björkman family sat in the third pew of the simple but spacious church. And the convalescent Hungarian girl, Lili Reich, sat with them. Their radiant faces turned towards the pulpit. Lili understood only a few words of Swedish so the sermon washed over her with the same solemnity as the organ fugue that followed it. Then she, too, kneeled in the line before the young priest with the piercing blue eyes, so he could place a wafer on her tongue.

> Dear Miklós,
>
> I'd like to ask you not to hurry so much next time you write, but rather to think over what you're writing and to whom. Our relationship isn't that close. Mind what you say to me! Yes, I'm a typical bourgeois girl. And if, among four hundred girls, 'about fifty' fit your description of them, why should you be surprised?

~

That same Sunday morning Miklós and Harry were sitting in front of a few scones and glasses of soda water in the Avesta canteen. They should have been celebrating the fact that they had the place to themselves, but Miklós was in such a bad mood that he didn't even notice.

'I've ruined it,' he muttered.

Harry waved him down. 'Of course you haven't. She'll calm down.'

'Never. I've got a feeling.'

'Then you can write to someone else.'

Miklós looked up, shocked. 'There isn't anyone else. It's either her or I die.' How could Harry be so insensitive?

Harry burst out laughing. 'Words, just words?'

Miklós dipped his finger in the glass of water and wrote 'LILI' on the wooden table. 'This'll dry up too,' he said sadly.

'Send her one of your poems!'

'Too late.'

'I don't like sorrowful Jews,' said Harry, getting up. 'I'll find you something sweet. I'll bribe someone or steal something for you. But wipe that glum look off your face.'

Harry crossed the dreary hall to the swing door and entered the kitchen. There was no one there either. He opened cupboards until he found a jar of honey buried deep in one of them.

He hurried back in triumph. 'No spoon. You'll have to dip your finger in, like this.'

My father was staring at the table. The stem of the second
'L' was still visible.

'Right.' Harry sucked his finger. 'Have you got paper and a
pencil? I'll dictate.'

'What?' asked Miklós, looking up at last.

'A letter. To her. Are you ready?' He dipped his finger in the
honey.

Puzzled, Miklós took some paper and a pencil out of his
pocket. Harry's cheerfulness had managed to strike a tiny crack
in the armour of his despair.

'Dear Lili,' Harry dictated, licking his finger, 'I have to
tell you that I despise and deride those stupid women who are
ashamed to talk about such things—'

Miklós slammed down his pencil. 'This is lunacy! You want
me to send this to Lili?'

'You've been writing to each other for a month now. It's
high time you became more intimate with her. I'm an outsider,
I can gauge things better.'

~

The following Sunday, after Sven Björkman had said grace,
and the two Björkman boys had more or less settled down, Mrs
Björkman began ladling out the soup with her usual precision.

'Where have you hidden your crucifix, Lili?' Björkman
asked, without so much as a glance at Lili.

Either he spoke little German or he wanted to test Lili's

knowledge of Swedish. When she looked at him blankly, he repeated the question, in Swedish, and pointed to the crucifix round his own neck.

Lili blushed. She fished the little silver cross out of her pocket and put it round her neck.

'Why did you take it off?' he asked, looking at her pleasantly. 'We gave it to you for you to wear. Always.'

The reproach was clear. The meal passed without further conversation.

> The tone and content of your last letter were rather
> strange but you seem like a kind man, so I'll answer
> this one too. On the other hand, I'm not sure that a
> 'bourgeois' girl like me is the right friend for you. This
> time I think you went too far.

~

It was dawn. Miklós felt for the thermometer in the drawer of his bedside table, and with his eyes still shut he stuck it in his mouth. Then he counted to 130. He opened his eyes for a split second: there was no need for him to study the delicate markings in detail. The fever, as stealthy as a thief, crept up, stole his confidence, and then vanished in the half-light of dawn. He put the thermometer in the drawer again, turned over and went back to sleep.

When he got up at eight o'clock his temperature was normal.

Dear Lili,

What a fool I am! I'm sorry. Why do I bother
you with all my stupid thoughts? I send you a warm
handshake.

Miklós

P.S.: Is that still allowed?

~

It took two days for a letter to arrive by Swedish mail train. When Miklós's apology arrived, Lili and Sára were huddled on Lili's bed.

"'P.S. Is that still allowed?'"

'Now you should forgive him,' said Sára after some thought.

'I already have.'

Lili scrambled across the bed and took an envelope from her bedside table.

'I purposely left it open,' she said as she searched for the bit she wanted to show Sára. 'Here it is: "Yes, Miklós, you really are a fool! But if you behave yourself we can be friends again."' She gave Sára a jubilant look.

'Men!' said Sára, smiling.

~

Four bicycles were kept in the entrance to Avesta, so patients could ride from the forest to the town. Now that the weather had turned cold and even the midday sunshine didn't melt the snow on the fir trees, Miklós and Harry had to rug up to prevent their ears and hands from freezing on the hour-long ride.

Even so, it took a long time, as they sat waiting at the post office, for the feeling to return to their fingers, though they tried to keep them warm under their thighs.

Miklós was anxious. From where they sat he could see the glass doors of the three telephone booths, which at that moment were all occupied. He was beside himself. It was his turn next.

After what seemed forever one of the booths became vacant. At the counter, an operator lifted the receiver to her ear. She looked at Miklós, said something into the phone and waved at him. He stood up and staggered into the vacant booth.

~

Judit Gold dashed up the stairs at full speed, practically knocking over the nurses and doctors hurrying in the opposite direction. Lili and Sára were reading in the open window of the ward. Judit stormed through the door. 'Lili! Lili!' she shouted. 'You've got a phone call!'

Lili gaped at her, not understanding.

'Hurry! Miklós is on the phone!'

Lili turned red and leapt off the windowsill. She flew downstairs to the basement, where a telephone room had been set up for patients. A nurse was on her way out of the room, and she looked at Lili in surprise. Lili saw the receiver lying on the table. She made herself slow down. She touched the receiver gingerly, and cautiously lifted it to her ear. 'It's me.'

In the post office Miklós gave a small cough, but his voice still came out an octave higher than its usual baritone. 'You sound exactly the way I imagined you would,' he managed to say. 'How mystical!'

'I'm out of breath. I ran. There's just one telephone, in the main building, and we…'

Miklós started to babble. 'Catch your breath. I'll do the talking, all right? Remember I told you how you can already send cables home? I'm calling because—just imagine—now we can send airmail letters too, via London or Prague. At last you can find your mother! Isn't it great! I thought I'd call and tell you right away.'

'Oh dear.'

'Did I say something wrong?'

Lili was clutching the receiver so tightly that her fingers had turned white. 'Mama…I don't know…I don't know her address…She had to leave our old flat and move to the ghetto… and now I don't know where she is living.'

Miklós's voice recovered its silky tone. 'Oh, I'm a fool. Of course you don't! But we can place a notice in a newspaper. We'll send her a message through *Világosság*. Everyone reads that. I've got a bit of money saved up. I'll arrange it.'

Lili was surprised. There was no way he could afford to do that on five kronor a week.

'How have you been able to save any money?'

'Didn't I tell you, my darling? Oh, sorry, have I gone too far? I'm sorry, Lili.'

Lili blushed furiously. Now her temperature had shot up. 'I wish I could see you.'

The post office felt like a palace to Miklós. Thrilled, he punched the air with his fist, signalling to Harry through the glass. 'Well, it's like this, what if I had a Cuban uncle…but that's a long story, I'll put it in a letter.'

No one spoke for a while. They pressed the receivers tightly to their ears.

'How are you?' Lili started up again. 'Your health, I mean.'

'Me? I'm fine. All my tests are negative. There was a tiny spot on my left lung. Some fluid. A touch of pleurisy. But not serious. I'm more or less in the middle of my treatment. And you?'

'I'm fine, too. Nothing hurts. I have to take iron tablets.'

'Have you got a temperature?' Miklós asked.

'Very slight. A kidney infection. Nothing to worry about. I've got a good appetite. I'm so looking forward to seeing you… seeing you both,' said Lili.

'Yes. I'm working on it. But in the meantime I've written you a poem.'

'Me?' Lili blushed again.

Miklós closed his eyes. 'Shall I recite it?'

'You know it by heart?'

'Of course.'

He had to think quickly. The truth was that he had already

written six poems for Lili, to Lili. Now he had to choose one. 'The title is "Lili". You still there?'

'Yes.'

Miklós leaned against the booth wall. He kept his eyes closed.

> *I stepped on an icy puddle*
> *the rime crunched under me.*
> *If you touch my heart, beware,*
> *a single move will be*
> *enough to crack apart*
> *my secret frozen sea.*

'Are you still there?'

Lili held her breath.

He couldn't hear her, but he could sense her presence.

'Yes.'

Miklós was frightened by something, too, or perhaps he was just hoarse. The distance made the receiver hiss, and the words of the poem sounded like breaking waves. 'I'll go on then,' he said.

> *So come to me gently,*
> *with the smiles that we lost.*
> *Seek out the places*
> *where pain has chilled to frost*
> *so the warmth of your caress*
> *melts to dew within my chest.*

Five

THE GROUND-FLOOR meeting room, which the hospital in Eksjö had made available to the Red Cross, was tiny and embarrassingly bare. It had no window. There was just room for a desk and a bentwood chair for visitors.

Madame Ann-Marie Arvidsson was the local Red Cross representative. She sharpened her pencil after almost every sentence she wrote. She spoke German slowly, enunciating every syllable to make it easier for Lili to understand the finer points. And she was set on explaining everything to this charming Hungarian girl. Even things that were out of her hands. Such as the risk Sweden had taken by allowing in so many sick people. Such as the fact that the International Red Cross never had enough money, because all sorts of unforeseeable expenses were always cropping up. She didn't even get to the question of accommodation. The main thing was, like it or not, she couldn't support this kind of private initiative.

'You ought to know, Lili, I don't agree with this type of visit even in principle.'

Lili tried again. 'Just a few days. What harm will that do anyone?'

'It won't do any harm. But what would be the point? To come from the other side of the country. That's a lot of money. And once the men are here? Among three hundred patients. This is a hospital, not a hotel! Have you considered that, Lili?'

'I haven't seen them for a year and a half.' She gave the woman an imploring look.

Madame Arvidsson thought she saw a speck of dust on the immaculate surface of the desk. She wiped it off. 'Let's say I give permission. What will your relatives eat? The Red Cross has no funds for extra food.'

'Something. Anything.'

'You are not facing facts, Lili. These men are patients too. I can't even imagine how they'll buy the tickets for the train.'

'We've got a Cuban relative.'

Ann-Marie Arvidsson raised an eyebrow. She jotted down a few words, then sharpened her pencil. 'And this relative is financing the visit, all the way from Cuba?'

Lili looked deep into Madame Arvidsson's eyes. 'We're a loving family...'

This, at last, made Madame Arvidsson laugh. 'I admire your determination. I'll try to do something. But I can't make any promises.'

Lili got up, leaned awkwardly over the desk and gave Madame Ann-Marie Arvidsson a kiss. Then she ran out of the room, knocking over her chair on the way.

Ann-Marie Arvidsson got up, set the chair on its legs, took out her handkerchief and wiped all trace of the kiss off her cheek.

~

A few days later Rabbi Emil Kronheim climbed briskly onto a train in Stockholm. The rabbi was an ascetic figure, small and thin, in an old grey suit. His hair was like a haystack. Ever since the Swedish government had called on him to give moral support to his fellow Jews in these hard times, his name and address had been pinned on the noticeboard of every rehabilitation centre in Sweden.

He travelled up and down the country for three weeks of each month. Sometimes he talked to people in groups. Other times he would listen to a single person for hours on end, hardly moving, giving strength with just the bat of an eyelid, until they were engulfed by the early evening twilight. He never grew tired.

His one excess was herring. It was almost comical. He couldn't resist pickled herring. Even on the train, reading the newspaper, while the snow-covered countryside raced past, he ate pieces of herring out of greasy paper.

At the station in Eksjö he clambered out of his carriage. It was pouring. He hurried across the wet platform.

According to his information there were three young Hungarian women in the hospital. A few days ago he had received a letter from one of them. A single soul is a soul. Without a moment's hesitation he had set out on the mind-numbing journey from Stockholm.

Now he was sitting in the same windowless room that had confined Madame Ann-Marie Arvidsson. He was concentrating on a fly that was crawling around the desk between the pencils, the sharpener.

There was a knock. Judit Gold stuck her head round the door. 'Can I come in?'

The rabbi smiled. 'Just as I imagined you. You see, dear—'

'I'm Judit Gold.'

'You see, dear Judit Gold, on the basis of your handwriting I formed a mental picture of you. Now comes my pat on the back: I've scored a bullseye. Incidentally the world is built on this kind of presentiment. Before the Battle of Waterloo, Napoleon…Oh, you look so pale. Can I get you some water?'

There was a jug on the desk. Rabbi Kronheim filled a glass.

Judit Gold drank greedily, then sat down. She spoke in a whisper. 'I'm ashamed of myself.'

'So am I. We all are. And we've reason to be. What's the reason for your shame, Judit?'

'I'm ashamed of writing you that letter. And of being forced to tell tales.'

'Don't tell tales then! Forget the whole thing.'

'I can't.'

'Of course you can. Shrug it off and throw what you wanted to tell me into the bin. Don't give it another thought. Forget it. Let's talk about something else. Let's talk about flies, for example. What's your attitude to flies?'

Emil Kronheim pointed to the fly buzzing over the desk.

'They disgust me.'

'You want to be careful with disgust. It can easily turn into hatred. And right after that comes conflict. Later, it becomes ideology. And in the end you'll be pursuing flies all your life.'

Judit couldn't take her eyes off the fly that had now landed on the rim of her glass. 'I've got a friend,' she said.

Judit paused. She was in need of a question or a gesture, but Kronheim seemed interested only in the fly, the crazy, fidgety fly.

She had to start somewhere. 'It's about my friend Lili. She's eighteen. Inexperienced and naïve.'

The rabbi shut his eyes. Was he listening at all?

'She has been completely ensnared by a man from Gotland. Well, he has now been transferred to Avesta. I can't stand by and do nothing. I can't bear seeing Lili getting all worked up about him. There's no way I can keep calm or stay out of this.'

The rabbi, who had been so chatty to start with, was now sitting still, his eyes closed. Had he fallen asleep?

Judit started crying. 'She is my best friend. I've grown to

love her. She was skin and bone when she arrived. She was so down. So alone. Then she started writing letters to this good-for-nothing. He's a gangster. He promises her everything under the sun. Right now he wants to come and visit her in the hospital. Sorry, I'm not making any sense. All I know is that Lili's too young.'

Judit felt that she had lost the thread. She should tell the story from the beginning. Tell him why she was anxious and why her fears were real. But, instead of helping her out, the rabbi was confusing her. He sat there with his eyes closed, his back straight. He wasn't paying attention.

A minute passed. Then Rabbi Kronheim ran his fingers through his untidy hair. So he hadn't been asleep.

Judit snivelled and sniffed. 'I've lived through so much horror. I've given up so many times. But I'm alive. I'm still here. And Lili is so young.'

Emil Kronheim put his hand in his pocket. 'I always have a clean handkerchief on me for such occasions. Here you are.'

~

Around this time Miklós began to figure out how he could trick fate. He had no illusions about his looks. Even though he now weighed fifty kilos, and the nasty warts were starting to disappear, he remained self-conscious.

Dr Lindholm was surprised by his request, but for once it wasn't about going to Eksjö, and it was something that would make Miklós happy, so he agreed right away. He went over to the cupboard and took out a small camera. Then he got a roll of film out of his desk drawer. He handed them both to Miklós, who was standing in the middle of the room, beaming.

Miklós, Harry and Tibor Hirsch headed across to a spacious, breezy tract of land between the barracks where hundred-year-old pine trees rose up high. Miklós solemnly handed the camera to Tibor, who at over fifty was the oldest of the patients. His hair didn't seem to want to grow; irregular-shaped purple patches could be seen on his scalp.

'You were a photographer,' Miklós said, looking at him. 'I trust you. My life's in your hands.'

Hirsch spent a long time examining the camera. 'I know this type. It'll be perfect, I promise.'

Miklós interrupted. 'No, it shouldn't be perfect.'

'What?'

'It should be fuzzy. That's what I want.'

Hirsch looked puzzled.

'That's why I asked you. Because you know what you're doing.'

'Only to a point. I'm an electronic radio technician and photographer's assistant. Or used to be. What *do* you want?'

Miklós now pointed at Harry. 'We both should be in the picture. Harry and me. Harry should be in focus. I should be blurred, somewhere in the background. Could you do that?'

'That's nuts!' Hirsch protested. 'Why on earth do you want to be out of focus?'

'Never you mind. Can you do it?'

Tibor Hirsch, electronic radio technician and photographer's assistant, hesitated. But Miklós was his friend, and was giving him begging looks, so he put aside his professional pride.

Within five minutes he had worked out how to take a photograph in which my father would be more or less unrecognisable. He posed Harry in the foreground. In half-profile, at the most flattering angle. A watery sun came out for the briefest moment. Hirsch positioned them with backlight for an artistic feel. He instructed Miklós to run up and down a few metres behind Harry. Hirsch took several shots while Miklós ran.

> Dear Lili,
>
> What a sorceress you are! You enchanted me on the telephone. Now I'm even more keen to see whether you are as I imagine you from your letters. There'll be trouble if you aren't, but even more trouble if you are. I've found a photo of myself and Harry, who's standing in the front. Granted I look like I've been crushed by some sort of Cyclops and I'm in a hurry to get to the smallest room in the house — but I'm sending it anyway.

An artificial palm with lush tropical foliage stood in front of an alcove window on the third-floor corridor of the Eksjö hospital. The three girls sat there, hidden from sight.

Lili was examining the photograph with a magnifying glass. She handed it to Sára and Judit. There was nothing wrong with their eyesight. But was that indistinct shape running away behind Harry's back, that almost unidentifiable figure, Miklós?

A shadow loomed over them. 'Ah ha, so that's why you needed my magnifier.'

The three girls jumped as one. Dr Svensson pointed to the photo. 'Men? Hungarians?'

Lili held out the photo in embarrassment. 'It's my cousin.'

Svensson took a good look. 'Handsome. An open face.'

Lili hesitated, but then she pointed at the hazy figure in the background. 'That's him, the one who seems to be running away.'

Dr Svensson lifted the photograph close to his eyes, trying to identify the young man loping out of the frame, but it was hopeless. 'I thought he was in the picture by mistake. How mysterious.'

Miklós's idea was a success. The mysterious figure had kept the promise of the future alive. The girls were laughing as Svensson handed back the photo in disappointment, and they returned his magnifying glass to him.

~

Now I'm going to be very cheeky, partly to you and partly to your friend Sára, to whom I send friendly greetings. You see, the thing is my friend Harry and I have acquired some rather ghastly muddy grey wool

that nimble-fingered girls could conjure into passable
sweaters. I'd like to ask you to do this for me—as soon
as possible, of course.

At dawn the next day Lili sat up in bed and took a handkerchief from under her pillow. She folded it carefully and slipped
it into the envelope on the bedside table.

Accept this trifle from me with love. I'm afraid it isn't
quite as fine as I'd have liked, and since I haven't got
an iron I had to press it under my pillow. How did you
find the wool? By the way, it's getting colder and colder
here, and since they haven't given us winter coats I
always put on two cardigans if I go out for a walk.

At that moment Judit Gold stuck her head out from beneath
her eiderdown and couldn't help but see Lili's look of peaceful
happiness. She wasn't a bit pleased.

~

The mail was distributed every afternoon after the men had
rested. It was usually Harry who went to get the letters from the
caretaker's office and he would read out the names. 'Misi, Adolf,
Litzman, Jenö Grieger, Jakobovits, Józsi, Spitz, Miklós…'

My father got lots of letters, perhaps too many, but only one
person's letters excited him. If he saw that Lili had written, he
didn't have the patience to wait until he was back in bed, but

greedily tore open the envelope on the way. Now a handkerchief slipped out onto the floor. He picked it up and smelled it over and over again.

> The fact that you pressed your handkerchief under your head just enhances its value for me…Tell me, why is it that your letters bring me more and more joy?
> Sorry about the pencil, but I wanted to write back straight away and someone has taken the ink.
> I send you a long warm handshake.
> Miklós

~

In Eksjö there was a hall on the ground floor of the hospital, with a yellow-sided platform where a red velvet curtain could be let down to make a stage. When Sára had the idea that they should give an evening concert, she and the girls hoped that the women living on the third floor would come and listen to them. In actual fact almost all of the two hundred chairs were taken up by the soldiers. The occasional Swedish nurse, with her braided hair, crisply starched cloak and bonnet, was squeezed in between them like a raisin in a bun.

The girls performed four numbers. Sára sang, while Lili accompanied her on the harmonium. After three Hungarian songs, Sára began to sing the Swedish national anthem. She was halfway through it when the soldiers, unshaven and in pyjamas, kicked back their two hundred chairs, jumped to their feet and joined in, none of them in tune.

> These Swedes are starting to get on my nerves. They expect us to sing their praises all the time. I am indescribably homesick!

Six

KLÁRA KÖVES arrived unexpectedly on the midday train. She had just enough money to buy a rail ticket from her camp near Uppsala to Avesta. That didn't worry her in the slightest—she was convinced that Miklós would take care of everything.

At the station she arranged a lift in the mail van, which meant that she travelled the last few kilometres in style. It was early afternoon when she arrived at the hospital.

Klára was a large girl—her friends called her 'bear woman'. Her walk was more like a trudge. Her handshake was like a man's. A good part of her body was covered with a silky down that, in a certain light, looked a lot like fur. She had full, sensuous lips, a hooknose and a mop of unruly, dark brown hair.

She blew into the barracks like a whirlwind. 'I'm here, dear Miklós!' she shouted. 'I've come to you!'

The men froze. Miklós couldn't connect this hefty woman with the amusing, quick-witted girl he'd been exchanging letters with for the past two months. There must be some misunderstanding.

Klára Köves, it turned out, was one of nine women apart from Lili with whom my father had been corresponding after he sent out his initial batch of 117 letters. He couldn't help himself. He took great joy in the process of writing; it helped him understand things, and he was genuinely curious about the lives of these girls. Of course the letters he wrote to the nine women were nothing like his outpourings to Lili. He and Klára, for instance, merely shared their views on world issues. Klára had distributed socialist pamphlets during the war—that's how she got caught.

She made a beeline for my father, threw her arms around him and kissed him on the lips. 'I've been wanting to do that for weeks.'

The other men hadn't moved an inch. What an entrance! A real flesh-and-blood woman, all ninety kilos of her, had materialised before them, despite all the regulations, restrictions and prohibitions. Their dreams had become three-dimensional.

Miklós shuddered, trapped in Klára's embrace. 'Wanting to do what?'

'To tie our lives together! What else?'

At last Klára let go of him. She took some letters out of her handbag and threw them in the air. She turned to the other men, who by this time were scrambling off their beds and gathering around her. 'Do you know who you've got in your midst? A new Karl Marx! A new Friedrich Engels!'

The letters fell like confetti. The men were enchanted.

Miklós wanted to die on the spot.

Klára took his arm and led him out of the barracks. My father signalled urgently for Harry to follow. The three of them set off down the path that led to the forest. It was as if Klára had taken possession of Miklós, as if she were hugging a doll. Harry walked behind them, hoping for his turn. It began to drizzle.

'Look here, Klára,' said Miklós in what he hoped was a quiet but authoritative voice. 'You should know that I write to other girls. Lots of them, in fact.'

Klára laughed. 'Are you trying to make me jealous, sweetie?'

'Heavens, no. I just want to be clear with you. Letter-writing is our only entertainment. Not only for me, but for the whole barracks. But it may have caused you to misunderstand certain things.'

'Misunderstanding, my foot! I've fallen for you, honey! You're as clever as they get. I look up to you. You'll be my teacher and my lover! You're full of hang-ups, but I'll be your saviour.'

'I write tons of letters. I want you to know that.'

'All geniuses are complex. I had two before the war, so I know. You don't mind my coming clean, do you? I'm not a virgin. Hell, no! I'm many things, but no virgin. But I will be faithful to you, I can feel it. The thoughts and ideas you come up with! I know them by heart. Would you like to test me?'

She grabbed Miklós by the waist and covered his face with kisses. His glasses misted up. But even through the fog he could see the desperation in her eyes, her fear of rejection.

This unexpected discovery had a soothing effect on Miklós. 'Could I get a word in, please, Klára,' he said calmly.

'I just wanted to say,' Klára raced on, 'that I'll nurse you if you need it. I've completely recovered. I'm going to work! I'll move to be near you. Now, what did you want to tell me?'

Miklós extricated himself from Klára's grasp and turned to her. 'All right. Now for the facts. I write many letters, but only because I've got beautiful handwriting. People have noticed it. The men in the barracks take advantage of it, so to speak. Your letters, I'm afraid, were composed by Harry, not me. He dictated them to me because my writing is so much better than his. That's the sad truth. You fell for Harry's brain through me.'

Klára's eyes widened. She spun around to Harry. The drizzle was getting heavier. 'So it turns out you're my genius. Is that right, sweetheart?'

Harry cottoned on. He hoped his lonely preparation for the manly tasks that lay ahead would prove sufficient. 'He…just did the writing,' he improvised, pointing to Miklós. 'The thoughts…' Harry gave his forehead a modest tap.

Klára looked from one man to the other. Miklós was short, wore glasses and had metal teeth. Harry was tall, with a neat moustache, and she must have detected the look of genuine desire in his eyes. She decided she was better off believing my father. She took Harry's arm.

'I'm going to get to know you, sweetheart. I don't give a damn about appearances. I don't care about the shape of a mouth, the colour of a man's eyes, whether he is handsome or not. It's the mind I go for, if you see what I mean. I get high on progressive, soaring ideas—I can't get enough of them.'

Harry turned the girl towards him, putting one hand on her ample bottom, and holding her chin in the other. 'I won't disappoint you,' he said boldly, and kissed her on the lips.

Miklós felt it was time to make his exit. At the end of the path he looked back and saw them locked in an embrace as they wandered towards the thick of the forest behind an increasingly heavy curtain of rain.

~

To atone for this episode with Klára, Miklós inflicted three days' penitence on himself. During this time he didn't write a word to Lili. On the fourth day, after getting the key from the caretaker, he ran a full bath of hot water in the only private bathroom on the grounds. It was in a separate building far from the barracks, so Miklós didn't bother to lock the door. He got into the bath, lit a cigarette and started bellowing out a workers' marching song. He wasn't exactly famous for his musical ear.

The door swung open. There was the tiny Márta, the head nurse, trying to wave the thick smoke away. In shock, Miklós tried to cover his penis with his left hand.

Márta was in a rage. 'What do you think you're doing here, Miklós? Hiding away to smoke in secret? You ought to be ashamed! How old are you? You're behaving like a naughty schoolboy!'

My father dropped his cigarette in the water. He tried to wave the smoke away with his right arm but only managed to stir it up. He was shy about being naked and in his embarrassment covered himself with both hands.

Márta, in her huge nurse's cap, came right over to the bath. 'For you, Miklós, every cigarette means death,' she shouted. 'Each one costs you a day of life. Is it worth it? Answer me, you foolish man! Is it worth it?'

> Lili, my dear little friend,
>
> It's time for a confession. Not the one that I'm afraid to write down — but another one. I have to tell you that my ear for music is atrocious and my singing voice is deplorable. But, like all pacifists, I belt out marching songs at the top of my voice in the bath.
>
> It's terrible the way they watch over us here. We have to keep to a strict daily routine: with silent rest times and other fun and games. The chief tyrant is Márta, the Mickey Mouse–like head nurse, Dr Lindholm's Hungarian wife. She's always fussing around us.

The Mickey Mouse–like head nurse stomped across the

garden. It was five minutes' walk to the caretaker's office, and Márta's anger grew with every step.

She practically tore the office door off its hinges.

Four days earlier, not least as a result of Klára Köves's patience, Harry had regained his lost masculinity. Although Klára went away slightly disappointed, they agreed to go on writing to each other. Harry, on the other hand, had worked up an appetite. This time it was big-boned Frida, the daytime caretaker—nicknamed 'baby elephant' by the men—who took his fancy. Harry meditated on the devious whims of his desire. It seemed that the days when only pale, wasp-waisted girls made an impression on him were inexplicably over.

When Márta appeared like an avenging angel in the caretaker's office, Frida and Harry (in his pyjamas) hadn't got past cuddling. But there was no time to break away from each other. Harry was grateful that the conversation took place in Swedish, of which he understood next to nothing.

'Did you sell Miklós cigarettes, Frida?'

Frida's plump arms held Harry in a tight clasp, which she didn't relax for a moment. 'Just two or three.'

'This is your last chance! If I catch you again I'll report you!' shouted Márta, and she turned on her heel, slamming the door behind her.

Of course, Frida was not just being generous by handing out cigarettes. The tiny mark-up she added went to supplement her meagre wages.

Honestly, I like a man who smokes, but you're an
exception now. Please don't overdo it. I don't smoke,
by the way.

~

Lili came into the ward like a sleepwalker. She sat down on her
bed without a word, radiating despair. Judit, who was in bed
reading *Tess of the d'Urbervilles* for the third time, closed the
book and sat up.

Sára was pouring herself a cup of tea. She hurried over to
Lili. 'Has anything happened? '

Lili, sitting there with drooping shoulders, didn't answer.

Sára put her hand on Lili's forehead. 'Your temperature's up
again. Where's the thermometer?'

Judit got out of bed to get the thermometer, which they kept
in a dish on the windowsill. Lili let the girls lift her arm then
press it tightly to her side. They sat opposite her on the bed and
waited.

The wind beat against the windowpane. Lili's soft voice
sounded like a lone violin over the beat of its thrumming and
creaking. 'Someone reported me.'

Judit straightened her back slightly. 'What?'

'I've just come from the Red Cross woman. She told me I'd
been lying…' Lili stared at her slippers.

Silence. Sára remembered her name. 'Ann-Marie
Arvidsson?' she queried.

'…That she knows Miklós isn't my cousin, he's an unknown letter-writer…'

Judit started to pace the room. 'Where did she get that from?'

'…and she's refusing to give permission. He can't come. Can't come!'

Sára kneeled down in front of Lili and kissed both her hands. 'We'll work something out. Get a hold on yourself, your temperature's up.'

Lili couldn't look up. 'She showed me a letter. It was written here, by one of us.'

'Who on earth?' Judit Gold was shouting now.

'She didn't say. She only told me it said that I had lied. Miklós isn't my cousin, as I had claimed, and that's why she is refusing permission for his visit.'

'We'll apply again,' Sára said. 'We'll go on putting in requests to receive visitors until they're sick of the sight of them.'

'Dearest Lili!' Judit collapsed at Lili's feet.

At last, Lili raised her head and looked at her friends. 'Who could hate me so much?'

Sára got up and took the thermometer from under Lili's arm. 'Thirty-nine point two. Get into bed this minute. We'll have to tell Svensson.'

The two girls laid Lili on her back and covered her with the eiderdown. She seemed incapable of moving on her own. They had to treat her like a baby.

'He's attracted to you,' remarked Judit by way of distraction.

Sára didn't understand at first. 'Who's attracted to Lili?'

'Svensson. You should see the looks he gives her.'

'Come off it!' Sára scoffed.

But Judit couldn't leave it alone. 'I'm never wrong in these matters.'

~

Miklós was standing on the iron girders of the bridge over the railway, staring at the tangle of tracks that snaked their way towards the horizon. The sky was steel grey.

A figure came into sight on the road. It was running. At the bridge it climbed the iron steps two at a time. Even so, Miklós only noticed it was Harry when he was standing beside him, puffing and panting.

'You going to jump?'

Miklós smiled. 'What makes you think that?'

'Your eyes. And the way you rushed off after we got the mail.'

A goods train pulled away below them. Its thick black smoke enveloped them like sorrow. Miklós grasped the bridge railings.

'No. I'm not going to jump.'

Harry leaned his elbows on the railings next to Miklós. They watched the departing train. When it had shrunk to a narrow streak in the distance, Miklós took a crumpled letter out of his pocket and handed it to Harry.

'I received this.'

Dear Sir,

In answer to your notice in today's *Szabad Nép*, I regret to inform you that your mother and father were the victims of a bombing raid on the Laxenburg camp in Austria on 12 February 1945…I knew them very well. It was me who guided them to the best place in the camp, the Coffee Factory, where they would be treated as humans and could get decent food and accommodation. I'm extremely sorry that I am the bearer of such sad news.

Andor Rózsa

Miklós had a confused and contradictory relationship with his father. The owner of Gambrinus, the famous bookshop in Debrecen, was a domineering character, prone to shouting and often to violence too. He didn't spare his wife—and he didn't even need to be drunk to attack her. Unfortunately he drank a lot. In spite of this, my grandmother often came into the bookshop with a sandwich or an apple or a pear for him.

My father always remembered a wonderful afternoon in spring when, as a small boy, perched on the top rung of the bookstore ladder, he became so engrossed in Alexei Tolstoy's *Peter the Great* that, spellbound by the intrigues of the tsar's court, his ears flaming red, he forgot all about the time.

In the evening his mother showed up, wearing a wide-brimmed maroon hat. 'Miki, it's seven o'clock. You forgot to come home for dinner. What are you reading?'

He looked up. The woman in the wide-brimmed maroon

hat was familiar, but he couldn't quite place her.

Harry folded the letter and gave it back to Miklós without a word. They leaned against the railings and kept their eyes on the tracks. Some birds were circling overhead.

> Dear Miklós,
> I am terribly sorry that the letter from Szolnok contained such dreadful news. I can't find the words to comfort you.

That afternoon Miklós rode a bike to the cemetery in Avesta. It started to rain. He wandered aimlessly along the headstones, sometimes leaning over an inscription to try to sound out the Swedish name.

> I'm sorry I'm so cold and that I'm taking this calamity so damn hard. Yesterday I went to the local cemetery. I hoped perhaps my loved ones, at the bottom of a mass grave, might be stirred by a cosmic memory... That's all.

~

Lili sat up in bed. It was late at night; the bulb above the door gave off a faint light. Her forehead was drenched in sweat. In the next bed Sára was lying uncovered in the foetal position. Lili slipped out of bed and knelt beside her.

'Are you asleep?'

Sára turned over, as if she had been expecting her. 'I can't sleep either!' she whispered back.

In a moment Lili was lying beside her; she held Sára's hand. Together they watched the strange patterns on the ceiling made by the birch tree swaying in the wind.

'He got some news,' Lili said. 'About his parents. They were bombed.'

Sára's eyes flickered; she could see the letter lying on Lili's bedside table. 'Good God!'

'I've worked it out. It's 373 days since I had any news of my mother or my father.'

With wide eyes they stared at the windblown expressionist images above them.

Seven

THE MAIL van arrived in Avesta soon after lunch. A man in a fur-collared coat jumped out, went round to the back, propped the door open and sorted the letters. It usually took him a few minutes. Then he went over to the yellow letterbox—which looked more like a large suitcase—opened the door at the bottom with a key and scooped all the outgoing mail into an empty canvas sack. After that he tipped all the incoming mail into the letterbox.

It was part of my father's daily routine to monitor this tedious ritual from beginning to end. He had to be absolutely convinced that his letter—as a result of some insidious plot—didn't fall out of the canvas sack.

> Lili, dear,
>
> I'm sure that, if not today, then tomorrow, you
> will get good news. The letter is sitting in your father's
> pocket, and he's waiting for the chance to try out
> this more or less impossible feat of sending a letter to
> Sweden.

~

In the Eksjö hospital there was one place you could smoke without getting caught. It was a bathroom on the second floor, which was used every morning for taking showers, but was then empty until the evening.

Judit Gold smoked at least half a pack a day; that's where all her pocket money went. But Sára, too, smoked three cigarettes a day. Lili went along to keep them company.

Sára inhaled pensively. 'We could go into town this afternoon. I begged for permission,' she announced after a while.

Judit was sitting on the edge of the shower cubicle, her legs drawn up under her. 'What for?'

'We could get a photo of Lili taken for Miklós.'

Lili was shocked. 'God forbid! He'll take one look and flee.'

Judit could blow excellent smoke rings. 'That's a good idea. A photo of the three of us, so we can remember all this, later on.'

'Later on when?' asked Sára.

'One day, when we're somewhere else. When we're happy.'

They meditated on this.

Then Lili said, 'I'm ugly. I don't want a photo.'

Sára smacked her hand. 'You're stupid, my friend, not ugly.'

Judit smiled enigmatically, her eyes following the smoke rings until they reached the ventilator.

~

In the post office Miklós leaned against the glass cubicle. He spoke in German to prevent any misunderstanding.

'I'd like to send a telegram.'

The clerk, who also wore glasses, gave him an encouraging look. 'Address?' she asked.

'Eksjö, Utlänningsläger, Korungsgården 7.'

She started to fill in the form. 'Message?'

'Two words. Two Hungarian words. I'll spell them.'

She took offence at that. 'Just say them, and I'll write them down.'

Miklós breathed in. He pronounced the words clearly, sylla-ble by syllable, in his melodious Hungarian. '*Sze-ret-lek, Li-li.*'

The girl shook her head. Quite a language. 'Spell them, please.'

Miklós went letter by letter. They progressed patiently. Then they got stuck. Whereupon Miklós reached under the glass, grabbed the girl's right hand and tried to guide her pencil.

It wasn't easy. At the capital L, the girl threw down her

pencil and shoved the form across to my father. 'You write it.'

Miklós crossed out the mishmash and in his gorgeous, swirling script wrote in Hungarian: *I love you, Lili!*

He pushed the form back.

The clerk look nonplussed at the unfamiliar word. 'What does it mean?'

Miklós hesitated. 'Are you married, miss?'

'I'm engaged.'

'Oh! Congratulations. Well, it means…it means…'

He knew exactly how to translate into German the simplest and most beautiful declaration in the world. Even so he was reluctant to give himself away.

The girl was adding up. 'That'll be two kronor. So, are you going to tell me?'

Miklós suddenly lost his nerve. He turned pale. 'Give it back, please!' he shouted at her. 'Give it back!'

She shrugged and pushed the form across the counter. Miklós grabbed it and tore it to pieces. He felt utterly stupid and cowardly. How could he explain? Instead he grinned in embarrassment, nodded at the girl and fled the post office.

~

Late that evening the men, wrapped in their blankets, sat around the wooden table in the courtyard. Many of them had their eyes closed in the drowsy silence, or stared vacantly at the bare red-brick wall opposite.

Miklós was standing with his back against the wall, his eyes closed, as if he were asleep.

> I won't send any new poems now, just a sonnet. I've got bigger plans: I'm working out the plot for a novel. It's about twelve people—men, women, children, German, French and Hungarian Jews, cultured people and peasants—travelling in various railway freight wagons to a German concentration camp. From the security of life to certain death. That would be the first twelve chapters. The next twelve would describe the moment of liberation. It's still rather vague, but I'm very keen on the idea.

Pál Jakobovits—who couldn't have been much more than thirty, though his hands were constantly shaking and the doctors no longer comforted him by saying that one day he would get better—rocked back and forth mumbling: 'Dear God, hear my prayers. Dear God, send me a girl, a beautiful dark girl, let her be dark, a beautiful blonde girl, let her be blonde.'

Tibor Hirsch, radio technician and photographer's assistant, could only take so much. From the other end of the table he lashed out at Jakobovits. 'You make yourself ridiculous with that prayer.'

'I can pray for whatever I like.'

'You're not a kid any more, Jakobovits. You're over thirty.'

Jakobovits looked down. He grasped his left hand in his right as if somehow to stop the shaking. 'What's it got to do with you?'

'A man of thirty doesn't drool over women.'

'What does he do then?' Jakobovits yelled. 'Jerk off?'

'Don't be vulgar.'

Jakobovits sank his nails into his arm to overcome the cursed shaking. 'What does a man of thirty do?' he wailed. 'I'm waiting for the answer!'

'He stifles his desires. He asks for bromide. He waits his turn.'

Jakobovits thumped the table. 'I'm not waiting any more! I've waited enough.' He rushed into the barracks.

Standing at the wall, Miklós winced. He kept his eyes shut.

> Lili, dearest,
>   I would swear like hell if I weren't so ashamed.
> That helps me cope with things in the way crying
> helps girls. We're getting dreadfully out of hand here.
> I'd like to get hold of a book by August Bebel for you,
> *Woman and Socialism*. I hope I'll manage it.

~

Lili was curled up under her eiderdown, sobbing. It was past midnight. Sára woke up to the sound of her weeping and climbed out of bed. She lifted the eiderdown and started to stroke Lili's hair.

'Why are you crying?'

'No reason.'

'Did you have a bad dream?'

Sára got into bed beside Lili. They stared at the ceiling—this was becoming a habit. And then Judit Gold appeared hovering over them.

'Is there room for me too?'

The two girls made room, and Judit slipped in with them.

'Who is this Bebel fellow?' asked Lili.

Judit made a face. 'Some sort of writer.'

Sára sat up. This was her field. At times like this she acted like a schoolmistress and even wagged her index finger. 'Not "some sort of writer"! He was a wonderful person.'

'Apparently he wrote a book, *Woman and Socialism*.' Lili dried her eyes.

Judit, who was irritated by Sára's schoolmarmy manner, and in any case loathed left-wing thinking, couldn't help being sarcastic. 'Judging by the title I'll be rushing off to read it. Try stopping me!'

'It's Bebel's finest book. I learned a lot from it,' Sára insisted.

Judit gave Lili's arm a squeeze under the eiderdown. But since she never allowed herself to be beaten in literary debates she opened a new front. 'I'll bet your poet keeps stuffing your head with leftist ideas.'

'He wants to send me this book as soon as he can.'

'Learn chunks of it by heart. That'll impress him.'

Sára was still sitting up with her index finger raised. 'In *Woman and Socialism* Bebel claims that in a just society women have equal rights with men. In love, in war, in everything.'

'Bebel is a prat. He never had a wife.' Judit gave a scathing smile. 'No doubt he had syphilis.'

This made Sára see red. All sorts of retorts churned around in her head, but she couldn't choose the right one. So she lay down again.

> I can't wait to receive the book. Sára has read it
> already, but she'll happily read it again.

~

In Avesta the patients had been given two board games and a chess set. The instructions for the board games were in Swedish and the games themselves seemed rather primitive, so after trying to play them once the men gave up.

The chess set, on the other hand, they fought over. Litzman and Jakobovits were the best players. Apparently Litzman had been chess champion in his home town. He and Jakobovits played for money, and this gave them certain prerogatives over the board. Litzman gave a running commentary on the game for the benefit of the onlookers. He picked up the bishop, drew circles with it in the air and chanted, 'I'll ta-ha-ha-hake it! Che-he-heck!'

Jakobovits thought about this for long minutes.

In the tense silence, Hirsch's exclamation hit them like the celebratory chime of a bell. 'She's alive!' Hirsch was sitting up in bed waving a letter. 'She's alive! My wife is alive!'

Everyone stared.

He stood up and looked around with a radiant face. 'Do you hear? She's alive!' He set out, marching between the beds, waving the letter like a flag above his head and shouting, 'She's alive! Alive! Alive!'

Harry was the first to join him. He fell in behind Hirsch with his hands on his shoulders, taking up the rhythm. They marched round and round between the beds, belting it out like the beat of a drum. 'She's alive! Alive! Alive!'

Then Fried, Grieger, Oblatt and Spitz joined in. There was no resisting the *joie de vivre* that swept them along, Miklós too, until all sixteen survivors were in a line. Hirsch led the way, holding the letter-flag up high, and behind him came the rest, Jakobovits and Litzman bringing up the rear.

They swirled around the room, finding different routes each time, like an endless snake. They clung to each other's shoulders and soon discovered they could tramp over everything, beds, tables, chairs—the main thing was not to break the rhythm.

'Alive! Alive! Alive! Alive! Alive! ALIVE! ALIVE! ALIVE!'

> Today one of my friends, Tibor Hirsch, got a letter
> from Romania. It said that his wife was alive and at
> home. Yet three people have already told me they are
> absolutely certain they saw her being shot in Belsen.

This triumphant episode inspired Miklós to make one last attempt to win permission for his journey.

He knew that Dr Lindholm spent Wednesday evenings working in his office in the main building. So he borrowed a coat to put on over his pyjamas, walked across the yard and knocked on his door.

Dr Lindholm motioned for him to sit down while he finished his sentence, and then looked up. The room was lit by a desk lamp, and its circle of light ended just under the doctor's eyes. This put Miklós off slightly.

'I'd like to speak to you about the soul, doctor.'

Lindholm's chin and nose were in the light. 'Yes, is a strange thing.'

My father took off his coat and threw it on the floor. He was sitting there in his frayed stripy pyjamas like a mediaeval saint. 'Sometimes it's more important than the body,' he said.

Dr Lindholm clasped his hands. 'A psychologist is coming next week.'

'No, I want to discuss this with you. Have you read *The Magic Mountain*?'

Dr Lindholm leaned back, his face disappearing in the darkness. He became headless. 'Yes, I have.'

'I'm a bit like Hans Castorp. The wry envy that I feel for the healthy almost hurts…'

'Is understandable.'

'Give me permission. Please.'

'How does that fit in?'

'If I could go and see my cousin, just for a few days. If I could pretend to myself that I was cured.'

Dr Lindholm interrupted. 'Is becoming obsessive, Miklós. Drop it, for goodness sake!'

'Drop what?'

'This travel madness! This stubborn behaviour. Come to senses!' Dr Lindholm was almost shouting. He got up and stepped out of the light.

Miklós jumped up too. He also raised his voice. 'I have come to my senses. I want to travel!'

'But you will die. You will die soon!'

Dr Lindholm's terrifying diagnosis circled them like a bird of prey. Miklós could see only the doctor's two well-lit legs in their suit trousers, and decided that his verdict could therefore be ignored.

In the ensuing silence only their rapid breathing could be heard.

Dr Lindholm turned round, ashamed, and went to the cupboard. He opened the door. Shut it. Opened it again. Shut it.

Miklós stood still, growing pale.

'I'm sorry. I'm sorry. I'm sorry,' Lindholm said softly in Swedish.

He opened the cupboard again, took out a file, went over to the backlit wall and flicked the switch there. The room was flooded with cold, sterile light. The doctor removed some X-rays from the file and held them in front of the pane of glass on the wall. There were six of them. He didn't turn round. He didn't catch my father's eye.

'By the way, where is your "cousin" being treated?'

'In Eksjö.'

'Take off pyjama jacket. I listen to your chest.'

Miklós slipped out of his jacket.

Lindholm took out his stethoscope. 'Deep breathings. In, out, in, out.'

They avoided each other's eyes. Miklós breathing. Dr Lindholm listening. He listened for a long time, as if he were enjoying some distant, celestial music.

'Three days,' Dr Lindholm said. 'To say goodbye.'

Miklós pulled on his pyjama jacket. 'Thank you, doctor.'

> Lili,
> Now you have to be quick and nimble because we're going to trick the Red Cross. I need a letter in Swedish from your doctor in which he recommends my visit on medical grounds. I've already managed to persuade my doctor!

Dr Lindholm fiddled awkwardly with his stethoscope. In the strange, intimate glow he was brave enough to take his wallet out of his back pocket. 'Finish with her. Is my opinion as a doctor, but what matters my opinion? The soul…sometimes you have to bury it.'

He took the X-rays down from the wall and put them back in the file. He switched off the backlit wall. Now, he took a small, creased photo out of his wallet and handed it to Miklós. It showed a fair-haired little girl with a ball in her hands, gazing warily into the lens.

'Who's that?' Miklós asked.

'My daughter. Not now. She die in an accident.'

My father hardly moved. Lindholm shifted from leg to leg. The floor creaked. His voice became husky. 'Life sometimes punish us.'

Miklós stroked the face of the little girl with a finger.

'Her name is Jutta. From my first marriage. Márta related second part of story to you. Jutta is first part.'

~

This time Lili and the others had planned a longer program. Sára sang eight songs with Lili accompanying her on the piano. They included two Hungarian songs, one Schumann, two Schubert and some of the popular songs from operettas.

The soldiers, in their pyjamas, and the nurses applauded loudly. On stage, Lili and Sára gave a modest and graceful bow after each song. It was to Lili's credit that Dr Svensson came too. He sat in the middle of the front row with a little girl on his lap, and after every song he stamped his feet.

At the end of the evening he went on stage to congratulate Lili, who was standing tensely by the piano. Lili looked longingly at the little girl, who hadn't been the slightest bit fidgety, but nor had she fallen asleep. In fact, she had clearly enjoyed the concert.

'Can I hold her?'

Svensson handed the girl over to Lili, and she chuckled as Lili hugged her.

Meanwhile Sára was surrounded by soldiers. It didn't take much asking for her to sing them an encore, just like that, unaccompanied. She chose 'Crane Bird High in the Sky'. A few soldiers wept, though they didn't understand a word.

Lili caught the mood too—a kind of sorrow overwhelmed her.

~

> One evening a few days ago I went into town and
> wandered around on my own in the snowy streets.

It was dusk. Miklós was tired by the time he reached the top of the hill and he couldn't pedal any more. He got off his bike, pushed it about twenty metres, then stopped.

There were no curtains in the windows of the house; from where he stood beside the fence he could easily look in. The scene was like a nineteenth-century realist painting. The man reading, the woman sitting at her sewing machine, and lying between them in a wooden cradle a young child. He could even see that the child was playing with a doll and smiling.

> I could see into a worker's home. I feel very tired.
> Twenty-five years and so many awful things. I can't
> look back on a good and harmonious family life: I
> never had one. Perhaps that's why I long for one so
> much. I couldn't bear to see them any more, and
> hurried away.

Eight

LILI KEPT hugging Dr Svensson's little girl. The soldiers, moved by Sára's song, still surrounded her.

> *Crane bird high in the sky*
> *Is flying homewards*
> *The gypsy boy is walking on his way*
> *His staff in his hand.*

Dr Svensson touched Lili's arm. 'I've received a letter from the Avesta rehab centre. A colleague of mine wrote it, the head doctor. He's got a Hungarian wife.'

Lili blushed and stammered something. 'Yes.'

'It was about your cousin.'

'Oh, yes.'

'I'm not quite sure how to tell you. It's a disturbing letter.'

The little girl suddenly felt heavy in Lili's arms. She put her down. 'We've been planning for him to come and visit me.'

The doctor took his daughter by the hand. 'That's what it's about. I agree with the visit. I shall certainly give my permission.'

Lili shrieked, and grabbed at Dr Svensson's hand to kiss it. The doctor did all he could to pull his hand away.

Down among the audience Sára was singing, 'If I could only be with you once more, I'd lie beside you on your violet couch.'

Svensson held his arm behind his back. 'But there's something you should know.'

'I know everything.'

'You don't know about this.' Svensson waited. 'Your cousin is seriously ill.'

'Is he?' Lili felt a tiny pang in her heart.

'It's his lungs. Very serious. Irreversible. Do you understand? Irreversible.'

'I do.'

'I was in two minds whether to tell you. But since he's family I think you should know. It's not contagious.'

'I see. It's not contagious,' repeated Lili, as she stroked the little girl's hair.

Sára had finished her song and there was a hush except for the sound of Svensson's daughter humming, the effect of which was like a fading echo. Svensson put his finger to her lips, and the echo died away too.

'Take care of yourself, dear Lili. You're not well either. Far from it.'

Lili's mouth was dry; she couldn't say anything.

~

Miklós tried to conceal it, but Lindholm's diagnosis nagged at him. He didn't really believe the doctor, but for his peace of mind he felt it would be good to get a second opinion. So he asked Jakobovits, who in peacetime had worked in a hospital as a theatre assistant, to assess the X-rays. That meant breaking into Lindholm's office. Harry happily joined the mission; he was up for anything that had the tang of adventure.

The narrow corridor of the main building was lit by the yellow glow of a night light. Miklós, Jakobovits and Harry crept towards Lindholm's office like three hobgoblins.

Harry was carrying a piece of wire. He often boasted of having belonged to a gang of thieves before the war. Apparently he was an expert at picking locks.

He fiddled about in the keyhole for ages, giving Miklós time to regret the whole idea. Their escapade seemed almost laughable. But eventually Harry succeeded in opening the door and they were inside.

They went into action like a crack military unit. Miklós gestured to Harry which cabinet to open, and Harry fiddled around with his wire once again. They didn't dare turn on the light, but there was a full moon and Lindholm's room was bathed in an unearthly phosphorescent glow. The three men might have felt like heroes in a fairytale.

The cabinet lock clicked. Miklós reached in and ran his fingers over the files; he remembered that his was somewhere around the middle. He breathed out when he found it, took the X-rays and handed them to Jakobovits.

Jakobovits settled himself comfortably in Lindholm's armchair and, holding the images up to the light of the moon, began to study them.

Someone flung the door open, flicked the switch and flooded the room with the unforgiving light of three hundred-watt bulbs.

Márta stood in the doorway, her tiny bosom heaving. 'What are you gentlemen doing here?'

The gentlemen, all wearing uniform striped pyjamas beneath their makeshift coats, leapt to their feet. The X-rays slipped out of Jakobovits's hands. No one answered. The situation spoke for itself. Márta added to the pantomime by strolling over to the X-rays and picking them up one by one.

Then she turned to the honourable company. 'You may go.'

The men began to tramp out in single file.

'You stay here, Miklós,' Márta said.

The relief felt by the other two was palpable. The door shut behind them. Miklós turned round with the most penitent expression he could summon. Márta had already taken up residence in Lindholm's armchair.

'What do you want to find out?'

'My friend Jakobovits is some kind of doctor,' Miklós stammered. 'Or used to be. I wanted him to take a look at the X-rays.'

'Didn't Erik assess them for you?'

Miklós looked down at his shoes with their sloppy laces. 'Yes.'

Márta stared at him for such a long time that he was forced to return her gaze. Then the head nurse nodded, as if she had taken note and understood. She stood up, put the X-rays back in the file and the file back in the cabinet. 'Erik does all he can for you. You are his favourite patient.'

'I always have a fever at dawn: thirty-eight point two.'

'New medicines are becoming available all over the world every week. Who knows what might happen?'

Something burst in my father. It happened so swiftly that he didn't even have time to turn away. It was as sudden as an earthquake. He collapsed to the floor and buried his face in his hands, sobbing.

Márta turned away discreetly. 'You've been through terrible things. You survived them. You survived, Miklós. Don't give up now, at the finishing post.'

Miklós couldn't speak. He wasn't crying any more—the sound he made now was more like the whimpering of a wounded animal. He tried to form intelligible words, but it was as if his voice had abandoned him.

At last, he said, 'I'm not giving up.'

Márta looked at him in despair. He was huddled on the floor, his arms covering his head. She stepped closer to him. 'Good. So now pull yourself together.'

They gave each other some time. Miklós was quiet now, but he was hiding behind his arms and had curled himself up even smaller.

'Right,' he said when he could speak normally again.

'Look at me, Miklós.' Márta crouched down beside him.

My father peered out between his two bony elbows.

Márta adopted her cold, bossy head-nurse voice. 'Take deep breaths.'

He attempted to breathe evenly.

Márta conducted. 'One, two. One, two. Deep breaths. Slowly.'

Miklós's chest was rising and falling regularly. One, two. One, two.

'Slowly. Deep breaths.'

> My dearest little Lili,
>   I'm not stupid, I know that the illness that keeps me here will gradually disappear. But I also know my fellow patients. I hear the terrible pity in their voices when they say, 'It's his lungs.'

~

It was November and an icy wind blew leaves around the Eksjö hospital. There was an open, circular pavilion in its grounds, an attractive building with a dark green wooden roof supported by graceful white pillars. For Lili, forbidden to leave the grounds during the week, this pavilion was a refuge. When she couldn't stand the smell of the hospital any longer she escaped there. On fine days she leaned against a column and bathed her face in the fitful sunshine.

But now, hostile winds were blowing. In their dejection, Lili and Sára were walking obsessively round and round the columns in their thick woollen uniforms.

> My dear Miklós,
>
> I am very cross with you! How can a serious, intelligent man of twenty-five be so foolish? Isn't it enough for you that I am fully aware of your illness and can hardly wait to meet you?

~

Late one afternoon, two men in suits and ties arrived in Avesta and were taken straight to the Hungarian section. It turned out they were from the Hungarian embassy. One of them held up a radio bound with a ribbon, and the other made an announcement.

'This radio has been sent to you, on loan, by the Orion factory in Hungary. Happy listening!'

Tibor Hirsch accepted the radio on behalf of the men. 'Thank you! News from home is more effective than any medicine.'

They put the radio on a table and my father looked for a

socket. Harry switched it on. The tuning eye glistened green, and the radio crackled and hissed.

'Search for Budapest,' ordered one of the suited men.

Within half a minute they could all hear Hungarian. 'Dear listeners, it is five minutes past five. We are transmitting a message to Hungarians abroad from Sándor Millok, Minister for Repatriation. "Every Hungarian scattered around the world who is listening to this program should know that we are thinking of them and have not forgotten them. In the next few minutes I will outline to them and to our listeners at home the regulations devised to simplify the administrative requirements for our compatriots' return home."'

That evening the men sat out in the courtyard with the radio on the long wooden table. The light bulb swung eerily in the wind. The men usually spent half an hour before bed in the open air. By now they had been playing the radio for six hours without a break. They had put on sweaters and coats over their pyjamas and wrapped blankets around themselves. They sat right up close to the radio. The green tuning light winked like the eye of an elf.

They were listening to Senator Claude Pepper talking from Washington. The Hungarian presenter whispered his translation every few sentences. Then they listened to the news from Budapest. The fragments of sound whirled around in their heads like the wind sweeping down from the North Pole.

The second transport of major war criminals had arrived at Keleti railway station.

The pontoon bridge at Boráros Square had been officially opened.

The training of the first unit of policewomen had been successfully completed.

A competition testing the skill of waiters had taken place on Nagy Körút.

In the second round of the boxing team championship Mihály Kovács, boxing for Vasas, had knocked out Rozsnyó from Csepel.

~

It was Sunday. The Björkmans' dark grey car swung round in front of the hospital, and Lili, who had been waiting in the caretaker's office, climbed into the back seat.

After mass the Björkmans took Lili home to Smålandsstenar. They sat at the table for lunch, and Sven Björkman said grace. Mrs Björkman ladled out the soup, and her husband was pleased to see Lili's silver cross sparkling around her neck. Language difficulties kept the conversation brief.

'No news from home, Lili?' Björkman asked her in Swedish.

Lili didn't look up. She understood every word. She shook her head.

Björkman took pity on her. 'You know what? Tell us something about your father!'

Lili winced. How could she possibly?

Björkman misunderstood: he thought Lili was struggling with his Swedish. Using his spoon for emphasis he hammered out the words. 'Your papa! YOUR PA-PA! Papa! Daddy! Father! Get it?'

Lili nodded. 'I could try to tell you in German, but I don't speak it well enough.'

'It doesn't matter,' Björkman said. He wasn't to be put off. 'Tell us in Hungarian. We'll listen. Believe me, we'll understand. Just tell us about him. In Hungarian. Come on! Fire away!'

The spoon was shaking in Lili's hand. The whole Björkman family was looking at her, even the two boys. Lili wiped her mouth on her napkin, put her spoon on the table and her hand in her lap. She glanced down at the cross hanging from her neck. 'My father, my dear father, has blue eyes...blue eyes that shine,' she said in her soft Hungarian. 'He's the kindest person in the world.'

The family listened, transfixed. Sven Björkman sat motionless, his head slightly to one side, enchanted by the music of the unfamiliar language. What did he understand in the melody, in the rhythm?

'My father isn't tall, but he isn't short either. He loves us dearly. He's a salesman by occupation. A suitcase salesman.'

Every Monday at dawn Lili's father, Sándor Reich, trudged down Hernád Street in Budapest carrying two huge Vulkan cabin-trunks. In each one, like the layers of an onion, dozens of smaller and smaller cases and bags lay one inside the other.

This picture was so vivid that, even without shutting her

eyes, Lili could see the shadow of her father creeping along the walls of the buildings in the spring sunshine.

'My father travels in the country all week. But at the weekend, on Fridays, he always comes home to us. We rented a flat to be near Keleti train station. On Monday mornings, Father sets out on foot with his wares and he walks down Hernád Street to the station. On Fridays, when he comes home, we are waiting for him.'

These words swept Lili into the past. They were sitting at the specially laid table in Hernád Street: Mother, Father and eight-year-old Lili. At the head of the table sat somebody else: an unshaven man, his scruffy coat buttoned up to hide his grimy, ragged shirt and torn trousers. Father had tried to take his coat from him, but he gave up. The stranger fingered the saltcellar with his dirty nails in embarrassment.

'On Friday evenings we always had a special supper to which Father invited a poor Jew. This was how he greeted the Sabbath. More often than not he invited a man from around the station.'

It was as if Sven Björkman understood Lili's words. A tear danced in the corner of his eye, but he remained hunched on his chair. His wife had an ecstatic smile on her face, and even the two boys were listening with wide eyes, between spoonfuls of soup.

'So every Friday evening we are a family of four.'

Lili didn't dare look down at the silver cross hanging round her neck.

In the evening, during the long drive back to Eksjö, Mrs Björkman described to Lili the complicated process of Swedish adoption. It didn't seem to bother her that Lili could not understand the subject of her excited monologue. She was simply relieved that at last she could speak out about what she and Sven had been planning for weeks.

The Björkman family was still waving goodbye to Lili long after she had disappeared behind the double wooden doors of the hospital.

> Dear Miklós,
>   Don't forget your promise to find a partner for my best friend Sára. She is older than I am. She has just turned twenty-two.

~

Crazed by nicotine deprivation, my father ran the short distance to the caretaker's office. He barged in without knocking. Frida and Harry shot apart.

'I just came for cigarettes,' Miklós said.

Frida leapt off Harry's lap and, not even doing up her blouse, went to the cupboard and took out a box. Its compartments were filled with various brands of cigarettes. She grinned, her breasts swinging all over the place. 'How many do you want?'

Miklós was ashamed, for her sake as well. He wanted four. Frida licked her fingers and picked out the cigarettes. Miklós fished out his coins. They swapped.

Harry embraced Frida from behind, kissing her neck. 'Give them to him free, darling. He's my best friend. It's thanks to him that I'm up to it again.'

Frida gave Miklós a coquettish look, shrugged and gave him back the coins.

> I'm really struggling with your request. There are
> sixteen of us Hungarians here, but there's not one that
> I'd choose for Sára. I wanted to take Harry with me to
> see you, for instance, but I've given up on that idea.

~

In Eksjö, the musical evenings were becoming more frequent. Dr Svensson even allowed Lili and Sára to skip half their afternoon rest. At two o'clock the girls shut themselves in the main hall and practised. The doctor had found some sheet music for them, too.

One of these albums included a selection of works by Leoncavallo. That week they performed his best known aria, 'Mattinata'. On the wings of this lofty song, Sára's soprano floated to the heights. She waved her arms about, enraptured. Lili took on this exaggerated romantic manner too, swooping down on the keys like a falcon.

It was a huge pity for them that they didn't have any suitable clothes to perform in. In fact they didn't have suitable clothes for any occasion. They took the stage in their hospital gowns, which were just long enough to cover their nightdresses.

Judit Gold sat among a row of soldiers, the only woman. She pulled herself up proudly; it felt good to be Hungarian.

> *L'aurora, di bianco vestita,*
> *Già l'uscio dischiude al gran sol.*
> *Dawn, dressed in white,*
> *Already opens the door to broad daylight.*

There must have been something in the atmosphere, because on the same evening in Avesta, hundreds of kilometres to the north, everyone was in high spirits.

Unaware of this synchronicity, the men began to sing the identical Leoncavallo aria. It was as if a celestial conductor had given a sign to his herald angels and called on his choir to sing the same song. Their rendition of 'Mattinata' in the barracks, at the suggestion of Jenö Grieger who spiced their performance with his accomplished guitar accompaniment, might have been slightly out of tune, but they gave the Italian everything they had.

For the soldiers in the Eksjö hospital the song's rousing power was irresistible. The hall was all smiles. Sára raised her arms high; Lili practically floated above the piano stool.

The men in the barracks were by now standing on beds and tables. Harry wormed himself in beside Grieger and conducted.

> *Ove non sei la luce manca,*
> *Ove tu sei nasce l'amor!*
> *There is no light where you are not,*
> *Love is born where you are!*

Miklós stood in the front row. He was flushed; the future seemed radiant. After all, 'Mattinata' was a hymn to love; he was certain that the others were celebrating *him* with this song.

~

I'm sending the wool, with our measurements. You don't mind, do you?

Miklós had hinted to Lili on the telephone that he wasn't short of funds, courtesy of a Cuban uncle. The truth was that Uncle Henrik was my grandmother's elder brother, and his claim to fame was that in 1932 he absconded with the family jewels and emigrated to Cuba. He mustn't have felt too many pangs of conscience, because as soon as he got to Havana he sent a postcard to the family in Hungary raving about the wonders of his new homeland.

As a little boy my father often studied that black-and-white picture of the crowded Havana harbour on a rainy afternoon. He could only vaguely remember Uncle Henrik's face. He seemed to think he had a jaunty moustache and sparkling eyes, and that now and then he wore a monocle, but he couldn't swear to that.

On the Havana postcard, which for years members of the family pointed at as proof of Uncle Henrik's unforgivable disloyalty, a three-funnelled ocean steamer was visible, as well as a number of Ford cars clustered on the dock. A few skinny stevedores loafing about gazed into the camera, so it was easy to identify them with Uncle Henrik's future. But my great-uncle had no intention of loading ships. Quite the contrary, as revealed by a more recent photograph, which he sent years later, with the obvious intention of tantalising his envious relations—a crystal-clear picture of Henrik embracing a mulatto woman with wide cheekbones and a dozen children underfoot.

In the photograph, Henrik and the woman are standing on a wooden veranda and Henrik has a cigar between his lips. On the back two lines were scribbled in his sloping hand: 'I'm fine. I've invested in a sugarcane plantation.'

When Miklós was struck by his passion for letter-writing, he immediately thought of his uncle as a potential source of cash. There was nothing to lose. He wrote to Henrik that he had managed to survive the war and was now being nursed in Sweden. He had an imaginary picture in his mind's eye. As a teenager he had often dreamed about Cuba after leafing through an album from the 1920s that he had found in his father's bookshop. In the picture he now imagined, his uncle was rocking in a hammock on the famous veranda. He had put on weight—he must have been at least 120 kilos. In my father's vision the veranda is set on a hillside overlooking the sea.

Whether or not Uncle Henrik lived like that or in even greater style history doesn't say. He didn't write a single word in reply to Miklós's letter, but three weeks later a cheque arrived to the tune of eighty-five dollars.

This became my father's capital. On the day it arrived, he gave some of it to an old man smelling of vinegar, who palmed off four skeins of mud-coloured wool in return.

Now the owner of the world's ugliest wool, Miklós wrote a touching ad and placed it in *Világosság* to help Lili find her mother in Hungary. Another portion of Uncle Henrik's now less-than-princely sum he spent on three little chocolate cupcakes from an Avesta café and had them wrapped in a smart parcel bound with gold twine. His most serious investment was three and a half metres of material for a winter coat, which, trembling with indecision, he took a great deal of time to choose. Now he was ready for his journey.

Nine

MY FATHER travelled for a whole day. He had to change trains several times. He sat in different compartments: sometimes by the window; sometimes, for lack of space, jammed up against the door. At times he removed his bulky overcoat, folding it up and laying it across his knees. At other times his glasses misted up from the heat so he fished Lili's handkerchief out of his trouser pocket to wipe them. He took the greatest care of his parcel of cakes. He found a safe place for it in every compartment—in no way was it to be damaged.

Occasionally he fell asleep; when he was awake he looked out of the window. The stations flashed by: Hovsta, Örebro,

Hallsberg, Motala, Mjölby.

Sometime after Mjölby he slipped as he entered his compartment and fell on his face. The left lens of his glasses was smashed to smithereens.

> I travelled to Stockholm so that I could buy my train ticket in person at the office for foreigners. You know what? I send you my kisses.
> Miklós

> There are two alcoves in the corridor. One of them is particularly secluded. We can sit all day under a huge artificial palm tree without anyone disturbing us. All right, then—I send you a kiss.
> Lili

> I want to tell you something the evening I arrive, just before we say goodnight for the first time. As for me, I send special kisses, heaps of them—not in that 'all right, then' mode.
> Miklós

> In Sára's repertoire there is another song that I'm sure you know—'The March of the Volunteers'. I'm so looking forward to seeing you! Till we meet, I send you many kisses.
> Lili

I'm glad about the alcove in the corridor because I

don't like talking in full view. I'm stroking your hair
in my thoughts (will you let me?) and sending lots of
kisses.

Miklós

This morning when I woke up my left eye was itching.
I told Sára it was a good sign. See you soon. Kisses.

Lili

I'm arriving on the first of December at 6.17 p.m. I
send my love many times over.

Miklós

~

On 1 December 1945 it was snowing hard in Eksjö. The platform
and tracks at the tiny station were not covered, but the entrance
was protected by a veranda.

Miklós was the only person to alight from the three-carriage
train. He didn't quite resemble Don Juan as he hobbled across
the platform. He leaned a little to the right because his shoulder
was dragged down by the weight of his suitcase, a dilapidated
number lent to him by Márta. It was tied up with string. In his
left hand he carried the cupcakes.

Lili and Sára were waiting outside the station. Lili clung
nervously to her friend's hand. Behind the girls stood a nurse in a
full-length black cloak and trademark peaked cap. She had been
instructed by Svensson to keep an eye on his patients.

Miklós spotted the reception committee in the distance and smiled. His metal teeth glimmered in the weak light of the platform lamps.

The girls glanced at each other in alarm, then looked guiltily back towards the platform where Miklós was advancing through the thick veil of snow. He had to rest for a moment while he coughed. The left lens frame of his glasses was stuffed with scrunched-up newspaper—that day's *Aftonbladet*—an operation he had performed in desperation half an hour earlier, leaving a crack free so that he could at least see a little. He drew nearer on the snow-covered platform; his borrowed winter coat, two sizes too big for him, floated around his ankles. He seemed to have tears in his visible eye, either from the cold or from excitement. Even from this distance and despite the thick lens, the girls could make that out. And he was smiling broadly, his iron teeth in full view.

Lili was scared stiff. In a matter of seconds he would be in earshot. 'He's yours! Let's swap!' she whispered to Sára out of the side of her mouth, with her teeth clenched, like someone who's had a stroke.

By now Miklós was a few steps away.

'You be Lili! I beg you!' she pleaded.

The nurse at the back of the little group was touched to see the skinny man in his funny coat reach her patients and set his battered case down in the snow.

My father had rehearsed thoroughly for this, the most important meeting of his life. He had put together a short but striking speech—three sentences in all—that he felt would have a magical effect. In the course of his seemingly endless journey, in the stuffy compartments, he had whispered it to himself a thousand times. But now he was struck dumb with happiness. He even seemed to have forgotten his name, but that was only because he was unable to suck air into his lungs. So all he did was extend his hand.

Sára took a quick look. At least his hand was all right. Long fingers, smooth palm. She grasped it. 'I'm Lili Reich,' she said.

Miklós gave her a firm handshake. He turned to Lili. She shook his hand vigorously.

'I'm Sára Stern, Lili's friend,' she said in a bright voice.

Miklós grinned with his metal teeth. He couldn't say a word.

They stood there. Eventually, Miklós handed the parcel of cakes bound with gold twine to Lili.

The nurse stepped forward and snatched the packet out of her hands. 'We must go!' she ordered, giving Miklós a compassionate look.

So they set out. Huge flakes of snow were falling. After a slight hesitation Sára took Miklós's arm. Lili walked beside them, her eyes on the ground. For a moment it occurred to her to take my father's other arm, but she felt it was too intimate. The nurse followed, carrying the elegant parcel of cupcakes.

To get to the hospital they had to cross an enormous park. As they trudged through the virgin snow, Miklós had one arm in Sára's. In his other hand he carried the suitcase tied up with string. Lili and the nurse were a few paces behind.

In the middle of the park, precisely eight minutes after his terrifying dumbness, as if a gift from God, Miklós got his voice back. He cleared his throat, then stopped. He put down the suitcase, withdrew his arm from Sára's and turned to Lili.

It had stopped snowing. The four of them resembled figures out of a Hans Christian Andersen fairytale: dark crumbs on an oval white china plate.

Miklós abandoned the speech he had practised. 'I always imagined you like this,' he said in his pleasant baritone, 'in my dreams. Hello, Lili.'

Lili stood there awkwardly. She nodded. The weight lifted from her; everything seemed natural. She took a step forward and so did Miklós. They hugged each other.

Sára and the nurse instinctively drew back.

Half an hour later Miklós and Lili were in the alcove behind the palm. Two worn upholstered armchairs stood opposite each other. My father draped his overcoat over the back of one of them and put his suitcase down.

They sat and looked at each other, not wanting to speak. At times they smiled. They were waiting.

Miklós took the suitcase onto his lap, undid the string and opened the lid. He had packed the coat fabric on top and now he smoothed it out. He lifted it up like a baby and handed it to Lili. 'I brought this for you.'

'What is it?'

'Material for a winter coat. You just have to get it made.'

'A coat?'

'You wrote that they hadn't given you a coat. Do you like it?'

Apart from the set of clothes she was given on her arrival in Sweden, Lili had one folksy skirt, a spinach-green waistcoat and a rust-red turban-like hat—all presents from the Björkmans. As she ran her hand down the thick, dark-brown, woollen fabric it reminded her of peacetime. She held back her tears.

'I took an hour choosing it,' Miklós added. 'I'm no expert when it comes to winter coats. Or summer coats for that matter.'

Lili again fingered the material, almost as if she were trying to decipher a secret code woven into it. Then she held it to her nose. 'It's got a nice smell.'

'I brought it in that old suitcase. I was afraid it'd get creased. But it hasn't, thank God. I borrowed the suitcase from the head nurse.'

Lili remembered everything. She had read each letter from Miklós at least five times. The first time hastily devouring it, then, escaping to the bathroom, twice more, thoroughly relishing every paragraph. Later, perhaps a day later, she would reread it twice, and behind each word she imagined other words. She knew a great deal about Márta.

'Mickey Mouse?'

'Yes.'

There was so much my father wanted to tell her. The sentences piled up in his head. Where to start?

He found a cigarette in his pocket. He took it out along with a box of matches. 'Do you mind?'

'Of course not. What about your lungs?'

'They're fine. All's well here inside,' he said pointing to his chest. 'It's just my heart! It wants to burst—it's beating so hard!'

Lili stroked the coat fabric with her fingertips.

Miklós lit up. Soon a cloud of grey smoke swirled above their heads.

At last they began to speak, eagerly, hardly finishing their sentences, cutting in on each other. They were excited and impatient, wanting to make up for everything all at once. But they never spoke about certain important things. Neither then, nor later.

~

My father never told Lili that for three months he burned bodies in Belsen concentration camp.

How could he have spoken of the suffocating stench that lingered over the mounds of the dead and clawed at his throat? Is there a word that could describe this work? A phrase that could describe the feeling as bare, scaly arms slipped from their grip, over and over, to land with a senseless thud on top of other frozen bodies?

Lili did not tell Miklós about the day of her liberation from Belsen.

It took her nine hours to drag herself from the barracks to the clothes depot, a distance of about a hundred metres. She was naked and the sun was scorching. The Germans had fled by then. All she could remember was that it was late afternoon when she made it. Then she was sitting in a German officer's tunic, leaning back against a wall and bathing her face in the light.

How did she come to be dressed in a German officer's uniform?

Miklós could never bring himself to tell her of his time, before he burned corpses, as an orderly in the typhoid barracks. In block seventeen, the most ghastly block in the camp, he doled out bread and soup to the half-dead. He had to wear the black band of the *Oberpfleger* on his arm. How could he possibly have told her about the time when Imre Bak knocked on the window? How Imre got down on all fours and barked like a rabid dog? Imre Bak was his best friend in Debrecen. He was hoping to get medicine from Miklós. Perhaps. Or at least a kind word. But he couldn't even walk into the typhoid death block. Through the filthy window, my father watched him topple over. His handsome, clever head landed in a puddle. He was dead.

And Lili never said a word—neither then nor later—about her twelve-day journey to Germany in a freight wagon. On the seventh day she discovered she could lick the condensation that had frozen overnight on the wall of the wagon. She was so thirsty, so dreadfully thirsty! Her friend Terka Koszárik had been screaming beside her nonstop for twenty hours. Perhaps Terka was the luckier of the two: she had gone completely mad.

And my father never described the murderous fight in the Belsen general hospital after the camp was liberated. He weighed twenty-nine kilos at the time. Someone had put him on the back of a truck, which took him to hospital. Afterwards, for weeks, he just lay on a bed. Three times a day a strapping German nurse picked up his featherweight body and poured cod-liver oil down his throat. Lying beside him was a dentist, a Polish Jew. He was thirty-five and spoke several languages. He could talk about Bergson, Einstein and Freud. Six weeks after liberation, this dentist beat an even more unfortunate Frenchman almost to death for half a kilo of butter. My father never spoke about that.

True, Lili never talked about the Belsen general hospital either. It was May, springtime, the war had just come to an end. She was lying there, not far from my father, as it happened, in the women's section. Lili was given paper and pencil. The task was to write down her name and date of birth. Lili thought hard. What was her name? She couldn't remember. Not for the life of her. She was devastated by the thought that she might never again remember her own name.

They didn't speak about any of these things.

Two hours later my father stroked Lili's hair, then got up awkwardly from his armchair and kissed the tip of her nose.

It was past midnight when a nurse took up position at a discreet distance, and Lili realised that it was time to say goodnight. The nurse accompanied Miklós down to the first floor and took him to a four-bed ward where he was to sleep for the next two nights.

Miklós undressed and got into his pyjamas. He was flooded with such happiness that for hours he paced the short distance from the window to the door and back again. Still exhilarated at 3.30 a.m., he had to force himself to get into bed. But he couldn't sleep.

After breakfast, at nine the next morning, they were sitting once more under the palm. When Judit Gold hurried down to the caretaker's office at 11 a.m. to bring up the mail for the women's section, she caught sight of Lili and Miklós in the alcove, their heads together, whispering. She turned away, ashamed of the spurt of breathless jealousy that took hold of her.

Lili was preparing to reveal her deepest secret. She took a breath. 'I've a terrible sin to confess. No one knows about it. Not even Sára, but I'm going to tell you.'

Miklós leaned forward and touched her hand. 'You can tell me anything. Everything.'

'I'm so ashamed…I…I…' Lili faltered.

'You've nothing to be ashamed of,' my father said confidently.

'I can't explain it…it's awful. When we had to give our personal details, before we got on the Swedish ship…I can't bear to tell you…'

'Of course you can!'

'I…I…Instead of my mother's name—her name is Zsuzsanna Herz—instead of her name, for some reason I can't understand, I was incapable of saying her name. I lied! I just couldn't give them my mother's name.'

Lili grabbed Miklós's hand and held it tight. Her face was so pale it seemed almost luminous. My father freed himself and lit a cigarette as he always did when he wanted to think hard.

'It's quite clear: you wanted to change your fate.'

Lili thought about this. 'That's right. What a lovely way of putting it! Changing one's fate. A solution presented itself on the spur of the moment, without my really preparing for it. To be different. Not Jewish. With just one word I was transformed.'

'From a frog to a princess.'

My father always loved images from fairytales. But, perhaps because he felt this was a bit trivial, he added, 'I felt the same way. But I was too much of a coward.'

'Lying on the stretcher there on the quay, I said my mother's name was Rozália Rákosi. Where on earth did I get that name from? Rákosi? I haven't a clue. Rozália Rákosi. That's what I said instead of my mother's real name.'

Miklós stubbed out his cigarette in the tin ashtray. 'Don't worry. It's over and done with.'

Lili shook her head. 'No, it isn't. You see, I also said that my father was a Jew but my mother was Roman Catholic. Not only that, I told them I was Catholic, too. Do you see? I wanted to be done with the whole thing. The Jewish business. Once and for all.'

'Quite understandable.'

Lili started to cry.

Miklós took out his precious handkerchief.

Lili hid her face in her hands. 'No, no, it's a terrible sin! Unforgivable! You are the first person I've ever told. And, if you want to know, every Sunday I go to a Swedish family for lunch. The Björkmans. Everyone thinks I go there because I want to. But that's not true, I go there because they are Catholics, too.

And I go to church with them. I've even got a cross!'

Lili pulled a creased envelope from the pocket of her gown. She unfolded it and took out the silver cross.

Miklós turned it over in his hand. 'That makes things clear.'

'Makes what clear?'

'Why your mother hasn't been in touch yet. Why she hasn't written to you.'

Lili took the cross, slipped it in the envelope and put it back in her pocket. 'Why hasn't she?'

'The list! The one that appeared in so many Hungarian newspapers. The official list. You would be on it as Lili Reich, mother's name Rozália Rákosi. That would be a different girl, not you. I imagine your mother read the list in Budapest and saw your name but didn't realise it was actually you. She was looking for a Lili Reich whose mother's name was Zsuzsanna Herz.

Lili stood up and raised her arms high, like a classical statue. A moment later she fell down on her knees in front of Miklós and started to kiss his hands. He stood up and hid his arms behind his back in embarrassment. Lili stayed kneeling, but she calmed down a little.

'This warrants a celebration!' she said in a whisper, looking up at my father. 'What a clever man you are!'

She was already flying down the corridor. 'Sára! Sára!' she shouted.

Ten

AT MIDDAY, in the cavernous and ugly yellow-tiled canteen where the girls ate their lunch half an hour after the men, Miklós felt that at last the hour had come for him to give an unforgettable account of his view of the world.

That winter twenty-three women were being treated on the third floor of the Eksjö hospital. They were all gathered around Miklós, including the three Hungarian girls, Lili, Sára and Judit. Using a small, sharp, wooden-handled knife Miklós sliced the three little chocolate cakes—gems of a confectioner in Avesta—into pieces. He first cut the cakes in half, then into quarters, then eighths. Soon twenty-four tiny pieces of cake were laid out in front of him, each one hardly bigger than a woman's fingernail.

Miklós stood on a chair—he was in his element. He removed his broken glasses. 'I will now explain communism to you,' he declared in an elevated form of German. 'At the core there is equality, fraternity and justice. What did you see a moment ago? Three small chocolate cakes. Three of you girls could have wolfed them down in no time. Instead, I cut up the three cakes—which, let's say, could stand for bread, milk, tractors or oil fields. I cut them into equal pieces. And, lo! Now I'll divide them among the people. Among you. Help yourselves.'

He pointed to the cakes on the table. It didn't really matter whether or not Miklós's wit had penetrated. Roused by the performance they reached for the plate, and everyone picked up a piece of cupcake. Lili looked at my father with pride.

The morsels of cake disappeared down their throats like breaths of air.

'No one has ever explained the essence of communism so beautifully,' remarked Sára, growing emotional.

Judit was the only one not to eat her now symbolic portion of cake. She turned it over in her hand until it had melted and the sticky, dark-brown goo dripped from her fingers.

~

In the early evening of 3 December, under the supervision of the cloaked nurse, Lili escorted my father to the railway station.

When the train set off, Miklós was hanging off the last step of the last carriage, and he didn't stop waving until the station had vanished.

Her eyes glistening, Lili remained on the snowy, frozen platform for a long time.

~

Miklós shut the door of the carriage behind him. He was on his way.

On the second night of his visit to Eksjö, in the four-bed ward, he had composed a love poem. On the following day, if he was on his own for a moment in the bathroom or the lift, he polished and corrected it. He hadn't dared recite it to Lili. But now, as the wheels of the train knocked against the joints in the tracks, the quickening clatter drew forth the music of his poem.

It yearned to come out of him. It wanted to burst out with such force that Miklós, even if he had wanted to, couldn't fight against it. He walked the length of the train, carrying his suitcase tied up with string. The newspaper jammed in his glasses was by this time in tatters; this didn't worry him in the slightest. He was reciting his poem. Out loud. In Hungarian.

The poem soared above the noise of the wheels. Miklós, like a cross between a troubadour and train conductor, marched the length of the carriages. He left half-empty compartments behind him without regret. He had no intention of sitting down. Instead he wanted to form some sort of bond with his fellow travellers, strangers who were staring in astonishment or sympathy at this passenger holding forth in an unfamiliar language. Maybe some of them could sense in him the lovesick minstrel. Maybe some thought he was a harmless madman. Miklós didn't give a damn; he walked on, reciting his poem.

> For thirty hours of endless trails
> My life has run on glowing rails
> I looked in the mirror seeing how
> Wonderfully happy I am now
> Thirty hours—the minutes don't linger
> Yet with each minute, my love grows stronger
> Promise to hold on and never let go
> Of my hand that you found thirty hours ago
> Arm in arm each storm we'll weather
> Smiling as in the alcove together.
> You'll be my conscience; you'll urge me to fight
> To stand up bravely for all that's right
> Justice bids me to battle for all
> I'm one of millions to answer the call
> With ease and conviction to each task I'll rise
> Helped by two stars, your beautiful eyes!

This was the poem that Miklós had been preparing for all his life. Yes, this was poetry itself. It had looped its way out from the pit of his stomach, spiced by the music of his heart and the precise mathematics of his brain. Once he had got to the end of the poem, he went back to the start. He recited it three times and the end flowed into the beginning. The Hungarian lines burning inside him flowed over the icy Swedish tracks.

Later, when he had calmed down, he settled into an empty compartment. He was convinced that the fire inside him was burning him up. Did he have a fever? Even his bones were hurting, and it was as if his skin had thinned, just as it had at dawn every day. He always kept his thermometer with him, in his pocket, in its handsome metal case. He took it out, put it in his mouth, shut his eyes and started counting. He was surprised to find that his symptoms had deceived him. The mercury stood at 36.3—there was nothing to be alarmed about.

Miklós looked through the window. Dark snowy fields and slim pine trees flashed by.

> My dearest, dearest Lili,
>   How can I thank you for those three wonderful days? They have meant more to me, much more, than anything else ever did.

All he had to do was shut his eyes to see himself and Lili shielded by the palm in the alcove of the corridor. The two armchairs with their worn upholstery. The overcoat lying over the back of one of the chairs, the fibre suitcase on the stone floor. The awkward silence of the first half-hour as they looked at each other, not wanting to speak.

> My darling little Lili,
>   Now I'm going to tell you about the impressions you left in me.

> First picture: the evening of the first of December.
> The palm, that indiscreet tree, waving its greenery
> as you smile and close your eyes. You're such a good
> person and so awfully charming!

Lili had suddenly thought of a question. If my father had had any talent for music he might even have been able to determine the tone.

'Is that today's paper?' she asked, as if she were a schoolteacher. Miklós wasn't sure what she meant. What paper?

Lili reached across and took off his glasses. She held them up and tried to make out the words on the scrap of scrunched-up newspaper. The awkwardness between them evaporated.

> The next day: your eyes beneath your red turban as
> we walk arm in arm along the street. Oh, for that little
> backstreet where the cinema is!

They had walked down the Kaserngatan in a howling wind, Miklós in the middle. Lili and Sára linked arms with him while he tried to explain things above the noise of the gale. He talked about his mother's special poppyseed pudding and the anthropomorphism of the German philosopher Feuerbach, and he finished up with the Swede Linnaeus's classification of plants. At last he could put to good use all those hours spent perched on the top rung of the ladder in the Gambrinus bookshop.

They were freezing by the time they plunged into the cinema. The remnants of Uncle Henrik's eighty-five dollars were nestled in Miklós's pocket. A soppy American film was playing, and my father felt the title was symbolic—*The Love Letters*. There was hardly anyone in the cinema. The three of them sat in the back row, Miklós between the two girls. He looked at the screen only for a moment or two. The *Aftonbladet* lens now proved a huge advantage: he could stare at Lili's profile, almost unnoticed, without employing any particular artifice. In a brave moment, when the dumb hero slipped on a patch of oil and slid on his bottom to the feet of his giggling love, Miklós tentatively touched Lili's hand. She squeezed his fingers in return.

> I won't write any more—it's suddenly hit me that it's all over. But afterwards, on the walk home, at the crossroads in the park, for a moment...

By the time they were in the park—at the centre of which, carved in stone, sat Carl Linnaeus himself—it was getting dark. Miklós made up his mind.

Sára tactfully walked two or three metres ahead, holding her palms out as if she were undertaking snowflake research for a meteorological institute. Miklós appreciated her tact. They walked past the gaze of Linnaeus's stone eyes. The snow was crisp beneath their boots, and the stars actually sparkled.

My father stopped Lili, stroked her face with his burning fingers—an inexplicable phenomenon in minus ten degrees without gloves—and kissed her on the lips. Lili snuggled into him and returned his kiss. Linnaeus was meditating above them.

Reassured that she could no longer hear the disappointing crunch of two pairs of feet behind her, Sára walked to the edge of the park. She began to count to herself. She was still alone when she got to 132, which gave her a good feeling. She smiled. Her heart, too, was beating hard.

> Monday. A quiet day. Only the photographer. I bet
> you, too, were wondering what your mother would say
> about our combined portrait.

The photography studio was at 38 Trädgårdsgatan. Miklós picked up the black-and-white leaflet advertising the place to save it for posterity. The photographer looked like Humphrey Bogart: a tall, handsome young man in a jacket and tie. He fiddled around with the positioning for a while, looking for the right angle. Miklós winced in jealousy every time Bogart gently touched Lili's knee to get her to move to the left or right. Then, from under the black cover behind his camera, he fussed for ages about how they should hold their heads. Eventually he emerged, rushed up to my father and started to read the news-paper stuffed into the frame of his glasses. He asked my father to take off his glasses, and then vanished under the cover again. For five or six minutes he positioned the camera at different angles. Then he came out once again, walked over to my father and whispered in his ear.

Miklós blushed. Bogart, using a very proper form of German, warned him that even if he, as the photographer, could discern that my father was aware of the problem, it didn't alter the fact that those somewhat uninviting metallic teeth were, in this powerful light, shining like mad. As a quality photographer, he felt that it was his responsibility to advise that an ideal family portrait might best be achieved if Lili were to laugh outright while my father was just beginning to form a smile. This is what he for his part would advise.

Half an hour later, the photographer of Trädgårdsgatan had finally taken my mother and father's first photo together.

> That evening you came downstairs with me, then you
> got into the lift, pulled the grating shut and, before it
> moved upwards, I leaned in once more.

The second night, Lili had made a foray down to the first floor for a goodnight kiss from Miklós. She was already in her nightdress and dressing-gown. She said goodnight to my father outside the lift, while the nurses were coming and going in the corridor. Lili got in. She pulled the iron grating across. Miklós managed to squeeze his head in between the bars, and in this hopeless position he tried to kiss her. In fact, he pressed his head towards her with such force that the white bars left their outline on his cheeks. The lift went up. Miklós couldn't bring himself to leave. He was still waiting for Lili's slippers to disappear when he felt a hand on his shoulder.

Dr Svensson was standing beside him in his white coat. 'You speak German, don't you?'

'I speak it and understand it.'

'Good. I'd like to call your attention to something.'

Miklós had no doubt what the doctor was referring to. But right now, at this rather special moment, he had no wish to launch into a discussion about the state of his health. 'I'm aware of everything, doctor. Currently my lungs are—'

'I wasn't thinking of you,' Svensson interrupted. 'You misunderstand me.'

Miklós breathed out.

'All I wanted was to ask you to take good care of Lili,' Svensson continued. 'She is no ordinary girl.' Dr Svensson took Miklós by the arm and guided him down the corridor. There was no one else around.

'You see, by a cruel stroke of fate, I happened to be on the international team of doctors present when the women's camp in Belsen was liberated. I'd like to forget that day. But it's impossible. We thought we'd found everyone who showed the tiniest sign of life. Only the dead remained, lying on the bare concrete...nearly three hundred childlike bodies, naked, or in rags. Skeletons weighing twenty kilos.'

Svensson stopped for a moment in the deserted hallway and stared into the distance. He seemed agitated. Miklós looked at him in surprise; the doctor's face was distorted into a strange grimace, as if he were in pain.

'We were on our way out. I looked back once more, just in case...I couldn't decide whether I was seeing things or...if a finger really did move. Do you understand, Miklós? Look...like the last flutter of a dove's wing…or the ripple of a leaf once the wind has died down.' Svensson raised his hand and crooked his index finger. His voice cracked. 'And so we brought Lili back among us.'

~

Years later, it always sent a chill down my father's spine when he recalled Svensson's expression and his hand held up with its quivering finger. And all this merged inseparably with another memory from his visit to Eksjö.

When the train puffed away and he was standing on the last step of the last carriage and waving until the station had disappeared, he was overjoyed that he could summon up Lili's true image. All he had to do was shut his eyes—his last glimpse of her was etched forever into his memory. Lili was waving on the snowy platform. She was crying. And her fingers—my father claimed that he had watched her delicate hand and those slender fingers almost as though they were in close-up on a cinema screen. This, of course, was impossible at such a distance, especially with his smashed glasses, but even so. He was clinging to the open carriage, the train was gaining speed and he, behind his closed eyelids, really did see Lili's fingers as they trembled in the wind like leaves.

~

'Take care of her. Love her,' Svensson instructed Miklós on that last evening in the hospital. 'It would be so good if...'

He fell silent for so long that Miklós wondered if he was searching for the appropriate word in German. 'What would be so good?' he asked.

Svensson still didn't speak. All at once it clicked—Svensson wasn't having trouble with his German. He had arrived at a boundary that he didn't want to cross. He never finished his sentence, but he gave Miklós a hug, which said more than any words could.

~

In Ervalla, Miklós changed trains. He found a window seat. In the foreground of the night landscape, his own tired, stubbly face was reflected in the glass.

> On Tuesday I got up in a bad mood: it was the last
> day. We walked again to Stadshotell Square like we
> had on Sunday evening. And I could only steal one or
> two furtive kisses from you on the way.

That last evening, they sat again in the two armchairs behind the palm. Lili was crying. Miklós held her hand; he couldn't think of anything encouraging to say.

'I dreamed about our flat last night,' Lili said. 'I saw Papa getting his suitcases ready. It was a Monday and just beginning to get light. I knew he would be setting off soon. In my dream I knew we wouldn't see him for a week. Isn't that odd?'

She forgot about crying and that she was in hospital in a foreign country. She talked as if she were recalling the previous day's picnic. When she was a child, her father's routine had seemed like a jigsaw puzzle. Sándor Reich, suitcase salesman, prepared his wares at dawn on Monday. He packed two medium-sized suitcases into two trunks, and the smaller cases into the medium-sized ones. And he crammed the briefcases and handbags into a red children's suitcase. It was quite incredible that all those leather goods could fit into two trunks.

The truth was that Lili's strong attachment to her parents disturbed Miklós. He had only one clear memory of his father. He couldn't quite decide whether the scene remained so vivid because he saw it once or because he saw it many times. Maybe every Sunday lunch had ended in this way.

My grandfather always tucked his damask napkin into the collar of his shirt. His thick hair shone with brilliantine. My grandmother, who always looked rather dishevelled, was taking a spoonful of soup. Pea soup, yes. A white china tureen of yellowy-green pea soup with globules of fat floating on the surface sat in the middle of the table. Beside it was a small dish piled with croutons. Miklós remembered every detail. He was just a boy, sitting opposite his mother in a black waistcoat. His father started shouting; he tore the napkin from his neck, jumped up and with a single movement yanked off the tablecloth.

My father never forgot it. The pea soup shot out of the tureen. The yellowy-green liquid flowed onto his knees, burning him, and the croutons dropped to the floor like tiny winged angels.

He told Lili this story, holding her hand, that evening under the palm.

Lili changed the subject. 'I don't want to be…'

'What don't you want to be?'

'It's so dreadful to say it. But I want to be different.'

'Different?'

'Different from Mama and Papa.'

Judit Gold appeared, carrying cups of tea. She couldn't help overhearing. 'What don't you want to be, Lili?'

Lili looked from her to Miklós. 'I don't want to be Jewish!' she replied in a quiet, resolute tone.

There might have been a hostile edge to her words.

'It's not a question of wanting or not wanting,' retorted Judit, wiping a drop of tea off the table with her finger. She marched off as if Lili had personally offended her.

Miklós was pensive. 'I know a bishop. We'll write to him. We'll apply for a conversion. All right?'

As usual, my father had exaggerated things a bit. He wasn't acquainted with any kind of bishop. But he was convinced that sooner or later, if he looked, he'd find one.

'You don't mind?' asked Lili, stroking my father's hand.

'It had occurred to me, too,' said my father equitably.

~

On the night train back to Avesta, as the stations flashed past, Miklós thought through the problem. For him the question of conversion was irrelevant. It didn't mean a thing to him that he was Jewish. As a teenager, he was so hooked on the new socialist ideology that there was no room left for anything antiquated. If conversion was important for Lili, if that was what she wanted, then he would get hold of a priest. Or a bishop. Or the pope himself, if it came to that.

He had gone through Örebro, Hallsberg, Lerbäck and Motala. Miklós was writing a letter.

> You can see, can't you, dearest Lili, what a devoted soldier I am in the cause of freedom and the oppressed, the cause that has awakened the sons and daughters of every nation. You'll be my companion in everyday life (you will, won't you?), so be my faithful companion in this, too! You were once a bourgeois girl — now you should become a tough and militant socialist! You do feel so inclined, don't you?
>
> I'll contact the bishop as soon as I get back to Avesta. I'm counting the days until Christmas when I hope I'll see you again!
>
> Many, many hugs and kisses,
> Miklós

Eleven

THE DAY after Miklós left Eksjö, at the end of the communal breakfast, Dr Svensson came in and tapped a spoon against a glass. The hum of chatter died away.

Svensson seemed nervous. 'I would like you all to remain patient and trusting. I have just received news that will bring certain changes to your lives. The Swedish Ministry of Health has decided to disband the Smålandsstenar rehabilitation hospital with immediate effect. This means that patients who have been cured in our hospital here in Eksjö will be permitted to leave. Others will be moving to another facility at Berga.'

Svensson wanted to say more, but no one could hear him

in the eruption of joy. The girls stood up on their chairs, some of them hugging each other, even screaming. Others tried to get close to Svensson, speaking to him in various languages. He tapped his glass to take control of the situation, but it was hopeless.

> This morning, in the midst of bedlam, they
> announced that the hospital here will be shut down,
> and we are moving to a vast rehab centre several
> hundred kilometres away—very soon. And it is my
> turn to visit you. But at least I'll be a bit nearer to you
> and won't have so far to travel when I come.

The three Hungarian girls went straight to their ward. They were about to start packing when Lili noticed the theft.

Half an hour later, a committee was trying to get the facts of the case, but Lili was in no condition to answer questions. She had one fit of crying after another, and finally she was given a sedative. She lay curled up on her side on her bed and didn't say a word.

So for the hundredth time Sára had to tell those concerned what had happened. 'I said that before. It was open,' she reported, pointing to the only cupboard, in the corner of the room.

The cupboard, which the girls had used to store their things, was still wide open and more or less empty.

A bespectacled man was whispering a translation of Sára's words into Swedish for the benefit of the local head of the Red Cross, a tall blond scowling fellow with amazingly pale skin.

Madame Ann-Marie Arvidsson was also there, writing the report. 'What did the material look like?' she asked.

Sára stroked Lili's curled back. 'What was it like, Lili? I only saw it once.'

But Lili just stared at the birch tree swaying in the breeze.

Sára did her best. 'It was brown fabric fit for a winter coat. Tweed, with a nap. She got it from her cousin.'

The man in glasses translated in a whisper. 'It must have happened while we were hearing the news in the dining hall. Everyone was downstairs.'

Ann-Marie Arvidsson put down her pen. 'There's never been a theft in this hospital before. I really don't know what to do,' she said.

'I do!' announced the stern, blond man from the Red Cross, striking the table. 'We'll find it and return it to the owner.'

~

When my father arrived back in Avesta he reported to the office, then walked across to the barracks to change. It was midday; everyone would be in the canteen.

Miklós caught sight of him immediately and backed away. The booted feet formed an arc above the middle row of beds. The suitcase slipped out of Miklós's hand. He took off his glasses and wiped the good lens. When he put his glasses back on, it was clear that he hadn't imagined it. From where he was standing one of the metal cupboards blocked his view of the upper part of the barracks. But when he moved forward he saw the torso too: the grey trousers and the belt around the waist.

It was Tibor Hirsch. He had hung himself. From a hook—a thick, bent nail near the overhead light. A letter lay on the ground beneath his body. Miklós's legs and hands began to tremble, he had to sit down. Minutes passed. He had an irresistible urge to read the letter. He had to overcome this trembling, this feeling of revulsion. He could see that the letter had an official stamp at the bottom. He knew what it would say even before he forced himself to stand up and shuffle over to the hanging body.

He was right, of course. He didn't need to pick it up; he could tell that the last letter in the life of the electronic radio technician and photographer's aide was a death notice. The death certificate of Mrs Tibor Hirsch, née Irma Klein.

It flashed through Miklós's mind that he had written to Lili about reports that Hirsch's wife had been shot in Belsen. That was when the triumphant conga line had taken over the barracks. What had made him suppress his misgivings? Why had he not hurried over to Hirsch and shaken him to wake him up to the truth? But when? When would he have had the chance?

Was it when Hirsch sat up in bed, waving the letter above his head? Or when he yelled out, 'She's alive! My wife's alive!'? Should he have rushed over and shaken him, shouting, 'No, she isn't alive, she's dead—three people saw her shot down like a rabid dog'?

Or could it have waited? Until when? When Hirsch set out between the beds holding up the message like a flag, turning the single word into a proclamation? Then? Or when Harry joined him, grasping his shoulders from behind, and together they began to chant their marching song?

What could he have done when their fears were transformed into a glorious eruption of words? Alive, alive, alive, alive, alive! How could he have stopped this volcano?

Should he have got up on the table and shouted above the chorus? What would he have shouted? *Come to your senses! Come to your senses, you idiots. You are alone now, they've died, they've gone. All those you loved have turned into smoke. I saw it happen. I know. She's not alive, not alive, not alive, not alive, not alive!*

But instead he had joined the line and become part of the snake, a part of the whole creature that wanted to abandon its common sense, to believe that nothing had changed.

And now, here was Hirsch's lifeless body hanging from the hook.

~

That evening, when the effect of the sedative had worn off, Lili walked down to the office with Sára and made a formal complaint. Two days later, when she got a letter from Miklós— who, within a couple of hours of learning of the theft, had found out what the usual Swedish procedures were in such a case—the investigation was already underway. But both of them knew very well that Lili wouldn't be wearing a decent overcoat that winter.

My one and only darling Lili!
    You must report the theft to the police saying that
the culprit is unknown. You must write a letter in
German in triplicate (one copy for the hospital, one
for the foreigners' office and one for the police) giving
exact details of the loss—three and a half metres of
brown material for a winter coat, etc.

More important things were taking place. On Tuesday
morning, nine girls who were convalescing at the Eksjö hospital, including the three Hungarians, were transported by bus to
Smålandsstenar railway station. It was chaos at the station, and
all the while it snowed.

Most of the Smålandsstenar patients were already on the
train. The arrivals from Eksjö hurried along the muddy platform
carrying bundles and suitcases. Dr Svensson and the nurses in
their black cloaks rushed up and down beside the train, like
a benevolent military brigade, trying to calm everyone down.
There was an abundance of tears, kisses and mud, all accompanied by rousing music played through a loudspeaker.

Lili, Sára and Judit Gold managed to find the carriage
where their friends from Smålandsstenar, whom they hadn't
seen for three months, were sitting. Screams of joy and much
hugging followed. Then they pulled down the windows, leaned
out and blew kisses to Dr Svensson. A nurse arrived on a bicycle
with a bulky leather bag on her shoulder containing that day's
post—a nice touch of organisation. She had tucked her cloak up
above her knees so it wouldn't get caught in the spokes. People

jumped aside when she rang her bell.

'Post! Post!' she called, getting off the bike in the middle of the platform, and letting it crash to the ground. She took a batch of envelopes from the bag and read out the names. She had to shout to be heard above the music.

'Scwarz, Vári, Benedek, Reich, Tormos, Lehmann, Szabó, Beck...'

Madame Ann-Marie Arvidsson, who was also fussing about on the platform and had a slight feeling of remorse about her treatment of Lili, pricked up her ears at 'Reich'. She took the envelope from the nurse and set out to find Lili in the crowd. She ran along beside the train, thinking it must be a letter from Miklós. She was calling Lili's name, but her chirpy voice was lost in the cacophony. Her coat was muddy up to the knees. Flushed and breathless, she held the letter above her head and shouted 'Reich, Reich'.

Then she spotted Lili hanging out of the window of a compartment a few metres away.

Lili saw her, too. 'Ann-Marie! Ann-Marie!' she yelled.

Madame Arvidsson was touched that Lili had called her by her first name. She held out the envelope and caught Lili's hand, giving it a squeeze.

'I expect it's your friend!' she said with a laugh, showing that she was on love's side.

But Lili glanced at the letter and blanched. The envelope had a Hungarian stamp and the address was written in a spidery hand. There was no mistaking it. Lili fell backwards into the compartment. Sára had to catch her to stop her falling to the floor.

'It's Mama's writing,' she whispered, clutching the letter and pressing it to her.

'It'll get terribly creased, let go!' demanded Sára, trying to prise the envelope from her hand. But Lili wouldn't let go.

Judit stuck her head out of the window and shouted to Svensson, who happened to be going past the carriage, 'Reich's got a letter from her mother!'

Dr Svensson stopped, along with his escort. The cloaked nurses surrounded him like a flock of crows, and they all clambered aboard.

There must have been at least fifteen people crammed into the tiny compartment. Lili still hadn't dared open the letter; she kept kissing and stroking it.

'Go on, open it, Lili!' urged Svensson.

'I don't dare,' she sobbed. She handed the letter to Sára. 'You open it.'

Sára didn't hesitate. She tore the envelope open and took out several densely filled pages, which she tried to give to Lili.

But Lili shook her head. 'You read it. Please!'

Svensson, who was now sitting next to Lili, held her hand between both of his. Somehow, news had got round about the letter from Budapest. More people had gathered in the corridor and on the platform. If Sára wanted to live up to the occasion she'd have to declaim the letter as if this were a theatre performance. She was aware of the singularity of the moment, but her voice let her down. She, who could easily get through Schumann's most difficult aria, now began to read in a scratchy, faltering tone.

"'My darling, one and only Lili! I saw your notice in *Világosság* under the headline, Three Hungarian Girls in Sweden Are Looking for Their Relatives.'"

Lili could see their building with its long balconies in Hernád Street, their dark-green front door and Mama's shabby dressing-gown. The bell rings. Mama opens the door wide. Her neighbour Bözsi is there, waving that day's *Világosság* above her head and shouting. Lili wasn't sure what she was shouting, but it didn't matter. There was no doubt, though, about the shouting—the muscles in her neck were tensed, and she was tapping the newspaper on the last page where the framed notice had been set in bold letters. Mama snatched the newspaper out of her hands, took a quick look at the notice, saw the name, her name, and fainted.

Lili distinctly heard what she said either before her collapse or after she came round. 'I always knew our little Lili was a clever girl!'

After her initial nervousness, Sára got her voice back.

"'Your miraculous news arrived after a dreadful year! I can't possibly describe to you what it means to me. I can only thank the Lord that I lived to see this day.'"

Svensson was still holding Lili's hand.

Bözsi dashed into the larder muttering to herself. 'Vinegar, vinegar, vinegar.'

She found it on the second shelf, drew the cork out with her teeth and sniffed it. Then she rushed back to Mama, who was still lying in the doorway, and splashed some vinegar on her face. Whereupon Mama sneezed and opened her eyes. She looked at Bözsi, but she was whispering to Lili.

"'I'm afraid your dear, good papa isn't home yet. After he was freed he was taken to hospital in Wels in Austria with enteritis. Since May I've heard nothing. I hope that with God's help he will come home soon so that we can live our lives together in happiness again.'"

Lili wasn't sure which bits Sára was reading, and which bits she was hearing in her mother's own voice, as if Mama was sitting in the stuffy compartment and taking over at the most important parts.

"'Since 8 June, when the husband of our dear cousin Relli came home from Auschwitz, I've been living with them, and I'll stay here until one of you returns. God willing, I hope it won't be too long now!'"

The penetrating smell of vinegar filled the flat. Mama wiped her face and got to her feet with Bözsi's help, then staggered over to the kitchen tap and washed her face. After that she sat on a stool, spread the newspaper on her knees and read the notice seven times running, until she was sure she'd remember its words as long as she lived.

"'I don't even know where to begin. What do you do all day? What do you get to eat? What do you look like? Are you very thin? Have you got enough underwear? I'm afraid we were robbed of everything. We got back nothing of what we sent to the country—no bed linen, no material, no winter coat, no clothes, nothing. But don't you worry about that, my girl.'"

Lili heard that last torrent of words in her mother's voice. Mama said 'my girl' in such an unmistakable way. My girl, my girl, my girl. God Almighty, how good that sounded!

Svensson didn't understand a syllable of the letter, but his face shone with as much happiness and pride as the faces of all the Hungarian girls in the compartment. Sára looked around, swallowed and went on reading.

"'Now for some good news. The new piano that you got from your dear father on your eighteenth birthday is safe and sound! I know you'll be very pleased about that, Lili.'"

Mama sat on the stool. She smoothed out the copy of *Világosság*, already composing the letter, smiling to herself. She started writing it down straightaway. In fact she had composed it in her head every night for the past ten months, so it was no effort now to put it on paper. She knew every comma and had checked the spelling over and over—she wasn't going to make mistakes in such an important document. She muttered and hummed while she wrote.

"'If you get the chance, my darling, use a sunray lamp on your hands and feet, even your head, because I suspect some of your beautiful wavy hair might have fallen out from lack of vitamins. You might even have had typhoid. So don't forget about that, sweetheart. When, with God's help, you come home, I want you to be just as radiant as you were before.'"

Someone, probably one of the nurses from Svensson's team,

rushed over to the stationmaster warning him not to let the train depart while the doctor was still aboard. Svensson himself didn't move. He was squeezing Lili's hand. The girls' bodies were pressed against each other in the compartment, their eyes shining. Sára's voice floated out through the open window onto the platform.

"'We've had no news of poor Gyúri, but all four of the Kárpátis are fine. Bandi Horn is apparently a prisoner of war in Russia. Zsuzsi isn't mentioned in your notice. What do you know about her, darling girl? You all set out together, after all.'"

The lump in Lili's throat began to swell. She and her cousin Zsuzsi were lying in each other's arms on the floor of the putrid barracks when Zsuzsi passed away—on butterfly wings, with a smile on her lips and a body scarred by millions of lice. When did she actually die? Lili would never speak to anyone about that.

In her kitchen smelling of vinegar, Mama seemed to sense that she had touched a raw patch. She became quiet: a drop of water fell from the tap. She looked at Bözsi and sobbed. Bözsi hugged her, and they cried together.

Lili could hear clearly what Mama said through her tears and with her head buried in Bözsi's neck.

"'If only I could hug you both. I've no other wish in life, but to live for that day. I'm longing for you and send you a million kisses, your adoring mama.'"

Lili was almost in a trance. She didn't notice Svensson and the nurses leave. Apparently they all hugged her and kissed her before they climbed down from the train. Later, Dr Svensson and his flock stood in the snow like statues on Eksjö platform until the train disappeared.

> My one and only darling Lili!
> I can't tell you how utterly happy your news made me! I told you so, didn't I? I knew you'd get a letter from your mother this week. I love you more and more every minute. You're such a sweet girl, and so good. And I'm such an uncouth boy. You'll make me better, won't you?

Twelve

TWO DAYS later, Miklós disappeared. No one noticed his absence until midday. The first to miss him were Harry and Frida, who were used to him slinking into the caretaker's office before lunch to buy his two cigarettes for the afternoon. When he didn't turn up, Harry asked Jakobovits when and where he'd last seen him.

By one o'clock, Dr Lindholm, too, had been informed that his favourite patient had evaporated like camphor. They counted the bicycles, but none was missing. When Miklós didn't show up for lunch, they started to worry.

Dr Lindholm despatched a car to town in case Miklós had

gone to the post office and been taken ill on the road. In the meantime he phoned all the possible places Miklós could have been—the post office, the café, the railway station. No one had seen him. In the late afternoon he notified the police and ordered a curfew.

Everyone linked Miklós's disappearance to Tibor Hirsch's suicide. Miklós had discovered the body, and he was there when they cut Hirsch down from the rope. In the days following he had sat silently on his bed. No one could cheer him up. Later, Harry suggested that he might have wandered off to escape Christmas, which was approaching fast. There was much talk about the festivities, though many of the patients, being Jews, had never observed Christmas. On the other hand, Jenö Grieger claimed Miklós was a socialist and couldn't care less about Christmas—there was no way a man like him would be undone by a religious holiday.

Márta came into the barracks and questioned everyone individually. She spent a long time in Miklós's corner, trying to decide whether she should sift through his correspondence. He kept all his letters in a cardboard box. There were about three hundred envelopes in it, in perfect order, including Lili's letters, which were bound separately with a yellow ribbon. Márta picked up the box, then resisted the temptation. She decided it was too soon. She would give him until the next morning.

At that moment, my father was wandering in the pine forest, lost in thought, seven kilometres away. He couldn't explain to himself why feelings of anxiety and depression had overwhelmed him that morning. It was no different from any other morning. He took his temperature at dawn, and then had breakfast. He wrote a letter to Lili. He played a game of chess with Litzman and then walked to Dr Lindholm's office for a quick check-up and to pester him about Lili visiting at Christmas.

Maybe that was it. The offhand glance with which Lindholm sent him on his way. The doctor listened to his lungs and shrugged. Shrugged!

Miklós stopped in the forest. There was a gentle breeze. Yes, it was Dr Lindholm's thoughtless response, like the first domino falling, that had set the whole thing off. He had come out of the doctor's office with a sinking heart. He had never believed in this stupid diagnosis. He'd always brushed it off as a mistake. Let the clever guys talk—he knew better!

But that morning, Lindholm's casual gesture had been like a blow to the stomach. It took his breath away. He was going to die! He was going to disappear like Tibor Hirsch. His cupboard would be emptied, his bed stripped. And that would be it.

So he left. He trudged through the gate and walked to the crossroads where, instead of turning left to go to town, he turned right towards the forest. He'd hardly ever walked that way before. The paved road soon gave way to a track, which narrowed into a path that had probably been made by deer. After a while it widened out into a large snow-covered meadow. By this time Miklós was completely lost. Not that it worried him. It felt good to walk, and he rather enjoyed keeping company with death. The Grim Reaper. So what if he was going to snuff it? He had lived and loved, and this was it. He'd fade away like the deer tracks. He repeated poems to himself, silently at first, then aloud and then at the top of his voice. He walked on between pine trees that reached towards the sky, reciting poetry the whole way—Attila József, Baudelaire, Heine.

By late afternoon, after a coughing attack, he began to feel sorry for himself. He was cold, his boots were wet through, and he was so tired that he had to sit down on a fallen tree trunk. He might have been reconciled to his fate, but he had no desire to freeze to death. So he set out north, imagining the barracks was in that direction, but not at all sure he was right.

~

At eight in the evening Lindholm phoned his colleague Svensson in Eksjö. He didn't know that the Smålandsstenar patients had been moved to Berga two days earlier. Svensson was surprised to hear of Miklós's disappearance; he couldn't imagine the reason for it but he, of course, gave Dr Lindholm the telephone number at Berga. Lindholm waited until 11 p.m. to call the Hungarian girl, who probably knew more about Miklós than anyone else. For some reason he phoned from the caretaker's office, perhaps because it allowed him to keep an eye on the road, down which he hoped Miklós would come any minute.

~

It was the girls' second day in the Berga rehab hospital. They were housed in a long, stark barracks like the one at Avesta. They were already in bed when a messenger came to summon Lili to the telephone in the main building. Lili got up, found a spare coat, and set out. Sára called after her. She had her misgivings, so she put on her boots and followed.

At the exact moment that Lindholm heard Lili's thin voice issue a hesitant 'hello', he caught sight of Miklós dragging himself towards the gate.

'Is that you, Lili? I have Miklós here on the line for you,' he yelled into the phone, though he reckoned it would take my father at least five minutes to shuffle up to the caretaker's lodge. 'Hold on. He'll be here in a moment.'

~

My father didn't think he would ever get back. He was trying to retrace his steps but it felt like he was going in circles. The imprint of his boots in the snow had faded; then his footprints seemed to double up. For a terrifying period he could have sworn he was following the tracks of a bear, but then he somehow found his own boot prints again.

He was completely flummoxed when the tracks he was following came to an end in the middle of the path. They were there one moment and gone the next, as if the track-maker had taken flight.

The sun had set and it was unbearably cold. Miklós was

suffering. His feet were blistered; his head throbbed. He kept coughing. The thin sickle of a moon barely lit the forest. He often fell, sinking to his knees in the powdery snow. He lost all hope. But he knew he mustn't stop. Gathering up his remaining strength, he concentrated on nothing but walking—one-two, one-two, one-two. But it felt hopeless. He could hear the call of an animal—a hoot, he imagined—but were there owls in Sweden in winter? 'The owl screeched death'—that was a good line, a good first line, but when would he get it down on paper? Never. Never more.

And then Miklós saw the caretaker's lodge, the fence and, behind the bars on the window, Lindholm holding the telephone. Perhaps he was dreaming.

It took him a good ten minutes to make the last fifty metres. He stumbled into the lodge. Lindholm looked at him and pressed the receiver into his hand. 'Lili Reich. You want talk to her, no, Miklós?'

Lili had no idea what to make of the long delay. Since the unknown man from Avesta kept reassuring her that he was about to connect Miklós, she assumed there must be some problem with the line. The receiver hissed and crackled in her ear.

After an eternity, she heard my father's faint voice: 'Yes?'

'Are you all right?'

'Fine. Great.' What could he say?

Lili was relieved. 'We've made a little corner for ourselves in the new place at Berga.'

'And?'

'You can't imagine. It's ghastly! I don't even want to write to you about it. Do you mind me complaining?'

Miklós's facial muscles were frozen. He had no breath. He could hardly form the words. 'Don't worry.'

He was playing for time. He tried to massage his face with stiff fingers. Dr Lindholm was suffocating him too, standing so close that Miklós had to hunch over in order not to touch him.

'What's it like? Tell me,' he asked.

'Wooden barracks, bumpy paths, awful…I can't sleep at night, it is so cold. I wake up with a sore throat and a temperature.'

'I see.'

'There isn't even anywhere in the barracks where we can sit. No chairs, no table! All day we just wander around the place like stray dogs.'

'I see.'

My father went blank. He felt empty. All he wanted to do was lie down and close his eyes.

Lili realised that Miklós wasn't himself. Most of the time she could hardly get a word in. Now there was a heavy silence. 'I've been in a bad mood and terribly uptight the whole day,' she tried again. 'All I want to do is cry. I don't know where I should be. I'm so homesick.'

'I see.'

That didn't sound like Miklós's voice. The tone was icy. Almost hostile. They both fell silent.

Yesterday's call—it was dreadful. I couldn't speak

> properly. I wanted to say how I love you beyond
> measure and feel for you. Forgive me if I didn't say
> that. Only a few days now and I'll be seeing you!

'Well, then,' Lili whispered.

'I see. I see.'

'Are you all right?'

'Yeah.'

Lili turned pale. 'I'd like you to write to my mother an airmail letter, now that we've got her address, and tell her everything about us,' she mumbled.

Lindholm could see that all my father wanted to do was sleep.

'Right. I'll do that.'

Silence.

> Yesterday when I put down the receiver I was
> overcome with a strange sensation…it was as if
> someone had thrown cold water on me! Your voice
> sounded so alien and icy that I couldn't help feeling
> that perhaps you don't love me any more.

Click. The line was cut. Lili was white as a sheet. Sára put her arm round her.

'His voice was so different. Something has happened.'

'His friend who committed suicide,' Sára said. 'That's what's behind it. He's got so much on his mind, poor thing.'

They walked back to the barracks arm in arm. Lili didn't sleep at all that night.

Thirteen

A DANCE was scheduled for the next day at Berga to celebrate the arrival of the new patients. A band was to play in the cavernous hall, which they jokingly called the snack bar. A three-piece playing Swedish tunes: a pianist, a drummer and a guy on the saxophone.

Some girls danced. It didn't seem to bother them that the musicians were the only men in the hall. Most of them, though, stared into space at the wooden tables that had been specially laid out for the occasion. Beer, scones and sausage were on offer.

Lili, Sára and Judit were sitting at a table on their own when two men came into the dining room and, after making enquiries, headed straight for them.

'Are you Lili Reich?' one asked in Swedish, taking off his hat.

Lili remained seated. 'Yes, that's me,' she replied in German.

The man pulled a thin strip of fabric out of his pocket. 'Do you recognise this?' he asked, switching to German.

Lili stood up and took the piece of material from him. 'Yes, I do!' She ran her hand over it, feeling the nap with her fingertips. 'Look,' she said, handing it to Sára, 'it's my coat material, isn't it?'

The other man took off his hat. 'Let me introduce myself, ladies. My name is Svynka, I'm the district representative from Eksjö. And this is the hospital caretaker, Mr Berg.'

Mr Berg nodded, and took over. 'During the investigation at the Eksjö hospital, we found three and a half metres of the cloth that you reported missing at the bottom of a cabinet in one of the corridors. Do you follow me, Miss?'

'Yes.'

'Good. The cloth had been cut into strips.'

He asked for the piece of fabric and held it up. Lili was stunned. The band was playing a slow number, and several girls were swaying around each other on the parquet floor.

Lili wanted to make sure she had understood. She turned to Sára. 'Did I hear right? It was cut into strips?'

Sára nodded, mystified.

'It seems the thief wasn't intending to keep the material, just to destroy it,' Svynka added.

The music had changed. A lively polka started up. Only a few girls were left on the floor, but they danced with gusto. Lili stared at the single strip of cloth dangling from the burly caretaker's fingers.

'It will be difficult to find the culprit at this stage. But, if you wish'—Berg made a sweeping gesture towards the other tables—'we'll question everyone.'

'It won't be easy, but if that's what you want,' Svynka continued.

Lili shook her head. She couldn't speak or take her eyes off the remnant of the never-to-be winter coat between the care-taker's thumb and index finger.

Without a word, the three girls tramped the paths between the barracks in the dark, their hands in the pockets of their quilted uniform jackets. It was freezing and the wind howled.

Lili stopped. 'Who can hate me that much?'

'Someone who envies you your luck,' said Sára, with a sympathetic smile.

Judit was angry. 'I wouldn't let it go if I were you. Make them investigate to find out which girl did it. I'd like to look her in the eye!'

'How could they find out?' asked Sára.

'How should I know? Question all the girls. Search their belongings.'

'Should they look for a pair of scissors? Or a knife?' asked Lili wryly.

Judit was adamant. 'Who knows? Scissors, knife, something!

Maybe a scrap of tweed!'

They walked on.

'Of course, the girl would have it on her! Next to her heart!' said Sára. 'Really, Judit, you're incredibly naïve.'

'All I'm saying is that this kind of thing should be sorted out. It shouldn't be left to fade away. That's my opinion.'

Lili was looking at the muddy, icy path. 'I have no wish to know. What would I say to her?'

'What it calls for. You'd spit on her,' Judit hissed.

'Me? Come off it! I'd feel sorry for her,' claimed Lili, even if she wasn't sure she would be so kind-hearted.

~

Dr Lindholm didn't ask Miklós where he'd gone on that desperately long day, or why. He prescribed a hot bath and something to bring his temperature down. Three days later, however, he felt it his duty to inform him, in person, of his final decision. They were sitting on the couch like old friends.

'I know this will be upsetting you, Miklós,' the doctor said, 'but I am forbidding your cousin to visit you at Christmas.'

'Why?'

'Is no room for her. Everywhere is full. But this only one reason.'

'And the other?'

'Last time I tell you, say goodbye to her, remember? But even if you were healthy, and you are not, I don't allow female visitor to male hospital. As a reading man you must understand that.'

'What should I understand?'

'You once mentioned *The Magic Mountain*? Sensuality is…how I put it…unsettling. Is dangerous.'

Miklós stood up and went to the door. Dr Lindholm's decision seemed irrevocable. What had changed in the last few days? How could Miklós have lost the doctor's sympathy? He urgently needed to do something different, something that would break Lindholm's resolve.

Gripping the doorhandle, he turned back. 'I'd like that in writing, please, Dr Lindholm.'

'Come on, Miklós, our relationship—'

'I don't care about our relationship,' said my father. 'I want your decision in writing, please. Three copies. I want to send your letter to a superior authority.'

Lindholm got to his feet. He lost his cool. 'Go to hell!' he yelled.

'I'm not going to hell; I'm going to the Hungarian embassy. You are restricting my rights. You are obliged to permit family visits. I'd like your opinion in writing.'

No one had ever spoken like this to Lindholm. He was stunned. He stared at my father. 'Get out!' he said.

Miklós slammed the door and set off down the long corridor. He had surprised himself with his quick thinking. A doctor was restricting his freedom of movement. This was a good argument, effective and true too, more or less. On the other hand, this country had taken him in. And was treating him. Dr Lindholm had every right to claim that restricting his freedom was in his medical interest. In reply, Miklós could point out that the International Red Cross was picking up the bill, not the Swedish state. In other words, he owed his thanks and accountability ultimately to the Red Cross. If he wanted, say, to spend Christmas in a nightclub in Stockholm, who could stop him?

But what, in fact, was his status here? It was confusing. Was he a patient, a refugee, a dissident or a temporary visitor? His status, yes, his status should be determined somehow. But who should determine it? The Swedish government? The Hungarian embassy? The hospital? Dr Lindholm?

Behind him, in the distance, a door opened and the doctor dashed out. 'Miklós! Come back. We talk it over,' Lindholm shouted down the corridor.

But my father had no intention of arguing his point.

My darling, my one and only Lili,
    I'm furious and depressed. But I won't give up. I'll
    think of something.

~

In the afternoons the canteen practically yawned with boredom. It was the only communal area in Berga. The girls didn't have much choice: they could stretch out on their beds in the barracks, go for walks in the biting wind or sit around in this hall crammed with tables and wait for supper.

That afternoon, Lili decided she would have a go at August Bebel's *Woman and Socialism*. Miklós had written to her about it a few times and it was now two months since he had sent her the paperback. Lili had stored it in different places to keep it out of sight. The cover wasn't very inviting: a woman with dilated pupils and bulging eyes, as if she were suffering from goitre, stared out at the reader, her long hair ruffled by the wind.

Lili read for ten minutes, and became more and more angry. By the fourth page, she was incensed. 'This is unreadable!' she said, banging the book shut and hurling it into the furthest corner of the hall.

Sára was knitting a pullover out of Miklós's ugly mud-grey wool, which she had brought with her from Eksjö. 'What's wrong with it?'

'Even the title irritates me. How can a book have a title like that? *Woman and Socialism*. Inside it's even worse.'

Sára put down her knitting and walked over to pick up the book. She dusted it off, returned to the table and handed it to Lili. 'It's a bit dry, I agree. But if you keep going—'

'No chance of that. I'm sick of it! I'd rather read nothing. Sick of it, you hear?'

'It could teach you a thing or two. How Miklós thinks, for example, if nothing else.'

Lili shoved the book away from her as if it were contagious. 'I know how he thinks. This book is unreadable.'

Sára gave up and went back to her knitting.

> Darling Miklós,
>   I'll be sending the Bebel book back shortly.
> Unfortunately the circumstances here—and my
> nerves—aren't conducive to my having the patience
> for a book like that.

Grey light filtered through the big, dusty windows of the canteen. Judit Gold peeped through to see whether Lili and Sára were in there together. Even like this, when they were having an argument, they clearly belonged together. Judit felt superfluous beside them, but her loneliness had never tugged at her heart as keenly as it did now. Would it always be like this? Would she never have anyone for herself? There'd be no men. Fair enough, she'd given up on them, but would she never have a girlfriend, a true, lifelong girlfriend? Would she always have to accommodate herself to other people? Humiliate herself for a caress? Be grateful for a kind word, a piece of advice, a hug? Who was this Lili Reich anyway?

Judit turned away from the window and hurried towards the barracks. Their dormitory was furnished with twelve iron beds. There were metal lockers in an anteroom. Judit walked over and unlocked one. She took out the yellow suitcase with its brass buckle that her cousin from Boston—her only surviving relative—had sent her in August, stuffed with tins of fish. All the sprats, mackerel and herrings had already been eaten or shared with the other girls, but now and then Judit took out the suitcase and ran her hands over it, imagining that one day she would carry it triumphantly down the main street of Debrecen. But perhaps she wouldn't return to Debrecen. Who of her friends and relatives there had survived? She might settle here in Sweden. She would find work, a husband, a home. Yes, a husband! Who knew? Fate is sometimes kind to the determined.

Judit was alone in the barracks. She took a purse out of one of the side pockets of the yellow suitcase where she had hidden it. And now she took the remnant out and clasped it in her hand. Why she had hidden it? Or kept it at all for that matter? It could have been discovered at any time. But she wasn't really worried about that. Who would dare search her suitcase? Unless! Unless those two unpleasant-looking guys from Eksjö were bent on getting to the bottom of the mystery. Better to get rid of it.

The fabric almost burned her palm—this expensive cloth she'd taken such delight in cutting up into strips. She had good reason for doing so. No one on earth could condemn her for that. No one!

Judit ran to the bathroom and locked the door. She took a last sniff of the material and threw it in the toilet, sighing as she pulled the chain. The rushing water hissed and frothed.

Fourteen

DR LINDHOLM had a few sleepless nights before he made up his mind to phone Lili. He shared his anxieties with Márta. Miklós's wandering off into the forest had disturbed her. She, too, felt that everything had got confused and a talk to clarify things wouldn't do any harm. Dr Lindholm asked Márta to be present as an impartial observer when he called Lili and to warn him, with a sign, if he went too far.

After the formalities, he began to make a little speech. 'Miklós's walk in the forest was part about wanting to escape, and part…'

Lili pressed the receiver to her ear in the caretaker's office at

Berga. She had hoped it was Miklós calling her and had sprinted for the phone. She waited for her heartbeat to slow after hearing Lindholm's voice. She wished he would get to the point.

'Part?'

'Part about facing facts. For five months have I now am treating him, dear Lili. Never, not once, has he faced up to how sick he really is. I mean it. I am going to say something cruel, Lili. Are you ready for it?'

'I'm ready for anything—and nothing, doctor. But, anyway, go ahead.'

Dr Lindholm was sitting in his comfortable armchair. He took a deep breath. 'Miklós must look death in the eyes. Four times we have to drain his lungs. We can treat his illness but we cannot cure it. Out of misconceived heroism he has ignored the diagnosis. As we doctors say, he is denying it. Are you there, Lili?'

'Yes, I am.'

'Now, when he went into the forest, is the first time for five months that he allowed reality to climb up the ivory tower he builds around himself. We have come to a turning place, Lili. Are you still there?'

'Yes, I am.'

'Unpredictable traumatic effects are normal. Can you help me in this, dear Lili? The answer is not to let Miklós cook his absurd pies in the sky. Are you still there, Lili?'

'Yes, I am.'

'This marriage that he is planning with you is not just absurd and sheer madness. At this stage it could even be damaging.

Miklós is no longer able to tell difference between reality and his imaginary world. You realise how symbolic this rambling was?'

'Symbolic? In what way?'

'A signal of alarm. A warning for me, his doctor, and for you who love him.'

'What do you expect from me?'

'You must end this foolishness. With sincerity. With love. With feeling.'

Lili was leaning against the wall in the caretaker's office, cradling the receiver. Now she pushed herself away from the wall. 'Look, doctor, I respect your exceptional expertise, your rich experience. The sensational achievements of medical research. The pills you prescribe, your X-rays, your cough mixtures, your syringes…I respect everything. But I implore you to leave us in peace. Leave us to dream. And not worry about science. I beg you on my knees. I pray and beseech you, doctor, let us get better! Are you still there?'

Lindholm had beckoned Márta to come over to him so she could hear Lili's passionate plea too. All he could manage now was a sorrowful 'Yes, I am'.

~

Two days before Christmas 1945, Miklós made a desperate decision. He persuaded Harry to go to Berga with him without permission or money.

He had weighed up his options. He would not seek official

approval—that would probably mean labyrinthine battles in an unfamiliar legal system. He knew he should stick to the straight and narrow, but his instincts were telling him otherwise.

To get to Berga, they would have to change trains three times. Three trains, three ticket collectors. Both Miklós and Harry were good at talking their way out of things. They were skinny, badly dressed, unwell. No official could help taking pity on them. They would ride their luck.

On Monday afternoon they walked to Avesta station and boarded a train.

> Dear Lili,
>   What do you think of this? We could place an announcement in the next issue of *Via Svecia* saying, 'We're engaged to be married'. Just that and our names.

> Dear Miklós,
>   Do write and tell Mama too. How will you get the money? Have you written to your acquaintance the bishop yet?

They were disqualified at the first hurdle. The ticket collector looked at them in surprise and asked them twice for their tickets.

Miklós smiled kindly at him. 'We don't have any. We don't have enough money. We're Hungarian patients from the Avesta rehabilitation centre.'

The ticket collector wasn't the slightest bit impressed. He put them off the train at the next station and reported them to the stationmaster.

They had travelled exactly seventeen kilometres. Someone arranged for a bus to transport the two fugitives back to Avesta. On this bus there would be no need for tickets.

In the meantime, a committee was convened to discuss the punishment for my father's wayward behaviour.

> My darling, one and only Lili,
>> Half an hour ago we were transported back here into the midst of a whopping hoo-ha. I can't describe the fuss they made.

~

Dr Lindholm X-rayed Miklós once again. The next day he sent for him to give him his assessment. Miklós sat down and, shutting his eyes, leaned back, balancing on the back two legs of his chair. Now all he had to do was concentrate, keep his balance, and he would find his centre of gravity. If he could keep the front two legs in the air for five seconds then he would be cured. Totally.

Dr Lindholm wanted to talk about his escape attempt. He was gentle today, understanding. 'You bungle that, Miklós. The director and governor of the centre are furious.'

Miklós got himself higher and further back on the chair. 'What can they do?'

'Transfer you.'

'Where?'

'To Högbo, probably. Is a village in the north. My medical opinion counts for nothing.'

'Why? Because I tried to go and see my cousin?'

'For breaking rules. Absence without leave. Don't forget, Miklós, you went missing twice recently. But please know I have nothing against you. Frankly, I understand you. You are thinking what difference it makes anyway?'

Miklós was nearing the tipping point. Was he going to topple over or not? That was the real question. 'What did you see on my lungs yesterday?' he asked.

'I wish I could give you good news but I can't. This X-ray confirms that—'

Crash. In anger Miklós let the front legs of the chair hit the floor. He looked up at the doctor. 'I'm going to get better!'

Lindholm winced at the thud. He avoided my father's gaze.

Lindholm got up and held out his hand. 'You are an odd chap, Miklós. Naïve and compulsive at the same time. Stubborn and a likeable fool. I am fond of you. Is pity we have to part.'

~

My father wasn't the least put out by his expulsion from Avesta, but was rattled to discover, when he looked up Högbo on the map, that it was forty-five kilometres further away from Berga. He walked over to the nurses' room. 'Could I borrow your suitcase again, please?'

Márta went up to my father without a word, stood on tiptoe and kissed his cheek.

'Don't forget to take your pills every morning,' she warned him. 'And give up smoking. Promise me. Let's shake on it.'

They shook hands.

In the afternoon, Miklós started packing. He decided to throw out everything that wasn't necessary, so he could cram his entire life into the battered suitcase. His clothes wouldn't take up much room, but he had a lot of books, notes and newspapers. And then there were all the letters, still in their envelopes, in the huge cardboard box.

Being kicked out of the barracks had created a symbolic opportunity. Now, at last, Miklós could jettison everything he had wanted to get rid of for ages. He took from the cardboard box a thick sheaf of letters tied up with silk ribbon. These were from Lili. He gathered up every other letter from the last five months—from Klára Köves, from a naïve sixteen-year-old girl from the north-east of Hungary, the floods of complaints from two divorced Transylvanian women—and set out with them to the shower room. The fact is, even after he came back from Eksjö in early December, after his three days with Lili, he was still writing to eight girls. He told them all that he was madly in love and soon to be married. Two wrote back to congratulate him.

Miklós took this distinguished bundle of letters out to the shower room and set fire to them. He watched all those words burn, and noted with satisfaction that he was also destroying the smooth-talking charmer who had written so many letters.

That was when he heard the sound of a violin. He waited until everything had turned to ashes and then walked back to the barracks. Harry was standing on a table in the centre of the dormitory playing the 'Internationale'. The men appeared from everywhere, from under beds, from behind cupboards, from behind the door. Ten of them lined up as if they were on a stage.

> Arise, you prisoners of starvation!
> Arise, you wretched of the earth!
> For justice thunders condemnation:
> A better world's in birth!

All my father's friends were singing: Laci, Jóska, Adi, Farkas, Jakobovits and Litzman. Harry's face was the picture of innocence as he played his violin.

> I'm being transferred to Högbo because I'm an
> undisciplined, subversive, disobedient trouble-maker.
> Ten of my friends announced right away that they
> wouldn't stay here for a moment without me. So Laci,
> Harry, Jakobovits and others are coming too.

The men marched out, taking Miklós with them. They paraded through the main building singing. Harry was in the lead with his violin, and the team followed him.

It is the final conflict
Let each stand in his place
The International Union
Shall be the human race.

Dozens of doctors, nurses and office workers poured out into the corridor. Only now were the men aware of the considerable army of people who were looking after them. There were a number of faces that Miklós didn't know. Most of them had never before heard this rousing, powerful song, especially not in Hungarian. But as the ten spirited young men marched and sang, arm in arm, it was victory itself.

My dear Miklós,

I'm devastated that our wanting to see each other again could be the cause of so much fuss.

Darling Lili,

Every minute we've spent together was a life for me. I love you so very much! You know, if I think that we've still got months and months to wait before we can be together forever, it puts me in the worst mood.

My one and only Miklós,

I'll try to get permission here in Berga to come and visit you.

~

The director of the Berga rehabilitation centre offered Lili a seat in her austerely furnished office. She was a thin, severe woman in glasses. Lili wondered if she'd ever smiled in her life. A cardboard box sat on her desk.

'Good to see you, Lili. I've just been speaking to Mr Björkman,' she said, indicating the telephone. 'He asked me to call him as soon as the parcel arrived.' She pushed the box across to Lili. 'It's yours. Go ahead and open it.'

Lili undid the string and tore the box open. She laid the contents out on the table. Two bars of chocolate, a few apples and pears, a pair of nylon stockings and a Bible.

The woman leaned back in her chair with satisfaction. 'Mr Björkman asked me to find a family for you here in Berga.'

Lili leafed through the Bible and saw to her disappointment that it was in Swedish—she wouldn't be able to read a word.

'I see you're wearing the present the Björkmans gave you.'

Lili put her hand on the silver cross. 'Yes.'

'Mr Björkman asked me to give you their love and tell you they remember you in their prayers. They are happy that you've been able to contact your mother. How would you feel if I were to let you spend the weekend with an excellent Catholic family?'

The right moment had come. Lili had planned not to beat around the bush or complicate things—she'd sweep the woman off her feet in a cavalry charge. 'I'm in love!' she declared.

The director was astonished. 'What has that got to do with it?'

'I need help, please! I've fallen in love with a man who is

about to be transferred from Avesta to Högbo. I'd like to visit him. I must!' At last it was out. She put on her most imploring expression.

The woman removed her glasses and, squinting fiercely, wiped them with a handkerchief. She must have been very short-sighted. 'One of the two men who went missing from Avesta last week?'

That sounded rather hostile.

'Yes, but they had reason—' Lili began.

'I disapprove of such behaviour,' the director said. She put her glasses back on and looked at Lili.

'I love him. And he loves me,' said Lili doggedly. 'We want to get married.'

The woman was taken aback. This new information required thought. 'How did you get acquainted?'

'Through letters! We've been writing to each other since September.'

'Have you ever met?'

'He came to visit me a few weeks ago in Eksjö. We spent three days together. I'm going to be his wife.'

The woman drew the Bible towards her and started to leaf through it. She was playing for time. When she looked up, there was so much sorrow in her expression that Lili almost felt pity for her.

'This must be a joke. After four months of letter-writing you want to tie your life to a stranger? I would expect more sense from you.'

Lili realised with dismay that she wouldn't be able to convince this woman. She made one last attempt. 'Are you married?'

'That's totally irrelevant.' The director shut the Bible, took off her glasses and looked down at her spindly fingers. 'I had a fiancé once. He was a great disappointment. An enlightening experience, but a great disappointment.'

Fifteen

RABBI EMIL Kronheim's home in Stockholm could hardly have been described as comfortable. But its dark, heavy furniture had served the rabbi's great-grandfather, grandfather and his father, too. The fraying and faded brocade curtains that hung from the massive windows might have been more than a hundred years old. The rabbi felt safe here. It never occurred to him to get the place painted or to move elsewhere.

There always seemed to be unwashed dishes piled up in the kitchen. Mrs Kronheim was no longer bothered by the smell of herring that hit visitors like an attack of mustard gas. But the rabbi always took a new, clean plate for his herring, and that was the source of frequent quarrels.

Mrs Kronheim was sitting in the kitchen staring at the dozens of oily plates scattered around the place.

'Listen to this,' the rabbi shouted to her from the dining-room table. '"Lili even wants to renounce her Jewishness. She and the man who has ensnared her with his letters are planning to convert. The man has a serious case of TB. On top of that he claims to know a bishop in Stockholm—which I'm sure is a lie. I beg you, Reb, please do something!'

The rabbi was reading out bits of the letter, while picking up and devouring pieces of herring without so much as a glance at his plate.

'Who wrote that?' Mrs Kronheim called from the kitchen.

The rabbi noticed, to his surprise, that stains from the salty liquid in which the herring was pickled were forming strange shapes on the tablecloth.

'A moon-faced girl with a moustache, by the name of'— he looked at the envelope on which oily traces of herring were already visible—'by the name of Judit Gold.'

Mrs Kronheim knew that sooner or later she would have to wash up and the thought gave her no pleasure. 'Do you know her?'

'Yes. I visited her in Eksjö months ago. We talked about flies.'

'One of your cautionary tales, no doubt.'

The rabbi demolished another herring. He smacked his lips. 'She is well meaning and emotional. Not afraid to cry.'

'Who is?' sighed Mrs Kronheim.

'This girl, Judit Gold. But deep inside, at the bottom of her heart, do you know what she's like?'

His wife got to her feet and began to gather up the plates, putting them disconsolately into a bowl.

'No, you tell me. You're such a clever man.'

'She's sad and disturbed,' he said, holding up the letter. 'That's what's she's like inside. This is her third letter. She keeps telling tales on her friend—and maybe not just to me.'

~

Miklós and his loyal friends were moved to a two-storey boarding house in Högbo, a couple of hundred kilometres north of Stockholm. They were greeted by Erik, a hefty man in a suit, who introduced himself as the superintendent and read out the house rules. Apart from being strict about meal times, he didn't really require anything of them. Once a week they would have to go to Sandviken for a check-up. My father had the distinct feeling that the whole thing was a waste of time.

He was even more dejected when they went upstairs to their rooms. Twenty men were housed in three dormitories, which meant that seven beds were crammed into rooms more suitable for a family weekend than a long-term stay. The cupboards had been moved out into the hallway. Erik watched from the doorway as they glumly selected their beds and sat with their suitcases on their laps. None of them was in a hurry to unpack.

Erik warned them that smoking in the rooms was forbidden and then disappeared.

> Seven of us live in a cubbyhole: Laci, Harry, Jóska, Litzman, Jakobovits, Farkas and me. So far we don't have a cupboard or a table. Luckily there's central heating. As for the beds! Straw mattresses and the kind of pillow I had in prison.

Miklós picked the bed under the window for himself. He tried not to let the pervasive gloom get a grip. He whistled as he unpacked the photo of Lili and himself from Eksjö. He put it on the sill, propping it up against the windowpane. When he woke up the next morning the first thing he'd see would be Lili's smile.

~

That afternoon Harry and Miklós took a bus into town to visit the jeweller. Harry had brought his violin with him in its case. Erik had warned them that the jeweller was a quibbling old man. Above the door of the shop hung a bronze bell that rang whenever someone entered.

The jeweller, contrary to expectations, was a kindly grey-haired gentleman who wore a purple bowtie.

My father had prepared his strategy. 'I would like to buy two gold wedding rings.'

The jeweller smiled. 'Do you know the sizes?'

Miklós fished a metal ring out of his pocket. He had taken it from a curtain rail in Eksjö. It fitted Lili's finger perfectly.

'This is my fiancée's size. The other one's for me.'

The old man took the ring, estimated its size, and pulled out a drawer in the cupboard behind him. He rummaged around a little.

'Here you are!' he said, holding up a gold ring. He took a gauge from under the counter, compared the two rings to his satisfaction, and slipped the gold ring into his pocket.

'Can I have your finger?' he asked.

He grasped my father's ring finger, pondered a moment, opened a different drawer and chose another ring. 'Try this one on,' he said holding it out to him.

Miklós slipped it on. It was an exact fit.

> I don't like gold; it always makes me think of all the alien, vulgar and wicked emotions associated with it. But I like these two rings; after all they connect your blood with mine.

Miklós and Harry exchanged glances. They'd arrived at the critical moment.

'How much do I owe you?' My father asked.

The old man deliberated. As if he too were brooding over the wicked emotions associated with such a trifle. 'Two hundred and forty kronor, the pair,' he announced.

Miklós didn't flinch. 'I'm living in a boarding house in Högbo—it's a rehabilitation centre.'

The old man straightened his bowtie. 'I've heard something about it.'

'I'd like to take you into my confidence. You see, I've been given an important job there.'

'Oh, a job. Excellent!' The jeweller gave him a friendly smile.

'Yes, and I'll get paid for it. Monthly. I reckon I can save 240 kronor in four months.'

Miklós wasn't making this up. That morning, after the small Hungarian colony, their suitcases on their laps, assessed their wretched situation, the men appointed my father their representative. He promised to stand up for them. And all of them, including the Poles and the Greeks, agreed to set aside a small part of their pocket money each month to pay Miklós for his efforts.

The old man seemed impressed. But he didn't want to be cheated. 'First of all, I congratulate you, young man. This could be the start of a fine career. But, for my part, I made a solemn vow to my mother. I was young at the time and perhaps it was a little rash of me. You know, our family has been in this business for two hundred years. I promised my mother that I would never on any account give credit to anyone. It might seem hard-hearted, but you must agree that a vow made to a mother is binding.'

Miklós, who had planned a two-pronged attack from the outset, nodded earnestly. 'I'm a Hungarian. I'd like you to look me in the eye. You don't think I'm a swindler, do you?'

The jeweller took a step back. 'Certainly not. I can smell swindlers a mile off. I can safely say that you are not the swindling type.'

The moment had come. Miklós gave Harry a kick. Harry sighed, laid his violin case on the counter and opened it. He picked up the violin tenderly and held it out to the old man.

'Well, I was pretty sure you wouldn't give credit to a stranger,' Miklós said, speaking with slow eloquence for heightened effect. 'What I had in mind was to leave this violin here as a pledge until I had saved enough money. It is worth at least four hundred kronor. I hope you'll accept it as security.'

The old man took out a magnifying glass and inspected the violin. It had been given to Harry by the Swedish Philharmonic Orchestra last summer, after a newspaper reported that a young violinist, a concentration camp survivor, was convalescing on the island of Gotland. It was worth a lot more than four hundred kronor. Even the old man's mother would have approved of this.

~

Rabbi Emil Kronheim stumbled off the bus. His legs were stiff from the long journey; it was beastly cold and now it had started to snow again. The rabbi asked where he could find the women's rehab hospital, drew his coat around him and set out.

~

Within a few days Miklós had the opportunity to prove how qualified he was for his elected post.

They were all sitting in the shabby dining room. The ten Hungarians, the Greeks, the Poles and the Romanians. The only sound was the angry beating of spoons as they struck the table in perfect time until Erik, the hefty superintendent, bustled in.

'What's the trouble, gentlemen?' he asked, afraid he wouldn't be heard above the din. Everybody stopped clanging. My father picked up a fork and rose to his feet.

> Just imagine, darling Lili, how grand I've become!
> I've been elected representative of our group. It's not
> much work, but I get paid 75 kronor a month.

Miklós pierced a piece of potato on the prong of his fork and held it up. 'This potato is rotten.'

Erik looked around in embarrassment. Then, since everyone was staring at him and he wanted to live up to his role as superintendent, he sauntered over to my father and put his nose to the potato. 'It smells of fish. What's the problem?' he said, trying not to make a face.

Miklós held the potato aloft as if it were an item of evidence.

'It's rotten. We had our suspicions about the potatoes yesterday, but today they are definitely off.'

A Greek kid, who kept his knitted hat on, even at night, stood up. 'I'll write to the International Red Cross!' he shouted in Greek.

'Pipe down, Theo,' Miklós admonished him. 'I'll deal with this.' He looked at Erik and politely pointed to a chair beside him. 'Sit with us.'

Erik hesitated.

'I'd like you to taste it,' said Miklós, drawing the chair back for him.

Erik sat down tentatively on the edge of the chair. Harry was already bringing him a plate and a knife and fork. My father eased the potato from his fork into the middle of the empty plate.

'Bon appétit,' Miklós said.

Erik looked around in dismay. There was no mercy. He bit into the potato. Miklós sat down beside him, studying him as he chewed and swallowed.

The superintendent tried to make a joke of it. 'It tastes a bit like shark. But I like shark. It's really quite nice.'

'Is that so? Well, if it's quite nice, have some more,' said Miklós with a deadpan expression as he stabbed another potato and put it on Erik's plate.

Erik knew he had to tackle this potato too. It was more difficult to get down, but somehow he managed it.

'Believe me, there's nothing wrong with it. Nothing on earth.'

'Nothing? Well, go on, have some more.'

Miklós sped up. He kept stabbing potatoes and piling them onto Erik's plate. The men were on their feet by this time, crowding around him.

My darling one and only Lili, just imagine, the
superintendent turned pale, but he led from the front
and right to the end he heroically maintained they
were edible.

Erik reckoned his best bet would be to get through this
circus as quickly as possible. So he wolfed the potatoes down.
'Quite edible. Not bad at all. Good, in fact.'

But now he was feeling sick. Drinking between every
mouthful, he bravely finished off the mound of potatoes. Then
he lurched to his feet, clutching the edge of the table to stop
himself falling.

Miklós grabbed his shoulders and tried to support him.
'As you very well know, every last potato peel is paid for by
the United Nations. I would be obliged if you did not treat us
inmates as beggars, expecting us to show our gratitude for every
last boiled potato.'

The men started clapping. This is what they were expecting
of my father, this tone. This was what he was being paid for.

Erik belched, clutching his stomach. 'You misunderstand
the situation,' he spluttered, and then collapsed with stomach
pains so severe he had to dig his nails into the floor to stop
himself crying out.

Sixteen

ONE HUNDRED and sixty girls ate lunch together in the Berga canteen, where all the tables had been pushed together to form three long rows. Two kitchen maids served the food, along with three patients elected each week to help. It took an hour and a half to serve everyone.

Emil Kronheim was escorted into the canteen by the unsmiling woman in charge—the director. The rabbi had grown accustomed to the bleak, military atmosphere of these places, but they still disheartened him. He had requested a room adjacent to the canteen be made available for him.

Judit Gold was sitting with Lili and Sára a long way from the door, but it was as if she sensed a change in the atmosphere. She couldn't say why she did it, but she glanced at the door just as it opened—and there was the rabbi. Judit turned pale and started to sweat. She willed herself to focus on her spoon as it dipped into the red soup.

The director came over and stopped right beside them. Judit almost buried her head in her soup bowl.

'You've got a visitor,' she whispered in a confidential tone.

Judit looked up. She found it strange that no one could hear her heart beating.

'Me?' asked Lili, getting to her feet.

'Rabbi Kronheim from Stockholm. He'd like to speak to you.'

'A rabbi? From Stockholm? Now?'

'He's in a hurry. He's got to catch the two o'clock train.'

Lili looked over the heads to the doorway where Emil Kronheim was standing. He gave her a friendly nod.

There was a small room next to the canteen, linked to it by a serving window. If Judit sat up straight, she could see into this room, and she couldn't resist peeking from time to time. She saw the two of them introduce themselves and sit at a table. Judit was trembling. She put her spoon down. She was sure the rabbi wouldn't betray her, but her remorse gnawed at her.

The rabbi had put his pocket watch on the table in the small room. He was relying on its quiet tick to create the right atmosphere. They had been listening to it for a while now—Lili had no intention of breaking the silence.

When Rabbi Kronheim felt that the tick-tock effect had been achieved, he leaned forward and looked into Lili's eyes. 'You have lost God.'

The pocket watch ticked away. Lili didn't ask how this stranger had the ability to see into her mind, but his powers of intuition didn't surprise her. 'No, God has lost me.'

'It's beneath you to split hairs on such a question.'

Lili was fiddling with the crocheted tablecloth. 'But what makes you think that about me?'

'It's not important at the moment. I just know.' The rabbi shifted his weight, making the chair creak. 'Have you got a cross, too?'

Lili blushed. How did he know? She felt in her pocket for the envelope where she kept the cross. Since she had come to Berga she had worn it only once, when she went to the director to beg for the visit. It hadn't helped. 'Yes. Yes, I do. It was a gift. Do you object?'

'Well, I'm not exactly thrilled,' he said sadly.

The pocket watch continued to tick.

'Look here, Lili, we are all filled with doubts. Big ones and lesser ones. But that doesn't mean we have to turn our backs.'

Lili thumped the table. The watch bounced like a rubber ball. 'Were you there? Did you come with us?' Lili was whispering, but her fist was clenched and her body was rigid. 'Were you there with us in the cattle wagon?'

The rabbi pointed to the others in the canteen beyond the window. 'I won't insult you by saying it was a test. I wouldn't dare tell you that, after all you've been through. God has lost you—all right. Or rather, it's not all right—I too have an issue with him about that. I'm angry. I don't forgive, either. How could he have done this to us? To you! To them!'

He put his watch away. It had served its purpose. He got to his feet and knocked his chair over. Taking no notice, he started pacing. It was four steps from wall to wall. He strode up and down, passionately waving his arms around.

'No, there can be no forgiveness for that. I, Rabbi Emil Kronheim, am telling you this. But…but! Millions of your brethren perished. Millions were murdered, like animals in a slaughterhouse. No, even animals are treated better than our fellow Jews were. But, for crying out loud, those millions aren't even cold in their graves yet! We haven't even finished the prayers for them. And you would leave us already? You would turn your back? Don't be fair to God; he doesn't deserve it. Be fair to the millions. You have no right to abandon them.'

From the canteen, Judit Gold could see Kronheim storming around the room and shouting. She felt lucky to be where she was. Here, she had only to put up with the hum of the dining room, the clatter of spoons, the quiet chatter of the girls. She had, however, lost her appetite. She was nauseated even by the thought of the risotto growing cold in her bowl.

~

Darling Miklós,

Today a rabbi came from Stockholm and gave me
a little moral sermon about our conversion. How on
earth did he hear about that? Could your bishop have
told him?

This part of the letter prodded my father into urgent action.
He decided to take a short cut with regard to the complicated
matter of their conversion. He looked up the phone number of
the nearest parish. The less significant the parish, he reckoned,
the less fuss there would be. A country priest would surely be
easier to convince than a bishop from the capital.

He discussed everything on the telephone and a few
days later caught a bus from Högbo to the nearby village of
Gävle.

In Gävle he found the friendly, simple wooden church that
he was secretly hoping for. The light flooded in through the
windows above the gallery. The priest was over eighty and his
head shook constantly. Miklós had gone to the public library
in Högbo the day before and buried himself in canon law in
preparation for the meeting. It was well worth the effort. When
he brought up the term *Congregationes religiosae* and explained
how he and Lili were Jews who wanted to be married in his
church, the old man's eyes shone with tears.

'How do you know about things like that?'

Miklós didn't respond; he went on in a rather self-important
way. 'The main thing is that, instead of taking a solemn vow, my

fiancée and I would only take a simple vow to bind us to the Catholic faith.'

The priest's hands were shaking too. He took out a handkerchief and wiped his eyes. 'I'm very touched by your fervour.'

Miklós was in full swing, and he began to quote, line by line, the relevant passages from the ecclesiastical literature. 'Do correct me if I'm wrong, Father, but as I understand it the simple vow is one-sided. It binds the party that takes the vow— that is, me and my fiancée—to the Church, but it doesn't bind the Church to us. On the other hand the solemn vow would be mutual, meaning that it couldn't be broken by either party.'

'How do you know all this?'

'We are serious about conversion, Father.'

The old man gathered his strength, got to his feet and began striding towards the sacristy. Miklós could hardly keep up with him. The priest took out an enormous leather-bound book and dipped his pen in the ink. Miklós was fascinated that the ink was green.

'You've convinced me. I have no doubts regarding the seriousness of your intentions. I'd like to write down your particulars. You should let me know when your fiancée can travel here from Berga. Once we have the date I will arrange for your baptism right away. I'll say one thing, Miklós, in all my time as a priest I've never come across such touching enthusiasm.'

~

Miklós and Lili now wrote to each other even more often. Sometimes they sent two letters in one day. On New Year's Eve, Miklós went up to his room. He didn't want to get drunk with the men in the boarding-house dining room downstairs. He lay on his bed, put Lili's photo on his chest and swore he would stay alive. He kept repeating this until he fell asleep. Towards dawn Harry and the others staggered in. They found my father lying on his back fully dressed, with tears trickling down his cheeks in his sleep and Lili's photo peeping out from under his hand.

> Darling Lili,
>   Damn the *Via Svecia*! I ordered the notice,
> sending in the exact wording, and they go and publish
> it with a shocking mistake. They mixed up the names!
> According to the notice, you asked for my hand! I
> hardly feel like sending it to you.

~

New Year's Eve in Berga began with Lili playing the piano and Sára singing. They had practised some songs from operettas— 'Péter Hajmási' from *The Csárdás Queen* was such a success they had to perform three encores. The rest of the evening was less cheerful. The three-piece band played, a lot of girls danced, and a lot cried, too. They had each been given a litre of red wine with supper.

> I thought of you today at lunchtime because we had
> tomato sauce, and I know you love that! Oh, how I
> love you, my little sweetie-pie!

~

On New Year's Day the men made resolutions. Ever since he'd been allowed to get out of bed, in July, Pál Jakobovits had been secreting a slice of bread into his pocket at every meal. He was aware of the stupidity of this; after all, there would always be bread here. But force of habit was stronger. On 1 January 1946, he resolved not to stuff his pocket with bread from that day on. Harry swore not to chat girls up unless he felt there was love involved. Litzman decided to emigrate to Israel. Miklós resolved to start learning Russian as soon as he got back to Hungary.

> When we daydream together, we think of everything,
> not only a self-serving love. We imagine a future
> together, working, following our vocations, in the
> service of mankind and society.

On the morning of New Year's Day in Berga the Hungarian girls sang the national anthem.

> My one and only darling Miklós,
> When are you going to the dentist in Stockholm?

~

A week later Miklós caught the bus to Sandviken, about half an hour away. He sat alone. It was one of the coldest winters for years—this day it was minus twenty-one degrees Centigrade. Thick ice coated the windows. The bus looked as if it had been wrapped in tin foil. It jolted along in its silver splendour.

> At home I only want to work for a left-wing newspaper and, if I can't find anything, I'll look around for some other occupation. I'm sick of the bourgeoisie.

On the same morning, in Berga, Lili refused to get out of bed. At about midday Sára and Judit pulled her up by force. They even dressed her, like a doll. They had found a sled somewhere, and they put Lili on it and took turns pulling her up and down the main pathway.

> My darling Miklós,
>   I've never ever felt as homesick as I do now. I'd give ten years of my life to be able to fly home.

My father sat on the bus like a forgotten chocolate in a box wrapped in silver paper. He could forget the outside world. The engine hummed. It was warm inside, the lighting was magical, and the springs rocked him. He put his hand in his pocket and felt something slim and pointed.

> I reached into my pocket and found a Mitzi Six carmine lipstick. I bought it the other day and forgot

> to send it to you. I'll be able to give it to you in
> person soon. First of all we'll check out whether it's
> kiss-proof. All right?

Lili was flying along on the sled. This time Sára and Judit were pulling it together. They were determined to cheer Lili up, and hoped that whizzing around in this clear, cold weather would have the desired effect.

> Your letter's in front of me and I've read it about
> twenty times. Every time, I discover something new in
> it, and every moment I am madder and madder with
> happiness.
> How I love you!!!
> Last night I had a dream that I can't get out of my
> mind. It was so clear. We had arrived home. Mama
> and Papa were at the train station to meet me. You
> weren't with me. I was alone.

In her dream Lili arrived at Keleti station in Budapest. Crowds of people were waiting but there was no pushing or shoving. People stood stiffly, staring straight ahead. The only movement in the dream was the train ceremoniously puffing its way alongside the covered platform. The smoke enveloped the crowd. Then it cleared, and in the grey light of dawn passengers began to step down from the train, carrying heavy suitcases. Those who were meeting them, several hundred, maybe several thousand, were waiting, transfixed.

Lili was wearing a red polka-dot dress and a wide-brimmed hat. She caught sight of her mother and father in the motionless crowd. She started running, but didn't get a step nearer to them. She was trying so hard to run that her mouth became dry and she could barely breathe. But she couldn't bridge the distance between them. It couldn't have been more than ten metres. Lili could see her mother's sad, lustreless eyes. Luckily, her father was laughing. He held his arms out wide to hug his little girl, but Lili couldn't reach him.

~

The X-ray room in Sandviken was very small; there was space only for the apparatus. By this time Miklós considered X-rays his personal enemy. He had pressed his narrow shoulders so many times against the cold pane of glass that he felt acute loathing if he even glanced at an X-ray machine.

He closed his eyes and tried to stifle his feeling of disgust.

It wasn't possible for Miklós to cultivate a close relationship with his new doctor, Irene Hammarström, as he had with Lindholm—though Irene was compassionate, softly spoken and delicately pretty. She always gave my father a searching look, as if she were trying to fathom his secret.

Now, she stood by the window and held the X-ray up to the light. Miklós played his usual game. He put his weight on the two back legs of the chair and pushed off. He didn't look at her; he was steering the chair into an increasingly precarious position.

'I can't believe my eyes,' gasped the doctor.

Miklós was at the point where a fraction of a millimetre mattered. If he miscalculated, he would crash down like a bowling pin.

Irene Hammarström didn't waste time. She walked over to the table and picked out an older X-ray from the file. She went back to the window and compared the two. 'Look, this is June. The patch is the size of a thumbnail,' she said to Miklós, who had eased himself back a smidgeon.

My father's act had reached its climax. The chair was balancing and his feet were dangling in the air.

'This is today. It's hardly visible. Miraculous! What did Dr Lindholm tell you?'

Miklós had reached his zenith. After all his practice he could balance on the chair between heaven and earth like a motionless falcon about to swoop.

'He said I had six months to live.'

'Somewhat brutal, but the truth. I wouldn't have been able to say anything different.'

My father's one-man show was still running. 'What do you mean by that?'

'Now I'm not quite sure, looking at this latest X-ray.'

'What do you mean?'

'Now, I'd probably encourage you. Tell you to keep up the good work. What about your high temperature? Your dawn fever?'

The show was over, but those five seconds would live on, in

the land of miracles. Miklós crashed backwards onto the floor.

'Good Lord!' Irene dropped the X-rays and rushed over to him.

My father had hit the back of his head pretty hard, but he was smiling. 'It's nothing, nothing. I made a bet with myself, that's all.'

Seeing Miklós's ghastly metal dentures, the doctor decided to refer her grinning patient to the district centre in the hope that they could sort out this amicable young Hungarian's teeth for a reduced price, or even for no fee.

~

It was a memorable day. When Miklós returned to the boarding house he found the men waiting for him upstairs, standing to attention. He couldn't imagine how they knew he was on the road to recovery. But as their faces were shining with pride and joy, he reckoned it must be the reason for this performance. He sat down on his bed and waited.

Then the men began to hum Beethoven's 'Ode to Joy'.

When the mystery of the ceremony became unbearable, when the humming chorus of the *Ninth Symphony* had reached its hymnal climax, when my father leaned back on his bed and with eyes shut started to soar, Harry brought out the newspaper. Without a word he held it up in front of Miklós.

There was the poem, in black and white. On page three of *Via Svecia*. In Swedish. In italics. *'Till en liten svensk gosse'* ('To a Little Swedish Boy'). Above it was the name of the poet: my father.

~

Miklós composed all his poems in his head. Days and weeks later, when he felt the poem was ready, all he had to do was write it out.

He had finished this poem, however, in about ten minutes. He was sitting in a deck chair on the ship, munching biscuits, savouring the taste of raspberry and vanilla. The ship's horn bellowed, and they drew away from the shore. The women on their bicycles were watching; not one of them stirred. There, an arm's length away, was the country that would take him in, for who knew how long. Miklós felt this sweet gift should be recip-rocated. He would write a poem for Swedish children. Advice about life, a warning that would draw its power from his infernal experiences.

He turned the crumbly biscuit in his mouth and set out the first two lines in his head. 'You have yet to learn, little brother, of the deep furrows ploughed across the forehead of a continent.' And now he could see the blond six-year-old child to whom his poem was addressed, who stood staring at him, hugging his teddy. The little Swedish boy.

The lines poured out; it was almost more difficult to remem-ber them than to create them. By the time the ship had turned round and reached the open sea, the poem was finished.

You have yet to learn, little brother,
of the deep furrows ploughed across the forehead of a
continent.
Here, in the north, you saw an aeroplane
dipped in starlight on a moonlit night.

You didn't know what air-raid warnings or bombs were,
or what it is to survive what's on the film —
the troubles of the world weren't washed
by evil waves onto the children, making them suffer.

Here you had points for clothes, meat rations and bread
tickets;
you could play sometimes, though, little brother!
But your skinny playmates were burnt in the flames,
and death grinned at its meagre bread.

By the time you grow up and become a man,
a kind, smiling blond giant,
all these falling tears will be clouds,
this age will be history, a hazy vision.

If you muse on this bloody age,
remember a pale little boy —
his plaything was a scrap of grenade,
his minders murderous weapons.

If you have a son, little brother, teach him
that the truth is never a gun or revolver;
and it's not the long range of the rocket
that relieves the suffering of the world.

And in the toyshop, little brother, don't buy
soldiers for your son; on the white toy shelf
let there be wooden blocks, so that in his childhood
he'll learn to build and not to kill.

Harry gave Miklós a pat on the shoulder. 'I took your career in hand. I sent your poem to a Swedish newspaper, anticipating your approval. I asked them to translate it, telling them not to commission any old translator with the task because this was the work of a great Hungarian poet. You. That was three months ago. And this morning it appeared in print. I had the translation checked. It's good.'

The others were still standing up straight, humming 'Ode to Joy'. Miklós got to his feet and gave Harry a hug, concentrating on holding back his tears. Crying wouldn't befit a great Hungarian poet.

~

This really was a fateful day—as Miklós was to discover.

It wasn't yet midnight. Someone was hammering on the door, calling my father's name—there was a man on the phone for him. Miklós woke up. For a moment he had no idea where he was. He found his way downstairs to reception in his pyjamas, his heart thumping.

'Did I wake you?' The voice on the line was unfamiliar.

'It doesn't matter.'

'I apologise. I'm Rabbi Kronheim from Stockholm. I want to speak to you on a matter of importance.'

Miklós's feet were cold; he pressed one sole against his calf. 'I'm listening.'

'Not over the phone! What are you thinking?'

'Sorry.'

'Listen, Miklós, I'm catching the train from Stockholm to Sandviken in the morning. I've got two hours before I have to catch the train back. Let's meet halfway.'

'I can meet you in Sandviken if you like.'

'No, no, I insist on halfway. Will Östanbyn be all right?'

Östanbyn was the first stop after Högbo on the bus to Sandviken. Miklós had passed through it many times.

'Where in Östanbyn?'

'Get off the bus and walk towards Sandviken. Take the first right and keep going until you come to a wooden bridge. I'll be waiting for you there. Got it?'

'Okay.' Miklós was in a daze. 'Could you tell me your name again, please?'

'Emil Kronheim. So, 10 a.m. at the wooden bridge. Don't be late.'

The rabbi hung up. It was all so fast that Miklós realised, with the receiver buzzing in his hand, that he had forgotten to ask what the rabbi wanted to discuss.

~

Miklós followed the rabbi's directions and got off the bus in Östanbyn. He took the first right. He must have been walking briskly for about twenty minutes before he saw the wooden bridge. At the far end a man in a black ankle-length coat was resting on a big stone. Miklós was amazed that anyone could sit still in this frozen world. In fact, he looked as if he were enjoying a summer picnic beside a lake.

'What's the news?' the rabbi yelled across the bridge in a cheerful tone.

Miklós stopped. Not only was the news good, it was positively splendid. But who knew what that grotesque figure over there was talking about?

'Rabbi Kronheim?'

'Who else? Who is this Catholic bishop? The one you promised to Lili? If it is the bishop of Stockholm, I know him well. He's a charming man.'

Lili's letter about a rabbi who lectured her on morality flashed into Miklós's mind. Of course, this was Emil Kronheim! Miklós understood everything! The rabbi had come to chastise him. To hell with it! To think he had made a pilgrimage to Östanbyn for that.

'We don't need the bishop any more.'

'I'll wager you've found someone else.'

The wooden bridge was at least thirty metres long. In the valley below, ancient pine trees were standing guard, silence frozen in the light on their snow-covered branches. There wasn't a breath of wind, no birdsong. The sublime beauty of the countryside was disturbed only by their shouting.

'Well guessed, Rabbi. An excellent old man in Gävle. He will baptise us.'

On the other side of the bridge, Kronheim ran his fingers through his wiry hair. 'Lili isn't so keen now on that silly idea.'

Miklós decided it was time to look the man in the eye. He walked across the bridge and held out his hand. 'She wrote just the opposite to me.'

'What did she write?'

'That a rabbi from Stockholm had preached her a sermon. Somehow or other he had sniffed out our intentions. Something like that.'

'Your lovely fiancée would never have used such a cynical expression. Sniffed out, indeed! I'm not a bloodhound.'

'Seriously, Rabbi, how did you find out? We haven't spoken to a soul about it.'

Kronheim took my father's arm and walked with him to the middle of the bridge. He leaned against the railing and gazed at the scene below.

'Have you ever seen anything as magnificent? It's looked like this for a hundred years. Even a thousand.'

The valley was eerily impressive. Dense pines as far as the eye could see, sprinkled all over with icing sugar.

Miklós decided it was time to leap the last hurdle. 'Look here, before the war I'd have considered this a way to escape. But now it's a clear and independent decision.'

Kronheim didn't look at my father. He had surrendered to

the wonder of nature. 'This landscape is utterly unspoilt.'

'I'm thinking of the fate of our unborn children,' said my father, determined to continue. 'In any case, I've never been a believer. I'm an atheist, and you can despise me for that. But I'd like you to know that our conversion has nothing to do with cowardice.'

The rabbi appeared not to have heard a word. 'It's been here from time immemorial. This bridge, for instance, was designed for people to admire the view. But they made sure to build it out of wood. Can you see any alien material here? Iron, glass or brass? You can't, can you, son?'

'Is this what you wanted to talk to me about, Reb, the wooden bridge at Östanbyn?'

'Among other things.'

Miklós was fed up with all this riddling talk. Just when he was getting the better of his misgivings, this little wiry-haired man turns up and preaches to him about the pristine country-side. He understood him, of course he understood him. Several thousand years—you bet! But if Lili wanted to convert, he would sweep away every worry or hesitation that lay in her path.

He bowed. 'I'm glad to have met you, Rabbi Kronheim. Our decision is final. No one can dissuade us. Goodbye.'

And he strode off in the direction he had come from. At the end of the bridge he turned round. It was as if Emil Kronheim had been waiting for him to do that. The rabbi pulled a letter out of his coat pocket and waved it.

'I hate myself for this,' he shouted. 'But as the scripture

says…or maybe it doesn't. Anyway, the main thing is I want to strike a dirty deal with you, son.'

Miklós stared at him, baffled.

'Come and see what I've got.' The rabbi was still holding the letter in the air.

Miklós reluctantly retraced his steps.

'I've written this request; it's so heartfelt that no eye will remain dry. You sign it and I'll take it to Stockholm today. They'll agree, have no worries about that. On one condition: I'd like to be the one who joins you in marriage at the synagogue in Stockholm. Naturally under a *chuppah*. I'll foot the bill for clothes, the ceremony and a reception for your friends. After that the Red Cross will be obliged to offer you, as newlyweds, a room of your own, say, in Berga.'

My father took the letter. It was written in Swedish. As far as he could make out it was addressed to the Stockholm headquarters of the Red Cross.

'They don't deal with cases like this.'

'Yes, they do. They'll be proud to. They'll pull out all the stops. Make good use of it. Get the story into the newspapers. After all, two young people under their patronage, struggling to live again after all but dying, have forged a commitment to a new life together. By the way, what does your doctor say?'

'About what?'

'Your TB.'

'So you know about that, too?'

'It's my duty to find out. That's what I'm paid for.'

'I'm getting better. The cavity is calcifying.'

'Thank God!' Kronheim gave my father a hug. 'Do we have a deal?' he whispered.

Miklós softened. He was already composing the letter to Lili in which he would explain that a grown-up person—especially if he's a socialist—doesn't quibble over trifling religious questions.

Seventeen

EVERYTHING HAPPENED quickly. The rabbi, as promised, procured the relevant permits. Within two months Lili and my father found themselves in the synagogue in Stockholm under the *chuppah*. Kronheim paid for the rental of a white taffeta dress for Lili and a dinner jacket for my father, and organised a reception after the wedding. The King of Sweden, Gustav V, sent a congratulatory telegram to the young couple who, having barely survived the concentration camp, were now about to swear their undying love.

In February 1946, before the wedding, my father suffered for weeks in a dentist's chair. Kronheim had insisted he swap his alloy teeth for porcelain.

'It can't be much fun kissing you, son,' he said one day. 'I've been talking to my congregation and they unanimously decided to raise the funds for the dental work. They collected six hundred kronor in three days. I've been in touch with a first-class man for the job. Here's his address.'

~

Emil Kronheim could have rubbed his hands. He really had pulled this whole thing off. But before the wedding, at the beginning of March, a visitor arrived to dampen his happiness.

It began with two long impatient rings of the doorbell. The rabbi was eating herring, as usual, and chuckling to himself as he read an American comic. His wife let the visitor into the flat and was so shocked by the stranger's distracted appearance that she led her into the main room without taking her coat, fur cap and snow-covered galoshes. The rabbi didn't even notice her as he lifted a bit of herring out of the brine.

Mrs Kronheim restrained herself from slapping his hand. 'You've got a visitor,' she hissed.

The rabbi stood up in embarrassment, wiping his hands on his trousers. Mrs Kronheim made a distressed sound. 'Your trousers! Dear God!'

There were snowflakes on the young woman's upper lip. She looked like a female Santa Claus.

'Ah, my conscientious letter writer! Sit down,' Kronheim

said, offering her a seat.

Judit sat, not even unbuttoning her coat. Mrs Kronheim left discreetly and went into the kitchen.

'I saw you in Berga, Rabbi. Thank you for not giving me away.'

'How about a little salted herring?' he asked, pushing the plate of fish towards her.

'No, thanks. I don't like it.'

'What is there not to like about salted herring? It's full of vitamins. Full of life. Now why would I have given you away, dear Judit? I'm grateful to you for the last-minute warning.'

The snow on Judit's galoshes was melting.

'No, the last minute is now!'

'Good God, did you come all the way to Stockholm to tell me that?'

Judit grabbed the rabbi's hand. 'We have to save Lili.'

'Save her? From whom? From what?'

'From marriage! I can't believe it. My friend wants to get married.'

Kronheim would have liked to withdraw his hand, but her grip was tight. 'Love is a wonderful thing,' he said. 'Marriage is its seal.'

'But the man who wants to marry her is a scoundrel. A marriage con man.'

'My gosh, that's no joke. What makes you think that, Judit?'

Mrs Kronheim came in with homemade vanilla biscuits and tea.

The rabbi hated anything sweet. 'Help yourself to tea. Relax. I'll stick to herring if you don't mind.'

Judit took no notice of the biscuits or the tea. Nor did she notice that the tile stove was pouring warmth into the room of imposing furniture. She didn't even loosen her scarf. 'Listen to me, Rabbi. You don't know everything, so just listen. Imagine a man who gets hold of the names and addresses of all the Hungarian girls convalescing in rehab hospitals in Sweden.'

'I can imagine him.'

'Now imagine that he sits down and writes a letter to each of them. Do you follow? To every single one of them.'

'I see a determined man before me,' said the rabbi, picking up another piece of herring.

'The letters are identical. The same sickly sweet wording. As if he'd made carbon copies. He then walks to the post office and posts the lot. Can you picture it?'

'Oh, that can't be true. Where did you hear that?'

Judit Gold gave the rabbi a triumphant look. Her moment had come. She took a crumpled letter out of her bag. 'Look at this. I got one too. In September last year. Of course I had no intention of replying. I saw through his tricks. What do you say to that? Lili received an identical letter. I saw it and read it. The only difference was the name. You can check it for yourself.'

Kronheim smoothed out the letter and studied it.

Dear Judit,
    You are probably used to strangers chatting you

up when you speak Hungarian, for no better reason
than they are Hungarian too. We men can be so
bad-mannered. For example, I addressed you by
your first name on the pretext that we grew up in the
same town. I don't know whether you already know
me from Debrecen. Until my homeland ordered
me to 'volunteer' for forced labour, I worked for
the *Independent* newspaper, and my father owned a
bookstore in Gambrinus Court.

'Very odd,' remarked the rabbi, shaking his head.

Judit was on the verge of tears. 'And Lili wants to tie the boat
of her life to this crook.'

Kronheim put another herring dreamily into his mouth.
'The boat of her life. How lyrical. Tie the boat of her life to him.'

~

More than fifty years later, when I questioned Lili, my mother,
about the moment she decided to reply to Miklós's letter, she
searched for a long time among her buried memories.

'I don't remember exactly. You know, in September, after
the ambulance took me from Smålandsstenar to Eksjö, during
my second week of being confined to bed, Sára and Judit turned
up in the ward. They brought some of my personal things from
Smålandsstenar—including your father's letter. Judit sat on my
bed and tried to persuade me to write back, prattling on about
how much that poor ill boy from Debrecen must be hoping for

a reply. Then the girls left and I was stuck in bed. I wasn't even allowed to go out to the bathroom. I lay there bored, with your father's letter beside me. Two or three days later I asked the nurses for pencil and paper.'

~

Lili and Miklós were assigned to the second transport of Hungarian returnees, in June 1946. They flew from Stockholm to Prague and caught a train to Budapest the same day.

They held hands in the crowded compartment. After they crossed the border into Hungary my father got up, with an apologetic smile, and made his way to the tiny, filthy toilet and locked the door. As usual his thermometer was in his pocket in its elegant metal case. The train rattled along on the newly repaired track. Miklós stuck the thermometer in his mouth, shut his eyes and clung to the doorhandle. He tried to count to 130 in time to the clattering of the wheels. When he got to ninety-seven he glanced up, and in the cracked mirror above the basin he saw a thin, unshaven man in glasses and an oversized jacket with a thermometer pressed between his lips. He peered closely at the mirror image. Was this what he'd see for the rest of his life? This cowardly looking fellow hooked on his thermometer?

He came to a decision. Without looking at the level of the quicksilver, he yanked the thermometer out of his mouth and chucked it down the toilet. He threw the metal case in as well. Then, determined and angry, he flushed twice.

By nine o'clock on that June evening in 1946 a huge crowd was gathered at Keleti station, even though this was a special train and its arrival hadn't been announced on the radio. But the word had got round. Lili's mother, for instance, heard about the train on the number six tram. A woman in a headscarf had yelled the news down the tramcar during the afternoon rush hour. She also had a daughter coming home after nineteen months away.

Lili was wearing a red polka-dotted dress; during the spring she had begun to put on weight and was now seventy kilos. Miklós's trousers still hung off him; he left Sweden weighing fifty-three kilos. They travelled in the last carriage.

My father stepped onto the platform first, carrying the two suitcases. Mama rushed over to Lili and they hugged each other without speaking. Then she hugged Miklós, who had no family to meet him.

Lili's mother hoped that her husband would make it back. The truth was, however, that Sándor Reich, suitcase salesman, returning home from Mauthausen concentration camp, found his way into a storeroom filled with food. He ate smoked sausage and bacon and was taken to hospital that same night. Two days later he died from a ruptured bowel.

It was a dusty, humid evening. Lili, her mother and Miklós wandered through the excited crowd. They couldn't stop looking at each other. They were at home together.

For the next two years I was in the making, silent and yearning.

Epilogue

MY PARENTS, Miklós and Lili, wrote to each other for six months, between September 1945 and February 1946, before they were married in Stockholm.

Until my father died in 1998, I had no idea the letters still existed. Then, with hope and uncertainty in her eyes, my mother gave me two neat bundles of envelopes bound in silk ribbon, one cornflower blue, the other scarlet.

I was familiar with the story of how they met. 'Your father swept me off my feet with his letters,' my mother would say, and make that charming wry face of hers. She might mention Sweden, that misty, icy enigmatic world at the edge of the map.

But for fifty years I did not know that their letters still existed. In the midst of political upheaval and the chaos of moving to new apartments, my parents had carted them around without ever talking about them. They were preserved by being invisible. The past was locked up in an elegant box it was forbidden to open.

Now I could no longer ask my father about what happened. My mother answered most of my questions with a shrug. *It was a long time ago. You know how shy your father was. We wanted to forget.*

Why? How could they forget a love so wonderfully uninhibited and so splendidly gauche that it still shines? If there were difficult moments in my parents' marriage—and every marriage has its share of them—why didn't they ever untie the ribbons to remind themselves of how they found each other? Or can we allow ourselves a more sentimental line of questioning? In their fifty-two-year relationship wasn't there a moment when time stood still? When the angels passed through the room? When one of them, out of pure nostalgia, longed to dig out the bundles hidden at the back of the bookcase, the testimony of how they met and fell in love?

Of course, I know the answer: there was no moment like that.

~

In one of his letters my father writes that he is planning a novel. He wanted to describe the collective horror of being transported to a German concentration camp—a book (*The Long Voyage*) Jorge Semprún later wrote instead of him.

Why didn't he ever get down to writing it?

I can guess the answer. My father arrived home in June 1946. His younger sister was his only living relative, and his parents' house had been bombed. His past had evaporated. His future, however, was taking shape. He became a journalist and started writing for a left-wing paper. Then, one day early in the 1950s, he found his desk had been moved outside the editorial office.

When exactly did my father lose his faith in communism? I don't know. But by the time of the show trial of László Rajk in 1949 it must have been shattered. And during the revolution in 1956 my parents were concerned primarily with the possibility of emigrating.

I remember my father standing in desperation in our kitchen, which was reeking as usual with the smell of boiling sheets. 'Do you want me to wash dishes for the rest of my life? Is that what you want?' he hissed at my mother.

They stayed.

During the Kádár era, between 1956 and 1988, my father became a respected foreign-affairs journalist. He was founder and deputy editor of *Magyarország*, a quality weekly newspaper. He never wrote the novel about the journey in the railway wagon, and he stopped writing poetry.

This leads me to record the sad fact that in my father's hands neither his own experiences nor those of his companions in distress became a literary work.

I'm convinced that the idea of a new future, the belief that grew into a religion at the beginning, was later cancelled out by his resigned submission to the political circumstances that undermined his aspirations as a writer too. This proves that talent alone is not enough. It doesn't hurt to have luck in life as well.

But my parents took great care of the letters. That's what matters. They kept them safe, until my mother's decision and my father's approving wave from the next world allowed them to reach me.

About the Author

Péter Gárdos is an award-winning Hungarian film director. *Fever at Dawn* is his first novel and is based on the true story of his parents. It has been made into a film in Hungary, and is being published in thirty territories around the world.

Fever at Dawn
Reading Group Questions

1. Discuss the author's decision to narrate the novel from Miklós's son's perspective. Why does the son narrate from his father's perspective? At what point do you know who the narrator's mother is? What kind of narrative distance does this create and how did it affect your reading?

2. The events of the novel are based on a true story. Did you know this before you started reading? How did it affect your reading of the story? Why do you think the author chose to write this as a novel instead of as nonfiction?

3. Did you learn anything new historically in reading this novel? What surprised you?

4. Why did Miklós persist in writing his letters? What did they mean to him?

5. The opening chapter depicts 'an army of women' on bicycles delivering freshly baked biscuits for the survivors arriving in Sweden. What other random acts of kindness are described in the novel? How do these contribute to the novel as a whole?

6. The author, Péter Gárdos, is also a filmmaker. Where could you see evidence of this in the writing?

7. The doctor gives Miklós very specific measures to guide him toward health: weight, temperature, X-ray results. How does this contrast with Miklós's nature as a poet? What does his temperature

each morning come to mean to him – i.e. why is the novel called 'Fever at Dawn'?

8. What are Miklós's politics before and after the war? Does Lili share these views? Do his fellow Hungarians, or the Swedes? (Does it matter?)

9. Talk about the idea of hope. What does it do for Miklós and Lili? How does hope help (or harm) us as humans in such extreme situations? Are there any other stories of hope that this story reminded you of?

10. After Lili and Miklós finally meet, the author writes, 'But they never spoke about certain important things. Neither then, nor later.' Why do you think they both silently, but mutually, agreed to do this? What do you think avoiding these topics meant for them and their relationship?

11. Lili and Miklós each have their own group of friends that they confide in about the letters. How did these friendships affect their letter-writing and relationship? And how were Lili and Miklós's friends influenced by their love story?

12. Why do you think Judit betrayed Lili to the Rabbi? Why didn't she want Lili and Miklós to get together? Were you sympathetic to her at all? How do you think the traumatic events she's suffered affect her choices here? How did their experiences of the war change – or not – all of these characters?

13. What role do you think humour plays in Lili and Miklós's relationship?

The Mistress of My Fate

Hallie Rubenhold

THE CONFESSIONS OF HENRIETTA LIGHTFOOT
There is much to be learned from a woman of her sort . . .

England, 1789. The Bastille has fallen, King George is mad, and Henrietta Lightfoot flees her home at Melmouth Park after a suspicious death, for which she is blamed. She has no life experience, little money and only her true love, Lord Allenham, to whom she can turn . . .

When he suddenly goes missing, Henrietta embarks on a journey through London's debauched and glittering underworld in the hope of finding him, but discovers more about herself and her mysterious past than she imagined. With the assistance of a sisterhood of courtesans, her skills at the card table and on the stage, the unstoppable Henrietta is ready to become mistress of her fate.

'A remarkable picture of a fascinating age'
DAILY EXPRESS

'A full-blooded historical romp'
INDEPENDENT

'Ricochets with energy, witty observation and rollicking pace'
EASY LIVING

The Ballroom

Anna Hope

1911: Inside an asylum at the edge of the Yorkshire moors, where men and women are kept apart by high walls and barred windows, there is a ballroom, vast and beautiful. For one bright evening every week, they come together and dance.

When John and Ella meet, it is a dance that will change two lives for ever.

'Moving, fascinating'
THE TIMES

'A tender and absorbing love story'
DAILY MAIL

'Heartbreaking and insightful'
SUNDAY EXPRESS

'Fiction at its finest . . . the reader is utterly transported'
IRISH INDEPENDENT

Longbourn

Jo Baker

'If Elizabeth Bennet had the washing of her own petticoats,' Sarah thought, 'she would be more careful not to tramp through muddy fields.'

It is wash-day for the housemaids at Longbourn House, and Sarah's hands are chapped and raw. Domestic life below stairs, ruled with a tender heart and an iron will by Mrs Hill the housekeeper, is about to be disturbed by the arrival of a new footman, bearing secrets and the scent of the sea.

'A triumph: a splendid tribute to Austen's original,
but, more importantly, a joy in its own right'
GUARDIAN

'A fascinating insight into the harsh working conditions
of life in a grand house two hundred years ago'
GOOD HOUSEKEEPING

'Superb . . . The lightest of touches by a highly accomplished
young writer of whom more, surely, will be heard'
MAIL ON SUNDAY

The Finding of Martha Lost

Caroline Wallace

Martha is lost.

She's been lost since she was a baby, abandoned in a suitcase on the train from Paris to Liverpool. Ever since, she's waited at the station lost property office for someone to claim her. It's been sixteen years, but she's still hopeful.

In the meantime, there are lost property mysteries to solve: a suitcase that may have belonged to the Beatles, for one. And that stuffed monkey that keeps appearing. But there is one mystery Martha has never been able to solve – until anonymous letters start to arrive, offering clues to the past she longs to know.

Time is running out, though. The authorities have found out about the girl in lost property, and if Martha can't discover who she really is, she will lose everything . . .

'Charming, magical and beautifully imagined'
CARYS BRAY

'A charming, quirky tale'
WOMAN & HOME

'If you love the films *Amelie* or *Hugo*, you will
adore this magical modern fairytale'
ESSENTIALS MAGAZINE

Five Rivers Met on a Wooded Plain

Barney Norris

'There exists in all of us a song waiting to be sung which is as heart-stopping and vertiginous as the peak of the cathedral. That is the meaning of this quiet city, where the spire soars into the blue, where rivers and stories weave into one another, where lives intertwine.'

One quiet evening in Salisbury, the peace is shattered by a serious car crash. At that moment, the lives of five people collide – a flower-seller, a schoolboy, an army wife, a security guard, a widower – all facing their own personal disasters. As one of those lives hangs in the balance, Norris draws the extraordinary voices of these seemingly ordinary people together into a web of love, grief, disenchantment and hope that is startlingly perceptive about the human heart.

'Wonderful . . . I was hooked from the first page. It's the real stuff'
MICHAEL FRAYN

'Remember the name Barney Norris. He's a new writer
in his mid-twenties, but already outstanding'
THE TIMES

The Book Thief

Markus Zusak

1939. Nazi Germany. The country is holding its breath. Death has never been busier.

Liesel, a nine-year-old girl, is living with a foster family on Himmel Street. Her parents have been taken away to a concentration camp. Liesel steals books.

This is her story and the story of the inhabitants of her street when the bombs begin to fall.

Features special bonus content, including manuscript pages, original sketches and pages from the author's notebook.

'Extraordinary'
Sunday Telegraph

'Brilliant and hugely ambitious'
New York Times

'This is a novel of breathtaking scope, masterfully told'
Guardian

The Boy in the Striped Pyjamas
John Boyne

What happens when innocence is confronted by monstrous evil?

Nine-year-old Bruno knows nothing of the Final Solution and the Holocaust. He is oblivious to the appalling cruelties being inflicted on the people of Europe by his country. All he knows is that he has been moved from a comfortable home in Berlin to a house in a desolate area where there is nothing to do and no one to play with. Until he meets Shmuel, a boy who lives a strange parallel existence on the other side of the adjoining wire fence and who, like the other people there, wears a uniform of striped pyjamas.

Bruno's friendship with Shmuel will take him from innocence to revelation. And in exploring what he is unwittingly a part of, he will inevitably become subsumed by the terrible process.

'An extraordinary tale of friendship and the horrors of war seen through the eyes of two young boys . . . raw literary talent at its best'
IRISH INDEPENDENT

'Overwhelmingly powerful . . . This is a story so exceptional and vivid that it cannot be erased from the mind'
CAROUSEL